CFIN

A South-Asian Perspective

2e

Scott Besley

University of South Florida, U.S.A

Eugene F. Brigham

University of Florida, U.S.A

N. R. Parasuraman

Shri Dharmasthala Manjunatheshwara Institute for Management Development (SDMIMD), Mysore

Cengage

Australia • Brazil • Canada • India • Mexico • Singapore • United Kingdom • United States

Cengage

CFIN 2e

Scott Besley
Eugene F. Brigham
N. R. Parasuraman

CFIN4, SE Package, Scott Besley and Eugene F. Brigham

This edition is reprinted with license from South-Western Cengage Learning, for sale in India, Pakistan, Bangladesh, Nepal, Bhutan, Sri Lanka and Maldives.

ISBN-13: 978-93-87511-00-2
ISBN-10: 93-87511-00-6

Cengage Learning India Pvt. Ltd.
T-303, 3rd Floor
DAV Complex, Plot 3
Mayur Vihar Phase 1
Delhi-110091

Printed by:
Rajiv Book Binding House
D-1518, DSIIDC Industrial Complex, Narela, New Delhi 110040

Printed in India
Print Number: 03 Print Year: 2023

Preface

4LTR Press, a Cengage Learning product, is a widely acclaimed concept of learning with a simple approach—creating an innovative teaching and learning solution built around today's learners and teachers. The idea behind bringing out this series of books is to introduce students and teachers in South Asia to an innovative concept in management studies. Since the launch, 4LTR Press has helped more than 1,800,000 college students at over 2,000 schools succeed worldwide. Every book in the series is built on the findings based on the inputs from discipline-specific focus groups, conversations, and surveys.

The books in this series present visually-engaging page layouts and succinct yet thorough topical coverage and are designed from the ground up to meet the needs of teachers and students. These books help increase students' classroom engagement and improve learning outcomes.

The books address a number of concerns, including the reality of the reading habits of the majority of today's students. 4LTR Press offers information in the formats students find engaging, while still providing the high-quality content instructors need. The chapters in these books are short and understandable. The text is easier to pay attention to, and the books are actually enjoyable to read. Everything is much more inviting than a regular textbook. The review pages at the end of each chapter serve a unique purpose: Students first go through the review page to preview the new concepts, then they read the chapter to understand the material, and finally they go through the review page again to make sure they have registered the key concepts.

We are sure that this series, a first of its kind in the South Asian market, will revolutionize the way students approach and become familiar with the concepts of business and economics.

Brief Contents

Contents

6 Bonds (Debt)—Characteristics and Valuation 120

7 Shares (Equity)—Characteristics and Valuation 146

8 Risk and Rates of Return 168

PART 4 Valuation—Real Assets (Capital Budgeting) 196

9 Capital Budgeting Techniques 196

10 Project Cash Flows and Risk 222

PART 5 Cost of Capital and Capital Structure Concepts 262

11 The Cost of Capital 262

12 Capital Structure 286

13 Distribution of Retained Earnings: Dividends and Stock Repurchases 314

PART 6 Working Capital Management 336

14 Working Capital Policy 336

15 Managing Short-Term Assets 356

16 Managing Short-Term Liabilities (Financing) 380

PART 7 Strategic Planning and Financing Decisions 400

17 Financial Planning and Control 400

Case Studies 424

Index 432

Equation Cards

PART 1

Introduction to Managerial Finance

CHAPTER 1

An Overview of Managerial Finance

Learning Outcomes

LO.1 Explain what finance entails and why everyone should have an understanding of basic financial concepts.

LO.2 Identify different forms of business organization as well as the advantages and disadvantages of each.

LO.3 Identify major goal(s) that firms pursue and what a firm's primary goal should be.

LO.4 Explain the roles that ethics and good governance play in successful businesses.

LO.5 Describe how foreign firms differ from U.S. firms and identify factors that affect financial decisions in multinational firms.

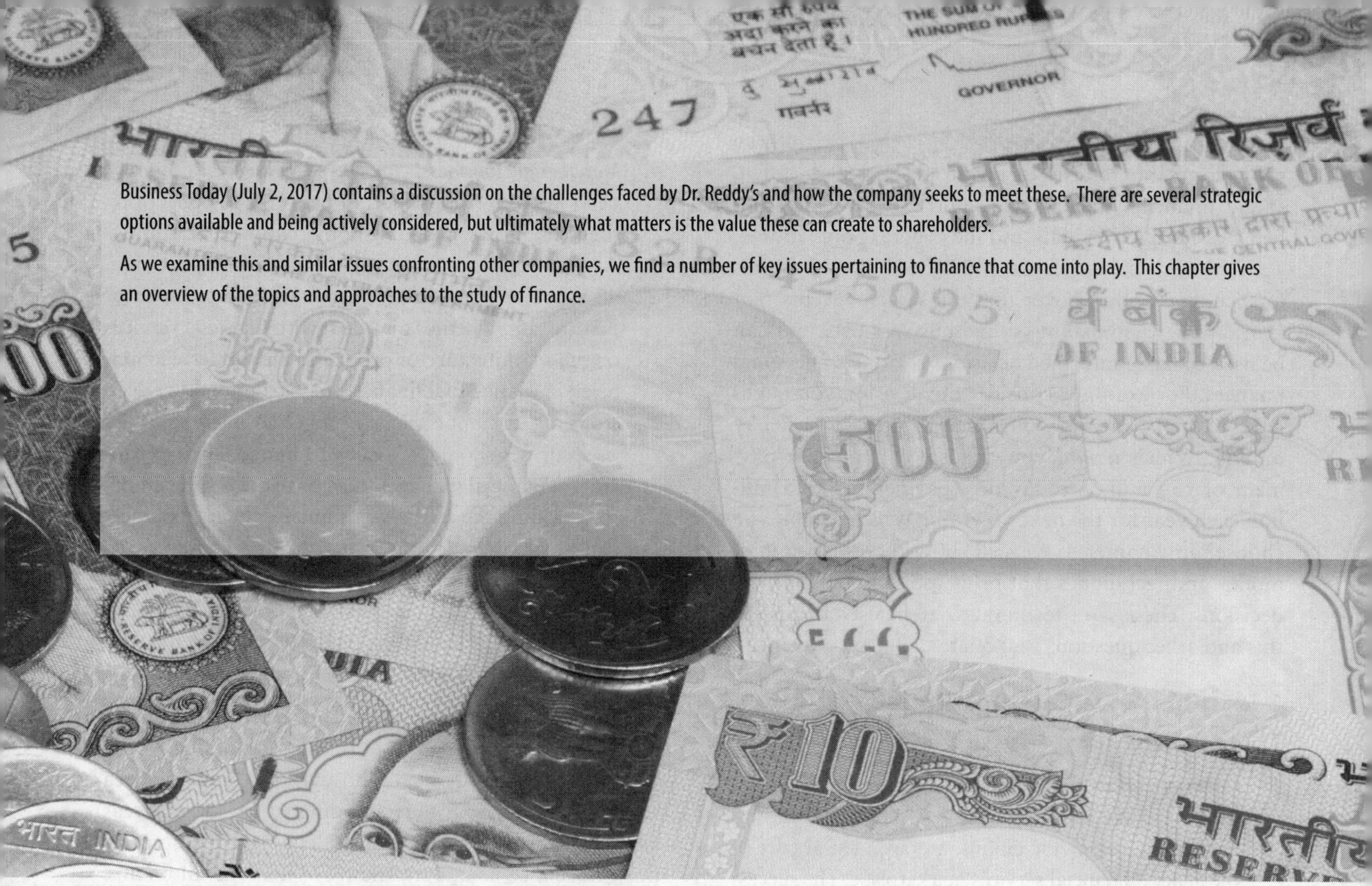

Business Today (July 2, 2017) contains a discussion on the challenges faced by Dr. Reddy's and how the company seeks to meet these. There are several strategic options available and being actively considered, but ultimately what matters is the value these can create to shareholders.

As we examine this and similar issues confronting other companies, we find a number of key issues pertaining to finance that come into play. This chapter gives an overview of the topics and approaches to the study of finance.

In this chapter, we introduce finance by providing you with (1) a description of the discipline and (2) an indication of the goals companies should attain, as well as the conduct that is acceptable when pursuing these goals. As you will discover, a company acts in the best interests of its owners (stockholders) when decisions are made that increase the firm's value, which in turn increase the value of its stock.

Study Tools

Problems are found at the end of this chapter

+

Login to **CourseMate** for **CFIN** at **CengageBrain.com** for additional problems and other study tools!

1-1 What is Finance?

In simple terms, finance is concerned with decisions about money. Financial decisions deal with how money is raised and used by businesses, governments, and individuals. To make sound financial decisions, you must understand three general, yet reasonable, concepts. Everything else equal, (1) more value is preferred to less; (2) the sooner cash is received, the more valuable it is; and (3) less risky assets are more valuable than (preferred to) riskier assets. These concepts are discussed in detail later in the book. At this point, we can state that firms that make decisions with these concepts in mind are able to provide better products to customers at lower prices, pay higher salaries to employees, and still provide greater returns to investors. In general, then, sound financial management contributes to the well-being of both individuals and the general population.

Although the emphasis in this book is on business finance, you will discover that the same concepts that firms apply when making sound business decisions can be used to make informed decisions relating to personal finances. For example, consider the decision you might have to make if you won a state lottery worth ₹54 million. Which *would* you choose: a lump-sum payment of ₹54 million today or a payment of ₹3.5 million each year for the next 30 years? Which *should* you choose? In Chapter 4, we will show the time value of money and techniques that firms use to make business decisions. These same techniques can be used to answer this and other questions that relate to personal finances.

1-1a General Areas of Finance

The study of finance consists of four interrelated areas:

1. ***Financial markets and institutions***—Financial institutions, which include banks, insurance companies, savings and loans, and credit unions, are an integral part of the general financial services marketplace. The success of these organizations requires an understanding of factors that cause interest rates and other returns in the financial markets to rise and fall, regulations that affect such institutions, and various types of financial instruments, such as mortgages, automobile loans, and certificates of deposit, that financial institutions offer.

2. ***Investments***—This area of finance focuses on the decisions made by businesses and individuals as they choose securities for their investment portfolios. The major functions in the investments area are (a) determining the values, risks, and returns associated with such financial assets as stocks and bonds and (b) determining the optimal mix of securities that should be held in a portfolio of investments.

3. ***Financial services***—*Financial services* refer to functions provided by organizations that deal with the management of money. Persons who work in these organizations, which include banks, insurance companies, brokerage firms, and similar companies, provide services that help individuals and companies determine how to invest money to achieve such goals as home purchase, retirement, financial stability and sustainability, budgeting, and so forth.

4. ***Managerial (business) finance***—*Managerial finance* deals with decisions that all firms make concerning their cash flows, including both inflows and outflows. As a consequence, managerial finance is important in all types of businesses, whether they are public or private, and whether they deal with financial services or the manufacture of products. The duties encountered in managerial finance range from making decisions about plant expansions to choosing what types of securities should be issued to finance such expansions. Financial managers also have the responsibility for deciding the credit terms under which customers can buy, how much inventory the firm should carry, how much cash to keep on hand, whether to acquire other firms (merger analysis), and how much of each year's earnings should be paid out as dividends versus how much should be reinvested in the firm.

Although our concern in this book is primarily with managerial finance, because all areas of finance are interrelated, an individual who works in any one area should have a good understanding of the other areas as well. For example, a banker lending to a business must have a basic understanding of managerial finance to judge how well the borrowing company is operated. The same holds true for a securities analyst, who must understand how a firm's current financial position can affect its future prospects and thus its stock price. At the same time, corporate financial managers need to know what their bankers are thinking and how investors are likely to judge their corporations' performances when establishing their stock prices.

1-1b The Importance of Finance in Non-Finance Areas

Everyone is exposed to finance concepts almost every day. For example, when you borrow to buy a car or house, finance concepts are used to determine the monthly payments you are required to make. When you retire, finance concepts are used to determine the amount of the monthly payments you receive from your retirement funds. Further, if you want to start your own business, an understanding of finance concepts is essential for survival. Thus, even if you do not intend to pursue a career in a finance-related profession, it is important that you have some basic understanding of finance concepts. Similarly, if you pursue a career in finance, it is important that you have an understanding of other areas in the

from company to company, the chief financial officer (CFO), who often has the title of vice president of finance, generally reports to the president. The financial vice president's key subordinates are the treasurer and the controller. In most firms, the *treasurer* has direct responsibility for managing the firm's cash and marketable securities, planning how the firm is financed and when funds are raised, managing risk, and overseeing the corporate pension fund. The treasurer also supervises the credit manager, the inventory manager, and the director of capital budgeting, who analyzes decisions related to investments in fixed assets. The *controller* is responsible for the activities of the accounting and tax departments.

1-2 Alternative Forms of Business Organization

There are three major forms of business organization in India: (1) proprietorships, (2) partnerships, and (3) corporations and partnerships (13–14 percent).[1] Because most key areas of business are conducted by corporations, we will focus on that form in this book. However, it is important to understand the differences among the three major forms of business, as well as the popular "hybrid" forms of business that have evolved from these major forms.

1-2a Proprietorship

A **proprietorship** is an unincorporated business owned by one individual. Starting a proprietorship is fairly easy—just begin business operations.

The proprietorship has three important advantages:

1. It is easily and inexpensively formed. Not much "red tape" is involved when starting such a business; generally, only licenses required by the state and the municipality in which the business operates are needed.
2. It is subject to few government regulations. Large firms that potentially threaten competition are much more heavily regulated than small so-called mom-and-pop businesses.
3. It is taxed like an individual, not like a corporation; thus, earnings are taxed only once. The double taxation of dividends is discussed later in the chapter.

The proprietorship also has four important limitations:

1. The proprietor has unlimited personal liability for business debts, because any debts of the business are considered obligations of the sole owner. With unlimited personal liability, the proprietor (owner) can potentially lose all of his or her personal assets, even those assets not invested in the business; thus, losses can far exceed the money that he or she has invested in the company. An explanation of this concept is given later in this chapter.
2. A proprietorship's life is limited to the time the individual who created it owns the business. When a new owner takes over the business, legally the firm becomes a new proprietorship (even if the name of the business does not change).
3. Transferring ownership is somewhat difficult. Disposing of the business is similar to selling a house in that the proprietor must seek out and negotiate with a potential buyer, which generally takes weeks or months to complete.
4. It is difficult for a proprietorship to obtain large sums of capital because the firm's financial strength generally is based only on the financial strength of the sole owner. A proprietorship's funds are derived from the owner's sources of credit, which include his or her credit cards, access to bank loans, loans from relatives and friends, and so forth. Unlike corporations, proprietorships cannot raise funds by issuing stocks and bonds to investors.

For these reasons, individual proprietorships are confined primarily to small business operations. However, most businesses start out as proprietorships and then convert to corporations when their growth causes the disadvantages of being a proprietorship—namely, unlimited personal liability and the inability to raise large sums of money—to outweigh the advantages.

proprietorship An unincorporated business owned by one individual.

[1]The statistics provided in this section are based on business tax filings reported by the Internal Revenue Service (IRS), which can be found on the IRS website at http://www.irs.ustreas.gov/taxstats/.

1-2b Partnership

A **partnership** is the same as a proprietorship, except that it has two or more owners. Partnerships can operate under different degrees of formality, ranging from informal, oral understandings to formal agreements filed with the secretary of the state in which the partnership does business. Most legal experts recommend that partnership agreements be put in writing.

The advantages of a partnership are the same as those of a proprietorship, except that most partnerships have more sources available for raising funds because there are more owners, with more relatives, more friends, and more opportunities to raise funds through credit. Even though they generally have greater capabilities than proprietorships to raise funds to support growth, partnerships still have difficulty in attracting substantial amounts of funds. This is not a major problem for a slow growing business. However, if a business' products really catch on and it needs to raise large amounts of funds to capitalize on its opportunities, the difficulty of attracting funds becomes a real drawback. For this reason, growth companies, such as Microsoft and Dell Computer, generally begin life as proprietorships or partnerships, but at some point find it necessary to convert to corporations.

Under partnership law, each partner is liable for the debts of the business. Therefore, if any partner is unable to meet his or her pro rata claim in the event the partnership goes bankrupt, the remaining partners must make good on the unsatisfied claims, drawing on their personal assets if necessary. Thus, the business-related activities of any of the firm's partners can bring ruin to the other partners, even though those partners are not direct parties to such activities.

1-2c Company

A **company** is a legal entity created by a state, which means that a corporation has the legal authority to act like a person when conducting business. It is separate and distinct from its owners and managers. Companies can be private limited with limited facilities for transfer of shares and calling for subscriptions from the public or public limited companies. The latter is more in vogue and all major ventures requiring huge outlay go in for this form of organization. In view of the large public stake involved, the Companies Act which governs the conduct of companies in India, has strict provisions for disclosure and procedure. This separateness gives the company four major advantages:

1. A company offers its owners *limited liability.* To illustrate the concept of limited liability, suppose you invested ₹10000 to become a partner in a business formed as a partnership that subsequently went bankrupt, owing creditors ₹1 million. Because the owners are liable for the debts of a partnership, as a partner you would be assessed for a share of the company's debt; you could even be held liable for the entire ₹1 million if your partners could not pay their shares. This is the danger of *unlimited liability*. On the other hand, if you invested ₹10000 in the stock of a company that then went bankrupt, your potential loss on the investment would be limited to your ₹10000 investment.[2]
2. Ownership interests can be divided into shares, which can be *transferred far more easily* than can proprietorship or partnership interests. Shares of stock can be bought and sold in minutes, whereas interests in proprietorships and partnerships generally cannot.
3. A company can continue after its original owners and managers no longer have a relationship with the business; thus it is said to have *unlimited life.* The life of a company is based on the longevity of its stock, not the longevity of those who own the stock (the owners).
4. The first three factors—limited liability, easy transferability of ownership interest, and unlimited life—make it much easier for companies than for proprietorships or partnerships to raise money in the financial markets. In addition, company can issue stocks and bonds to raise funds, whereas proprietorships and partnerships cannot.

Even though the corporate form of business offers significant advantages over proprietorships and partnerships, it does have two major disadvantages:

1. Setting up a company, as well as periodic filings of returns stipulated in the Companies Act, is more complex and time-consuming than for a proprietorship or a partner-

partnership An unincorporated business owned by two or more persons.

corporation A legal entity created by a state, separate and distinct from its owners and managers, having unlimited life, easy transferability of ownership, and limited liability.

[2]In the case of small companies, the limited liability feature is often a fiction because bankers and credit managers frequently require personal guarantees from the stockholders of small, weak corporations.

FIGURE 1.1 Value of the Firm

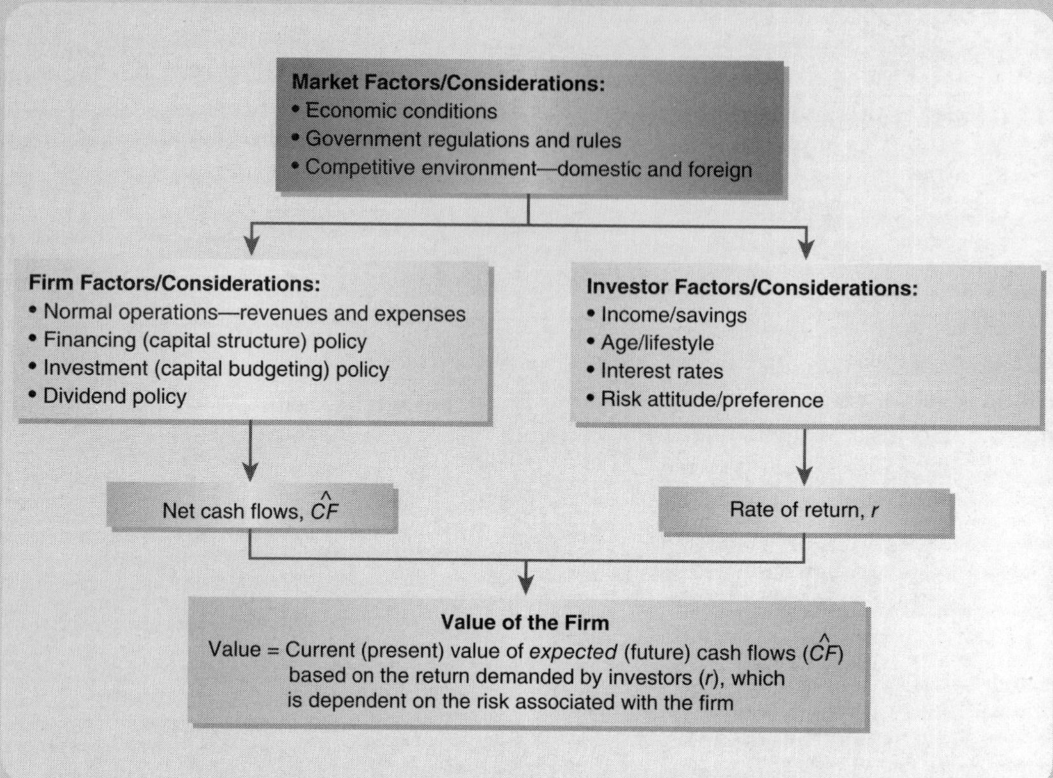

that maximizing earnings in the current period has on either future earnings (timing) or the firm's future risk position.

First, consider the *timing of the earnings*. Suppose a company has a project that will cause earnings per share to rise by ₹0.20 per year for five years, or ₹1 in total, whereas another project would have no effect on earnings for four years but would increase EPS by ₹1.25 in the fifth year. Which project is better? In other words, is ₹0.20 per year for five years better or worse than ₹1.25 in Year 5? The answer depends on which project contributes the most to the value of the firm, which in turn depends on the time value of money to investors. Thus, timing is an important reason to concentrate on wealth as measured by the price of the stock rather than on earnings alone.

Second, consider *risk*. Suppose one project is expected to increase EPS by ₹1, while another is expected to increase earnings by ₹1.2 per share. The first project is not very risky. If it is undertaken, earnings will almost certainly rise by approximately ₹1 per share. However, the other project is quite risky. Although our best guess is that earnings will rise by ₹1.2 per share, we must recognize the possibility that there might be no increase whatsoever or that the firm might even suffer a loss. Depending on how averse stockholders are to risk, the first project might be preferable to the second.

In many instances, firms have taken actions that increased earnings per share, yet the stock price decreased because investors believed that either the higher earnings would not be sustained in the future or the risk level of the firm would be increased substantially. Of course, the opposite effect has been observed as well. We see, then, that the firm's stock price, and thus its value, is dependent on (1) the cash flows the firm is expected to provide in the future, (2) when those cash flows are expected to occur, and (3) the risk associated with those cash flows. As we proceed through the book, you will discover that every significant corporate decision should be analyzed in terms of these factors and their effects on the firm's value, and hence the price of its stock.

1-3c Managers' Roles as Agents of Stockholders

Because they generally are not involved in day-to-day

operations, stockholders of large corporations "permit" (empower) the executives to make decisions about how the firms are run. Of course, the stockholders want the managers to make decisions that are consistent with the goal of wealth maximization. However, managers' interests can potentially conflict with stockholders' interests.

An *agency relationship* exists when one or more individuals, who are called the *principals,* hire another person, the *agent,* to perform a service and delegate decision-making authority to that agent. If a firm is a proprietorship, there is no agency relationship because the owner–manager operates the business in a fashion that will improve his or her own welfare, with welfare measured in the form of increased personal wealth, more leisure, or perquisites.[3] However, if the owner–manager incorporates and sells some of the firm's stock to outsiders, potential conflicts of interest immediately arise. For example, the owner–manager (agent) might now decide not to work as hard to maximize shareholder (principals') wealth because less of the firm's wealth will go to him or her, or he or she might decide to take a higher salary or enjoy more perquisites because part of those costs will fall on the outside stockholders. This potential conflict between two parties—the principals (outside shareholders) and the agents (managers)—is an **agency problem**.

The potential for agency problems is greatest in large corporations with widely dispersed shareholding—because individual stockholders own extremely small proportions of the companies and managers have little, if any, of their own wealth tied up in these companies. For this reason, managers might be more concerned about pursuing their own agendas, such as increased job security, higher salaries, or more power, than about maximizing shareholder wealth.

Mechanisms used by large corporations to motivate managers to act in the shareholders' best interests include:

1. ***Managerial compensation (incentives)***—A common method used to motivate managers to operate in a manner consistent with stock price maximization is to tie managers' compensation to the company's performance. Such compensation packages should be developed so that managers are rewarded on the basis of the firm's performance over a long period of time, not on its performance in any particular year. For example, a company might implement a compensation plan where managers earn 100 percent of a specified reward when the company achieves a targeted growth rate. If the performance is above the target, higher rewards can be earned, whereas managers receive lower rewards when performance is below the target. Often the reward that managers receive is the stock of the company. If managers own stock in the company, they are motivated to make decisions that will increase the firm's value and thus the value of the stock they own.

   All incentive compensation plans should be designed to accomplish two things: (1) Provide inducements to executives to act on those factors under their control in a manner that will contribute to stock price maximization. (2) Attract and retain top-level executives. Well-designed plans can accomplish both goals.

2. ***Shareholder intervention***—A number of wealthy individuals in India invest directly in stocks. Along with such institutional stockholders as pension funds and mutual funds, individual stockholders often "flex their muscles" to ensure that firms pursue goals that are in the best interests of shareholders rather than that of the managers (where conflicts might arise). In addition, many institutional investors routinely monitor top corporations to ensure that managers pursue the goal of wealth maximization. When it is determined that action is needed to realign management decisions with the interests of investors, these institutional investors exercise their influence by suggesting possible remedies to management or by sponsoring proposals that must be voted on by stockholders at the annual meeting. Stockholder sponsored proposals are not binding, but the results of the votes are noticed by corporate management.

   In situations where large blocks of the stock are owned by a relatively few large institutions that have enough clout to influence a firm's operations, these institutional owners often have enough voting power to overthrow management teams that do not act in the best interests of stockholders. Examples of major corporations whose managements have been ousted in past years include Coca-Cola, General Motors, and United Airlines.

3. ***Threat of takeover***—**Hostile takeovers**, instances in which management does not want the firm to be taken over, are most likely

agency problem A potential conflict of interest between outside shareholders (owners) and managers who make decisions about how to operate the firm.

hostile takeover The acquisition of a company over the opposition of its management.

[3]Perquisites (or "perks") are executive fringe benefits, such as luxurious offices, use of corporate planes and yachts, personal assistants, and general use of business assets for personal purposes.

publicly traded, whereas others are privately held.

Like corporations in the United States, most large companies in England and Canada are *open,* which means their stocks are widely dispersed among a large number of different investors, both individuals and institutions. On the other hand, in much of continental Europe, stock ownership is more concentrated; major investor groups include families, banks, and other corporations. In Germany and France, for instance, other domestic companies represent the primary group of shareholders, followed by families. Although banks in these countries do not hold large numbers of shares of stock, they can greatly influence companies because many shareholders assign banks their **proxy votes** for the directors of the companies. In addition, often the family unit has concentrated ownership and thus represents a major influence in many large companies in developed countries such as these. The ownership structures of these firms and many other large non-U.S. companies often are concentrated in the hands of a relatively few investors or investment groups. Such firms are considered *closed* because shares of stock often are not publicly traded, relatively few individuals or groups own the stock, and major stockholders generally are involved in the firms' daily operations.

The primary reason non-U.S. firms are likely to be more closed, and thus have more concentrated ownership, than U.S. firms results from the universal banking relationships that exist outside the United States. Financial institutions in other countries generally are less regulated than in the United States, which means foreign banks can provide businesses with a greater variety of services than U.S. banks can, including short-term loans, long-term financing, and even stock ownership. As a result, non-U.S. firms tend to have close relationships with individual banking organizations that also might take ownership positions in the companies. What this means is that banks in countries like Germany can meet the financing needs of family-owned businesses, even if they are very large. Therefore, such companies do not need to go public, and thus relinquish control in order to finance additional growth. The opposite is true in the United States, where large firms do not have comparable "one-stop" financing outlets. Hence, their growth generally must be financed by bringing in outside owners, which results in more widely dispersed ownership.

proxy votes Voting power that is assigned to another party, such as another stockholder or institution.

industrial groups Organizations of companies in different industries with common ownership interests, which include firms necessary to manufacture and sell products; networks of manufacturers, suppliers, marketing organizations, distributors, retailers, and creditors.

In some parts of the world, firms belong to **industrial groups**, which are organizations composed of companies in different industries that have common ownership interests and, in some instances, shared management. Firms in an industrial group are linked by a major lender, typically a bank, which often also has a significant ownership interest, along with other firms in the group. The objective of an industrial group is to create an organization that ties together all the functions of production and sales from start to finish by including firms that provide the materials and services required to manufacture and sell the group's products. Thus, an industrial group encompasses firms involved in manufacturing, financing, marketing, and distribution of products: suppliers of raw materials, production organizations, retail stores, and creditors. A portion of the stocks of firms that are members of an industrial group might be traded publicly, but the lead company, which is typically a major creditor, controls the management of the entire group. Industrial groups are most prominent in Asian countries. In Japan, an industrial group is called a *keiretsu,* while it is called a *chaebol* in Korea. Well-known *keiretsus* include Mitsubishi, Toshiba, and Toyota, while Hyundai probably is the most recognizable *chaebol*. The success of industrial groups in Japan and Korea has inspired the formation of similar organizations in developing countries in Latin America and Africa as well as in other parts of Asia.

The differences in ownership concentration of non-U.S. firms might cause the behavior of managers, and thus the goals they pursue, to differ. For instance, often it is argued that the greater concentration of ownership of non-U.S. firms permits managers to focus more on long-term objectives, especially wealth maximization, than on short-term earnings, because these firms have easier access to credit in times of financial difficulty. In other words, creditors who also are owners generally have greater interest in supporting both short-term and long-term survival. On the other hand, it also has been argued that the ownership structures of non-U.S. firms create an environment where it is difficult to change managers, especially if they are significant stockholders. Such entrenchment could be detrimental to firms if management is inefficient. Whether the ownership structure of non-U.S. firms is an advantage or a disadvantage is debatable. What we do know is that the greater concentration of ownership in non-U.S. firms permits greater monitoring and control by individuals or groups than do the more dispersed ownership structures of U.S. firms.

In India, the Companies Act and rules framed thereunder have elaborate provisions regarding the following, among other things:

- Name of the company
- The contents and revision of Memorandum of Association
- The contents and revision of Articles of Association
- Procedure for making a public issue of shares
- Transfer of shares from one person to another
- Transmission of shares in the event of the death of the shareholder
- Types of shares and rules thereof
- Distinction between private and public limited companies
- Provisions regarding deemed public companies, when private companies who grow beyond a level are treated as public companies for all practical purposes
- Raising of debt instruments called debentures
- Conduct of general meetings of shareholders
- Conduct of board meetings
- Constitution of the Board of Directors of the company
- Disclosure of accounts by companies
- Audit of accounts of companies
- Payment of dividends
- Buy-back of shares
- Issue of bonus shares
- Complaints from minority shareholder

1-5a Multinational Corporations

Large firms, both in the United States and in other countries, generally do not operate in a single country; rather, they conduct business throughout the world. Because large **multinational companies** are involved in all phases of the production process, from extraction of raw materials, through the manufacturing process, to distribution to consumers throughout the world, managers of such firms face a wide range of issues that are not present when a company operates in a single country.

U.S. and foreign companies "go international" for the following major reasons:

1. ***To seek new markets***—After a company has saturated its home market, growth opportunities often are better in foreign markets. As a result, such home-grown firms as Coca-Cola and McDonald's have aggressively expanded into overseas markets, and foreign firms such as Sony and Toshiba are major competitors in the U.S. consumer electronics market.
2. ***To seek raw materials***—Many U.S. oil companies, such as ExxonMobil, have major subsidiaries around the world to ensure that they have continued access to the basic resources needed to sustain their primary lines of business.
3. ***To seek new technology***—No single nation holds a commanding advantage in all technologies, so companies scour the globe for leading scientific and design ideas. For example, Xerox has introduced more than 80 different office copiers in the United States that were engineered and built by its Japanese joint venture, Fuji Xerox.
4. ***To seek production efficiency***—Companies in countries where production costs are high tend to shift production to low-cost countries. The ability to shift production from country to country has important implications for labor costs in all countries. For example, when Xerox threatened to move its copier rebuilding work to Mexico, its union in Rochester, New York, agreed to work rule and productivity improvements that kept the operation in the United States.
5. ***To avoid political and regulatory hurdles***—Many years ago, Japanese auto companies moved production to the United States to get around U.S. import quotas. Now, Honda, Nissan, and Toyota all assemble automobiles or trucks in the United States. Similarly, one of the factors that prompted U.S. pharmaceutical maker SmithKline and U.K. drug company Beecham to merge in 1989 was the desire to avoid licensing and regulatory delays in their largest markets. Now, GlaxoSmithKline, as the company is known, can identify itself as an inside player in both Europe and the United States.

The substantial growth that has occurred in multinational business during the past few decades has created an increasing degree of mutual influence and interdependence among business enterprises and nations, to which the United States is not immune. Political and social developments

multinational companies Firms that operate in two or more countries.

3. EPS is
   - a. Net income/ Number of shares
   - b. Total sales turnover / Number of shares
   - c. Dividends/ Number of shares
   - d. Both a and c

4. The following aspects differentiate multinational finance from managerial finance
   - a. Cultural differences
   - b. Language differences
   - c. Higher profits
   - d. Both a and c

5. Compared to U.S firms, foreign firms have
   - a. Higher number of owners
   - b. Lower number of owners
   - c. No owners
   - d. None of the above

6. Firms that pursue ethical practices
   - a. Always perform better than other companies in the long run
   - b. Sometimes perform better than other companies
   - c. Make lesser profits
   - d. Have larger number of employees

7. The chief aim of the finance manger ought to be to
   - a. Bring about ethical practices
   - b. Maximize profits
   - c. Both a and b
   - d. None of the above

8. Financial decisions involve
   - a. Profits and cash flows
   - b. Cash flows and ethics
   - c. Profits and ethics
   - d. None of the above

9. Finance and Economics are connected in that
   - a. Many finance theories have evolved from Economics
   - b. Many economic theories have evolved from Finance
   - c. Both a and b
   - d. None of the above

10. Finance is concerned principally with
   - a. Decisions relating to employee welfare
   - b. Decisions relating to shareholder welfare
   - c. Decisions relating to money
   - d. Both a and b

Answers:

1.	(a)	2.	(a)	3.	(a)	4.	(a)	5.	(b)
6.	(a)	7.	(c)	8.	(a)	9.	(c)	10.	(c)

PROBLEMS

For more problems, login to CourseMate for CFIN at CengageBrain.com

1-1 What is finance? What types of decisions do people in finance make?

1-2 Why should persons who pursue careers in business have a basic understanding of finance even if their jobs are in areas other than finance, such as marketing or personnel?

1-3 What does it mean to maximize the value of a corporation?

1-4 In general terms, how is value measured? What three factors determine value? How does each factor affect value?

1-5 What is the difference between stock price maximization and profit maximization? Under what conditions might profit maximization not lead to stock price maximization?

1-6 What are some actions that stockholders can take to ensure that management's interests and those of stockholders coincide? What are some other factors that might influence management's actions?

1-7 If you were the owner of a proprietorship, would you make decisions to maximize the value of your business or your personal satisfaction?

1-8 Suppose you are the president of a large corporation located in Mumbai. How do you think the stockholders will react if you decide to increase the proportion of the company's assets that is financed with debt from 35 percent to 50 percent? In other words, what if the firm used much more debt to finance its assets.

1-9 What is corporate governance? How does corporate governance affect the returns generated for stockholders?

1-10 Why do corporations go international?

1-11 What are the factors that make financial decision making more complicated for firms that operate in foreign countries than for purely domestic firms?

1-12 Describe the four general areas included in the study of finance. Why is it important for a person who works in the financial markets to understand the responsibilities of a person who works in managerial finance?

1-13 Describe the major differences among the three primary forms of business organization (a proprietorship, a partnership, and a corporation).

1-14 Why do you think hybrid forms of business, such as limited liability partnerships and limited liability companies, have evolved over time?

1-15 What does it mean to be ethical in business dealings? Should unethical business behavior be encouraged by business owners (stockholders) if such behavior increases the value of the stock they own in the short term?

CHAPTER 1 REVIEW

Chapter 1 Key Managerial Finance Concepts

- Financial decisions deal with cash flows, both inflows and outflows. To make sound financial decisions, students must understand three general, yet reasonable, concepts. Everything else equal, (1) more value is preferred to less; (2) the sooner cash is received, the more valuable it is; and (3) less risky assets are more valuable than (preferred to) riskier assets.
- The primary goal of the financial manager should be to maximize the value of the firm.
- The managers of a firm are the decision-making agents of its owners (stockholders in a corporation). When managers do not make decisions that are in the best interests of the owners, agency problems exist. Agency problems can be mitigated by rewarding managers for making decisions that help maximize the firm's value.
- Firms that are ethical and have good governance policies generally perform better than firms that are less ethical and have poor governance policies.
- Firms "go international" for a variety of reasons, including to operate in new markets, to search for raw materials, to attain production efficiency, and to avoid domestic regulations.
- Foreign firms generally are less open—that is, have fewer owners (stockholders)—than U.S. firms.

Key Terms

LO.1

proprietorship An unincorporated business owned by one individual. *p. 4*

partnership An unincorporated business owned by two or more persons. *p. 5*

corporation A legal entity created by a state, separate and distinct from its owners and managers, having unlimited life, easy transferability of ownership, and limited liability. *p. 5*

corporate charter A document filed with the secretary of the state in which a business is incorporated that provides information about the company, including its name, address, directors, and amount of capital stock. *p. 6*

bylaws A set of rules drawn up by the founders of the corporation that indicates how the company is to be governed; includes procedures for electing directors, rights of stockholders, and how to change the bylaws when necessary. *p. 6*

limited liability partnership (LLP) A partnership wherein at least one partner is designated as a *general partner* with unlimited personal financial liability, and the other partners are *limited* partners whose liability is limited to amounts they invest in the firm. *p. 6*

limited liability company (LLC) Offers the limited personal liability associated with a corporation; however the company's income is taxed like that of a partnership. *p. 6*

LO.3

stockholder wealth maximization The appropriate goal for management decisions; considers the risk and timing associated with expected cash flows to maximize the price of the firm's common stock. *p. 7*

value The present, or current, value of the cash flows that an asset is expected to generate in the future. *p. 8*

agency problem A potential conflict of interest between outside shareholders (owners) and managers who make decisions about how to operate the firm. *p. 10*

hostile takeover The acquisition of a company over the opposition of its management. *p. 11*

LO.4

business ethics A company's attitude and conduct toward its stakeholders (employees, customers, stockholders, and community). Ethical behavior requires fair and honest treatment of all parties. *p. 11*

corporate governance Deals with the set of rules that a firm follows when conducting business; these rules identify who is accountable for major financial decisions. *p. 12*

stakeholders Those who are associated with a business, including managers, employees, customers, suppliers, creditors, stockholders, and other parties with an interest in the firm's well-being. *p. 12*

LO.5

proxy votes Voting power that is assigned to another party, such as another stockholder or institution. *p. 13*

industrial groups Organizations comprised of companies in different industries with common ownership interests, which include firms necessary to manufacture and sell products; a network of manufacturers, suppliers, marketing organizations, distributors, retailers, and creditors. *p. 13*

multinational companies Firms that operate in two or more countries. *p. 14*

exchange rates The prices at which the currency from one country can be converted into the currencies of other countries. *p. 15*

PART 2

Essential Concepts in Managerial Finance

CHAPTER 2

Analysis of Financial Statements

Learning Outcomes

LO.1 Describe the basic financial information that is produced by corporations and explain how the firm's stakeholders use such information.

LO.2 Describe the financial statements that corporations publish and the information that each statement provides.

LO.3 Describe how ratio analysis should be conducted and why the results of such an analysis are important to both managers and investors.

LO.4 Discuss potential problems (caveats) associated with financial statement analysis.

Tata Steel Ltd. Industry : Steel - Large			
Year ended	Mar 15	Mar 16	Mar 17
Key Ratios			
Debt-Equity Ratio	0.44	0.52	0.61
Long Term Debt-Equity Ratio	0.37	0.42	0.5
Current Ratio	0.54	0.55	0.55
Turnover Ratios			
Fixed Assets	1.13	0.87	0.77
Inventory	6.63	5.63	6.13
Debtors	73.8	52.56	33.93
Interest Cover Ratio	4.14	2.61	3.19
PBIDTM (%)	21.86	18.24	22.77
PBITM (%)	17.57	11.3	16.12
PBDTM (%)	17.62	13.91	17.72
CPM (%)	14.44	9.94	13.77
APATM (%)	10.16	3.0	7.12
ROCE (%)	8.38	5.17	10.01
RONW (%)	7.4	2.26	7.87

SOURCE: http://www.capitaline.com

The above table shows key ratios pertaining to Tata Steel Ltd. The executives and analysts of the company will study the ratios of past few years, as well as compare these with the corresponding ratios of competitors to identify areas for improvement. This chapter explains the computation and the limitations of these ratios.

Financial statement analysis involves evaluation of a firm's financial position to identify its current strengths and weaknesses and to suggest actions that the firm might pursue to take advantage of those strengths and correct any weaknesses to accomplish its goal of wealth maximization. In this chapter, we discuss how to evaluate a firm's current financial position using its financial statements. In later chapters, we examine actions that a firm can take to improve its financial position in the future, thereby increasing the price of its stock.

Study Tools

Problems are found at the end of this chapter

+

Login to **CourseMate** for **CFIN** at **CengageBrain.com** for additional problems and other study tools!

2-1 Financial Reports

Of the various reports that corporations provide to their stockholders, the **annual report** probably is the most important. This report provides two types of information:

1. ***Discussion of operations***—describes the firm's operating results during the past year and discusses new developments that will affect future operations.

2. ***Basic financial statements***—include (a) the balance sheet, (b) the income statement, (c) the statement of cash flows, and (d) the statement of retained earnings. Taken together, these statements give an accounting picture of the firm's operations and its financial position. Detailed data are provided for the two most recent years, along with historical summaries of key operating statistics for the past five to 10 years.[1]

The quantitative and verbal information contained in the annual report are equally important. The financial statements indicate what actually happened to the firm's financial position and to its earnings and dividends over the past few years, whereas the verbal statements attempt to explain why things turned out the way they did and how management expects the firm to perform in the future. To illustrate how annual reports can prove helpful, we will use data taken from Ashok Leyland Limited.

2-2 Financial Statements

Before we analyze how Ashok Leyland's financial position compares to other firms, let's take a look at the financial statements the company publishes.

annual report A report issued by a corporation to its stockholders that contains basic financial statements, as well as the opinions of management about the past year's operations and the firm's future prospects.

balance sheet A statement that shows the firm's financial position—assets and liabilities and equity—at a specific point in time.

2-2a The Balance Sheet

The **balance sheet** represents a picture taken *at a specific point in time (date)* that shows a firm's assets and how those assets are financed (debt or equity). Figure 2.1 shows the general set up for a simple balance sheet. Table 2.1 shows Ashok Leyland's balance sheets on March 31 for the years 2014 and 2015. March 31 is the end of the financial year, which is when the company "takes a snapshot" of its existing assets, liabilities, and owners' equity to construct the balance sheet. In this section, we concentrate on the more recent balance sheet—that is, March 31, 2015.

Assets, which represent the firm's investments, are classified as either short term (current) or long term (see Figure 2.1). Current assets generally include items that the firm expects to liquidate and thus convert into cash within one year, whereas long-term, or fixed assets include investments that help generate cash flows over longer periods.

To finance its assets, a firm uses debt, equity (stock), or both forms of financing. Debt represents the loans the firm has outstanding, and it generally is divided into two categories—short-term debt and long-term debt (see Figure 2.1). Short-term debt, which is labelled "current liabilities," represents debt that is due to be paid off within one year, and includes accounts payable (amounts owed to suppliers), accruals (amounts owed to employees and state and federal governments), and notes payable (amounts owed to banks).

Equity represents stockholders' ownership, which, unlike debt, does not have to be paid off. Total equity is the amount that would be paid to stockholders if the firm's assets could be sold at the values reported on the balance sheet and its debt could be paid off in the amounts reported on the balance sheet. Thus, the company's **common stockholders' equity**, or **net worth**, equals total assets minus total liabilities.

Note that in Table 2.1, the assets are listed in the descending order of their liquidity, or the length of time it typically takes to convert them to cash. The claims (liabilities and equity) are listed in the order in which they must be paid. For example, accounts payable generally must be paid within 30 to 45 days, accruals are payable within 60 to 90 days, and so on, right up to the stockholders' equity accounts, which represent ownership that never needs to be repaid.

FIGURE 2.1 Simple Balance Sheet Format

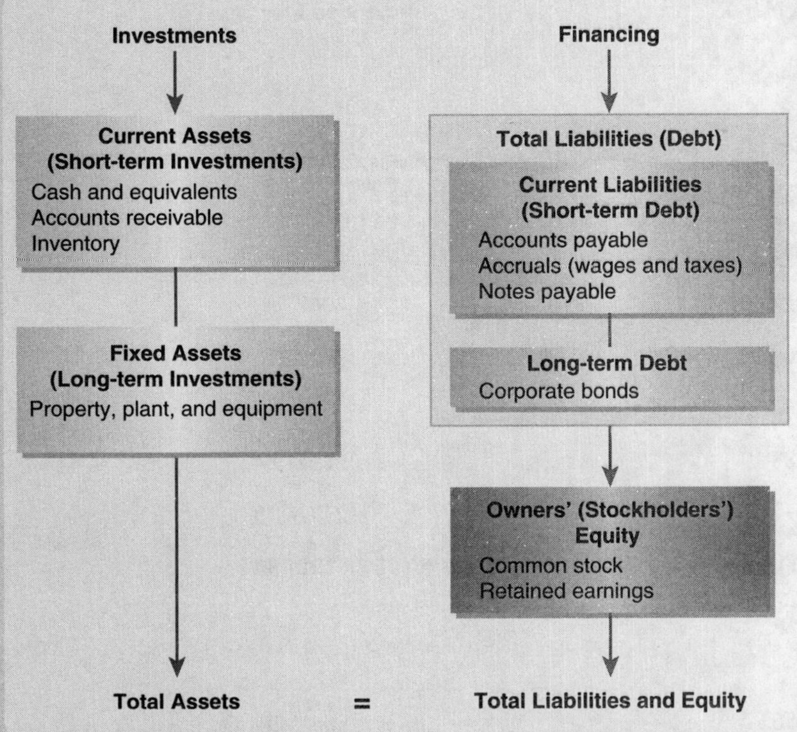

Some additional points about the balance sheet are worth noting.

1. ***Cash and equivalents versus other assets***—Although the assets are all stated in terms of rupees, only the "Cash and equivalents" account represents actual money that can be spent. The other noncash assets should produce cash over time, but they do not represent cash in hand. The amount of cash they would bring in if sold today could be either higher or lower than the values that are reported on the balance sheet.

2. ***Accounting alternatives***—Not every firm uses the same method to determine the account balances shown on the balance sheet. Accounting standards insist that these are uniform across the years so that comparison becomes easy.

   In some cases, a company might use one accounting method to construct financial statements provided to stockholders and another accounting method for tax purposes, internal reports, and so forth. For example, a company generally uses the most accelerated method permissible to calculate depreciation for tax purposes because accelerated methods lower taxable income in the early years of the asset's life, which means lower taxes are paid. The same company might use straight-line depreciation for constructing financial statements reported to stockholders because this method results in a higher net income. There is nothing illegal or unethical about this practice, but when evaluating firms, users of financial statements must be aware that more than one accounting alternative is available for constructing financial statements.

3. ***Breakdown of the common equity account***—The equity section of Ashok Leyland 's balance sheet contains two accounts: common stock and retained earnings. The amount shown in the **retained earnings** account effectively represents the total amount of income that was saved and reinvested in assets rather than was paid out as dividends since the firm started business. According to Table 2.1, Ashok Leyland has kept ₹48341.06 million of all the income generated presently and in the past as reserve. This amount could have been paid to stockholders as dividends over the years, but Ashok Leyland instead decided to use these funds to finance growth in assets.

   The common equity section might include three accounts: common stock at par, paid-in capital, and retained earnings. For example, if Ashok Leyland's common stock had a par value equal to Re.1 per share, then the funds raised through the stock issue would have to be reported in two accounts: "Common stock at par" and "Paid-in capital". The amount reported in the "Common stock at par" account would equal the

common stockholders' equity (net worth) The funds provided by common stockholders—common stock, paid-in capital, and retained earnings.

retained earnings The portion of the firm's earnings that have been reinvested in the firm rather than paid out as dividends.

TABLE 2.1 Balance Sheet of Ashok Leyland

₹ in Millions	Year ended Mar 15 Amount	Year ended Mar 14
Sources Of Funds		
Common stock	2845.88	2660.68
Reserves	48341.06	41818.16
Long-term borrowings	25663.36	32965.05
Defered tax liabilities	5102.669	4067.669
Other long term liabilities	20.604	23.712
Long term provisions	786.136	678.662
Accounts payables	28283.19	22141.54
Other Current liabilities	22072.01	23724.48
Total Liabilities	**133114.9**	**128080**
Application Of Funds		
Fixed Assets:	53756.97	58413.94
Non-current Investments	22403.81	24053.11
Long-term Advances	9829.176	10014.63
Other Non-current Assets	194.996	330.899
Current Investments	4084.52	3843.748
Inventories	13985.27	11887.03
Accounts Receivable	12576.93	12990.11
Cash and Bank Balance	7512.879	116.906
Short-term Advances	5688.217	4720.134
Other Current Assets	3082.139	1709.45
Total Assets	133114.9	128080
Market price as on March 31, 2015	₹76.1	

Source: http:// www.capitaline.com

total value of the stock issue stated in terms of its par value, and it would be computed as follows:

The breakdown of the common equity accounts shows whether the company actually earned the funds reported in its equity accounts or generated the funds mainly from selling (issuing) stock. This information is important to both creditors and stockholders. For instance, a potential creditor would be interested in the amount of money that the owners (stockholders) put up, and stockholders would want to know the form of stockholders' funds.

$$\begin{aligned} \text{Common stock at par} &= \text{Total shares issued} \times \text{Per share par value} \\ &= 2845.88 \text{ million shares} \times \text{Re.}1 \\ &= ₹2845.88 \text{ million} \end{aligned}$$

4. ***Book values versus market values***—The values, or accounting numbers, that are reported on the balance sheet are called *book values*, and they are generated using generally accepted accounting principles (GAAP). In many cases, the book values of the assets are not the same as the prices (values) for which they can actually be sold in the marketplace. For instance, when Ashok Leyland bought its assets at various points of time during its life, the value of the assets originally was to the tune of ₹81360 million. Today, the book value of the fixed assets is ₹53756.96 million.

   The **book values** of assets often are not equal to their **market values**, especially long-term assets. On the other hand, because most debt represents a contractual obligation to pay a certain amount at a specific time, the book values of a firm's debt generally are either equal to or very close to the market values of the firm's liabilities. The equity section of the balance sheet, which represents the book value of the firm's equity, must equal the book value of assets minus the book value of liabilities (see Figure 2.1).
5. ***The time dimension***—The balance sheet can be thought of as a snapshot of the firm's financial position *at a particular point in time*. The balance sheet changes every day as inventories are increased or decreased, as fixed assets are added or retired, as liabilities are incurred or paid off, and so on. Companies whose businesses are seasonal, experience especially large changes in their balance sheets during the year. As a result, firms' balance sheets will change over the year, depending on the date on which the statements are constructed.

2-2b The Income Statement

The **income statement**, which is also referred to as the *profit and loss statement*, presents the results of business operations *during a specified period of time* such as a quarter or a year. It summarizes the revenues generated and the expenses incurred by the firm during the accounting period. Table 2.2 gives the 2014 and 2015 income statements for Ashok Leyland. Net sales are shown at the top of the statement, followed by various costs, including income taxes, which are subtracted to determine the net income (earnings) available to common stockholders. A report on earnings and dividends per share appears at the bottom of the statement. In managerial finance, earnings per share (EPS) is called "the bottom line" because EPS is often considered the most important item on the income statement. Ashok Leyland earned ₹1.20 per share in 2015.

Should Firms with Identical Assets/Operations Report the Same Net Income?

The obvious answer is yes. However, although two firms have identical operating structures—that is, facilities, employees, and production methods—they might be financed differently. For example, one firm might be financed with a substantial amount of debt, whereas the other firm is financed only with stock. Interest payments to debt holders are tax deductible; while dividend payments to stockholders are not. The firm that is financed with debt will have greater tax-deductible expenses as a result of the interest expense and thus will report a lower net income than the firm that is financed with equity only. For this reason, when comparing the operations of two firms, analysts often examine the *net operating income (NOI)*, also known as the *earnings before interest and taxes (EBIT)*, because this figure represents the result of normal operations before considering the effects of the firm's financing choices (financial structure). Ashok Leyland's EBIT was ₹8357 million in 2015. A firm that has the same operating structure (and follows the same accounting procedures) as Ashok Leyland should have reported EBIT around the same level, even if it does not use the same amount of debt as Ashok Leyland does to finance its assets.

Does Net Income Determine Value?

Investors often focus on the net income when determining how well a firm has performed during a particular time period. However, *if investors are concerned with whether management is pursuing the goal of maximizing the firm's stock price, net in-*

book values Amounts reported in financial statements—accounting numbers.

market values Values of items—asset, liability, and equity—in the marketplace outside the firm.

income statement A statement summarizing the firm's revenues and expenses over an accounting period, generally a quarter or a year.

TABLE 2.2 Profit & Loss account of Ashok Leyland in ₹ in Millions

	Year ended Mar 15	Year ended Mar 14
Income		
Sales Turnover	135621.84	99434.27
Other Income	1244.71	1161.95
Total Income	136866.55	100596.22
Expenditure		
Cost of Materials	86266.35	59096.95
Traded Goods Purchased	13911.87	12690.28
Changes in Invenotry	–526.13	4238.71
Employee Cost	11840.04	9996.72
Depreciation	4163.37	3770.36
Other Expenses	13863.36	12242.74
Interest	3935.08	4529.25
Total Expenses	133453.94	106565.00
PBDIT	11511.05	2330.83
Depreciation	–4163.37	-3770.36
Exceptional Items	1009.36	5056.59
EBIT	8357.04	3617.06
Interest	–3935.08	–4529.25
Profit Before Tax	4421.97	–912.19
Tax	–1073.91	1206.00
Net Profit (PAT)	3348.06	293.81
Equity Dividend	1280.60	0.00
Corporate Dividend Tax	260.70	0.00
Per Share Data (annualized)	0.00	0.00
Shares in Issue (Millions)	2845.88	2660.68
Earning Per Share (₹)	1.20	0.11

Source: http:// www.capitaline.com

come might not be the appropriate measure to examine.

Recall from your accounting courses that, for most corporations, the income statement is generated using both the accrual method of accounting and the matching principle. That is, revenues are recognized when they are earned, not when the cash is received, and expenses are recognized when they are incurred, not when the cash is paid. As a result, not all of the amounts shown on the income statement represent cash flows. However, as we mentioned in Chapter 1, the value of an investment, such as the firm's stock price, is determined by the cash flows it generates. Therefore, although the firm's net income is important, cash flows are even more important because cash is needed to continue normal business operations, including the payment of financial obligations, the purchase of assets, and the payment of dividends. As a result, in finance we focus on *cash flows* rather than net income.

One item on Ashok Leyland's income statement that we know is a noncash item is *depreciation*. The cash payment for a fixed asset, such as a building, occurs when the asset is originally purchased. However, because the asset is used to generate revenues and its life extends for more than one year, depreciation is the method that is used to match the expense associated with the decrease in the value of an asset to the years in which revenues are generated by its use. For example, Table 2.2 shows that Ashok Leyland's net income for 2015 was ₹ 3348 million and the depreciation expense for the year was ₹4163 million. Depreciation was not an expense that required a cash payment during the year. Ashok Leyland's net cash flow must be higher than the Profit After Tax that is reported as net income. If the only noncash item on its income statement is depreciation, then the net cash flow that Ashok Leyland generated in 2015 was ₹7511 lakh.

When a firm sells all of its products for cash and pays cash for all of the expenses reported on its income statement except depreciation and amortization, its net cash flow can be computed using Equation 2.1:

= ₹3348 million + ₹4163 million
= ₹ 7511 million

Managers and analysts often use this equation to estimate the net cash flow generated by a firm, even when some customers have not paid for their purchases or the firm has not paid all of the bills for supplies, employees' salaries, and the like. In such cases, Equation 2.1 often is used to get a rough estimate of the firm's net cash flow. To get a better estimate of net cash flow, as well as to examine in detail which of the firm's actions provided cash and which actions used cash, a statement of cash flows should be constructed. We discuss the statement of cash flows in the next section.

For our purposes, it is useful to divide cash flows into two categories: (1) operating cash flows and (2) other cash flows. **Operating cash flows** arise from normal operations, and they represent, in essence, the difference between cash collections and cash expenses, including taxes paid, that are associated with the manufacture and sale of inventory. Other cash flows arise from borrowing, from the purchase or sale of fixed assets, from the sale or repurchase of common stock, and from paying dividends. Our focus here is on operating cash flows.

We know that operating cash flows can differ from **accounting profits** (or operating income) when a firm sells on credit, some operating expenses are not cash costs, or both situations occur. For example, we know that depreciation and amortization expenses represent costs that do not use cash in the current period. For this reason, analysts often compute a firm's *earnings before interest, taxes, depreciation, and amortization (EBITDA)* when evaluating its operations. Because both depreciation, which recognizes the decline in the values of tangible assets (buildings, equipment, and so forth), and amortization, which recognizes the decline in the values of intangible assets (patents, trademarks, and so forth) are noncash expenses, EBITDA provides an indication of the cash flows that are generated by normal operations. Ashok Leyland's EBITDA was ₹12520 million in 2015. This is higher than the reported EBIT of ₹8357 million because the depreciation expense was ₹4163 million. Ashok Leyland has no amortization expense.

2-2c Statement of Cash Flows

The **statement of cash flows** is designed to show how the firm's operations have affected its cash position by

2.1

Net cash flow = Net income + Depreciation and amortization

operating cash flows Those cash flows that arise from normal operations; the difference between cash collections and cash expenses associated with the manufacture and sale of inventory.

accounting profits A firm's net income as reported on its income statement.

examining the firm's investment decisions (uses of cash) and financing decisions (sources of cash). The information contained in the statement of cash flows can help answer questions such as the following: Is the firm generating the cash needed to purchase additional fixed assets for growth? Does it have excess cash flows that can be used to repay debt or to invest in new products? Because this information is useful for both financial managers and investors, the statement of cash flows is an important part of the annual report.

Constructing a statement of cash flows involves looking at individual items in the balance sheet and working with the changes in this in the current year compared to those in the previous year. In many companies, some of the reported revenues have not been collected, and some of the reported expenses have not been paid at the time the income statement is constructed. To adjust the estimate of cash flows obtained from the income statement and account for cash flow effects not reflected in the income statement, we need to examine the changes in the balance sheet accounts during the period in question. To accomplish this, we look at the changes in the balance sheet accounts from the beginning to the end of the year to identify which items provided cash (*sources*) and which items used cash (*uses*) during the year. To determine whether a change in a balance sheet account was a source of cash or a use of cash, we follow these simple rules:

Sources of Cash	Uses of Cash
Increase in a Liability or Equity Account	***Decrease in a Liability or Equity Account***
Borrowing funds or selling stock provides cash.	Paying off a loan or buying back stock uses cash.
Decrease in an Asset Account	***Increase in an Asset Account***
Selling inventory or collecting receivables provides cash.	Buying fixed assets or buying more inventory uses cash.

The cash flow effect shown in Table 2.3 is classified as resulting from (1) operations, (2) long-term investments, or (3) financing activities. Operating cash flows are those associated with the production and sale of goods and services. The estimate of cash flows obtained from the income statement is the primary operating cash flow, but changes in accounts payable, accounts receivable, inventories, and accruals are also classified as operating cash flows because these accounts are directly affected by the firm's day-to-day operations. Investment cash flows arise from the purchase or sale of plant, property, or equipment. Financing cash inflows result when the firm issues debt or common stock; financing cash outflows occur when the firm pays dividends, repays debt (loans), or repurchases stock. The cash inflows and outflows from these three activities are summed to determine their effect on the firm's liquidity position, which is measured by the change in the cash and equivalents account from one year to the next.

TABLE 2.3 Ashok Leyland Limited Statement of cash flows for the period ended 31st March, 2015 (₹ In Millions)

Cash Flows from Operating Activities	
Additions	
Increase in accounts payable	6141.65
Increase in other current liabilities	-1652.48
Increase in long-term provisions	107.47
Subtractions	
Increase in accounts receivable	-413.18
Increase in inventory	2098.24
Increase in other non-current assets	-135.90
Increase in short-term advances	968.08
Increase in other current assets	1372.69
	0.00
NET cash flow from operating activites	706.72
Cash flow from Investing actvities	
Additions	
Decrease in fixed assets	4656.98
Decrease in long-term advances	185.45
Decrease in non-current investments	1649.30
Subtractions	
Less: increase in current investment	240.77
NET flow from investing activities	6250.96
Cash flow from Financing actvities	
Additions	
Increase in common stock	185.20
Increase in long-term borrowings	-7301.69
Increase in deferred tax liabilities	1035.00
Increase in long-term liabilities	-3.11
Increase in reserves	6522.90
Net flow from financing activities	438.30
Total flow from all activities	7395.98
Add opening balance of cash	116.91
Results in our getting	
Closing balance of cash	7512.89

Source: http:// www.capitaline.com

2-3 Financial Statement (Ratio) Analysis

As we discovered in previous sections, financial statements provide information about a firm's position at a specific point in time, as well as its operations over some past period. Nevertheless, the real value of financial statements lies in the fact that they can be used to help predict the firm's financial position in the future and to determine expected earnings and dividends. From an investor's standpoint, *predicting the future is the purpose of financial statement analysis;* from management's standpoint, *financial statement analysis is useful both as a way to anticipate future conditions and, more importantly, as a starting point for planning actions that will influence the firm's future course of events.*

The first step in a financial analysis typically includes an evaluation of the firm's ratios, which are designed to show relationships between financial statement accounts *within* firms and *between* firms. Translating accounting numbers into relative values, or *ratios*, allows us to compare the financial position of one firm with the financial position of another firm, even if their sizes are significantly different.

Table 2.4 shows the solutions for various ratios for Ashok Leyland in 2015. In this section, we discuss the five categories of ratios shown in this table and evaluate Ashok Leyland 's financial results in relation to the industry averages. Note that all rupee amounts used in the ratio calculations given in the table are in millions, except where per-share values are used. Also note that there are literally hundreds of ratios that are used by management, creditors, and stockholders to evaluate firms; we show only a few of the most-often used ratios in Table 2.4.

2-3a Liquidity Ratios

A **liquid asset** is one that can be easily converted to cash without significant loss of its original value. Converting assets—especially current assets such as inventory and receivables—to cash is the primary means by which a firm obtains the funds needed to pay its current bills. Therefore, a firm's *liquidity position* deals with the question of how well the company is able to meet its current obligations, which include amounts owed to suppliers (accounts payable), amounts owed to employees (wages payable), and so forth. Short-term, or *current*, assets are more easily converted to cash (more liquid) than are long-term assets. In general, then, one firm is considered more liquid than another firm if it has a greater proportion of its total assets in the form of current assets.

According to its balance sheet, Ashok Leyland has current liabilities totaling ₹50355.20 million that must be paid off within the coming year. Will it have trouble satisfying those obligations? A full liquidity analysis requires the use of cash budgets (described in Chapter 15). Nevertheless, by relating the amount of cash and other current assets to the firm's current obligations, ratio analysis provides a quick, easy-to-use measure of liquidity. Two commonly used **liquidity ratios** are discussed next.

$$\textbf{Current ratio} = \frac{\textbf{Current assets}}{\textbf{Current liabilities}}$$

Current assets normally include cash and equivalents, accounts receivable, and inventories, and current liabilities consist of accounts payable, short-term notes payable, long-term debt that matures in the current period (current maturities of long-term debt), accrued taxes, and other accrued expenses (principally wages). Because the current ratio provides the best single indicator of the extent to which the claims of short-term creditors are covered by assets that are expected to be converted to cash fairly quickly, it is the most commonly used measure of short-term solvency. When a company experiences financial difficulty, it pays its bills (e.g., accounts payable) more slowly, borrows more from its bank, and so forth. If current liabilities are rising more rapidly than current assets, the current ratio will fall, which could spell trouble.

$$\textbf{Quick ratio} = \frac{\textbf{Current assets- Inventories}}{\textbf{Current liabilities}}$$

Inventories typically are the least liquid of a firm's current assets, so they are the assets on which losses are most likely to occur in the event of an "emergency" liquidation. Therefore, having a measure of the firm's ability to pay off short-term obligations without relying on the sale of inventories is important.

Evaluation. Evaluation of ratios is done based on two parameters

liquid asset An asset that can be easily converted into cash without significant loss of the amount originally invested.

liquidity ratios Ratios that show the relationship of a firm's cash and other current assets to its current liabilities; they provide an indication of the firm's ability to meet its current obligations.

TABLE 2.4 Ashok leyland Ltd.
Summary of Financial Ratios

Ratio	Formula for calculation	Ratio value
Curent	Current Assets/Current liabilities	0.86
Quick	(Current assets -Inventory)/Current liabilities	0.57
Inventory turnover	Cost of goods sold/Inventory	7.16
DSO	Receivables /(Sales/360)	33.38
Fixed assets turnover	Sales/Fixed Assets	2.52
Total assets turnover	Sales/Total Assets	1.02
Debt ratio	Debt/Total Assets	0.61
TIE	EBIT/Interest	2.12
Net profit margin	PAT/Sales	2.47%
ROA	PAT/Total Assets	2.52%
ROE	PAT/Total Equity	6.54%

- the comparison with similar ratios on a year to year basis, as well as comparison with the industry average or the corresponding figures of the closest competitor.

2-3b Asset Management Ratios

Firms invest in assets to generate revenues both in the current period and in future periods. To purchase their assets, Ashok Leyland and other companies must borrow or obtain funds from other sources. If firms have too many assets, their interest expenses will be too high; hence, their profits will be depressed. On the other hand, because production is affected by the capacity of assets, if assets are too low, profitable sales might be lost due to the firm's inability to manufacture enough products.

Asset management ratios measure how effectively the firm is managing its assets. These ratios are designed to answer the following question: Does the total amount of each type of asset as reported on the balance sheet seem reasonable, too high, or too low in view of current and projected sales levels? A few asset management ratios are discussed in this section.

$$\textbf{Inventory turnover} = \frac{\textbf{Cost of goods sold}}{\textbf{Inventory}}$$

provides an indication of how well the firm is managing its inventory.[2] On average, each item of Ashok Leyland's inventory is sold and restocked, or turned over, 7.16 times per year (approximately every 51 days).

asset management ratios A set of ratios that measure how effectively a firm is managing its assets.

You should use care when calculating and using the inventory turnover ratio, because purchases of inventory (and thus the cost of goods sold) occur over the entire year, whereas the inventory figure applies to one point in time (perhaps March 31). For this reason, it is better to use an average inventory measure.[3] If the firm's business is highly seasonal, or if a strong upward or downward sales trend has occurred during the year, it is essential to make such an adjustment. To maintain comparability with industry averages, however, we did not use the average inventory figure in our computations.

$$\textbf{Days Sales outstanding (DSO)} = \frac{\textbf{Accounts receivable}}{\textbf{[Annual sales/360]}}$$

also called the *average collection period (ACP)*, is used to evaluate the firm's ability to collect its credit sales

[2] *Turnover* is a term that originated many years ago with the old Yankee peddler, who would load up his wagon with goods, then go off on his route to peddle his wares. The merchandise was his working capital because it was what he actually sold, or turned over, to produce his profits. His turnover was the number of trips that he took each year. Annual sales divided by inventory equaled turnover, or trips per year. If the peddler made 10 trips per year, stocked 100 pans, and made a gross profit of ₹5 per pan, his annual gross profit would be 100 × ₹5 × 10 = ₹5,000. If the peddler went faster and made 20 trips per year, his gross profit would double, if other things held constant.

[3] Preferably, the average inventory value should be calculated by dividing the sum of the monthly figures during the year by 12. If monthly data are not available, you could add the beginning-of-year and end-of-year figures and divide by 2; this calculation will adjust for growth but not for seasonal effects.

[4] To compute DSO using this equation, we must assume that all of the firm's sales are on credit. We usually compute DSO in this manner because information on credit sales is rarely available. Because not all firms have the same percentage of credit sales, the days sales outstanding could be misleading. Also, note that by convention, much of the financial community uses 360 rather than 365 as the number of days in the year for purposes such as this. The DSO is discussed further in Chapters 14 and 15.

in a timely manner.[4] The DSO represents the average length of time that the firm must wait after making a credit sale before receiving cash—that is, its average collection period. Ashok Leyland has about 33 days of sales outstanding,

$$\textbf{Fixed assets turnover} = \frac{\textbf{Sales}}{\textbf{Net fixed assets}}$$

measures how effectively the firm uses its plant and equipment to help generate sales. Ashok Leyland's of 2.52 × appears reasonable.

$$\textbf{Total assets turnover} = \frac{\textbf{Sales}}{\textbf{Total assets}}$$

measures the turnover of all of the firm's assets. Ashok Leyland's ratio is 1.02. To become more efficient, Ashok Leyland might consider increasing its sales, disposing some assets, or pursuing a combination of these steps.

Evaluation Again, a true evaluation of these ratios will be based on past performance on one side and performance of competitors on the other side.

2-3c **Debt Management Ratios**

The extent to which a firm uses debt financing has three important implications:

1. By raising funds through debt, the firm avoids diluting stockholder ownership.
2. Creditors look to the equity, or owner-supplied funds, to provide a margin of safety. If the stockholders have provided only a small proportion of the total financing, the risks of the enterprise are borne mainly by its creditors.
3. If the firm earns more on investments financed with borrowed funds than it pays in interest, the return on the owners' capital is magnified, or *leveraged.*

© iStockphoto.com/danleap

Financial leverage, or borrowing, affects the expected rate of return realized by stockholders for two reasons. First, the interest on debt is tax deductible, whereas dividends are not, so paying interest lowers the firm's tax bill, everything else being equal. Second, if the firm has healthy operations, it typically invests the funds it borrows at a rate of return that is greater than the interest rate on its debt. In combination with the tax advantage that debt offers compared to stock, the higher investment rate of return produces a magnified positive return to the stockholders. Under these conditions, leverage works to the advantage of the firm and its stockholders. Unfortunately, however, financial leverage is a double-edged sword. When the firm experiences poor business conditions, typically sales are lower and costs are higher than expected, but the cost of borrowing, which generally is contractually fixed, still must be paid. Therefore, the required interest payments might impose a very significant burden on a firm that has liquidity problems. In fact, if the interest payments are high enough, a firm with a positive operating income could end up with a negative return to stockholders. Under these conditions, leverage works to the detriment of the firm and its stockholders.

In general, then, we can conclude that firms with relatively high debt ratios have higher expected returns when business is normal or good but are exposed to risk of loss when business is poor. Conversely, firms with low debt ratios are less risky, but they also forgo the opportunity to leverage up their returns on equity. The prospects of high returns are desirable, but the average investor is averse to risk. Therefore, decisions about the use of debt require firms to balance the desire for higher expected returns against the increased risk that results from using more debt. Determining the optimal amount of debt for a given firm is a complicated process, and we will defer discussion of this topic until Chapter 12. Here, we will simply look at two procedures that analysts use to examine the firm's debt in a financial statement analysis: (1) examining balance sheet ratios to determine the extent to which borrowed funds have been used to finance assets and (2) evaluating income statement ratios to determine how

financial leverage The use of debt financing.

well operating profits can cover fixed charges such as interest. These two sets of ratios are complementary, so analysts use both types. A few **debt management ratios** are discussed next.

$$\textbf{Debt ratio} = \frac{\textbf{Total liabilities}}{\textbf{Total assets}}$$

measures the percentage of the firm's assets financed by borrowing (loans). Total liabilities (debt) includes both current liabilities and long-term debt. Creditors prefer low debt ratios, because the lower the ratio, the greater the cushion against creditors' losses in the event of liquidation of the firm. The owners, on the other hand, can benefit from leverage because it magnifies earnings, thereby increasing the return to stockholders. However, too much debt often leads to financial difficulty, which eventually could cause bankruptcy.

$$\textbf{Times interest earned (TIE)} = \frac{\textbf{EBIT}}{\textbf{Interest charges}}$$

measures the extent to which a firm's operating earnings—before interest and taxes (EBIT), also called *net operating income (NOI)*—, can decline before these earnings are no longer sufficient to cover annual interest costs. Failure to meet this obligation can bring legal action by the firm's creditors, possibly resulting in bankruptcy. Note that EBIT, rather than net income, is used in the numerator because interest is paid with pre-tax rupees.

Evaluation. In evaluating Ashok Leyland's leverage levels, one should examine the standard level of borrowing in the industry as well as the extent of borrowing that Ashok Leyland has had over the years.

2-3d Profitability Ratios

Profitability is the net result of a number of policies and decisions. The ratios examined thus far provide some information about the way the firm is operating, but the **profitability ratios** discussed in this section show the combined effects of liquidity management, asset management, and debt management on operating results.

debt management ratios Ratios that provide an indication of how much debt the firm has and whether the firm can take on more debt.

profitability ratios A group of ratios showing the effect of liquidity, asset management, and debt management on operating results

market value ratios A set of ratios that relate the firm's stock price to its earnings and book value per share.

$$\textbf{Net profit margin} = \frac{\textbf{Net profit}}{\textbf{Sales}}$$

measures the profit (earnings) per rupee of sales.

$$\textbf{Return on total assets (ROA)} = \frac{\textbf{Net income}}{\textbf{Total assets}}$$

measures how effectively the firm uses its assets and provides an indication of the return that the firm generates on its investment in assets; that is, the average return that is generated on funds provided by all shareholders (both creditors and stockholders).

$$\textbf{Return on equity (ROE)} = \frac{\textbf{Net income}}{\textbf{Common equity}},$$

or the *rate of return on stockholders' investment*, measures the return that the firm generates on the funds provided only by common stockholders (the owners of the firm).

Evaluation. Ashok Leyland's net profit margin of 2.47 percent does not appear to be high enough. It may be that the liquidity position and overall asset usage had a say in the profitability figures.

2-3e Market Value Ratios

The **market value ratios** relate the firm's stock price to its earnings and book value per share. These ratios give management an indication of what *investors* think of the company's future prospects based on its past performance. If the firm's liquidity ratios, asset management ratios, debt management ratios, and profitability ratios are all good, then its market value ratios will be high and its stock price will probably be as high as can be expected. Of course, the opposite also is true.

$$\textbf{Price/Earning (P/E) ratio} = \frac{\textbf{Market price per share}}{\textbf{Earnings per share}}$$

shows how much investors are willing to pay for the firm's stock for each rupee of reported profits. Ashok Leyland's shares had a price of ₹76.10 in March, 2015. Taking this figure as the basis, the EPS of 1.20 translates to a PE ratio of 63.42.

If other things hold constant, P/E ratios are higher for firms with high growth prospects and lower for riskier firms.

$$\textbf{Market/Book (M/B)} = \frac{\textbf{Market price per share}}{\textbf{Book value per share}}$$

gives another indication of how investors regard the company. The stocks of companies with relatively high rates of return on equity generally sell at higher multiples of book value than do those with low returns.

Evaluation. Ashok Leyland's M/B ratio is calculated as the market value per one share divided by the net worth for one share. The market value per share has been taken as ₹76.10 based on the highest price in March, 2015. The net worth of ₹51186 million when divided by 2846 million shares of the company gives a per share book value of ₹17.99.

Thus, the market to book ratio comes to be (76.10/17.99), i.e., 4.23. One approach used to determine the direction in which a firm is headed is to evaluate the trends of the ratios over the past few years and thereby answer the following question: Is the firm's financial position improving or deteriorating?

2-3f Comparative Ratios (Benchmarking) and Trend Analysis

Our analysis of Ashok Leyland 's ratios indicates that the firm's current financial position is poor compared to the industry norm. The type of analysis we completed in the previous sections is called **comparative ratio analysis**—that is, the ratios calculated for Ashok Leyland were compared with those of other firms in the same industry at the same point in time.[10] Comparative ratio analysis indicates how well the firm is currently performing, but it does not tell us whether the company is in a better or a worse financial position now than it was in previous years.

To forecast the direction in which the firm is headed, we must analyze trends in ratios. By examining the paths taken in the past, **trend analysis** provides information about whether the firm's financial position is more likely to improve or to deteriorate in the future. A simple approach to trend analysis is to construct graphs containing both the firm's ratios and the industry averages for the past five years. Using this approach, we can examine both the direction of the movement in, and the relationships between, the firm's ratios and the industry averages. If we were to graphically compare a good trend.

2-3g Summary of Ratio Analysis: The DuPont Analysis

Management and analysts often evaluate ratios using the DuPont approach, named after the company whose managers developed the evaluation technique. The idea is to attain greater detail by dissecting a single ratio into two or more related ratios. For example, using the basic DuPont approach we can compute the return on assets (ROA) by multiplying the net profit margin by total assets turnover as shown in Equation 2.2:

2.2

$$\text{ROA} = \text{Net profit margin} \times \text{Total assets turnover}$$
$$= \frac{\text{Net income}}{\text{Sales}} \times \frac{\text{Sales}}{\text{Total assets}}$$
$$= \frac{\text{Net income}}{\text{Total assets}}$$

In 2015, Ashok Leyland made 2.47 percent, or ₹2.47, on each ₹100 of sales, and assets were turned over 1.02 times during the year, which indicates that every ₹1 that was invested in total assets generated ₹1.02 in sales. The company earned a return of 2.52 percent on its assets. Applying the DuPont equation, ROA can be restated as follows:

$$\text{ROA} = \frac{33480.60}{1356218.36} \times \frac{1356218.36}{1331149.02}$$
$$= 2.52\%$$

If the company were financed only with common equity—that is, if it had no debt—the ROA and the ROE would be the same, because total assets would equal the amount of common equity such that (Net income)/(Total assets) = (Net income)/(Owners' equity). However, Ashok Leyland has debt. Because ROA shows the average return that is earned by both debt holders and stockholders (that is, all investors), ROE, which shows the return to common stockholders only, must be greater than the ROA of 6.4 percent. To translate the ROA into the ROE, we must multiply ROA by the *equity multiplier*, which is the number of times by which the total assets exceed the amount of common equity. (It is also the inverse of the proportion of total assets that is financed with equity.) Using this approach, we can write ROE as

comparative ratio analysis An analysis based on a comparison of a firm's ratios with those of other firms in the same industry at the same point in time.

trend analysis An evaluation of changes (trends) in a firm's financial position over a period of time, perhaps years.

2.3

$$\begin{aligned} ROE &= \quad ROA \quad \times \text{Equity miltiplier} \\ &= \frac{\text{Net income}}{\text{Total asssts}} \times \frac{\text{Total assets}}{\text{Common equity}} \end{aligned}$$

shown in Equation 2.3:

$$= \quad 2.52\% \quad \times \quad \frac{133114.90 \text{ million}}{51186.94 \text{ million}}$$

$$= 6.54\%$$

We can combine Equations 2.2 and 2.3 to form the *extended DuPont equation*, which is written as shown in Equation 2.4:

2.4

$$\begin{aligned} ROE &= \left[\begin{pmatrix}\text{Profit}\\\text{margin}\end{pmatrix}\right] \times \begin{pmatrix}\text{Total assets}\\\text{turnover}\end{pmatrix} \times \begin{pmatrix}\text{Equity}\\\text{multiplier}\end{pmatrix} \\ &= \left[\frac{\text{Net income}}{\text{Sales}} \times \frac{\text{Sales}}{\text{Total assets}}\right] \times \frac{\text{Total assets}}{\text{Common equity}} \end{aligned}$$

Ashok Leyland's management can use the DuPont analysis to evaluate ways to improve the firm's performance. Focusing on the net profit margin, Ashok Leyland's marketing personnel can study the effects of raising prices (or lowering them to increase volume); of selling new products or moving into markets with higher margins; and so forth. The company's cost accountants can study various expense items and, working with engineers, purchasing agents, and other operating personnel, seek ways of holding down costs. To improve the turnover of assets, Ashok Leyland's financial analysts, working with both production and marketing personnel, can investigate ways of minimizing its investment in various types of assets. At the same time, its treasury staff can analyze the effects of alternative financing strategies, seeking to hold down interest expense and the risk of debt while still using leverage to increase the rate of return on equity.

2-4 Uses and Limitations of Ratio Analysis

Although ratio analysis can provide useful information concerning a company's operations and financial condition, it does have inherent problems and limitations that necessitate care and judgment. Some potential problems follow.

Picturenet/Blend Images/Getty Images

1. Many large firms operate a number of divisions in very different industries. In such cases, it is difficult to develop a meaningful set of industry averages for comparative purposes. Consequently, ratio analysis tends to be more useful for small, narrowly focused firms than for large, multidivisional ones.

2. Most firms want to be better than average, so merely attaining average performance is not necessarily good. As a target for high-level performance, it is best to focus on the industry leaders' ratios. Thus, the industry average is not a magic number that all firms should strive to maintain. If a firm's ratios are far removed from the average for its peers or the industry, however, an analyst should question why this deviation has occurred.

3. Inflation might distort firms' balance sheets. Because many recorded values are historical, they could be substantially different from the "true" values. For example, if we are comparing an old firm that acquired its fixed assets many years ago at low prices with a new company that acquired its fixed assets only recently, we probably would find that the old firm has a higher fixed assets turnover ratio due to the lower values. Furthermore, because inflation affects both depreciation charges and inventory costs, it also affects profits. For these reasons, a ratio analysis for one firm over time, or a comparative analysis of firms of different ages, must be carefully interpreted with judgment.

4. Seasonal factors can distort a ratio analysis. For example, the inventory turnover ratio for a textile firm will be radically different if the balance sheet figure used for inventory is the one just before the fall fashion season rather than the one just after the close of the season. You can minimize this problem by using monthly averages for inventory (and receivables) when calculating ratios such as turnover.

5. Firms can employ **window-dressing techniques** to make their financial statements look stronger. To illustrate, consider a builder company which borrowed on a five-year basis on March 30, 2015, held the proceeds of the loan as cash for a few days, and then paid off the loan ahead of time on April 10, 2015. This activity improved the company's current and quick ratios, and it made the firm's 2014-15 balance sheet look good. The improvement was strictly window dressing, however; one week later, the balance sheet was back at the old level.

6. Different accounting practices can distort comparisons. As noted earlier, inventory valuation and depreciation methods can affect financial statements. The fact that different methods can be used to measure the same event makes comparisons among firms difficult.

7. It is difficult to generalize about whether a particular ratio is "good" or "bad." For example, a high current ratio might indicate a strong liquidity position, which is good, or excessive cash, which is bad (because excess cash in the bank is a nonearning asset). Similarly, a high fixed asset turnover ratio might denote either a firm that uses its assets efficiently or one that is undercapitalized and cannot afford to buy enough assets.

8. A firm might have some ratios that look good and others that look bad, making it difficult to tell whether the company is, on balance, strong or weak. Statistical procedures can be used to analyze the net effects of a set of ratios and thereby clarify the situation. No matter what method is used to interpret ratios, however, you should perform a complete analysis of the firm's financial statements before reaching conclusions. Do not form opinions about a firm's financial position based on only a few ratios.

Ratio analysis is useful, but analysts should be aware of these problems and make adjustments as necessary. When conducted in a mechanical, unthinking manner, this type of analysis is dangerous. Used intelligently and with good judgment, however, it can provide useful insights into a firm's operations. Probably *the most important and most difficult input to successful financial statement (ratio) analysis is the judgment used when interpreting the results to reach an overall conclusion about the firm's financial position.*

window-dressing techniques
Techniques employed by firms to make their financial statements look better than they actually are.

KEY FINANCIAL STATEMENT ANALYSIS CONCEPTS

To conclude this chapter, we summarize some financial statement analysis concepts that were discussed.

- The information provided in financial reports is used by the firm's managers, its creditors and stockholders, potential creditors and stockholders, and other stakeholders and interested parties.
- If a financial analyst could use only one of the financial statements mentioned in this chapter, he or she probably would choose the statement of cash flows because it provides information about how a firm generated funds during the year and how those funds were used.
- Although ratio analysis provides information about a firm's current financial position, the primary purpose of such an analysis is to provide an indication of the direction the firm's operations are headed in the future.
- When evaluating the financial position of a firm, an analyst must be aware that different accounting techniques exist to measure the same event; that the firm might use techniques to "dress up" its financial statement; that the effects of inflation can distort values from different time periods; and so forth. The most important ingredient in financial statement analysis is the judgment the analyst uses when interpreting the results.

MULTIPLE CHOICE QUESTIONS

1. If there is an increase in inventory, other factors remaining same,

a. Current ratio will go up

b. Quick ratio will go up

c. Both current ratio and quick ratio will go up

d. There will be no change in these ratios

2. There will be improvement in the assets turnover ratio if

a. Sales go up more than proportionately in relation to the assets

b. Assets come down and sales remain the same

c. Sales come down for the same level of assets

d. Both a and b

3. Profit after tax is the numerator in

a. Calculation of ROA

b. Calculation of ROE

c. Calculation of profit on sales

d. All of the above

4. ROA and ROE will be different

a. If there are taxes

b. If there is debt in the structure

c. If there is depreciation

d. None of the above

5. Inventory turnover ratio is

a. Inventory / Sales

b. Inventory / (Sales / 365)

c. Sales / Inventory

d. None of the above

6. Days sales outstanding is

a. Receivables / 365

b. Sales / 365

c. Receivables / (Sales / 365)

d. None of the above

7. Debt ratio is

a. Debt / Total assets

b. Debt / Equity

c. Debt / Profits

d. Short-term debt / Long-term debt

8. Market to book ratio is

a. A good indication of profitability

b. A good indication of asset use

c. A good indication of market acceptance of company's policies

d. None of the above

9. PE ratio is

a. Used as a relative valuation measure

b. A function of the EPS

c. A function of market price

d. All of the above

10. EPS is

a. Net income divided by common stock and reserves

b. Net income divided by reserves

c. Net income divided by share capital

d. None of the above

Answers:

1.	(a)	2.	(d)	3.	(d)	4.	(b)	5.	(c)
6.	(c)	7.	(a)	8.	(c)	9.	(d)	10.	(c)

PROBLEMS

For more problems, login to CourseMate for CFIN at CengageBrain.com

2-1 What kind of financial information is a publically traded company required to provide to its stockholders? Which financial statement do you think provides the best information for investors?

2-2 Differentiate (compare) among the information that is provided in each of the following financial statements: (1) balance sheet, (2) income statement, and (3) statement of cash flows.

2-3 Discuss some of the limitations associated with performing ratio (financial statement) analysis. What is the most important ingredient (input) in completing ratio analysis? Explain why.

2-4 Rashmi Robots (RR) recently issued 100,000 shares of common stock at ₹7 per share. The stock has a par value equal to ₹3 per share. What amount of the ₹700,000 that RR raised should be reported in the "common stock at par" account, and what amount should be reported in the "Paid-in capital" account?

2-5 Chattisgarh Golf's 2014 income statement shows that net income was ₹90,000, depreciation was ₹25,000, and taxes were ₹60,000. What was Chattisgarh Golf's net cash flow in 2014?

2-6 Heera Wireless just published its 2014 income statement, which shows net income equal to ₹240,000. The statement also shows that operating expenses were ₹500,000 before including depreciation, depreciation was ₹100,000, and the tax rate was 40 percent. If Heera has no debt, what were its sales revenues in 2014? What was its 2014 net cash flow?

2-7 Credit Card of Assam (CCA) has a current ratio of 3.5 and a quick ratio of 3.0. If its total current assets equal ₹73,500, what are CCA's (a) current liabilities and (b) inventory?

2-8 At the end of the year, Wodle Free Laundry (WFL) had ₹150,000 in total assets. (a) If WFL's total assets turnover was 2.0, what were its sales revenues? (b) If WFL's return on assets was 6 percent, what were its net income *and* net profit margin?

2-9 The balance sheet for Paupathy Open Pictures (POP) shows ₹300,000 in total assets and ₹200,000 in total liabilities. POP's return on assets (ROA) is 5 percent. Compute POP's (a) net income for the year and (b) its return on equity (ROE). POP has no preferred stock.

2-10 Leema's Cleaning has a debt ratio equal to 40 percent, total assets equal to ₹750,000, return on assets (ROA) at 6 percent, and total assets turnover of 3.0. (a) If it has no preferred stock, what amount of common equity does Leema have? (b) What is Leema's net profit margin?

2-11 At the end of the year, Water Works International (WWI) had ₹10,000 in total assets. Its total assets turnover was 2.5, and its return on assets (ROA) was 4 percent. What were WWI's (a) sales revenues and (b) net profit margin?

2-12 Last year, Deepika Desserts had a quick ratio of 1.8, a current ratio of 5.0, an inventory turnover of 7, total current assets of ₹340,000, and cash and equivalents of ₹43,000. If the cost of goods sold equaled 80 percent of sales, what were Deepika Desserts' annual sales and DSO?

2-13 Worlewala's Wilderness pays 6 percent interest on its outstanding debt, which equals ₹200,000. The company's sales are ₹540,000, its tax rate is 40 percent, and its net profit margin is 4 percent. (a) What is Worlewala's TIE? (b) If Worlewala's wants to maintain a TIE equal to 6.0, what must its sales equal?

2-14 The most recent balance sheet of Indira Information Systems (IIS) shows that the company has ₹35 million of common equity and 7 million shares of common stock outstanding. The company's common stock has a market value equal to ₹8 per share. IIS's net income was ₹14 million. What are IIS's (a) P/E ratio and (b) M/B ratio?

2-15 Sarovar BBQ has a total assets turnover equal to 2.0, a return on equity (ROE) equal to 15 percent, and a debt ratio equal to 60 percent. If Sarovar is financed with debt and common stock, what are its (a) return on assets (ROA) and (b) net profit margin?

2-16 Deena Boutique's total assets are ₹440,000, its return on assets (ROA) is 8 percent, and its debt ratio is 20 percent. What are Deena's (a) net income and (b) return on equity (ROE)?

2-17 Hariram's current assets equal ₹260,000. The company's return on assets (ROA) is 4 percent, its net income is ₹140,000, its long-term debt equals ₹1,755,000, and 35 percent of its assets are financed with common equity. Hariram's has no preferred stock. Compute the company's current ratio.

2-18 Fine Dog Spa's financial statements show that its total assets equal ₹100,000, its return on assets (ROA) is 3 percent, and its return on equity (ROE) is 5 percent. (a) Compute the company's net income. (b) What portion of total assets is financed with debt? Fine has no preferred stock.

2-19 Sixty (60) percent of Ennappa Well Drilling's assets are financed with common equity, which is the only type of equity financing the company has. Ennappa's current ratio is 5.0, its total assets turnover is 4.0, current assets equal ₹150,000, and its sales equal ₹1,800,000. What amount of Ennappa's total liabilities is long term, and what amount is short term?

2-20 Uthar Airlines generated the following information from its financial statements: (1) P/E ratio equals 15.0, (2) common stock market price per share is ₹30, (3) fixed assets turnover equals 8.0, (4) current ratio equals 5.0, (5) current liabilities equal ₹300,000, (6) net profit margin equals 4 percent, and (7) 60,000 shares of common stock are outstanding. What are Uthar's (a) return on assets (ROA) and (b) total assets turnover?

Analysis of Financial Statements

Learning Outcomes

LO.1 Describe the basic information that is produced by corporations and explain how the firm's stakeholders use such information.

- A corporation must provide stockholders with a report on its operations each year. This annual report generally includes (1) a discussion of the operations and (2) basic financial statements. Stakeholders—stockholders, bondholders, and others—use information provided by the firm to form opinions and make decisions about the future success of its operations.

LO.2 Describe the financial statements that corporations publish and the information that each statement provides.

- The financial statements that are published by a firm include (1) the balance sheet, which gives a picture, as of a specific date, of the firm's assets and how the assets are financed (liabilities and equity); (2) the income statement, which shows the results of operations by summarizing the revenues that the firm generates and the expenses that it incurs over a particular time period; (3) the statement of cash flows, which shows the firm's financing activities (sources of funds) and investment activities (uses of funds) during a specified period; and (4) the statement of retained earnings, which provides information about the changes in the common equity accounts between balance sheet dates, including the effects of the firm's operations on retained earnings.

LO.3 Describe how ratio analysis should be conducted and why the results of such an analysis are important to both managers and investors.

- Financial statement analysis (ratio analysis) generally consists of an examination and interpretation of various ratios to determine the future financial position of a firm. Ratios that should be evaluated can be classified in one of five categories: (1) liquidity ratios, which give an indication as to how well the firm can meet its current obligations; (2) asset management ratios, which show how efficiently the firm utilizes its assets (investments) to generate revenues; (3) debt management ratios, which give an indication of how well the firm is servicing its current debt and whether the firm can take on more debt; (4) profitability ratios, which show the combined effects of liquidity management, asset management, and debt management on operating results; and (5) market value ratios, which give an indication of what stockholders think of the firm's future prospects based on its past performance.
- Two general types of analyses should be completed when examining ratios: (1) comparative analysis, which is a comparison of how the firm's current financial position compares to that of its peers (or some benchmark); and (2) trend analysis, which is an examination of the firm's financial position during the most recent three to five years to determine whether its financial position is likely to improve or deteriorate in the future.

LO.4 Discuss potential problems (caveats) associated with financial statement analysis.

- Some potential problems that are associated with ratio analysis include: (1) many large firms operate a number of divisions in very different industries, which makes it difficult to develop a meaningful set of industry averages for comparative purposes; (2) most firms want to be better than average, so merely attaining average performance is not necessarily good; (3) because many values on a balance sheet are historical, inflation might distort the figures; (4) seasonal factors can distort a ratio analysis; (5) firms can employ "window dressing" to make their financial statements look stronger than they really are; (6) use of different accounting practices can distort comparisons among firms; (7) at times it is difficult to generalize about whether a particular ratio is "good" or "bad"; and (8) a firm might have some ratios that look "good" and others that look "bad," making it difficult to tell whether the company is, on balance, strong or weak.

CHAPTER 2 REVIEW

Chapter 2 Key Financial Statement Analysis Concepts

- The information provided in financial reports is used by the firm's managers, its creditors and stockholders, potential creditors and stockholders, and other stakeholders and interested parties.
- If a financial analyst could use only one of the financial statements mentioned in this chapter, he or she probably would choose the statement of cash flows because it provides information about how a firm generated funds during the year and how those funds were used.
- Although ratio analysis is used to determine the current financial position of a firm, it is primarily used to indicate the direction the firm's operations are headed in the future.
- When evaluating the financial position of a firm, an analyst must be aware that different accounting techniques exist to measure the same event, that the firm might use techniques to "dress up" its financial statements, that the effects of inflation can distort values from different time periods, and so forth. Probably the most important ingredient in financial statement analysis is the judgment the analyst uses when interpreting the results.

Key Terms

LO.1

annual report A report issued by a corporation to its stockholders that contains basic financial statements, as well as the opinions of management about the past year's operations and the firm's future prospects. *p. 19*

LO.2

balance sheet A statement that shows the firm's financial position—assets and liabilities and equity—at a specific point in time. *p. 19*

common stockholders' equity (net worth) The funds provided by common stockholders—common stock, paid-in capital, and retained earnings. *p. 20*

common size balance sheet Rupee amounts on the balance sheet are stated as a percent of total assets. *p. 21*

retained earnings The portion of the firm's earnings that has been reinvested in the firm rather than paid out as dividends. *p. 22*

book values Amounts reported in financial statements—accounting numbers. *p. 22*

market values Values of items—asset, liability, and equity—in the marketplace outside the firm. *p. 22*

income statement A statement summarizing the firm's revenues and expenses over an accounting period, generally a quarter or a year. *p. 23*

operating cash flows Those cash flows that arise from normal operations; the difference between cash collections and cash expenses associated with the manufacture and sale of inventory. *p. 24*

accounting profits A firm's net income as reported on its income statement. *p. 25*

statement of cash flows A statement that reports the effects of a firm's operating, investing, and financing activities on cash flows over an accounting period. *p. 25*

statement of retained earnings A statement reporting the change in the firm's retained earnings as a result of the income generated and retained during the year. The balance sheet figure for retained earnings is the sum of the earnings retained for each year that the firm has been in business. *p. 27*

LO.3

liquid asset An asset that can be easily converted into cash without significant loss of the amount originally invested. *p. 28*

liquidity ratios Ratios that show the relationship of a firm's cash and other current assets to its current liabilities; they provide an indication of the firm's ability to meet its current obligations. *p. 28*

asset management ratios A set of ratios that measures how effectively a firm is managing its assets. *p. 30*

financial leverage The use of debt financing. *p. 31*

debt management ratios Ratios that provide an indication of how much debt the firm has and whether the firm can take on more debt. *p. 31*

profitability ratios A group of ratios showing the effect of liquidity, asset management, and debt management on operating results. *p. 32*

market value ratios A set of ratios that relate the firm's stock price to its earnings and book value per share. *p. 33*

comparative ratio analysis An analysis based on a comparison of a firm's ratios with those of other firms in the same industry. *p. 33*

trend analysis An evaluation of changes (trends) in a firm's financial position over a period of time, perhaps years. *p. 33*

LO.4

window-dressing techniques Techniques employed by firms to make their financial statements look better than they actually are. *p. 35*

CHAPTER 3

The Financial Environment: Markets, Institutions, and Investment Banking

Learning Outcomes

LO.1 Describe the role that financial markets play in improving the standard of living in an economy.

LO.2 Describe how various financial markets are differentiated.

LO.3 Discuss the role that an investment banking house plays in the financial markets.

LO.4 Describe the role that financial intermediaries play in the financial markets, and explain why there are so many different types of intermediaries.

LO.5 Describe how financial markets and financial intermediaries in the United States differ from those in other parts of the world.

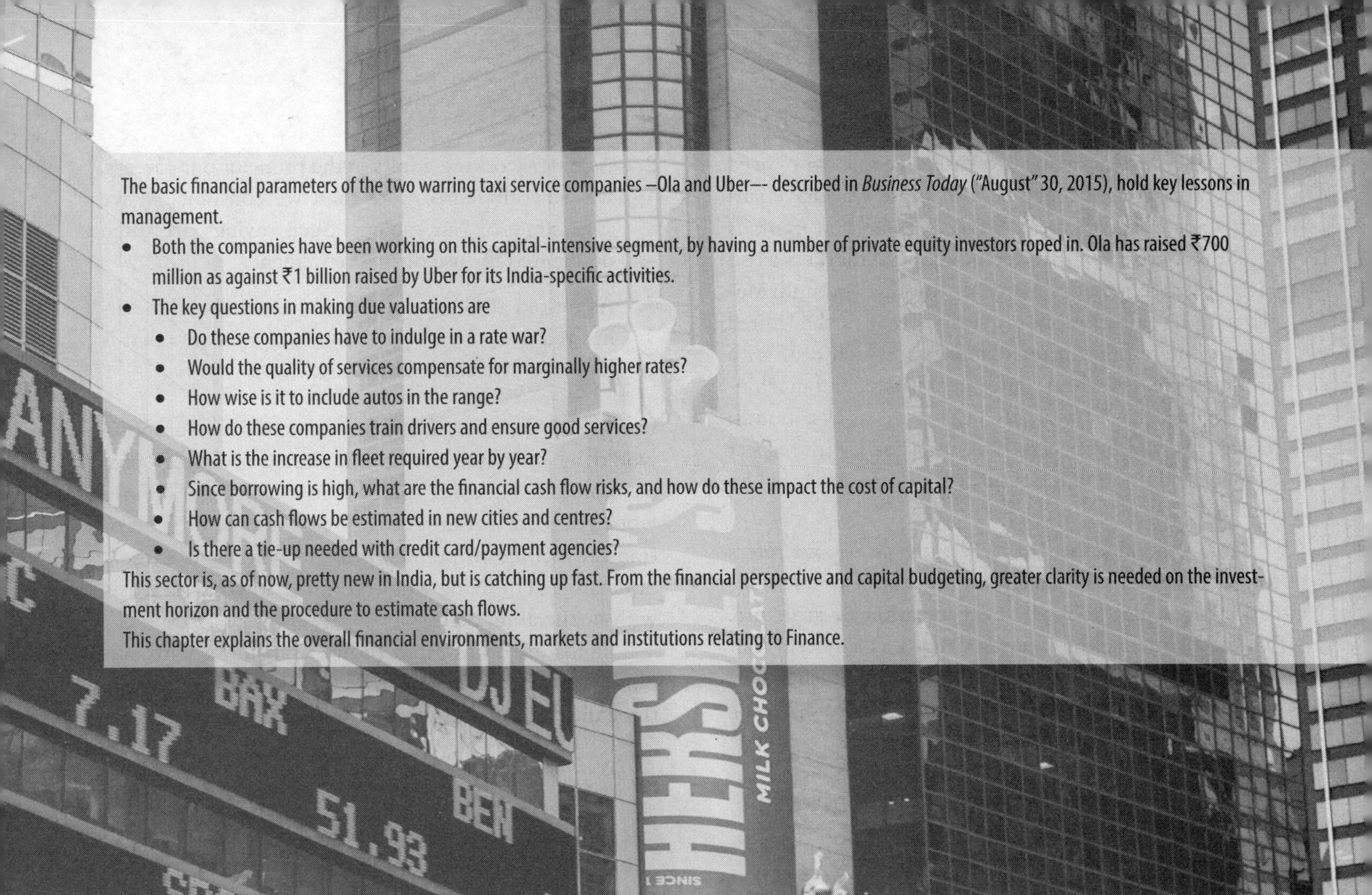

The basic financial parameters of the two warring taxi service companies –Ola and Uber–- described in *Business Today* ("August" 30, 2015), hold key lessons in management.

- Both the companies have been working on this capital-intensive segment, by having a number of private equity investors roped in. Ola has raised ₹700 million as against ₹1 billion raised by Uber for its India-specific activities.
- The key questions in making due valuations are
  - Do these companies have to indulge in a rate war?
  - Would the quality of services compensate for marginally higher rates?
  - How wise is it to include autos in the range?
  - How do these companies train drivers and ensure good services?
  - What is the increase in fleet required year by year?
  - Since borrowing is high, what are the financial cash flow risks, and how do these impact the cost of capital?
  - How can cash flows be estimated in new cities and centres?
  - Is there a tie-up needed with credit card/payment agencies?

This sector is, as of now, pretty new in India, but is catching up fast. From the financial perspective and capital budgeting, greater clarity is needed on the investment horizon and the procedure to estimate cash flows.

This chapter explains the overall financial environments, markets and institutions relating to Finance.

© iStockphoto.com/aaM Photography, Ltd

Study Tools

Problems are found at the end of this chapter

+

Login to **CourseMate** for **CFIN** at **CengageBrain.com** for additional problems and other study tools!

Businesses, individuals, and governments often need to raise funds to finance operations or to invest in assets. For example, suppose Florida Power & Light (FP&L) forecasts an increase in the demand for electricity in Florida, and the company decides to build a new power plant. Because FP&L almost certainly will not have the hundreds of millions of rupees necessary to pay for the plant, the company will have to raise these funds in the financial markets. This chapter examines the markets where such funds are raised, securities are traded, and the prices for stocks and bonds are established.[1]

3-1 What Are Financial Markets?

Although some individuals and firms need funds, others have funds to invest because their incomes are greater

[1]Throughout much of this chapter, we primarily refer to corporations as the users, or issuers, of such financial assets as debt and equity. In reality, governments, government agencies, and individuals also issue debt. For example, an individual "issues" a mortgage when he or she finances the purchase of a house. Because corporations issue a variety of debt instruments and can also issue equity, we will identify them as the issuers more often than governments or individuals in the examples.

than their current living expenses. People who need money are brought together with those who have surplus funds in the *financial markets*. Note that *markets* is plural; a great many different financial markets exist, each of which includes many institutions and individuals, in a developed economy such as that of the United States. Unlike *physical asset markets*, which deal with products such as wheat, autos, real estate, and machinery, *financial asset markets* deal with stocks, bonds, mortgages, and other *claims on real assets* with respect to the distribution of the future cash flows generated by such assets.

In a general sense, the term *financial market* refers to a conceptual mechanism rather than a physical location or a specific type of organization or structure. We usually define the **financial markets** as a system that includes individuals and institutions, instruments, and procedures that bring together borrowers and savers, no matter the location.

3-1a **Importance of Financial Markets**

The primary role of financial markets is to facilitate the flow of funds *from* individuals and businesses that have surplus funds *to* individuals, businesses, and governments that have needs for funds in excess of their incomes. The more efficient the flow of funds process is, the more productive the economy is, in terms of both manufacturing and financing.

3-1b **Flow of Funds**

The financial markets allow us to consume amounts different from our current incomes by providing *mechanisms* that help us transfer income through time.[2] When we borrow, for example, we sacrifice future income to increase current income; when we save, or invest, we sacrifice current income in exchange for greater expected income (spending) in the future. The ability to transfer income to different time periods allows us to pass through three financial phases during our lives that would not be possible without financial markets.

1. As young adults, we generally consume more than our incomes to buy such items as houses and cars. To do so, we borrow based on our ability to generate future income that will be used to pay off the debt.

financial markets A system consisting of individuals and institutions, instruments, and procedures that bring together borrowers and savers.

2. As older working adults in the prime of our careers, we generally earn more than we consume, so we save some of our income. Such savings are often designated for use during retirement.
3. As retired adults, we use funds accumulated in earlier years to at least partially replace income that is lost when we retire from our careers.

In the absence of financial markets, consumption would be restricted to income earned each year plus any amounts put aside (perhaps in a coffee can) in previous years. As a result, because it would be difficult to transfer income to periods prior to when it is earned, our standard of living would be much lower than exists with financial markets.

Funds are transferred (flow) from those with surpluses (savers) to those with needs (borrowers) by the three different processes diagrammed in Figure 3.1.

1. A *direct transfer* of money and securities, as shown in the top section, occurs when a business sells its stocks or bonds directly to savers (investors) without going through any type of intermediary or financial institution. The business delivers its securities to savers, who in turn provide the firm with some of the money it needs.
2. As shown in the middle section, a transfer can also go through an *investment banking house,* which serves as a middleman that facilitates the issuance of securities by firms that need to raise funds. The firm's securities and the savers' money merely "pass through" the investment banking house. The investment banking process is described later in this chapter.
3. Transfers can also be made through a *financial intermediary,* such as a bank or a mutual fund. In this case, the intermediary obtains funds from savers and then uses the money to lend out or to purchase another company's securities. The existence of intermediaries greatly increases the efficiency of the financial markets. More information concerning the

[2] Throughout this chapter, we often refer to the parties involved in financial market transactions as borrowers or lenders, which implies that only loans are traded in the financial markets. In reality, stocks, options, and many other financial assets also are traded in the financial markets. In our general discussions, we will use the term borrowers to refer to parties such as individuals and government units that raise needed funds through various types of loans, as well as corporations that use both loans and stock issues to raise needed funds. We will use the term lenders to refer to those parties who provide funds by investing in such instruments as stocks (equity) and bonds (debt).

FIGURE 3.1 Diagram of the Capital Formation Process

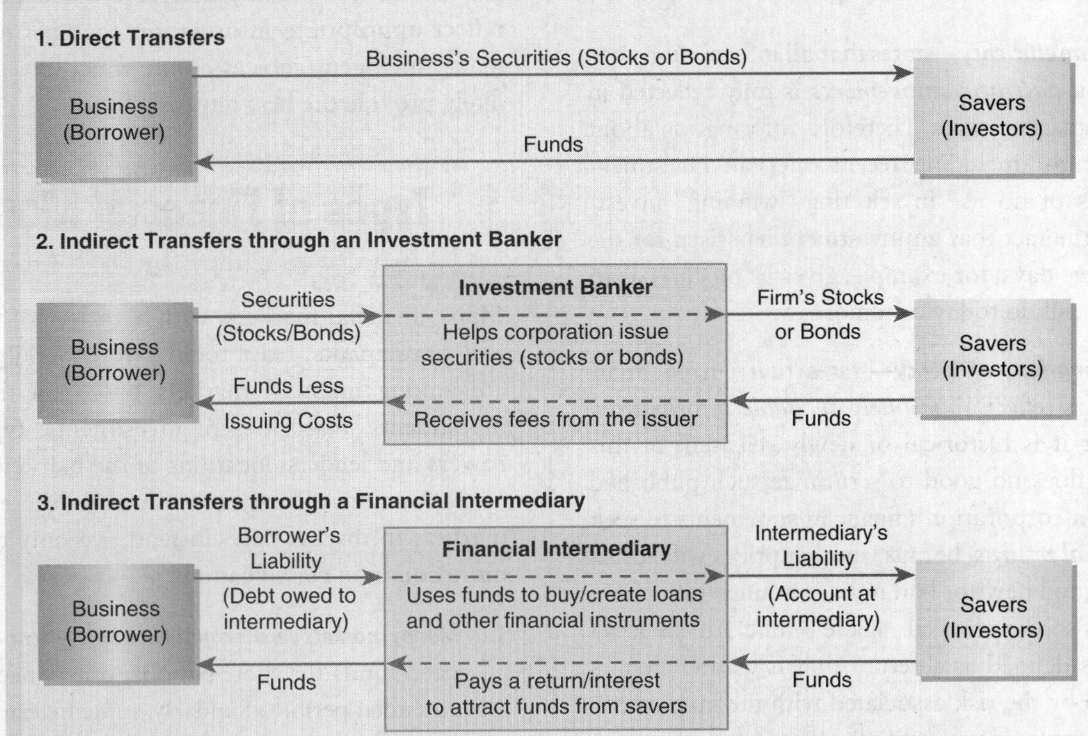

roles and descriptions of financial intermediaries is provided later in this chapter.

Direct transfers of funds from savers to borrowers are possible and do occur on occasion. Generally, however, corporations and government entities use investment bankers to help them raise needed capital in the financial markets, whereas individuals use financial intermediaries to help them borrow (raise) needed funds. Individuals also use financial intermediaries to help them save to meet such future financial goals as retirement.

3-1c Market Efficiency

If the financial markets did not provide efficient funds transfers, the economy simply could not function as it does now. Because Florida Power & Light would have difficulty raising needed capital, Miami's citizens would pay more for electricity. Likewise, you would not be able to buy the house you want when you want it or earn a decent rate on funds you save. Clearly, the level of employment and productivity, and hence our standard of living, would be much lower. Therefore, it is essential that our financial markets function efficiently—not only quickly, but also at a low cost. When we speak of *market efficiency*, we generally mean either economic efficiency or informational efficiency.

Economic Efficiency. The financial markets are said to have achieved **economic efficiency** if funds are allocated to their optimal use at the best costs (interest rates). In economically efficient markets, businesses and individuals invest their funds in assets that yield the highest returns, and the costs of searching for such opportunities are lower than those observed in less efficient markets.

Informational Efficiency. The prices of investments bought and sold in the financial markets are based on available information. If these prices reflect existing information and adjust very quickly when new information becomes available, then the financial markets have achieved **informational efficiency.** When the financial markets have a large number of participants in search of the

economic efficiency Funds are allocated to their optimal use at the lowest costs in the financial markets.

informational efficiency The prices of investments reflect existing information and adjust quickly when new information enters the markets.

most profitable investments, informational efficiency generally exists. Informational efficiency typically is classified into one of the following three categories:

1. ***Weak-form efficiency***—states that all information contained in *past price movements* is fully reflected in current market prices. Therefore, information about past trends (including recent ones) in investment prices is of no use in selecting "winning" investments; the fact that an investment has risen for the past three days, for example, gives us no clues as to what it will do today or tomorrow.
2. ***Semistrong-form efficiency***—states that current market prices reflect all *publicly available information,* whether it is historical or newly released. In this case, it does no good to scrutinize such published data as a corporation's financial statements to seek *abnormal returns*, because market prices will adjust to any good news or bad news contained in such reports as soon as they are made public. An **abnormal return** is defined as a return that is greater than is justified by the risk associated with the investment. For example, if you and all of your friends invest in similar-risk securities, you should all earn about the same return. However, if you earn a 20 percent return and your friends earn a 12 percent return on investments with the same risk, the additional 8 percent is considered an abnormal return.
3. ***Strong-form efficiency***—states that current market prices reflect *all pertinent information*, whether it is publicly available or privately held. If this form of efficiency holds, even company insiders would find it impossible to earn abnormal returns in the financial markets.

The informational efficiency of the financial markets has received a great deal of attention. The results of most market efficiency studies suggest that the financial markets are highly efficient in the weak form and reasonably efficient in the semistrong form, but strong-form efficiency does not appear to hold.

abnormal return Return that exceeds what is justified by the risk associated with the investment.

money markets The segments of the financial markets where the instruments that are traded have maturities equal to one year or less.

capital markets The segments of the financial markets where the instruments that are traded have maturities greater than one year.

Generally, when financial markets are informationally efficient, they are also economically efficient. This situation arises because investors can expect prices to reflect appropriate information that permits them to make intelligent choices about which investments will likely provide the best returns.

3-2 Types of Financial Markets

Many financial markets, with a variety of investments and participants, exist today. We generally differentiate among financial markets based on the types of investments, maturities of investments, types of borrowers and lenders, locations of the markets, and types of transactions. There are too many different financial markets to discuss here. Instead, we only describe the more common classifications.

1. ***Money markets versus capital markets***—Some borrowers need funds for short periods; others need funds for extended periods. Similarly, some investors prefer to invest for short periods, but others prefer to invest for longer periods. The markets for short-term financial instruments are termed the *money markets,* and the markets for long-term financial instruments are called the *capital markets*. More specifically, the **money markets** include debt instruments that have maturities equal to one year or less when originally issued, and the **capital markets** include instruments with original maturities greater than one year. By definition, then, money markets include only debt instruments, because stocks (equities) have no specific maturities, whereas capital markets include both equity instruments and such long-term debt instruments as mortgages, corporate bonds, and government bonds.

   The money markets and capital markets provide us with financial instruments with different maturities that permit us to better match our cash inflows with cash outflows. The primary function of the money markets is to provide liquidity to businesses, governments, and individuals so that they can meet their short-term needs for cash, because, in most cases, the receipt of cash inflows does not coincide exactly with the payment of cash outflows. The primary function of the capital markets is to provide us with the opportunity to transfer cash surpluses or deficits to future years. For example, individuals transfer income through time so that they can afford to buy houses with mortgages that are paid off as income is generated in the future.

2. ***Debt markets versus equity markets***—Simply stated, the **debt markets** are where loans are traded, and the **equity markets** are where stocks are traded. A debt instrument is a contract that specifies how and when a borrower must repay a lender. In contrast, equity represents "ownership" in a corporation that entitles the stockholder to share in future cash distributions generated by the firm.

   Debt markets generally are described (labeled) according to the characteristics of the debt that is traded. In many cases, the segmentation of the debt markets is based on the maturity of the instrument (money or capital market instruments), the type of debt (consumer, government, or corporate), and the participant (borrowers and investors). Characteristics of stock markets are discussed later in the chapter.

3. ***Primary markets versus secondary markets***—The *primary markets* are where "new" securities are traded, and the *secondary markets* are where "used" securities are traded. **Primary markets** are the markets in which corporations raise new capital. The corporation selling a newly created stock receives the proceeds from the sale (less issuing costs) in a primary market transaction. **Secondary markets** are markets in which existing, previously issued securities are traded among investors. The corporation whose securities are traded in the secondary market is not involved in the transaction and, therefore, does not receive any funds from the transaction; rather, funds are transferred from one investor to another investor.

4. ***Derivatives markets***—Options, futures, and swaps are some of the securities traded in the **derivatives markets.** These securities are called *derivatives* because their values are determined, or derived, directly from other assets. For example, a *call option* allows the option buyer (owner) to purchase a certain number of shares of stock (or some other security) from the option seller at a specific price—say, ₹50—for a particular period of time—say, 60 days. Because the option contract fixes the purchase price of the stock, the value of the call option changes as the *market value* of the stock on which the option is written changes. For example, if the per-share price of the "underlying" stock increases to ₹60 (decreases to ₹45), the value of the option increases (decreases) because the person who owns the option can "exercise" his or her right to purchase the stock for the contracted ₹50 per share from the option seller regardless of the existing market price of the stock.

   Although many investors use derivatives to speculate about the movements of prices in the financial markets, these instruments are typically employed to help manage risk. Individuals, corporations, and governments use derivatives to *hedge* risk by contracting to set (fix) future prices, which offsets exposures to uncertain price changes in the future.

3-2a Stock Markets

During the past couple of decades, individuals have expressed greater interest in stocks than ever before. A major reason for this increased interest is the fact that the stock markets generated record-breaking returns during the 1990s. Although the markets slowed and many investors experienced substantial losses in their investments during the beginning of the twenty-first century, the popularity and intrigue of the stock markets is still evident. For this reason, we describe some of the characteristics of stock markets in this section.

3-2b Types of General Stock Market Activities

We generally classify basic stock market activities into three distinct categories:

1. ***Trading in the outstanding, previously issued shares of established, publicly owned companies: the secondary market***—If the owner of 100 shares of Infosys sells his or her stock to another investor, the trade

debt markets Financial markets where loans are traded.

equity markets Financial markets where corporate stocks are traded.

primary markets Markets in which various organizations raise funds by issuing new securities.

secondary markets Markets where financial assets that have previously been issued by various organizations are traded among investors.

derivatives markets Financial markets where options and futures are traded.

is said to have occurred in the *secondary market*. The company (e.g., Infosys) receives no new money when sales occur in this market.

2. ***Additional shares sold by established, publicly owned companies: the primary market***—If Infosys decides to sell (or issue) new shares to raise funds for expansion, this transaction is said to occur in the *primary market*. In this case, the company receives the funds that are raised when its securities are sold (issued), less any issuing costs.
3. ***New public offerings by privately held firms: the initial public offering (IPO) market; the primary market***—When a privately held corporation raises funds by issuing stock to the public for the first time, the company is said to be *going public*, and the market for stocks in companies that have recently gone public is called the **initial public offering (IPO) market.**

©: iStock/Thinkstock

Most of the time stock markets function as secondary markets. In the United States, these secondary stock markets generally are categorized either as physical stock exchanges or as part of the more general over-the-counter market.

3-2c Physical Stock Exchanges[3]

The **physical stock exchanges** are tangible physical entities. They include national exchanges, such as the National Stock Excange (NSE), and the Bombay Stock Exchange (BSE). The prices of stocks listed on the physical stock exchanges are determined by auction processes whereby investors (through their brokers) bid for stocks.

Until the late 1990s, most physical stock exchanges were not-for-profit organizations that were owned by their members, who were said to hold "seats" on the exchanges (although everyone stood up). These seats, which were bought and sold, gave the holder the right to trade on the exchange.[5] Organizations such as these, which are owned and operated by their members, are said to have *mutual ownership* structures. Although most stock exchanges were set up as mutual ownership structures when they were started many decades ago, the recent trend has been to convert stock exchanges from not-for-profit mutual ownership organizations to for-profit organizations that are owned by outside stockholders and are publicly traded. The process of converting an exchange from a mutual ownership organization to a stock ownership organization is called *demutualization*.

initial public offering (IPO) market Market consisting of stocks of privately held companies that have recently gone public for the first time.

physical stock exchanges Formal organizations with physical locations that facilitate trading in designated ("listed") securities. The major U.S. stock exchange is the New York Stock Exchange (NYSE).

listing requirements Characteristics a firm must possess to be listed on a stock exchange.

Listing Requirements. For a stock to be traded on an exchange, it must be *listed*. Each exchange has established **listing requirements**, which indicate the quantitative and qualitative characteristics that a firm must possess to be listed. Table 3.1 provides examples of the listing requirements for some U.S. exchanges. The primary purpose of these requirements is to ensure that investors have some interest in the company so that the firm's stock will be actively traded on the exchange.

A listed firm pays a relatively small annual fee to the exchange to receive such benefits as the marketability offered by continuous trading activity and the publicity and prestige associated with being an exchange-listed firm. Many people believe that listing has a beneficial

TABLE 3.1 Listing Requirements for Stock Exchanges and the NASDAQ

	NYSE	Regional Exchanges	NASDAQ
Round-lot (100 shares) shareholders	400	800	400
Number of public shares (Millions)	1.1	0.5	1.1
Market value of public shares (₹ in Millions)	₹100	₹3	₹15
Assets (₹ in Millions)	₹75	₹4	₹50
Pre-tax income (₹ in Millions)	₹2.00	₹0.75	₹1.00

Sources: Information for the listing requirements was taken from the websites of the New York Stock Exchange (https://nyse.nyx.com/), the Chicago Stock Exchange (http://www.chx.com/index.asp), and NASDAQ (http://www.nasdaq.com/).

effect on the sales of the firm's products and that it is advantageous in terms of lowering the return investors demand when they buy the firm's common stock. Investors respond favorably to a listed firm's increased information and liquidity, and they have confidence that its quoted price is not being manipulated.

3-2d The Over-the-Counter (OTC) Market

If a security is not traded on an organized exchange, it has been customary to say that it is traded in the **over-the-counter (OTC) market**, which is a trading system that consists of a network of brokers and dealers around the country. Traditionally, the OTC market has been defined as including all of the facilities needed to conduct securities transactions not conducted on the physical exchanges. These facilities consist of (1) the *dealers* who hold inventories of OTC securities and who are said to "make a market" in these securities, (2) the *brokers* who act as *agents* in bringing the dealers together with investors, and (3) the *electronic networks* that provide a communications link between dealers and brokers. Unlike physical exchanges, the OTC market generally does not operate as an auction market. The dealers who make a market in a particular stock continuously quote a price at which they are willing to buy the stock (the *bid price*) and a price at which they will sell shares (the *asked price*). Each dealer's prices, which are adjusted as supply and demand conditions change, can be read off computer screens across the country. The spread between the bid and asked prices (called the *dealer's spread*) represents the dealer's markup, or profit.

NSE National Stock Exchange (NSE) in India is an online trading platform for stocks and shares which has become extremely popular over the last 20 years or so. From being just a stock exchange, NSE now trades in bonds and derivatives. It facilitates in trading in more than 3000 securities and has a daily turnover of ₹43 million. All details about the products and trading rules in NSE are available at http://www.nseindia.com/.

3-2e Electronic Communications Networks (ECN)

Today many trades are executed electronically using trading systems known as electronic communications networks (ECN). ECNs, which are registered with the **Securities and Exchange Board of India (SEBI)** are electronic systems that quickly transfer information about securities transactions to facilitate the execution of orders at the best available prices. ECNs automatically match the buy and sell orders by price for a large number of investors. Investors use ECNs through accounts they have at brokerage firms that offer online trading services and subscribe to ECNs. When an order (buy or sell) is placed electronically, the process is seamless in the sense that investors have no indication that an ECN is used to execute their transactions. ECNs provide an alternative trading medium, which has increased competition with the stock exchanges.

over-the-counter (OTC) market
A collection of brokers and dealers, connected electronically by telephones and computers, that provide for trading in securities not listed on the physical stock exchanges.

3-2f Competition Among Stock Markets

Competition among the major stock markets has become increasingly fierce in recent years. In the United States, the major stock markets, especially the NYSE and NASDAQ, continuously explore ways to improve their competitive positions. Two factors have changed the competitive arena of the stock markets. First, whereas many years ago stocks could be listed and traded on only one stock exchange, today many popular stocks are *dual listed*. A stock with a **dual listing** is eligible (registered) to be traded in more than one stock market. Dual listing increases liquidity because a stock has more exposure through a greater number of outlets than if it were listed on only one market. Various stock markets compete to list stocks that are actively traded because increased trading activity translates into increased profits.

Second, in 2005, the Securities and Exchange Commission adopted Regulation NMS (National Market Structure), which mandates that the *trade-through rule* be used when securities are traded. The trade-through rule states that a stock trade should be executed at the best price that is available in all of the stock markets. In other words, a trade order continues to pass through the markets until the best price is reached.

As a result of the increased competition among the stock markets, both the NYSE and NASDAQ have taken actions to improve their competitive positions. For example, we mentioned earlier that in 2006 the NYSE merged with ArcaEX to form the NYSE Group. The "new and improved" NYSE Group effectively consists of two distinct stock (securities) exchanges. The physical stock exchange called the NYSE still exists, and the products and services that it offers are similar to those offered prior to the merger. In addition, the NYSE Group offers a fully electronic exchange through NYSE Arca. In 2007, the NYSE Group merged with Euronext, which includes leading stock markets throughout Europe, to form NYSE Euronext. And in 2008, NYSE Euronext acquired the American Stock Exchange (AMEX), the second largest national stock market in the United States at the time, to broaden its offerings of financial instruments. Clearly, NYSE Euronext has positioned itself as a leader in global financial markets.

Soon after the announcement of the NYSE-ArcaEx merger in 2005, NASDAQ acquired Instinet, an electronic exchange that improved the technology and efficiency of NADAQ trading and helped it compete better with NYSE. In addition, since 2005, NASDAQ has acquired regional stock exchanges (Philadelphia Stock Exchange and the Boston Stock Exchange) and the OMX, which operates stock exchanges in northern Europe.

dual listing When stocks are listed for trading in more than one stock market.

A recent example of the "stock market wars" took place at the beginning of 2011, when NASDAQ made a bid to take over the NYSE. In May of 2011, however, the U.S. Justice Department denied the hostile takeover attempt because it felt that investors (competition) would be hurt by the consolidation of the two markets. And, in 2012, an attempt to merge the NYSE and a German stock market company named Deutsche Börse was also blocked by regulators because it was felt the megamarket that would be created would stifle competition. Even so, increased competition among global stock markets assuredly will result in alliances among various exchanges and markets in the future. Clearly, the playing field on which the exchanges compete will be much different in the future.

Competition among stock markets in India The Bombay Stock Exchange (BSE) is the oldest stock exchange in Asia having been set up in 1875. With a market capitalization of listed companies of ₹9470 million, and more than 4000 companies listed therein, BSE is an important exchange in India. In terms of products, and index, it runs a close competition with NSE.

3-2g Regulation of Securities Markets

Sales of new securities, such as stocks and bonds, as well as operations in the secondary markets, are regulated. For the most part, the SEBI regulations are intended to ensure that investors receive fair disclosure of financial and nonfinancial information from publicly traded companies and to discourage fraudulent and misleading behavior by firms' investors, owners, and employees who might contemplate manipulating stock prices.

The primary elements of SEBI regulations include (1) jurisdiction over most interstate offerings of new securities to the general investing public, (2) regulation of national securities exchanges, (3) power to prohibit manipulation of securities prices (deliberate manipulation of securities prices is illegal), and (4) control over stock trades by corporate *insiders*, which include the officers, directors, and major stockholders of a company.[6]

Regulation of securities markets in India: In India, the Securities and Exchange Board of India (SEBI) is the regulating authority for the capital

[6]Insiders must file monthly reports of changes in their holdings of the corporation's stock, and any *short-term* profits from trading in the stock must be handed over to the corporation.

markets in the country. In addition, the Ministry of Finance through its Department of Economic Affairs formulates policies and guidelines for the orderly functioning of the capital markets. SEBI is responsible for protecting investor interests and in taking up cases and complaints against companies and intermediaries in respect of public offers, trading and related issues

3-3 The Investment Banking Process

When a business needs to raise funds in the financial markets, it generally enlists the services of an **investment banker** (see the middle panel in Figure 3.1). Such organizations perform three tasks: (1) They help corporations design securities with the features that are most attractive to investors, given existing market conditions; (2) they generally buy these securities from the corporations; and (3) they resell the securities to investors (savers). Although the securities are sold twice, this process is actually one primary market transaction, with the investment banker acting as a middleman (agent) as funds are transferred from investors (savers) to businesses. The major investment banking houses often are divisions of large financial service corporations that engage in a wide range of activities (e.g., Bank of America/Merrill Lynch).

In this section we describe the general procedures that are followed when stocks and bonds are issued in the financial markets with the aid of investment bankers.

3-3a Raising Capital: Stage I Decisions

A corporation that needs to raise funds makes some preliminary decisions on its own, including the following:[7]

1. ***Amount to be raised***—How much new capital is needed?
2. ***Type of securities used***—Should stock, bonds, or a combination of these instruments be used?
3. ***Competitive bid versus negotiated deal***—Should the company simply offer a block of its securities for sale to the investment banker that submits the highest bid of all interested investment bankers, or should it sit down and negotiate a deal with a single investment banker? These two procedures are called *competitive bids* and *negotiated deals (purchases)*, respectively. Only a handful of the largest firms, whose securities are already well known to the investment banking community, are in a position to use the competitive bid process.
4. ***Selection of an investment banker***—If the issue is to be negotiated, which investment banker should the firm use? Older corporations that have "been to market" before will already have established relationships with investment bankers. A firm that is going public for the first time will have to choose an investment banker, and different investment banking houses are better suited for different companies. Some investment bankers deal mainly with large companies such as IBM, whereas others specialize in more speculative issues such as initial public offerings (IPOs).

[7]For the most part, the procedures described in this section also apply to government entities. Governments issue only debt, however; they do not issue stock.

3-3b Raising Capital: Stage II Decisions

Stage II decisions, which are made jointly by the firm and its selected investment banker, include the following:

1. ***Reevaluating the initial decisions***—The firm and its investment banker will reevaluate the initial decisions about the size of the issue and the type of securities to use to determine whether revisions are needed, given current market conditions.
2. ***Best-efforts or underwritten issue***—The firm and its investment banker must decide whether the investment banker will work on a best-efforts basis or underwrite the issue. In an **underwritten arrangement**, the investment banker generally assures the company that the entire issue will be sold, so *the investment banker bears significant risks* in such an offering. With this type of arrangement, the investment banking firm typically buys the securities from the issuing firm and then sells the securities in the primary markets, hoping to make a profit. In a **best-efforts arrangement**, the issue is handled on a contingency basis so

investment banker An organization that underwrites and distributes new issues of securities; it helps businesses and other entities obtain needed financing.

underwritten arrangement Agreement for the sale of securities in which the investment bank guarantees the sale by purchasing the securities from the issuer, thus agreeing to bear any risks involved in selling the securities in the financial markets.

best-efforts arrangement Agreement for the sale of securities in which the investment bank handling the transaction gives no guarantee that the securities will be sold.

that the investment banker receives a commission based on the amount of the issue that is sold. The investment banker essentially promises to exert its best efforts when selling the securities, which means *the issuing firm takes the chance* that the entire issue will not be sold and that all needed funds will not be raised.

3. ***Issuance (flotation) costs***—The investment banker's fee must be negotiated, and the firm must estimate the other expenses that it will incur in connection with the issue, including lawyers' fees, accountants' costs, printing and engraving costs, and so forth. The investment banker will buy the issue from the company at a discount below the price at which the securities are to be offered to the public. This *underwriter's spread* covers the investment banker's costs and provides for a profit. Generally, the issuing costs, called **flotation costs**, associated with public issues are higher for stocks than for bonds, and they are also higher for small issues than for large issues (because certain fixed costs exist).

To show how flotation costs affect decisions firms make when issuing securities to raise new funds, suppose a firm needs ₹475,000 to support its growth. The firm plans to raise the needed funds by issuing new common stock, which will require it to pay flotation costs equal to 5 percent of the issue's value. If the firm needs exactly ₹475,000 for its growth, perhaps to purchase a piece of land, then it must issue more than ₹475,000 in common stock to ensure that ₹475,000 is left over after covering flotation costs. How much common stock does the firm need to issue? We can answer this question by recognizing that the amount of funds the firm will net from the stock issue is computed as follows:

$$\begin{aligned}\text{Net proceeds} &= \text{Amount of issue} - \text{Flotation costs}\\ &= \text{Amount of issue} \times (1 - F)\end{aligned}$$

where F represents the flotation costs stated in decimal form.

If we plug into the preceding equation the information we know for our example, we have

$$₹475{,}000 = \text{Amount of issue} \times (1 - 0.05)$$

$$\text{Amount of issue} = \frac{₹475{,}000}{0.95} = ₹500{,}000$$

If the firm issues ₹500,000 in common stock, the flotation costs will be ₹25,000 = ₹500,000(0.05); thus ₹475,000 will be left over after flotation costs are paid.

flotation costs The costs associated with issuing new stocks or bonds.

Equation 3.1 generalizes the relationship we discussed here. This equation can be used to determine the amount a firm must issue to net a specific rupee amount after paying flotation costs.

3.1

$$\text{Amount of issue} = \frac{\text{NP}}{(1-\text{F})}$$

Here NP represents the net proceeds from the issue, which is the amount that the firm receives (needs) after paying flotation costs, and F is the flotation costs stated in decimal form.

4. ***Setting the offering price***—If the company is already publicly owned, the *offering price* will be based on the existing market price of the stock or the yield on the firm's existing bonds. An investment banker has an easier job of selling the issue if it carries a relatively low price, but the issuer of the securities naturally wants as high a price as possible. Therefore, an inherent conflict of interest on price exists between the investment banker and the issuer. If the issuer is financially sophisticated and its stock is actively traded, however, the investment banker will be forced to price the issue close to the market price.

The stock of a company that is going public for the first time (an IPO) will not have an established price. Consequently, the investment banker must estimate the equilibrium price at which the stock will sell after it is issued. If the offering price is set below the true equilibrium price, the stock price will rise sharply after issue, and the company and its original (founding) stockholders will have "given away" too many shares to raise the required capital. If the offering price is set above the true equilibrium price, either the issue will fail, or, if the investment bankers succeed in selling the stock, their clients will be unhappy when the price subsequently falls to its equilibrium level. For these reasons, it is important that the equilibrium price be estimated as accurately as possible.

3-3c Raising Capital: Selling Procedures

Once the company and its investment banker have decided how much money to raise, the types of securities to issue, and the basis for pricing the issue, they will prepare and file a registration statement and prospectus with the SEC. The **registration statement** provides financial, legal, and technical information about the company, whereas the **prospectus** summarizes the information in the registration statement and is provided to prospective investors for use in selling the securities. When the SEC approves the registration statement and the prospectus, it merely validates that the required information has been furnished; it does not judge the quality or value of the issue.

The final price of the stock (or the interest rate on a bond issue) is set at the close of business on the day the issue clears the SEC, and the securities are then offered to the public on the following day. Typically, investment bankers sell the stock within a day or two after the offering begins. On occasion, however, they are unable to quickly move the issue at a good price, so they hold it for a longer period.

Underwriting Syndicate. Because investment bankers are exposed to large potential losses, an investment banker typically does not handle the purchase and distribution of an issue alone unless it is fairly small. Often an investment banker will form an **underwriting syndicate** whereby the issue is distributed to a number of investment firms around the country in an effort to minimize the amount of risk that is carried by each firm. The investment banking house that sets up the deal is called the *lead*, or *managing, underwriter.*

In addition to the underwriting syndicate, larger offerings might require the services of still more investment bankers as part of a *selling group*. The selling group, which handles the distribution of securities to individual investors, includes all members of the underwriting syndicate plus additional dealers who take relatively small *participations* (shares of the total issue) from the syndicate members. Members of the selling group act as selling agents and receive commissions for their efforts. The number of investment banking houses in a selling group depends partly on the size of the issue.

Shelf Registrations. The selling procedures described here apply to many securities sales. However, a large, well-known public company (called a *seasoned* company) that frequently issues securities will often file a master registration statement with the SEC and then update it with a short-form statement just prior to each individual offering. In such a case, the company could decide at 10 a.m. to sell registered securities and have the sale completed before noon. This procedure is known as **shelf registration** because, in effect, the company puts its new securities "on the shelf" and then sells them to investors when it thinks the market is right.

Maintenance of the Secondary Market. In the case of a large, established firm, the investment banking firm's job is finished once it has issued the stock and the net proceeds have been turned over to the company. But, if a company is going public for the first time, the investment banker has an obligation to maintain a market for the shares after the issue has been completed. Such stocks typically are traded in the OTC market, and the lead underwriter generally agrees to "make a market" in the stock and keep it reasonably liquid. The issuing company wants a good market to exist for its stock, as do its stockholders. Therefore, if the investment banking house wants to do business with the company in the future, to keep its own brokerage customers happy, and to have future referral business, it will hold an inventory of the shares and help maintain an active secondary market in the stock.

3-4 Financial Intermediaries and Their Roles in Financial Markets

Financial intermediaries include such financial services organizations as commercial banks, savings and loan associations, pension funds, and insurance companies. In simple terms, **financial intermediaries** facilitate the transfer of funds from those who have funds (savers) to those who need funds (borrowers) by *manufacturing* a variety of financial products. When intermediaries accept funds (generally called *deposits*) from savers, they issue *securities* with such names

registration statement A statement of facts filed with the SEC about a company that plans to issue securities.

prospectus A document describing a new security issue and the issuing company.

underwriting syndicate A group of investment banking firms formed to spread the risk associated with the purchase and distribution of a new issue of securities.

shelf registration Registration of securities with the SEC for sale at a later date. The securities are held "on the shelf" until the sale.

financial intermediaries Organizations that create various loans and investments from funds provided by depositors.

as savings accounts, money market funds, and pension plans, that represent claims, or liabilities, against the institutions. The funds received by intermediaries are, in turn, lent to businesses and individuals via debt instruments created by these institutions, which include automobile loans, mortgages, commercial loans, and similar types of debt. The process by which financial intermediaries transform funds provided by savers into funds used by borrowers is called *financial intermediation*. The lower panel of Figure 3.1 illustrates the financial intermediation process. The arrows at the top portion of the boxes (pointing to the right) indicate the changes in the balance sheets of savers, borrowers, and intermediaries that result from the intermediation process. The arrows at the bottom portion of each box (pointing to the left) show the flow of funds from savers to borrowers through intermediaries.

Without financial intermediaries, savers would have to provide funds directly to borrowers, which would be a difficult task for those who do not possess such expertise; such loans as mortgages and automobile financing would be much more costly, so the financial markets would be much less efficient economically. Clearly, the presence of intermediaries improves economic well-being. In fact, financial intermediaries were created to reduce the inefficiencies that would otherwise exist if users of funds could get loans only by borrowing directly from savers.

Improving economic well-being is only one of the benefits associated with intermediaries. Following are other benefits:

1. ***Reduced costs***—Without intermediaries, the net cost of borrowing would be greater, and the net return earned by savers would be less, because individuals with funds to lend would have to seek out appropriate borrowers themselves, and vice versa. Intermediaries are more cost-efficient than individuals because they (a) create combinations of financial products that better match the funds provided by savers with the needs of borrowers and (b) spread the costs associated with these activities over large numbers of transactions, thus achieving economies of scale.

2. ***Diversification (risk)***—The loan portfolios of intermediaries generally are well diversified, because they provide funds to a large number and variety of borrowers by offering many different types of loans. Thus, intermediaries spread their risks by "not putting all their financial eggs in one basket."

3. ***Funds divisibility/pooling***—Intermediaries can pool funds provided by individuals to offer loans or other financial products with different denominations and different maturities. For example, an intermediary can offer a large loan to a single borrower by combining the funds provided by many small savers, and vice versa.

4. ***Financial flexibility***—Because intermediaries offer a variety of financial products—that is, different types of loans and savings instruments—savers and borrowers have greater choices, or financial flexibility, than can be achieved with direct placements with respect to denominations, maturities, and other characteristics.

5. ***Related services***—A system of specialized intermediaries offers more than just a network of mechanisms to transfer funds from savers to borrowers. Many intermediaries provide other financial services, such as check clearing services, insurance, retirement funds, and trust services.

3-4a Types of Financial Intermediaries

In the United States, a large set of specialized, highly efficient financial intermediaries has evolved. Although each type of intermediary originated to satisfy a particular need in the financial markets, recent competition and government policy have created such a rapidly changing arena that different institutions currently offer financial products and perform services that previously were reserved for others. This trend has caused the lines among the various types of intermediaries to become blurred. Still, some degree of institutional identity persists, and these distinctions are discussed in this section.

Commercial Banks. *Commercial banks*, commonly referred to simply as *banks*, are the traditional "department stores of finance"—that is, they offer a wide range of products and services to a variety of customers. Originally, banks were established to serve the needs of commerce, or business—hence the name "commercial banks." Today, commercial banks, which represent one of the largest types of financial intermediaries, still represent the primary source of business loans. Historically, banks were the institutions that handled checking accounts and provided mechanisms for clearing checks. Also, they traditionally provided the medium through which the supply of money was expanded or contracted. Today, however, several other institutions provide checking and check clearing services and significantly influence the money supply. At the same time, banking companies offer a greater range of services than before.

Credit Unions. A *credit union* is a depository institution that is owned by its depositors, who often are members of a common organization or association, such as an occupation, a religious group, or a community. Credit unions operate as not-for-profit businesses and are managed by member depositors elected by other members.

The purpose of the original credit unions, which were established in Europe more than 160 years ago, was to create savings pools that could be used to provide credit to neighboring farmers who suffered temporary losses of income due to crop failures or other catastrophes. The common bonds possessed by the members generated a help-thy-neighbor attitude within the savings pools. Today, credit unions differ significantly from their earliest forms: They are much larger and hence less personal. Nevertheless, the spirit of credit unions remains unchanged—to serve depositor members. Members' savings are still loaned to other members, but the loans are primarily for automobile purchases, home improvements, and the like. Because credit unions are not-for-profit organizations, loans from these intermediaries often are the cheapest source of funds for individual borrowers.

Thrift Institutions. *Thrift institutions*, also known as *savings and loan associations* or *S&Ls*, cater to savers, especially individuals who have relatively small savings or need long-term loans to purchase houses. Thrifts were originally established because the services offered by commercial banks were designed for businesses rather than individuals, who have substantially different financial needs. S&Ls were first set up so that depositors could pool their savings to create loans that helped other depositors build houses in a particular geographic area. Each savings association was eventually liquidated when the building goals were achieved and all of the loans were repaid. Today, S&Ls not only take the funds of many small savers and then lend this money primarily to home buyers, but also to other types of borrowers.

Mutual Funds. *Mutual funds* are *investment companies* that use funds provided by savers to buy various types of financial assets, including stocks and bonds. These organizations pool investors' funds, reducing risks through diversification. They also achieve economies of scale, which lower the costs of analyzing securities, managing portfolios, and buying and selling securities.

Literally hundreds of different types of mutual funds exist, offering a variety of instruments to meet the objectives of many different types of savers. Investors can find mutual funds to meet almost any financial goal. For example, investors who prefer to receive current income can invest in *income funds*, which are comprised of financial instruments that generate fairly constant annual incomes. Investors who are willing to accept higher risks in hopes of obtaining higher returns can invest in *growth funds*, which include investments that generate little or no income each year but exhibit high growth potential that can result in significant increases in the values of the investments (that is, capital gains) in the future.

Whole-Life Insurance Companies[8]. Broadly speaking, the purpose of life insurance is to provide a beneficiary, such as a spouse or other family members, with protection against financial distress or insecurity that might result from the premature death of a breadwinner or other principal wage earner. In a general sense, life insurance can be labeled either term insurance or whole-life insurance. *Term life insurance* is a relatively short-term contract that provides financial protection for a temporary period—perhaps for one year or for five years at a time—and it must be renewed each period to continue such protection. On the other hand, *whole-life insurance* is a long-term contract that provides lifetime protection.

The cost of term insurance, called the *premium*, generally increases with each renewal, because the risk of premature death increases as the insured ages. In contrast, the premiums associated with whole-life insurance policies are fixed payments computed as an average of the premiums required over the expected life of the insured person. As a consequence, the premiums in the early years exceed what is needed to provide the appropriate coverage, whereas the premiums in the later years are less than what is needed. The excess amounts in the early years are invested to make up for the deficits in later years. These invested amounts provide savings features that create cash values for the whole-life insurance policies. In contrast, term life insurance policies do not provide such savings features because the premiums are fixed for only a short time period (generally five years or less); for this reason, the premiums are based on the existing risks only and change at renewal when risks change. Thus, whole-life polices offer both insurance coverage and a savings feature, whereas term life policies do not.[9]

Pension Funds. *Pensions* are retirement plans funded by corporations or government agencies for their workers. Pension plans are administered primarily by the trust departments of commercial banks or by life insurance companies. Probably the most famous pension plan is Social Security, which is a government-sponsored plan established in 1935 that is funded by tax revenues collected by the federal government. Most state and municipal governments and large corporations also offer pension plans to their employees. Many of these plans have been established to accept both employer and employee contributions, which often are shielded from taxes until the assets are withdrawn from the plan. These contributions are invested by pension fund managers, primarily in long-term investments (stocks and bonds) that will provide retirement income at some later date.

3-5 International Financial Markets[10]

Financial markets have become much more global during the past few decades. As the economies of developing countries have grown, greater numbers of investors have provided funds to these financial markets. In 1970, U.S. stocks accounted for nearly two-thirds of the value of worldwide stock markets. Today, U.S. stock markets represent slightly more than 30 percent of the total value worldwide. But the markets in the United States are still much larger than individual stock markets in any country. During the past decade, the areas of greatest worldwide growth lay in the emerging markets of China, India, and Brazil. In addition, although fairly small in size, the financial markets of countries that were previously part of the Soviet Union—for example, Russia, Serbia, and Ukraine—have experienced substantial growth in recent years.

Even with the expansion of stock markets internationally, exchanges in the United States continue to account for the greatest numbers of trades, with respect to both volume and value. U.S. trading activity accounts for nearly 50 percent of worldwide trading activity each year.

The international market for bonds has experienced growth similar to that of the international stock markets. Even so, the bond markets in the United States and in the countries that comprise Euroland continue to dominate the international bond markets, with approximately 65 percent of the total value (United States, 40 percent; Euroland, 25 percent).[11]

The financial markets truly are global in nature, as can be seen by how recent economic events in the United States have affected economies around the world, and vice versa, especially in Europe and Asia.

While the globalization of financial markets continues and international markets offer investors greater frontiers of opportunity, investing overseas can be challenging due to restrictions imposed or barriers erected by foreign countries. In many cases, individual investors find it difficult or unattractive to invest directly in foreign stocks. Many countries prohibit or severely limit the ability of foreigners to invest in their financial markets, or make it extremely difficult for such investors to access reliable information concerning the companies that are traded in their stock markets.

3-5a Financial Organizations in Other Parts of the World

Two notable factors distinguish financial institutions in the United States from those in other countries. These differences can be traced to the regulatory climate that has existed historically in the United States. Generally speaking, U.S. financial institutions have been much more heavily regulated and faced greater limitations than have their foreign counterparts with regard to expansion (branching), the services that could be offered, and relationships with nonfinancial businesses. Such regulations have imposed an organizational structure

[8]Insurance is intended to reduce the consequences of risk by transferring some of the economic consequences to others—namely insurance companies—that are better able to absorb such risk. Insurance companies achieve risk reduction by *pooling*, or diversifying, the risks of individuals, companies, and governments.

[9]Premiums charged by other insurance companies, such as health insurance, property and casualty insurance, and the like, are based only on the risks faced and are changed over time as the risks change. In other words, they reflect the cost of the peril (risk) that is insured at the time at which the premium is paid. There is no savings function, because individuals pay only for the insurance services offered by such companies. Such insurance companies do not perform the same intermediary function as whole-life insurance companies.

[10]Information about worldwide stock markets can be found in *Standard & Poor's Global Stock Markets Factbook, 2013*. The value given for U.S. stock exchanges is based on the combined values of the New York Stock Exchange, the American Stock Exchange, and NASDAQ. Information about worldwide bond markets can be found on the Bank for International Settlements website in the publication *BIS Quarterly Review*, June 2013, which is available at http://www.bis.org /publ/quarterly.htm.

[12]The term *Euroland* refers to the countries that comprise the European Monetary Unit (EMU), which officially was born on January 1, 1999 with 11 member countries. The original 11 countries included in Euroland were Austria, Belgium, Finland, France, Germany, Ireland, Italy, Luxembourg, the Netherlands, Portugal, and Spain. Even though it was not one of the original 11 countries, Greece is now part of Euroland. Euroland members created a common currency (the *euro*) and a common debt instrument that is denominated in the euro and traded in a unified financial market called the *Euromarket*. The emergence of Euroland was intended to reduce or eliminate the effects of country boundaries with respect to member countries' economic and trading policies.

and competitive environment that have long curbed the ability of individual financial intermediaries in the United States to grow.

©: iStock/Thinkstock

First, past regulation restricted the ability of financial institutions, especially intermediaries, to operate through branches. As a result, the U.S. banking system traditionally has been characterized by a large number of independent financial institutions of various sizes, rather than the few very large institutions that might exist if branching was not restricted. Consider, for example, that there are approximately 14,000 individual banks, credit unions, and thrift institutions in the United States (in 2013), whereas Japan has fewer than 150 licensed banks; there are about 20 Australian-owned banks (four of which are considered large commercial banks), and Canada has only 70 chartered banks (seven of which operate both nationally and internationally). Even India, which has a population about four times larger than that of the United States, has fewer than 300 individual banks. In India and other countries, however, each financial intermediary generally has many branches. For instance, the State Bank of India alone has more than 10,000 offices (branches). The financial institutions of nearly every other country in the world have been allowed to branch with few, if any, limitations, and as a result, their banking systems include far fewer individual, or unit, institutions than exist in the United States.

Second, most foreign financial institutions are allowed to engage in nonbanking (nonfinancial) business activities, whereas the nonbanking activities of U.S. intermediaries have been severely restricted until recently. Developed countries such as the United Kingdom, France, Germany, and Switzerland, to name a few, permit financial firms and commercial businesses to interact without restriction; banking firms can own commercial firms, and vice versa. Other countries, including Canada, Japan, and Spain, allow the mixing of financial institutions and commercial firms with some restrictions.

In the past, regulations that restricted the nonbanking activities of U.S. financial institutions put these organizations at a competitive disadvantage internationally. However, Congress has shown that it is willing to remove existing competitive restraints to allow U.S. institutions to better compete in the global financial arena. To be more like their international counterparts, U.S. financial intermediaries must have the ability to engage in more aspects of multilayer financial deals, which means that these organizations must be able to offer such services as investment banking, commercial lending, insurance, and other necessary financial services. Being able to operate as a company's lender, owner, investment banker, and insurer permits foreign financial organizations to be a "one-stop shop" for financial services and products. Because a single financial institution can offer such financial products as a package, it is possible to reduce the aggregate costs associated with financial services.

It should not be surprising that foreign banks dominate international banking activities. In recent years, however, the presence of U.S. banks in international banking has grown rapidly. At the same time, the limitations that overseas banking operations face in the United States have not discouraged the entry of foreign banks, especially in California, where large Japanese banks have claimed significant market shares. As the world continues to become more globally oriented, so will the banking industry.

3-5b **Recent Legislation of Financial Markets in U.S.**

During 2007–2008, financial markets worldwide experienced substantial declines, some to the point of near collapse. For example, the U.S. stock markets lost more than 50 percent of their total value from November 2007 through February 2009. Much of the blame for this financial crisis was directed toward the actions of financial institutions, especially with regard to some of their lending practices. As a result, governments around the world imposed new regulations to rein in the powers of financial institutions and to provide accountability to world financial systems. Recent major legislative actions include:

Dodd-Frank Wall Street Reform and Consumer Protection Act. Passed in the summer of 2010, this legislation represents the most significant revision of financial regulations in the United States since the 1930s. The purpose of the Act was to restore confidence in the financial markets by requiring accountability and limiting the actions of all participants. Major provisions include:

- Created new organizations to: (1) Help (a) provide consumers clear and accurate information related to credit so that better-informed decisions can be made and (b) protect consumers from unreasonable credit fees. (2) Monitor rules associated with the capital, liquidity, and risk of institutions to help prevent future failures of mega financial organizations.
- Restricts the ability of the U.S. government to use taxpayers' funds to bail out large financial institutions.
- Requires greater transparency for trading exotic securities, such as derivatives and hedge funds. Nearly all complex, risky securities transactions must now be monitored.
- Permits stockholders to have a say on corporate governance, including executive compensation, through nonbinding votes.
- Strengthens the supervision of banks, S&Ls, and bank holding companies.

Basel III Accord (2010). Representatives from 27 countries agreed to increase their banks' capital requirements in an effort to reduce the risk that mega bank failures will cause future financial crises.

Emergency Economic Stabilization Act of 2008. (1) Permitted the U.S. government to purchase up to $700 billion in troubled mortgages in an attempt to improve liquidity in the financial markets (called the Troubled Asset Relief Program, or TARP). (2) Extended certain tax incentives to encourage capital spending. (3) Extended some protections for homeowners whose houses were valued lower than their mortgages. (4) Limited salaries of executives whose companies received TARP funds.

Microfinance in India—Some Observations Microfinance refers to the provision and administration of financial services to rural and unorganized sectors, where access to regular banking is limited. Essentially, microfinance seeks to address the gap created by conventional banks following elaborate procedures and rules before granting loans, which would in most cases make poor people ineligible. This is because of the cost involved in processing absence of collaterals and guarantors and the absence of clear-cut projections regarding repayment of interest and principal.

Microfinance has seen shifts in emphasis over the years. In the early days of microfinance, the ways and means of augmenting self-help programs were the focal points. Now, the emphasis is on total solutions and also on how to make this a working model for both the financing organization and the beneficiary. In some circles, this is being viewed as a huge business opportunity as well.

A country like India surely needs a perfect system of microfinance. It is not that there is dearth of government-sponsored schemes for the rural poor or those intended to boost agriculture and the cottage industry. But, by and large, these schemes are concentrated on specific activities and the conditions for availing these facilities do not always meet the specific requirement of a rural trader.

Among the several questions that have been debated over the years is which one is the correct type of organization to meet this requirement. Arguments have ranged from having a devoted cooperative system to having banks extend their wings in a more pronounced way. The role of rural finance entities has also been examined by the regulators from time to time.

In a fast-developing economy such as India, we certainly need a well-regulated and transparent system which can address the needs, the processes and the servicing and final benefit from financing in a schematic manner. While a number of steps have been taken in this direction, there is still a lot to be achieved. Microfinance institutions draw money from commercial banks, donors and philanthropists and support organizations as they transmit these to ultimate beneficiaries. In India, 70% of the population lives in rural areas. 60% of the population depends directly or indirectly on agriculture. Coupled with this, rural people have low accessibility to structured credit. There are more than 1000 microfinance companies operating in India. Some estimates say that while the total requirement of rural credit is of the order of several trillion, only around ₹700 million crore is being catered to. The impact of microfinance touches at the personal level, the community segment and entire regions.

In India, microfinance is sought by small farmers, rural artisans and other economic weak sections. Women are an important segment in this. The present banking system in the country requires proof regarding the credentials and residence, which the rural poor is unable to furnish.

The microfinance sector with all its growth potential is also facing a number of challenges. Capital is not easy to come by. There is a lot of competition and operational issues including communicating and monitoring. This would, in turn, need microfinance institutions to submit themselves for tighter control and surveillance. Several microfinance institutions have now been recognized as small banks under recent changes in policy by the government.

KEY FINANCIAL ENVIRONMENT CONCEPTS

To conclude this chapter, we summarize some essential concepts that were discussed.

- Financial markets represent the system, or mechanisms, by which borrowers and lenders are brought together.
- Financial markets permit companies and individuals to move income from one time period to another—income is moved from future periods to the current period through borrowing, whereas income is moved from the present period to future periods through investing.
- Corporations generally use the services of investment banking houses when raising funds through issues of stocks and bonds. Investment bankers provide advice and help firms issue securities to raise needed funds.
- Financial intermediaries, which include banks, credit unions, pension funds, and so forth, are important factors in the financial markets. Such intermediaries generally take deposits and create loans (perhaps through investments) that are needed by individuals and businesses. If financial intermediaries did not exist, our standard of living would be much lower because the financial markets would not be able to bring together borrowers and lenders as efficiently as they currently do.
- Even though foreign financial markets have increased their prominence during the past couple of decades, U.S. financial markets continue to dominate financial markets around the world.
- On a relative basis, in most developed countries, there are many fewer individual banks, which are larger, than the number of banks in the United States. In addition, foreign banks often are permitted to engage in nonbanking business activities that U.S. banks are prohibited from doing.

MULTIPLE CHOICE QUESTIONS

1. A primary market means

a. A market between two individuals

b. An unorganized market

c. Invitation by a company to the general public

d. None of the above

2. A secondary market means

a. An initial public offer

b. An underwriting contract

c. Trading of securities in an exchange

d. None of the above

3. Money market instruments are

a. Generally of very long-term duration

b. Generally of very short-term duration

c. Do not have any specific tenure

d. Issued by companies

4. Derivatives are

a. Instruments issued by companies

b. Specific rights on specific assets traded in the exchange

c. Non-tangible assets

d. None of the above

5. Capital markets are necessary

a. As a source of funds mobilization for companies

b. As a source of trading in the secondary market

c. To ensure liquidity for investors

d. All of the above

6. The soundness of a financial system can be assessed by

a. The volume of transactions therein

b. The extent of default in transactions

c. The number and variety of products under trade

d. All of the above

7. A stock exchange

a. Enables buying and selling of shares

b. Stands guarantee to individual transactions

c. Is a source of liquidity for investors

d. All of the above

8. Mutual funds help

a. In gathering funds from banks and in investing them

b. In gathering funds from companies and in investing them

c. In gathering funds from small investors and in investing them

d. None of the above

9. Trading in bonds

a. Is useful for enabling individual investors to earn fixed return on their portfolio

b. Is useful for investors when interest rates in the market keep changing

c. Enables investors to have a wide portfolio

d. All of the above

10. Structured products

a. Are a combination of derivatives and fixed-income securities

b. Are carved out of a group of assets

c. Require a good financial institution to act as intermediary for issue and liquidity

d. All of the above

Answers:

1.	(c)	2.	(c)	3.	(b)	4.	(b)	5.	(d)
6.	(d)	7.	(d)	8.	(c)	9.	(d)	10.	(d)

PROBLEMS

For more problems, visit CourseMate for CFIN at CengageBrain.com

3-1 How do financial markets that run freely and efficiently affect the standard of living in a country?

3-2 What does it mean for a financial market to be considered (a) informationally efficient and (b) economically efficient?

3-3 Do you think investors can earn abnormal returns in financial markets that are at least semistrong-form efficient?

3-4 What economic functions do financial intermediaries perform?

3-5 Do you think that the financial services industry will be more reregulated or deregulated in the future? Explain.

3-6 How do you think intermediaries' characteristics will change in the future?

3-7 How do financial institutions in the United States differ from financial institutions in other parts of the world? Why?

3-8 Eashwar Courier (EC) needs ₹141 million to support future growth. If it issues common stock to raise the needed funds, EC will have to pay its investment banker 6 percent of the issue's total value. If EC can issue common stock at a market price of ₹80 per share, how many shares must be issued so that the company has ₹141 million *after* flotation costs to fund the planned growth?

3-9 Jaiswal Regal Cars (JRC) must raise ₹240 million to support operations. To do so, JRC plans to issue new bonds. Investment bankers have informed JRC that the flotation costs will be 4 percent of the total amount issued. If the market value of each bond is ₹1,000, how many bonds must JRC sell to *net* ₹240 million *after flotation costs*? Assume that fractions of bonds cannot be issued.

3-10 Bhama Rugs needs ₹115 million to build a new distribution center. If it issues common stock to raise the funds, the issuance costs will be 8 percent of the total amount issued. If Bhama can issue stock at ₹40 per share, how many shares of common stock must be issued so that it has ₹115 million *after* flotation costs to use to fund the construction of its distribution center?

3-11 Parashar Rugs needs ₹600 million to support growth next year. If it issues new common stock to raise the funds, the flotation (issuance) costs will be 4 percent. If Parashar can issue stock at ₹125 per share, how many shares of common stock must be issued so that it has ₹600 million *after* flotation costs to use for its planned growth?

3-12 Gana Morris Corporation (GM) plans to issue bonds to raise ₹95 million. GM's investment banker will charge flotation costs equal to 5 percent of the total amount issued. The market value of each bond at issue time will be ₹1,000. How many bonds must GM sell to *net* ₹95 million *after flotation costs*? Assume that fractions of bonds cannot be issued. Show how much of the total amount issued will consist of flotation costs and how much GM will receive after flotation costs are paid.

3-13 Grameen Energy Corporation (GE) plans to issue bonds to raise ₹345 million. GE's investment banker will charge flotation costs equal to 8 percent of the total amount issued. The market value of each bond at issue time will be ₹1,000. How many bonds must GE sell to net ₹345 million *after flotation costs*? Assume that fractions of bonds cannot be issued. Show how much of the total amount issued will consist of flotation costs and how much GE will receive after flotation costs are paid.

3-14 Bharath Emporium (BE) must raise ₹225 million. To do so, BE expects to issue new common stock. BE's Investment banker will charge issuing costs equal to 10 percent of the total amount issued. If the stock can be issued for ₹160 per share, how many shares must BE sell to *net* ₹225 million *after flotation costs*. Show how much of the issue will consist of flotation costs and how much BE will receive after the flotation costs are paid.

3-15 Bhimashankar Mowing needs ₹360 million to support growth. If it issues new common stock to raise the funds, the flotation (issuance) costs will be 4 percent. If Bhimashankar can issue stock at ₹60 per share, how many shares of common stock must be issued so that it has ₹360 million *after* flotation costs? Show how much of the issue will consist of flotation costs and how much Bhimashankar will receive after flotation costs are paid.

3-16 Mama's Motel Corporation (MM) plans to issue bonds to raise ₹175 million that it needs to support future operations. MM's investment banker will charge 2.5 percent of the total amount issued to help MM raise the funds. In addition, MM will incur other costs associated with the issue that equal ₹500,000. The market value of each bond at issue time will be ₹1,000. How many bonds must MM sell to *net* ₹175 million *after flotation costs*? Assume that fractions of bonds cannot be issued.

3–17 Udbhav Uninsured Underwriters (U^3) needs to raise ₹192 million. If it issues new common stock to raise the funds, the flotation costs will be 8 percent. The new issue will also require U^3 to pay ₹280,000 in fees to its lawyers, the printer, and others associated with the issue. U^3 can issue stock at ₹25 per share. How many shares of common stock must be issued so that it has ₹192 million *after* flotation costs? Show how much of the total rupee amount will be flotation costs and how much U^3 will receive after the flotation costs are paid.

3–18 Janaki Flowers must raise ₹345 million for its future expansion. To do so, Janaki expects to issue new common stock. Investment bankers have informed the company that the flotation costs will be 6.5 percent of the total amount issued and that the company will incur another ₹576,000 in costs associated with the issue. Janaki can issue its stock for ₹55 per share. Determine how many shares Janaki must sell to *net* ₹345 million *after flotation costs.*

3–19 Wadge World (WW) needs to raise ₹84 million in debt. To issue the debt, WW must pay its underwriter a fee equal to 3 percent of the issue. The company estimates that other expenses associated with the issue will total ₹487,000. If the face value of each bond is ₹1,000, how many bonds must be issued to net the needed ₹84 million? Assume that the firm cannot issue a fraction of a bond.

The Financial Environment: Markets, Institutions, and Investment Banking

Learning Outcomes

LO.1 Describe the role that financial markets play in improving the standard of living in an economy.

- Financial markets facilitate the transfer of funds from savers (investors) to borrowers. Financial markets that provide an efficient flow of funds provide lower interest rates to borrowers than do inefficient financial markets. At the same time, efficient markets provide good returns (interest rates) to investors who supply the funds that borrowers use. The more efficient the process of the flow of funds, the more productive the economy is in terms of both manufacturing and financing. As a result, financial markets help improve the standard of living in an economy by providing opportunities to borrow and invest at good rates, which provides businesses with opportunities to be more productive than they could be without financial markets. Greater productivity provides more employment and higher salaries than would otherwise exist.

LO.2 Describe how various financial markets are differentiated.

- Some of the categories into which financial markets are classified include:
  - o Money markets versus capital markets—short-term investments (initial maturities of one year or less) are traded in the money markets, whereas long-term investments are traded in the capital markets.
  - o Debt markets versus equity markets—loans are traded in the debt markets and stocks are traded in the equity markets.
  - o Primary versus secondary markets—firms issue new securities in the primary markets to raise funds, whereas already issued, outstanding securities are traded in the secondary markets.
  - o Derivatives markets—securities, such as options and futures, that "derive" their values from other assets are traded in the derivatives markets.

LO.3 Discuss the role that an investment banking house plays in the financial markets.

- Investment banking houses are companies that specialize in assisting corporations when they issue stocks and bonds to raise funds.
- Investment bankers help companies determine how and when to raise funds. The investment banking house generally buys the issue from the company and then resells the securities to investors in the financial markets.

LO.4 Describe the role that financial intermediaries play in the financial markets, and explain why there are so many different types of intermediaries.

- Financial intermediaries are organizations that facilitate the transfer of funds from savers to borrowers. Intermediaries "manufacture" financial products, such as savings accounts, money market funds, and pension funds to attract money that is then loaned to individuals and businesses in the form of debt instruments such as automobile loans, commercial loans, mortgages, and similar types of debt.
- There are many different types of intermediaries, including commercial banks, credit unions, mutual funds, and so forth; each was formed to meet a particular need of borrowers, investors, or both. For example, commercial banks generally provide services used by businesses.

LO.5 Describe how financial markets and financial intermediaries in the United States differ from those in other parts of the world.

- Financial markets and intermediaries have become much more globalized during the past few decades. Most U.S. financial markets and institutions are more heavily regulated than their foreign counterparts. As a result, the largest financial intermediaries in the world generally reside outside the United States.

CHAPTER 3 REVIEW

Chapter 3 Key Financial Environment Concepts

- Financial markets represent the system, or mechanism, by which borrowers and lenders are brought together.
- Financial markets permit companies and individuals to "move" income from one time period to another—income is moved from future periods to the current period through borrowing, whereas income is moved from the present period to future periods through investing (saving).
- Corporations generally use the services of investment banking houses when raising funds through issues of stocks and bonds. Investment bankers provide advice and help firms issue securities to raise needed funds.
- Financial intermediaries, which include banks, credit unions, pension funds, and so forth, are important "players" in the financial markets. Such intermediaries generally take deposits and create loans (perhaps through investments) that are needed by individuals and businesses. If financial intermediaries did not exist, our standard of living would be much lower because bringing together borrowers and lenders would be more difficult and more costly than is possible when such markets exist.
- Even though foreign financial markets have increased their prominence during the past couple of decades, U.S. financial markets continue to dominate financial markets around the world.

Key Terms

LO.1

financial markets A system consisting of individuals and institutions, instruments, and procedures that bring together borrowers and savers. *p. 39*

economic efficiency Funds are allocated to their optimal use at the lowest costs in the financial markets. *p. 40*

informational efficiency The prices of investments reflect existing information and adjust quickly when new information enters the markets. *p. 41*

abnormal return Return that exceeds what is justified by the risk associated with the investment. *p. 41*

LO.2

money markets The segments of the financial markets where the instruments that are traded have original maturities equal to one year or less. *p. 41*

capital markets The segments of the financial markets where the instruments that are traded have original maturities greater than one year. *p. 41*

debt markets Financial markets where loans are traded. *p. 42*

equity markets Financial markets where corporate stocks are traded. *p. 42*

primary markets Markets in which various organizations raise funds by issuing new securities. *p. 42*

secondary markets Markets where financial assets that have previously been issued by various organizations are traded among investors. *p. 42*

derivatives markets Financial markets where options and futures are traded. *p. 42*

initial public offering (IPO) market Market consisting of stocks of privately held companies that have recently gone public for the first time. *p. 43*

physical stock exchanges Formal organizations with physical locations that facilitate trading in designated ("listed") securities. The major U.S. stock exchange is the New York Stock Exchange (NYSE). *p. 43*

listing requirements Characteristics a firm must possess to be listed on a stock exchange. *p. 44*

over-the-counter (OTC) market A collection of brokers and dealers, connected electronically by telephones and computers, that provides for trading in securities not listed on the physical stock exchanges. *p. 44*

dual listing When stocks are listed for trading in more than one stock market. *p. 45*

LO.3

investment banker An organization that underwrites and distributes new issues of securities; it helps businesses and other entities obtain needed financing. *p. 46*

underwritten arrangement Agreement for the sale of securities in which the investment bank guarantees the sale by purchasing the securities from the issuer, thus agreeing to bear any risks involved in the transaction. *p. 47*

best-efforts arrangement Agreement for the sale of securities in which the investment bank handling the transaction gives no guarantee that the securities will be sold. *p. 47*

flotation costs The costs associated with issuing new stocks or bonds. *p. 47*

registration statement A statement of facts filed with the SEC about a company that plans to issue securities. *p. 48*

prospectus A document describing a new security issue and the issuing company. *p. 48*

underwriting syndicate A group of investment banking firms formed to spread the risk associated with the purchase and distribution of a new issue of securities. *p. 48*

shelf registration Registration of securities with the SEC for sale at a later date. The securities are held "on the shelf" until the sale. *p. 49*

LO.4

financial intermediaries Organizations that create various loans and investments from funds provided by depositors. *p. 49*

CHAPTER 4

Time Value of Money

Learning Outcomes

- LO.1 Identify various types of cash flow patterns (streams) seen in business.
- LO.2 Compute (a) the future value of different cash flow streams. Explain the results.
- LO.3 Compute the present value of different cash flow streams. Explain the result.
- LO.4 Compute (a) the return (interest rate) on an investment (loan) and (b) how long it takes to reach a financial goal.
- LO.5 Explain the difference between the annual percentage rate (APR) and the effective annual rate (EAR). Explain when each is more appropriate to use.
- LO.6 Describe an amortized loan. Compute (a) amortized loan payments and (b) the amount that must be paid on an amortized loan at a specific date during the life of the loan.

Business Today (July 2, 2017) contains coverage on the ways Ruias are seeking to restructure the highly debt-ridden Essar. In 1999, Essar Steel became the first company to default on its international debt obligations. Once debt gets high, servicing is a challenge and then the negative impact on the profits adds pressure. This chapter describes the major techniques used in finance to evaluate the amounts spent and received at various points of time and the impact of interest rates on these.

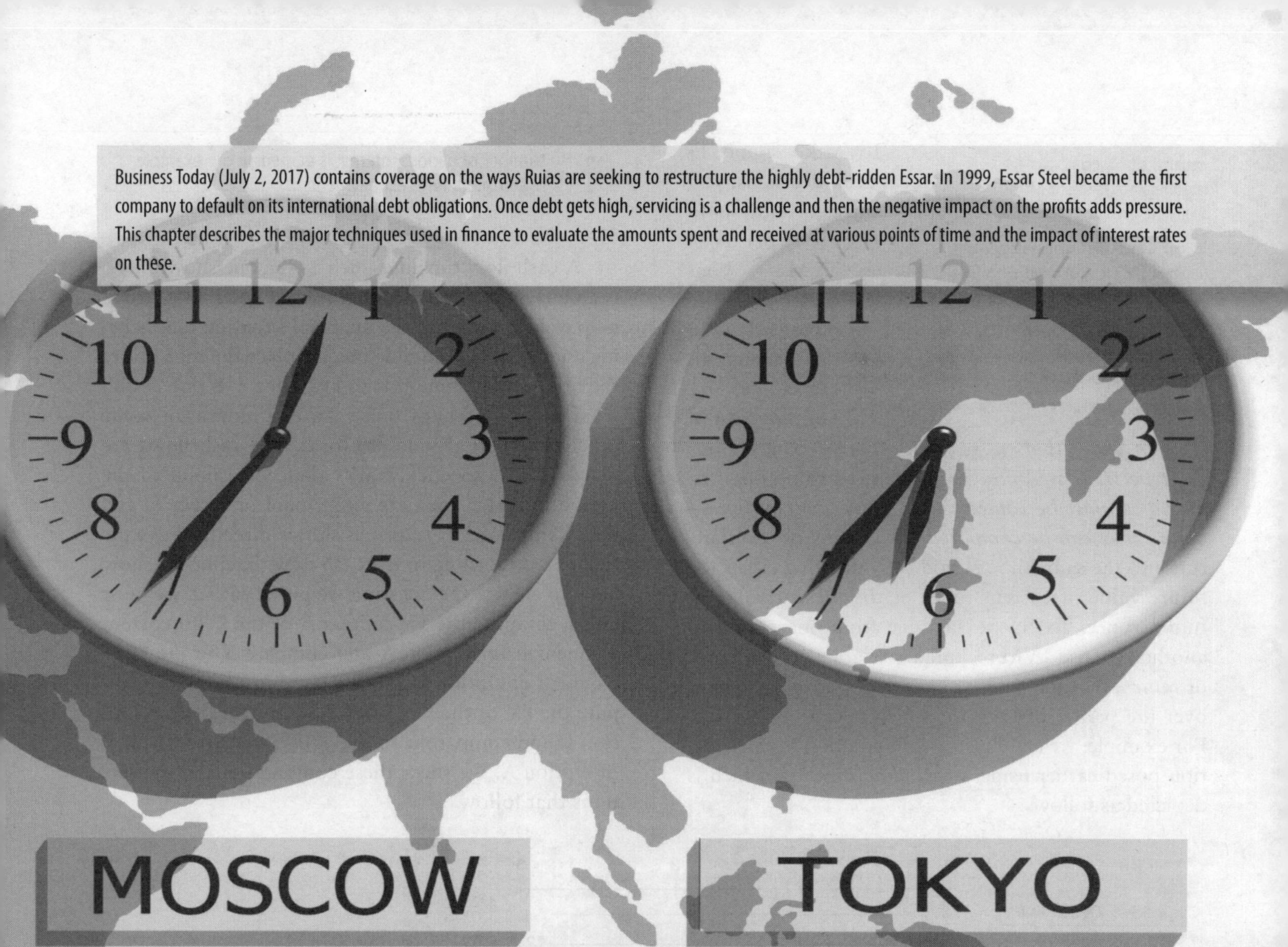

Yakobchuk Vasyl/Shutterstock.com

A basic financial principle states that, all else equal, the sooner cash is received, the more valuable it is. The logic is simple—*the sooner a rupee is received, the more quickly it can be invested to earn a positive return*. So does this mean that receiving ₹700 today is better than receiving ₹935 in three years? Not necessarily because the ₹935 payoff in three years is much greater than the ₹700 payoff today. To determine which payoff is more valuable, the rupee payoffs of each option must be compared at the same point in time. For example, we can restate (revalue) the future payoff of ₹935 in terms of current (today's) rupees and then compare the result to the ₹700 payoff today. The concept used to revalue payments from different time periods, such as the ones described here, is termed the **time value of money (TVM)**.

Study Tools

Problems are found at the end of this chapter

+

Login to **CourseMate** for **CFIN** at **CengageBrain.com** for additional problems and other study tools!

time value of money (TVM) The principles and computations used to revalue cash payoffs from different times so they are stated in rupees of the same time period.

opportunity cost rate The rate of return on the best available alternative investment of equal risk.

lump-sum amount A single payment (received or made) that occurs either today or at some date in the future.

annuity A series of payments of an equal amount at fixed, equal intervals for a specified number of periods.

To make sound financial decisions, you must understand fundamental TVM concepts that are presented in this chapter. To begin, *an important TVM concept states that rupee from different time periods must be translated into the same* time value—*that is, all rupee must be valued at the same point in time—before they can be compared.* We restate, or translate, rupee to the same time period by computing either the future value of current rupee or the present value of future rupee. To "move" a value from one period to another, we use TVM techniques to adjust the interest, or *return*, that the amount has the opportunity to earn over the period of time for which it can be invested. For example, we can illustrate the solution to the question posed earlier using a *cash flow timeline*, which is depicted as follows:

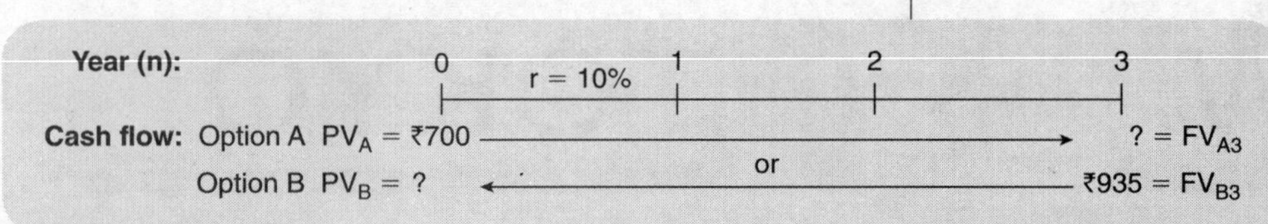

Following are the definitions of the variables shown in the cash flow timeline:

PV =	*Present value*, or beginning amount, that can be invested. PV also represents the current value of some future amount. In our example, the PV of Option A is ₹700 because this is the amount that will be paid today. At this point, we do not know the PV of Option B.
FV_n =	*Future value*, which is the value to which an amount invested today will grow at the end of n periods (years, in this case), after accounting for interest that can be earned during the investment period. In our example, the FV of Option B in Year 3 is ₹935. At this point, we do not know the FV of Option A in Year 3.
r =	Rate of return, or interest rate, that is paid each period. The interest earned each period is based on the balance in the account at the beginning of each period, and we assume that it is paid at the end of the period. In our example, we assume that all investors can earn a 10 percent rate of return each year—that is, the **opportunity cost rate** is 10 percent. Thus, r = 10% or, expressed as a decimal, r = 0.10.
n =	Number of periods interest is earned. In our example, n = 3 years (interest payments).

A cash flow timeline, such as the one shown here, is an essential TVM tool that is used much like a road map to help visualize the financial situation that is being analyzed. On the timeline, we place the time above the line so that Time 0 is today, Time 1 is one period from today—perhaps one year, one month, or some other time period—and so forth. The cash flows are placed below the tick marks that correspond to the period in which they are either paid or received, and the interest rate, or *return*, is shown directly above the timeline. According to the cash flow timeline we show here, to answer the question we posed earlier, we must either compute the FV in Year 3 of the ₹700 current payment from Option A and compare it to the ₹935 payment of Option B to be received in Year 3, or compute the PV of the ₹935 payment in Year 3 from Option B and compare it to the ₹700 PV (current value) of Option A. We show these computations in the sections that follow.

4-1 Cash Flow Patterns

The three cash flow patterns that we normally see in business include:

- ***Lump-sum amount***—A single, or one-time, payment (received or made) that occurs either today or at some date in the future. The cash flows given in the earlier examples and shown in the previous cash flow timeline are lump-sum amounts.
- ***Annuity***—Multiple payments of the same amount over equal time periods. For example, an investment of ₹400 in each of the next three years represents an annuity. If the payment is made at the end of

the period, the annuity is referred to as an **ordinary annuity** because this is the way most payments are made between businesses. On the other hand, if the payment is made at the beginning of the period, the annuity is referred to as an **annuity due**, because in such situations a business has paid for, and is due to receive, certain products or services.

- ***Uneven cash flows***—Multiple payments of different amounts over a period of time. For example, investments of ₹400 this year, ₹300 next year, and ₹250 the following year represent an uneven cash flow stream.

4-2 Future Value (FV)

To compute the **future value** of an amount invested today (a current amount), we "push forward" the current amount by *adding interest* for each period the money can earn interest in the future. This process is called **compounding.** Following is a cash flow timeline that shows how we "push forward" the current ₹700 payment from Option A in our example by adding annual interest (at a 10 percent rate) to determine its value at the end of Year 3.

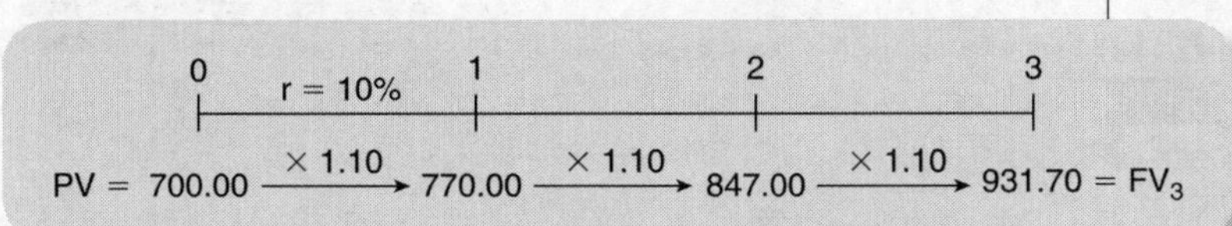

This example shows that if you invest ₹700 today at a 10 percent annual return (interest), your money will grow to ₹770 in one year, to ₹847 in two years, and to ₹931.70 in three years. Using this information, we can now answer the question that was posed earlier: Assuming that all future payments are guaranteed, you should prefer to receive the ₹935 payment from Option B in three years rather than the ₹700 payment from Option A today. The logic is simple: If you take the ₹700 payment today from Option A and invest it at a 10 percent annual return, it will grow to only ₹931.70 in three years, which is ₹3.30 less than the ₹935 you would receive with Option B at the same point in time—that is, at the end of three years.

4-2a FV of a Lump-Sum Amount—FV_n

The computations given on the cash flow timeline show that we can determine the future value of a ₹700 investment that is made today by multiplying the value of the investment at the beginning of each of the three years by (1 + r) = (1.10). As a result, in our example, we would get the same ending balance of ₹931.70 if we multiplied the initial ₹700 investment by (1.10) × (1.10) × (1.10) = $(1.10)^3$. That is,

$$FV_3 = ₹700(1.10)^3 = ₹700(1.33100) = ₹931.70$$

When this concept is generalized, the future value of an amount invested today can be computed by applying Equation 4.1.

4.1

$$FV_n = PV(1 + r)^n$$

Equation 4.1 shows that the future value (FV) of an amount invested today (PV) is based on the multiple by which the initial investment will increase in the future, $(1 + r)^n$. As you can see, this multiple depends on both the interest rate (r) and the length of time (n) interest is earned—that is, $(1 + r)^n$; it is greater when r (interest rate) is higher, when n (investment time period) is greater, or when both conditions exist.

Equation 4.1 shows one approach that can be used to solve a TVM problem—the equation solution. Such problems can also be solved using a financial calculator or a spreadsheet. Each approach gives the same answer to a particular problem, because each performs the same computation. In this chapter, we primarily show the equation solutions and the financial calculator solutions to the problems that are presented.

FV of a Lump-Sum Amount—Equation Solution. The equation solution to our current situation was shown in the previous section with the application of Equation 4.1; that is, FV = $700(1.10)^3$ = 700(1.33100) = 931.70.[1]

ordinary annuity An annuity with payments that occur at the end of each period.

annuity due An annuity with payments that occur at the beginning of each period.

uneven cash flows Multiple payments of different amounts over a period of time.

future value (FV) The amount to which a cash flow or series of cash flows will grow over a given period of time when compounded at a given interest rate.

compounding The process of determining the value to which an amount or a series of cash flows will grow in the future when compound interest is applied.

FV of a Lump-Sum Amount—Financial Calculator Solution. Equation 4.1 and most other TVM equations have been programmed directly into *financial calculators*. These calculators have five keys that correspond to the five most commonly used TVM variables. On a Texas Instruments BAII PLUS financial calculator, which is the calculator we use throughout this book, N = number of periods interest is paid, I/Y = interest rate paid each period, PV = present (today's) value of some amount, FV = future value of an amount, and PMT = amount of an annuity payment (if the problem includes such a cash flow pattern).

Following is an illustration of the financial calculator solution for the current example:

Inputs:	3	10	−700	0	?
	N	I/Y	PV	PMT	FV
Output:					= 931.70

Throughout the book, we show the values that must be entered into the calculator above the illustrations of the TVM keys and show the result of the computation below the keys. Note that financial calculators require all cash flows to be designated as either inflows or outflows, because the computations are based on the fact that we generally pay money, which is a *cash outflow* (a negative cash flow), to receive a benefit, which is a *cash inflow* (a positive cash flow). When entering the cash flows into the calculator, you must designate a cash outflow with a negative sign. In our illustration, because the initial ₹700 is invested today—that is, an investment is purchased—PV is entered as −700. If you forget the negative sign and enter 700, then the calculator assumes you receive ₹700 in the current period and that you must pay it back with interest in the future, so the FV solution would appear as −931.70, a cash outflow.

FV of a Lump-Sum Amount—Spreadsheet Solution. You probably will use a financial calculator to solve the TVM problems assigned in class. Because most businesses use spreadsheets to solve such problems, however, you should have some familiarity with the TVM functions that are programmed into spreadsheets. As a result, we briefly discuss how to set up a spreadsheet to solve the current TVM problem. To solve the problems that we discuss in the remainder of this chapter, similar setups are used; you simply use the appropriate spreadsheet TVM function.

To access the TVM functions that are programmed into Microsoft Excel 2013, you must click on the Insert Function option, which is designated f_x and can be found in the Formulas menu on the toolbar at the top of the spreadsheet.[2] Each preprogrammed function is standardized so that numbers must be entered in a specific order to solve the problem correctly. Figure 4.1

FIGURE 4.1 Using Excel's FV Function to Compute the Future Value of a Lump-Sum Amount, FV

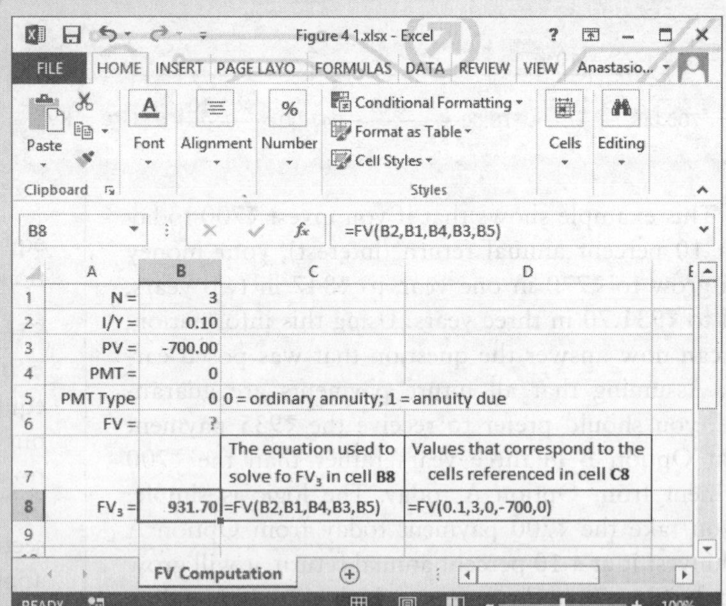

Note: According to the equation shown in cell **C8**, the input values must be entered in a specific order: I/Y, N, PMT, PV, and PMT type (not used for this problem). It is a good idea to set up a table that contains the data needed to solve the problem, and then refer to the cell where each number is located when you apply the FV equation. If you follow this technique, you can change any number in the table you set up and the result of the change will immediately show in the cell where the equation is located. For example, if the current problem is changed so that ₹500 rather than ₹700 is deposited in a bank account, you would change the value in cell **B3** to -500, and the result of 665.50 would appear in cell **B8**.

[2]The Insert Function selection can also be found on the Home menu under the summation sign (Σ).

shows the setup and the results of using the FV function to compute the future value in three years of ₹700 invested today at 10 percent. Because a spreadsheet and a financial calculator have similar functions to solve TVM problems, the labels given in Row 1 through Row 4 of Column A in Figure 4.1 correspond to the TVM keys on a financial calculator. Note that the ₹700 that is invested today is entered into the spreadsheet as a negative value, just as it is when using a financial calculator to solve the problem. Values should be entered in the spreadsheet in the same way as they are entered in the financial calculator, except for the interest rate. The interest rate is entered as a percentage (10 in our example) in the financial calculator, whereas it is entered as a decimal (0.10 in our example) in the spreadsheet.

4-2b FV of an Ordinary Annuity—FVA_n

Suppose Alice decides to deposit ₹400 each year for three years in a savings account that pays 5 percent interest per year. If Alice makes the first deposit one year from today, how much will be in the account when she makes the final deposit? Because the first deposit is at the end of the year (one year from today), the series of deposits represents an *ordinary annuity*. One way to determine the future value of this annuity, which we designate FVA_n, is to compute the future value of *each* individual payment using Equation 4.1 and then sum the results. Using this approach, we find that FVA_3 = ₹1,261.

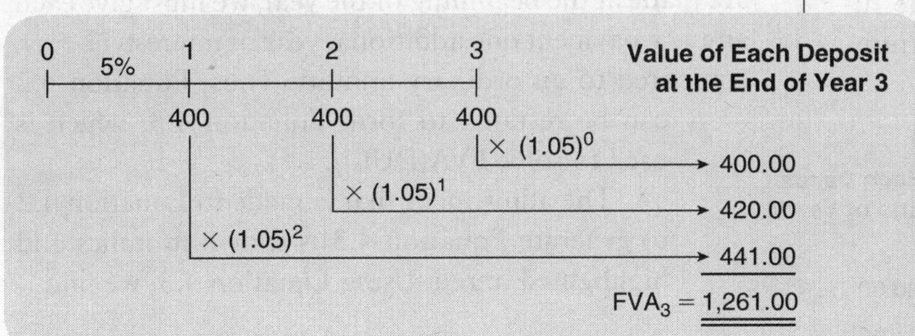

FVA_n—Equation Solution. The timeline solution shows that we can compute the future value of this ₹400 ordinary annuity as follows:

$$\begin{aligned} FVA_3 &= 400(1.05)^2 + 400(1.05)^1 + 400(1.05)^0 \\ &= 400[(1.05)^2 + (1.05)^1 + (1.05)^0] \\ &= 400(1.1025 + 1.0500 + 1.0000) \\ &= 400(3.1525) = 1{,}261.00 \end{aligned}$$

[3]The version of Equation 4.2 given on the third line is derived from the equation given on the first line by applying the algebra of geometric progressions.

Because an annuity represents a *series of equal payments*, we can generalize this computation to obtain Equation 4.2 to solve for the FVA of any ordinary annuity.

4.2

$$\begin{aligned} FVA_n &= PMT\,[(1+r)^{n-1} + (1+r)^{n-2} + \cdots + (1+r)^0] \\ &= PMT\sum_{t=0}^{n-1}(1+r)^t \\ &= PMT\left[\frac{(1+r)^n - 1}{r}\right] \end{aligned}$$

Here the symbol Σ indicates summation, which means that $\sum_{t=0}^{n-1}(1+r)^t = (1+r)^0 + (1+r)^1 + \cdots + (1+r)^{n-1}$ in Equation 4.2. The same interpretation applies to equations that include Σ in the remainder of the book.

Entering the information from our example into Equation 4.2, we have the following solution:[3]

$$FVA_3 = 400\left[\frac{(1.05)^3 - 1}{0.05}\right] = 400(3.15250) = 1{,}261.00$$

FVA_n—Financial Calculator Solution. To solve for FVA_n using a financial calculator, we use the PMT (annuity) key. In our example, we input PMT = −400 because Alice will deposit ₹400 each year in the bank account; this deposit is considered a cash outflow. Thus, the inputs and the result are as follows:

	N	I/Y	PV	PMT	FV
Inputs:	3	5	0	−400	?
Output:					= 1,261.00

Using MS Excel. we will be using the same FV formula that we used for getting the future value of a lump-sum, but here we will be having an entry against the Pmt row. The Pmt row refers to periodic payments and against this we enter (-400). We will not be entering anything against the Pv row, and we get the answer as ₹1261.

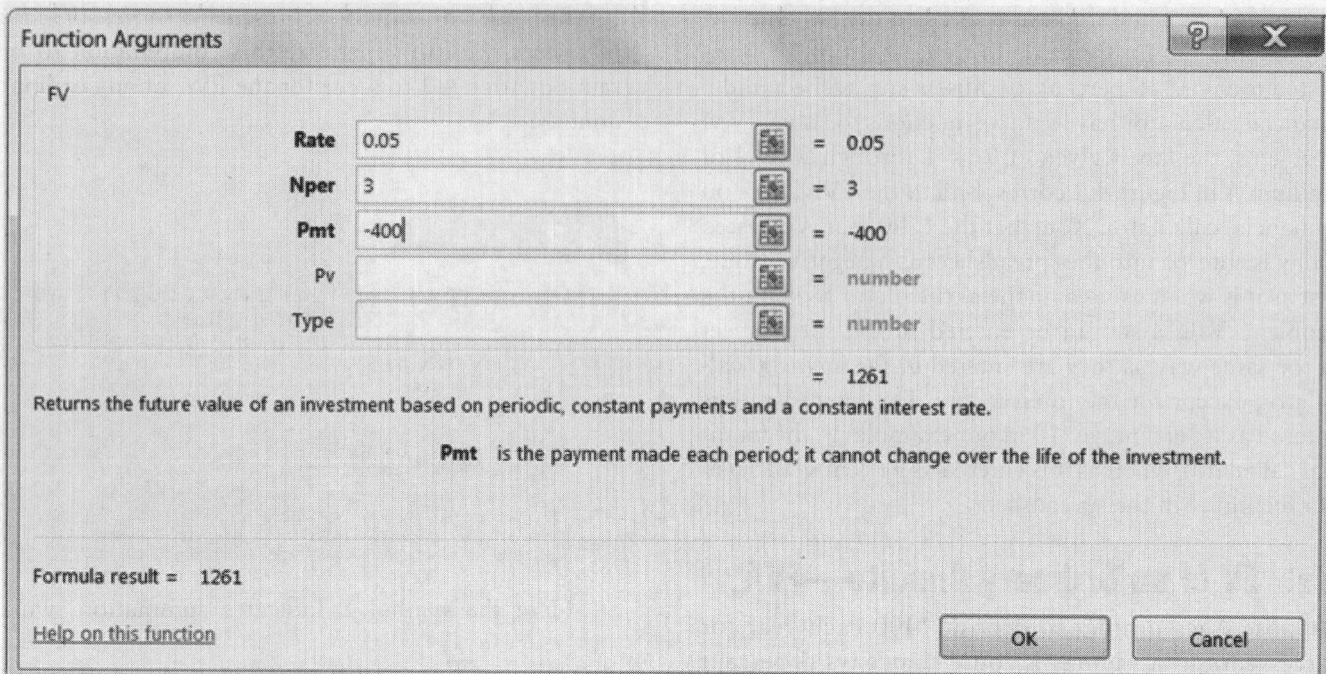

4-2c FV of an Annuity Due—$FVA(DUE)_n$

Now suppose Alice's twin brother, Alvin, thinks that his sister's savings plan is a good idea, so he decides to copy her by also depositing ₹400 each year for three years in a savings account that pays 5 percent interest per year. However, Alvin plans to make his first deposit today rather than one year from today, which means that his series of deposits represents an *annuity due*. Using Equation 4.1 to solve for the future value of the individual payments for this annuity, which we designate $FVA(DUE)_n$, we find

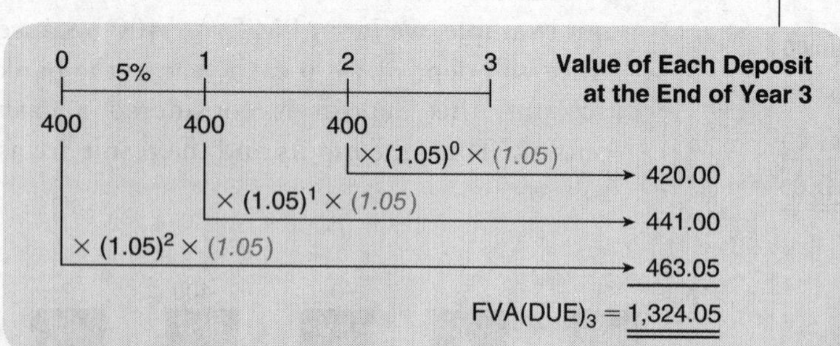

$FVA(DUE)_n$—Equation Solution. As you can see from the cash flow timeline, the future value of Alvin's deposits—$FVA(DUE)_3$ = ₹1,324.05—is greater than the future value of Alice's deposits—FVA_3 = ₹1,261.00. Even though both annuities have the same total amount (cash flows) deposited over the three-year period, each year Alvin makes his deposit at the beginning of the year (annuity due), whereas Alice makes her deposit at the end of the year (ordinary annuity). As a result, each of Alvin's deposits earns one additional year's worth of interest compared to Alice's deposits, which amounts to ₹63.05 additional interest (= ₹1,324.05 − ₹1,261.00).

As the cash flow timeline shows, Equation 4.2, which we used to solve for FVA, must be adjusted to solve for $FVA(DUE)_n$. Specifically, because the payments are made at the beginning of the year, we must give each annuity payment one additional year of interest, $(1 + r)$, compared to an ordinary annuity. Thus, Equation 4.2 can be restated to form Equation 4.3, which is used to solve $FVA(DUE)_n$.

The adjustment that is made to Equation 4.2 to generate Equation 4.3 is shown in italics and highlighted in red. Using Equation 4.3, we find

$$FAV(DUE)_3 = 400\left\{\left[\frac{(1.05)^3 - 1}{0.05}\right] \times (1.05)\right\}$$

$$= 400(3.31013) = 1,324.05$$

4.3

$$FVA(DUE)_n = PMT\sum_{t=0}^{n-1}(1 + r)^t\ (1 + r)$$

$$= PMT\left\{\left[\frac{(1 + r)^n - 1}{r}\right] \times (1 + r)\right\}$$

FVA(DUE)$_n$—Financial Calculator Solution. Financial calculators have a switch, or key, generally marked DUE or BGN, that allows you to designate whether annuity cash flows are end-of-period payments (ordinary annuity) or beginning-of-period payments (annuity due). When the beginning mode is activated on the Texas Instruments BAII PLUS calculator, the letters "BGN" appear in the upper right corner of the display. Thus, to deal

					BGN
Inputs:	3	5	0	−400	?
	N	I/Y	PV	PMT	FV
Output:					= 1,324.05

with annuities due, switch your calculator to BGN and proceed as before:[4]

Because most problems specify end-of-period cash flows—that is, ordinary annuities—*you should always switch your calculator back to the END mode after you work an annuity due problem.*

This can be calculated with MS Excel by using the same FV formula, but by adding "1" to the row "Type", as shown below:

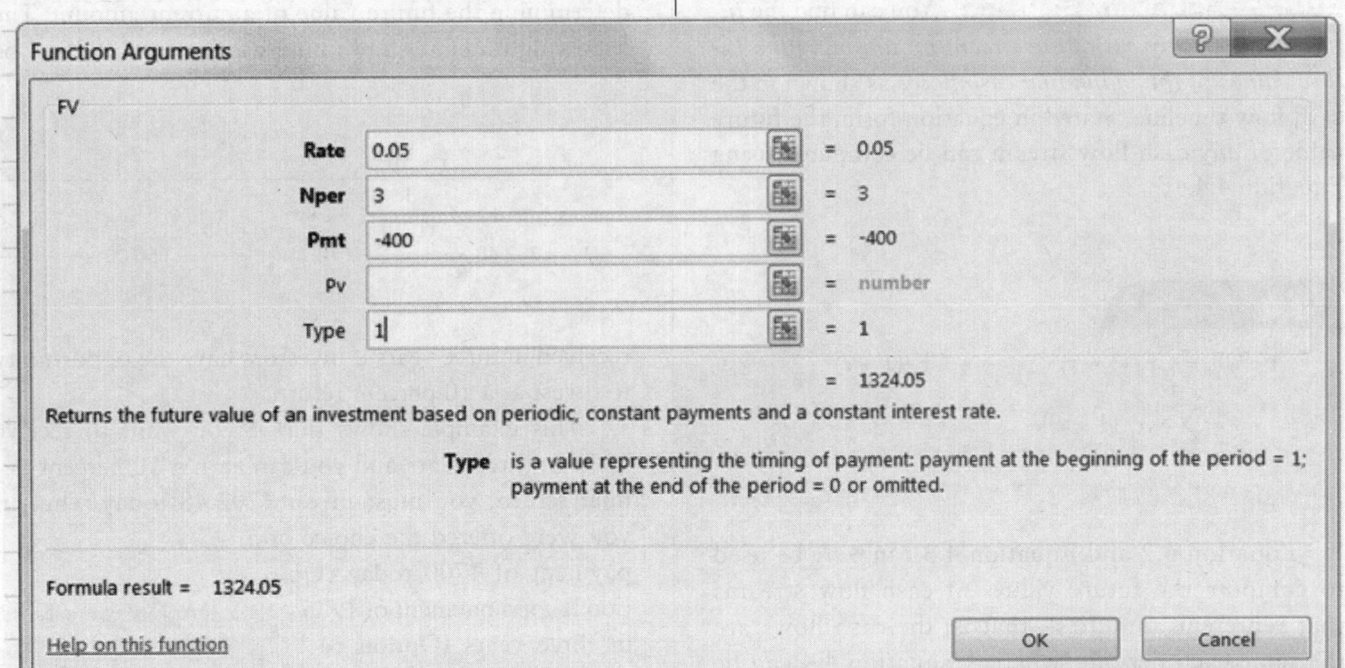

[4]See the operating instructions for the financial calculator you are using to determine how to switch to the "begin" mode.

4-2d FV of an Uneven Cash Flow Stream—FVCF$_n$

The definition of an annuity includes the words *constant*, or *equal, amount*, because annuities consist of payments that are the same for every period. Because some important financial decisions involve uneven, or *nonconstant*, cash flows, it is necessary to extend our TVM discussion to include *uneven cash flow streams*.

Throughout the book, we use the term **payment (PMT)** to identify situations where the cash flows are constant such that the cash flow pattern represents an annuity, and we use the term **cash flow (CF)** to denote a cash flow series in general, which *includes both uneven cash flows and annuities*. When all cash flows in a series are nonconstant, $CF_1 \neq CF_2 \neq CF_3 \neq \ldots \neq CF_n$, which represents an uneven cash flow stream; when all cash flows in a series are equal, $CF_1 = CF_2 = \ldots = CF_n = PMT$, which represents an annuity.

payment (PMT) This term designates constant cash flows—that is, the amount of an annuity payment.

cash flow (CF) This term designates cash flows in general, including uneven cash flows.

The future value of an uneven cash flow stream, sometimes called the **terminal value**, is found by compounding each payment to the end of the stream and then summing the future values. For example, suppose that rather than depositing ₹400 each year in her bank account, Alice managed to deposit ₹400 at the end of the first year, ₹300 at the end of the second year, and ₹250 at the end of the third year. If the account earns 5 percent interest each year, the future value of this uneven cash flow stream is

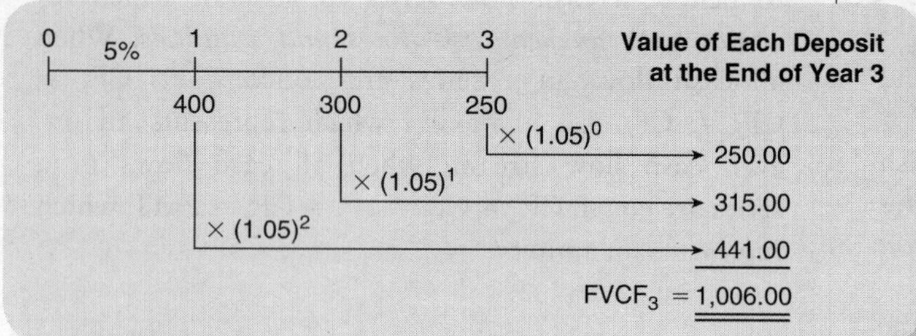

FVCF$_n$—Equation Solution. You can find the *future value of any cash flow stream by summing the future values of the individual cash flows* as shown in the cash flow timeline. Stated in equation form, the future value of *any* cash flow stream can be computed using Equation 4.4.

4.4

$$FVCF_n = CF_1(1+r)^{n-1} + \cdots + CF_n(1+r)^0 = \sum_{t=0}^{n-1} CF_t(1+r)^t$$

Equation 4.2 and Equation 4.3 can *only* be used to compute the future values of cash flow streams that represent annuities—that is, the cash flows are the same each period—whereas Equation 4.4 can be used to find the future value for *any* cash flow stream (annuity or uneven). Because the cash flows shown in the previous cash flow timeline are not equal, Equation 4.4 cannot be simplified further for our example. Thus, to compute the future value of an uneven cash flow stream, you must compute the future value of each cash payment and then sum the results. In our example, the computation is

$$\begin{aligned} FV_3 &= 400(1.05)^2 + 300(1.05)^1 + 250(1.05)^0 \\ &= 400(1.1025) + 300(1.0500) + 250(1.0000) \\ &= 1{,}006.00 \end{aligned}$$

This process can be quite tedious if the uneven cash flow stream covers many years. Fortunately, financial calculators have *cash flow registers* that can be used to make such computations more manageable. We will discuss use of the cash flow register on the financial calculator to compute the future value of an uneven cash flow stream at the end of the next section.

4-3 Present Value (PV)

To compute the **present value** of a future amount, we "bring back" the future amount by *taking interest out* for each future period that the money has the opportunity to earn interest; that is, we "de-interest" the future amount. This process, which is called **discounting**, is essentially the opposite of determining the future value of a current amount. The following timeline shows how we discount ₹935 to be

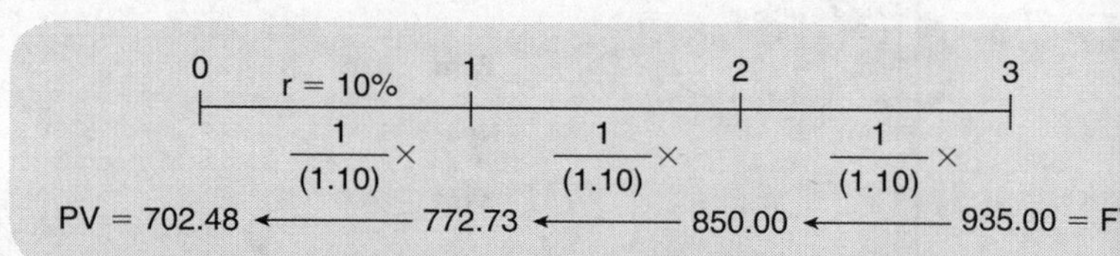

received in three years if investors have the opportunity to invest at a 10 percent return.

This example shows that if you want to receive ₹935 in three years and you can earn a 10 percent annual return, you must invest ₹702.48 today. Thus, if you were offered the choice of a payment of ₹700 today (Option A) or a payment of ₹935 in three years (Option B) and you have the opportunity to earn a 10 percent return (the situation we described at the beginning of the chapter), everything else equal, you

terminal value The future value of a cash flow stream.

present value (PV) The value today—that is, the current value—of a future cash flow or series of cash flows.

discounting The process of determining the present value of a cash flow or a series of cash flows to be received (paid) in the future; the reverse of compounding.

should choose the payment of ₹935 in three years because it has a current (present) value that is greater than ₹700. Another interpretation is to view the present value as either the current cost or the selling price of the future amount. In our example, the cost to produce ₹935 in three years if investors can earn a 10 percent return is ₹702.48; thus, anyone who owns the right to receive ₹935 in three years should be able to sell it today for ₹702.48, which is ₹2.48 greater than the option to receive ₹700 today.

4-3a PV of a Lump-Sum Amount—PV

The timeline solution shows that we compute the present value of the ₹935 payment in three years by taking away three years worth of interest from ₹935, which can be accomplished by *dividing* the value of the investment at the end of each of the three years by $(1 + r) = (1.10)$. As a result, in our example, we would get the same present value of ₹702.48 if we divided the ₹935 to be received in three years by $(1.10)^3$, which discounts the ₹935 by the 10 percent interest that it will earn over the next three years. That is,

$$PV = \frac{935}{(1.10)^3} = 935\left[\frac{1}{(1.10)^3}\right]$$
$$= 935(0.751315) = 702.48$$

PV of a Lump-Sum Amount—Equation Solution. When we generalize the process shown in the previous computation and in the cash flow timeline, the present value of a future lump-sum payment can be computed by applying Equation 4.5:

4.5

$$PV = \frac{FV_n}{(1+r)^n} = FV_n\left[\frac{1}{(1+r)^n}\right]$$

According to Equation 4.5, to compute the present value (PV) of a future amount (FV), we must discount the future amount by the interest that it could earn from the present period until some future period. This discount factor, $1/(1 + r)^n$, depends on both the interest rate (r) and the length of time (n) interest is earned. The PV is lower when r (interest) is higher, when n (time) is greater, or when both conditions exist.

Applying Equation 4.5, we find the solution to our current problem is

$$PV = 935\left[\frac{1}{(1.10)^3}\right] = 935(0.751315) = 702.48$$

PV of a Lump-Sum Amount—Financial Calculator Solution. When solving this problem using a financial calculator, input the known information into the appropriate TVM locations and solve as follows:

Inputs:	3	10	?	0	935
	N	I/Y	PV	PMT	FV
Output:			= −702.48		

Present Value can be calculated in MS Excel by using the "PV" formula as shown below:

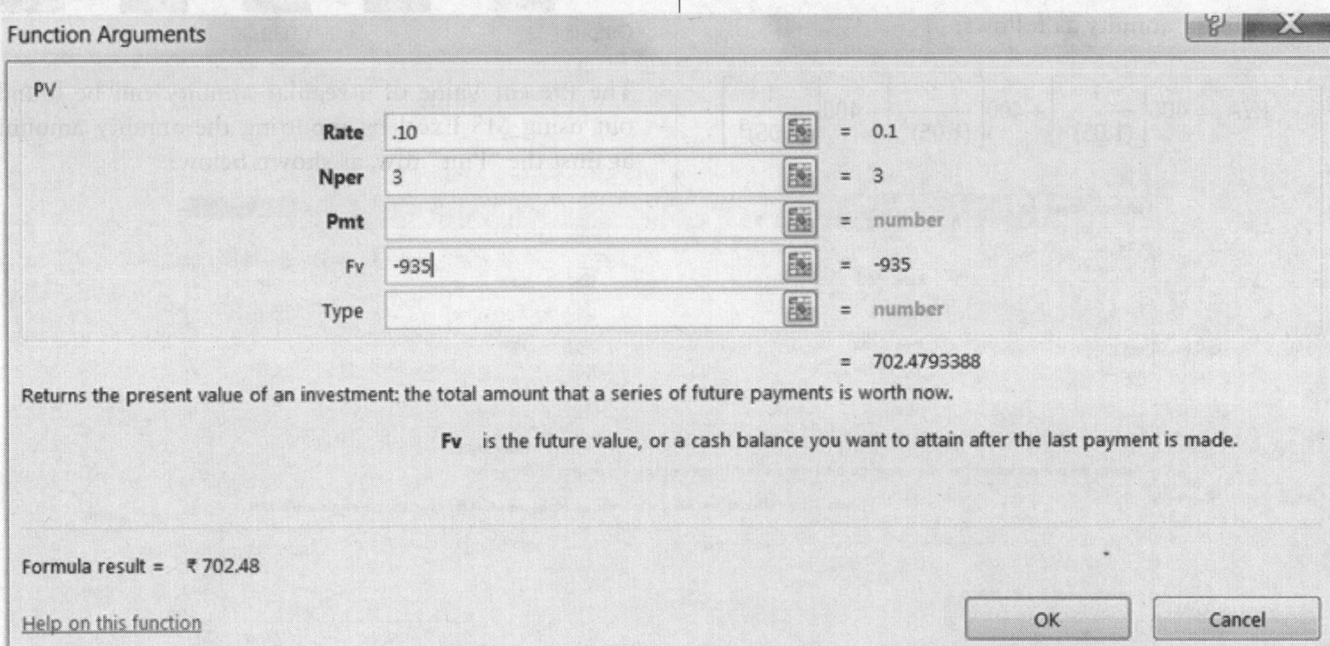

4-3b PV of an Ordinary Annuity—PVA_n

Suppose that Alice, whom we introduced earlier, has decided that she wants to pay herself—that is, take out of savings—₹400 each year for the next three years rather than deposit these amounts in her savings account. If she can invest a lump-sum amount in a savings account that pays 5 percent per year, how much money does she need to deposit today to accomplish her goal? Alice would make the first ₹400 withdrawal from the savings account at the end of this year, which means that the series of cash flows represents an ordinary annuity. Using Equation 4.5, we can compute the present value of each of Alice's annual withdrawals and sum the results to determine the present value of this ordinary annuity, which we designate PVA_n.

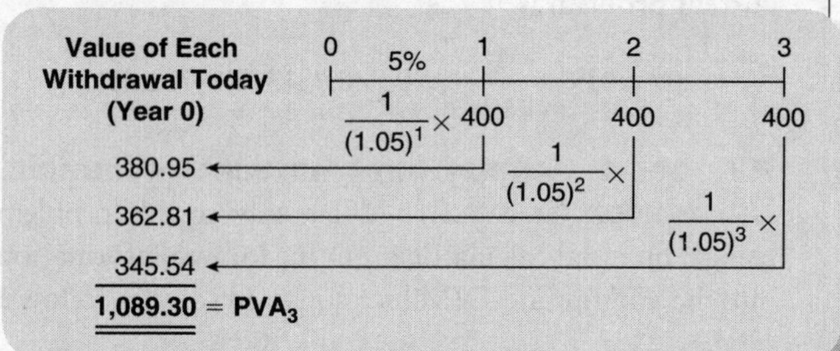

This result indicates that if Alice deposits ₹1,089.30 today in a savings account that pays 5 percent interest per year, she will be able to pay herself (withdraw) ₹400 at the end of each of the next three years.

PVA_n—Equation Solution. According to the timeline solution, we can compute the present value of this ₹400 ordinary annuity as follows:

$$PVA_3 = 400\left[\frac{1}{(1.05)^1}\right] + 400\left[\frac{1}{(1.05)^2}\right] + 400\left[\frac{1}{(1.05)^3}\right]$$

$$PVA_3 = 400\left[\frac{1}{(1.05)^1} + \frac{1}{(1.05)^2} + \frac{1}{(1.05)^3}\right]$$

$$= 400(0.95238 + 0.90703 + 0.86384)$$

$$= 400(2.72325) = 1{,}089.30$$

When this concept is generalized, the present value of an ordinary annuity can be computed by applying Equation 4.6:

4.6

$$PVA_n = PMT\left[\sum_{t=1}^{n}\frac{1}{(1+r)^t}\right] = PMT\left[\frac{1-\frac{1}{(1+r)^n}}{r}\right]$$

Entering the information from our example into Equation 4.6, we find that

$$PVA_3 = 400\left[\frac{1-\frac{1}{(1.05)^3}}{0.05}\right] = 400\,(2.72325) = 1{,}089.30$$

PVA_n—Financial Calculator Solution. To solve for PVA_3 in our example using a financial calculator, the inputs and the result are

	N	I/Y	PV	PMT	FV
Inputs:	3	5	?	400	0
Output:			= −1,089.30		

The Present Value of a regular annuity can be found out using MS Excel by inputting the annuity amount against the "Pmt" row, as shown below:

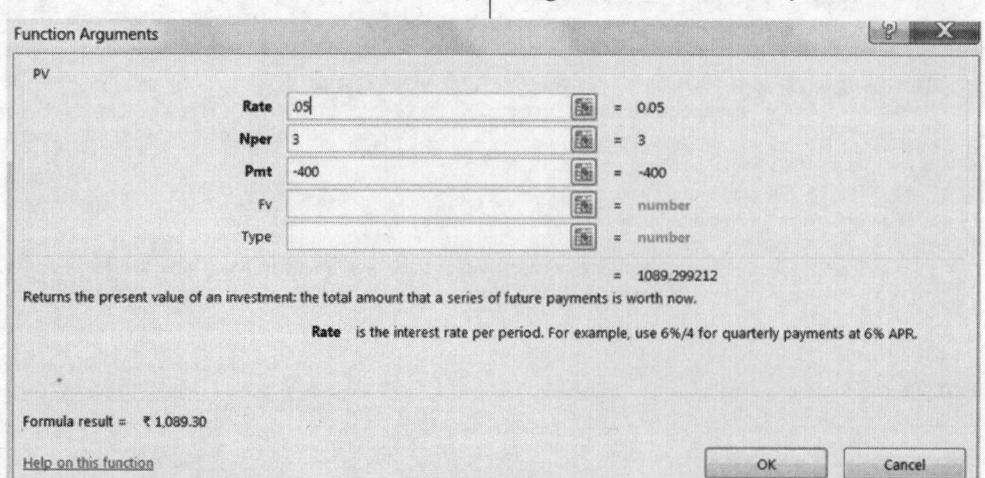

4-3c PV of an Annuity Due—PVA(DUE)$_n$

Suppose that Alice's twin brother, Alvin, again wants to copy his sister. However, Alvin plans to make the first ₹400 withdrawal from his savings account today rather than one year from today. The series of deposits now represents an *annuity due*. Using Equation 4.5, we can compute the PVs of the individual payments and sum the results to find the PV of the annuity due, which we designate PVA(DUE)$_n$.

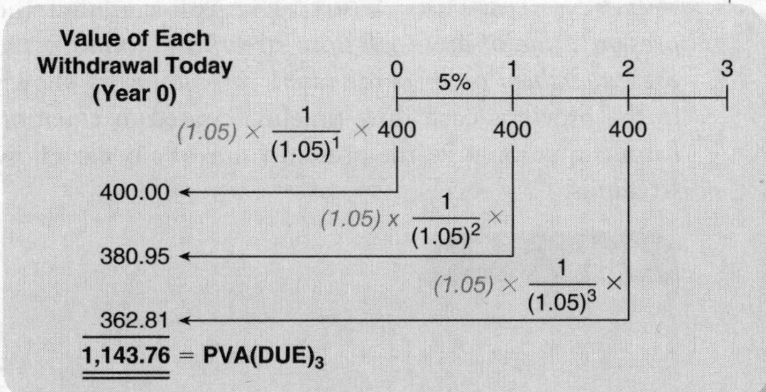

Note that the PV of Alvin's annuity (₹1,143.76) is greater than the PV of Alice's annuity (₹1,089.30). You should have expected this result because Alvin will need to deposit more money today if he wants to pay himself each of the ₹400 withdrawals one year earlier than Alice pays herself. In other words, Alvin's money earns less interest because it is invested for a shorter time than Alice's money, which means he must start with a greater amount to withdraw the same total amount as his sister over the three years.

PVA(DUE)$_n$—Equation Solution. Because an annuity due payment is made at the beginning of the year, to compute PVA(DUE)$_n$, we adjust Equation 4.6 to reflect the fact that each annuity payment must be "given" one additional year of interest (one less year of interest can be earned) compared to an ordinary annuity. Thus, the equation is now stated as Equation 4.7:

4.7

$$\text{PVA(DUE)}_n = \text{PMT}\left\{\sum_{t=1}^{n}\left[\frac{1}{(1+r)^t}\right](1+r)\right\}$$

$$= \text{PMT}\left\{\left[\frac{1-\dfrac{1}{(1+r)^n}}{r}\right]\times(1+r)\right\}$$

The adjustment that is made to Equation 4.6 to generate Equation 4.7 is shown in italics and highlighted in red. Applying Equation 4.7 to our example, we find

$$\text{PVA(DUE)}_3 = 400\left\{\left[\frac{1-\dfrac{1}{(1.05)^3}}{0.05}\right]\times(1.05)\right\}$$

$$400(2.85941) = 1{,}143.76$$

PVA(DUE)$_n$—Financial Calculator Solution. As described earlier, to deal with annuities due, you must switch your calculator to the BGN mode. The inputs and the result for the current situation are

					BGN
Inputs:	3	5	?	400	0
	N	I/Y	PV	PMT	FV
Output:			= −1,143.76		

In case of Annuity due, the excel input will also include a "1" against "Type" row as shown below:

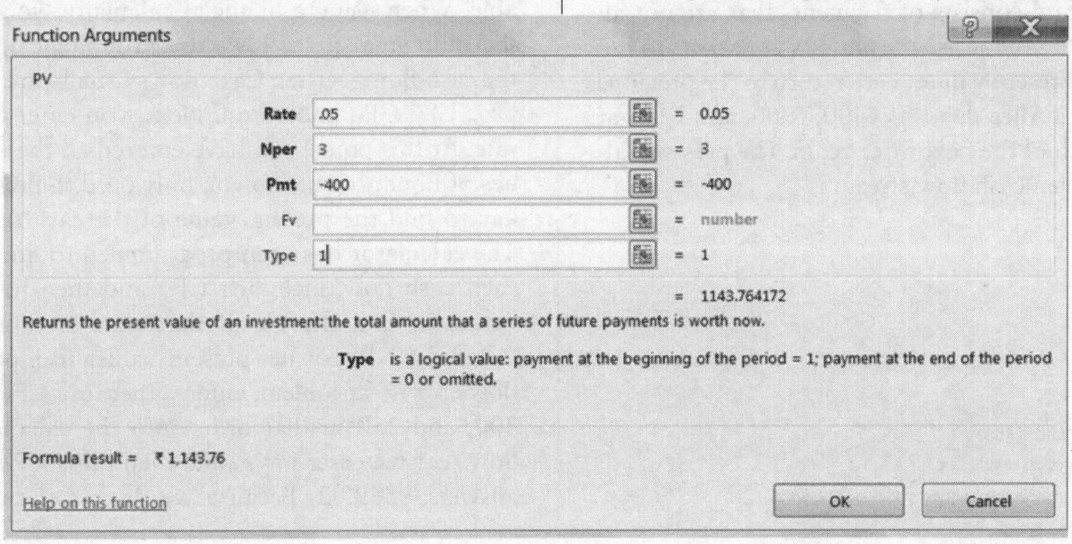

4-3d **Perpetuities**

Although most annuities call for payments to be made over some limited period of time, some annuities go on indefinitely, or perpetually. These *perpet*ual ann*uities* are called **perpetuities.** The present value of a perpetuity is found by applying Equation 4.8, which is simply Equation 4.6 when n = ∞:

4.8

$$PVT = PMT\left[\frac{1}{r}\right] = \frac{PMT}{r}$$

Suppose an investment promises to pay ₹100 per year in perpetuity. What is this investment worth if the opportunity cost rate is 5 percent? The answer is ₹2,000:

$$PVP = \frac{100}{0.05} = 2{,}000$$

Suppose the interest rate increases to 10 percent. What would happen to the investment's value? The value would drop to ₹1,000:

$$PVP = \frac{100}{0.10} = 1{,}000$$

We see that the value of a perpetuity changes dramatically when interest rates change. This example demonstrates an important financial concept: Everything else equal, when the *interest rate changes, the value of an investment changes in an opposite direction.*

4-3e **PV of an Uneven Cash flow Stream—PVCF$_n$**

We mentioned earlier that an uneven, or nonconstant, cash flow stream consists of payments that are not all equal; thus, we cannot use the annuity equations to determine their present values. Let's return to the previous example where Alice deposits ₹400, ₹300, and ₹250 at the end of each of the next three years. The present value of this uneven cash flow stream is

perpetuities Streams of equal payments that are expected to continue forever.

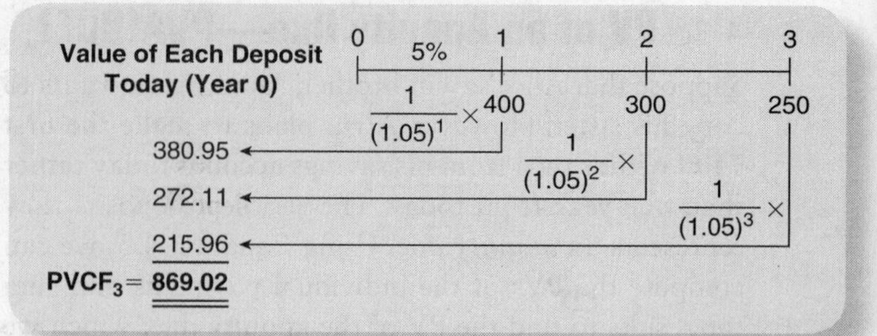

PVCF$_n$—Equation Solution. You can find the *present value of any cash flow stream by summing the present values of the individual cash flows* as shown in the previous cash flow timeline. Stated in equation form (Equation 4.9), the present value of any cash flow stream is:

4.9

$$PVCF_n = CF_1\left[\frac{1}{(1+r)^1}\right] + \cdots + CF_n\left[\frac{1}{(1+r)^n}\right]$$

$$= \sum_{t=1}^{n} CF_t\left[\frac{1}{(1+r)^t}\right]$$

Because the cash flows shown in the previous cash flow timeline are not equal, Equation 4.9 cannot be simplified further for our situation. Thus, to compute the present value of an uneven cash flow stream, you must compute the present value of each cash payment and then sum the results as shown in the cash flow timeline.

PVCF$_n$—Financial Calculator Solution. Financial calculators have "cash flow registers" that can be used to make the computation of PVCF$_n$ more manageable. When using a financial calculator, you first input the individual cash flows in chronological order into the cash flow register. Cash flows usually are designated CF_0, CF_1, CF_2, and so on. Next, you enter the interest rate. At this point, you have entered all the known values of Equation 4.9, so you only need to press the NPV key to find the present value of the cash flow stream. The calculator has been programmed to find the PV of each cash flow, including CF_0, and then to sum these values to find the PV of the entire stream, which is called the NPV, or net present value. To input the cash flows for this problem, enter 0 (because $CF_0 = 0$), 400, 300, and 250 in that order into the calculator's cash flow register, enter I = 5, and then press NPV to get the answer, −869.02. Because we discuss the application of this function in much greater detail in Chapter 9, we will wait until then to describe in more detail the process of solving for NPV using a financial calculator.

After computing the present value of an uneven cash flow stream, we can use either Equation 4.1 or a financial calculator to determine its future value. For the current situation, $FVCF_3$ = ₹869.02$(1.05)^3$ = ₹1,006. This is the same result we found earlier using Equation 4.4.[5]

4-3f Comparison of Future Value with Present Value

In the previous sections, we showed that if, beginning in one year, Alice deposits ₹400 per year in a savings account that pays 5 percent interest annually, her account will have a balance of ₹1,261 at the end of three years. We also discovered that Alice must deposit ₹1,089.30 today in a savings account that pays 5 percent interest annually if she wants to pay herself ₹400 per year for the next three years, assuming that she withdraws the first ₹400 from the account in one year.

Suppose you win a raffle that allows you to choose from one of three prizes: ₹1,089.30 that will be paid to you today, ₹1,261 that will be paid to you in three years, or three payments of ₹400 at the end of each of the next three years. If your opportunity cost is 5 percent, which prize *should* you choose? Believe it or not, you should flip a coin to make your choice, because each prize is equally desirable. Whichever prize you receive can be transformed into one of the other prizes. For example, let's assume that you don't have a choice and you are given the prize that pays you ₹1,089.30 today. If you don't need the money, you can invest the ₹1,089.30 at 5 percent, and it will grow to ₹1,261 in three years. That is, FV_3 = ₹1,089.30$(1.05)^3$ = ₹1,261.00. Conversely, if you are given the prize that pays you ₹1,261 in three years, you can sell the prize today for its present value of ₹1,089.30, because PV = ₹1,261.00/$(1.05)^3$.

What if you need money today to pay your rent? Shouldn't you want the prize that pays you ₹1,089.30 today? The answer is the same as before: It doesn't matter which prize you get because you can convert the payoff you receive from one prize into the payoff that you would receive from either of the other two prizes. In other words, even if you receive the prize

Stephen Stickler/Taxi/Getty Images

with the future payoff, you should be able to turn it into cash today (immediately) by selling it. Moreover, if you want the annuity payment, as discussed earlier, you can invest ₹1,089.30 at 5 percent annual interest and pay yourself ₹400 at the end of each of the next three years. Table 4.1 shows that this statement is indeed correct.

This simple example shows that when we work TVM problems, we simply translate (restate) rupees (values) from one time period into their *equivalent* rupees (values) at some other point in time. To determine the future value of a current amount, we *add interest* that can be earned over the investment period; to determine the present value of a future amount, we *take out interest* that can be earned over the investment period.

4-4 Solving for Interest Rates (r) or Time (n)

The equations that we presented in the previous sections include variables labeled PV, FV, r, n, and PMT. If we know the values of all these variables except one, we can solve for the value of the unknown variable. To this point, we have solved for present values and future

[5] Some financial calculators are programmed to compute both the net present value, NPV, and the net future value, NFV. The NFV is the future value of the cash flows from Period 0 through Period n; that is, NFV = $NPV(1 + r)^n$.

TABLE 4.1 Creating a ₹400 Annuity Payment

Year	Balance at the Beginning of the Year	Annual Interest Earned @ 5%[a]	Balance at the End of the Year	Withdrawal at the End of the Year
1	₹1,089.30	₹54.47	₹1,143.77	₹400.00
2	743.77	37.19	780.96	400.00
3	380.96	19.05	400.01[b]	400.00

[a]Annual interest is computed by multiplying the balance at the beginning of the year by 0.05. For example, the interest earned in the first year is ₹54.47 = ₹1,089.30 × 0.05.
[b]There is a ₹0.01 difference due to rounding.

values. In many situations, however, we need to solve for either r or n. In this section, we give a couple of situations where we might want to solve for these variables. We show the financial calculator solutions only, because the algebraic (equation) solutions are more complicated.

4-4a Solving for r

Suppose you can buy a security at a price of ₹78.35 that will pay you ₹100 after five years. What annual rate of return will you earn if you purchase the security? Here you know PV, FV, and n, but you do not know r, the interest rate that you will earn on your investment. The timeline setup is:

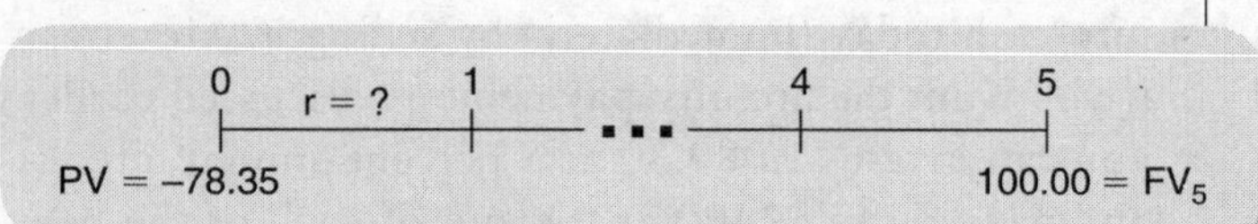

Using your financial calculator, enter the known values into the appropriate locations—that is, N = 5, PV = −78.35, PMT = 0, and FV = 100—and then solve for the unknown value.

	N	I/Y	PV	PMT	FV
Inputs:	5	?	−78.35	0	100.00
Output:		= 5.00			

4-4b Solving for n

Suppose you know that a security will provide a return of 10 percent per year, it will cost ₹68.30 to purchase, and you want to keep the investment until it grows to a value of ₹100. How long will it take the investment to grow to ₹100? In this case, we know PV, FV, and r, but we do not know n, the number of periods.

annual compounding The process of determining the future (or present) value of a cash flow or series of cash flows when interest is paid once per year.

semiannual compounding The process of determining the future (or present) value of a cash flow or series of cash flows when interest is paid twice per year.

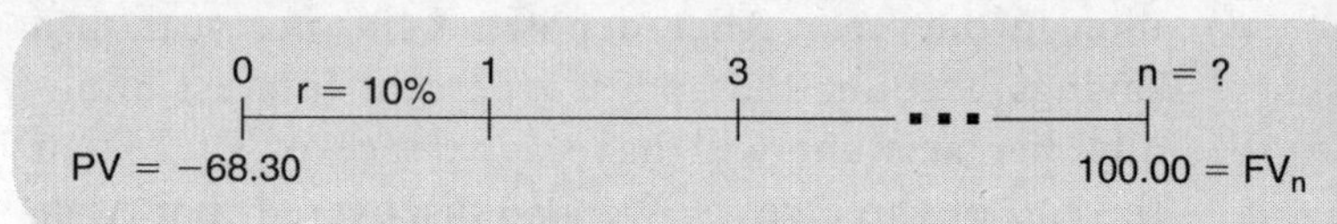

Using your financial calculator, enter I/Y = 10, PV = −68.30, PMT = 0, and FV = 100; then solve for n = 4.

	N	I/Y	PV	PMT	FV
Inputs:	?	10	−68.30	0	100.00
Output:	= 4.0				

The same steps can be applied to solve for r and n for annuities. We will discuss how to determine r for an uneven cash flow stream later in the book.

4-5 Annual Percentage Rate (APR) and Effective Annual Rate (EAR)

In all of our examples to this point, we assumed that interest was compounded once per year or annually. This is called **annual compounding.** Suppose, however, that you earn interest more often than once per year—say, twice per year **(semiannual compounding)**, four times per year (quarterly compounding), or every day (daily compounding). In this section, we compare the rate of return that is earned when interest is paid once per year (annually) with the rate that is earned when interest is paid more than once per year.

4-5a Semiannual and Other Compounding Periods

To illustrate semiannual compounding, let's return to the example we introduced at the beginning of the

FIGURE 4.2 Timeline: Semiannual Compounding

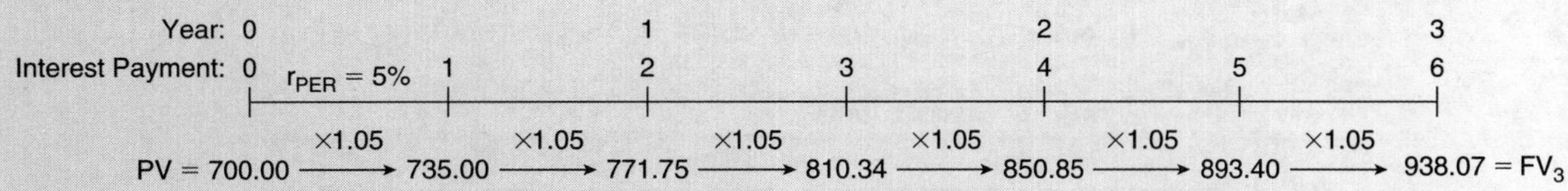

chapter: Assume that ₹700 is invested at an annual interest rate of 10 percent for a period of three years. Earlier we showed what happens when interest is *compounded annually*: The interest that is earned will grow the investment to ₹931.70 at the end of three years.

How would the future value change if interest is paid twice each year, that is, semiannually? Look at the timeline in Figure 4.2 on the next page.

To find the future value, we apply Equation 4.1, generally after making the two adjustments that are shown on the cash flow timeline: (1) convert the annual interest rate to a rate per period (*periodic rate*) and (2) convert the investment period from the number of years to the number of interest payments (compounding periods) during the life of the investment. These conversions are as shown in Equations 4.10 and 4.11:

4.10

$$\text{Periodic rate} = r_{PER} = \frac{\left(\begin{array}{c}\text{Stated annual}\\ \text{interest rate}\end{array}\right)}{\left(\begin{array}{c}\text{Number of interest}\\ \text{payments per year}\end{array}\right)} = \frac{r_{SIMPLE}}{m}$$

4.11

$$\text{Number of interest periods} = n_{PER} = \left(\begin{array}{c}\text{Number}\\ \text{of years}\end{array}\right) \times \left(\begin{array}{c}\text{Number of interest}\\ \text{payments per year}\end{array}\right) = n_{YRS} \times m$$

Here m is the number of interest payments per year, r_{SIMPLE} is the simple (noncompounded) annual interest rate, r_{PER} is the rate of interest that is paid *each* compounding period, n_{YRS} is the number of years interest is earned, and n_{PER} is the total number of interest payments during the n_{YRS} years (periods). Note that $r_{PER} = r_{SIMPLE}$ and $n_{PER} = n_{YRS}$ only when interest is compounded annually; when interest is compounded more than once per year, $r_{PER} < r_{SIMPLE}$ and $n_{PER} > n_{YRS}$.

In our current example, if interest is paid semiannually there are $n_{PER} = 2 \times 3 = 6$ interest payments during the life of the investment, and interest is paid at a rate equal to $r_{PER} = r_{SIMPLE}/m = 10\%/2 = 5\%$ every six months. If we make these adjustments and apply Equation 4.1, we find:

$$FV_3 = ₹700\left(1+\frac{0.10}{2}\right)^{3\times2} = ₹700(1.05)^6$$

$$= ₹700(1.34010) = ₹938.07$$

The financial calculator solution is

	N	I/Y	PV	PMT	FV
Inputs:	6	5	−700	0	?
Output:					= 938.07

Relevance of periods of compounding

The periodicity of compounding has a bearing on the final result, whether it is future value, future value of an annuity, present value or the present value of an annuity.

Suppose we wish to find the value of ₹5,000 invested for one year at 8% interest (see Exhibit 1).

We get the answer to be ₹5,400. In the same example, if the interest rates were to be compounded half-yearly, all we have to do is to modify the formula as indicated in Exhibit 2.

EXHIBIT 1

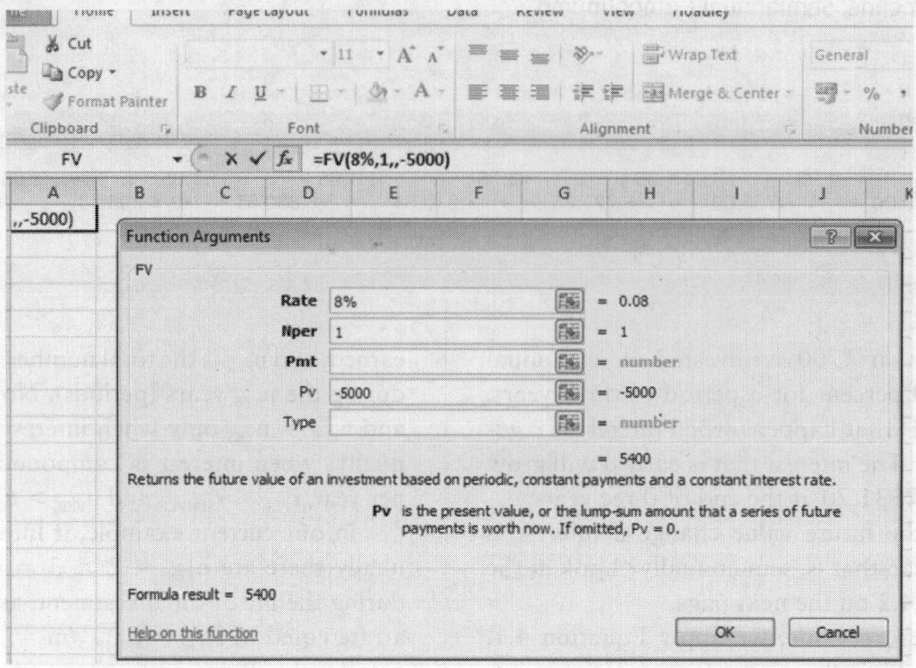

Notice that the rate has been changed to the relevant percentage divided by two (to indicate half-yearly interest) and the number of periods has correspondingly gone up to two. The result is ₹5408, which understandably is greater than the one obtained under annual compounding.

In the same, way we can compute the value in case the compounding is quarterly (see Exhibit 3).

The result is ₹5412.16. Similarly, we can calculate the value for compounding for other frequencies by inputting the following particulars against the Rate and Nper rows, resultantly getting the values indicated in the last column (see Table 4.2).

EXHIBIT 2

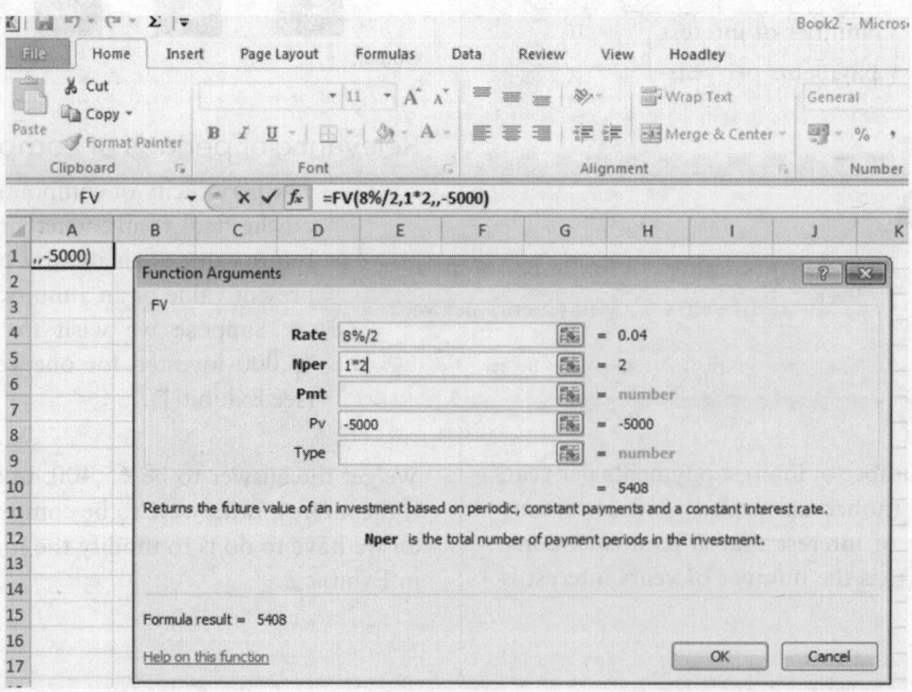

EXHIBIT 3

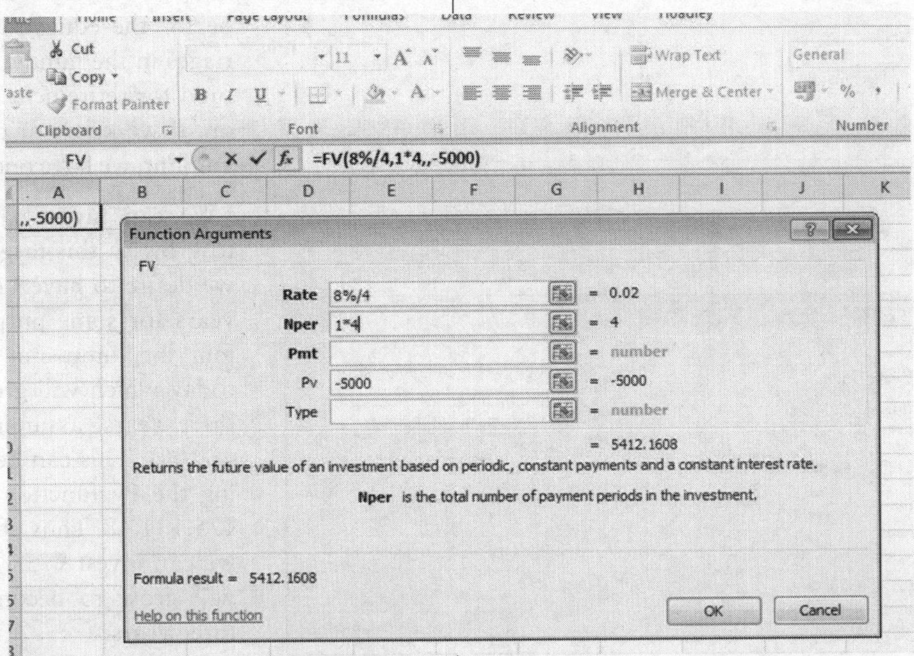

TABLE 4.2		
Monthly compounding	Rate 8%/12 Nper 1 × 12	₹5415.00
Fortnightly compounding	Rate 8%/24 Nper 1 × 24	₹5415.71
Daily compounding	Rate 8%/365 Nper 1 × 365	₹5416.39

Effective Interest Rates

Another way of looking at the phenomenon would be to see the increase in effective interest rates consequent to increase in the compounding frequency. The interest rate for half-yearly compounding becomes effectively higher than the one for yearly compounding. The interest rate for quarterly compounding is effectively higher than the one for half-yearly compounding and so on. It should be remembered that interest rate per annum is the same in all cases, but because of the increase in the frequency of compounding, the interest rate effectively goes up as the periodicity of compounding increases.

Mathematically, the effective interest rate for various compounding periods can be found out by the formula

$$= \left(1 + \frac{i}{n}\right)^n - 1$$

i = stated annual interest rate

n = number of compounding periods

If the yearly rate of interest is 12%, the corresponding effective rate of interest for various other frequencies of compounding will be as given below.

The effective interest rate tells us that if the compounding is, say, half-yearly, it is as good as having an annual interest rate of 12.36%.

Calculations with MS Excel

The above calculation can be made in MS Excel by using the EFFECT formula as shown in Exhibit 4.

The row Nominal_rate refers to the annual interest rate for annual compounding. Npery refers to the number of compounding per year. Thus, a half-yearly compounding (shown above) has two compounding per year, quarterly compounding has four, monthly has twelve and so on.

By filling up the two relevant rows as shown in Table 4.3, we get the same results as those under the EFFECT formula.

Periodicity of compounding	Formula	Result
Half-yearly compounding	((1 + (.12 / 2))2) – 1	0.1236 or 12.36%
Quarterly compounding	((1 + (.12 / 4))4) – 1	0.1255 or 12.55%
Monthly compounding	((1 + (.12 / 12))12) – 1	0.1268 or 12.68%
Fortnightly compounding	((1 + (.12 / 24))24) – 1	0.1272 or 12.72%
Daily compounding	((1 + (.12 / 365))365) – 1	0.1275 or 12.75%

EXHIBIT 4

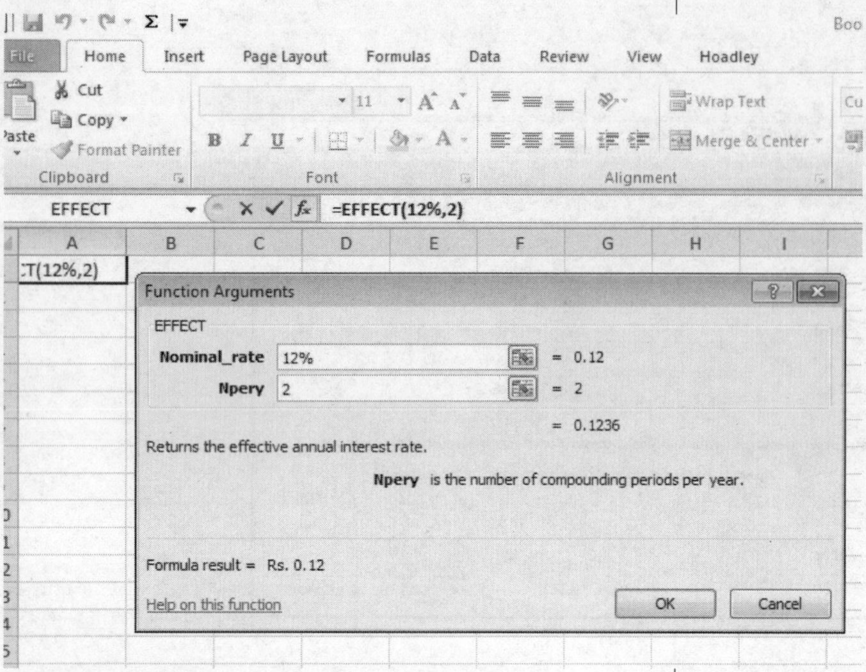

TABLE 4.3

Periodicity of compounding	Inputs in effect Formula	Result
Half-yearly compounding	Nominal_rate: 12% Npery: 2	0.1236 or 12.36%
Quarterly compounding	Nominal_rate: 12% Npery: 4	0.1255 or 12.55%
Monthly compounding	Nominal_rate: 12% Npery: 12	0.1268 or 12.68%
Fortnightly compounding	Nominal_rate: 12% Npery: 24	0.1272 or 12.72%
Daily compounding	Nominal_rate: 12% Npery: 365	0.1275 or 12.75%

Sinking Fund

With MS Excel

There can be many situations where we may wish to invest specific amounts periodically so that these grow to a target amount. On an individual front, these could be for the education of children, marriages in the family, having an adequate fund for retirement or a holiday and so on. If we know or decide on the target amount, we have one of the two choices:

- We can invest a lump-sum amount to grow to this target amount. Thus, if we desire to have ₹1,00,000 after three years for some purpose, we can ascertain the lump-sum investment needed today which will grow to ₹1,00,000 in three years, assuming an interest rate of 10%. This can be ascertained by using the Pv function and the answer is ₹75,131.48. Thus, if we have the funds, we can invest ₹75,131.48 today, which will grow to become ₹1,00,000 after three years.

- Alternatively, we can ascertain the equated annual amount required every year starting now, which will grow to become ₹1,00,000 after three years. This is ascertained by using the PMT function as shown in Exhibit 5.

EXHIBIT 5

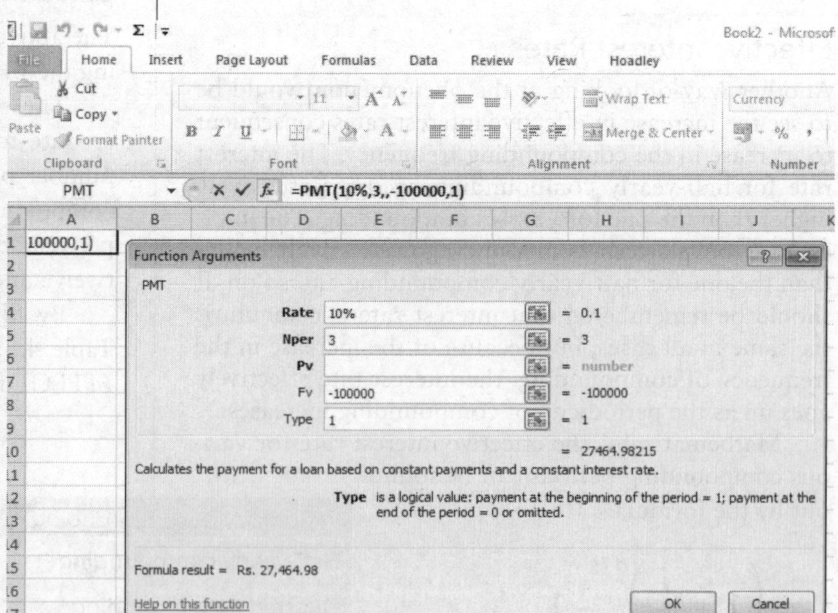

Notice that the target amount under Fv can be put as a negative figure, in which case we will get a positive answer. Alternatively, this can be put without a minus sign, in which case the answer will show a negative figure. Also notice that Type has been given as 1, which indicates that it is an annuity due, since the first instalment is to be paid now. The answer is ₹27464.98. This means that if we are to invest ₹27,464.98 every year starting from now at an interest rate of 10%, we will have ₹1,00,000at the end of the third year.

The timeline for this and the computation which will verify this is shown in Table 4.4.

TABLE 4.4

Timeline with T = Year and amount in ₹			
T0	T1	T2	T3
−27464.98	−27464.98	−27464.98	
			100000

The verification is shown in Table 4.5.

TABLE 4.5

Year	Opening balance of investment	Interest	Investment now	Closing balance of investment
0	0.00	0.00	27464.98	27464.98
1	27464.98	2746.50	27464.98	57676.46
2	57676.46	5767.65	27464.98	90909.08
3	90909.08	9090.91	0	100000

Table 4.5 shows how the yearly instalments earn interest year after year and ultimately grow to reach the target.

Given the number of periods it takes for a periodical investment to grow to a given target, we can ascertain the implied interest rate. Thus, if we have a yearly payment of ₹2000 (starting now) for 5 years and this accumulates to become ₹15000 after 5 years, we can ascertain the implied interest by using the RATE function as shown in Exhibit 6 below. We input the number of periods, the periodical payment (against PMT row) and the final amount in FV. As in the case of all such Excel functions, either the PMT amount or the final FV amount has to have a minus sign. We get the answer as 13.83%. In case the periodical payments have commenced at the end of each year, we would have indicated this as TYPE 0 or leave the TYPE row blank. If instead of periodically payments an initial lump-sum is invested, we would have indicated this against the PV row in the RATE function window and left the PMT row blank.

EXHIBIT 6

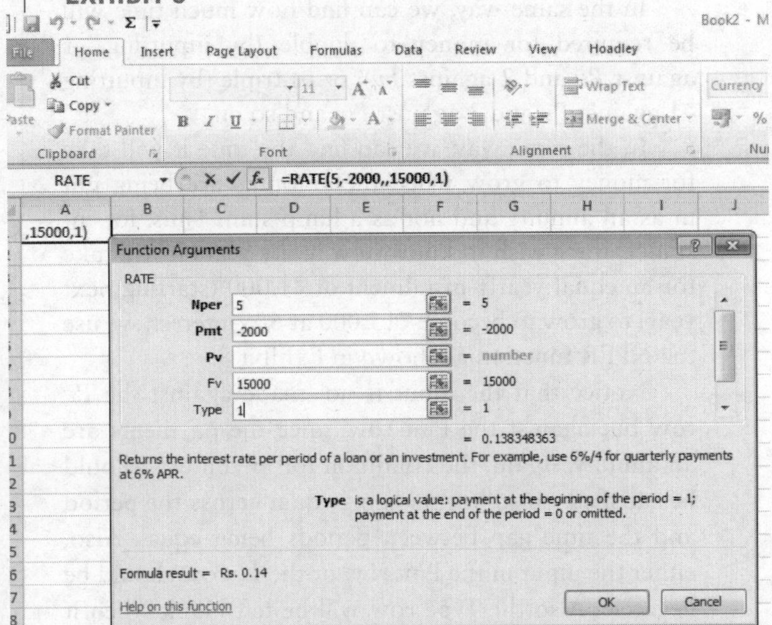

Calculating the Time Required

MS Excel Function

The time required for money to grow can be determined in MS Excel by using the NPER formula. Suppose we wish to know the time required for ₹1,000 to become ₹2,500 at 8% interest, we call for the NPER function and input as data as shown in Exhibit 7.

EXHIBIT 7

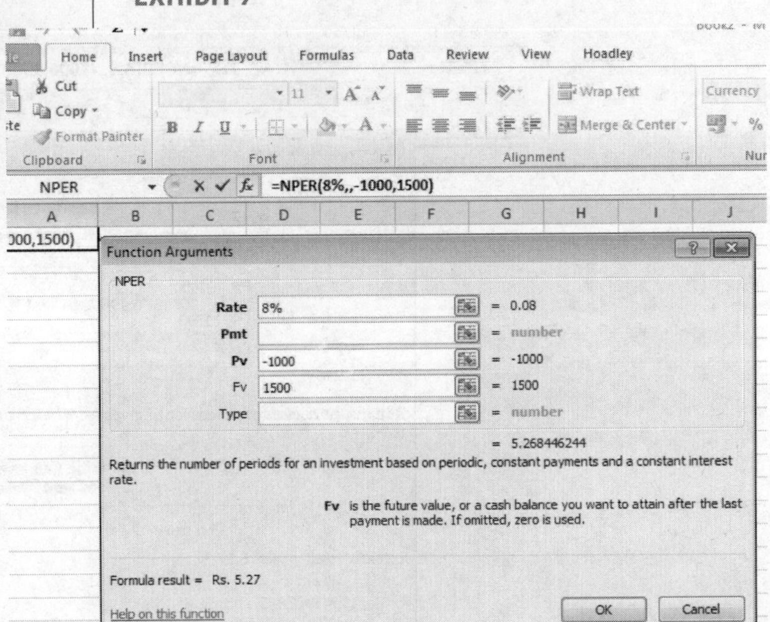

We input the amount of investment against the *Pv* row and the final amount against the *Fv* row. One of the two rows will have to be negative. We get the answer as 5.27 years.

In the same way, we can find how much time will be required for money to double (by inputting –1 against *Pv* and 2 against *Fv*); or to triple (by inputting –1 against *Pv* and 3 against *Fv*) and so on.

In the same way, we can find the time it will take for money to grow when the amounts are being put in as an annuity and not as a lump-sum. Thus, for instance, if we wish to know how many years it will take for an equal yearly instalment of ₹1,000 (starting next year) to grow to become ₹15,000 at 6% interest, we use the NPER function as shown in Exhibit 8.

Notice that the input is not made against the *Pv* row but against the Pmt row, since the payments are an annuity. Again, the condition for an annuity should be satisfied—instalments being equal across the period and the time gap between periods being equal. Also, either the input in the Pmt row or the *Fv* row should be negative. Also the Type row will be left blank when it is a regular annuity or filled as 1 when it is an annuity due.

EXHIBIT 8

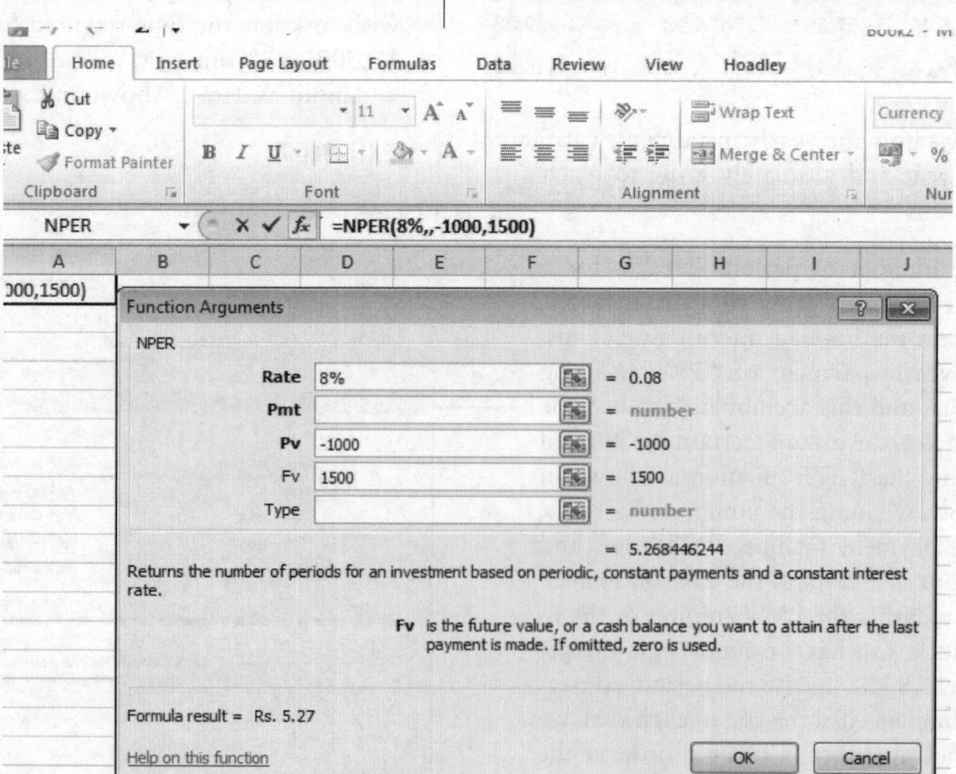

Loan Amortization

With Excel Functions

Another common application of the time value of money is the determination of the equated annual instalment required to repay a loan. The equated annual instalment is a system by which the person who takes the loan repays it in equal instalments—yearly, quarterly, monthly, or such other periods as mutually agreed upon. The instalments are equal across the tenure and at the end of the tenure the borrower will have repaid both the principal and interest for the loan.

Suppose we take a personal loan of ₹5,00,000 at 12% interest, and the bank calls for repayment in equal annual instalments over four years with the first instalment starting one year from now. The amount of the instalment can be found out using the PMT formula as shown in Exhibit 9.

Again notice that the minus entry under *Pv* will give the answer as positive. If we had put a positive entry against *Pv*, our answer would have been negative. Also, we have left Type blank to indicate that the annuity is a regular one. If the first instalment were to be paid now, we would have entered 1 against Type to indicate that it is an annuity due.

EXHIBIT 9

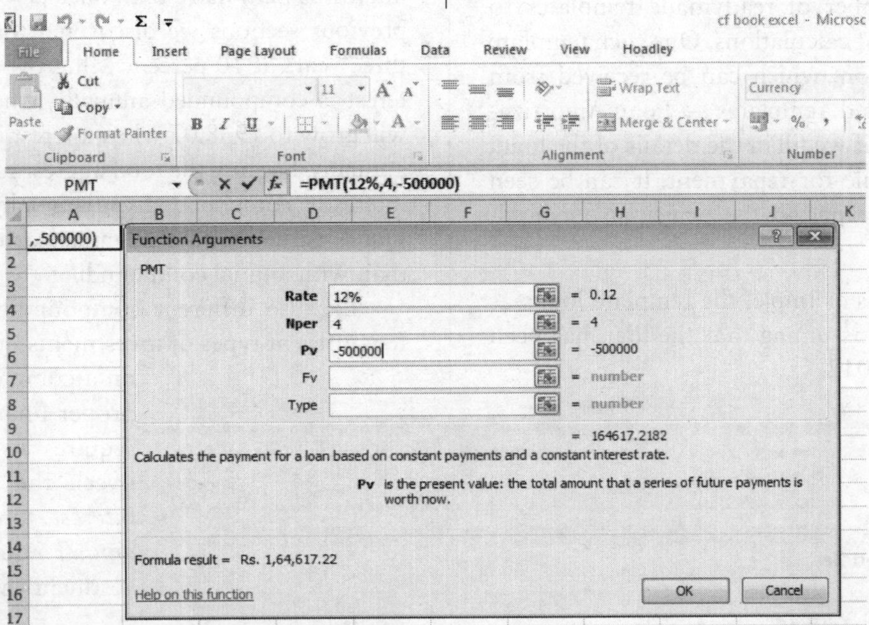

We get the answer as ₹164617.22. This can be verified with Table 4.6.

Table 4.6

Year	Opening balance of loan	Interest	Repayment now	Closing balance of loan
1	500000.00	60000.00	–164617.22	395382.8
2	395382.78	47445.93	–164617.22	278211.5
3	278211.49	33385.38	–164617.22	146979.7
4	146979.65	17637.56	–164617.22	0

Table 4.6 shows how the equal instalments paid year after year go towards the payment of interest and principal in such a way that at the end of the period the whole repayment process is over.

This function can also be used for ascertaining monthly or other instalments. Suppose we take a housing loan for ₹20,00,000 for 10 years at 10% interest. The equated monthly instalment (EMI) needed to repay the loan in ten years is found out by using the PMT function as shown in Exhibit 10.

We get the instalment to be ₹26430.15. You can see the verification of this in the next section.

EXHIBIT 10

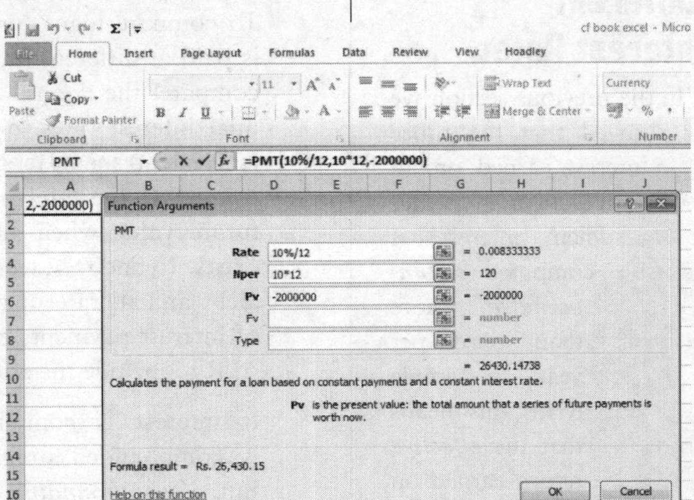

With MS Excel Template

MS Excel has a number of readymade templates to facilitate many types of calculations. One such template is on loan amortization, which can be received from File → New → Installed Templates → Loan Amortization. In this template, if we fill in the details of the loan, we get the full schedule for repayment. It can be seen that at the end of the period the principal outstanding reduces to zero.

Using the previous example, the template looks as shown in Exhibit 10, assuming that the loan has been taken on January 1, 2012.

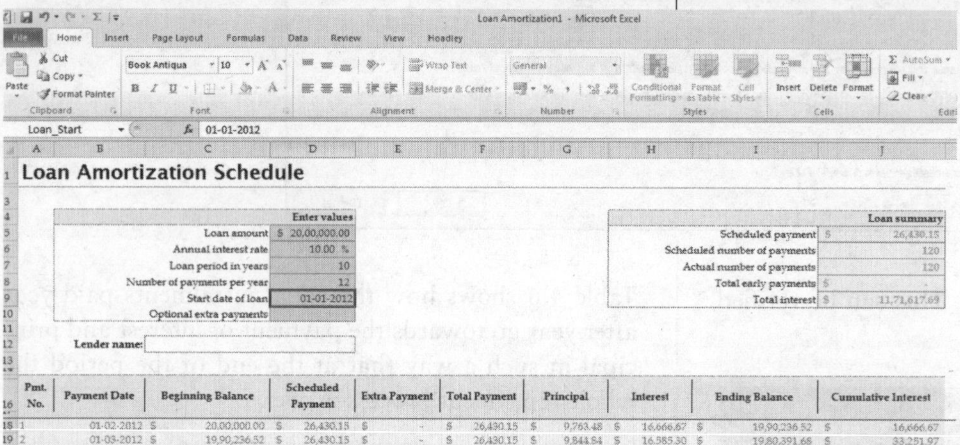

Exhibit 11

The template table also gives us the details of the total interest that would be paid over the life and date-wise due dates for repayment, full working as to how much of the instalment paid goes towards repayment of the principal and how much towards interest is also clearly given.

4-5b Comparison of Different Interest Rates

In the previous section we showed that the rupee interest earned on an investment is greater when interest is computed *(compounded)* more than once per year. In simple terms, this means that the *effective* return earned on an investment is higher than the stated, or simple, return (r_{SIMPLE}) when interest is paid more than once per year. For example, in previous sections we discovered that ₹700 invested for three years at 10 percent will grow to ₹931.70 when interest is compounded annually, whereas the same ₹700 will grow to ₹938.07 when interest is compounded semiannually. Because the total interest earned is greater when interest is compounded semiannually, the effective return that is earned with semiannual compounding is greater than with annual compounding.

Because different compounding periods are used for different types of investments, we must state returns on a comparable basis to make proper financial decisions. This requires us to distinguish between the *simple* (or *quoted*) *interest rate* and the *effective annual rate (EAR)* that an investment earns.

- In our example, the **simple,** or **quoted, interest rate,** which we designate r_{SIMPLE}, is 10 percent. Often interest is quoted as a simple annual rate along with an indication of the number of times interest will be paid during the year. In our current example, the quoted rate is *10 percent, compounded semiannually*. The simple rate is also called the **annual percentage rate**, or **APR**, and it is generally one of the rates that is reported to you by lenders when you borrow money. The APR is a noncompounded interest rate because it does not consider the effect of compounding when interest is paid more than once per year.
- To compare loans (or investments) when interest is paid at different times during the year, we must compare the loans' (investments') effective annual interest rates, not their APRs. The **effective (equivalent) annual rate**, which we designate (r_{EAR}), is defined as the rate that would produce the same future value when annual interest compounding exists. To find r_{EAR}, we convert the APR to its equivalent annual rate of return based on the number of interest payments each year—that is, we adjust APR to include the effects of compounded interest.
- If interest is computed once each year—that is, compounded annually—$r_{EAR} = r_{SIMPLE} = APR$. But, *if compounding occurs more than once per*

simple (quoted) interest rate (r_{SIMPLE}) The annual, noncompounded rate, quoted by borrowers and lenders; it is used to determine the rate earned per compounding period (periodic rate, r_{PER}).

annual percentage rate (APR) Another name for the simple interest rate, r_{SIMPLE}; does not consider the effect of interest compounding.

effective (equivalent) annual rate (r_{EAR}) The annual rate of interest actually being earned, as opposed to the quoted rate; considers the compounding of interest.

year, the effective annual rate is greater than the simple, or quoted, interest rate; that is, $r_{EAR} > r_{SIMPLE}$.

In our example, r_{EAR} is the rate that will grow a ₹700 investment today to ₹938.07 at the end of three years if interest is paid once per year rather than twice per year. Thus, we have the following situation:

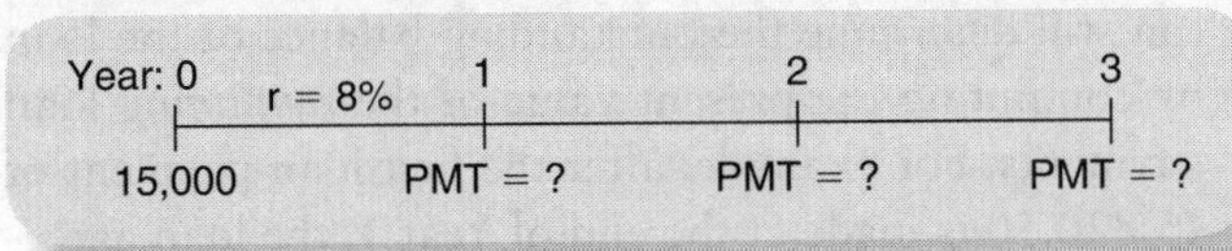

Using a financial calculator, enter N = 3, PV = −700, PMT = 0, and FV = 938.07; then solve for I/Y = 10.25 = r_{EAR}.

We can compute the effective annual rate, given the simple rate, r_{SIMPLE}, and the number of compounding periods per year, m, by solving Equation 4.12:

4.12

$$\text{Effective annual rate(EAR)} = r_{EAR} = \left(1 + \frac{r_{SIMPLE}}{m}\right)^m - 1.0$$

$$= (1 + r_{PER})^m - 1.0$$

Using Equation 4.12 to find the r_{EAR} if the simple rate is 10 percent and interest is paid semiannually, we have:

$$rEAR = \left(1 + \frac{0.10}{2}\right)^2 - 1.0$$

$$= (1.05)2 - 1.0 = 1.1025 - 1.0$$

$$= 0.1025 = 10.25\%$$

To compute r_{EAR} for this situation using a financial calculator, enter N = 2 = number of interest payments each year, I/Y = 5 = interest rate for each interest payment, PV = −1 (assume ₹1 is invested today), and PMT = 0; then solve for FV = 1.1025. The result indicates to what amount an investment of ₹1 will grow in one year. We compute the return that would be earned during the year by subtracting 1.0 and converting the result to a percentage; that is, r_{EAR} = 1.1025 – 1.000 = 0.1025 = 10.25%.

Now let's determine to what amount an investment of ₹700 will grow if it earns 10.25 percent interest that is *compounded annually* for three years:

$$FV_3 = ₹700(1.1025)^3 = ₹700(1.34010) = ₹938.07$$

Using a financial calculator, enter N = 3, I/Y = 10.25, PV = −700, and PMT = 0; then solve for FV = 938.07.

Note that when ₹700 is invested for three years at 10.25 percent compounded annually, the future value is the same as when ₹700 is invested for three years at 10 percent compounded semiannually. As a result, we can conclude that the investment that pays 10 percent compounded semiannually earns the same rate of return as the investment that pays 10.25 percent compounded annually. This means that both investments have an *effective*, or actual, rate of return that equals 10.25 percent—that is, r_{EAR} = 10.25%. Also, note that the answer to the question that was posed at the beginning of the chapter is different if interest is compounded more than once per year. We discovered earlier that you should choose a payment of ₹935 in three years rather than a payment of ₹700 today if your opportunity cost is 10 percent compounded annually, because the ₹700 would grow to only ₹931.70 if it were invested for three years. However, the current example shows that when interest is compounded semiannually, this same ₹700 would grow to ₹938.07 in three years, which is greater than the ₹935 payment that Option B promises. Thus, when interest is compounded semiannually, Option A, which pays ₹700 today, is preferable to Option B.

4-6 Amortized Loans

One of the most important applications of compound interest involves loans that are paid off in installments over time. Included in this category are automobile loans, home mortgages, student loans, and some business debt. If a loan is to be repaid in equal periodic amounts (monthly, quarterly, or annually), it is said to be an **amortized loan.**[6]

To illustrate, suppose that you borrow ₹15,000 for a business that you own, and the loan is to be repaid in three equal payments at the end of each of the next three years. The lender will charge 8 percent interest on the amount of the loan balance that is outstanding at the beginning of each year. Our first task is to determine the amount that you must repay each year; that is, the annual loan payment.

amortized loan A loan that requires equal payments over its life; the payments include both interest and repayment of the debt.

[6]The word *amortized* comes from the Latin *mors*, meaning death, so an amortized loan is one that is "killed off" over time.

To find this amount, recognize that the ₹15,000 represents the present value of an annuity of PMT rupees per year for three years, discounted at 8 percent.

Using a financial calculator, the solution is

Inputs:	3	8	15,000	?	0
	N	I/Y	PV	PMT	FV
Output:				= –5,820.50	

The payments represent an ordinary annuity because each payment is made at the end of the year. Each payment on an amortized loan consists partly of interest and partly of repayment of the amount borrowed *(principal)*. This breakdown is given in the **amortization schedule** shown in Table 4.7. Note that the interest component is largest in the first year, and it declines as the outstanding balance of the loan decreases. For tax purposes, a business borrower reports the interest component shown in Column 3 as a deductible cost each year, whereas the lender reports this amount as taxable income. The same logic that is presented in Table 4.7 can be used to create amortization schedules for home mortgages, automobile loans, and other amortized loans.[7]

Column 5 in Table 4.7 shows the outstanding balance that is due for our illustrative loan at the end of each year. If you do not have an amortization schedule, you can still determine the outstanding balance of the loan by computing the present value of the *remaining* loan payments. For example, after the first loan payment of ₹5,820.50 is made at the end of Year 1, the loan agreement calls for two more payments equal to ₹5,820.50 each. Remember that a portion of each ₹5,820.50 payment includes a payment for interest on the amount of the loan that has not been repaid; the remainder of the ₹5,820.50 represents repayment of the loan. Thus, to determine the total amount of these payments that represents repayment of the loan only, you must take out the portion of each payment that represents interest. We can "de-interest" the future payments by computing the present value of the two remaining payments. Using a financial calculator, enter N = 2, I/Y = 8, PMT = –5,820.50, and FV = 0; then solve for PV = 10,379.49 = PVA_1, which is the remaining balance at the end of Year 1 that is shown in Column 5 in Table 4.7 (there is a rounding difference in the table).

TABLE 4.7 Loan Amortization Schedule; ₹15,000 Loan at 8 Percent Interest Rate

Year	Beginning of Year Balance (1)	Payment (2)	Interest @ 8%[a] (3) = (1) × 0.08	Repayment of Principal[b] (4) = (2) – (3)	Remaining Loan Balance[c] (5) = (1) – (4)
1	₹15,000.00	₹5,820.50	₹1,200.00	₹4,620.50	₹10,379.50
2	10,379.50	5,820.50	830.36	4,990.14	5,389.36
3	5,389.36	5,820.50	431.15	5,389.35	0.01

[a]Interest is calculated by multiplying the loan balance in Column 1 by the interest rate (0.08). For example, the interest in Year 2 is ₹10,379.50 x 0.08 = ₹830.36.

[b]Repayment of principal (shown in Column 4) is equal to the payment of ₹5,820.50 in Column 2 minus the interest charge for each year in Column 3. For example, the repayment of principal in Year 2 is ₹5,820.50 – ₹830.36 = ₹4,990.14.

[c]The ₹0.01 remaining balance at the end of Year 3 results from a rounding difference.

amortization schedule A schedule showing precisely how a loan will be repaid. It gives the payment required on each payment date and a breakdown of the payment, showing how much is interest and how much is repayment of principal.

[7]Financial calculators and spreadsheets are programmed to calculate amortization tables—you simply enter the data and apply the appropriate built-in function. If you have a financial calculator, it is worthwhile to read the appropriate section of the manual and learn how to use its amortization feature. Similarly, it is worth your time to learn how to set up an amortization table using a spreadsheet.

KEY TIME VALUE OF MONEY CONCEPTS

To conclude this chapter, we summarize some TVM concepts (rules) that were discussed.

- Before making financial decisions, rupees from different time periods must be stated in the same "time value"—that is, all rupees must be valued at the same time period before they can be compared.
- Everything else equal, an amount that is invested at a higher rate or for a longer time period will grow to a greater future amount (future value), because a greater amount of interest is earned.
- The further in the future an amount is received (paid) or the higher the interest rate, the lower the present value of the future amount; less money must be invested today to accumulate the future amount because more interest is earned during the investment period. Based on this TVM rule, we know that, everything else equal, the current value of an investment is lower the higher the interest rate it earns in the future. This is an important financial concept that we will discuss throughout the book.
- Everything else equal, the greater the number of compounding periods per year, the greater the effective rate of return that is earned on an investment. In other words, the total rupee amount of interest that is earned on an investment is greater when interest is compounded more often during the year.

MULTIPLE CHOICE QUESTIONS

1. PV has the following relationship with the interest rate

a. Higher the interest rate, higher the PV
b. Higher the interest rate, lower the PV
c. Lower the interest rate, lower the PV
d. Both a and c

2. PV of an annuity due will be

a. Higher than the PV of a regular annuity
b. Lower than the PV of a regular annuity
c. Equal to the PV of a regular annuity
d. Having no relationship with the PV of a regular annuity

3. If the interest rate is higher,

a. The number of years it takes for money to double will come down
b. The number of years it takes for money to double will go up
c. No impact on the number of years it takes to double the money
d. Unless tenure is given, no conclusion can be drawn

4. A timeline assumes

a. That all receipts and payments occur at the start of the year
b. That receipts occur at the start of the year and payments at the end of the year
c. That both receipts and payments occur at the end of the year
d. That receipts occur at the end of the year and payments at the start of the year

5. If I require an amount after five years,

a. It is better to put in small amounts every year to make them grow to the target amount at the end of five years
b. It is better to put in a lump-sum amount to make it grow to the target amount at the end of five years
c. Either a or b
d. b will be better than a

6. If I take a three-year loan and it has to be repaid in three equated annual installments,

a. The instalment amount will have a high interest in the beginning and a low repayment of principal
b. The instalment amount will have a low interest in the beginning and a high repayment of principal
c. The instalment amount will carry a principal repayment element which is equal across the years
d. Both a and c

7. I have a choice of repaying a loan in ten instalments or fifteen instalments. If I choose to repay in fifteen instalments,

a. I will end up paying lesser instalment amount
b. I will end up paying lesser interest overall
c. I will end up paying higher interest overall
d. Both a and c

8. If I have a target amount in mind to be accumulated after six years,

a. The equated amount will be like an annuity which will grow to the target

b. The equated amount will be like a series of lump-sums that will grow to the target

c. Both a and b

d. Neither a nor b

9. When a loan is taken, the total amount repaid with interest will be

a. Higher when the period of the loan is long

b. Lower when the period of the loan is long

c. The same regardless of the period

d. We need figures to get a correct answer

10. After an equated monthly instalment (EMI) has been determined for a housing loan, the borrower pays a lump-sum amount in partial repayment. Now the EMI will

a. Come down if the period of the loan remains the same

b. Go up if the loan period is the same

c. Be higher or lower depending on whether the loan is a fixed rate or a floating rate loan

d. Depend on the interest rate now prevailing in the market

Answers:

1.	(b)	2.	(a)	3.	(a)	4.	(c)	5.	(c)
6.	(a)	7.	(d)	8.	(c)	9.	(a)	10.	(a)

PROBLEMS

For more problems, login to CourseMate for CFIN at CengageBrain.com

4-1 If Sarada invests ₹700 today in an account that pays 4 percent interest compounded annually, how much will she have in her account four years from today?

4-2 Fifteen (15) years ago, your parents purchased an investment for ₹2,500. If the investment earned 6 percent interest each year, how much is it worth today?

4-3 Feema plans to invest ₹500 later today. She wants to know to what amount her investment will grow in 20 years if she earns 12 percent interest compounded (a) annually, (b) quarterly, and (c) monthly.

4-4 Sheela invested ₹950 five years ago. Her investment paid 7.2 percent interest compounded monthly. Sheela's twin sister Seema invested ₹900 at the same time. But Seema's investment earned 8 percent interest compounded quarterly. How much is each investment worth today?

4-5 What is the present value of ₹1,500 due in 14 years at a (a) 5 percent interest rate and (b) 10 percent rate. Explain why the present value is lower when the interest rate is higher.

4-6 Mohan is considering the purchase of an investment that will pay him ₹12,500 in 12 years. If Mohan wants to earn a return equal to 7 percent per year (annual compounding), what is the maximum amount he should be willing to pay for the investment today?

4-7 What is the present value (PV) of an investment that will pay ₹2,500 in five years if the opportunity cost rate is 9 percent compounded (a) annually, (b) quarterly, and (c) monthly? Explain why the PV is lowest when interest is compounded monthly.

4-8 If Qasy can invest at an opportunity cost rate equal to 12 percent compounded monthly, what lump-sum amount should he invest today so that he has ₹2200000 to buy a new car in three years?

4-9 Suppose you invest ₹385 at the end of each of the next eight years. (a) If your opportunity cost is 7 percent compounded annually, how much will your investment be worth after the last ₹385 payment is made? (b) What will be the ending amount if the payments are made at the beginning of each year?

4-10 At the end of each of the past 14 years, Vamana deposited ₹450 in an account that earned 8 percent compounded annually. (a) How much is in the account today? (b) How much would be in the account if the deposits were made at the beginning each year rather than at the end of each year?

4-11 Suppose your opportunity cost is 11 percent compounded annually. (a) How much must you deposit in an account today if you want to pay yourself ₹230 at the end of each of the next 15 years? (b) How much must you deposit if you want to pay yourself ₹230 at the beginning of each of the next 15 years?

4-12 Compute the amount Amala must deposit in an account today so that she can pay herself ₹450 per month for the next nine years if her opportunity cost is 8.4 percent compounded monthly. How much must Amala deposit today if she wants to pay herself at the beginning of each month?

4-13 Kajal plans to deposit ₹100 in an account at the end of each month for the next five years so that she can take a trip. (a) If Kajal's opportunity cost is 6 percent compounded monthly, how much will she have in the account in five years? (b) How much will be in the account if the deposits are made at the beginning of each month?

4-14 Ratna would like to set up an account to supplement her parents' retirement income for the next 15 years. (a) If the account earns 7.2 percent compounded monthly, how much will Ratna have to deposit today so that her parents are paid ₹15000 at the end of each month? (b) How much would she have to deposit if her parents wanted to receive the ₹15000 payment at the beginning of each month?

4-15 If the opportunity cost is 7.5 percent, what is the present value of an investment that pays ₹500 at the end of this year, ₹400 at the end of the next year, and ₹300 at the end of the following year? What is the present value if the payments are made at the beginning of each year?

4-16 Suppose Jayanthi deposits ₹500 in an account at the end of this year, ₹400 at the end of the next year, and ₹300 at the end of the following year. If her opportunity cost is 7.5 percent, how much will be in the account immediately after the third deposit is made? How much will be in the account at the end of three years if the deposits are made at the beginning of each year?

4-17 Compute the present value (PV) of an annuity that pays ₹320 forever if the opportunity cost is (a) 4 percent, (b) 8 percent, and (c) 10 percent. Why does the PV decrease as the opportunity cost increases?

4-18 Ten years ago, Bhardwaj invested ₹1,250. Today, the investment is worth ₹3,550. If interest is compounded annually, what annual rate of return did Bhardwaj earn on his investment?

4-19 Tamara owes ₹12,000 on her automobile loan, which has an interest rate equal to 4.8 percent compounded monthly. If Tamara pays ₹526 at the end of each month, how long will it take her to repay the loan?

4-20 Mayank wants to take a trip that costs ₹4,750, but currently he only has ₹2,260 saved. If Mayank invests this money at 7 percent compounded annually, how long will it take for his investment to grow to ₹4,750?

4-21 CanAm Financial offers investments that pay 12 percent interest compounded monthly, whereas UniMex Financial offers investments that pay 12.25 percent interest compounded semiannually. Which investment offers the better effective annual return?

4-22 Yelahanka bank advertises a savings investment that pays 6 percent compounded monthly. What is the investment's (a) annual percentage rate (APR) and (b) effective annual rate (r_{EAR})?

4-23 Warna recently graduated from NFA University. While at NFA, Warna took out a ₹50,000 student loan. His loan requires him to make monthly payments for a 10-year period. (a) If the simple annual interest is 4.2 percent, what are Warna's monthly payments? (b) To the nearest rupee, how much will Warna owe on his student loan after he makes payments for three years?

4-24 When Sana purchased her house 12 years ago, she took out a 30-year mortgage for ₹5000000. The mortgage has a fixed interest rate of 9.5 percent compounded monthly. (a) Compute Sana's monthly mortgage payments. (b) If Sana wants to pay off her mortgage today, for how much should she write a check? She made her most recent mortgage payment earlier today.

4-25 Nayana purchased a new car earlier today for ₹3200000. She financed the entire amount using a five-year loan with a 9 percent interest rate (compounded monthly). (a) Compute the monthly payments for the loan. (b) How much will Nayana owe on the loan after she makes payments for two years (i.e., after 24 payments)?

4.26 Bank A offers a new deposit scheme by which an amount of ₹50000 invested today grows to ₹125000 in 8 years. If the compounding frequency is quarterly, what interest rate does this translate into?

4.27 A bank offers 6.5% interest. How many years will it take for an investment of ₹50000 to grow to ₹300000, if the compounding frequency is quarterly?

4.28 X is planning to retire after 15 years. He presently has an investible corpus of ₹275000. He is prepared to put aside a monthly amount of ₹10000 from the next month for 15 years. The interest rate for this is 6.25% per annum. At the end of 15 years, X wants to join a pension plan which will pay him an equated monthly instalment for 12 years starting from the month after the retirement. What will be the pension amount if the pension fund reckons an interest rate of 6% per annum for its calculations?

4.29 A charity organization is soliciting donations for a new midday meal scheme. Under this, 300 children will be fed every day for 250 days in a year for all time to come. To be part of the donor team for this scheme, a person has to deposit ₹500000 per year for the next 20 years. If the applicable interest rate is 8%, what is the cost of a meal?

4.30 A non-banking company is offering a deposit scheme by which a growing yearly interest will be paid to the depositors. If the interest amount for the first year is ₹5000 and this will grow in perpetuity at 3% every year, and the general interest rate in the market is 8%, how big must the deposit be?

4.31 An investment scheme promises a payment of ₹10000 per year for all time to come starting from the 6th year from now. For this, the depositor has to make quarterly deposits of ₹5000 from now for a 5-year period. If the interest rate for the quarterly deposits was 7%, what is the implied interest rate for the payment to be made by the investment scheme from the 6th year?

Time Value of Money (TVM)

Learning Outcomes

LO.1 Identify various types of cash flow patterns (streams).

- Cash flows can take the form of (a) lump-sum, or single payment, amounts; (b) annuities, which represent equal payments over equal time periods; or (c) uneven cash flows, which represent different rupee amounts over multiple periods.

LO.2 Compute the future value of different cash flow streams. Explain the results.

- The future value (FV) and present value (PV) are computed to restate rupees from one time period into rupees at different time periods. FV is the amount to which a lump-sum investment (or a series of cash flows) will grow in the future, based on the return it earns over time. To compute the FV of a current amount, interest that can be earned during the life of the investment (or loan) is "added to" the current amount.

LO.3 Compute the present value of different cash flow streams. Explain the results.

- PV is the amount that must be invested today to accumulate a specific amount (or a series of cash flows) in the future based on the return that will be earned during the investment period. To compute the PV of a future amount, interest that can be earned during the life of the investment (or loan) is "taken out" of the FV amount.

LO.4 Compute (a) the return (interest rate) on an investment (loan) and (b) how long it takes to reach a financial goal.

- TVM techniques can be used to determine the percentage return (r) an investment earns over time. The techniques can also be used to determine the length of time (n) it will take to reach a financial objective. Both of these pieces of information are important in financial decisions.

LO.5 Explain the difference between the annual percentage rate (APR) and the effective annual rate (EAR). Explain when each is more appropriate to use.

- APR represents an annual rate of return that does not consider the compounding of interest, whereas EAR is the return that recognizes interest compounding. Investors and borrowers should use the EAR to make financial decisions, because this figure represents the "true" return on an investment (or loan). EAR > APR, except when interest is compounded annually.

LO.6 Describe an amortized loan. Compute (a) amortized loan payments and (b) the amount that must be paid on an amortized loan at a specific point during the life of the loan.

- An amortized loan is repaid in equal periodic payments. Each payment includes both repayment of a portion of the outstanding amount that is owed on the loan and payment of interest on the outstanding balance.
- To compute an amortized loan payment, you simply compute the annuity that you could pay yourself each period from the amount that is borrowed, assuming that you can invest the borrowed amount at the same rate as the interest charged on the loan.
- To compute the amount that is owed on an amortized loan before the last payment is made, you must "take out" any interest that is associated with the future loan payments (because you shouldn't have to pay this interest). That is, you find the present value of all remaining loan payments.

Chapter 4 Key TVM Concepts

- Before making financial decisions, rupees from different time periods must be stated in the same "time value," which means that all rupees must be valued at the same time period before they can be compared.
- An amount that is invested at a higher rate or for a longer time period will grow to a greater future amount (future value) because a greater amount of interest is earned.
- The further in the future an amount is received (paid) or the higher the opportunity cost rate, the lower the present value of the future amount—that is, the less money that must be invested today to accumulate the future amount. Based on this TVM rule, we know that, everything else equal, the current value of an investment is lower the higher the interest rate it earns in the future. This is an important financial concept that we will discuss throughout the book.
- Everything else equal, the greater the number of compounding periods per year, the greater the effective rate of return that is earned on an investment. In other words, the total rupee amount of interest that is earned on an investment is greater when interest is compounded more often during the year

Key Terms

time value of money (TVM) The principles and computations used to revalue cash payoffs from different times so they are stated in rupees of the same time period. *p. 57*

opportunity cost rate The rate of return on the best available alternative investment of equal risk. *p. 57*

LO.1

lump-sum amount A single payment (received or made) that occurs either today or at some date in the future. *p. 57*

annuity A series of payments of an equal amount at fixed, equal intervals for a specified number of periods. *p. 57*

ordinary annuity An annuity with payments that occur at the end of each period. *p. 58*

annuity due An annuity with payments that occur at the beginning of each period. *p. 58*

uneven cash flows Multiple payments of different amounts over a period of time. *p. 58*

LO.2

future value (FV) The amount to which a cash flow or series of cash flows will grow over a given period of time when compounded at a given interest rate. *p. 58*

compounding The process of determining to what value an amount or a series of cash flows will grow in the future when compound interest is applied. *p. 58*

payment (PMT) This term designates constant cash flows—that is, the amount of an annuity payment. *p. 61*

cash flow (CF) This term designates cash flows in general, including uneven cash flows. *p. 61*

terminal value The future value of a cash flow stream. *p. 62*

LO.3

present value (PV) The value today—that is, the current value—of a future cash flow or series of cash flows. *p. 62*

discounting The process of determining the present value of a cash flow or a series of cash flows received (paid) in the future; the reverse of compounding. *p. 62*

perpetuities Streams of equal payments that are expected to continue forever. *p. 65*

LO.5

annual compounding The process of determining the future (or present) value of a cash flow or series of cash flows when interest is paid once per year. *p. 67*

semiannual compounding The process of determining the future (or present) value of a cash flow or series of cash flows when interest is paid twice per year. *p. 67*

simple (quoted) interest rate (r_{SIMPLE}) The rate, quoted by borrowers and lenders, that is used to determine the rate earned per compounding period (periodic rate, r_{PER}). *p. 68*

annual percentage rate (APR) Another name for the simple interest rate, r_{SIMPLE}; does not consider the effect of interest compounding. *p. 69*

effective (equivalent) annual rate (r_{EAR}) The annual rate of interest actually being earned, as opposed to the quoted rate; considers the compounding of interest. *p. 69*

LO.6

amortized loan A loan that requires equal payments over its life; the payments include both interest and repayment of the debt. *p. 70*

amortization schedule A schedule showing precisely how a loan will be repaid. It gives the payment required on each payment date and a breakdown of the payment, showing how much is interest and how much is repayment of principal. *p. 70*

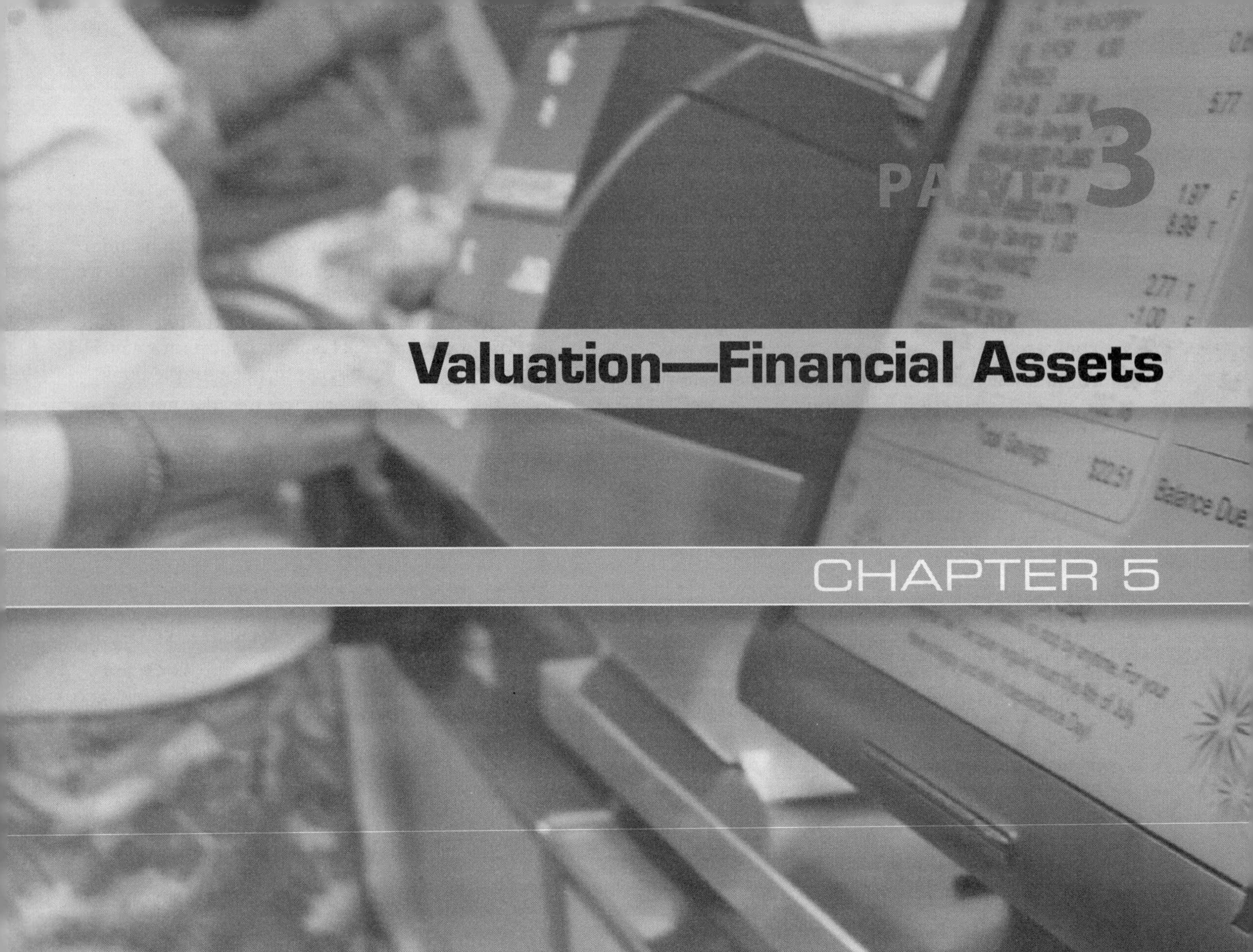

© iStockphoto.com/Tom Hahn

PART 3

Valuation—Financial Assets

CHAPTER 5

The Cost of Money (Interest Rates)

Learning Outcomes

LO.1 Describe the cost of money and factors that affect the cost of money (interest rates).

LO.2 Describe how interest rates are determined.

LO.3 Describe a yield curve and discuss how a yield curve might be used to determine future interest rates.

LO.4 Discuss how government actions and general business activity affect interest rates.

LO.5 Describe how changes in interest rates (returns) affect the values of stocks and bonds.

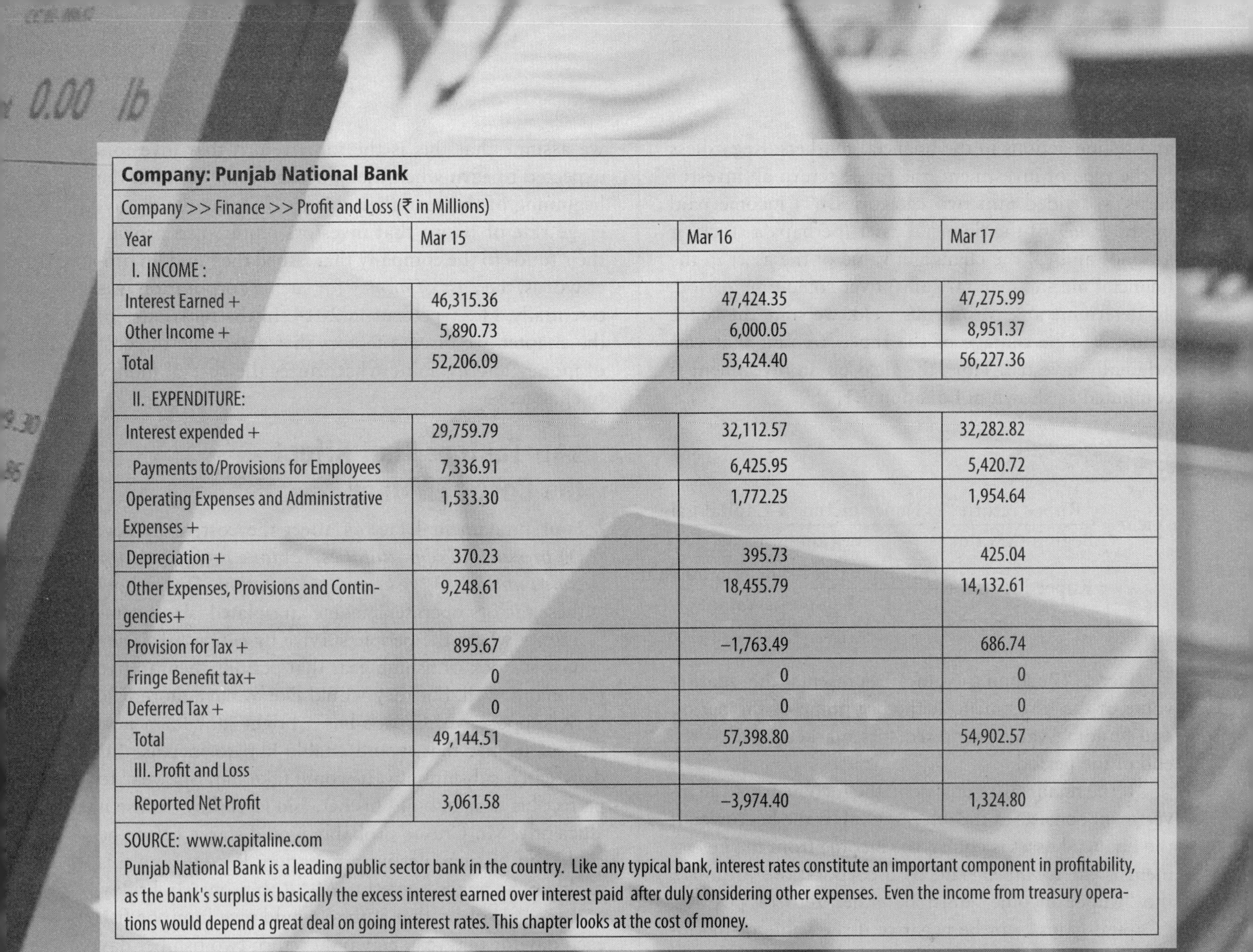

Company: Punjab National Bank			
Company >> Finance >> Profit and Loss (₹ in Millions)			
Year	Mar 15	Mar 16	Mar 17
I. INCOME :			
Interest Earned +	46,315.36	47,424.35	47,275.99
Other Income +	5,890.73	6,000.05	8,951.37
Total	52,206.09	53,424.40	56,227.36
II. EXPENDITURE:			
Interest expended +	29,759.79	32,112.57	32,282.82
Payments to/Provisions for Employees	7,336.91	6,425.95	5,420.72
Operating Expenses and Administrative Expenses +	1,533.30	1,772.25	1,954.64
Depreciation +	370.23	395.73	425.04
Other Expenses, Provisions and Contingencies+	9,248.61	18,455.79	14,132.61
Provision for Tax +	895.67	−1,763.49	686.74
Fringe Benefit tax+	0	0	0
Deferred Tax +	0	0	0
Total	49,144.51	57,398.80	54,902.57
III. Profit and Loss			
Reported Net Profit	3,061.58	−3,974.40	1,324.80

SOURCE: www.capitaline.com

Punjab National Bank is a leading public sector bank in the country. Like any typical bank, interest rates constitute an important component in profitability, as the bank's surplus is basically the excess interest earned over interest paid after duly considering other expenses. Even the income from treasury operations would depend a great deal on going interest rates. This chapter looks at the cost of money.

Study Tools

Problems are found at the end of this chapter

\+

Login to **CourseMate** for **CFIN** at **CengageBrain.com** for additional problems and other study tools!

In a free economy such as that of the United States, the excess funds of lenders are allocated to borrowers in the financial markets through a pricing system that is based on the supply of and the demand for funds. This system is represented by interest rates, or the *cost of money*, which permits those borrowers who are willing to pay the rates that prevail in the financial markets to use funds provided by others. In this chapter, we describe basic concepts associated with interest rates, including factors that affect rates and methods for forecasting them.

5-1 The Cost of Money

In this section, we explain what the cost of money is and discuss general factors that affect interest rates (the cost of money). The discussion is meant to provide only a simple overview of the cost of money.

5-1a Realized Returns (Yields)

Investors determine rates of return through their buying

and selling actions in the financial markets. Regardless of the type of investment, the rupee return an investor earns is divided into two categories: (1) income paid by the *issuer* of the financial asset (perhaps a stock or a bond) and (2) the change in value of the asset in the financial market (capital gains) over some time period. To determine an investment's yield, we state the rupee return as a percentage of the rupee amount that was originally invested. Thus, the yield on an investment is computed as shown in Equation 5.1:

5.1

$$\text{Yield} = \frac{\text{Rupee return}}{\text{Beginning value}} = \frac{\text{Rupee income} + \text{Capital gains}}{\text{Beginning value}}$$

$$= \text{Rupee income} + \frac{(\text{Ending value} - \text{Beginning value})}{\text{Beginning value}}$$

Here, "Beginning value" represents the market value of the investment at the beginning of the period and "Ending value" represents its market value at the end of the period.

If the financial asset is debt, the income from the investment consists of the *interest* paid by the borrower. If the financial asset is equity, the income from the investment is the *dividend* paid by a corporation. Although the "Rupee income" must be either zero or positive, "Capital gains" can be negative if the value of the investment decreases during the period it is held.

To illustrate the concept of yield, consider the return that you would earn if you purchased a corporate bond on January 2, 2014, for ₹980 and sold it one year later for ₹990.25. If the bond paid ₹100 interest on December 31, 2014, the bond's one-year yield, or *percentage return*, would be

$$\begin{array}{c}\text{Yield}\\ (\%\text{return})\end{array} = \frac{₹100.00 + (₹990.25 - ₹980.00)}{₹980.00}$$

$$= \frac{₹110.25}{₹980.00}$$

In this example, investors who purchased the bond at the beginning of 2014, and held it for one year would have earned a one-year holding-period return equal to 11.25 percent. If we assume that this is the same return that investors expected to earn when they purchased the bond at the beginning of the year, then this yield represents the average rate of return that investors required to provide their funds to the company that issued the bond. In other words, the *cost of money* for such a corporation was essentially 11.25 percent in 2014. In the remainder of the chapter, we discuss factors that determine the cost of money and examine what causes the cost of money to change.

production opportunity The return available within an economy from investment in a productive (cash-generating) asset.

time preference for consumption The preference of a consumer for current consumption as opposed to saving for future consumption.

5-1b Factors That Affect the Cost of Money

Four fundamental factors affect the cost of money: (1) *production opportunities*, (2) *time preferences for consumption,* (3) *risk,* and (4) *inflation.* To see how these factors operate, imagine an isolated island community where the people survive by eating fish. They have a stock of fishing gear that permits them to live reasonably well, but they would like to have more fish. Now suppose Mr. Crusoe has a bright idea for a new type of fishnet that would enable him to increase his daily catch substantially. It would take him one year to perfect his design, build his net, and learn how to use it efficiently. Mr. Crusoe probably would starve before he could put his new net into operation. Recognizing this problem, he might suggest to Ms. Robinson, Mr. Friday, and several others that if they would give him one fish each day for one year, he would return two fish per day during all of the following year. If Ms. Robinson accepted the offer, then the fish that she gave to Mr. Crusoe would constitute *savings* that she is willing to *invest* in the fishnet, and the extra fish the net produced in the future would constitute a *return on the investment.* Obviously, the more productive Mr. Crusoe thought the new fishnet would be—that is, the higher the **production opportunity**—the higher his expected return on the investment would be, and the more he could afford to offer potential investors to attract their savings. In this example, we assume that Mr. Crusoe thinks he will be able to pay, and thus has offered to give back two fish for every one fish he receives, which is a 100 percent rate of return. He might have tried to attract savings for less—say, 1.5 fish next year for every one fish he receives this year.

The attractiveness of Mr. Crusoe's offer to a potential saver would depend in large part on the saver's **time preference for consumption**. For example, Ms. Robinson might be thinking of retirement, and she might be willing to trade fish today for fish in the future on a

FIGURE 5.1 Interest Rates as a Function of Supply and Demand

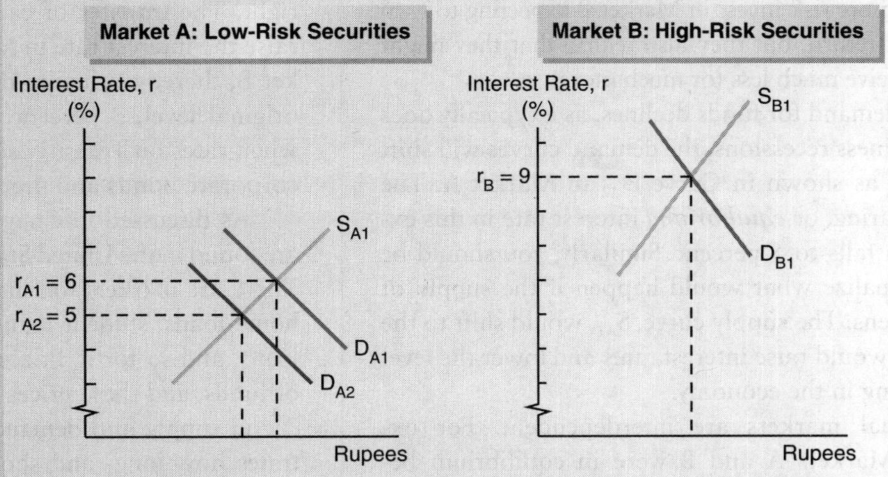

one-for-one basis, whereas Mr. Friday might be unwilling to "lend" a fish today for anything less than three fish next year because he has a wife and several young children to feed with his current fish. Mr. Friday is said to have a *high time preference for consumption*, whereas Ms. Robinson has a *low time preference for consumption*. Note also that if the entire population is living at the subsistence level, time preferences for current consumption would necessarily be high, aggregate savings would be low, interest rates would be high, and capital formation would be difficult.

The **risk** inherent in the fishnet project, and thus in Mr. Crusoe's ability to repay the loan, also affects the return required by investors: The higher the perceived risk, the higher the required rate of return. For example, if Mr. Crusoe has a history of not always following through with his ideas, those who are interested in Mr. Crusoe's new fishnet would consider the investment to be fairly risky, and thus they might provide Mr. Crusoe with one fish per day this year only if he promises to return four fish per day next year. In addition, a more complex society includes many businesses like Mr. Crusoe's, many goods other than fish, and many savers like Ms. Robinson and Mr. Friday. Furthermore, most people use money as a medium of exchange rather than bartering with fish. When a society uses money, its value in the future, which is affected by inflation, comes into play. That is, the higher the expected rate of **inflation**, the greater the return required to compensate investors for the loss in purchasing power caused by the inflation.

This simple illustration shows that the interest rate paid to savers depends in a basic way on (1) *the rate of return that producers expect to earn on their invested capital,* (2) *savers' time preferences for current consumption versus future consumption,* (3) *the riskiness of the loan,* and (4) *the expected future rate of inflation.* The returns that borrowers expect to earn by investing borrowed funds set an upper limit on how much they can pay for such funds. In turn, consumers' time preferences for consumption establish how much consumption they are willing to defer, and hence how much they will save at different levels of interest offered by borrowers. Higher risk and higher inflation also lead to higher interest rates.

5-1c Interest Rate Levels

Funds are allocated among borrowers by interest rates. Firms with the most profitable investment opportunities are willing and able to pay the most for capital, so they tend to attract it away from less-efficient firms or from firms whose products are not in demand. Of course, our economy is not completely free in the sense of being influenced only by market forces. As a result, the federal government supports agencies that help designated individuals or groups obtain credit on favorable terms. Among those eligible for this kind of assistance are small businesses, certain minorities, and firms willing to build facilities in areas characterized by high unemployment. Even with these government interventions, most capital in the U.S. economy is allocated through the price system.

Figure 5.1 shows how supply and demand interact to determine interest rates in two capital markets. Markets A and B represent two of the many capital markets in existence. The going interest rate, which we designate as r for this discussion, initially is 6 percent for the low-risk securities in Market A. That is, borrowers whose credit is strong enough to qualify for this market can obtain funds at a cost of 6 percent, and investors who want

risk In a financial market context, the chance that a financial asset will not earn the return promised.

inflation The tendency of prices to increase over time.

to put their money to work without much risk can obtain a 6 percent return. Riskier borrowers must borrow higher-cost funds in Market B. Investors who are willing to take on more risk invest in Market B expecting to earn a 9 percent return, but they also realize that they might actually receive much less (or much more).

If the demand for funds declines, as it typically does during business recessions, the demand curves will shift to the left, as shown in Curve D_{A2} in Market A. The market-clearing, or *equilibrium*, interest rate in this example then falls to 5 percent. Similarly, you should be able to visualize what would happen if the supply of funds tightens: The supply curve, S_{A1}, would shift to the left, which would raise interest rates and lower the level of borrowing in the economy.

Financial markets are interdependent. For example, if Markets A and B were in equilibrium before the demand shifted to D_{A2} in Market A, it means that investors were willing to accept the higher risk in Market B in exchange for a *risk premium* of 3% = 9% − 6%. After the shift to D_{A2}, the risk premium would initially increase to 4% = 9% − 5%. In all likelihood, this larger premium would induce some of the lenders in Market A to shift to Market B, which in turn would cause the supply curve in Market A to shift to the left (or up) and the supply curve in Market B to shift to the right. The transfer of capital between markets would raise the interest rate in Market A and lower it in Market B, thereby bringing the risk premium closer to the original level, 3 percent. We know, for example, that when rates on Treasury securities increase, the rates on corporate bonds and mortgages generally follow suit.

As discussed in Chapter 3, many financial markets are found in the United States and throughout the world. There are markets for short-term debt, long-term debt, home loans, student loans, business loans, government loans, and so forth. Prices are established for each type of funds, and these prices change over time as shifts occur in supply and demand conditions. Figure 5.2 illustrates how long- and short-term interest rates paid by business borrowers have varied over the years. Notice that short-term interest rates are especially prone to rise during booms and then fall during recessions. (The tall blue-shaded areas of the chart indicate recessions.) When the economy is expanding, firms need capital, and this demand for capital pushes rates higher. Inflationary

FIGURE 5.2 Long- and Short-Term Interest Rates, 1990–2013

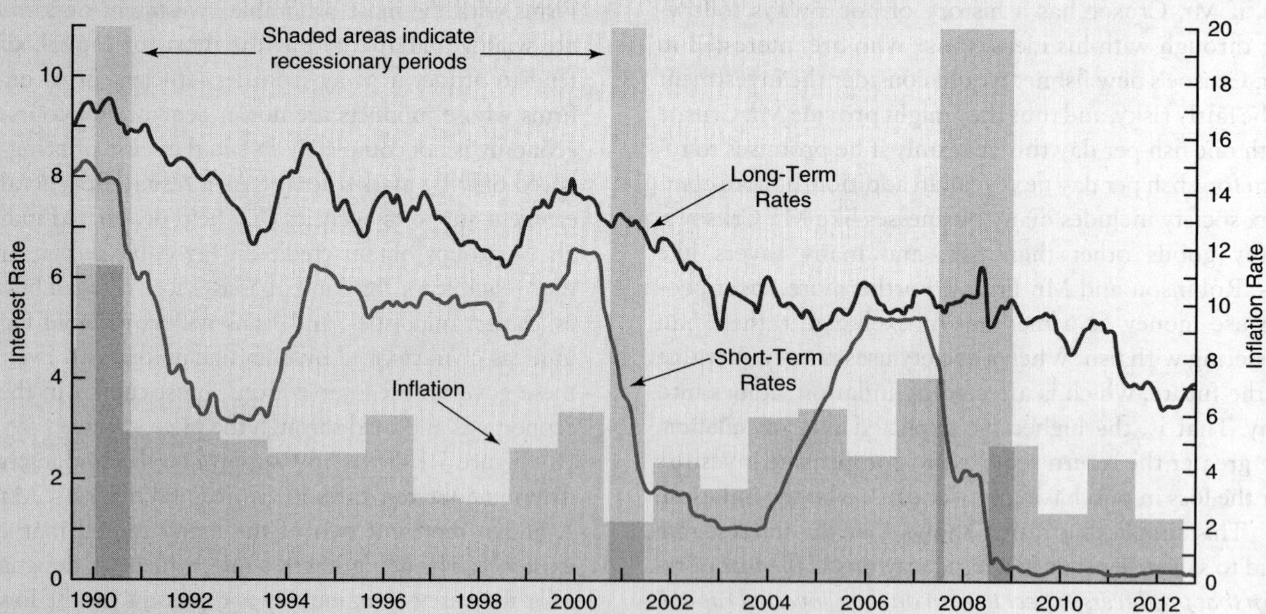

Notes:

1. Short-term interest rates are measured by three-month loans to very large, strong corporations, and long-term rates are measured by AAA corporate bonds.
2. Tick marks on the X-axis represent the middle of the year—that is, July 1.

Sources: Interest rates are found at the Federal Reserve website at www.federalreserve.gov/; information about recessions can be found at the National Bureau of Economic Research website at www.nber.org/cycles.html/, and CPI data are found at the website of the U.S. Department of Labor, Bureau of Labor, at www.bls.gov.

pressures are strongest during business booms, which also exert upward pressure on rates. Conditions are reversed during recessions, such as the ones during 2001 and 2007–2009. In these periods, a slowdown in business reduces the demand for credit, the rate of inflation falls, and thus interest rates generally decline.

These tendencies do not hold exactly. For example, the price of oil fell dramatically in 1985 and 1986, reducing inflationary pressures on other prices and easing fears of serious long-term inflation. In earlier years, these fears had pushed interest rates to record high levels (e.g., greater than 15 percent in 1982). From 1984 to 1987, the economy was fairly strong, but dwindling fears about inflation more than offset the normal tendency of interest rates to rise during good economic times, and the net result was lower interest rates.[1]

5-2 Determinants of Market Interest Rates

In general, the quoted (or nominal) interest rate, r, on *any* security traded in the financial markets is composed of a risk-free rate of interest plus a premium that reflects the riskiness of the security. This relationship can be expressed as shown in Equation 5.2:

5.2

$$\text{Rate of return} = r = \left(\text{Risk-free rate}\right) + \left(\text{Risk premium}\right)$$

This relationship is illustrated in Figure 5.3, which shows that investors require greater returns to invest in securities with greater risks. Although we discuss risk and return in detail in Chapter 8, the discussion in this section will give you an indication as to the general factors that affect interest rates on such debt securities as bonds.

The interest on *debt* can be expressed as shown in Equation 5.3:

5.3

$$r = r_{RF} + RP$$
$$= r_{RF} + [DRP + LP + MRP]$$

FIGURE 5.3 Rate of Return (Interest Rate)

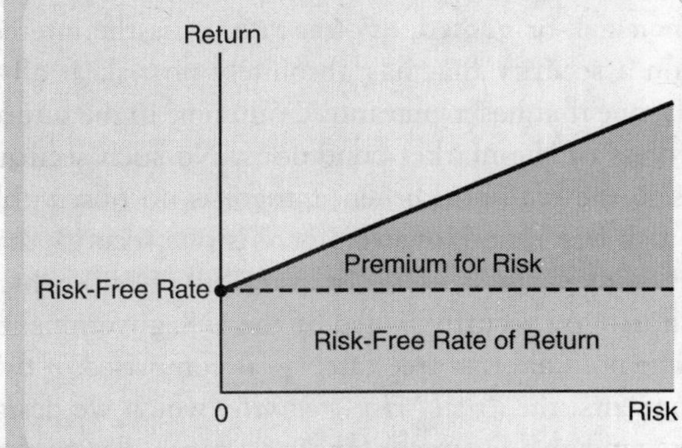

The variables in Equation 5.3 are defined as follows:

r =	the quoted, or *nominal*, rate of interest on a given security.[2] There are many different securities with different levels of risk; hence, there are many different quoted interest rates.
r_{RF} =	the quoted risk-free rate of return. Theoretically, this rate is the return associated with an investment that has a guaranteed outcome in the future—that is, it has no risk.
RP =	risk premium, which is the return that exceeds the risk-free rate of return, r_{RF}, and thus represents payment for the risk associated with an investment. $RP = r - r_{RF} = DRP + LP + MRP$.
DRP =	default risk premium, which reflects the chance that the borrower—that is, the issuer of the security—will not pay the debt's interest or principal on time.
LP =	liquidity, or marketability, premium, which reflects the fact that some investments are more easily converted into cash on short notice at a reasonable price than are other securities.
MRP =	maturity risk premium, which accounts for the fact that longer-term bonds experience greater price reactions to interest rate changes than do short-term bonds.

We discuss the components whose sum makes up the quoted, or *nominal*, rate on a given security in the following sections.[3]

[1]Short-term rates respond to current economic conditions, whereas long-term rates primarily reflect long-run expectations for inflation. As a result, short-term rates are sometimes higher than and sometimes lower than long-term rates. The relationship between long-term and short-term rates is called *term structure of interest rates*. This topic is discussed later in the chapter.

[2]The term *nominal* as it is used here means the *stated* rate as opposed to the *real* rate, which is adjusted to remove the effects of inflation. If you bought a 10-year Treasury bond in August 2013, the quoted, or nominal, rate was about 2.9 percent, but because inflation was expected to average 1.5 percent over the next 10 years, the real rate was 1.4% = 3.9% − 1.5%.

[3]Clearly, relationships exist among the components that we include in Equation 5.3, which means that they are not strictly additive. To simplify our discussion, however, we assume that these components are additive (independent).

5-2a The Nominal, or Quoted, Risk-Free Rate of Interest, r_{RF}

The **nominal**, or **quoted**, **risk-free rate**, r_{RF}, is the interest rate on a security that has absolutely no risk at all—that is, one that has a guaranteed outcome in the future, regardless of the market conditions. No such security exists in the real world; hence, there is no observable truly risk-free rate. However, there is one security that is free of most risks: a U.S. Treasury bill (T-bill), which is a short-term security issued by the U.S. government.

The nominal risk-free rate, r_{RF}, is comprised of two components: the *"real" risk-free rate,* which we designate r*, and an adjustment for the average inflation that is expected during the life of the investment, which we designate IP, or the *inflation premium.* As a result, $r_{RF} = r^* + IP$ in Equation 5.3.

The **real risk-free rate of interest, r***, is defined as the interest rate that would exist on a risk-free security *if inflation is expected to be zero* during the investment period. It can be thought of as the rate of interest that would exist on short-term U.S. Treasury securities in an *inflation-free world.* The real risk-free rate changes over time depending on economic conditions, especially (1) the rate of return corporations and other borrowers are willing to pay to borrow funds and (2) people's time preferences for current versus future consumption. It is difficult to measure the real risk-free rate precisely, but most experts think that r* fluctuates in the range of 2 to 4 percent in the United States.

No matter what investments they make, all *investors are affected by inflation.* For this reason, the minimum rate earned on any security, *no matter its risk,* must include compensation for the loss of purchasing power (due to inflation) that is expected during the life of the investment. Thus, r_{RF} must include a component for the average inflation, or purchasing power loss, that investors expect in the future.

5-2b Inflation Premium (IP)

Inflation has a major effect on interest rates because it erodes the purchasing power of the rupee and thus lowers the real rate of return on investments. To illustrate, suppose you invested ₹1,000 in a certificate of deposit that matures in one year and pays 4.5 percent interest. At the end of the year you will receive ₹1,045: your original ₹1,000 plus ₹45 of interest. Now suppose the inflation rate during the year is 10 percent and that it affects all items equally. If pizza cost ₹1.00 per slice at the beginning of the year, it would cost ₹1.10 at the end of the year. Therefore, your ₹1,000 could buy ₹1,000/₹1.00 = 1,000 slices of pizza at the beginning of the year but only ₹1,045/₹1.10 = 950 slices at year's end. *In real terms,* therefore, you would be worse off at the end of the year: You would receive ₹45 in interest, but that amount would not be sufficient to offset the effect of inflation. In this case, you would be better off buying 1,000 slices of frozen pizza (or some other storable asset such as land, timber, apartment buildings, wheat, or gold) than investing in the certificate of deposit.

nominal (quoted) risk-free rate, r_{RF} The rate of interest on a security that is free of all risk; r_{RF} is proxied by the T-bill rate and includes an inflation premium.

real risk-free rate of interest, r* The rate of interest that would exist on default-free U.S. Treasury securities if no inflation were expected.

inflation premium (IP) A premium for expected inflation that investors add to the real risk-free rate of return.

Investors are well aware of the effect of inflation. When they lend money, therefore, they build in an **inflation premium (IP)** equal to the *average inflation rate expected over the life of the security.* Thus, if the real risk-free rate of interest, r*, is 3 percent, and if inflation is expected to be 2 percent during the next year (and hence IP = 2%), then the quoted rate of interest on one-year T-bills would be $r_{RF} = 3\% + 2\% = 5\%$.[4]

It is important to note that the rate of inflation built into interest rates is the *rate of inflation expected in the future,* not the rate experienced in the past. Note also that the inflation rate reflected in the quoted interest rate of an investment is the *average inflation expected over the life of the investment.* Consequently, the inflation rate that is built into a one-year bond is the expected inflation rate for the next year, but the inflation rate built into a 10-year bond is the average rate of inflation expected over the next 10 years.

5-2c Default Risk Premium (DRP)

The risk that a borrower will *default* on a loan—that is, not pay the interest or the principal according to the loan contract—also affects the market interest rate on a security: The greater the default risk, the higher the interest rate that lenders charge (demand). Treasury securities have no default risk because everyone believes that the U.S. government will pay its debt on time. For corporate bonds, the better the bond's overall credit rating

[4]In reality, we should recognize that the purchasing power of the real risk-free rate is also affected by inflation. As a result, it is more appropriate to compute the nominal risk-free rate as $r_{RF} = (1 + r^*)(1 + IP) - 1$, which means that the appropriate rate in our example is $r_{RF} = (1.03)(1.02) - 1 = 0.0506 = 5.06\%$. The additional 0.06 percent represents the increase in the nominal rate associated with the real risk-free rate, r*, that is needed to ensure investors' wealth actually increases by 3 percent.

(AAA is the best), the lower its default risk and consequently the lower its interest rate.[5] Following are some representative interest rates on 10-year bonds that existed in August 2013:[6]

Type of Debt	Amount of Risk	Rate, r	DRP = r − r_{RF}
RBI rediscounting rate	No default risk, r_{RF}	2.9%	—
AAA corporate bond	Default risk greater than T-bonds	4.7	1.8%
BBB corporate bond	Default risk greater than AAA corporate bonds	5.6	2.7
CCC corporate bond	Default risk much greater than BBB corporate bonds	6.9	4.0

Assuming that these bonds have identical provisions, the only reason their rates differ is because their default risks differ. As a result, the difference between the quoted interest rate on a T-bond and that on a corporate bond with similar maturity, liquidity, and other features is the **default risk premium (DRP)**. Thus, if the bonds listed here were otherwise similar, the default risk premium would be DRP = $r_{\text{Corporate bond}} - r_{\text{T-bond}}$. Default risk premiums vary somewhat over time. Because investors were uncertain about the future of the economy in August 2013, the figures shown in the table are somewhat higher than normal.

5-2d Liquidity Premium (LP)

Liquidity generally is defined as the ability to convert an asset into cash on short notice and reasonably capture the amount initially invested. The more easily an asset can be converted to cash at a price that substantially recovers the initial amount invested, the more liquid it is considered. Clearly, assets have varying degrees of liquidity, depending on the characteristics of the markets in which they are traded. For instance, such financial assets as government securities trade in very active and efficient secondary markets, whereas the markets for real estate are much more restrictive. In addition, it generally is easier to convert an asset into cash at a "good" price the closer the asset's life is to its maturity date. Thus, financial assets generally are more liquid than real assets, and short-term financial assets generally are more liquid than long-term financial assets.

Because liquidity is important, investors evaluate liquidity and include a **liquidity premium (LP)** when the market rate of a security is established. Although it is difficult to accurately measure liquidity premiums, a differential of at least two, and perhaps four or five, percentage points exists between the least liquid and the most liquid financial assets of similar default risk and maturity.

5-2e Maturity Risk Premium (MRP)

The prices of long-term bonds decline (increase) sharply whenever interest rates rise (decline). Because interest rates can and do occasionally rise, *all* long-term bonds—even Treasury bonds—have an element of risk called *interest rate risk*. As a general rule, the bonds of any organization have more interest rate risk the longer the maturity of the bonds.[7] Therefore, the required interest rate must include a **maturity risk premium (MRP)**, which is higher the longer the time to maturity. Such a premium, like the other types of premiums, is extremely difficult to measure. Nevertheless, two things seem clear: (1) The MRP appears to vary over time, rising when interest rates are more volatile and uncertain, then falling when interest rates are more stable; (2) the MRP on T-bonds with 20–30 years to maturity normally is in the range of one or two percentage points.[8]

To illustrate the effect of time to maturity on the prices of bonds, consider two investments that are identical except for their maturity dates. Both investments promise to pay ₹1,000 at maturity, but Investment A matures in two years, whereas Investment B matures in 10 years.

default risk premium (DRP) The difference between the interest rate on a U.S. Treasury bond and a corporate bond of equal maturity and marketability; compensation for the risk that a corporation will not meet its debt obligations.

liquidity premium (LP) A premium added to the rate on a security if the security cannot be converted to cash on short notice at a price that is close to the original cost.

maturity risk premium (MRP) A premium that reflects interest rate risk; bonds with longer maturities have greater interest rate risk.

[5]Bond ratings, and bonds' riskiness in general, are discussed in more detail in Chapter 6. For this example, note that bonds rated AAA are judged to have less default risk than are bonds rated BBB, and BBB bonds are less risky than CCC bonds.

[6]Sources: http://www.federalreserve.gov/releases/h15/data.htm, http://finance.yahoo.com/bonds/composite_bond_rates, and http://www.bloomberg.com.

[7]For example, if you had bought a 30-year Treasury bond for ₹1,000 in 1972, when the long-term interest rate was 7 percent, and held it until 1981, when the long-term T-bond rate was 14.5 percent, the value of the bond would have declined to ₹514. That decrease would represent a loss of almost half the money, and it demonstrates that long-term bonds—even U.S. Treasury bonds—are not riskless. If you had purchased short-term T-bills in 1972 and subsequently reinvested the principal each time the bills matured, however, you would still have ₹1,000. This point will be discussed in Chapter 6.

[8]The total MRP from long-term government securities has averaged 1.5–2.0 percent over the last 65–70 years. Thus, the MRP per additional year of maturity has averaged 0.05–0.07 percent. See *Ibbotson SBBI Classic Yearbook: Market Results for Stocks, Bonds, Bills, and Inflation 1926–2012* (Chicago: Morningstar, 2013).

To simplify this example, let's assume that there currently is no MRP so that the return on both investments is the same. When interest rates are 10 percent and 12 percent, the values of the two bonds are shown here:

Investment	Maturity	Value @ 10%	Value @ 12%	₹ Change in Value	% Change in Value
A	2 years	₹826.45	₹797.19	−₹29.26	−3.5%
B	10 years	385.54	321.97	−63.57	−16.5

Note that both the rupee change and the percentage change are greater for the investment with the longer term to maturity—that is, Investment B. This simple example, which illustrates the general concept of maturity risk, shows why investors normally demand higher MRPs for investments with longer terms to maturity.

Although long-term bonds are heavily exposed to interest rate risk, short-term investments are more vulnerable to *reinvestment rate risk*. When short-term investments mature and the proceeds are reinvested, or *rolled over*, a decline in interest rates would necessitate reinvestment at a lower rate, and hence would lead to a decline in interest income. Thus, although investing short-term preserves one's principal, the interest income provided by short-term investments varies from year to year, depending on reinvestment rates. The implications of interest rate risk and reinvestment rate risk are discussed in greater detail in Chapter 6.

5-3 The Term Structure of Interest Rates

A study of Figure 5.2 reveals that at certain times, such as in 2002–2004 and 2008–2010, short-term interest rates are lower than long-term rates. At other times, such as in 2007, short-term rates are higher than long-term rates. The relationship between long- and short-term rates, which is known as the **term structure of interest rates**, is important to corporate treasurers, who must decide whether to borrow by issuing long- or short-term debt, and to investors, who must decide whether to buy long- or short-term bonds. For these reasons, it is important to understand (1) how long- and short-term rates are related, and (2) what causes shifts in their relative positions.

term structure of interest rates The relationship between yields and maturities of securities.

yield curve A graph showing the relationship between yields and maturities of securities on a particular date.

normal yield curve An upward-sloping yield curve.

inverted (abnormal) yield curve A downward-sloping yield curve.

The relationship between long- and short-term bonds varies and generally is dependent on the supply-and-demand relationship that exists for these bonds at a particular point in time. For example, the tabular section of Figure 5.4 includes interest rates for different maturities on three different dates. The set of data for a given date, when plotted on a graph such as that in Figure 5.4, is called the **yield curve** for that date. The yield curve provides a snapshot of the relationship between short- and long-term rates on a particular date. The yield curve changes both in position and in slope over time. For example, in November 2006 the yield curve was *downward sloping* (although not substantially); but, in August 2013, all rates were substantially lower, and long-term rates were higher than short-term rates, so the yield curve at that time was *upward sloping*.[9] In January 2007, rates were similar to those in November 2006, but short- and long-term rates did not differ much, so the yield curve was fairly *flat*, or *horizontal*.

Historically, long-term rates have generally been higher than short-term rates, so the yield curve normally has been upward sloping. For this reason, people often refer to an upward-sloping yield curve as a **normal yield curve**. On the other hand, because a downward-sloping yield curve is pretty rare, we normally refer to this type of curve as an **inverted**, or **abnormal, yield curve**. Thus, in Figure 5.4, the yield curve for November 2006 was inverted, but the yield curve for August 2013 was a normal shape (even though all rates were low). In the next section, we discuss three explanations for the shape of the yield curve and explain why an upward-sloping yield curve is considered normal.

5-3a Why Do Yield Curves Differ?

It is clear from Figure 5.4 that the shape of the yield curve at one point in time can be significantly different from the yield curve at another point in time. For example, the yield curve was downward sloping in 2006 whereas it was upward sloping in 2013. Remember that interest rates consist of (1) a risk-free return, r_{RF}, which includes the real risk-free return (r^*) and an adjustment for expected inflation (IP)

[9]The yield curve exhibited a fairly dramatic downward slope in March 1980, when short-term rates hovered around 16 percent and long-term rates were approximately 12 percent. During this recessionary period, interest rates remained at historically high levels for several months.

FIGURE 5.4 Indian Treasury Bonds: Interest Rates on Different Dates (Yield Curves)

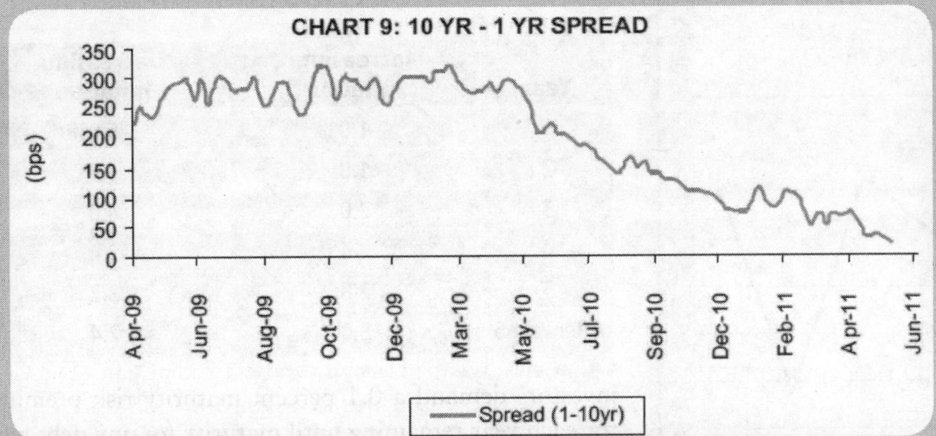

SOURCE: http://capitalmind.in/2011/06/inverting-yield-curves-in-india-and-brazil/ viewed on 11th October, 2015

and (2) a risk premium that rewards investors for various risks, including default risk (DRP), liquidity risk (LP), and maturity risk (MRP). Although the real risk-free rate of return, r*, does change at times, it generally is relatively stable from period to period. As a result, when interest rates shift to substantially different levels, it generally is because investors have changed either their expectations concerning future inflation or their attitudes concerning risk. Because changes in investors' risk attitudes generally evolve over time (years), *inflation expectations represent the most important factor in the determination of current interest rates,* and thus the shape of the yield curve.

To illustrate how inflation impacts the shape of the yield curve, let's examine interest rates on U.S. Treasury securities. First, the rate of return on these securities can be written as in Equation 5.4:

5.4

$$r_{Treasury} = r_{RF} + MRP = r^* + IP + MRP$$

This equation is the same as Equation 5.3, except that neither the default risk premium (DRP) nor the liquidity premium (LP) is included because we generally consider Treasury securities to be liquid (marketable), default-free investments. As a result, DRP = 0 and LP = 0. The maturity risk premium (MRP) is included in the equation because Treasury securities vary in maturity from as short as a few days to as long as 30 years. All else equal, *investors generally prefer to hold short-term securities* because such securities are less sensitive to changes in interest rates and provide greater investment flexibility than longer-term securities. As a result, investors will generally accept lower yields on short-term securities, which leads to relatively low short-term rates. *Borrowers,* on the other hand, *generally prefer long-term debt* because short-term debt exposes them to the risk of having to refinance the debt under adverse conditions (e.g., higher interest rates). Accordingly, borrowers want to lock into long-term funds, which means they are willing to pay higher rates, other things held constant, for long-term funds than for short-term funds, which also leads to relatively low short-term rates. Taken together, these two sets of preferences imply that under normal conditions, a positive maturity risk premium (MRP) exists, and the MRP increases with years to maturity, causing the yield curve to be upward sloping. In economics, the general theory that supports this conclusion is referred to as the **liquidity preference theory**, which simply states that long-term bonds normally yield more than short-term bonds, all else equal, primarily because MRP > 0 and MRP increases with time to maturity.

During the past decade, we have observed three basic shapes for the yield curve associated with Treasury securities. Each of the three shapes is shown in Figure 5.4: a normal, or upward-sloping, yield curve; an inverted, or downward-sloping, yield curve; and a flat yield curve. For this reason, although MRP > 0, which supports the *liquidity preference theory*, it appears that this theory does not fully explain the shape of the yield curve. Remember that the nominal risk-free rate of return, r_{RF}, consists of two components: the real risk-free rate of return, r*, which is considered to be relatively constant from one year to the next, and an adjustment for the inflation expectations of investors, IP—that is, $r_{RF} = r^* + IP$. Expectations about future inflation do vary over time. However, the inflation premium, IP, that is included in interest rates

liquidity preference theory The theory that, all else being equal, lenders prefer to make short-term loans rather than long-term loans; hence, they will lend short-term funds at lower rates than they lend long-term funds.

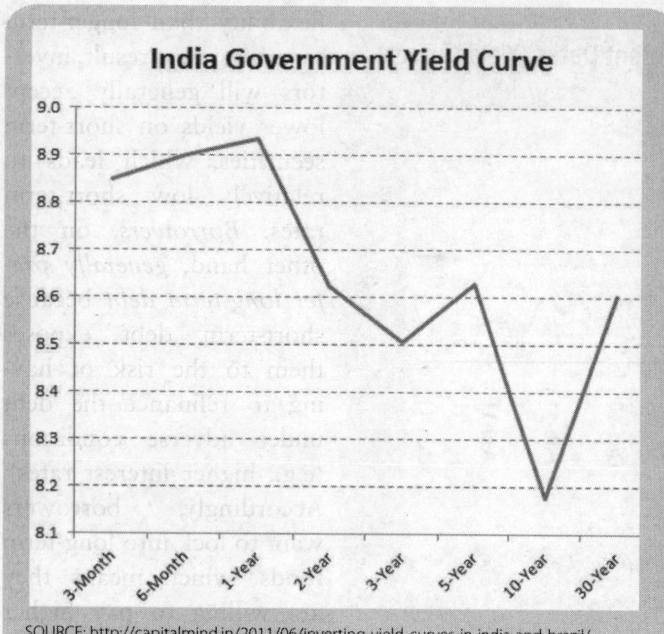

SOURCE: http://capitalmind.in/2011/06/inverting-yield-curves-in-india-and-brazil/ viewed on 11th October, 2015

is somewhat predictable because it is the average of the inflation rates that are expected to occur during the life of the investment (a Treasury security in this case). In fact, the yield curve is often used as an aid when forecasting future interest rates because both investors and borrowers base their current decisions on expectations regarding which way interest rates will move in the future. For example, because interest rates were at historically low levels in 2012 and 2013, most people believed rates most certainly would have to increase in the future. The attitude was that rates could not possibly drop any lower. During this time, many homeowners refinanced their houses to take advantage of, and thus "lock in," the low rates, whereas investors primarily purchased short-term securities in hopes that rates would increase in the future, at which time they would be able to lock in the higher rates. Clearly, the expectations of the participants in the financial markets—that is, investors and borrowers—greatly impact interest rates. The **expectations theory** states that the shape of the yield curve depends on *expectations* concerning future inflation rates. More specifically, the yield curve should be upward sloping when investors expect inflation, and thus interest rates, to increase, and vice versa. We illustrate how expectations can be used to help *forecast* interest rates in the next section.

expectations theory The theory that the shape of the yield curve depends on investors' expectations about future inflation rates.

Let's consider the impact of inflation expectations on the determination of interest rates when inflation is expected to (1) increase in the future and (2) decrease in the future. For both situations, assume the real risk-free rate, r*, is 2 percent and that investors demand a 0.1 percent maturity risk premium for each year remaining until maturity for any debt with a term to maturity greater than one year, with a maximum value of 1 percent. Thus, if a Treasury bill matures in one year, MRP = 0; but, if a Treasury bond matures in five years, MRP = 0.5%, and bonds that mature in 10 years or longer will have MRP = 1.0%. Also, suppose that inflation expectations are as follows for the two situations:

Year	Increasing Inflation	Decreasing Inflation
1	1.0%	5.0%
2	1.8	4.2
3	2.0	4.0
4	2.4	3.4
5	2.8	3.2
After Year 5	3.0	2.4

Note that these two situations are not related; that is, we are not assuming that these two patterns of expected inflation can exist at the same time; rather, they are mutually exclusive.

Using this information, we can compute the interest rates for Treasury securities with any term to maturity. To illustrate, consider a bond that matures in five years. For the case in which inflation is expected to *increase*, the interest rate, or yield, on this bond should be 4.5% = 2% + 2% + 0.5% because r* = 2%, IP = 2.0% = (1.0% + 1.8% + 2.0% + 2.4% + 2. 8%)/5, and MRP = 0.5% = 0.1% × 5 years. Note that IP is the average of the inflation rates that investors expect each year during the bond's five-year life. Had we evaluated a 10-year bond, IP would have been the average of the inflation rates that investors expect each year during the next 10 years (IP = 2.5%) and MRP would have been 1 percent (MRP = 0.1% × 10); thus r = 2% + 2.5% + 1% = 5.5%.

Figure 5.5 shows the yield curves for both inflationary situations. The yields are given in the tables in the figure. As the graphs show, when inflation is expected to increase, the yield curve is upward sloping, and vice versa. In either case, economists often use the yield curve to form expectations about the future of the economy. For example, when inflation is high and expected to decline, as Panel B of Figure 5.5 indicates, the yield curve generally is downward sloping. In many cases a downward-sloping yield curve suggests that the economy will weaken in the

FIGURE 5.5 Illustrative Yield Curves for Treasury Securities

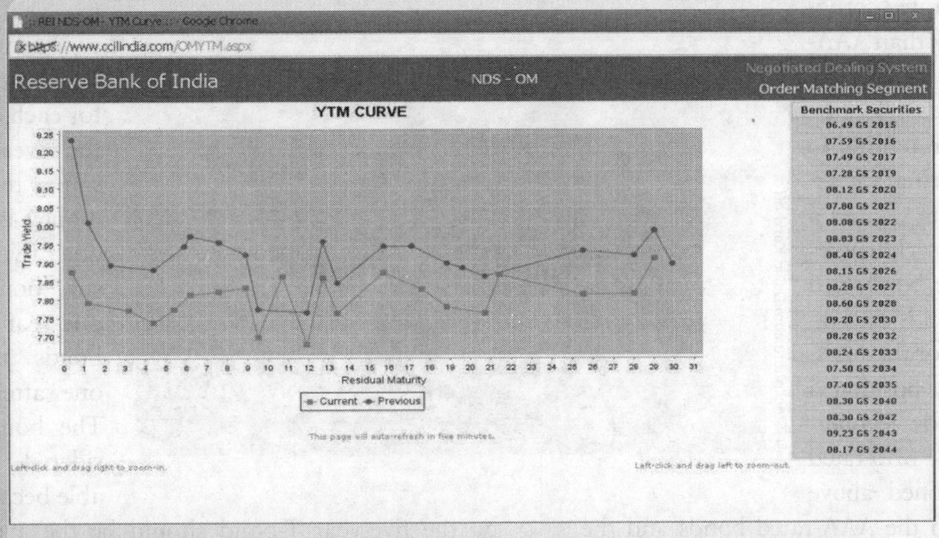

SOURCE:http://freefincal.com/rbi-rate-cut-india/page viewed on 11th October, 2015

future: Consumers delay purchases because they expect prices to decline in the future, borrowers wait to borrow funds because they believe rates will be lower in the future, and investors provide more long-term funds to the financial markets in an effort to capture (lock in) higher current long-term rates. All of these actions lead to long-term rates that are lower than short-term rates in the current period.

There are times when the yield curve exhibits either humps or dips for bonds in a particular range of terms to maturity because the supply/demand condition in one range of maturities is significantly different from those in other maturity ranges. When such a situation exists, interest rates for bonds in the affected maturity range are either substantially higher or substantially lower than rates in the maturity ranges on either side. In such cases, the resulting yield curve is not smooth or uniform; rather, there is a hump in the yield curve if rates are higher, and a dip if rates are lower. The reason these humps and dips occur is because there are instances when investors and borrowers prefer bonds with specific maturity ranges. For example, a person borrowing to buy a long-term asset like a house, or an electric utility borrowing to build a power plant, would want a long-term loan. However, a retail firm borrowing in September to build its inventories for Christmas would prefer a short-term loan. Similar differences exist among savers. For example, a person saving to take a vacation next summer would want to lend (save) in the short-term market, but someone saving for retirement 20 years hence would probably buy long-term securities.

According to the **market segmentation theory** that has been developed by economists, the slope of the yield curve depends on supply/demand conditions in the long- and short-term markets. Thus, the yield curve could at any given time be flat, upward sloping, or downward sloping, and could have humps or dips. Interest rates would be high in a particular segment compared to other segments when there was a low supply of funds in that segment relative to demand, and vice versa. The slight hump in the January 2007 yield curve shown in Figure 5.4 for bonds with a maturity of one year suggests that the demand for one year loans was high relative to the supply; that is, in relative terms, borrowers demanded more one-year loans than longer-term loans, fewer investors bought bonds that matured in one year, so the supply of short-term funds was relatively low, or both conditions existed.

In this section, we use Treasury securities to illustrate concepts relating to the shape of the yield curve. The same concepts apply to corporate bonds. To include corporate bonds in the illustration, we would have to determine the default risk premium, DRP, and the liquidity premium,

market segmentation theory
The theory that every borrower and every lender has a preferred maturity, and that the slope of the yield curve depends on the supply of and the demand for funds in the long-term market relative to the short-term market.

LP, associated with such bonds. In Chapter 6, we discuss bond ratings, which provide an indication of the default risk, and thus the DRP, associated with a bond. In bond-rating terminology, BBB-rated corporate bonds have more risk than AAA-rated corporate bonds, which have more risk than T-bonds. Because investors demand higher returns to purchase riskier investments, we expect that $r_{BBB} > r_{AAA} > r_{Treasury}$. As a result, if we were to add yield curves for AAA-rated corporate bonds and BBB-rated corporate bonds to Figure 5.4, the yield curves for the AAA-rated bonds would be positioned above the yield curves for T-bonds, and the yield curve for the BBB-rated bonds would be positioned above the yield curves for both the AAA-rated bonds and the T-bonds.

© iStockphoto.com/David Kerkhoff

5-3b Does the Yield Curve Indicate Future Interest Rates?

It was mentioned earlier that the *expectations theory* states that the shape of the yield curve depends on expectations concerning future inflation rates. It was also mentioned that the primary reason interest rates change is because investors change their expectations concerning future inflation rates. If this is true, can we use the yield curve to help forecast future interest rates? In this section, we examine Treasury securities to illustrate how interest rates might be forecast using information provided by a yield curve. Because there are many factors that affect interest rates in the real world, models that are used to forecast interest rates are very complex and not always very accurate. Therefore, the discussion in this section is very much oversimplified; significantly more analysis than examining a yield curve is needed to forecast interest rates.

Although we know that Treasury securities are exposed to maturity risk, to simplify the discussion here, we assume that MRP = 0 in the determination of interest rates for these securities. If MRP = 0, then all Treasury securities have the same risk, regardless of their terms to maturity, and neither investors nor borrowers should have a preference for securities with particular maturities because all securities are interchangeable. In other words, a person who wants to invest for a five-year period should not care whether the funds are invested in a Treasury bond that matures in five years or a Treasury bond that matures in one year that can be turned over in each of the next five years. The Treasury securities should be perfect substitutes for each other so that the investor earns the same return if the money is invested in one five-year Treasury bond or in five one-year Treasury bonds that mature one after the other. The bonds are considered interchangeable because the yield on the five-year T-bond should be the average of the yields on the five one-year T-bonds.

To illustrate, suppose that on January 2, 2015, the real risk-free rate of interest was r* = 3% and expected inflation rates for the next three years are as shown here:[10]

Year	Expected Annual (One-Year) Inflation Rate	Expected Average Inflation Rate from January 2, 2015 to December 31 of Indicated Year
2015	2.0%	$IP_1 = (2\%)/1 = 2.0\%$
2016	4.0	$IP_2 = (2\% + 4\%)/2 = 3.0\%$
2017	6.0	$IP_3 = (2\% + 4\% + 6\%)/3 = 4.0\%$

Given these expectations, the following table shows the interest rate pattern that should exist:

Bond Type	Real Risk-Free Rate (r*)		Inflation Premium (IP_t) = Average Expected Inflation Rate		Nominal Rate for Each Type of Bond (r_{RF})
1-year bond	3.0%	+	2.0%	=	5.0%
2-year bond	3.0%	+	3.0%	=	6.0%
3-year bond	3.0%	+	4.0%	=	7.0%

If the yields on these hypothetical bonds were plotted, the yield curve would be upward sloping, similar to the August 2013 yield curve in Figure 5.4. Had the pattern

[10]In this example, we compute simple *arithmetic* average. Technically, we should be using *geometric* average, but the differences are not material in this example.

of expected inflation rates been reversed, with inflation expected to fall from 6 percent to 2 percent during the three-year period, the pattern of interest rates would have produced an inverted yield curve like the November 2006 yield curve shown in Figure 5.4, except the downward slope would have been much more pronounced.

Because the yield on any bond is the average of the annual, or one-year, interest rates that are expected during its life, we know the relationship shown in Equation 5.5 exists:

5.5

$$\text{Yield (\%) on an } n\text{-year bond} = \frac{R_1 + R_2 + \cdots + R_n}{n}$$

Here, R_1 is the interest rate expected only during the first year of the bond's remaining life (Year 1), R_2 is the interest rate expected only during the second year of its remaining life (Year 2), and so forth.

We should be able to reverse the averaging process shown in Equation 5.5 to forecast the interest rate expected in each year (R_1, R_2, and so forth) by examining the yields that currently exist on bonds with various maturities. For example, suppose that currently the yield on a one-year T-bill is 5 percent and the yield on a two-year T-bond is 6 percent. Plugging in the known information, we have

$$6\% = \frac{5\% + R_2}{2}$$

Solving for R_2, we have

$$5\% + R_2 = 6\%(2) = 12\%,$$

$$\text{so} \quad R_2 = 12\% - 5\% = 7\%$$

Therefore, if today were January 2, 2015, according to this example, investors would expect the interest rate to be 5 percent in 2015 and 7 percent in 2015. If this were true, then the average yield over the next two years would be 6% = (5% + 7%)/2. You can see that the yield curve is upward sloping whenever interest rates are expected to increase in future years because the *average yield* increases as higher interest rates are included in the computation.

This information can also be used to determine the expected inflation rate. In the current example, the interest rate consists of the real risk-free rate, r*, which is constant, and an adjustment for inflation. Therefore, to determine the expected inflation rate each year, we simply subtract r* from the nominal interest rate that is expected to occur during the year. Remember that we assumed the real risk-free rate, r*, is 3 percent per year. As a result, in the current example, investors expect inflation to be 2% = 5% − 3% in 2014 and 4% = 7% − 3% in 2015. These results are the same as the expected inflation rates that were reported earlier.

5-4 Other Factors That Influence Interest Rate Levels

Factors other than those discussed earlier also influence both the general level of interest rates and the shape of the yield curve. The four most important factors are discussed here.

Reserve Bank of India and monetary policy

In India, regulation of banks and financial institutions is carried out by the Reserve Bank of India (RBI). The central board of RBI is constituted for administrative purposes and has a tenure of 4 years. Among other things, RBI performs the following key functions:

1. Formulation of the monetary policy of the country, including deciding on key interest rates.
2. Regulation and supervision of the overall financial system in the country. This includes deciding on banking regulations, having new licenses and general norms for financial activities.
3. Management of the country's foreign exchange. This includes managing the foreign exchange reserves and also occasionally indulging in open market operations.
4. Overseeing the developmental activities pertaining to the financial sector including being the banker for the Central Government.
5. Acting as a lender of last resort for the banking sector and the Government.
6. Monitoring the exchange rate of the rupee.
7. Overseeing the agricultural and rural credit in the country including microfinance.

5-4a Federal Reserve Policy

You probably learned two important points in your economics courses: (1) The money supply has a major effect on both the level of economic activity and the rate of inflation; (2) in the United States, the Federal Reserve (the Fed) controls the money supply. If the Fed wants to slow (control) growth in the economy, it slows growth in the money supply. Such an action initially causes interest rates to increase and inflation to stabilize. The opposite effect occurs when the Fed loosens the money supply.

The most important tool used by the Fed to manage the supply of money is **open market operations**, which involve buying or selling U.S. Treasury securities to change bank reserves. When the Fed wants to increase the money supply, it *purchases* government securities from *primary dealers* who have established trading relationships with the Federal Reserve. The Fed pays for the securities by sending funds to the banks where the primary dealers have accounts. This action increases the deposit balances of the dealers, which in turn increases the overall reserves of the banking system. Banks have additional funds to lend, so the money supply increases, which causes interest rates to decline. To increase rates, the Fed would decrease the money supply by *selling* government securities. The Fed carries out "normal" open market operations on a continuous basis to maintain economic activity within defined limits, and it shifts its open market strategies toward heavier-than-normal buying or selling when more substantial adjustments are required.

5-4b Federal Deficits

If the federal government spends more than it takes in from tax revenues, it runs a *deficit*. Deficit spending must be covered either by borrowing or by printing money. If the government borrows, the added demand for funds pushes up interest rates. If it prints money, the expectation is that future inflation will increase, which also drives up interest rates. Thus, other things held constant, the larger the federal deficit, the higher the level of interest rates. Whether long- or short-term rates are affected to a greater extent depends on how the deficit is financed. Consequently, we cannot generalize about how deficits will influence the slope of the yield curve.

open market operations
Operations in which the Federal Reserve buys or sells Treasury securities to expand or contract the U.S. money supply.

5-4c International Business (Foreign Trade Balance)

Businesses and individuals in the United States buy from and sell to people and firms in other countries. If Americans import more than they export (buy more than they sell), the United States is said to be running a *foreign trade deficit*. When trade deficits occur, they must be financed, and the main source of financing is debt.[11] Therefore, the larger the trade deficit, the more the United States must borrow. As the country increases its borrowing, interest rates are driven up. In addition, foreigners are willing to hold U.S. debt only if the interest rate on this debt is competitive with interest rates in other countries. Therefore, if the Federal Reserve attempts to lower interest rates in the United States, causing U.S. rates to fall below rates abroad, foreigners will sell U.S. bonds. This activity will depress bond prices and cause U.S. interest rates to increase. As a result, the existence of a deficit trade balance hinders the Fed's ability to combat a recession by lowering interest rates.

5-4d Business Activity

We can return to Figure 5.2 to see how business conditions influence interest rates.

1. During periods of inflation, the general tendency is toward higher interest rates.
2. During recessions, both the demand for money and the rate of inflation tend to fall. At the same time, the Federal Reserve tends to increase the money supply in an effort to stimulate the economy. As a result, interest rates typically decline during recessions.
3. When the U.S. economy shows signs of expanding too quickly, the Fed normally takes actions to increase interest rates to discourage too much expansion and to control future growth so that it does not result in high inflation.
4. During recessions, short-term rates decline more sharply than do long-term rates. This situation occurs for two reasons. First, the Fed operates mainly in the short-term sector, so its intervention has the strongest effect here. Second, long-term rates reflect the average expected inflation rate over the next

[11]The deficit could also be financed by selling assets, including gold, corporate stocks, entire companies, or real estate. The United States has financed its massive trade deficits by all of these approaches, but the primary method has been by borrowing.

20 to 30 years. This expectation generally does not change much, even when the current rate of inflation is low because of a recession.

5-5 Interest Rate Levels and Stock Prices

Interest rates have two effects on corporate profits. First, because interest is a cost, the higher the rate of interest, the lower a firm's profits, other things held constant. Second, interest rates affect the level of economic activity, and economic activity affects corporate profits. Interest rates obviously affect stock prices because of their effects on profits. Perhaps even more important, they influence stock prices because of competition in the marketplace between stocks and bonds. If interest rates rise sharply, investors can obtain higher returns in the bond market, which induces them to sell stocks and transfer funds from the stock market to the bond market. A massive sale of stocks in response to rising interest rates obviously would depress stock prices. Of course, the reverse would occur if interest rates decline. Indeed, the 11 percent increase in the Dow Jones Industrial Index in October 2002 was the result of a sharp drop in long-term interest rates during the prior few months. On the other hand, at least to some extent, the poor performance exhibited by the market in 2000, when the prices of common stocks declined, resulted from increases in interest rates.

5-5a The Cost of Money as a Determinant of Value

In this chapter, we have discussed some of the factors that determine the cost of money. For the most part, these same factors also affect other rates of return, including rates earned on stocks and other investments. In Chapter 1, we mentioned that the value of an asset is a function of the cash flows it is expected to generate in the future and the *rate of return* at which investors are willing to provide funds to purchase the investment. We know that many factors, including conditions in the economy and financial markets, affect the determination of the expected cash flows and the rate people demand when investing their funds; thus, the process of determining value can be fairly complex. In Chapter 4, however, you should have discovered that the value of an asset can be stated in simple mathematical terms as the present value of the future cash flows that the asset is expected to generate during its life. Thus, to compute the value of an asset, you must solve Equation 5.6:

5.6

$$\text{Value of an asset} = \frac{\widehat{CF}_1}{(1+r)^1} + \frac{\widehat{CF}_2}{(1+r)^2} + \cdots + \frac{\widehat{CF}_n}{(1+r)^n} = \sum_{t=1}^{n} \frac{\widehat{CF}_t}{(1+r)^t}$$

In this equation, $\widehat{CF}_t$ is the cash flow that the asset is expected to generate in Period t, and r represents the cost of funds. As a result, you can see that mathematically, as r increases, the denominator in Equation 5.6 increases, which decreases the present value. In general, then, when the cost of money increases, the value of an asset decreases. Let's consider the logic of this statement with a simple example. Suppose that you are offered an investment that will pay you a constant ₹100 per year forever (a perpetuity). If you want to earn a 10 percent return on this investment, you should be willing to pay ₹1,000 = ₹100/0.10 to purchase it. But would the amount you are willing to pay for the investment be different if interest rates on similar investments increase to 12 percent before you have a chance to purchase the perpetuity? Because the ₹100 annual payment that you will receive from the investment does not change, you must change the amount that you are willing to pay for the perpetuity if you want to earn the higher 12 percent return. To earn the higher return, you must lower the price you are willing to pay for the investment to ₹833.33 = ₹100/0.12. In other words, if you purchase the investment for ₹833.33, you will earn 12 percent because ₹100 is 12 percent of ₹833.33.

As you can see, the cost of money—that is, the interest rate (return)—affects the prices of investments. In general, *when rates in the financial markets increase, the prices (values) of financial assets decrease.* In the next couple of chapters, we discuss the valuation of stocks and bonds to give you a better understanding of this fundamental valuation concept.

KEY COST OF MONEY (INTEREST RATE) CONCEPTS

To conclude this chapter, we summarize some cost-of-money concepts that were discussed.

- ▶▶ The yield, or return, that is earned on an investment is comprised of two components: (1) income paid by the *issuer* of the financial asset and (2) the change in the market value of the financial asset over some time period.
- ▶▶ The cost of money (interest rates) is based on (1) the rate of return that borrowers expect to earn on their investments, (2) savers' preferences to spend income in the current period rather than delay consumption until some future period, (3) the risks associated with investments/loans, and (4) expected inflation.
- ▶▶ In general, the rate of return on an investment, or the interest rate on a loan, includes a minimum payment for delaying consumption until some future date, which is termed the risk-free rate of return, r_{RF}, and payment for the risk associated with the investment/loan which is termed a risk premium, RP. Risks can include the risk that the borrower will default on the loan, the risk associated with the liquidity of the investment, and so forth.
- ▶▶ In most instances, long-term interest rates are greater than short-term interest rates; that is, the yield curve is upward sloping. However, there are rare instances when the yield curve is inverted, or downward sloping, which occurs when long-term interest rates are lower than short-term interest rates. An inverted yield curve is likely to appear when the economy is in a recession.
- ▶▶ Everything else equal, when interest rates (returns) increase, the prices (values) of investments decrease. In other words, when investors want to receive higher returns, they lower the amount they are willing to pay for investments.

MULTIPLE CHOICE QUESTIONS

1. The yield of a security is comprised of

a. The periodic amount paid by the issuer of the security

b. The increase in the market value of the security

c. Both a and b

d. None of the above

2. In computing the cost of money, the following items matter

a. The risk of the security

b. The return that borrowers expect to earn on this

c. Both a and b

d. None of the above

3. When long-term interest rates are higher than short-term interest rates,

a. The yield curve is downward sloping

b. The yield curve is flat

c. The yield curve is upward sloping

d. The yield curve does not depend on this

4. When short-term interest rates are higher than long-term interest rates,

a. The yield curve is downward sloping

b. The yield curve is flat

c. The yield curve is upward sloping

d. The yield curve does not depend on this

5. When interest rates in the market go up, the

a. Price investors are prepared to pay as the investment goes up

b. Price investors are prepared to pay as the investment goes down

c. Price investors are prepared to pay as the investment does not change

d. We need more data to be able to tell

6. Generally speaking,

a. Companies prefer long-term borrowing to short-term borrowing

b. Companies prefer short-term borrowing to long-term borrowing

c. Companies decide on borrowing long-term or

short-term, based on the predictions given by the yield curve

d. None of the above

7. Yield curves differ from time to time because

a. Companies decide on their own to change interest rates

b. Macro-economic conditions decide interest rates

c. Inflation is a factor in interest rates

d. Both b and c

8. According to the Liquidity Preference theory,

a. Long-term bonds yield less than short-term bonds

b. Long-term bonds yield more than short-term bonds

c. Long-term bonds yield the same as short-term bonds

d. None of the above

9. According to the Expectations theory,

a. Long-term bonds yield less than short-term bonds

b. Long-term bonds yield more than short-term bonds

c. This would depend on supply/demand conditions in the market

d. This would depend on inflation expectations

10. According to the Segmentation theory,

a. Long-term bonds yield less than short-term bonds

b. Long-term bonds yield more than short-term bonds

c. This would depend on inflation expectations

d. This would depend on supply/demand conditions in the market

Answers:

1.	(c)	2.	(c)	3.	(c)	4.	(a)	5.	(b)
6.	(c)	7.	(d)	8.	(d)	9.	(b)	10.	(d)

PROBLEMS

For more problems, login to CourseMate for CFIN at CengageBrain.com

5–1 Yesterday Deepak sold 1,000 shares of stock that he owned for ₹29 per share. Deepak purchased the stock one year ago for ₹28 per share. During the year, Deepak received a quarterly dividend equal to ₹0.10 per share. What return (yield) did Deepak earn during the time he owned the stock?

5–2 One year ago, Pawan purchased 40 shares of common stock for ₹10 per share. During the year, he received one dividend payment in the amount of ₹0.50 per share. If the stock currently is worth ₹9 per share, what yield did Pawan earn on his investment for the year?

5–3 One year ago, Smitha purchased ₹1,050 worth of Elite Electrician's common stock for ₹42 per share. During the year, Smitha received two dividend payments, each equal to ₹0.05 per share. The current market value of the stock is ₹44 per share. What yield did Smitha earn on her investment during the year?

5–4 Pooja just sold all the shares of International Inns stock that she owned for ₹156 per share. She purchased the stock one year ago for ₹150 per share. If Pooja did not receive any dividend payments during the year, what yield did she earn on her investment?

5–5 Yesterday Ramya sold 1,000 shares of stock that she owned for ₹45 per share. When she purchased the stock two years ago, Ramya paid ₹50 per share. Every three months during the time that she held the stock, Ramya received a quarterly dividend equal to ₹0.50 per share. A total of eight dividends were received. (a) What return (yield) did Ramya earn during the two years she held the stock? (b) If the price of the stock was ₹45 per share one year ago, what return did Ramya earn in *each* year she held the stock?

5–6 Earlier today, Krishna sold 200 shares of stock he owned. He purchased the stock three years ago for ₹28 per share. Following is a table that shows the market value of the stock at the end of each year and the amount of the dividend that Krishna received during the year:

Year	Market Value (per share)	Dividend (per share)
1	₹26	₹0.60
2	28	0.60
3	32	0.60

(a) What total return (yield) did Krishna earn during the three-year period he held the stock? (b) What return did Krishna earn for *each* year he held the stock?

5-7 Suppose the yield on a two-year Treasury bond is 5 percent and the yield on a one-year Treasury bond is 4 percent. If the maturity risk premium (MRP) on these bonds is zero (0), what is the expected one-year interest rate during the second year (Year 2)?

5-8 The interest rate on one-year Treasury bonds is 1.0 percent, the rate on two-year T-bonds is 0.9 percent, and the rate on three-year T-bonds is 0.8 percent. Using the expectations theory, compute the expected *one-year* interest rates in (a) the second year (Year 2 only) and (b) the third year (Year 3 only).

5-9 The interest rate on one-year Treasury bonds is 0.4 percent, the rate on two-year T-bonds is 0.8 percent, and the rate on three-year T-bonds is 1.1 percent. Using the expectations theory, compute the expected *one-year* interest rates in (a) the second year (Year 2 only) and (b) the third year (Year 3 only).

5-10 The interest rate on five-year Treasury bonds is 3.1 percent, the rate on six-year T-bonds is 2.9 percent, and the rate on seven-year T-bonds is 2.6 percent. Using the expectations theory, compute the expected *one-year* interest rates in (a) Year 6 only and (b) Year 7 only.

5-11 The interest rate on two-year Treasury bonds is 1.2 percent, the rate on three-year T-bonds is 1.4 percent, and the rate on four-year T-bonds is 1.9 percent. Using the expectations theory, compute the expected *one-year* interest rates in (a) the third year (Year 3 only) and (b) the fourth year (Year 4 only).

5-12 The rate of inflation for the next 12 months (Year 1) is expected to be 1.4 percent; it is expected to be 1.8 percent the following year (Year 2); and it is expected to be 2.0 percent every year after Year 2. Assume the real risk-free rate, r*, is 3 percent for all maturities. What should be the yield to maturity on risk-free bonds that mature in (a) one year, (b) five years, and (c) 10 years.

5-13 Economists expect the inflation rate to be 1.5 percent for the coming year and the following year, and then after Year 2 inflation will settle at a constant rate greater than 1.5 percent. The yield is the same on one-year bonds and two-year bonds; the yield on three-year bonds is 0.5 percent greater than on one-year and two-year bonds. The real risk-free rate is 2 percent for all bonds. If the bonds are risk-free, what rate of inflation is expected in Year 3 and beyond?

5-14 Today is January 1, 2014, and investors expect the *annual* risk-free interest rates in 2014 through 2016 to be:

Year	One-Year Rate (r_{RF})
2014	2.2%
2015	1.8
2016	2.9

What is the yield to maturity for Treasury bonds that mature at the *end* of (a) 2015 (a two-year bond) and (b) 2016 (a three-year bond)? Assume the bonds have no risks.

5-15 Suppose today is January 1, 2014, and investors expect the *annual* inflation rates in 2014 through 2016 to be:

Year	One-Year Inflation Rate
2014	2.1%
2015	1.5
2016	0.9

To yield a real risk-free rate, r*, equal to 2 percent, what would the average nominal rate be on a (a) one-year bond, (b) two-year bond, and (c) three-year bond? Assume the bonds are risk-free.

5-16 Suppose today is January 3, 2014, and investors expect the *annual* risk-free interest rates in 2018 and 2019 to be:

Year	One-Year Rate (r_{RF})
2018	4.5%
2019	2.3

Currently a four-year Treasury bond that matures on December 31, 2017 has an interest rate equal to 2.5 percent. What is the yield to maturity for Treasury bonds that mature at the end of (a) 2018 (a five-year bond) and (b) 2019 (a six-year bond)? Assume the bonds have no risks.

5-17 *The Wall Street Journal* reports that the yield on a nine-month Treasury bond is 2.3 percent, the yield on a three-year Treasury bond is 2.9 percent, and the yield on a 10-year Treasury bond is 4.3 percent. Although no liquidity premium is associated with Treasury securities, there is a maturity risk premium (MRP) for Treasuries with maturities equal to one year or greater. What is the MRP?

5-18 Currently, a six-month Treasury bill is yielding 3.2 percent. Company F's three-year bond has a yield equal to 5.0 percent, and its seven-year bond has a yield equal to 5.8 percent. Although none of the bonds has a liquidity premium, any bond with a maturity equal to one year or longer has a maturity risk premium (MRP). Except for their terms to maturity, the characteristics of the bonds are the same. Compute the (a) *annual* MRP and (b) default risk premium (DRP) associated with the bonds.

5-19 Suppose economists expect that the nominal risk-free rate of return, r_{RF}, which is also the rate on a one-year Treasury note, will be 3.2 percent long into the future. You are evaluating two corporate bonds that are identical except for their terms to maturity. The bonds have the same default risk, and neither bond has a liquidity premium. Bond T matures in five years and has a yield equal to 5.3 percent, whereas Bond Q matures in eight years and has a yield equal to 5.9 percent. Compute (a) the annual maturity risk premium (MRP) and (b) the bond's default risk premium (DRP).

5-20 Economists expect that the nominal risk-free rate of return, r_{RF}, on one-year Treasury bonds will be 2.4 percent long into the future. General Machinery's (GM) one-year bond has a yield equal to 4.8 percent. The yield on the GM bond includes a liquidity premium equal to 0.3 percent. Suppose the maturity risk premium (MRP) for all bonds with maturities *greater* than one year is 0.15 percent per year. Based on this information, what should be the yield on GM's five-year bonds?

The Cost of Money (Interest Rates)

Learning Outcomes

LO.1 Describe the cost of money and factors that affect the cost of money (interest rates).

- The cost of money, which refers to interest rates, is effectively the cost of "renting" (borrowing) funds from savers (investors). Factors that affect interest rates include production opportunities, time preference for consumption, risk, and inflation. All else equal, when there are more profitable production opportunities, greater time preference for funds, higher risk, and higher inflation expectations, interest rates are higher, and vice versa.
- Interest rates are determined by factors that affect the supply of and the demand for funds. Everything else equal, if demand increases or supply decreases, the general levels of interest rates increase.

LO.2 Describe how interest rates are determined.

- Interest rates represent the returns on investments. The return on any investment is equal to the nominal risk-free rate of return plus a premium for the risk that is associated with the investment. The nominal risk-free rate consists of the real risk-free return plus a return that compensates investors for the average rate of inflation they expect during the life of the investment. The risk premium includes an additional return that pays investors for taking the risks that are associated with the investment, which include default risk, maturity risk, and liquidity risk.

LO.3 Describe a yield curve and discuss how a yield curve might be used to determine future interest rates.

- The yield curve shows the relationship between long-term and short-term interest rates at a particular point in time. Some experts believe that the shape of the yield curve indicates in which direction interest rates will move in the future. For instance, suppose that you think interest rates are going to increase. As an investor, should you invest your funds in long-term or short-term securities? Like other investors, you should invest short term, and wait until interest rates increase to lock up your money in long-term investments. Everything else equal, buying pressure on (demand for) short-term securities will increase prices, and thus decrease rates in the short-term markets. The opposite activity will occur in the long-term markets. As a result, when investors expect interest rates to increase, short-term interest rates should be lower than long-term rates, which will produce an upward-sloping yield curve. Such logic has been applied when using the yield curve to forecast future rates.

LO.4 Discuss how government actions and general business activity affect interest rates.

- The government affects interest rates through open market operations, its spending policies, and the balance of trade. Through open markets operations the Federal Reserve buys government securities when it wants to increase the money supply and thus decrease interest rates, and vice versa. When the government runs a deficit because it spends more money than it collects, it must borrow, which, everything else equal, increases demand for funds and thus increases interest rates. When imports are greater than exports, a trade deficit must be financed, which increases interest rates because the demand for funds in the financial markets is higher than it would be otherwise. In addition, as business activity increases in the economy, so do interest rates on loans that are used to finance these expanded activities.

LO.5 Describe how changes in interest rates (returns) affect the values of stocks and bonds.

- Higher interest rates indicate that investors demand higher returns. Everything else equal, the only way investors can earn higher returns is if they can purchase securities for lower prices. Thus, interest rates (returns) and prices are inversely related.

CHAPTER 5 REVIEW

Chapter 5 Key Cost of Money (Interest Rate) Concepts

- The yield, or return, that is earned on an investment is comprised of two components: (1) income paid by the *issuer* of the financial asset and (2) the change in the market value of the financial asset over some time period (called capital gains).
- The cost of money (interest rates) is based on (1) the rate of return that borrowers expect to earn on their investments, (2) savers' preferences to spend income in the current period rather than delay consumption until some future period, (3) the risks associated with investments/loans, and (4) expected inflation.
- In general, the rate of return on an investment, or the interest rate on a loan, includes a minimum payment for delaying consumption until some future date, which is termed the risk-free rate of return, r_{RF}, and payment for the risk associated with the investment/loan, RP, which is termed a risk premium. Risks can include the risk that the borrower will default on the loan, the risk associated with the liquidity of the investment, and so forth.
- In most instances, long-term interest rates are greater than short-term interest rates—that is, the yield curve is upward sloping. However, there are rare instances when the yield curve is inverted, or downward sloping, which occurs when long-term interest rates are lower than short-term interest rates. An inverted yield curve is likely to appear when the economy is in a recession.
- Everything else equal, when interest rates (returns) increase, the prices (values) of investments decrease. In other words, when investors want to receive higher returns, they lower the amount they are willing to pay for investments.

Key Terms

LO.1

production opportunity The returns available within an economy from investment in a productive (cash-generating) asset. *p. 74*

time preference for consumption The preference of a consumer for current consumption as opposed to saving for future consumption. *p. 75*

risk In a financial market context, the chance that a financial asset will not earn the return promised. *p. 75*

inflation The tendency of prices to increase over time. *p. 75*

LO.2

nominal (quoted) risk-free rate, r_{RF} The rate of interest on a security that is free of all risk; r_{RF} is proxied by the T-bill rate and includes an inflation premium. *p. 78*

real risk-free rate of interest, r* The rate of interest that would exist on default-free U.S. Treasury securities if no inflation were expected. *p. 78*

inflation premium (IP) A premium for expected inflation that investors add to the real risk-free rate of return. *p. 78*

default risk premium (DRP) The difference between the interest rate on a U.S. Treasury bond and a corporate bond of equal maturity and marketability; compensation for the risk that a corporation will not meet its debt obligations. *p. 79*

liquidity premium (LP) A premium added to the rate on a security if the security cannot be converted to cash on short notice at a price that is close to the original cost. *p. 79*

maturity risk premium (MRP) A premium that reflects interest rate risk; bonds with longer maturities have greater interest rate risk. *p. 79*

LO.3

term structure of interest rates The relationship between yields and maturities of securities. *p. 80*

yield curve A graph showing the relationship between yields and maturities of securities on a particular date. *p. 80*

normal yield curve An upward-sloping yield curve. *p. 80*

inverted (abnormal) yield curve A downward-sloping yield curve. *p. 80*

liquidity preference theory The theory that, all else being equal, lenders prefer to make short-term loans rather than long-term loans; hence, they will lend short-term funds at lower rates than they lend long-term funds. *p. 81*

expectations theory The theory that the shape of the yield curve depends on investors' expectations about future inflation rates. *p. 82*

market segmentation theory The theory that every borrower and lender has a preferred maturity, and that the slope of the yield curve depends on the supply of and the demand for funds in the long-term market relative to the short-term market. *p. 83*

LO.4

open market operations Operations in which the Federal Reserve buys or sells Treasury securities to expand or contract the U.S. money supply. *p. 85*

CHAPTER 6

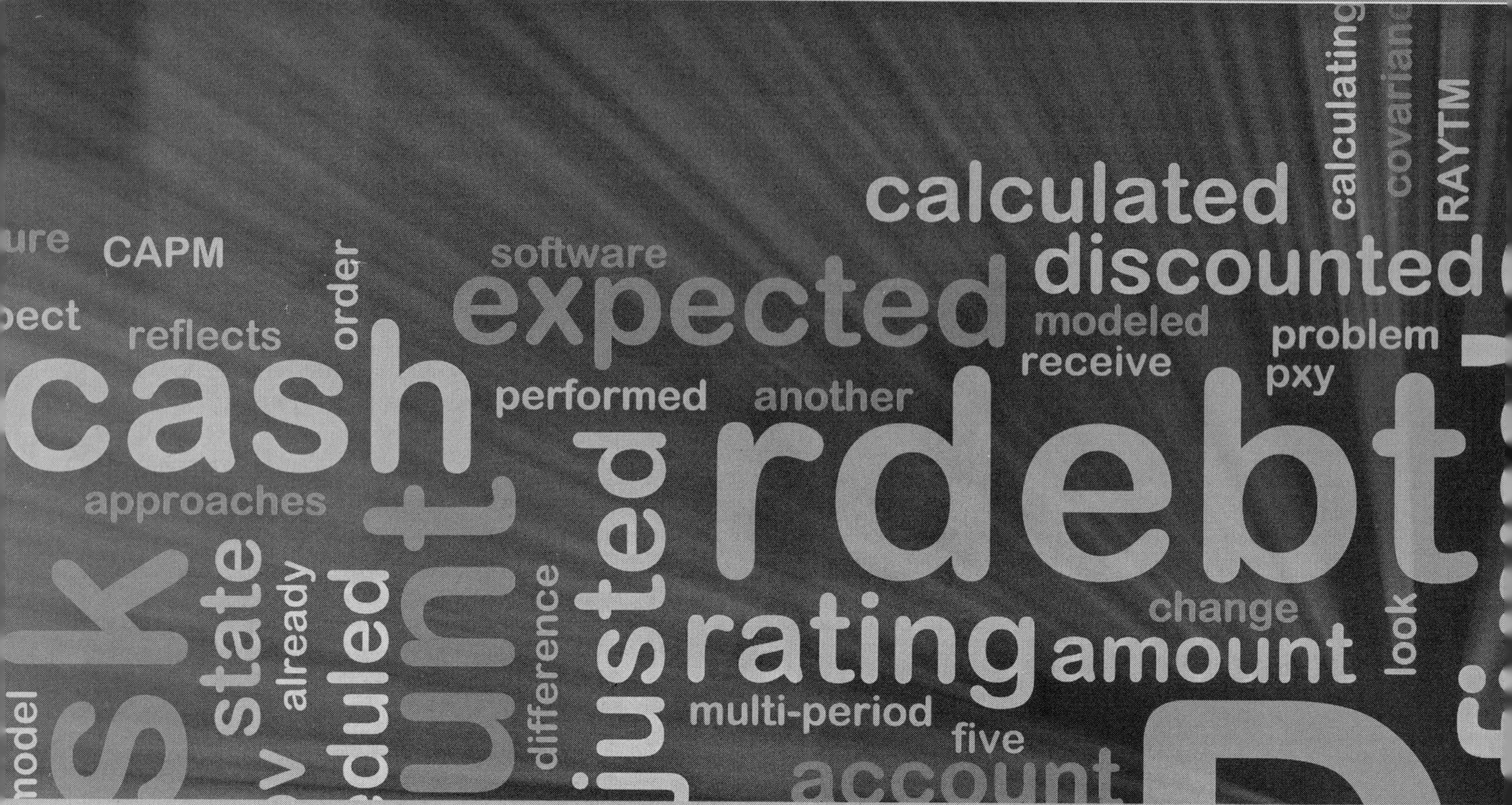

Bonds (Debt)—Characteristics and Valuation

Learning Outcomes

LO.1 Describe the basic characteristics of debt and some of the different types of debt.

LO.2 Discuss bond ratings and the information that they provide to investors.

LO.3 Explain how bond prices are determined.

LO.4 Explain how bond yields (market rates) are determined.

LO.5 Describe the relationship between bond prices and interest rates, and explain why it is important for investors to understand this relationship.

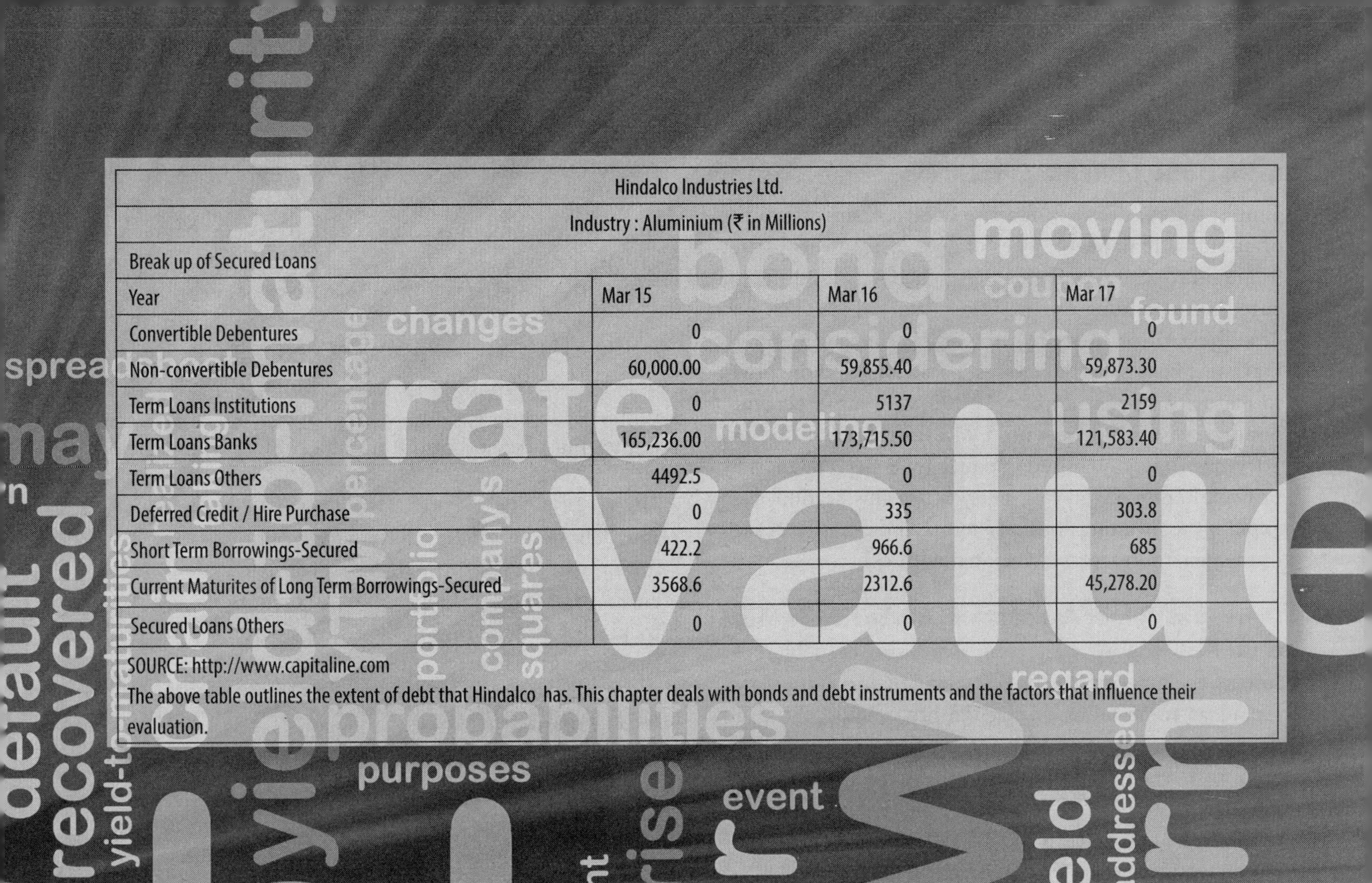

Hindalco Industries Ltd.			
Industry : Aluminium (₹ in Millions)			
Break up of Secured Loans			
Year	Mar 15	Mar 16	Mar 17
Convertible Debentures	0	0	0
Non-convertible Debentures	60,000.00	59,855.40	59,873.30
Term Loans Institutions	0	5137	2159
Term Loans Banks	165,236.00	173,715.50	121,583.40
Term Loans Others	4492.5	0	0
Deferred Credit / Hire Purchase	0	335	303.8
Short Term Borrowings-Secured	422.2	966.6	685
Current Maturites of Long Term Borrowings-Secured	3568.6	2312.6	45,278.20
Secured Loans Others	0	0	0

SOURCE: http://www.capitaline.com

The above table outlines the extent of debt that Hindalco has. This chapter deals with bonds and debt instruments and the factors that influence their evaluation.

In this chapter, we discuss debt. First, we describe the general characteristics and features of debt. Then, we show how bonds are valued and discuss factors that affect the values of bonds. It is important to understand the valuation concepts presented in this and the next few chapters because they represent the general foundations of finance.

Study Tools

Problems are found at the end of this chapter

+

Login to **CourseMate** for **CFIN** at **CengageBrain.com** for additional problems and other study tools!

Kheng Guan Toh/Shutterstock.com

6-1 Characteristics and Types of Debt

In this section, we describe some of the characteristics of debt. Far too many types of debt with different features exist to cover everything here; thus, we only include the most common types of debt and the features associated with those debt instruments.

6-1a Debt Characteristics[1]

Simply stated, **debt** is a loan to a firm, a government, or an individual. Many types of debt instruments exist: home mortgages, commercial paper, bonds, and unsecured notes, among others. Often, we identify debt by describing three of its features: the principal amount that must be repaid, the interest payments, and the time to maturity. For instance, a ₹1,000, 10-year, 8 percent bond consists of debt with a ₹1,000 principal due in 10 years that pays interest equal to 8 percent of the principal amount, or ₹80, per year. In this section, we explain the meanings of these terms and describe some of the general features associated with debt.

Principal Value, Face Value, Maturity Value, and Par Value. The *principal value* of debt represents the amount owed to the lender, which must be repaid at some point during the life of the debt. For much of the debt issued by corporations, the principal amount is repaid at the maturity date. Consequently, we also refer to the principal value as the *maturity value*. In addition, the principal value generally is written on the face, or outside cover, of the debt contract, so it is sometimes called the *face value*. When the market value of debt is the same as its face value, it is said to be selling at *par;* thus, the principal amount is also referred to as the *par value*. For most debt, therefore, the terms *par value, face value, maturity value,* and *principal value* are used interchangeably to designate the borrowed amount that must be repaid by the borrower.

Interest Payments. In many cases, owners of (investors in) debt instruments receive periodic payments of interest, which are computed as a percentage of the principal amount. But some debt does not pay interest; to generate a positive return for investors, such financial assets must sell for less than their par, or maturity, values. Securities that sell for less than their par values when issued are called **discounted securities**.

Maturity Date. The maturity date represents the date on which the principal amount of a debt is due. As long as interest has been paid when due, once the total principal amount is repaid, the debt obligation has been satisfied. Some debt instruments, called *installment loans*, require the principal amounts to be repaid in several payments during the lives of the loans. In such cases, the maturity date is the date the last installment payment is due.

debt A loan to a firm, government, or individual.

discounted securities Securities selling for less than par value.

Treasury bills(T-bills) Discounted debt instruments issued by the U.S. government.

Priority to Assets and Earnings. Corporate debt holders have priority over stockholders with regard to distribution of earnings and liquidation of assets; that is, they must be paid before any stockholders can be paid.

Control of the Firm (Voting Rights). Corporate debt holders do not have voting rights, so they cannot attain control of the firm. Nevertheless, debt holders can affect the management and operations of a firm by placing restrictions on the use of the funds as part of the loan agreement.

6-1b Types of Debt

Many types of debt instruments exist, some of which we describe in this section. Whereas most long-term debt instruments pay interest, most short-term debt instruments do not; rather, they are sold as discounted securities when issued, so that the difference between their purchase prices and maturity values represent the rupee returns earned by investors.

6-1c Short-Term Debt

Short-term debt refers to debt instruments with original maturities of one year or less. Some of the more common short-term debt instruments are described here.

Treasury Bills. Treasury bills (T-bills) are discounted securities issued by the U.S. government to finance its operations and programs. When the U.S. Treasury issues T-bills, the prices are determined by an auction process: interested investors and investing organizations submit competitive bids to purchase T-bill issues.[2] T-bills are issued electronically with face values ranging from ₹1,000 to ₹5 million, and with maturities that range from a few days to 52 weeks at the time of issue.

[1]In this chapter, we primarily discuss bonds (debt) from the perspective of a corporation. Most of the characteristics we describe for corporate debt also apply to government debt.

[2]The U.S. Treasury also sells T-bills on a noncompetitive basis to investors or investment organizations offering to buy a certain rupee amount. In such cases, the purchase price is based on the average of the competitive bids received by the Treasury.

Repurchase Agreements (Repos). A **repurchase agreement** (also called a *repo*) is an arrangement whereby a firm that needs funds sells some of its financial assets to another firm that has excess funds to invest, with a promise to *repurchase* the securities at a higher price at a later date. The price at which the securities will be repurchased is agreed to at the time the *repo* is arranged. Although some repos last for days or even weeks, most repos last only a few hours, which means they are essentially overnight agreements.

Federal Funds. Often referred to simply as *fed funds*, **federal funds** represent loans from one bank to another. Banks generally use the fed funds market to adjust their reserves: Banks that need additional funds to meet the reserve requirements of the Federal Reserve borrow from banks with excess reserves. The interest rate associated with such debt is known as the *federal funds rate.* Federal funds have very short maturities, often overnight.

Banker's Acceptances. A **banker's acceptance** might be best described as a postdated check. More accurately, a banker's acceptance is a *time draft,* which is an instrument issued by a bank that obligates it to pay a specified amount to the holder of the draft at some future date. Generally used in international trade, a banker's acceptance arrangement is established between a bank and a firm to ensure the firm's international trading partner that payment for goods and services is essentially guaranteed at some future date, which allows sufficient time to verify the completion of the transaction. A banker's acceptance is generally sold at a discount by the original owner before its maturity to raise immediate cash.

Commercial Paper. **Commercial paper** is a type of *promissory note,* or "legal IOU," issued by large, financially sound firms. Like a T-bill, commercial paper does not pay interest, so it is issued at a discount. The maturity on commercial paper varies from one to nine months, with an average of about five months.[3] Generally, commercial paper is issued in denominations of ₹100,000 or more, so few individuals can afford to directly invest in the commercial paper market. Instead, commercial paper is sold primarily to other businesses, including insurance companies, pension funds, money market mutual funds, and banks.

[3]The maximum maturity without SEC registration is 270 days. In addition, commercial paper can be sold only to sophisticated investors; otherwise, SEC registration would be required even for maturities of less than 270 days.

Certificates of Deposit (CDs). A **certificate of deposit** represents a time deposit at a bank or other financial intermediary. Traditional CDs, which generally earn periodic interest, must be kept at the issuing institution for a specified time period. To liquidate a traditional CD prior to maturity, the owner must return it to the issuing institution, which normally applies an interest penalty (lower interest) to the amount paid out. *Negotiable CDs,* however, can be traded to other investors prior to maturity because they can be redeemed by whoever owns them at maturity. Often called *jumbo CDs,* these investments typically are issued in denominations of ₹1 million to ₹5 million, and they have maturities that range from a few months to a few years.

Eurodollar Deposits. A **Eurodollar deposit** is a deposit in a bank outside the United States that is not converted into the currency of the foreign country; instead, it is denominated in U.S. dollars. Such deposits are not exposed to *exchange rate risk,* which is the risk associated with converting dollars into foreign currencies. Eurodollar deposits earn rates offered by foreign banks and are not subject to the same regulations imposed on deposits in U.S. banks. Consequently, the rate that can be earned on Eurodollars is sometimes considerably greater than the rate that can be earned in the United States.

Money Market Mutual Funds. **Money market mutual funds** consist of investment dollars that are pooled to purchase large amounts of short-term financial (money market) assets, such as those described here. The mutual funds are professionally managed by firms, called *investment companies*, that specialize in investing money that is provided by many individual investors. These funds offer individual investors the ability to in-

repurchase agreement An arrangement where one firm sells some of its financial assets to another firm with a promise to *repurchase* the securities at a later date.

federal funds Overnight loans from one bank to another.

banker's acceptance An instrument issued by a bank that obligates the bank to pay a specified amount at some future date.

commercial paper A discounted instrument that is a type of promissory note, or "legal" IOU, issued by large, financially sound firms.

certificate of deposit An interest-earning time deposit at a bank or other financial intermediary.

Eurodollar deposit A deposit in a foreign bank that is denominated in U.S. dollars.

money market mutual funds Pools of funds managed by investment companies that are primarily invested in short-term financial assets.

directly invest in such short-term securities as T-bills, commercial paper, and Eurodollars, which they otherwise would not be able to purchase because such investments either are sold in denominations that are too large or are not available to individual investors.

6-1d Long-Term Debt

Long-term debt refers to debt instruments with maturities greater than one year. Owners of such debt generally receive periodic payments of interest. This section describes common types of long-term debt.

Term Loans. A **term loan** is a contract under which a borrower agrees to make a series of interest and principal payments to the lender on specific dates. Term loans usually are negotiated directly between the borrowing firm and a financial institution, such as a bank, an insurance company, or a pension fund. For this reason, they are often referred to as *private debt.* Although term loans' maturities vary from two years to 30 years, most maturities are in the three- to 15-year range.[4]

Hiroshi Watanabe/Photodisc/Getty Images

Term loans have three major advantages over public debt offerings such as corporate bonds: *speed, flexibility,* and *low issuance costs.* Because they are negotiated directly between the lender and the borrower, formal documentation is minimized. The key provisions of a term loan can be worked out much more quickly than can those for a public issue, and it is not necessary for the loan to go through the Securities and Exchange Commission (SEC) registration process because it is not sold to the public. In addition, unlike typical corporate bonds that have many different bondholders, a company often can sit down with the lender in a term loan arrangement and work out mutually agreeable modifications to the contract if necessary. The interest rate on a term loan can be either fixed for the life of the loan or it can be variable.

term loan A loan, generally obtained from a bank or insurance company, on which the borrower agrees to make a series of payments consisting of interest and principal.

bond A long-term debt instrument.

coupon rate Interest paid on a bond or other debt instrument stated as a percentage of its face (maturity) value.

government bonds Debt issued by a federal, state, or local government.

municipal bonds Bonds issued by a state or local government.

Bonds. A **bond** is a long-term contract under which a borrower (issuer) agrees to make payments of interest and principal on specific dates to the bondholder (investor). The interest payments are determined by the **coupon rate,** which represents the total interest paid each year, stated as a percentage of the bond's face value. Typically, interest is paid semiannually, although bonds that pay interest annually, quarterly, and monthly also exist, and the principal amount is generally paid in a lump-sum amount at the end of the bond's life (maturity date).

Some of the more common bonds issued by both governments and corporations are listed below.

1. **Government bonds** are issued by the U.S. government, state governments, and local or municipal governments. U.S. government bonds are issued by the U.S. Treasury and are called either *Treasury notes* or *Treasury bonds.* Both types of debt pay interest semiannually. The primary difference between Treasury notes and Treasury bonds is that the original maturity on T-notes can be from more than one year to 10 years, whereas the original maturity on T-bonds exceeds 10 years.

   Municipal bonds, or *munis,* are similar to Treasury bonds, except they are issued by state and local governments. The two principal types of munis are revenue bonds and general obligation bonds. *Revenue bonds* are used to raise funds for projects that will generate revenues that contribute to payment of interest and the repayment of the debt, such as a roadway that generates revenues through tolls. *General obligation bonds* are backed by the government's ability to tax its citizens; special taxes or tax increases are used to generate the funds needed to

[4]Most term loans are *amortized,* which means that they are paid off in equal installments over the life of the loan. Amortization protects the lender against the possibility that the borrower will not make adequate provisions for the loan's retirement during the life of the loan. (Chapter 4 reviews the concept of amortization.) In addition, if the interest and principal payments required under a term loan agreement are not met on schedule, the borrowing firm is said to have *defaulted,* and it can then be forced into bankruptcy.

service such bonds. Generally, the income that an investor earns from munis is exempt from federal taxes.

2. As the name implies, **corporate bonds** are issued by businesses called *corporations*. A corporate bond issue generally is advertised, offered to the public, and sold to many different investors. The interest rate typically remains fixed, although the popularity of floating-rate bonds has grown during the past couple of decades. Several types of corporate bonds exist, the more important of which are discussed in the remainder of this section.

3. With a **mortgage bond,** the corporation pledges certain tangible assets as security, or *collateral*, for the bond. In addition to original, or *first,* mortgages, firms can issue *second-mortgage bonds* secured by the same assets. In the event of liquidation, the holders of these second mortgage bonds (called *junior mortgages)* would have a claim against the property, but only after the first-mortgage (called *senior-mortgage*) bondholders have been paid off in full.

4. A **debenture** is an unsecured bond; as such, it provides no lien, or *claim*, against specific property as security for the obligation. Therefore, debenture holders are general creditors whose claims are protected by property not otherwise pledged as collateral. A **subordinated debenture** is an unsecured bond that ranks below, or is inferior to, other debt with respect to claims on cash distributions made by the firm. In the event of bankruptcy, for instance, *subordinated debt* has claims on assets only after senior debt has been paid off. Debentures are often issued by companies, such as large mail-order houses, that are in industries in which it would not be practical to provide security through a mortgage on fixed assets.

4. Several other types of corporate bonds are used sufficiently often to merit mention.

   - **Income bonds** pay interest only when the firm generates sufficient income to cover the interest payments. As a consequence, when income is insufficient, missing interest payments on these securities cannot bankrupt a company. From an investor's standpoint, these bonds are riskier than bonds that require fixed interest payments.

   - **Putable bonds** are bonds that can be turned in to the firm prior to maturity in exchange for cash at the bondholder's option if the firm takes some specified action—for example, if the firm is acquired by a weaker company or its outstanding debt increases substantially.

   - **Indexed,** or **purchasing power, bonds** pay interest based on an inflation index, such as the consumer price index (CPI). The interest paid rises automatically when the inflation rate rises, thereby protecting bondholders against inflation.

   - **Floating-rate bonds** are similar to *indexed bonds* except the coupon rates on these bonds float with market interest rates rather than with the inflation rate. Thus, when interest rates rise, the coupon rates increase, and vice versa. In many cases, limits are imposed on how high and low the rates on such debt can go (referred to as caps and collars, respectively).

5. *Original issue discount bonds (OIDs),* commonly referred to as **zero coupon bonds,** were created during the 1980s. These securities were offered at substantial discounts below their par values because they paid little or no coupon interest. OIDs have since lost their attraction for many individual investors, primarily because the interest income that must be reported each year for tax purposes includes any cash interest actually received, which is ₹0 for zero coupon bonds, plus the annual *prorated* capital appreciation that would be received if the bond were held to maturity. Thus, capital appreciation is taxed before it is actually received. For this

corporate bonds Long-term debt instruments issued by corporations.

mortgage bond A bond backed by tangible assets. First-mortgage bonds are senior in priority to second-mortgage bonds.

debenture A long-term bond that is not secured by a mortgage on specific property.

subordinated debenture A bond which, in the event of liquidation, has a claim on assets only after the senior debt has been paid off.

income bond A bond that pays interest to the holder only if the interest is earned by the firm.

putable bond A bond that can be redeemed at the bondholder's option when certain circumstances exist.

indexed (purchasing-power) bond A bond that has interest payments based on an inflation index to protect the holder from loss of purchasing power.

floating-rate bond A bond whose interest rate fluctuates with shifts in the general level of interest rates.

zero coupon bond A bond that pays no annual interest but sells at a discount below par, thus providing compensation to investors in the form of capital appreciation.

reason, most OID bonds currently are held by institutional investors, such as pension funds and mutual funds, rather than by individual investors.

6. Another innovation from the 1980s is the **junk bond,** a high-risk, high-yield bond often issued to finance a management buyout (MBO), a merger, or a troubled company. In junk bond deals, firms generally have significant amounts of debt, so bondholders must bear as much risk as stockholders normally would. The high yields on these bonds reflect this fact.

6-1e Bond Contract Features

A firm's managers are concerned with both the effective cost of debt and any restrictions in debt contracts that might limit the firm's future actions. This section discusses the features that generally are included in bond contracts, which can affect the firm's cost of debt and its future financial flexibility.

Bond Indenture. An **indenture** is a document that spells out the legalities of the bond issue, including any features or legal restrictions associated with the bond and the rights of the bondholders (lenders) and the corporation (bond issuer). A *trustee,* usually a bank, is assigned to represent the bondholders and to guarantee that the terms of the indenture are carried out. The indenture, which could be several hundred pages long, includes *restrictive covenants* that cover such points as the conditions under which the issuer can pay off the bonds prior to maturity, the levels at which various financial measures (such as the ability to pay interest) must be maintained if the company is to sell additional bonds, and restrictions on the payment of dividends to stockholders when earnings do not meet certain specifications. The Securities and Exchange Commission approves indentures for publicly traded bonds and verifies that all previous indenture provisions have been met before allowing a company to sell new securities to the public.

junk bond A high-risk, high-yield bond; used to finance mergers, leveraged buyouts, and troubled companies.

indenture A formal agreement (contract) between the issuer of a bond and the bondholders.

call provision A provision in a bond contract that gives the issuer the right to redeem the bonds under specified terms prior to the normal maturity date.

sinking fund A required annual payment designed to amortize a bond issue.

conversion feature Permits bondholders to exchange their investments for a fixed number of shares of common stock.

Call Provision. Most corporate bonds contain a **call provision**, which gives the issuing firm the right to "call in" the bonds for redemption prior to maturity. A call provision generally states that the company must pay the bondholders an amount greater than the bond's par value when it is called. This additional amount, which is termed a *call premium,* typically equals one year's interest if the bond is called during the first year in which a call is permitted; the premium declines at a constant rate each year thereafter. Bonds usually are not callable until several years (generally five to 10) after they are issued; bonds with such *deferred calls* are said to have *call protection.* Call provisions allow firms to refinance debt, much as individuals might refinance mortgages on their houses: when interest rates decline, firms can *recall* (refund) high-cost debt that is outstanding and replace it with new, lower-cost debt.

Sinking Fund. A **sinking fund** is a provision that facilitates the orderly retirement of a bond issue. Typically, the sinking fund provision requires the firm to retire a portion of the bond issue each year. On rare occasions, the firm might be required to deposit money with a trustee, which invests the funds and then uses the accumulated sum to retire the bonds when they mature. Often the firm has the right to handle the sinking fund in two ways: by randomly calling for redemption (at par value) a certain percentage of the bonds each year or by purchasing the required amount of bonds in the open market. The firm will choose the lower-cost method. A sinking fund call does not require the company to pay a call premium, but only a small percentage of the issue is normally callable in any one year.

Convertible Feature. A **conversion feature** permits the bondholder (investor) to exchange, or *convert,* the bond into shares of the company's common stock at a fixed price. Investors have greater flexibility with a *convertible bond* than with a straight (regular) bond because they can choose whether to hold the company's bond or convert the bond into its stock. Once the conversion is made, investors cannot convert back to bonds.

An important provision of a convertible bond is the *conversion ratio,* which is defined as the number of shares of stock that the bondholder receives upon conversion. Related to the conversion ratio is the *conversion price,* which is the price that is effectively paid for the common stock obtained by converting a bond into stock. For example, a ₹1,000 convertible bond with a conversion ratio of 20 can be converted into 20 shares of common stock, so the conversion price is ₹50 = ₹1,000/20. If the market value of the stock rises above ₹50 per share, it would be beneficial for the bondholder to convert his or her bonds into stock (ignoring any costs associated with conversion).

6-1f Foreign Debt Instruments

Any debt sold outside the country of the borrower is called *international debt*. Two important types of international debt exist:

1. **Foreign debt** is debt sold by a foreign borrower, but it is denominated in the currency of the country in which the issue is sold. For instance, Bell Canada might need U.S. dollars to finance the operations of its subsidiaries in the United States. If it decides to raise the needed capital in the U.S. bond market, the bond will be underwritten by a syndicate of U.S. investment banking firms, denominated in U.S. dollars, and sold to U.S. investors in accordance with SEC and applicable state regulations. Except for the foreign origin of the borrower (Canada), this bond is indistinguishable from bonds issued by equivalent U.S. corporations. Foreign bonds often are labeled according to the country in which they are issued. For example, if foreign bonds are issued in the United States, they are called *Yankee bonds;* if they are issued in Japan, they are called *Samurai bonds;* and if they are issued in the United Kingdom, they are called *Bulldog bonds.*
2. The term **Eurodebt** is used to designate any debt sold in a country other than the one in whose currency it is denominated. An example of a *Eurobond* is a bond issued by Ford Motor Company in Germany that remains denominated in U.S. dollars. The institutional arrangements by which Eurobonds are marketed are different from those for most other bond issues, with the most important distinction being a far lower level of required disclosure than normally applies to bonds issued in domestic markets, particularly in the United States. Governments tend to be less strict when regulating securities denominated in foreign currencies than they are with home-currency securities because the bonds' purchasers generally are sophisticated investors. The lower disclosure requirements result in lower total transaction costs for Eurobonds. In addition, Eurobonds generally are issued in bearer form rather than as registered bonds, so the names and nationalities of investors are not recorded. Individuals who desire anonymity, whether for privacy reasons or for tax avoidance, find Eurobonds to their liking. Similarly, most governments do not withhold taxes on interest payments associated with Eurobonds.

Other types of *Eurodebt* include *Eurocredits, Euro-commercial paper (Euro-CP),* and *Euronotes.* Eurocredits are bank loans that are denominated in the currency of a country other than that where the lending bank is located. Many of these loans are very large, so the lending bank often forms a loan syndicate to help raise the needed funds and to spread out some of the risk associated with the loan. Euro-CP is similar to commercial paper issued in the United States, except that there is not as much concern about the credit quality of Euro-CP issuers as there is about U.S. commercial paper issuers. Euronotes, which represent medium-term debt, typically have maturities ranging from one to 10 years. The general features of Euronotes closely resemble those of longer-term debt instruments like bonds. The principal amount is repaid at maturity, and interest often is paid semiannually.

Interest rates on short-term Eurodebt typically are tied to a standard rate known by the acronym **LIBOR**, which stands for *London Interbank Offered Rate.* LIBOR is the rate of interest offered by the largest and strongest London banks on deposits of other large banks of the highest credit standing.

6-2 Bond Ratings

Bonds are often assigned quality ratings that reflect their probabilities of going into default. The two major rating agencies are Moody's Investors Service (Moody's) and Standard & Poor's Corporation (S&P). Table 6.1 shows these agencies' rating designations and gives an indication of the investment risk that is associated with the particular ratings.[5]

6-2a Bond Rating Criteria

Bond ratings are based on both qualitative and quantitative factors. Factors considered by the bond rating agencies include the financial strength of the company as measured by various ratios, collateral provisions, the seniority of the debt, restrictive covenants, such

foreign debt Debt sold by a foreign borrower but denominated in the currency of the country where it is sold.

Eurodebt Debt sold in a country other than the one in whose currency the debt is denominated.

LIBOR The London Interbank Offered Rate; the interest rate offered by the best London banks on deposits of other large, very creditworthy banks.

[5]In the discussion to follow, a reference to the S&P code is intended to imply the Moody's code as well. Thus, "triple-B bonds" means both BBB and Baa bonds; "double-B bonds" means both BB and Ba bonds; and so on.

TABLE 6.1 Moody's and Standard & Poor's (S&P) Bond Ratings

Investment Risk	High Quality Low		Investment Grade Medium		Junk Bonds: Substandard High		Junk Bonds: Speculative Extremely High	
Moody's	Aaa	Aa	A	Baa	Ba	B	Caa	C
S&P	AAA	AA	A	BBB	BB	B	CCC	D

Note: Both Moody's and S&P use modifiers for bonds rated below triple-A. S&P uses a plus and minus system; that is, A+ designates the strongest A-rated bonds, and A− indicates the weakest. Moody's uses a 1, 2, or 3 designation, with 1 denoting the strongest and 3 the weakest; thus, within the double-A category, Aa1 is the best, Aa2 is average, and Aa3 is the weakest.

provisions as a sinking fund or a deferred call, litigation possibilities, regulation, and so on. Representatives of the rating agencies have consistently stated that no precise formula is used to set a firm's rating; all the factors listed, plus others, are taken into account, but not in a mathematically precise manner.

6-2b Importance of Bond Ratings

Bond ratings are important to both issuers and investors for several reasons. First, because a bond's rating serves as an indicator of its default risk, the rating has a direct, measurable influence on the bond's interest rate and the firm's cost of using such debt. As we discussed in Chapter 5, the greater a bond's default risk, the greater the *default risk premium (DRP)* associated with the bond. Second, most bonds are purchased by institutional investors rather than individuals, and many institutions are restricted to *investment-grade,* or high-quality, securities. If a firm's bonds fall below a BBB rating, it will therefore have a difficult time selling new bonds because many potential purchasers will not be allowed to buy them. As a result of their higher risk and more restricted market, lower-grade bonds offer higher returns than high-grade bonds. Figure 6.1 illustrates this point. In each of the years shown on the graph, U.S. government bonds (least amount of risk) have the lowest yields, AAA-rated corporate bonds have the next lowest, and BBB-rated corporate bonds (riskiest) have the highest yields. The figure also shows that the gaps between yields on the three types of bonds vary over time, indicating that the cost differentials, or *risk premiums,* fluctuate as well.

FIGURE 6.1 Yields on Selected Long-Term Bonds, 1990–2013

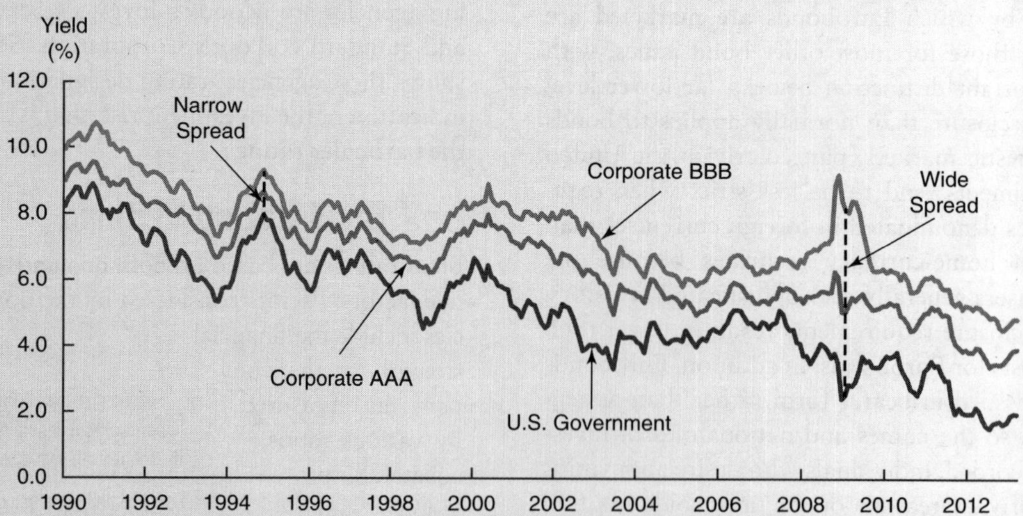

Note: The yields for the U.S. government bonds are based on bonds with 10-year maturities.
Source: Federal Reserve; http://www.federalreserve.gov.

6-2c Changes in Ratings

Changes in a firm's bond rating affect both its ability to borrow long-term capital and the cost of such funds. Rating agencies review outstanding bonds on a periodic basis, occasionally upgrading or downgrading a bond as a result of its issuer's changed financial circumstances. For example, firms that were financially distressed by the poor economic conditions that existed from 2007 through 2011 saw their bond ratings downgraded. Not even the U.S. government is immune to ratings changes; its debt was downgraded from AAA to AA+ at the end of July 2011 due to concerns about its financial stability. Firms that had their credit ratings downgraded discovered that their costs of raising funds in the financial markets increased because their bankruptcy risks were perceived by investors to be higher than they were prior to the downgrades.

6-3 Valuation of Bonds

Suppose that on January 2, 2014, Genesco Manufacturing borrowed ₹25 million by selling 25,000 individual bonds for ₹1,000 each. Genesco received the ₹25 million, and it promised to pay the holders of each bond interest equal to ₹100 per year and to repay the ₹25 million at the end of 15 years.[6] The lenders (investors), who wanted to earn a 10 percent return on their investment, were willing to provide Genesco ₹25 million, so the value of the bond issue was ₹25 million. But how did investors decide that the issue was worth ₹25 million?

As we will see, a bond's market price is determined by the cash flows that it generates: both the interest that is paid over its life, which depends on the coupon interest rate, and the principal amount that must be repaid at maturity (₹1,000 per bond in our example). At the time a bond is issued, the coupon rate generally is set at a level that will cause the market price of the bond to equal its par value. With a lower coupon rate, investors would not be willing to pay ₹1,000 for the bond. With a higher coupon rate, investors would clamor for the bond and bid its price up over ₹1,000. As a result, a new bond's coupon rate of interest normally is set to equal the market yield on similar-risk bonds that exist at the time the new bond is issued. *After it is issued, however, the value of the outstanding bond can vary widely from its par value.* Annual interest payments that bondholders receive are fixed (constant). Consequently, when economic conditions change, a bond that sold at par when it was issued will sell for more or less than par, depending on the relationship between the prevailing market rates and the bond's coupon rate.

6-3a The Basic Bond Valuation Model

The value of any financial asset is based on the cash flows that investors expect the asset to generate during its life. In the case of a bond, the cash flows consist of interest payments during the life of the bond plus a return of the principal amount borrowed (the par value) when the bond matures. In a cash flow timeline format, here is the situation:

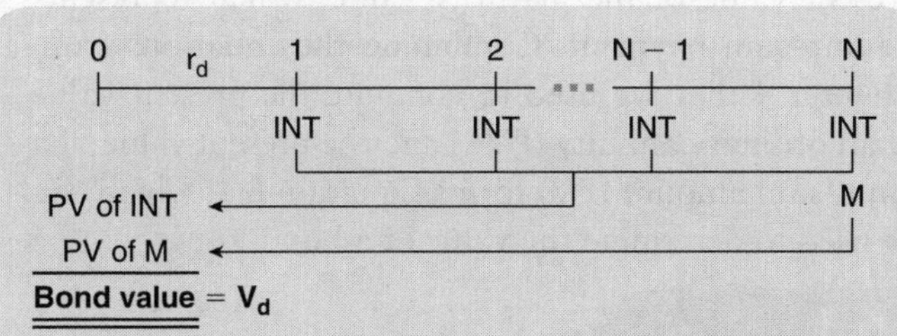

Here,

r_d = the average rate of return investors require to invest in the bond (the letter *d* stands for "debt"). For the Genesco Manufacturing bond issue, r_d = 10%.[7]

N = the number of years before the bond matures. For the Genesco bonds, N = 15. Note that N declines each year the bond is outstanding, so a bond that had a maturity of 15 years when it was issued (original maturity = 15) will have N = 14 after one year, N = 13 after two years, and so on.

M = maturity value, which is the principal amount that must be paid off at maturity; M = ₹1,000 per bond in our example.

INT = rupees of interest paid each year = C × M; where C is the coupon rate of interest stated as a decimal and M is the bond's maturity value. In our example, each bond requires an interest payment equal to ₹100, which means that the coupon rate is 10 percent because ₹100 = 0.10(₹1,000). In financial calculator terminology, INT = PMT = 100.

[6]Actually, Genesco would receive some amount less than ₹25 million because of costs associated with issuing the bond, such as legal fees, investment banking fees, and so forth. For our discussion here, we choose to ignore issuing costs to simplify the explanations. Chapter 3 describes the topics of issuing costs and the investment banking process.

[7]The appropriate interest rate on debt securities was discussed in Chapter 5. The bond's riskiness, liquidity, and years to maturity, as well as supply and demand conditions in the capital markets, all influence the interest rates on bonds.

We can now redraw the cash flow timeline for Genesco's bond to show the numerical values for all variables except the bond's current value:

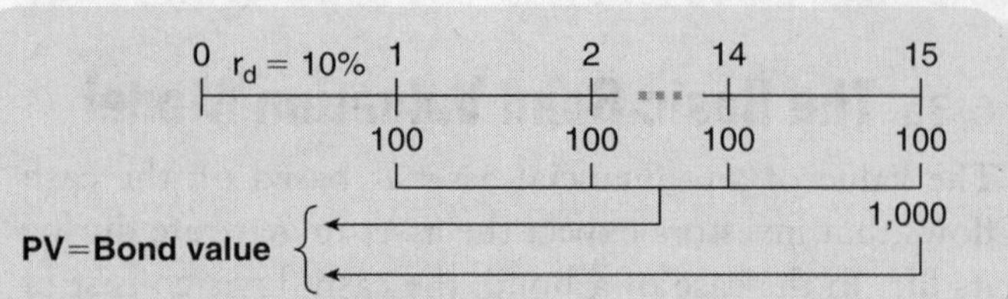

As the timeline shows, the value of a bond is determined by computing the present value of the interest payments, which represent an ordinary annuity, and the present value of the maturity value, which represents a lump-sum payment. Combining the equations from Chapter 4 that we used to compute the present value of an ordinary annuity (PVA) and the present value of a lump-sum amount (PV) forms Equation 6.1, which can be used to determine the value of a bond.

6.1

$$\text{Bond value} = V_d = \text{INT}\left(\frac{1-\dfrac{1}{(1+r_d)^N}}{r_d}\right) + M\left(\frac{1}{(1+r_d)^N}\right)$$

Inserting the values relevant to Genesco's bond into Equation 6.1, we find:[8]

$$V_d = ₹100\left(\frac{1-\dfrac{1}{(1.10)^{15}}}{0.10}\right) + ₹1{,}000\left(\frac{1}{(1.10)^{15}}\right)$$

$$= ₹100(7.60608) \quad + ₹1{,}000(0.23939) = ₹1{,}000$$

The value of the bond can be computed using any of the three approaches discussed in Chapter 4: (1) equation (numerical) solution, which requires us to use Equation 6.1 as shown here; (2) financial calculator solution, which requires use of all five of the calculator's time-value-of-money (TVM) keys; or (3) spreadsheet solution, which is essentially the same as using a financial calculator. In this chapter, we primarily use the financial calculator to compute the value of a bond.[9] For Genesco's bond, the setup on the financial calculator is:

	N	I/Y	PV	PMT	FV
Inputs:	15	10	?	100	1,000
Output:			= −1,000.00		

Input N = 15, I/Y = 10, PMT = 100, and FV = 1,000; then solve for PV = −1,000. Because the PV is an outflow to the investor, it is shown with a negative sign.

6-3b Bond Values with Semiannual Compounding

Although some bonds pay interest annually, *most* pay interest semiannually. To evaluate semiannual payment bonds, we must modify the bond valuation equation just as we did in Chapter 4 when we discussed interest compounding that occurs more than once per year. In this case, we use Equation 6.2, which is a simply modified version of Equation 6.1:

6.2

$$V_d = \left(\frac{\text{INT}}{2}\right)\left(\frac{1-\dfrac{1}{\left(1+\dfrac{r_d}{2}\right)^{2\times N}}}{\left(\dfrac{r_d}{2}\right)}\right) + \frac{M}{\left(1+\dfrac{r_d}{2}\right)^{2\times N}}$$

To illustrate, assume that Genesco's bonds pay ₹50 interest every six months rather than ₹100 at the end of each year. Each interest payment is now only half as large as before, but there are twice as many payments. When the going (simple) rate of interest is 8 percent with semiannual compounding and, there are 14 years remaining until maturity, the value of the bond is found as follows:[10]

	N	I/Y	PV	PMT	FV
Inputs:	28	4	?	50	1,000
Output:			= −1,166.63		

Input N = 28 = 14 × 2, I/Y = 4 = 8/2, INT = PMT = 50 = 100/2, and M = FV = 1,000; compute PV = −1,166.63.

[8]The bond prices quoted by brokers are calculated as described. If you bought a bond between interest payment dates, however, you would have to pay the basic price plus accrued interest. Thus, if you purchased a Genesco bond six months after it was issued and market rates had not changed, your broker would send you an invoice stating that you must pay ₹1,000 as the basic price of the bond plus ₹50 interest, representing one-half the annual interest of ₹100. The seller of the bond would receive ₹1,050. If you bought the bond the day before its interest payment date, you would pay ₹1,000 − (364/365)(₹100) = ₹1,099.73. Of course, you would receive an interest payment of ₹100 at the end of the next day. Throughout the chapter, we assume that the bond is being evaluated immediately after an interest payment date. Some financial calculators include a built-in calendar that permits the calculation of exact values between interest payment dates.

[9]Although we do not show the spreadsheet solutions, you can set up a spreadsheet to compute the present value of cash flows, that is, use the PV function that is programmed into the spreadsheet.

[10]We also assume a change in the effective annual interest rate, from 8 percent with annual compounding to EAR = $(1.04)^2 - 1 = 0.0816$ = 8.16% with semiannual compounding. Most bonds pay interest semiannually, which means effective annual rates for most bonds are somewhat higher than the quoted rates, which, in effect, represent the APRs for the bonds.

6-4 Finding Bond Yields (Market Rates): Yield to Maturity and Yield to Call

Suppose that you were offered a 10-year, 8 percent coupon, ₹1,000 par value bond at a price of ₹875. Interest from this bond is paid semiannually. What rate of interest, or *yield*, would you earn if you bought this bond? In this section, we show you how to compute the yield, or return, you would earn if you purchase a bond with these characteristics.

6-4a Yield to Maturity (YTM)

If you buy a bond and hold it until it matures, the average rate of return you will earn per year is called the bond's **yield to maturity (YTM)**. To find the yield to maturity, we solve Equation 6.1 or Equation 6.2 for r_d. For the current situation, we know that investors who buy the bond today and hold it to maturity will receive ₹40 = (0.08 × ₹1,000)/2 interest every six months for the next 10 years and a ₹1,000 principal payment when the bond matures in 10 years. Because investors have determined that this bond is currently worth ₹875, based on Equation 6.2, we know the following relationship exists:

$$V_d = \frac{₹40}{\left(1+\frac{r_d}{2}\right)^1} + \frac{₹40}{\left(1+\frac{r_d}{2}\right)^2} + \cdots + \frac{₹40 + ₹1{,}000}{\left(1+\frac{r_d}{2}\right)^{20}}$$

$$= \frac{₹40}{\left(1+\frac{YTM}{2}\right)^1} + \frac{₹40}{\left(1+\frac{YTM}{2}\right)^2} + \cdots + \frac{₹40 + ₹1{,}000}{\left(1+\frac{YTM}{2}\right)^{20}} = ₹875$$

Using a financial calculator, input N = 2 × 10 = 20, PV = −875 (this is a cash outflow when you buy the bond), INT = PMT = 80/2 = 40, and M = FV = 1,000, and then compute I/Y = 5.0, which represents the yield *per interest payment period* (six months in our example).

	N	I/Y	PV	PMT	FV
Inputs:	20	?	−875	40	1,000
Output:		= 5.0			

In this case, the yield is 5 percent per six months; thus the annual yield to maturity for this bond is r_d = 10.0% = 5.0% × 2. Note that the YTM is stated as an annual return, and it is not a compounded return; rather, it is an APR as described in Chapter 4.

For this bond, the going rate of return, or yield, is 10 percent (YTM = 10.0% = 5.0% × 2). Thus, an investor who purchases this bond today for ₹875 and holds it until it matures in 10 years will receive an *average* of 10 percent return each year.

Notice that YTM = 10% > coupon = 8%. When the bond was issued, which might have been five years ago, the yield for similar bonds was 8 percent. We know that this is the case because a firm sets the coupon rate on a bond immediately before it is issued so that the bond's issuing price equals its face (par) value. However, as market conditions change, the bond's yield to maturity changes, which causes its market price to change. In our example, market interest rates have increased since the time the bond was issued, so the price (value) of the bond has decreased below its face value. In reality, the calculated YTM and thus the price of a bond will change frequently before it matures because market conditions change frequently. We will discuss the relationship between YTM changes and price changes in greater detail later in the chapter.

Let us take a bond with a face value of ₹1,000 issued at par, and it is to be redeemed at par after five years. The coupon rate is 11%. The timeline will be as shown in Table 6.2.

TABLE 6.2

Year 0	1	2	3	4	5
−1000	110	110	110	110	1110

Notice that the final year flow includes both the interest and the redemption amount.

The yield to maturity (YTM) of this stream is the internal rate of return that is represented by the flows. Using MS Excel we can find the IRR in one of the two ways shown in Exhibits 1 and 2.

In Exhibit 1, we get 11% as the answer.

The other method would be to use the RATE function as shown in Exhibit 2.

It is to be noted that under *Fv*, we have to feed in only it is to be noted is that under Fv we have to feed in only the face value and not the interest relating to last year, since that is already factored in the Pmt row.

In the above example, the initial amount paid by the investor and the final amount to be received were the same. The following example shows the position when these are different.

yield to maturity (YTM) The average rate of return earned on a bond if it is held to maturity.

EXHIBIT 1

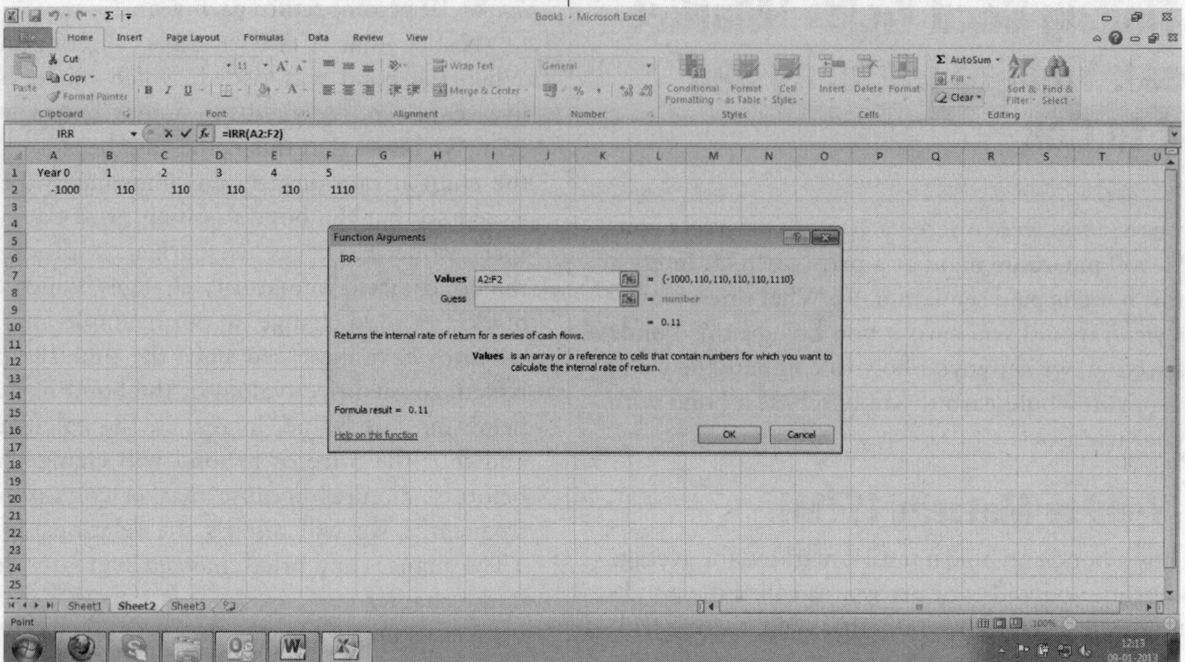

EXHIBIT 2

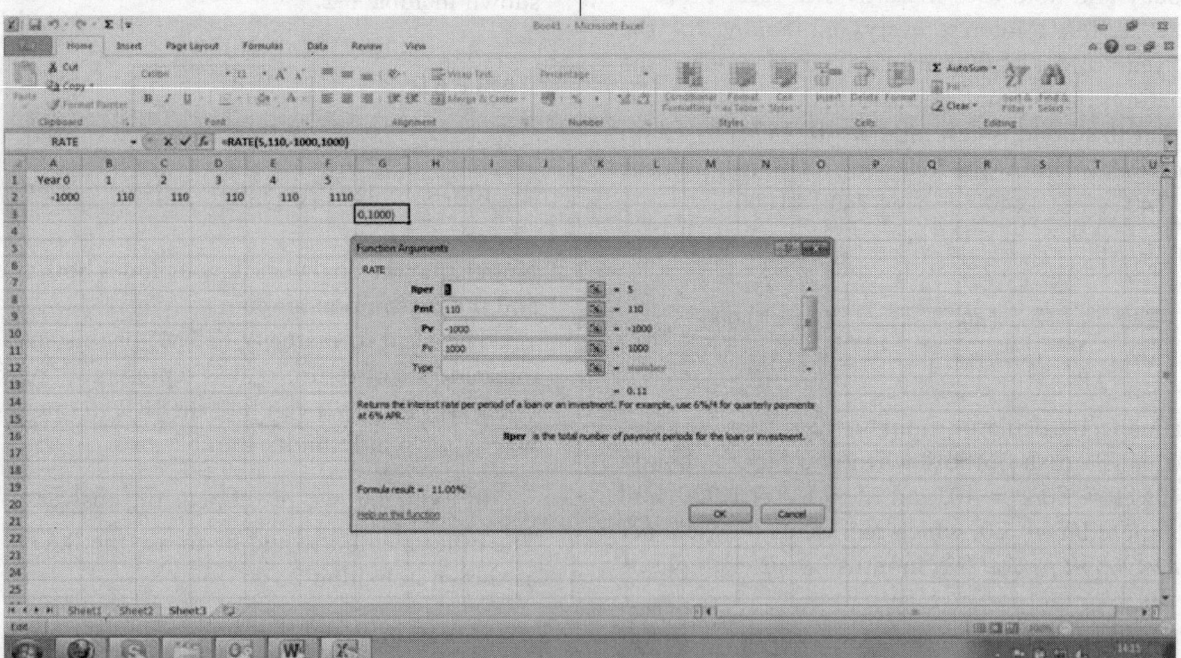

Let us take the case of ₹1000 bond issued at a discount of ₹50, carrying a coupon of 12%, having a tenure of ten years, on which the final redemption value is the face value of ₹1,000.

Using the RATE formula, YTM can be determined as shown in Exhibit 3.

We calculate the YTM to be 12.92%.

YTM changes with changes in initial price paid, the coupon and the quantum of the final amount. When the initial amount and the final amount are the same, as in a bank loan, the YTM will be equal to the coupon rate.

EXHIBIT 3

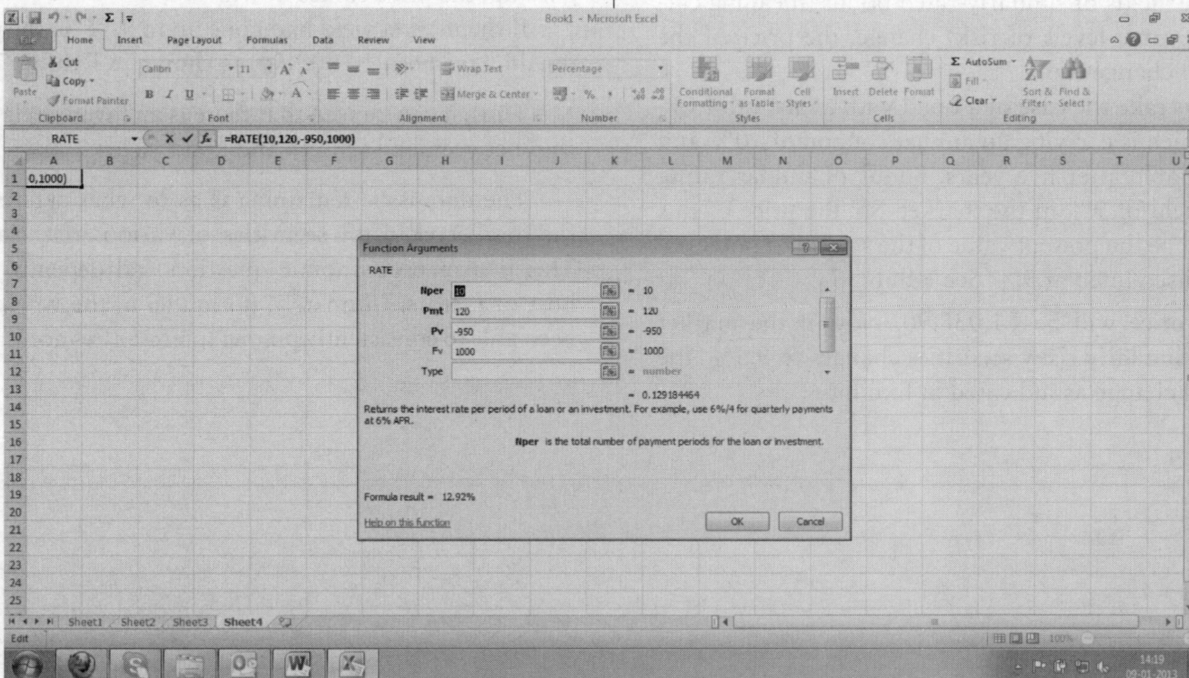

Yield and Price The price of a bond at a given point of time is the present value of the coupon flow and final redemption flow that it enjoys. The present value is calculated by discounting the potential inflows with the yield to maturity.

Suppose the market YTM for AAA bonds now is 8%. Let us find the price of a bond which has a 9% annual coupon, a tenure of 12 years and will be redeemed on the par value of ₹1000. See Exhibit 4.

EXHIBIT 4

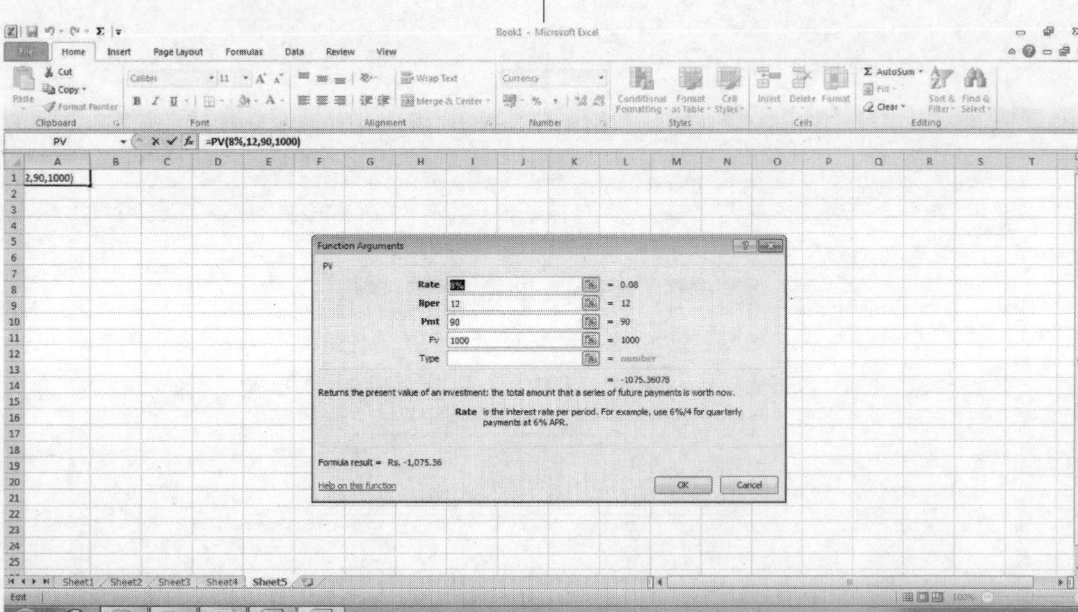

We get the answer as 1,075.36, which ought to be the price of the bond in the market today. If it is selling at a cheaper value, then the buyer has the chance to earn a higher yield than the corresponding yield for a bond of the same risk (AAA). If it is selling at a higher rate, it means that the yield on this bond is lower than those given by other AAA securities, and so it is not worthwhile investing here.

Changes in Yield

When the yields of similarly-rated bonds (meaning carrying the same levels of risk) change, the price of the bond will change too.

Let us take the case of a bond with a face value of ` 1,000 which is carrying an annual coupon of 10% and is redeemable after five years. Bonds of similar rating have a yield of 9% in the market. So, the price of this bond will be the present value of the stream of potential inflows discounted at 9%. See Exhibit 5.

The price will be ₹1,038.90. Now if the market yield for similarly risky securities changes to 9.5%, the price will change as indicated in Exhibit 6.

The new price will be ₹1,019.20. So when the yield goes up, the price comes down.

If the market yield had gone up to 9.75%, the price would have been ₹ 1009.54, as shown in Exhibit 7.

Thus, it can be seen that there is an inverse relationship between bond prices and bond yields.

The only issue remaining is as to what determines the market yield for securities of various risk classes. This is a macroeconomic question and depends on a host of factors. Ultimately, no model in the world has been able to consistently predict interest rates accurately.

EXHIBIT 5

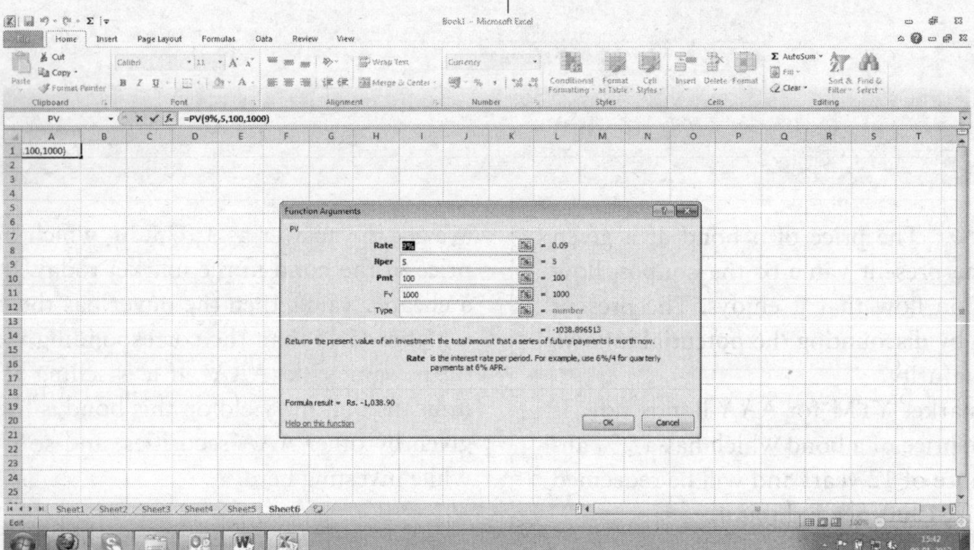

EXHIBIT 6

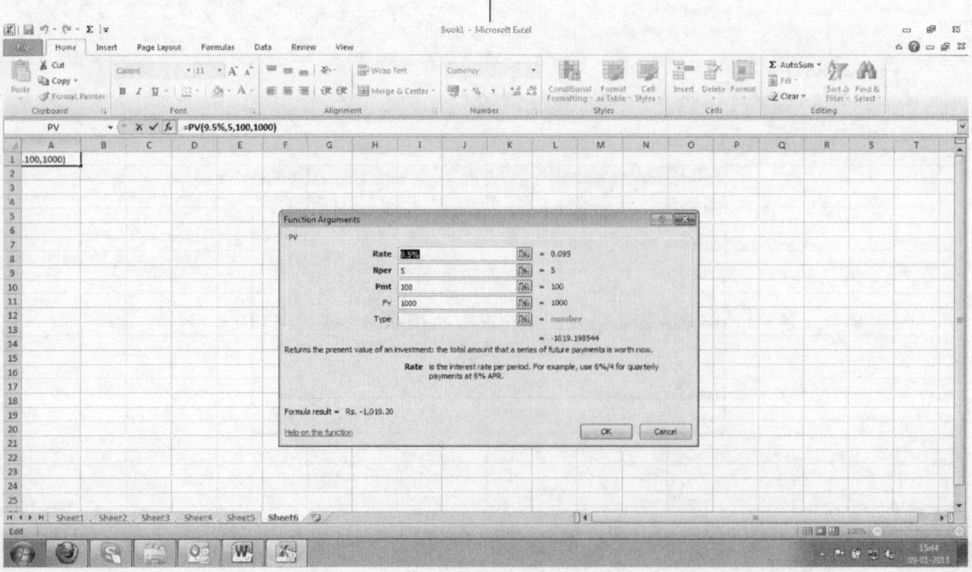

EXHIBIT 7

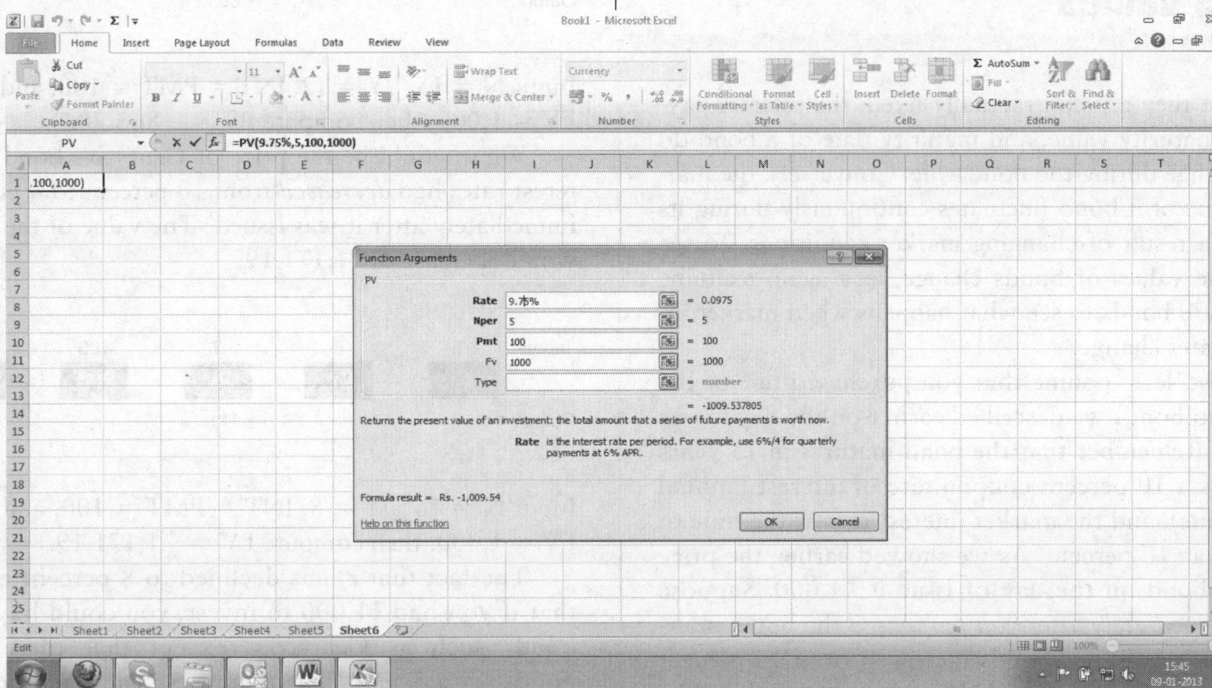

6-4b Yield to Call (YTC)

Bonds that contain call provisions (*callable bonds*) often are called by the firm prior to maturity. In cases where a bond issue is called, investors do not have the opportunity to earn the yield to maturity because the bond issue is retired before its maturity date arrives. Thus, for callable bonds, we generally compute the **yield to call (YTC)** rather than the YTM. The computation for the YTC is the same as that for the YTM, except that we substitute the *call price* of the bond for the maturity (par) value and the number of years until the bond can be first called for the years to maturity. To calculate the YTC for a bond with annual interest payments, then, we modify Equation 6.1, and solve the following equation for r_d:

$$V_d = \frac{\text{INT}}{(1+r_d)^1} + \frac{\text{INT}}{(1+r_d)^2} + \cdots + \frac{\text{INT} + \text{Call price}}{(1+r_d)^{N_c}}$$

$$= \frac{\text{INT}}{(1+\text{YTC})^1} + \frac{\text{INT}}{(1+\text{YTC})^2} + \cdots + \frac{\text{INT} + \text{Call price}}{(1+\text{YTC})^{N_c}}$$

Here N_c is the number of years until the company can first call the bond; "Call price" is the price that the company must pay to call the bond on the first call date; and r_d now represents the YTC. To solve for the YTC, we proceed just as we did to solve for the YTM of a bond.

Suppose the bond we are currently examining has a call provision that kicks in four years from today—that is, the bond is callable six years before it matures. If it calls the bond on the first date possible, the firm will have to pay a call price equal to ₹1,080. Using a financial calculator, you would find the YTC equals 13.7 percent:

Inputs:	8	?	−875	40	1,080
	N	I/Y	PV	PMT	FV
Output:		= 6.87			

Input N = 2 × 4 = 8, PV = −875 (this is a cash outflow if you buy the bond), INT = PMT = 40 = 80/2, and Call price = FV = 1,080, and then compute I/Y = 6.87, which is the six-month yield. As a result, YTC = 6.87% × 2 = 13.7%. Thus, investors who purchase the bond today expect to earn an average annual return equal to 13.7 percent if the bond is called in four years, which is likely to occur.

yield to call (YTC) The average rate of return earned on a bond if it is held until the first call date.

6-5 Interest Rates and Bond Values

Because they are contractually fixed, the interest payment, maturity value, and maturity date of a bond do not change during the bond's life. Conversely, the market value of a bond fluctuates continuously during its life as a result of changing market conditions. To see why the values of bonds change, let's again examine Genesco's bonds to see what happens when market interest rates change.

First, let's assume that you purchased one of the Genesco bonds we described earlier on the day it was issued. Remember that the bond matures in 15 years and has a 10 percent coupon rate of interest (annual payments), and the market interest rate at the time of issue was 10 percent. As we showed earlier, the price of the bond on the day of issue is ₹1,000. Suppose that *immediately after you purchased* the bond, interest rates on similar bonds increased from 10 percent to 12 percent. How would the value of your bond be affected?

Because the cash flows associated with the bond—that is, interest payments and principal repayment—remain constant, the value of the bond will decrease when interest rates increase. In present value terms, the decrease in value makes sense. If you want to mimic the Genesco bond—that is, pay yourself ₹100 each year for 15 years and then pay yourself ₹1,000 at the end of the fifteenth year—and your opportunity cost is 10 percent, you must deposit ₹1,000 in a savings account. However, if you found a savings account that pays 12 percent interest annually, you could deposit some amount less than ₹1,000 and pay yourself the same ₹100 each year and receive ₹1,000 in 15 years because your deposit would earn greater interest. The same logic applies when we consider how an interest rate change affects the value of Genesco's bond.

If market rates *increase* from 10 percent to 12 percent immediately after you purchase Genesco's bond, the value of the bond would decrease to ₹863.78 (assuming annual interest payments):

Inputs:	15	12	?	100	1,000
	N	I/Y	PV	PMT	FV
Output:			= − 863.78		

Input N = 15, I/Y = 12, INT = PMT = 100, and M = FV = 1,000; then compute PV = −863.78.

What would be the price of Genesco's bond if interest rates had *decreased* from 10 percent to 8 percent immediately after it was issued? The value of the bond would increase to ₹1,171.19:

Inputs:	15	8	?	100	1,000
	N	I/Y	PV	PMT	FV
Output:			= −1,171.19		

Input N = 15, I/Y = 8, INT = PMT = 100, and M = FV = 1,000; then compute PV = −1,171.19.

The fact that r_d has declined to 8 percent means that if you had ₹1,000 to invest, you could buy *new* bonds such as Genesco's, except that these new bonds would pay ₹80 of interest each year rather than the ₹100 interest paid by Genesco. Naturally, you would prefer ₹100 to ₹80, so you would be willing to pay more than ₹1,000 for Genesco's bonds to get its higher interest payments. Because all investors would recognize these facts, the Genesco Manufacturing bonds would be bid up in price to ₹1,171.19. At that price, the Genesco bonds would provide the same rate of return to potential investors as the new bonds: 8 percent.

Following is a table that summarizes the relationship between the value of Genesco's bond and its yield to maturity.

Relationship of Market Rate, r_d, with Coupon Rate, C = 10%	Bond Value, V_d (N = 15, PMT = 100, FV = 1,000, and I/Y = r_d)	Relationship of Market Price, V_d and Maturity Value, M = ₹1,000
$r_d = 10\% = C$	₹1,000.00	$V_d = M$; bond sells at par
$r_d = 12\% > C$	863.78	$V_d < M$; bond sells at a discount
$r_d = 8\% < C$	1,171.19	$V_d > M$; bond sells at a premium

These same relationship exists for all bonds. When the market yield (r_d = YTM) and the coupon rate of interest are equal, the bond sells for its par value; when the market yield is greater than the coupon rate of interest, the bond sells for less than its par value, or at a *discount*. When the market yield is less than the coupon rate of interest, the bond sells for greater than its par value, or at a *premium*.

6-5a Changes in Bond Values over Time

Let's again assume that immediately after Genesco issued its bond interest rates in the economy fell from 10 to 8 percent. In the previous section, we showed that the price of the bond would increase from ₹1,000 to ₹1,171.19. Assuming that interest rates remain constant at 8 percent for the next 15 years, what will happen to the value of Genesco's bond as time passes and the maturity date approaches? It will decrease gradually from ₹1,171.19 at present to ₹1,000 at maturity, when Genesco will redeem each bond for ₹1,000. We can illustrate this point by calculating the value of the bond one year from now, when it has 14 years remaining to maturity:

Inputs:	14	8	?	100	1,000
	N	I/Y	PV	PMT	FV
Output:			= −1,164.88		

As you can see, the value of the bond will decrease from ₹1,171.19 to ₹1,164.88, or by ₹6.31. If you were to calculate the bond's value at other future dates using $r_d = 8\%$, its price must decline as the maturity date approaches—when N = 13, V_d = ₹1,158.08, when N = 12, V_d = ₹1,150.72, and so on. At maturity, the value of the bond must equal its par value of ₹1,000 (as long as the firm does not go bankrupt).

Suppose that Sherman purchased a Genesco bond *just after* the market rate dropped to 8 percent, so he paid ₹1,171.19 for the bond. If he sold the bond one year later for ₹1,164.88, Sherman would realize a capital *loss* of ₹6.31, or a total rupee return of ₹93.69 = ₹100.00 – ₹6.31. The percentage rate of return that Sherman would earn on the bond consists of an *interest yield* (called the **current yield**) plus a **capital gains yield.** These yields are calculated using Equation 6.3:

6.3

$$\text{Bond yield} = \text{Current yield} + \text{Capital gains yield}$$
$$= \frac{INT}{V_{d,Begin}} + \frac{V_{d,End} - V_{d,Begin}}{V_{d,Begin}}$$

Here, $V_{d,Begin}$ represents the value of the bond at the beginning of the year (period) and $V_{d,End}$ is the value of the bond at the end of the year (period).

The yields Sherman would earn by holding Genesco's bond for one year are computed as follows:

Current yield	= ₹100.00/₹1,171.19 =	0.0854 =	8.54%
Capital gains yield	= −₹6.31/₹1,171.19 =	−0.0054 =	−0.54%
Total rate of return (yield)	= ₹93.69/₹1,171.19 =	0.0800 =	8.00%

Had interest rates risen from 10 to 12 percent rather than fallen immediately after issue, the value of the bond would have immediately decreased to ₹863.78. In this case, because the bond's value must equal the principal, or par, amount at maturity (as long as bankruptcy does not occur), its value will gradually increase from the current price of ₹863.78 to its maturity value of ₹1,000. The value of the bond would increase to ₹867.44 at N = 14, to ₹871.53 at N = 13, to ₹876.11 at N = 12, and so forth. The total expected future yield on the bond would again consist of a current yield and a capital gains yield. However, now the capital gains yield would be positive, and the total yield on the bond would be 12 percent (assuming market rates remain constant).

Figure 6.2 graphs the value of Genesco's bond over time, assuming that interest rates in the economy (1) remain constant at 10 percent, (2) fall to 8 percent immediately after issue and then remain constant at that level, or (3) rise to 12 percent immediately after issue and remain constant at that level. Of course, if interest rates do not remain constant, the price of the bond will fluctuate. However, regardless of what interest rates do in the future, *the bond's price will approach its face value (₹1,000) as it nears its maturity date* (barring bankruptcy, in which case the bond's value might drop to zero).

6-5b Interest Rate Risk on a Bond

As we saw in Chapter 5, interest rates change over time. Furthermore, changes in interest rates affect bondholders in two ways. First, as shown earlier, an increase in interest rates leads to a decline in the values of outstanding bonds. (At $r_d = 10\%$, the value of Genesco's 15-year bond was ₹1,000; at $r_d = 12\%$, V_d = ₹863.78.)

current (interest) yield The interest payment divided by the market price of the bond.

capital gains yield The percentage change in the market price of a bond over some period of time.

FIGURE 6.2 Time Path of the Value of a 10% Coupon, ₹1,000 Par Value Bond When Market Interest Rates Are 8%, 10%, and 12%

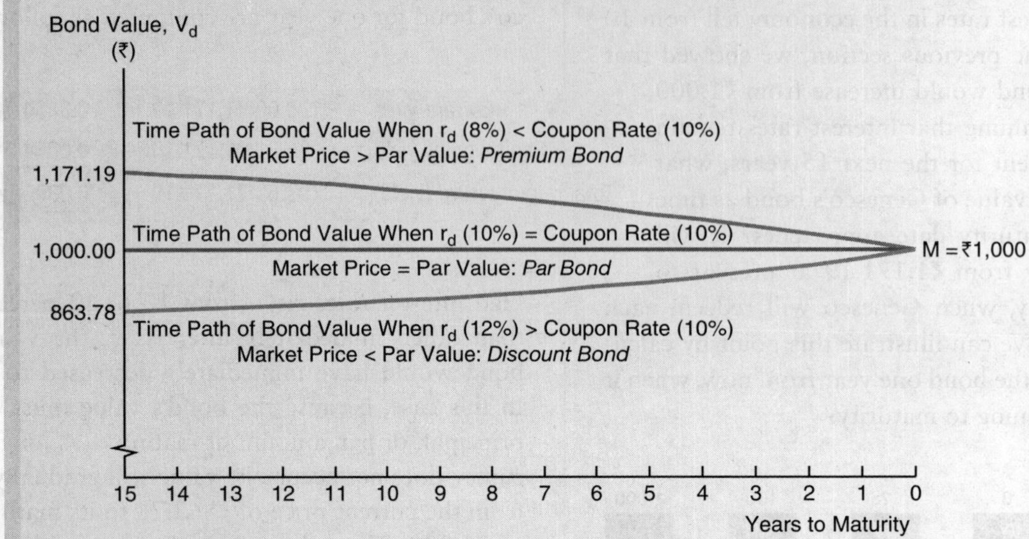

Years to Maturity	r_d = 8%	r_d = 10%	r_d = 12%
15	₹1,171.19	₹1,000.00	₹863.78
14	1,164.88	1,000.00	867.44
⋮	⋮	⋮	⋮
0	1,000.00	1,000.00	1,000.00

Thus, because interest rates can rise, bondholders face the risk of suffering losses in the market values of their bond portfolios. This risk is called **interest rate price risk**. Second, many bondholders buy bonds to build funds for some future use. These bondholders reinvest each interest payment when it is received (generally every six months) and the principal repayment when it is received at maturity (or when the bond is called). If interest rates decline—say, from 10 percent to 8 percent—the bondholders will earn a lower rate of return on *reinvested cash flows*, which will reduce the future values of their portfolios relative to the values they would have accumulated if interest rates had not fallen. This risk is called **interest rate reinvestment risk.**

We can see, then, that any given change in interest rates has two separate effects on bondholders: (1) It changes the current market values of their portfolios (price risk), and (2) it changes the rates of return at which the cash flows from their portfolios can be reinvested (reinvestment risk). These two risks tend to offset one another. For example, an increase in interest rates will lower the current value of a bond portfolio. However, the future value of the portfolio will increase because the cash flows produced by the portfolio can be reinvested at the higher rates of return.

interest rate reinvestment risk The risk that income from a bond portfolio will vary because cash flows must be reinvested at current market rates.

interest rate price risk The risk of changes in bond prices to which investors are exposed as the result of changing interest rates.

An investor's exposure to interest rate price risk is greater on bonds with long maturities than on those that will mature in the near future. We can demonstrate this fact by considering how the value of a one-year bond with a 10 percent coupon fluctuates with changes in r_d and then comparing these changes with the effects on a 15-year bond, as calculated previously. Figure 6.3 shows the values for a one-year bond and a 15-year bond at several different market interest rates, r_d. The values for the bonds were computed assuming that the coupon interest payments for the bonds occur annually. Notice how much more sensitive the price of the long-term bond is to changes in interest rates. At a 10 percent

FIGURE 6.3 Value of Long-Term and Short-Term 10% Annual Coupon Rate Bonds at Different Market Interest Rates (r_d)

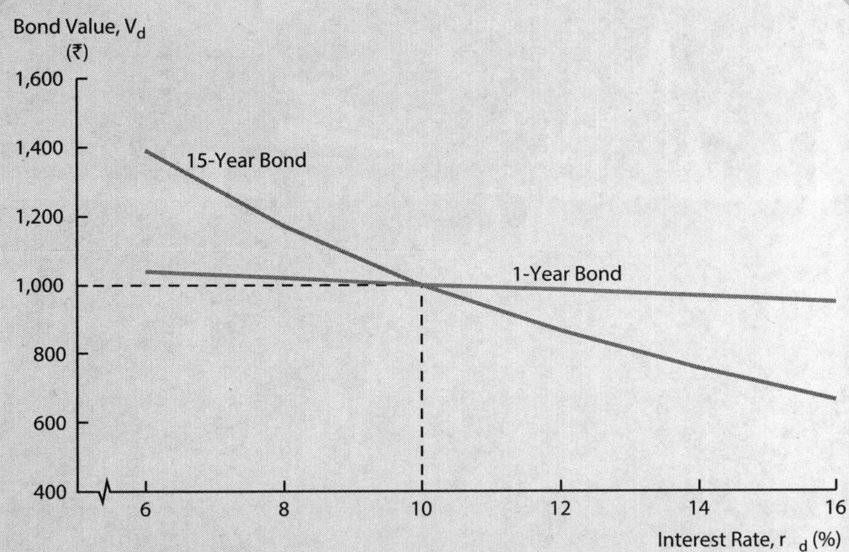

	Value of	
Current Market Interest Rate, r_d	**1-Year Bond**	**15-Year Bond**
6%	₹1,037.74	₹1,388.49
8	1,018.52	1,171.19
10	1,000.00	1,000.00
12	982.14	863.78
14	964.91	754.31
16	948.28	665.47

interest rate, both the long- and short-term bonds are valued at ₹1,000. When rates rise to 12 percent, the value of the long-term bond decreases to ₹863.78, or by 13.6 percent, but the value of the short-term bond falls to only ₹982.14, which is a 1.8 percent decline.

For bonds with similar coupons, this differential sensitivity to changes in interest rates always holds. *The longer the maturity of the bond, the more significantly its price changes in response to a given change in interest rates.* Thus, if two bonds have exactly the same risk of default, the bond with the longer maturity typically is exposed to more price risk from a change in interest rates.[11]

The logical explanation for this difference in interest rate price risk is simple. Suppose that you bought a 15-year bond that yielded 10 percent, or ₹100 per year. Now suppose that interest rates on comparable-risk bonds increased to 12 percent. You would be stuck with only ₹100 of interest for the next 15 years. On the other hand, had you bought a one-year bond, you would have received a low return for only one year. At the end of the year, you would get your ₹1,000 back, and you could then reinvest it and receive 12 percent, or ₹120 per year, for the next 14 years. As you can see, interest rate price risk reflects the length of time one is committed to a given investment. As we described in Chapter 5, the longer a bond's term to maturity, the higher its maturity risk premium (MRP), which accounts for its higher interest rate risk.

Although a one-year bond has less interest rate price risk than a 15-year bond, the one-year bond exposes the buyer to more interest rate reinvestment risk. Suppose that you bought a one-year bond that yielded 10 percent, and then interest rates on comparable-risk bonds fell to 8 percent so that newly issued bonds now pay ₹80 interest. After one year, when you get your ₹1,000 back, you would have to invest your funds at only 8 percent. As a result, you would lose ₹100 – ₹80 = ₹20 in annual interest. Had you bought the 15-year bond, you would have continued to receive ₹100 in annual interest payments even if rates fell. If you reinvested those coupon payments, you would have to accept a lower reinvestment rate of return, but you would still be much better off than if you had been holding the one-year bond.

6-5c Bond Prices in Recent Years

From Chapter 5, we know that interest rates fluctuate. We have also just seen that the prices of outstanding bonds rise and fall inversely with changes in interest rates. When interest rates fall, many firms refinance by issuing new, lower-cost debt and using the proceeds to repay higher-cost debt. In 2003, interest rates dropped to levels that had not been seen in more than 45 years. Not surprisingly, firms that had issued higher-cost debt in earlier years refinanced much of their debt at that time. In 2012 and 2013, rates were at historically low levels, which enticed many firms to refinance their bonds once again.[12]

[11] If a 10-year bond were plotted in Figure 6.3, its curve would lie between the curves for the 15-year and one-year bonds. The curve of a one-month bond would be almost horizontal, indicating that its price would change very little in response to an interest rate change. A perpetuity would have a very steep slope.

[12] In some cases, corporate bonds could not be refinanced at the lower rates due to restrictions that existed in the debt contracts or because firms (issuers) were not financially sound.

© iStockphoto.com/Nikada

Suppose that you bought a five-year bond that a corporation issued on January 2, 2009, when the average interest rate on AAA-rated bonds was 4.8 percent. Because the bond would have a coupon rate equal to 4.8 percent, you would have received ₹24 every six months (₹48 per year) until the bond matured on December 30, 2013. The following table shows the market price of the bond on the first trading day of January until it matured in 2013:

Note that because market rates were close to the bond's coupon rate, the bond's market price was at or near its par value each year. The total yield shown in the far right column indicates the yield you would have earned if you bought the bond on the first trading day of January in a particular year and then sold it the following January. For example, if you bought the bond January 3, 2009, and sold it on January 4,

Date	Years to Maturity	Market Rate of Return (%)	Market Price	Current Yield (%)	Capital Gain Yield (%)	Total Yield(%)
January 2, 2009	5	4.8%	₹1,000.00			
January 4, 2010	4	5.4	978.67	4.80%	−2.13%	2.67%
January 3, 2011	3	4.9	997.24	4.90	1.90	6.80
January 3, 2012	2	3.8	1,019.08	4.81	2.19	7.00
January 2, 2013	1	3.8	1,009.72	4.71	−0.92	3.79
December 31, 2013	0	3.8	1,000.00	4.75	−0.96	3.79

2010, you would have earned 2.67 percent return. The return for this one-year period is lower than the bond's coupon rate because market rates increased in 2009 from 4.8 percent to 5.4 percent, which decreased the bond's value by ₹21.33 and resulted in a 2.13 percent capital loss. Also, note that by the maturity date of the bond, interest rates had dropped to 3.8 percent, which means the rate at which you could reinvest the ₹1,000 maturity value that you received on December 31, 2013 was 3.8 percent. In other words, AAA-rated corporate bonds issued on December 31, 2013 had a coupon rate of interest equal to 3.8 percent, thus any new bonds you bought on that date paid ₹38 interest per year (compared to ₹48 in 2009).

Although market rates might differ when you read this book, this illustration shows that (1) bond prices change as market rates change (in an opposite direction) and (2) the value of a bond approaches its par value as the maturity date gets closer (assuming the firm is financially healthy).

KEY BOND VALUATION AND CHARACTERISTICS CONCEPTS

To conclude this chapter, we summarize some bond valuation concepts (rules) that were discussed.

- Other things held constant, the higher the coupon rate, the higher the market price of a bond.
- When interest rates change, the values of bonds change in an opposite direction; that is, when rates increase, bond prices decrease, and vice versa.
- Whenever the going rate of interest, r_d, equals the coupon rate, a bond will sell at its par value; whenever r_d is greater than the coupon rate, a bond's price will fall below its par value (a discount bond); whenever r_d is less than the coupon rate, a bond's price will rise above its par value (a premium bond).
- The going rate of interest, r_d, which represents the return that investors earn when buying and holding a bond to its maturity, is comprised of a return that is associated with (1) the annual interest payment, which is called the current yield, and (2) the annual change in the market value of the bond, which is called the capital gains yield.
- The market value of a bond will always approach its par value as its maturity date approaches, provided that the firm does not go bankrupt.

MULTIPLE CHOICE QUESTIONS

1. A bond is

a. A debt instrument

b. An equity instrument

c. Neither a nor b

d. Both a and b

2. In bond terminology, coupon means

a. Yield to maturity

b. Market interest rate

c. Periodic interest rate paid on the bond

d. None of the above

3. The face value of a bond is

a. The final amount paid on the bond

b. The initial amount paid for the bond

c. The amount on which the coupon is calculated

d. Both a and c

4. Yield to maturity will be equal to the coupon rate when

a. The tenure is shorter than three years

b. The market interest rates do not fluctuate

c. The initial price and the final redemption value are the same

d. Will never be equal

5. The yield to maturity of a zero coupon bond is obtained by

a. Dividing the final value by the initial value

b. Dividing the initial value by the final value

c. Finding the rate for discounting the final value to the initial value

d. Cannot be found

6. When the final value is less than the initial price,

a. There will be a high coupon

b. There will be no coupon

c. Yield to maturity cannot be calculated

d. None of the above

7. In respect of bonds, which of the following is true?

a. The YTM once determined remains steady for life.

b. YTM cannot be determined without reference to market forces.

c. YTM is based on initial intermittent and terminal flows.

d. When in doubt, coupon can be taken as YTM.

8. A buy and hold investor

a. Will always realize, YTM, if bond is held to maturity

b. Will always realize, YTM, if it is a zero coupon bond

c. Will never realize YTM, if market yield falls

d. Will realize YTM, if held to maturity and it is a zero coupon bond

9. A bond's value

a. Depends on market interest rates

b. Depends on the bond coupon

c. Depends on bond YTM

d. Does not depend on any of the above

10. Which of the following statements is right?

a. A bond is safer than a stock

b. Generally a bond gives higher returns than a stock

c. A bond cannot be sold in the market

d. Both a and c

Answers:

1.	(a)	2.	(c)	3.	(d)	4.	(c)	5.	(c)
6.	(d)	7.	(c)	8.	(a)	9.	(c)	10.	(a)

PROBLEMS

For more problems, login to CourseMate for CFIN at CengageBrain.com

6-1 Kedarnath Bicycles plans to issue convertible bonds to finance its future growth. Each convertible bond has a face value equal to ₹1,000 and can be converted into 25 shares of common stock. What is the minimum stock price that would make it beneficial for bondholders to convert their bonds?

6-2 Many years ago, Bharath Matha Maps issued a convertible bond with a conversion ratio equal to 40. The bond's face value is ₹1,000. (a) For how many shares of stock can a bondholder convert each bond? (b) At what stock price should bondholders convert?

6-3 Suppose you own a convertible bond that has a conversion ratio equal to 50. Each convertible bond has a face value equal to ₹1,000. The current market value of the company's common stock is ₹19, and the bond is selling for ₹980. If you want to liquidate your position today because you need money to pay your rent, should you sell the bond or should you convert the bond into common stock and then sell the stock?

6-4 Haryana Electric's outstanding bond has a ₹1,000 maturity value and a 4.5 percent coupon rate of interest (paid *semiannually*). The bond, which was issued five years ago, matures in 10 years. If investors require a return equal to 6 percent to invest in similar bonds, what is the current market value of Haryana Electric's bond?

6-5 Eleven years ago, Dakshin Elements issued a 15-year bond with a ₹1,000 face value and a 5 percent coupon rate of interest (paid semiannually). If investors require a return equal to 7 percent to invest in similar bonds, what is the current market value of Dakshin Elements' bond?

6-6 Priyadarshini Fishing Lures (PFL) has an outstanding bond with a ₹1,000 face value and a 9 percent coupon rate of interest (paid *semiannually*). The bond, which was issued 22 years ago, matures in eight years. If investors require a return equal to 4 percent to invest in similar bonds, what is the market value of PFL's bond?

6-7 Harbhajan Manufacturers issued a 10-year bond six years ago. The bond's maturity value is ₹1,000, and its coupon interest rate is 6 percent. Interest is paid *semiannually*. The bond matures in four years. If investors require a return equal to 5 percent to invest in similar bonds, what is the current market value of Harbhajan Manufacturers' bond?

6-8 Somnath Corp.'s outstanding bond, which has a coupon rate equal to 8 percent and a ₹1,000 face value, matures in six years. If investors require a rate of return equal to 12 percent on similar bonds and interest is paid *semiannually*, what should be the market price of Somnath Corp.'s bond?

6-9 The Vishnu Company has two bonds outstanding. Both bonds pay ₹100 *annual* interest plus ₹1,000 at maturity. Bond L matures in 15 years, whereas Bond S matures in one year. One interest payment remains on Bond S. What will be the values of these bonds when the going rate of interest is (a) 5 percent and (b) 7 percent?

6-10 Padmini Farm Equipment's five-year zero coupon bond is currently selling for ₹621. The bond's maturity value is ₹1,000 bond. What is the bond's yield to maturity (YTM)?

6-11 Meenakshi Company's bond has four years remaining to maturity. Interest is paid *semiannually*, the bonds have a ₹1,000 par value, and the coupon interest rate is 9 percent. Compute the yield to maturity for the bonds if the current market price is (a) ₹851 and (b) ₹1,105.

6-12 Surya Interiors has an outstanding bond with a ₹1,000 maturity value and a 5.5 percent coupon rate of interest that was issued 20 years ago. Interest is paid *semiannually*. The bond, which matures in five years, is currently selling for ₹1,022. What is the bond's yield to maturity?

6-13 Four years ago Chandra House Painting issued a 20-year bond with a ₹1,000 maturity value and a 4 percent coupon rate of interest. Interest is paid *semiannually*. The bond is currently selling for ₹714. (a) What is the bond's yield to maturity? (b) If the bond can be called in three years for a redemption price of ₹1,040, what is the bond's yield to call?

6-14 Three years ago, Bhimsen's Automotive Jacks issued a 20-year callable bond with a ₹1,000 maturity value and a 8.5 percent coupon rate of interest. Interest is paid *semiannually*. The bond is currently selling for ₹1,046. (a) What is the bond's yield to maturity? (b) If the bond can be called in four years for a redemption price of ₹1,085, what is the bond's yield to call?

6-15 Narayan Archery's bond currently is selling for ₹1,005; its value one year ago was ₹990. The bond has a ₹1,000 maturity value and a coupon rate equal to 7 percent, and it matures in eight years. Interest is paid *annually*. Compute (a) the current yield and capital gains yield Narayan Archery's bondholders earned during the year and (b) the bond's yield to maturity today.

6-16 City Garage issued a bond with a 10-year maturity, a ₹1,000 par value, a 10 percent coupon rate, and *semiannual* interest payments. Two years after the bond was issued, the going rate of interest on similar-risk bonds fell to 6 percent. Suppose the market rate stays at this level for the remainder of the bond's life. Compute the (a) current yield and (b) capital gains yield that the bond will generate in the third year (Year 3) of its life.

6-17 Five years ago Namkin Systems issued a 15-year bond with a ₹1,000 par value and a 7 percent coupon rate. Interest is paid *semiannually*. Today the going interest rate is 10 percent, and it is expected to remain at this level for many years in the future. Compute the (a) current yield and (b) capital gains yield that the bond will generate in the fifth year (Year 5) of its life.

6-18 One year ago, Mitti Honey issued a 10-year bond for ₹1,000. The bond's coupon rate of interest is 4 percent, and interest is paid *annually*. If the current value of the bond is ₹929, what are (a) the current yield and capital gains yield Mitti Honey's bondholders earned during the year and (b) the bond's yield to maturity today.

6-19 Eight years ago, Sab-se-Bada Trampolines issued a 15-year bond with a ₹1,000 par value and a 6 percent coupon rate (interest is paid *annually*). Today the going rate of interest on similar bonds is 6 percent. (a) What is the bond's current value? If the market rate stays at 6 percent for the remainder of the bond's life, what (b) current yield and (c) capital gains yield will bondholders receive during the next two years (i.e., Years 9 and 10)?

6-20 Many years ago, Hamesa Knives issued a zero coupon bond with a ₹1,000 face value. The bond matures in three years. If the current market rate on similar bonds is 11 percent, (a) what is the bond's current value? Suppose the market rate stays at 11 percent for the next three years. What (b) current yield and (c) capital gains yield will bondholders receive each year during the remainder of the bond's life?

Bonds (Debt)—Characteristics and Valuation

Learning Outcomes

LO.1 Describe the basic characteristics of debt and some of the different types of debt that exist.

- Debt can have many different characteristics, which generally are outlined in the bond contract (called the indenture). Some of the characteristics include (1) the coupon rate, which specifies the annual interest that is paid; (2) the maturity date; and (3) whether the bond has a call provision, a sinking fund, or a conversion feature. In addition, there are various types of debt that are generally identified by the original term to maturity or by the issuer. Short-term debt instruments have original maturities equal to one year or less, and long-term debt instruments have original maturities greater than one year. Some of the different types of debt are government debt and corporate bonds. Different types of instruments with different characteristics exist in each of these categories.

LO.2 Discuss bond ratings and the information that they provide to investors.

- Bond ratings provide investors with an indication as to the risks that are associated with debt instruments. Risk is an important factor that investors consider when determining the rates of return that they require to purchase different debt instruments.

LO.3 Explain how bond prices are determined.

- Bond prices are based on two fundamental factors: (1) the future cash flows generated by the bonds and (2) the rates of return that investors require to purchase the bonds. The price of a bond is determined by computing the present value of the future cash flows that the bond is expected to generate during its life. A bond's cash flows include the annual interest that is paid and the repayment of the principal (maturity value).

LO.4 Explain how bond yields (market rates) are determined.

- The yield (return) on a bond is "set" by investors who participate in the financial markets. Investors determine the price at which the bond sells. The yield on the bond can be determined by computing the rate that equates the bond's current selling price with the present value of the cash flows it will generate during its life.

LO.5 Describe the relationship between bond prices and interest rates, and explain why it is important for investors to understand this relationship.

- Interest rates and bond prices are inversely related. Because the cash flows that a bond generates are contractually fixed, the only way investors can earn higher returns is by paying a lower price for a bond.
- The inverse relationship between prices and rates of return exists for *all* investments. It is important that all investors understand this concept.

CHAPTER 6 REVIEW

Chapter 6 Key Bonds Valuation Concepts

- Other things held constant, the higher *the coupon rate, the higher the market price of a bond.*
- When interest rates change, the values of bonds change in an opposite direction—that is, when rates increase, bond prices decrease, and vice versa.
- Whenever the going market rate of interest, r_d, equals the coupon rate, a bond will sell at its par value; whenever r_d is greater than the coupon rate, a bond's price will fall below its par value (a discount bond); whenever r_d is less than the coupon rate, a bond's price will rise above its par value (a premium bond). The market rate of interest, r_d, which represents the return that investors earn when buying and holding a bond to its maturity (also called the yield to maturity, or YTM), is comprised of a return that is associated with (1) the annual interest payment, which is called the current yield, and (2) the annual change in the market value of the bond, which is called the capital gains yield.
- The market value of a bond will always approach its par value as its maturity date approaches, provided that the firm does not go bankrupt.

Key Terms

LO.1

debt A loan to a firm, government, or individual. *p. 91*

discounted securities Securities selling for less than par value. *p. 91*

Treasury bills (T-bills) Discounted debt instruments issued by the U.S. government. *p. 91*

repurchase agreement An arrangement where one firm sells some of its financial assets to another firm with a promise to *repurchase* the securities at a later date. *p. 92*

federal funds Overnight loans from one bank to another. *p. 92*

banker's acceptance An instrument issued by a bank that obligates the bank to pay a specified amount at some future date. *p. 92*

commercial paper A discounted instrument that is a type of promissory note, or "legal" IOU, issued by large, financially sound firms. *p. 92*

certificate of deposit An interest-earning time deposit at a bank or other financial intermediary. *p. 92*

Eurodollar deposit A deposit in a foreign bank that is denominated in U.S. dollars. *p. 92*

money market mutual funds Pools of funds managed by investment companies that are primarily invested in short-term financial assets. *p. 92*

term loan A loan, generally obtained from a bank or insurance company, on which the borrower agrees to make a series of payments consisting of interest and principal. *p. 93*

bond A long-term debt instrument. *p. 93*

coupon rate Interest paid on a bond or other debt instrument stated as a percentage of its face (maturity) value. *p. 93*

government bonds Debt issued by federal, state, or local governments. *p. 93*

municipal bonds Bonds issued by state or local governments. *p. 93*

corporate bonds Long-term debt instruments issued by corporations. *p. 94*

mortgage bond A bond backed by fixed assets. First-mortgage bonds are senior in priority to claims of second-mortgage bonds. *p. 94*

debenture A long-term bond that is not secured by a mortgage on specific property. *p. 94*

subordinated debenture A bond which, in the event of liquidation, has a claim on assets only after the senior debt has been paid off. *p. 94*

income bond A bond that pays interest to the holder only if the interest is earned by the firm. *p. 94*

putable bond A bond that can be redeemed at the bondholder's option when certain circumstances exist. *p. 94*

indexed (purchasing-power) bond A bond that has interest payments based on an inflation index to protect the holder from loss of purchasing power. *p. 94*

floating-rate bond A bond whose interest rate fluctuates with shifts in the general level of interest rates. *p. 94*

zero coupon bond A bond that pays no annual interest but is sold at a discount below par, thus providing compensation to investors in the form of capital appreciation. *p. 94*

junk bond A high-risk, high-yield bond used to finance mergers, leveraged buyouts, and troubled companies. *p. 95*

indenture A formal agreement (contract) between the issuer of a bond and the bondholders. *p. 95*

call provision A provision in a bond contract that gives the issuer the right to redeem the bonds under specified terms prior to the normal maturity date. *p. 95*

sinking fund A required annual payment designed to amortize a bond issue. *p. 95*

conversion feature Permits bondholders to exchange their investments for a fixed number of shares of common stock. *p. 95*

foreign debt Debt sold by a foreign borrower but denominated in the currency of the country where it is sold. *p. 96*

Eurodebt Debt sold in a country other than the one in whose currency the debt is denominated. *p. 96*

LIBOR The London Interbank Offered Rate; the interest rate offered by the best London banks on deposits of other large, very creditworthy banks. *p. 96*

LO.4

yield to maturity (YTM) The average rate of return earned on a bond if it is held to maturity. *p. 100*

yield to call (YTC) The average rate of return earned on a bond if it is held until the first call date. *p. 100*

LO.5

current (interest) yield The interest payment divided by the market price of the bond. *p. 102*

capital gains yield The percentage change in the market price of a bond over some period of time. *p. 102*

interest rate price risk The risk of changes in bond prices to which investors are exposed as the result of changing interest rates. *p. 103*

interest rate reinvestment risk The risk that income from a bond portfolio will vary because cash flows must be reinvested at current market rates. *p. 103*

CHAPTER 7

Shares (Equity)—Characteristics and Valuation

Learning Outcomes

LO.1 Explain what equity is, and identify some of the features and characteristics of (a) preferred stock and (b) common stock.

LO.2 Describe how stock prices (values) are determined when (a) dividends grow at a constant rate and (b) dividend growth is nonconstant.

LO.3 Describe some approaches (techniques) other than strict application of time value of money models that investors use to value stocks.

LO.4 Identify factors that affect stock prices.

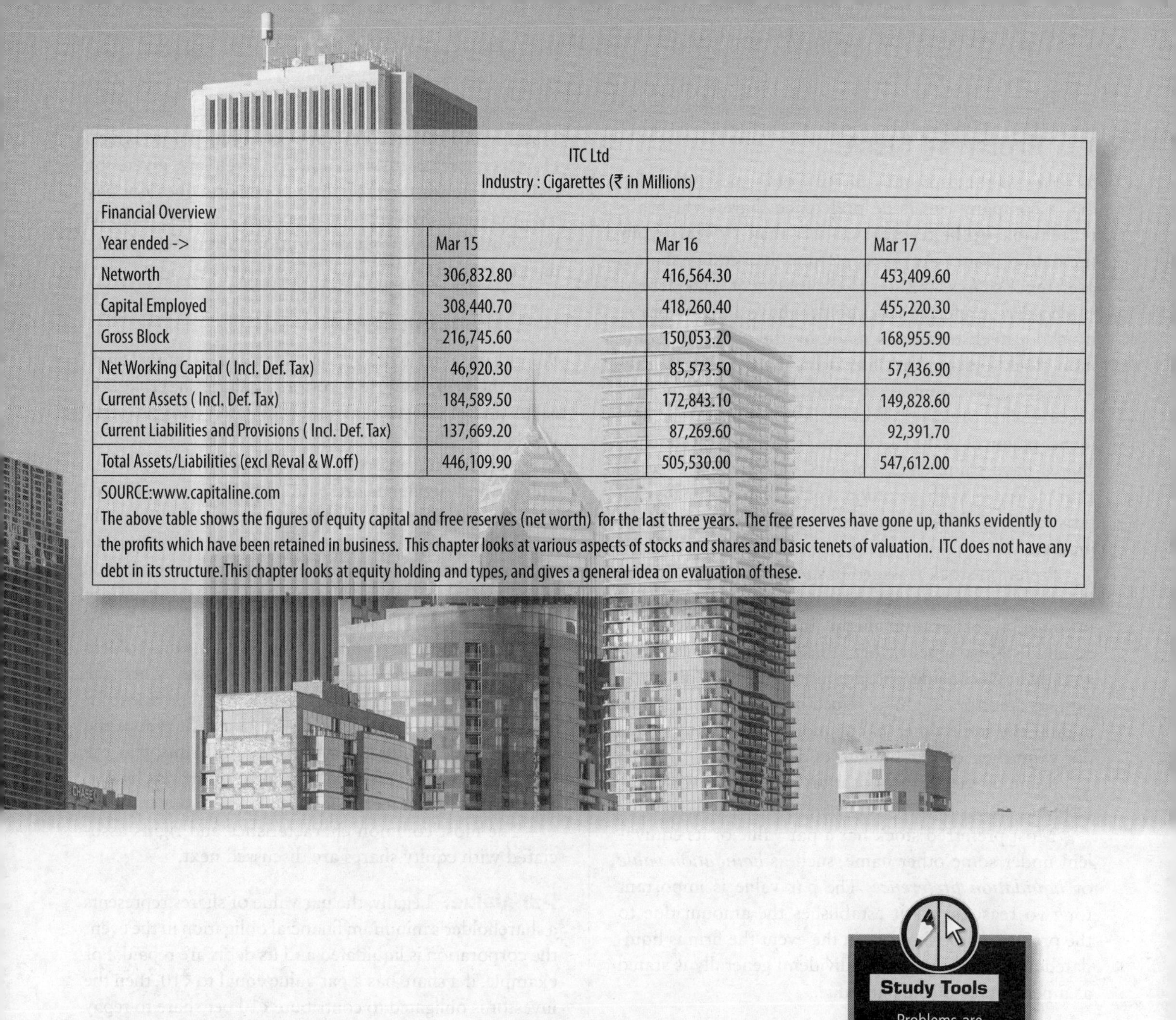

ITC Ltd Industry : Cigarettes (₹ in Millions)			
Financial Overview			
Year ended ->	Mar 15	Mar 16	Mar 17
Networth	306,832.80	416,564.30	453,409.60
Capital Employed	308,440.70	418,260.40	455,220.30
Gross Block	216,745.60	150,053.20	168,955.90
Net Working Capital (Incl. Def. Tax)	46,920.30	85,573.50	57,436.90
Current Assets (Incl. Def. Tax)	184,589.50	172,843.10	149,828.60
Current Liabilities and Provisions (Incl. Def. Tax)	137,669.20	87,269.60	92,391.70
Total Assets/Liabilities (excl Reval & W.off)	446,109.90	505,530.00	547,612.00

SOURCE:www.capitaline.com

The above table shows the figures of equity capital and free reserves (net worth) for the last three years. The free reserves have gone up, thanks evidently to the profits which have been retained in business. This chapter looks at various aspects of stocks and shares and basic tenets of valuation. ITC does not have any debt in its structure.This chapter looks at equity holding and types, and gives a general idea on evaluation of these.

Dan Kosmayer/Shutterstock.com

Study Tools

Problems are found at the end of this chapter

\+

Login to **CourseMate** for **CFIN** at **CengageBrain.com** for additional problems and other study tools!

Each company issues at least one type of share, or equity, called *common shares*. Some companies issue more than one type of share, and some issue *preference shares* in addition to equity shares. As the names imply, most equity takes the form of equity shares, and preference shareholders have preference over common shareholders when a firm distributes funds to stockholders. In this chapter, we discuss the general characteristics of both preferred stock and common stock and then give an indication as to how equity is valued.

7-1 Types of Equity

In this section, we describe some of the characteristics of equity. Far too many types of stock with different features exist to cover everything here; thus, we include only the most common features associated with preferred stock and common stock.

7-1a Preferred Stock

In terms of the provsions of the Companies Act in India, a company can issue preference shares which are redeemable (to be repaid) not later than 20 years from the date of issue. At the same time, like equity shares, preference shares are safer to use than debt. Like debentureholders, preferred stockholders have a higher priority claim to distributions made by the firm than common stockholders. And, like debt, if the firm is highly successful, the common stockholders do not share that success with preferred stockholders because their dividend payment is fixed. We see, then, that preference shares have some characteristics with debt and some characteristics with common stock; that is, the characteristics of preferred stock fall between debt and common stock.

Preferred stock is issued in situations where neither debt nor common stock is entirely appropriate. For instance, a corporation might find preferred stock to be an ideal instrument when it needs to raise funds and already has a considerable amount of debt. In this situation, its creditors might be reluctant to lend more funds, and, at the same time, its common stockholders might not want their ownership shares diluted.

Some of the features that are associated with preferred stock are described next.

Most preferred stock has a par value or its equivalent under some other name, such as *liquidation value* or *liquidation preference*. The par value is important for two reasons: (1) it establishes the amount due to the preferred stockholders in the event the firm is liquidated and (2) the preferred dividend generally is stated as a percentage of the par value.

Priority to Assets and Earnings. Preferred stockholders have priority over common stockholders, but not debt holders, with regard to earnings and assets. Thus, dividends must be paid on preferred stock before they can be paid on common stock, and, in the event of bankruptcy, the claims of the preferred shareholders must be satisfied before the common stockholders receive anything. To reinforce these features, most preferred stocks have coverage requirements similar to those placed on bonds. These restrictions limit the amount of preferred stock that a company can use, and they require a minimum level of retained earnings before the firm can pay any dividends to common stockholders.

Control of the Firm (Voting Rights). Nearly all preferred stock is *nonvoting stock*, which means that preferred stockholders neither elect the members of the board of directors nor vote on corporate issues. However, preferred stockholders often are given the right to vote for directors if the company does not pay the preferred dividend for a specified period, such as two years. Some sample declarations of dividend by Indian companies

7-1b Common Stock

We usually refer to common shareholders as the owners of the firm, because investors in shares have certain rights and privileges generally associated with property ownership. Shareholders are entitled to any earnings that remain after interest payments are made to bondholders and dividends are paid to preferred stockholders. Because debt and preference shares are generally *fixed-payment* securities, shareholders do not have to share earnings that exceed the amounts that the firm is required to pay to these shareholders. As a result, equity shareholders benefit when the firm performs well. On the other hand, the payments due to debenture holders and preference stockholders do not change when the company performs poorly. In this case, payment of mandatory fixed financial obligations might reduce the common stockholders' (owners') equity. Thus, it is the common stockholders who bear most of the risk associated with a firm's operations.

The most common characteristics and rights associated with equity shares are discussed next.

Par Value. Legally, the par value of shares represents a shareholder's minimum financial obligation in the event the corporation is liquidated and its debts are repaid. For example, if a share has a par value equal to ₹10, then the investor is obligated to contribute ₹10 per share to repay the firm's debt upon liquidation. If a newly issued share is purchased for more than ₹10 per share, the investor's obligation is satisfied; but if the share is purchased for less than ₹10—say, for ₹6—then the shareholder is required to make up the difference—₹4 in this case—if the firm goes bankrupt and additional funds are needed to repay creditors. In nearly every instance, new shares are sold for more than its par value, so investors generally are not concerned with a share's par value. As you will discover later in this chapter, the par value and market value of a share are not related—that is, *par value does not determine market value, and vice versa*.

Dividends. Dividends refer to the amounts paid by the company to its shareholders from out of the profits of the company. This is paid to shareholders in proportion to their holding of capital in the company. Dividend is paid after the accounts of the financial year are prepared, audited and approved by the company in a general meeting. The prerogative for declaration of dividend rests with the general meeting. The shareholders of preference shares are paid at the pre-stipulated fixed rate.

TABLE 7.1

Co_Name	Year End[Latest]	Dividend-Amount (₹ in Crores)	Div. Yield-%[Latest]	Dividend-%[Latest]
ACC	201412	638.34	2.43	340
Adani Ports	201503	227.71	0.36	55
Ambuja Cem.	201412	774.61	2.19	250
Asian Paints	201503	585.12	0.75	610
Axis Bank	201503	1090.44	0.82	230
B H E L	201503	283.92	0.49	58
B P C L	201503	1626.94	2.78	225
Bajaj Auto	201503	1446.84	2.48	500
Bank of Baroda	201503	709.7	1.97	160
Bharti Airtel	201503	1539	0.98	77
Bosch	201503	266.9	0.33	850
Cairn India	201503	1687.31	4.21	90
Cipla	201503	160.59	0.28	100
Coal India	201503	13074.88	5.71	207
Dr Reddy's Labs	201503	340.8	0.57	400
GAIL (India)	201503	761.08	1.54	60
Grasim Inds	201503	165.33	0.5	180
H D F C	201503	2362.05	1.14	750
HCL Technologies	201406	700.27	0.67	500
HDFC Bank	201503	2005.2	0.78	400
Hero Motocorp	201503	1198.12	2.27	3000
Hind. Unilever	201503	3245.32	1.72	1500
Hindalco Inds.	201503	206.52	0.77	100
ICICI Bank	201503	2898.81	1.59	250
Idea Cellular	201503	226.94	0.34	6
IndusInd Bank	201503	212.01	0.45	40
Infosys	201503	5111	2.01	1190
ITC	201503	5009.7	1.92	625
Kotak Mah. Bank	201503	82.07	0.08	18
Larsen & Toubro	201503	1510.54	0.95	812.5
Lupin	201503	337.12	0.37	375
M & M	201503	745.31	1.01	240
Maruti Suzuki	201503	755.2	0.68	500
NTPC	201503	2061.38	1.7	25
O N G C	201503	8127.72	3.1	190
Power Grid Corpn	201503	1046.32	1.38	20
Punjab Natl.Bank	201503	612	2.29	165
Reliance Inds.	201503	2944	1.1	100
St Bk of India	201503	2613	1.31	350
Sun Pharma.Inds.	201403	310.67	0.26	150

TABLE 7.1

Co_Name	Year End[Latest]	Dividend-Amount (₹ in Crores)	Div. Yield-%[Latest]	Dividend-%[Latest]
Tata Motors	201503	0	0	0
Tata Power Co.	201503	351.99	1.69	1.3
Tata Steel	201503	776.97	2.52	80
TCS	201503	15473.87	3.1	7900
Tech Mahindra	201503	576.5	0.95	120
UltraTech Cem.	201503	246.96	0.31	90
Vedanta	201503	1215.6	2.16	410
Wipro	201503	2963.6	1.91	600
Yes Bank	201503	375.96	1.1	90
Zee Entertainmen	201503	216.1	0.66	225

Maturity. Like preferred stock, equity shares have no specified maturity; that is, it is perpetual. At times, however, companies repurchase shares of their common stock in the financial markets. Share buy-back might be undertaken when (1) the firm has excess cash but no good investment opportunities; (2) the price of the firm's stock is undervalued; or (3) management wants to gain more ownership control of the firm by repurchasing stock from *other* investors, thereby increasing the percentage owned by management. These are done subject to limits and conditions stiplulated under the Companies Act and rules framed thereunder.

©: iStock/Thinkstock

Priority to Assets and Earnings. Shareholders can be paid dividends only after interest on debt and preferred dividends are paid. In the event the company is liquidated, shareholders are last to receive any of the proceeds from the liquidation. Thus, as investors, the shareholders are last in line to receive any cash distributions from the corporation.

rights shares A provision that gives existing common stockholders the right to purchase new issues of common stock on a pro rata basis before any shares can be offered to other investors.

Control of the Firm (Voting Rights). The shareholders have the right to elect the firm's Board of directors, who in turn appoint the officers who manage the business. Shareholders also vote on proposals, mergers, and changes in the firm's charter. In a small firm, the major shareholder typically assumes the positions of Chairman of the board of directors. In a large, publicly owned firm, the managers typically own some shares, but their personal holdings are insufficient to provide voting control. Thus, if shareholders decide that the management team of a large, publicly owned company is not effective, they must join together when voting to remove the executives.

Provisions of the Companies Act give details on how shareholders can exercise control over the affairs of the company. Companies must hold elections of directors at their annual meetings. Each share normally has one vote, so the owner of 1,000 shares has 1,000 votes. Managers who do not have majority control (more than 50 percent of their firms' stock) are very much concerned about proxy fights and takeovers from other companies, and many attempt to get shareholder approval for changes in their corporate charters that would make takeovers more difficult.

Rights shares A **rights share** requires a firm to offer existing shareholders shares of a new share issue in proportion to their current ownership holdings before such shares can be offered to other investors. The purpose of the preemptive right is twofold. First, it protects the power of control of shareholders. If not for this safeguard, the management team of a corporation could prevent the shareholders from removing the managers from office by issuing a large number of additional shares and purchasing these shares themselves. Second, and more importantly, a preemptive right protects stockholders against the dilution of value that would occur if new shares were sold at relatively low prices.

7-1c Equity Instruments in International Markets

For the most part, the financial securities of companies in other countries are similar to those in the United States. Some differences do exist, however, as discussed in this section.

American Depository Receipts. In the United States, most foreign stock is traded through **American depository receipts (ADRs)**. ADRs are not foreign stocks; rather, they are certificates that represent ownership in stocks of foreign companies held in trust by a bank that created the ADRs and is located in the country where the stock is traded. ADRs provide U.S. investors with the ability to invest in foreign companies with less complexity and difficulty than might otherwise be possible.

In many cases, investors can purchase foreign securities directly, but such investments might be complicated by legal issues, the ability to take funds such as dividends out of the country, and translation of value and information into domestic terms. ADRs enable investors to participate in the international financial markets without having to bear risks greater than the risks associated with the corporations in which the investments are made. Each ADR certificate represents a certain number of shares of stock of a foreign company, and it entitles the owner to receive any dividends paid by the company in U.S. dollars. ADRs are traded in the stock markets in the United States, which often are more liquid than foreign markets. All financial information, including value, is denominated in dollars and stated in English, thereby eliminating potential problems with exchange rates and language translations.

Foreign Equity (Stock). The primary difference between stocks of foreign companies and stocks of U.S. companies is that U.S. regulations provide greater protection of stockholders' rights than do the regulations of most other countries. In the international markets, equity generally is referred to as either *Euro stock* or *Yankee stock*. With the exception of stock traded in the United States, any stock that is traded in a country other than the issuing company's home country is called **Euro stock**. Thus, if the stock of a Japanese company is sold in Germany, it would be considered a Euro stock. On the other hand, **Yankee stock** is issued by foreign companies and traded in the United States. For example, if a Japanese company sells its stock in the United States, it is termed a Yankee stock in the international markets.

7-2 Stock Valuation—The Dividend Discount Model (DDM)

A stock's value is found in the same manner as the values of other assets; by determining the present value of the expected future cash flow stream. The expected future cash flows that an investor receives as the result of purchasing a stock consist of dividends, which include regular dividends, *special* dividends (not regularly scheduled), or *liquidating* dividends (paid when a firm liquidates its assets and after its debts are paid).

Before we present the general stock valuation model, let's define some terms and notations that we use in the remainder of the chapter.

$\hat{D}_1$ = pronounced "D hat t"; the dividend stockholders expect to receive at the end of Year t. We designate expected value by placing a hat (^) above the variable. D_0 is the most recently paid dividend, which already has been paid; $\hat{D}_1$ is the next dividend that is expected to be paid at the end of this year; $\hat{D}_2$ is the dividend expected at the end of Year 2; and so forth. Because D_0 has already been paid, its value is known, and thus we do not place a hat over the D.

American depository receipts (ADRs) "Certificates" created by organizations such as banks; represent ownership in stocks of foreign companies that are held in trust by a bank located in the country where the stock is traded.

Euro stock Stock traded in countries other than the home country of the company, not including the United States.

Yankee stock Stock issued by foreign companies and traded in the United States.

$\hat{P}_0 =$	$V_s =$ the *actual* **market price (value)** of the stock today.
$\hat{P}_1 =$	the *expected* price of the stock at the end of each Year t. $\hat{P}_0$ is the **intrinsic**, or **theoretical, value** of the stock today as seen by a particular investor; 0 $\hat{P}_1$ is the price *expected* at the end of Year 1; and so on. Note that $\hat{P}_0$ is the intrinsic value of the stock today based on a particular investor's estimate of the stock's expected dividend stream and the riskiness of that stream. Whereas P_0 is fixed and is identical for all investors because it represents the actual price at which the stock currently can be purchased in the stock market, $\hat{P}_0$ can differ among investors depending on what they feel the firm (stock) actually is worth. An investor would buy the stock only if his or her estimate of $\hat{P}_0$ is equal to or greater than the current selling price, P_0; that is, the stock is a good investment if $\hat{P}_0 \geq P_0$.
$g =$	the expected **growth rate** in dividends as predicted by an average investor. If we assume that dividends are expected to grow at a constant rate, then g is also equal to the expected rate of growth in the stock's price (*capital gains*).
$r_s =$	the minimum acceptable, or **required, rate of return** on the stock that investors demand, considering both its riskiness and the returns available on other investments. The determinants of r_s are discussed in detail in Chapter 8.
$\dfrac{\hat{D}}{P_0} =$	the expected **dividend yield** on the stock during the coming year.
$\dfrac{\hat{P}_1 - P_0}{P_0} =$	the expected **capital gains yield** on the stock during the coming year; it is the expected change in the stock's value stated as a percentage.
$\hat{r}_s =$	the **expected rate of return**, which is the return that an investor who buys the stock *expects* to receive. The value of $\hat{r}_s$ could be above or below the required rate of return, r_s, but an investor should buy the stock only if $\hat{r}_s$ is equal to or greater than r_s; that is, a stock is considered a good investment if $\hat{r}_s \geq r_s$.

market price (value), P_0 The price at which a stock currently sells in the market.

intrinsic (theoretical) value, P The value of an asset that, in the mind of a particular investor, is justified by the facts; $\hat{P}_0$ can be different from the asset's current market price, its book value, or both.

intrinsic (theoretical) value, $\hat{P}$ The value of an asset that, in the mind of a particular investor, is justified by the facts; $\hat{P}_0$ can be different from the asset's current market price, its book value, or both.

growth rate, g The expected rate of change in dividends per share.

required rate of return, r_s The minimum rate of return that stockholders consider acceptable on a common stock.

dividend yield The next expected dividend divided by the current price of a share of stock, $\hat{D}_1/P_0$.

capital gains yield The change in price (capital gain) during a given year divided by the price at the beginning of the year; $(\hat{P}_1 - P_0)/P_0$.

expected rate of return, $\hat{r}_s$ The rate of return that an individual stockholder expects to receive on a common stock. It is equal to the expected dividend yield plus the expected capital gains yield,

$\hat{r}_s = \hat{D}_1/P_0 + (\hat{P}_1 - P_0)/P_0$.

7-2a Expected Dividends as the Basis for Stock Values

In our discussion of bonds, we found that the value of a bond is the present value of the interest payments over the life of the bond plus the present value of the bond's maturity (par) value. Stock prices are likewise computed as the present value of a stream of cash flows, and the basic stock valuation equation resembles the bond valuation equation shown in Chapter 6 (Equation 6.1).

To determine the cash flows that corporations provide to their stockholders, think of yourself as an investor who buys a stock with the intention of holding it (in your family) forever. In this case, all that you (and your heirs) will receive from your investment in the stock is a stream of dividends. Thus, the value of the stock today is calculated as the present value of an infinite stream of dividends (we assume the firm remains in business forever), which is depicted on a cash flow timeline as follows:

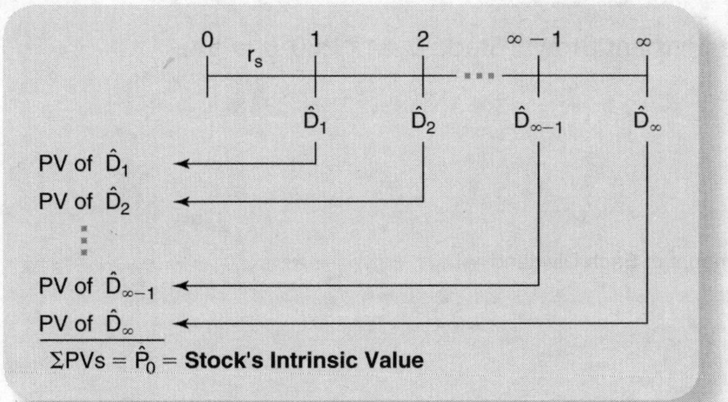

This cash flow timeline shows that the general equation to compute the value of a stock can be stated as Equation 7.1:

7.1

$$\text{Stock value} = V_s = \hat{P}_0 = \frac{\hat{D}_1}{(1+r_s)^1} + \cdots + \frac{\hat{D}_\infty}{(1+r_s)^\infty} = \sum_{t=1}^{\infty} \frac{\hat{D}_t}{(1+r_s)^t}$$

According to Equation 7.1, the value of a stock is determined by computing the present value of the dividends that the corporation is expected to pay stockholders during its life, which we generally assume is infinite for a going concern. From an investor's viewpoint, however, a stock's expected cash flows consist of two elements: (1) the dividends expected in each year the stock is held and (2) the price that is received when the stock is sold. So how do you determine the value of $\hat{P}_0$ when you plan to hold the stock for a specific (finite) period and then sell it, which is the typical scenario followed by investors? Unless the company is likely to be liquidated, and therefore disappear, *the value of the stock is still determined by Equation 7.1*. To see why, recognize that for any individual investor, the expected cash flows consist of expected dividends plus the expected price of the stock when it is sold. However, the sale price that the current investor receives depends on the dividends that the *future investor expects* to be paid by the company from that point forward. As a consequence, for all present and future investors, expected cash flows include *all* of the expected future dividends. Put another way, unless the corporation is liquidated or sold to another concern, *the cash flows that it provides stockholders will consist only of a stream of dividends*. Therefore, the value of a share of stock must equal the present value of the dividend stream that the company is expected to pay throughout its life.

The general validity of Equation 7.1 can be confirmed by considering the following scenario: Suppose you buy a stock and expect to hold it for one year. You will receive dividends during the year plus the value of the stock when you sell it at the end of the year. The value of the stock at the end of the year—that is, $\hat{P}_1$— equals the present value of the dividends during Year 2 plus the stock price at the end of that year, which in turn is determined as the present value of another set of future dividends and an even more distant stock price. This process can be continued forever, with the ultimate result being Equation 7.1.

Equation 7.1 is a generalized stock valuation model in the sense that over time the value of $\hat{D}_t$ can follow any pattern: $\hat{D}_t$ can be rising, falling, or constant, or it can even fluctuate randomly, and Equation 7.1 will still hold. Often, however, the projected stream of dividends follows a systematic pattern, in which case we can develop a simplified (easier to apply) version of the stock valuation model expressed in Equation 7.1. In the following sections, we show how to apply Equation 7.1 when the firm grows at a constant rate as well as when the firm's growth rate is not constant.

7-2b Valuing Stocks with Constant, or Normal, Growth (g)

Even though expected growth rates vary from company to company, for many firms it is not uncommon for investors to expect dividend growth to continue for the foreseeable future at about the same rate as that of the *nominal gross national product* (real GNP plus inflation). On this basis, we might expect the dividend of an average, or "normal," company to grow at a rate of 3–5 percent per year. Thus, if the last dividend paid by such a normal, or constant, growth company was D_0, the firm's dividend in any future Year t can be forecast as $\hat{D}_t = D_0$

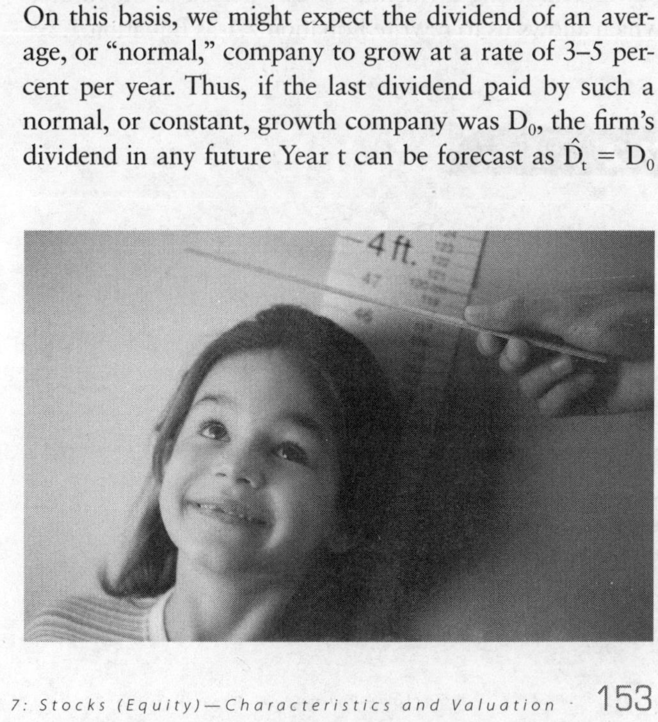

Stockbyte/Jupiter Images

FIGURE 7.1 Present Value of Dividends of a Constant Growth Stock: D_0 = ₹1.60, g = 5%, r_s = 20%

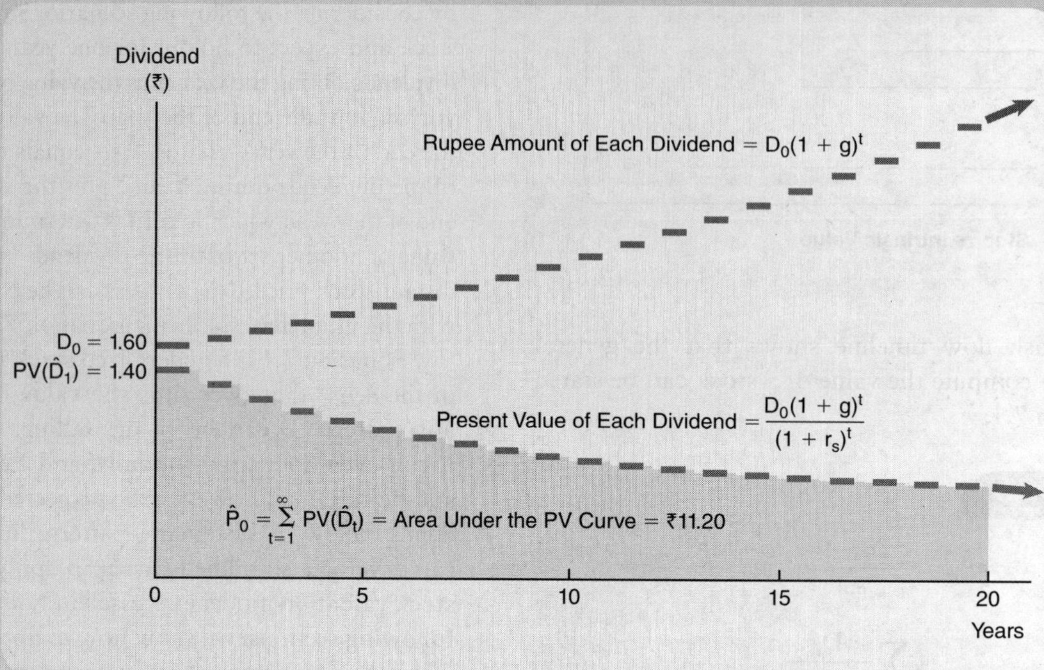

$(1 + g)^t$, where g is the constant expected rate of growth each year. For example, if a firm just paid a dividend of ₹1.60—that is, D_0 = ₹1.60—and investors expect a 5 percent growth rate, the estimated dividend one year hence would be $\hat{D}_1$ = ₹1.60(1.05) = ₹1.68; $\hat{D}_2$ would be ₹1.60$(1.05)^2$ = ₹1.764; and so on. When g is constant such that $g = g_1 = g_2 = \cdots = g_\infty$, we can use this method for estimating dividends for any period in the future, which allows us to rewrite Equation 7.1 as Equation 7.2:[1]

7.2

$$\hat{P}_0 = \frac{D_0(1+g)^1}{(1+r_s)^1} + \frac{D_0(1+g)^2}{(1+r_s)^2} + \cdots + \frac{D_0(1+g)^\infty}{(1+r_s)^\infty}$$

$$= \frac{D_0(1+g)}{r_s - g} = \frac{D_1}{r_s - g}$$

= value of a constant growth stock

constant growth model Also called the Gordon model, it is used to find the value of a stock that is expected to experience constant growth.

The form of the equation given in the second line of Equation 7.2, which is often referred to as the **constant growth model**, is merely a simplification of Equation 7.1 under the condition that dividends grow at a constant rate, g.[2] Note that for the simplified form of Equation 7.2 (shown in the second line) to yield meaningful results, r_s must be greater than g. In situations where $r_s < g$, the results are meaningless because the denominator in the simplified form of Equation 7.2 is negative—that is, $(r_s - g) < 0$—which gives a negative value for $\hat{P}_0$. $\hat{P}_0 < 0$ doesn't make sense in the world of finance.

Inserting values from our illustrative stock, we find that when investors require a 20 percent return, the value of the stock should be ₹11.20:

$$\hat{P}_0 = \frac{₹1.60(1.05)}{0.02 - 0.05} = \frac{₹1.68}{0.15} = ₹11.20$$

Figure 7.1 illustrates the concept underlying the valuation process for this constant growth stock. Dividends are growing at the rate g = 5%. Because $r_s > g$, however, the present value of each future dividend is declining. For example, the dividend in Year 1 is $\hat{D}_1 = D_0(1 + g)^1$

[1]The second line in Equation 7.2 is derived by applying the algebra of geometric progressions.

[2]The constant growth model as set forth in the last term of Equation 7.2 is often called the *Gordon model*, after Myron J. Gordon, who did much to develop and popularize it.

$= ₹1.60(1.05) = ₹1.68$. The present value of this dividend, discounted at 20 percent, is $PV(\hat{D}_1) = ₹1.68/(1.20)^1 = ₹1.40$. The dividend expected in Year 2 grows to $\hat{D}_2 = ₹1.68(1.05) = ₹1.764$, but the present value of this dividend falls to $PV(\hat{D}_2) = ₹1.225$. Continuing, $\hat{D}_3 = ₹1.8522$ and $PV(\hat{D}_3) = 1.0719$, and so on. As you can see, the expected future dividends are growing, but the present value of each successive dividend is declining because the dividend growth rate, 5 percent, is less than the rate used for discounting the dividends to the present, 20 percent.

If we summed the present values of each future dividend, this summation would equal the value of the stock, $\hat{P}_0$. When g is constant, this summation is equal to $\hat{D}_1/(r_s-g)$, as shown in Equation 7.2. Therefore, if we extended the lower step function curve in Figure 7.1 to infinity and added up the present values of all future dividends, the summation would be identical to the value given by solving Equation 7.2; that is, ₹11.20.

Growth in dividends occurs primarily as a result of growth in *earnings per share (EPS)*. Earnings growth, in turn, results from a number of factors, including the amount of earnings that is *reinvested*, or plowed back into the firm. If the firm's earnings are not all paid out as dividends—that is, if the firm retains some fraction of its earnings—the rupees of investment behind each share will increase over time, which should lead to growth in future earnings and dividends. On the other hand, when all earnings are paid out as dividends, the firm retains nothing for reinvestment; thus, everything else equal, the growth rate equals zero.

Special Case of Constant Growth: g = 0. Equation 7.2 is sufficiently general to encompass the case where $g = 0$; that is, there is no growth, so constant growth is equal to 0 percent. When $g = 0$, which is simply a special case of constant growth, the simplified form of Equation 7.2 becomes:

$$\hat{P}_0 = \frac{D_0(1+g)}{r_s - g} = \frac{D}{r_s}$$

We eliminated the subscript and the hat for D, because all future dividends will be same as the most recently paid dividend, which means that $D_0 = \hat{D}_1 = \hat{D}_2 = \cdots = \hat{D}_\infty = D$. This stream of dividends represents a perpetuity, and the equation given here is the same as the equation given in Chapter 4 to compute the present value of a perpetuity. This equation can be used to determine the value of preferred stock, because the constant preferred dividend represents a perpetuity.

Expected Rate of Return on a Constant Growth Stock. We can solve Equation 7.2 for r_s, again using the hat to denote that we are dealing with an expected rate of return (Equation 7.3):[3]

7.3

$$\begin{matrix}\text{Expected rate of return}\end{matrix} = \text{Expected dividend yield} + \text{Expected growth rate, or capital gains yield}$$

$$\hat{r}_s = \frac{\hat{D}_1}{P_0} + g$$

For example, imagine that you buy a stock for a price $P_0 = ₹11.20$, and that you expect the stock to pay a dividend $\hat{D}_1 = ₹1.68$ at the end of the year and to grow at a constant rate of $g = 5\%$ in the future. In this case, your expected rate of return will be 20 percent:

$$\hat{r}_s = \frac{₹1.68}{₹11.20} + 0.05 = 0.15 + 0.05 = 0.20 = 20.0\%$$

In this form, we see that $\hat{r}_s$ is the *expected total return* and that it consists of an *expected dividend yield*, $\hat{D}_1/P_0 = 15\%$, plus an *expected growth rate or capital gains yield*, $g = 5\%$.

Suppose we had conducted this analysis on January 2, 2014. In other words, $P_0 = ₹11.20$ is the January 2, 2014, stock price and $\hat{D}_1 = ₹1.68$ is the dividend expected at the end of 2014 (December 31). What would be the expected stock price at the end of 2014 (or the beginning of 2015)? We would again apply Equation 7.2, but this time we would use the expected 2015 dividend, $\hat{D}_2 = \hat{D}_1(1+g) = \hat{D}_{2015} = \hat{D}_{2014}(1+g) = ₹1.68\ (1.05) = ₹1.764$, and solve for $\hat{P}_1$.

$$\hat{P}_1 = \hat{P}_{1/2/15} = \frac{\hat{D}_{12/13/15}}{r_s - g} = \frac{₹1.764}{0.20 - 0.05} = ₹11.76$$

Notice that $\hat{P}_1 = ₹11.76$ is 5 percent greater than $\hat{P}_0$, the ₹11.20 price on January 2, 2014; that is, $\hat{P}_{1/2/15} = ₹11.20(1.05) = ₹11.76$. In this case, we would expect to make a capital gain of $₹0.56 = ₹11.76 - ₹11.20$ during the year, which represents a capital gains yield of 5 percent:

$$\text{Capital gains yield} = \frac{\text{Capital gain}}{\text{Beginning price}} = \frac{P_1 - P_0}{P_0}$$

[3]The r_s value of Equation 7.2 is a *required* rate of return. When we transform this equation to obtain Equation 7.3, we are finding an *expected* rate of return. Obviously, the transformation requires that $r_s = \hat{r}_s$. This equality holds if the stock market is in equilibrium, a condition discussed in Chapter 8.

$$\begin{matrix}\text{Expected} & & \text{Expected} & & \text{Expected growth} \\ \text{rate of} & = & \text{dividend} & + & \text{rate, or capital} \\ \text{return} & & \text{yield} & & \text{gains yield}\end{matrix}$$

$$= \frac{₹0.56}{₹11.20} = 0.05 = 5.0\%$$

Here P_0 represents the actual stock price at the beginning of the period, and $\hat{P}_1$ represents the expected price of the stock at the end of one period (one year in this case).

We could extend this analysis further, if desired. In each future year the expected capital gains yield would equal g = 5%, the expected dividend growth rate. Continuing, we could estimate the dividend yield in 2015 as follows:

$$\text{Dividend yield}_{2015} = \frac{\hat{D}_1}{P_0} = \frac{\hat{D}_{12/13/15}}{P_{1/2/15}} = \frac{₹1.764}{₹11.76}$$

$$= 0.15 = 15.0\%$$

We could also calculate the dividend yield for 2016, which would again be 15 percent. Thus, for a constant growth stock, the following conditions must hold:

1. The dividend is expected to grow forever at a constant rate, g. The stock price is expected to grow at this same rate, g. As a result, the expected capital gains yield is also constant, and it is equal to g.
2. The expected dividend yield is a constant, such that $\hat{D}_1/P_0, = \hat{D}_2/P_1, = \cdots = \hat{D}_\infty/P_{\infty-1}$.
3. The expected total rate of return, $\hat{r}_s$, is equal to the expected dividend yield plus the expected growth rate: $\hat{r}_s = \hat{D}_1/P_0 + g$.

We should clarify the meaning of the term *expected* here. It means expected in a probabilistic sense: the statistically expected outcome. Thus, if we say the growth rate is expected to remain constant at 5 percent, we mean that the best prediction for the growth rate in any future year is 5 percent. We do not literally expect the growth rate to be exactly equal to 5 percent in each future year. In this sense, the constant growth assumption is a reasonable one for many large, mature companies.

7-2c Valuing Stocks with Nonconstant Growth

Firms typically go through *life cycles*. During the early parts of their lives, their growth greatly exceeds that of the economy as a whole. Later, their growth matches the economy's growth. In the final stage of its life, a firm's growth lags behind that of the economy.[4] Automobile manufacturers in the 1920s, computer software firms such as Microsoft in the 1990s, and the Wi-Fi (which stands for *wi*reless *fi*delity) industry in the 2000s are examples of firms in the early part of their cycles. On the other hand, firms, such as those in the tobacco industry or coal industry, are currently in the waning stages of their life cycles. That is, their growth is not keeping pace with the general economic growth. (In some cases, their growth actually is negative.) Firms with growth rates that are not essentially the same each year are called **nonconstant growth** firms.

nonconstant growth The part of the life cycle of a firm in which its growth is either much faster or much slower than that of the economy as a whole.

Because it is applicable only when *all* the future dividends grow at a constant rate, g, Equation 7.2 cannot be used to estimate the value of a nonconstant growth stock. But we can easily estimate the value of a nonconstant growth stock if we assume that, at some point during its life, the firm stops growing at a nonconstant rate and begins to grow at a constant rate. With this assumption, we can follow these three steps to determine the current value of a nonconstant growth stock:

- **Step 1**—Start computing the dividends that are expected to be paid during the nonconstant growth period; continue computing dividends until you compute the last dividend that is affected by nonconstant growth. Using the investors' required rate of return, r_s, compute the present values of all the nonconstant growth dividends, and sum these present values.
- **Step 2**—Compute the first dividend that is affected by the constant, or normal, growth rate, and use this dividend to compute the value of the stock at the *end of the nonconstant growth period*. Because at this point all future dividends will grow at a constant rate, which we designate g_{norm}, we can use the modified version of Equation 7.2 shown in Equation 7.4 to compute the value of the stock at the end of the nonconstant growth period, $\hat{P}_t$:

7.4

$$\hat{P}_t = \frac{\left(\begin{matrix}\text{First constant} \\ \text{growth dividend}\end{matrix}\right)}{r_s - g_{norm}} = \frac{\hat{D}_t(1 + g_{norm})}{r_s - g_{norm}} = \frac{\hat{D}_{t+1}}{r_s - g_{norm}}$$

[4]The concept of a life cycle could be broadened to include a *product cycle*, which would include small start-up companies and large companies such as IBM that periodically introduce new products that boost sales and earnings. We should also mention *business cycles*, which alternately depress and boost sales and profits. The growth rate just after a major new product has been introduced, or just after a firm emerges from the depths of a recession, is likely to be much higher than the expected long-run average growth rate, which is the proper value to use for evaluating the project.

$\hat{D}_t$ is the last nonconstant growth dividend the firm is expected to pay, and $\hat{D}_{t+1}$ represents the first dividend that grows at the constant rate, g_{norm}. As a result, $\hat{P}_t$, which is the expected value of the stock in Year t, represents the value of all the dividends that are expected to be paid in Year t + 1 and beyond. That is, $\hat{P}_t$ represents the value of all the future constant growth dividends at the end of Year t because $\hat{D}_{t+1}$, $\hat{D}_{t+2}$, ... $\hat{D}_\infty$ are all dividends that grow at the same rate, g_{norm}.

After computing $\hat{P}_t$, find its present value: PV of $\hat{P}_t = \hat{P}_t/(1 + r_s)^t$.

- **Step 3**—To determine the current intrinsic value of the stock, add the present value of the nonconstant growth dividends computed in Step 1 to the present value of the future stock price computed in Step 2. In other words, $\hat{P}_0$ = (PV of nonconstant growth dividends) + (PV of $\hat{P}_t$).

To illustrate the valuation of a nonconstant growth stock using these steps, let's suppose that the dividends paid by a firm are expected to grow at a 20 percent rate for the next three years, and then the growth rate is expected to fall to 5 percent and remain at that level for the remainder of the firm's life. Clearly, the growth rate for this firm is not constant, because different growth rates are expected during the remainder of the firm's life (i.e., $g_1 = g_2 = g_3 = 20\%$, but $g_4 = g_5 = \cdots = g_\infty = 5\%$). In this example, even though the growth rate is not the same for all future years, the stock becomes a constant growth stock at the end the period of supernormal growth, which is at the end of Year 3 because, after that point in time, the firm grows at a constant rate forever.

To determine the current value of the stock for our example, let's assume that investors require a 15 percent return to invest in the company's stock. If the last (most recent) dividend paid by the company was ₹1.00, we can follow the steps outlined previously to find the current value of the stock.

- **Step 1**—Compute the values of the nonconstant growth dividends, and then compute the sum of the present values of these dividends. The computations and the results of this step are shown in the following table:

Year	Growth Rate, g_t	Dividend, $\hat{D}_t = \hat{D}_{t-1}(1 + g_t)$	(PV of $\hat{D}_t$) = $\hat{D}_t\,(1 + r_s)^t$
1	20.0%	₹1.2000 = ₹1.00(1.20)	₹1.0435 = ₹1.2000/(1.15)^1
2	20.0	1.4400 = 1.20(1.20)	1.0888 = 1.4400/(1.15)^2
3	20.0	1.7280 = 1.44(1.20)	1.1362 = 1.7280/(1.15)^3
			Σ(PV of $\hat{D}_t$) = ₹3.2685

- **Step 2**—Using Equation 7.4, compute the value of the stock at the end of the nonconstant growth period. In our example, because nonconstant growth ends after the Year 3 dividend, $\hat{D}_3$, is paid, we have

$$\hat{P}_3 = \frac{\hat{D}_3(1+g_{norm})}{r_s - g_{norm}} = \frac{\hat{D}4}{r_s - g_{norm}}$$

$$= \frac{₹1.7280(1.05)}{0.15-0.05} = \frac{₹1.8144}{0.10} = ₹18.1440$$

This result indicates that in Year 3 the value of the constant growth dividends $\hat{D}_4$, $\hat{D}_5$, ..., D_∞ is ₹18.14. In other words, the stock should be selling for ₹18.14 at the end of Year 3, after the last nonconstant growth dividend, $\hat{D}_3$, is paid.

Compute the present value of $\hat{P}_3$: (PV of $\hat{P}_3$) = ₹18.1440/(1.15)^3 = ₹11.9300.

- **Step 3**—To determine the current intrinsic value of the stock, sum the result of Step 1 and the result of Step 2. Thus, $\hat{P}_0$ = ₹3.2685 + ₹11.9300 = ₹15.1985 ≈ ₹15.20. Figure 7.2 shows the cash flow timeline with the actual cash flows and the results we found for our example. Note that at the end of the last year of nonconstant growth two cash flows are included: (1) the last nonconstant dividend, which is $\hat{D}_3$ in our example, and (2) the value of the stock after nonconstant growth ends, $\hat{P}_3$, which represents the value of the constant growth dividends that will be paid during the remainder of the firm's life, Year 4 through Year ∞ in our example.

If you think about the steps we followed to determine the value of the stock in our example, we can summarize the process of computing the intrinsic value of a nonconstant growth stock in simple terms: When valuing a nonconstant growth stock, assume that you buy the stock and hold it only for the nonconstant growth period, and then you sell the stock to another investor immediately after the last nonconstant growth dividend is paid. With this scenario, you would receive all of the nonconstant growth dividends ($\hat{D}_1$, $\hat{D}_2$, and D_3 in our example), and then you would sell all of the constant growth dividends to another investor (in our example, $\hat{P}_3$ represents all the future

FIGURE 7.2 Determining the Value of a Nonconstant Growth Stock

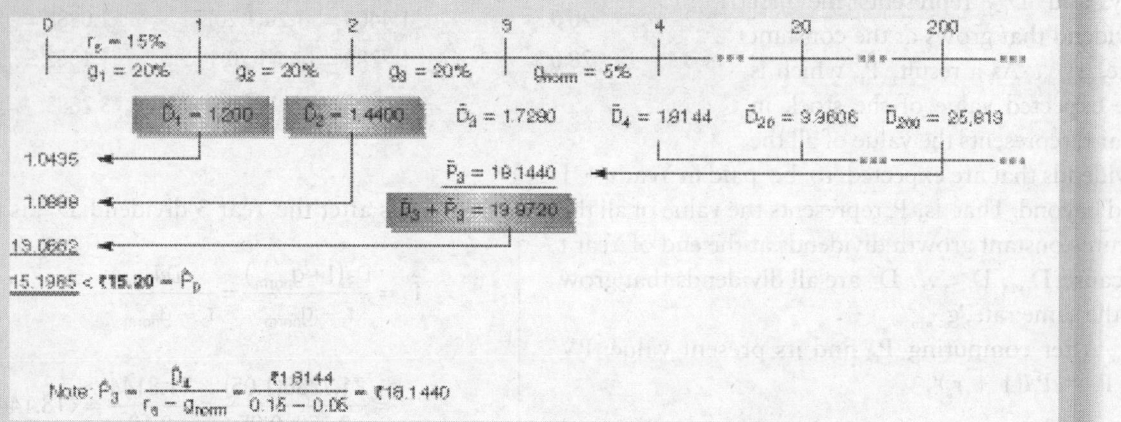

constant dividends valued at the end of the nonconstant growth period, Year 3). In this case, the value of the stock today is the present value of all of the future nonconstant growth dividends you receive from owning the stock plus the present value of the future price for which you can sell the stock when nonconstant growth ends.

To give a different perspective of the valuation process presented in Steps 1–3, let's assume that the same situation exists for the stock that we are currently evaluating, except investors expect the company to pay dividends for the next 50 years and then go bankrupt (at which point its stock is worthless) rather than continue to pay dividends forever. Table 7.2 shows the dividend that would be paid each year, as well as the present value of all of the dividends that would be paid during the 50-year period. Notice that the present value of the dividends equals ₹15.0326, which is about ₹0.17 less than the result we computed earlier (shown in Figure 7.2). Because the only difference between the result shown in Table 7.2 and the result shown in Figure 7.2 is that Table 7.2 excludes the dividends that would be received beyond Year 50, ₹0.17 represents the present value of the dividends from Year 51 to infinity. This is a small value.

Clearly, it is very easy to compute the dividends and their present values for 50 years (or even 1,000 years), using a spreadsheet if we know the annual growth rates. However, it is easier to compute the dividends during the nonconstant growth period, use Equation 7.4 to compute the value of the stock at the point when nonconstant growth ends, and then add the present values of these future cash flows to determine $\hat{P}_0$ (as illustrated in Figure 7.2).

P/E ratio The current market price of a stock divided by the earnings per share; P_0/EPS_0.

7-3 Other Stock Valuation Methods

Investors often use more than one method to determine (estimate) the value of a stock. In this section, we describe two other valuation methods that are popular with investors. It is important to keep in mind that to apply any model literally, certain assumptions must be met. There are few, if any, instances where all the assumptions associated with a model are met in the real world. Therefore, models such as those described in this chapter should be used as guidance when determining the value of a stock; that is, the results should not be taken to mean that a stock should be selling for precisely the same price that a model predicts.

7-3a Valuation Using P/E Ratios

Many analysts consider the P/E ratio, or *earnings multiplier*, to be a good indicator of the value of a stock in relative terms. The **P/E ratio** mentioned here is the same as that described in Chapter 2; it is computed by dividing the current market price per share, P_0, by the firm's earnings per share, EPS_0. The higher (lower) the P/E ratio, the more (less) investors are willing to pay for each rupee earned by the firm.

TABLE 7.2 Present Value of the Dividends Received from a Stock Investment During a 50-Year Period

Year	Growth Rate, g_t	Dividend $\hat{D}_t = \hat{D}_{t-1}(1+g_t)$	PV of Dividend $= \hat{D}_t/(1.15)^t$	Year	Growth Rate, g_t	Dividend $\hat{D}_t = \hat{D}_{t-1}(1+g_t)$	PV of Dividend $= \hat{D}_t/(1.25)^t$
1	20	1.2000	1.0435	26	5	5.3076	0.1402
2	20	1.4400	1.0888	27	5	5.5730	0.1280
3	20	1.7280	1.1362	28	5	5.8516	0.1169
4	5	1.8144	1.0374	29	5	6.1442	0.1067
5	5	1.9051	0.9472	30	5	6.4514	0.0974
6	5	2.0004	0.8648	31	5	6.7740	0.0890
7	5	2.1004	0.7896	32	5	7.1127	0.0812
8	5	2.2054	0.7210	33	5	7.4683	0.0742
9	5	2.3157	0.6583	34	5	7.8417	0.0677
10	5	2.4315	0.6010	35	5	8.2338	0.0618
11	5	2.5530	0.5488	36	5	8.6455	0.0565
12	5	2.6807	0.5010	37	5	9.0778	0.0515
13	5	2.8147	0.4575	38	5	9.5317	0.0471
14	5	2.9555	0.4177	39	5	10.0083	0.0430
15	5	3.1032	0.3814	40	5	10.5087	0.0392
16	5	3.2584	0.3482	41	5	11.0341	0.0358
17	5	3.4213	0.3179	42	5	11.5858	0.0327
18	5	3.5924	0.2903	43	5	12.1651	0.0299
19	5	3.7720	0.2650	44	5	12.7734	0.0273
20	5	3.9606	0.2420	45	5	13.4120	0.0249
21	5	4.1586	0.2210	46	5	14.0826	0.0227
22	5	4.3666	0.2017	47	5	14.7868	0.0208
23	5	4.5849	0.1842	48	5	15.5261	0.0189
24	5	4.8141	0.1682	49	5	16.3024	0.0173
25	5	5.0549	0.1536	50	5	17.1175	0.0158
							$\sum$ PV of Dividends = ₹15.0326

Information: Last dividend payment, D_0 = ₹1.00
Dividend growth rates: $g_{super} = g_1 = g_2 = g_3 = 20\%$; $g_{norm} = g_4 = \cdots = g_{50} = 5\%$
Required rate of return, $r_s = 15\%$

In a sense, the P/E ratio gives an indication of a stock's "payback period." For example, if a firm's P/E ratio is 12, then, assuming that the firm distributes all of its earnings as dividends, it would take 12 years for an investor to recover his or her initial investment. If we view P/E ratios as measures of payback, all else equal, lower earnings multipliers are better. In fact, it has been suggested that firms with low P/E ratios relative to other firms in their industries can earn above-average risk-adjusted returns, and vice versa. The rationale is that if a company's P/E ratio is too low relative to that of similar firms, its earnings have not been fully captured in the existing stock value; thus the price will be bid up. Similarly, if the firm's P/E ratio is too high relative to that of similar firms, the market has overvalued its current earnings, and its stock price must decrease.

Generally, investors examine whether a stock's P/E ratio is higher or lower than "normal" to decide whether the price is too high or too low. If we can determine what value is appropriate for the P/E ratio, we can then multiply that value by the firm's EPS to estimate the appropriate stock price. Determining the appropriate P/E requires judgment, so analysts do not always agree as to what the preferred P/E ratio for a firm should be.

7-3b Evaluating Stocks Using the Economic Value Added Approach

Economic value added (EVA) is an approach, developed by Stern Stewart Management Services, that is based on the concept that the earnings generated by a company must be sufficient to compensate investors who provide its funds. EVA measures by how much a firm's economic value is increased based on the decisions it makes. The change in a firm's economic value, or its EVA, is determined by decreasing its after-tax operating income by the costs associated with both the debt and the equity issued by the firm. Equation 7.5 gives the basic EVA equation:

7.5

$$\text{Economic value added} = \text{EVA} = \text{EBIT}\,(1 - \text{T}) - \left[\left(\begin{array}{c}\text{Average cost}\\ \text{of funds}\end{array}\right) \times \left(\begin{array}{c}\text{Invested}\\ \text{capital}\end{array}\right)\right]$$

In this equation, EBIT represents the earnings before interest and taxes as reported on the firm's income statement, T is the firm's marginal tax rate, "Invested capital" is the amount of funds provided by investors (both debt and equity), and "Average cost of funds" is the average interest rate, or percentage return, that the firm pays for its debt and equity (invested capital). We discuss the cost of funds in detail in Chapter 11. For the purposes of our discussion here, we simply define the percentage cost of funds as the *average* rate of return that must be paid to investors—both bondholders and stockholders—who provide funds to the firm. As a result, when EVA is greater than zero, the firm's value should increase because its operating earnings exceed the amount that must be paid to investors who have provided the funds that the firm uses to finance its assets.

To illustrate the use of the EVA approach, suppose the following information has been gathered from the financial statements of a company:

Operating income, EBIT	₹15.0 million
Total invested capital = long-term debt + equity	₹60.0 million
Marginal tax rate	40%
Number of outstanding shares of common stock	2.5 million
Average cost of funds	7.0%

If we apply Equation 7.5, we find the company's EVA as follows:

EVA = [₹15.0 million × (1 – 0.4)] – (0.07 × ₹60.0 million)

= ₹9.0 million – ₹4.2 million – ₹4.8 million

According to this computation, the EVA approach suggests that investors demanded ₹4.2 million in compensation for providing funds to the firm. Because the firm generated ₹9 million in net operating profits after taxes to cover the compensation associated with financing, we can conclude that it was able to use its funds to earn higher returns than those demanded by investors. Thus, the firm should be attractive to investors. The company's stock should be especially attractive to common stockholders, because they have the right to any amounts earned in excess of their required rate of return.

We can use the EVA concept to determine the maximum dividend per share that can be paid to stockholders before we would expect the firm's current value to be threatened. The computation is simple: Divide the computed EVA by the number of outstanding shares. For our illustrative firm, the maximum dividend suggested by EVA is ₹1.92 = (₹4.8 million) ÷ (2.5 million shares).

The EVA approach has gained attention as a valuation technique because it is based on the fundamental principle of wealth maximization, which should be the goal of every firm. Prospective EVA users should be aware that to obtain a precise estimate of the economic performance of a firm, it might be necessary to make many adjustments to the accounting numbers contained in the firm's financial statements. For instance, Stern Stewart indicates that it has identified more than 160 possible adjustments to accounting values contained in financial statements that can be made to provide a better estimate of the true economic value of a firm's performance. Knowing how to apply such adjustments often takes considerable expertise.

7-4 Changes in Stock Prices

Stock prices are not constant: They sometimes change significantly, as well as very quickly. For example, on October 19, 1987, the Dow Jones Industrial Average (DJIA) dropped 508 points, and the average stock lost about 23 percent of its value in just one day. Some stocks lost more than half of their values on that day. More recently, the DJIA decreased by nearly 1,880 points the week of October 6, 2008, through October 10, 2008; the average stock lost nearly 25 percent of its value during the week. On the following Monday, October 13, 2008, however, the DJIA rebounded, increasing by almost 940 points and the value of the average stock increased by more than 11 percent. To see how such changes can occur, assume you own the stock of a company that just paid a ₹2.50 dividend (D_0 = ₹2.50). The company's growth has been constant for many years, so it is expected that the company will continue to grow at the same rate, 6 percent, in the future (g = 6%). Currently, investors require a return equal to 15 percent for such investments. Therefore, the expected value of the company's stock should be:

$$\hat{P}_0 = \frac{\text{₹}2.50(1.60)}{0.15 - 0.06} = \frac{\text{₹}2.65}{0.09} = \text{₹}29.44$$

Now consider what would happen to the stock price if the value of any of the variables used to compute the current price changes. For instance, how would the price be affected if investors demand a higher rate of return—say, 18 percent? If we change the value for r_s to 18 percent in the previous equation, we find that the expected value of the stock becomes:

$$\hat{P}_0 = \frac{\text{₹}2.50(1.60)}{0.18 - 0.06} = \frac{\text{₹}2.65}{0.12} = \text{₹}22.08$$

The new price is lower (−25%) because investors demand a higher return for receiving the same future cash flows.

How will the price change if the future cash flows differ from the expected cash flows, but the required return is 15 percent? Consider the effect if the company's growth rate is 4 percent rather than 6 percent:

$$\hat{P}_0 = \frac{\text{₹}2.50(1.04)}{0.15 - 0.04} = \frac{\text{₹}2.60}{0.11} = \text{₹}23.64$$

Again, the new price is lower (−19.7%) than the original price of ₹29.44. In this case, however, the price is lower because the cash flows that the stock is expected to provide are smaller than previously expected.

From this simple example, you should have concluded that changes in stock prices occur for two reasons: (1) investors change the rates of return they require to invest in stocks and (2) expectations about the cash flows associated with stocks change. From the preceding example, we can generalize about how such changes affect stock prices: *Stock prices move opposite changes in rates of return, but they move in the same direction as changes in cash flows expected from the stock in the future.* Therefore, if investors demand higher (lower) returns to invest in stocks, then prices should fall (increase). If investors expect their investments to generate lower (higher) future cash flows, then prices should also fall (increase).

Of course, we generally do not know (cannot compute) the "true" (intrinsic) price of a stock, because it is unlikely that (1) the company's future growth pattern is exactly as analysts forecast and (2) all the assumptions of the model that is used to estimate the equilibrium value are met. However, the various valuation techniques we discussed in this chapter give some indication of a stock's *equilibrium*, or intrinsic, value.

Evidence suggests that stocks—especially those of large NYSE companies—adjust rapidly to disequilibrium situations. Consequently, equilibrium ordinarily exists for any given stock, and, in general, required returns (r) and expected returns ($\hat{r}$) are equal. Stock prices certainly change, sometimes violently and rapidly, but these changes simply reflect different conditions and expectations. We discuss stock market equilibrium in greater detail in Chapter 8.

KEY STOCK VALUATION CONCEPTS

To conclude this chapter, we summarize some stock valuation concepts that were discussed.

- The current value of a stock is based on the stream of dividends investors expect the firm to pay during its life (generally considered to be infinite).
  - a. The current value of a stock is computed as the present value of the dividends the stock is expected to generate during the remainder of its life. If a company's dividends grow at a constant rate, its stock can be valued using a simple equation: $\hat{P}_0 = [D_0(1 + g)]/(r_s - g)$.
  - b. When a person sells stock that he or she owns, the investor who purchases the stock pays for the dividends that the stock is expected to generate in the future (during the remainder of the firm's life).
- Everything else equal, if the dividends that are expected to be paid in the future increase, the value of a stock also increases.
- Everything else equal, when investors demand higher rates of return—that is, when market rates increase—stock prices decrease. In other words, to earn higher rates of return, investors lower the prices they are willing to pay for their investments (stocks in this case).
- Investors often use P/E ratios to estimate the intrinsic values of stocks. The value of a stock can be estimated by multiplying a "normal" P/E ratio by the firm's earnings per share (EPS).
- The economic value added (EVA) approach can be used to determine whether the actions taken by a firm are sufficient to generate the funds that are needed to pay investors (stockholders and bondholders) who provide funds to the firm. If the firm generates more operating profits than are needed to pay its taxes and cover its costs of funds, then its economic value increases.

MULTIPLE CHOICE QUESTIONS

1. The real owners of a company are:

a. Preference shareholders

b. Equity shareholders

c. Lenders until the debt is repaid and equity shareholders

d. Preference shareholders and equity shareholders

2. When profits are sufficient to repay debt interest,

a. Preference shareholders get the next priority up to the promised dividends

b. Preference shareholders get the next priority up to 10%

c. Equity shareholders and preference shareholders share the rest in proportion to the holding percentage

d. None of the above

3. If the company goes bankrupt,

a. Preference shareholders get the next priority up to the promised dividends

b. Preference shareholders get the next priority up to 10%

c. Equity shareholders and preference shareholders share the rest in proportion to the holding percentage

d. None of the above

4. When the profits are not sufficient to repay debt interest,

a. Lenders, preference shareholders and equity shareholders share whatever is there in proportion to their holding percentage

b. Lenders, preference shareholders and equity shareholders share whatever is there in equal proportion

c. Lenders and preference shareholders get this in equal proportion

d. Debt gets priority and the entire amount is paid to the lenders

5. The following stakeholders have voting rights:

a. Equity holders

b. Preference shareholders

c. Lenders

d. Both a and b

6. A convertible preference share can be
   a. Converted to equity at any time chosen by the preference shareholder
   b. Converted at a time to be decided by the company
   c. Converted after all debt obligations have been met
   d. This depends on the terms of issue of preference shares
7. The dividend discount model assumes
   a. A growing perpetuity
   b. A simple perpetuity
   c. A no-growth stream
   d. None of the above
8. In a constant growth model:
   a. The growth rate is higher than the discount rate
   b. The discount rate is higher than the growth rate
   c. It can be either way
   d. Growth rate has to be equal to discount rate
9. The PE ratio involves:
   a. Calculating the price as a ratio of EBIT
   b. Calculating the price as a ratio of PAT
   c. Calculating the price as a ratio of sales
   d. None of the above
10. The PE ratio must be:
   a. The same across all major companies in an industry
   b. The same across all companies – major and minor – in an industry
   c. Higher for major companies than for the minor companies
   d. Depends on a variety of factors

Answers:

1.	(d)	2.	(a)	3.	(a)	4.	(d)	5.	(d)
6.	(d)	7.	(a)	8.	(b)	9.	(d)	10.	(d)

PROBLEMS

For more problems, login to CourseMate for CFIN at CengageBrain.com

7–1 One year ago, Prakash bought XYZ Computer common stock for ₹20 per share. Today the stock is selling for ₹19 per share. During the year, Prakash received four dividend payments, each in the amount of ₹0.20 per share. (a) What rate of return did Prakash earn during the year? (b) What were the (1) dividend yield and (2) the capital gains yield associated with the stock for the year?

7–2 Last year, Nema Saran bought one share of common stock for ₹950. During the year, Nema Saran received a ₹47.50 dividend. Earlier today, she sold the stock for ₹988. (a) What rate of return did Nema Saran earn on her investment? (b) What were the (1) dividend yield and (2) the capital gains yield associated with holding the stock?

7–3 Teji Center's (TC) preferred stock, which has a par value equal to ₹110 per share, pays an annual dividend equal to 9 percent of the par value. If investors require a 15 percent return to purchase TC's preferred stock, what is the stock's market value?

7–4 The Kush Company's preferred stock pays an annual dividend equal to ₹16.50. If investors demand a return equal to 11 percent to purchase Kush Company's preferred stock, what is its market value?

7–5 Dekh-Nai-Saktha Telecommunications has preferred stock outstanding with a par value of ₹40 per share that pays an annual dividend equal to 5 percent. (a) If investors who purchase similar investments require a 10 percent return, what is the market value of preferred stock? (b) What would be the market value of the stock if investors require an 8 percent return?

7–6 Your broker offers to sell you shares of Nithya & Company common stock, which paid a dividend of ₹2 *yesterday*. You expect the dividend to grow at a rate of 5 percent per year into perpetuity. If the appropriate rate of return for the stock is 12 percent, what is the market value of Nithya & Company stock?

7–7 Archana Ski Resort has grown at a constant rate, which equals 4 percent, for as long as it has been in business. This growth rate is expected to continue long into the future. A couple of days ago, Archana Ski Resort paid common stockholders a dividend equal to ₹3 per share. If investors require a 10 percent rate of return to purchase Archana Ski Resort's common stock, what is the market value of its common stock?

7-8 Since it started business 10 years ago, Acha Company has paid a constant ₹1.20 per share dividend to its common stockholders. Next year and every year thereafter, the company plans to increase the dividend at a constant rate equal to 2.5 percent per year. If investors require a 15 percent rate of return to purchase Acha's common stock, what is the market value of its common stock?

7-9 Suppose your company is expected to grow at a constant rate of 6 percent long into the future. In addition, its dividend yield is expected to be 8 percent. If your company expects to pay a dividend equal to ₹1.06 per share at the end of the year, what is the value of your firm's stock?

7-10 Prem Company's stock is currently selling for ₹19.50 per share. At the end of the year, the company plans to pay a dividend equal to ₹2.34 per share. For the remainder of the company's life, dividends are expected to grow at a constant rate, and investors are expected to require a 16 percent return to invest in Prem's stock. What should be the value of Prem's stock five years from now?

7-11 Since it has been in business, Phaneesh Jewelry has never paid a dividend. The company will not pay a dividend at the end of this year. However, two years from today—at the end of Year 2—Phaneesh Jewelry expects to pay a dividend equal to ₹0.50 per share, which it plans to increase by 6 percent each year thereafter for the remainder of the company's life. If investors require a 14 percent rate of return to purchase its common stock, what should be the market value of Phaneesh Jewelry stock today?

7-12 Mitra Company has never paid a dividend, and there are no plans to pay dividends during the next three years. But, in four years—that is, at the end of Year 4—the company expects to start paying a dividend equal to ₹3 per share. This same dividend will be paid for the remainder of Mitra Company's existence. If investors require a 10 percent rate of return to purchase the company's common stock, what should be the market value of Mitra Company's stock today?

7-13 Since it has been in business, Asan Company has paid a ₹1 per share annual dividend. The company plans to pay a ₹1 dividend for the next two years. Beginning in three years, however, Asan Company plans to increase the dividend by 8 percent each year for the remainder of the company's life. If investors require a 17 percent rate of return to purchase Asan Company's common stock, what should be the market value of its stock today?

7-14 Phool Company has never paid a dividend. But, the company plans to start paying dividends in two years—that is, at the end of Year 2. The first dividend is expected to equal ₹2 per share. The second dividend and every dividend thereafter are expected to grow at a 5 percent rate. If investors require a 15 percent rate of return to purchase Phool's common stock, what should be the market value of its stock today?

7-15 Excellent Artifacts has not paid a dividend during the past 10 years. However, at the end of this year, the company plans to pay a ₹1.50 dividend and a ₹2 dividend the following year (Year 2). Starting in three years, the dividend will begin to grow by 5 percent each year for as long as the firm is in business. If investors require an 11 percent rate of return to purchase Excellent Artifacts' common stock, what should be the market value of its stock today?

7-16 Smaran Jewelers expects to pay dividends (per share) of ₹0.60, ₹0.90, ₹2.40, and ₹3.50 during the next four years. Beginning in the fifth year, the dividend is expected to grow at a rate of 4 percent indefinitely. If investors require a 20 percent return to purchase Smaran's stock, what is the current value of the company's stock?

7-17 Ganaras Motorcars common stock normally sells for 19 times its earnings; that is, its P/E ratio equals 19. If GM's earnings per share are ₹3.70, what should be its stock price under normal circumstances?

7-18 For the past 15 years, the P/E ratio of North/South Travel has been between 28 and 30. If North/South's earnings per share equal ₹4, in what price range would you estimate its stock should be selling?

7-19 RJS generated ₹65,000 *net* income this year. The firm's financial statements also show that its interest expense was ₹40,000, its marginal tax rate was 35 percent, and its invested capital was ₹800,000. If its average cost of funds is 12 percent, what was RJS's economic value added (EVA) this year?

7-20 Bacha Beer Brewers (BBB) just announced that the current fiscal year's *net* income was ₹1.2 million. BBB's marginal tax rate is 40 percent, its interest expense for the year was ₹1.5 million, it has ₹8 million of invested capital, and its average cost of funds was 10 percent. What is BBB's economic value added (EVA) for the current year?

Stocks (Equity)—Characteristics and Valuation

Learning Outcomes

LO.1 Explain what equity is and identify some of the features and characteristics of (a) preferred stock and (b) common stock.

- Equity in a corporation comes in two forms: (1) preferred stock and (2) common stock.
- Some of the characteristics that are associated with preferred stock include (1) fixed dividend payment, (2) no maturity, (3) cash dividends that are paid prior to distributions to common stockholders, and (4) no voting rights. Some preferred stock (1) is convertible into the firm's common stock; (2) is callable by the firm; or (3) has a sinking fund, which permits the firm to repurchase and retire a preferred issue.
- Some of the characteristics of common stock include (1) dividends that, if paid, are distributed to common stockholders after interest is paid to bondholders and preferred stock dividends are paid; (2) no maturity date; (3) voting rights, which allow common stockholders to elect the firm's board of directors; and (4) in some common stock issues, a preemptive right, which requires the firm to offer existing stockholders shares of a new stock issue before offering them to other investors.

LO.2 Describe how stock prices (values) are determined when (a) dividends grow at a constant rate and (b) dividend growth is nonconstant.

- The value of a common stock is determined by computing the present value of the cash distributions (dividends) that the firm is expected to pay during its life.
- When a firm is expected to grow at a constant rate long into the future, the value of its stock can be computed using the constant growth dividend discount model.
- When a firm is expected to experience nonconstant growth in the future, to compute the value of its stock, (1) compute each dividend that grows at a nonconstant rate; (2) assume that the firm will begin to grow at a constant rate at some point in the future so that the constant growth model can be applied to determine the value of the stock at that time; (3) compute present values of the nonconstant dividends and the future stock price; and (4) sum the results.

LO.3 Describe some approaches (techniques) other than strict application of time value of money models that investors use to value stocks.

- Investors also evaluate stocks using P/E ratios and the economic value added (EVA) approach.
- The P/E ratio is an earnings multiplier that can be used to estimate a stock's current value by multiplying a benchmark, or "normal," P/E ratio by the firm's earnings per share (EPS).
- The EVA approach recognizes that to increase its value, the firm must produce earnings that are sufficient to cover the cost of the funds investors (bondholders and stockholders) provide.

LO.4 Identify factors that affect stock prices.

- Stock prices fluctuate continuously because conditions in the financial markets change. Investors react to changing market conditions by altering their expectations of (1) the risk associated with the investment, which affects the return that they require to purchase a stock, and (2) the cash distributions that the firm will make in the future, which are dependent on the firm's future growth rate(s). If investors require a return that exceeds the return they expect the firm to generate, they will not purchase the company's stock or they will sell the shares that they own. Such activity will tend to lower the price of the stock, and thus increase its expected return. The opposite reaction will occur if investors' expected return is greater than their required return.

CHAPTER 7 REVIEW

Chapter 7 Key Stocks Valuation Concepts

- The current value of a stock is based on the stream of dividends investors expect the firm to pay during its life (generally considered to be infinite).
  - The current value of a stock is computed as the present value of the dividends the stock is expected to generate during the remainder of its life. If a company's dividends grow at a constant rate, its stock can be valued using a simple equation: $P_0 = [D_0(1 + g)]/(r_s - g)$.
  - When a person sells stock that he or she owns, the investor who purchases the stock pays for the dividends that the stock is expected to generate in the future (during the remainder of the firm's life).
- Everything else equal, if the dividends that are expected to be paid in the future increase, the value of a stock also increases.
- Everything else equal, when investors demand higher rates of return—that is, when market rates increase—stock prices decrease. In other words, to earn higher rates of return, investors lower the prices they are willing to pay for their investments (stocks in this case).
- Investors often use P/E ratios to estimate the intrinsic values of stocks. The value of a stock can be estimated by multiplying a "normal" P/E ratio by the firm's existing earnings per share (EPS).
- The economic value added (EVA) approach can be used to determine whether the actions taken by a firm are sufficient to generate the funds that are needed to pay investors (stockholders and bondholders) who provide funds to the firm. If the firm generates more operating profits than are needed to pay taxes and cover its costs of funds, then its economic value increases.

Key Terms

LO.1

cumulative dividends A protective feature on preferred stock that requires preferred dividends previously not paid to be disbursed before any common stock dividends can be paid. *p. 109*

call premium The amount in excess of par value that a company must pay when it calls a security. *p. 110*

income stocks Stocks of firms that traditionally pay large, relatively constant dividends each year. *p. 110*

growth stocks Stocks that generally pay little or no dividends so as to retain earnings to help fund growth opportunities. *p. 110*

proxy A document giving one person the authority to act for another; typically it gives him or her the power to vote shares of common stock. *p. 111*

preemptive right A provision in the corporate charter or bylaws that gives existing common stockholders the right to purchase new issues of common stock on a pro rata basis. *p. 111*

American depository receipts (ADRs) "Certificates" created by organizations such as banks; represent ownership in stocks of foreign companies that are held in trust by a bank located in the country where the stock is traded. *p. 112*

Euro stock Stock traded in countries other than the home country of the company, not including the United States. *p. 113*

Yankee stock Stock issued by foreign companies and traded in the United States. *p. 113*

LO.2

market price (value), P_0 The price at which a stock sells in the market. *p. 113*

intrinsic (theoretical) value, $\hat{P}_0$ The value of an asset that, in the mind of a particular investor, is justified by the facts; $\hat{P}_0$ can be different from the asset's current market price, its book value, or both. *p. 113*

growth rate, g The expected rate of change in dividends per share. *p. 113*

required rate of return, r_s The minimum rate of return on a common stock that stockholders consider acceptable. *p. 113*

dividend yield The expected dividend divided by the current price of a share of stock, $\hat{D}_1/P_0$. *p. 113*

capital gains yield The change in price (capital gain) during a given year divided by the price at the beginning of the year, $(\hat{P}_1 - P_0)/P_0$. *p. 113*

expected rate of return, $\hat{r}_s$ The rate of return that an individual stockholder expects to receive on a common stock. It is equal to the expected dividend yield plus the expected capital gains yield, $\hat{r}_s = \hat{D}_1/P_0 + (\hat{P}_1 - P_0)/P_0$. *p. 113*

constant growth model Also called the Gordon model, it is used to find the value of a stock that is expected to experience constant growth. *p. 115*

nonconstant growth The part of the life cycle of a firm in which its growth is either much faster or much slower than that of the economy as a whole. *p. 117*

LO.3

P/E ratio The current market price of a stock divided by the earnings per share; P_0/EPS_0. *p. 120*

economic value added (EVA) An analytical method that seeks to evaluate the earnings generated by a firm to determine whether they are sufficient to compensate the suppliers of funds—both the bondholders and the stockholders. *p. 120*

CHAPTER 8

Risk and Rates of Return

Learning Outcomes

LO.1 Explain what it means to take risk when investing.

LO.2 Compute the risk and return of an investment, and explain how the risk and return of an investment are related.

LO.3 Identify relevant and irrelevant risk, and explain how irrelevant risk can be reduced.

LO.4 Describe how to determine the appropriate reward—that is, rate of return—that investors should earn for purchasing an investment.

LO.5 Describe actions that investors take when the return they require to purchase an investment is different from the return they expect the investment to produce.

LO.6 Identify different types of risk, and classify each as relevant or irrelevant with respect to determining an investment's required rate of return.

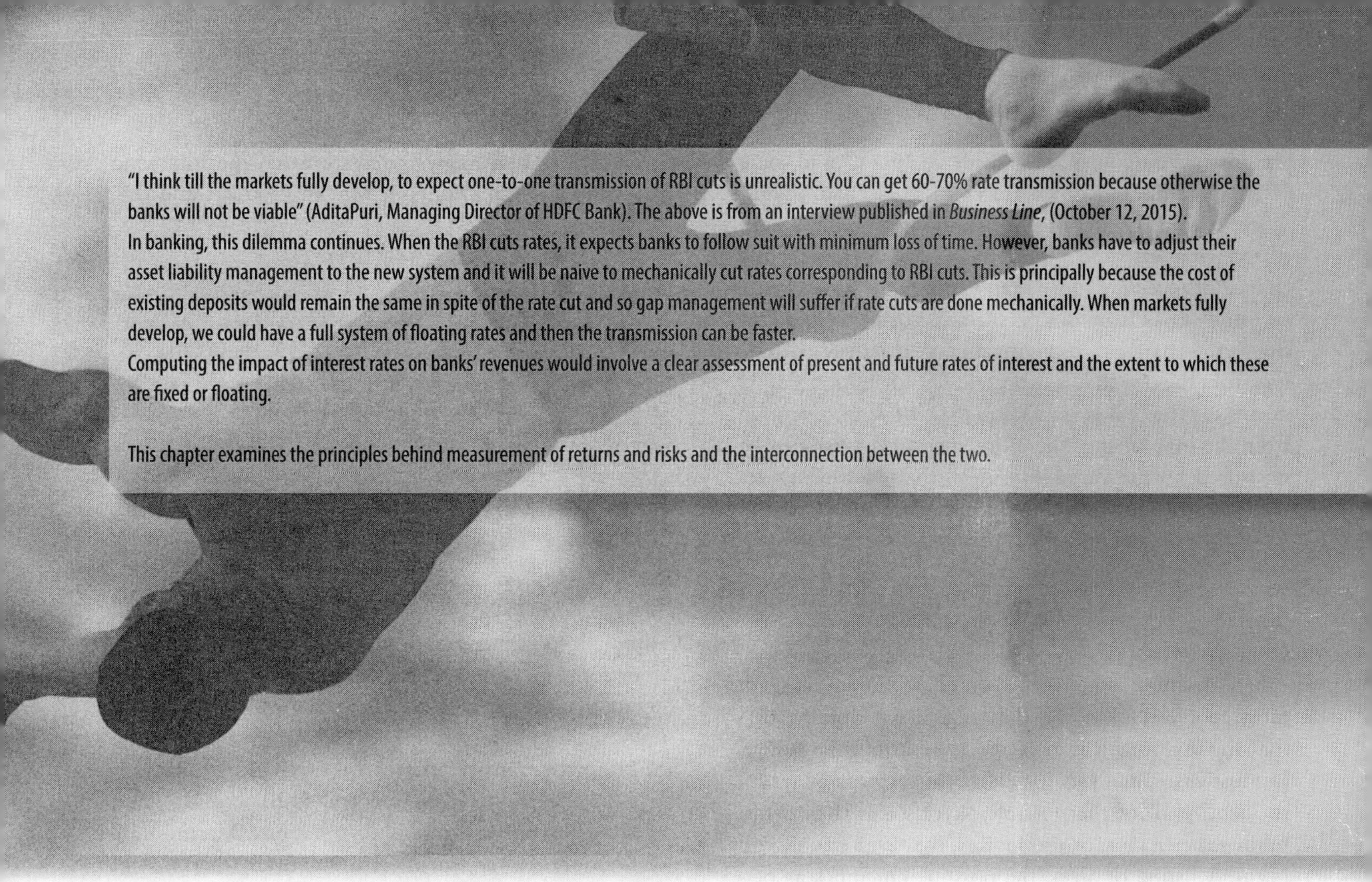

"I think till the markets fully develop, to expect one-to-one transmission of RBI cuts is unrealistic. You can get 60-70% rate transmission because otherwise the banks will not be viable" (AditaPuri, Managing Director of HDFC Bank). The above is from an interview published in *Business Line*, (October 12, 2015).

In banking, this dilemma continues. When the RBI cuts rates, it expects banks to follow suit with minimum loss of time. However, banks have to adjust their asset liability management to the new system and it will be naive to mechanically cut rates corresponding to RBI cuts. This is principally because the cost of existing deposits would remain the same in spite of the rate cut and so gap management will suffer if rate cuts are done mechanically. When markets fully develop, we could have a full system of floating rates and then the transmission can be faster.

Computing the impact of interest rates on banks' revenues would involve a clear assessment of present and future rates of interest and the extent to which these are fixed or floating.

This chapter examines the principles behind measurement of returns and risks and the interconnection between the two.

John Lund/Drew Kelly/Blend Images /Jupiter Images

Earlier in the book, we showed that the return (interest rate) on debt is equal to the nominal risk-free rate, r_{RF}, plus several premiums that reflect the riskiness of the debt instrument in question (Chapter 5). In this chapter, we define the term *risk* more precisely in terms of how it relates to investments in general, we examine procedures used to measure risk, and we discuss the relationship between risk and return.

Study Tools

Problems are found at the end of this chapter

\+

Login to **CourseMate** for **CFIN** at **CengageBrain.com** for additional problems and other study tools!

8-1 Defining and Measuring Risk

Although most people view risk as a chance of loss, in reality *risk occurs any time we cannot be certain about the future outcome of a particular activity or event*. Consequently, risk results from the fact that an action such as investing can produce *more than one outcome in the future*. When multiple outcomes are possible, some of the possible outcomes are considered "good" and some of the possible outcomes are considered "bad." Thus, when we think of investment risk, along with the chance of receiving less than expected, we should consider the chance of receiving more than expected. If we consider investment risk from this perspective, then we can define **risk** as the chance of receiving an actual return that differs from the one that is expected. This definition simply means that there is *variability in the returns* or outcomes from the investment. Therefore, investment risk can be measured by the variability of all the investment's returns, both "good" and "bad." *The greater the variability of the possible outcomes, the riskier the investment.*

8-1a **Probability Distributions**

When deciding whether to purchase an investment, most people think about the range of possible payoffs that the investment is expected to return in the future. In most cases, analysts formalize this process by trying to identify all of the possible payoffs and then determining the chance, or probability, that each payoff will occur. A listing of all of the possible outcomes associated with an investment along with their probabilities is called a **probability distribution.**

To illustrate probability distributions, let's consider two fictitious companies—Martin Products, Inc. and U.S. Electric. Martin Products manufactures equipment that is used in the data transmission industry, which is quite cyclical; that is, the firm's profits generally rise and fall with business cycles. On the other hand, U.S. Electric supplies electricity, which is considered an essential service, and thus its profits are fairly stable and predictable.

Suppose that analysts have created the following probability distributions for Martin Products and U.S. Electric:

		Rate of Return on the Stock if the Economic State Occurs	
State of the Economy	**Probability of This State Occurring**	**Martin Products**	**U.S. Electric**
Boom	0.2	110%	20%
Normal	0.5	22	16
Recession	0.3	−60	10
	1.0		

This probability distribution indicates that there is a 20 percent chance of a booming economy, in which case both companies will have high returns, there is a 50 percent probability that the two companies will operate in a normal economy and offer moderate returns, and there is a 30 percent chance of a recession, which will mean low returns will be generated by the companies.[1]

Although the general pattern of returns is the same for both companies, notice that there is a fairly high probability that the value of Martin's stock will vary substantially, possibly resulting in a loss of 60 percent or a gain of 110 percent; conversely, there is no chance of a loss for U.S. Electric, and its maximum gain is 20 percent.[2] Thus, according to the probability distributions, Martin's rate of return could vary far more dramatically than that of U.S. Electric. Based on our definition of risk, then, Martin Products seems to be a riskier investment than U.S. Electric.

risk The chance that an outcome other than the expected one will occur.

probability distribution A listing of all possible outcomes or events, with a probability (chance of occurrence) assigned to each outcome.

expected rate of return $\hat{r}$ The rate of return expected to be realized from an investment, which is the mean value of the probability distribution of possible results.

8-2 **Expected Rate of Return**

The probability distribution given in the previous section shows that the most likely outcome is for the economy to be normal, in which case Martin Products will return 22 percent and U.S. Electric will return 16 percent. Because other outcomes are also possible, however, we need to summarize all of the information contained in the probability distributions into a single measure that can be used to make decisions. That measure is called the expected value, or **expected rate of return**, and it is

[1]The probability distributions given in the table are called *discrete*, because the number of outcomes is limited, or finite. In reality of course, the state of the economy could actually range from a deep depression to a fantastic boom, with an unlimited number of possible states in between. The probability distribution for such a situation is called *continuous* because the number of possible outcomes is infinite within a particular range.

[2]It is, of course, completely unrealistic to think that any stock has no chance of a loss. Only in hypothetical examples could this situation occur.

TABLE 8.1 Calculating Martin Products' Standard Deviation

Payoff r_i (1)		Expected Return $\hat{r}$ (2)		Deviation $r_j - \hat{r}$ (1) − (2) = (3)	$(r_j - \hat{r})^2$ = (4)	Probability (5)	$(r_j - \hat{r})^2 Pr_i$ (4) × (5) = (6)
110%	−	15%	=	95	9,025	0.2	9,025 × 0.2 = 1,805.0
22	−	15	=	7	49	0.5	49 × 0.5 = 24.5
−60	−	15	=	−75	5,625	0.3	5,625 × 0.3 = 1,687.5
							Variance = σ^2 = 3,517.0

Standard deviation = $\sigma = \sqrt{\sigma^2} = \sqrt{3{,}517} = 59.3\%$

measured by computing the *weighted average* of the outcomes using the probabilities as the weights. The expected rate of return, $\hat{r}$, can be calculated using Equation 8.1:

8.1

$$\text{Expected rate of return} = \hat{r} = Pr_1r_1 + \cdots + Pr_nr_n = \sum_{i=1}^{n} Pr_ir_i$$

Here r_i is the *i*th possible outcome, Pr_i is the probability that the *i*th outcome will occur, and n is the number of possible outcomes. Applying Equation 8.1, the expected returns for Martin Products and U.S. Electric are

$$\hat{r}_{Martin} = 0.2(110\%) + 0.5(22\%) + 0.3(-60\%) = 15.0\%$$

$$\hat{r}_{US} = 0.2(20\%) + 0.5(16\%) + 0.3(10\%) = 15.0\%$$

Notice that neither expected rate of return equals any of the possible payoffs given in the probability distributions. Simply stated, the expected rate of return represents the *average payoff* that investors will receive if the probability distributions do not change over a long period of time. For example, if the probability distribution for Martin Products is correct, then 20 percent of the time the economy will be booming and investors will earn a 110 percent rate of return, 50 percent of the time the economy will be normal and investors will earn 22 percent, and 30 percent of the time the economy will be in a recession and investors will earn −60 percent. On average, then, Martin Products' investors should earn 15 percent over some period of time, say, 10 years.

Other terminologies in Return

Every person who invests money would like to have the maximum possible return therefrom. An investment involves foregoing the immediate use of money for compensation, which is the return. At the time of investment, returns can only be estimated. Any promise of an assured return is a good estimate of the return that will eventually come, but it is only an estimate at the time of making the investment. The following aspects regarding return merit attention.

Holding Period Yield

This refers to the return that an investor will get over the tenure of an investment. During the tenure, the investor will get periodic returns and at the end of the tenure will get a capital appreciation as well. Suppose an investor has a one-year horizon and invests ₹100. The company gives him a dividend or interest of ₹ 8 and at the end of the year, the price of the security is ₹103. Here, the periodic return is 8% and capital appreciation is 3%. The total return is 11%.

The formula for arriving at the return is

$$((P1 - P0) + D) / P0$$

where,

*P*1 is the price at the end of the tenure.

*P*0 is the price at the beginning.

D is the periodic return.

In the above example, this will translate to

((103 − 100) + 8) / 100, which is 11%.

It is easier to comprehend returns when the holding period is one year. When the holding period is greater than one year, the translation into an annual return is not straightforward. For instance, if the holding period return for a two-year investment is 20%, the annual return is not 10%, since the element of compounding will have to be reckoned. Similarly, a half-yearly return of 6% does not come to an annual return of 12%, again because of the compounding effect.

Example Let us take the case of a security. At the start, when it was bought the price was ₹ 5,468. At the end of Year 1, it became ₹ 5,998. At the end of Year 2, the price rose to ₹ 6,354 and at the end of Year 3 to ₹ 6,998.

Here the holding period return for each particular year (assuming that the security was held only for one year at a time) would be ((End price – Start price) / Start price).

The holding period yield for various individual periods is given below:

Year	Start	End	HPY
1	5468	5998	0.096928
2	5998	6354	0.059353
3	6354	6998	0.101353
4	6998	7010	0.001715
		AM	0.064837
		GM	0.064075

Arithmetic mean is just the average of the holding period yields and is found by using the AVERAGE formula in MS Excel.

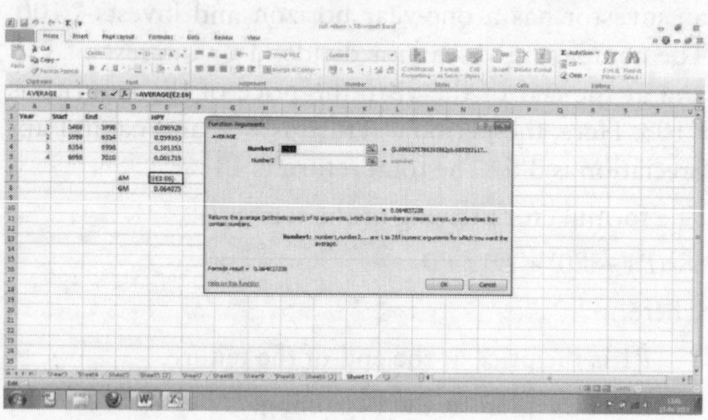

Similarly, geometric mean can be found in MS Excel using the formula GEOMEAN as follows:

First, we find the return relatives. This is just the end return / start return. Then we use the formula as shown below.

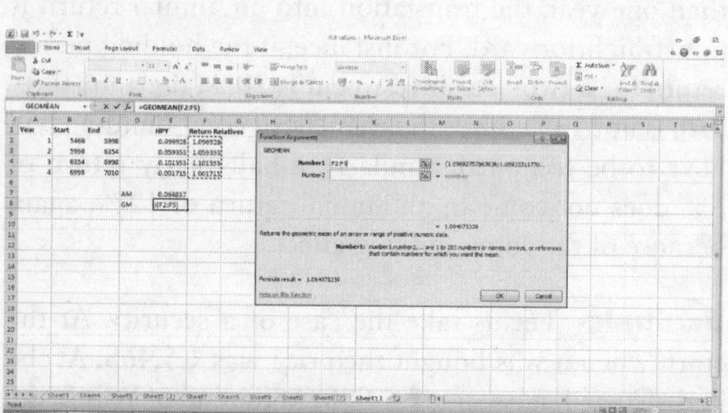

Note that we have to deduct 1 from the answer obtained by the GEOMEAN formula. Thus we get 1.0640 from the formula and deducting 1 we get the geometric mean as 0.0640. This can be done by deducting 1 from the formula in the formula bar itself, as shown below. The formula in cell E8 will appear as follows:

= GEOMEAN (F2:F5) – 1

Arithmetic Mean vs. Geometric Mean

Calculating returns by using the arithmetic mean is intuitive. However, the geometric mean approach is strictly more accurate. Let us discuss this with an example.

A person invests ₹60 and this amount appreciates to ₹ 70 after one year and ₹ 80 after two years. The return for the first year is ((70 – 60) / 60) = 16.67%. For the second year, the return is ((80 – 70) / 70) = 14.29%. The average annual return is (16.67% + 14.29%) / 2 = 15.48%. This is the arithmetic mean approach.

Under the geometric mean approach, we multiply the two period return relatives and find the square root to get the annual return. The return relative for 16.67% return in the first year is 1.1667 and that for 14.29% return in the second year is 1.1429.

Square root of 1.1667 multiplied by 1.1429 is 1.1548. Thus, the geometric mean return also is 15.48%.

There does not appear to be any difference here. But, take the case of an investment of ₹200 which became ₹400 after one year and then became ₹200 after two years. The first year return is 100% ((400 – 200) / 200). The second year return is minus 50% ((200 – 400 / 400). The average arithmetical mean return is ((100% + (–50%)) / 2 = 50%.

The investor started with ₹200 and ended after two years with ₹200. Yet the arithmetic mean calculation shows that the investor got an annual return of 50%. This is obviously wrong.

The geometric mean answer would be square root of the two return relatives. The return relative of the first year is (1 + First year return), and for the second year it is (1 + Second year return). Thus, the first year return relative is 1 and the second year return relative is -0.5. Multiplying the two we get 1, the square root of which is also 1, meaning that the geometric mean return is 0.

First year return = 100%

First year return relative (1 + First year return) = (1 + 100%) = 2

Second year return = (–50%)

Second year return relative (1 + Second year return) = (1 + (–50%)) = 0.5

Geometric mean return is the square root of first year return relative × Second year return relative

$= \sqrt{(2 \times 0.5)}$.

Square root of 1 is 1.

So geometric mean is (1-1) = 0%, which fully reflects the reality.

In spite of the above difference, geometric mean is not as popular as the arithmetic mean because of the simplicity of calculation of the latter and its intuitive appeal.

Geometric mean will always be lower than the arithmetic mean, and at best can be equal.

Daily Return and Annual Return

When analyzing stocks, it is a usual practice to find daily returns. Here we apply the formula

$(P1 - P0) / P0$

where,

$P1$ is the price on Day 1.

$P0$ is the price on Day 0.

We use the above formula to find the return for Day 1. In the same way, the return for each day can be drawn up and the average return for the entire period can be computed. This average is, of course, the average daily return, which when multiplied by 365 roughly approximates to the corresponding annual return.

There are two variations to this. Many academics and trading institutions use the 252-day convention for conversion of returns from daily to annual and back. Thus, approximately, a daily return multiplied by 252 will give the annual return. Strictly, this is not correct as it ignores the compounding effect. The correct annual return will be $((1 + \text{Daily return})^{252}) - 1)$.

Example Upon analysis, it is found that a security has an average daily return of 0.06%. What is the annual return?

Assuming a 252-day year convention, the annualized return will be

$((1 + 0.0006)^{252}) - 1)$

Notice that 0.06% has to be written in decimals as 0.0006.

We get the answer as 16.32%.

8-2a Measuring Total (Stand-Alone) Risk: The Standard Deviation (σ)

Because we have defined risk as the variability of returns, we can measure it by examining the tightness of the probability distribution associated with the possible outcomes. In general, the width of a probability distribution indicates the amount of *scatter*, or variability, of the possible outcomes. The measure we use most often to evaluate variability is the **standard deviation**, the symbol for which is **σ**, the Greek letter *sigma*. *The smaller the standard deviation*, the tighter the probability distribution, and, accordingly, *the lower the total risk associated with the investment*. The standard deviation of returns can be calculated using Equation 8.2:

8.2

$$\text{Standard deviation} = \sigma = \sqrt{(r_1 - \hat{r})^2\, Pr_1 + \cdots + (r_n - \hat{r})^2\, Pr_n}$$

$$= \sqrt{\sum_{i=1}^{n} (r_i - \hat{r})^2 Pr_i}$$

Equation 8.2 shows that the standard deviation is a weighted average deviation from the expected value, which gives an idea as to how far above or below the expected value the actual value is likely to be. Note that the standard deviation is the square root of the variance—that is, Standard deviation $= \sigma = \sqrt{\sigma^2} = \sqrt{\text{Variance}}$.

Table 8.1 shows the steps you should follow to compute $\sigma_{\text{Martin}} = 59.3\%$. Using these same procedures, we find U.S. Electric's standard deviation to be 3.6 percent. The larger standard deviation for Martin Products indicates a greater variation of returns for this firm, and hence a greater chance that the actual, or realized, return will differ significantly from the expected return. Consequently, according to this measure of risk, Martin Products is considered a riskier investment than U.S. Electric.

To this point, the example we have used to compute the expected return and standard deviation has been based on data that take the form of a known probability distribution, which includes estimates of all future outcomes and the chances that these outcomes will occur in a particular situation. In many cases, however, the only information we have available consists of data

standard deviation, σ A measure of the tightness, or variability, of a set of outcomes.

over some *past period*. For example, suppose we have observed the following returns associated with a common stock during the past six years ($\ddot{r}$ = historical returns):

Year	$\ddot{r}_t$	Year	$\ddot{r}_t$
2014	16%	2011	20%
2013	13	2010	17
2012	−5	2009	23

We can use this information to *estimate* the risk associated with the stock by estimating the standard deviation of returns. The estimated standard deviation can be computed using a series of past, or *observed*, returns to solve Equation 8.3:

8.3

$$\text{Estimated } \sigma = s = \sqrt{\frac{\sum_{t=1}^{n}(\ddot{r}_t - \bar{r})^2}{n-1}}$$

Here $\ddot{r}_t$ represents the past realized rate of return in Period t, and $\bar{r}$ (pronounced "r bar") is the arithmetic average of the annual returns earned during the last n years. We compute $\bar{r}$ using Equation 8.4:

8.4

$$\bar{r} = \frac{\ddot{r}_1 + \ddot{r}_2 + \cdots + \ddot{r}_n}{n} = \frac{\sum_{t=1}^{n}\ddot{r}_t}{n}$$

Continuing with our current example, we compute the arithmetic average and *estimate* the value for σ as follows:[3]

$$\bar{r} = \frac{16\% + 13\% + (-5\%) + 20\% + 17\% + 23\%}{6} = \frac{84\%}{6} = 14.0\%$$

$$\text{Estimated } \sigma = s$$

$$= \sqrt{\frac{(16\% - 14\%)^2 + (13\% - 14\%)^2 + (-5\% - 14\%)^2 + (20\% - 14\%)^2 + (17\% - 14\%)^2 + (23\% - 14\%)^2}{6-1}}$$

$$= \sqrt{\frac{492}{5}} = \sqrt{98.4} = 9.9\%$$

The historical standard deviation is often used as an estimate of the future standard deviation because $s \approx \sigma$. On the other hand, the historical return generally is not used as an estimate of the expected return because the past *level* of returns generally will not be repeated in the future; that is, $\bar{r} \neq \hat{r}$, especially for young, high-growth firms.

Other aspects of risk

The standard deviation has significance only with reference to the mean. If in relation to the mean, the standard deviation is high, then the risk is high. If the analysis follows a normal distribution, then 69% of the distribution will be within one standard deviation on either side of the mean, 95% of the distribution within two standard deviations and 99% within three standard deviations. If the data in the above analysis conform to a normal distribution, we can conclude as follows:

	Between	and
Mean return	0.1525	
Standard deviation	0.0193	
69% probability + or -1 standard deviation from mean	0.1718	0.1332
95% probability + or - 2 standard deviation from mean	0.1911	0.1139
99% probability + or - 3 standard deviation from mean	0.2104	0.0946

From the above analysis, we know that 99% times the return can range from 9.46% to 21.04%. It is very unlikely for the return to be lower than 9.46% or

[3]You should recognize from statistics courses that a sample of six observations is not sufficient to make a good estimate. We use six observations here only to simplify the illustration.

higher than 21.04%. This shows us the extent of risk we are taking in the investment.

FIGURE 8.1 Normal distribution curve

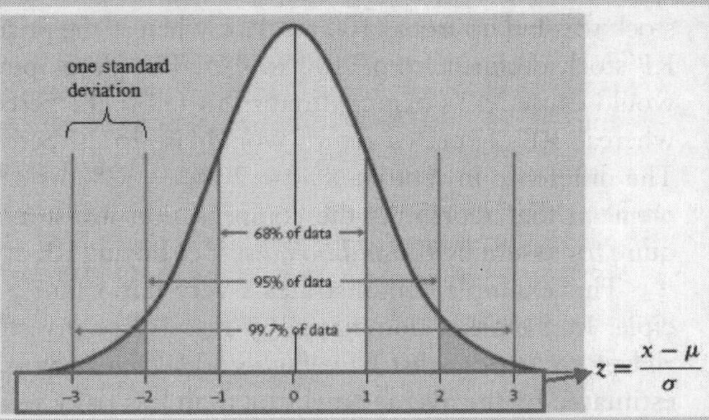

Of course, this analysis using standard deviation is applicable only if the data conform to a normal distribution. The formula on the right of the chart (see Figure 8.1) is the one used to find out the area under the normal distribution, given the value of the variable, the mean of the population and the standard deviation of the population.

Daily Standard Deviation and Annualized Standard Deviation

The standard deviation of returns computed for daily returns can be converted into an annualized standard deviation by multiplying it with the square root of 252. This is when we assume that the year has 252 trading days. If we follow the 365-day convention, we have to multiply the daily standard deviation by the square root of 365 to get the annualized standard deviation.

Example An analyst discovers that the mean daily return of a security is 0.0575% and the standard deviation thereof is 0.013%. Find the annualized standard deviation.

If we assume that the analyst is following the 252-day convention, then the annualized return and standard deviation are

Annualized return = (1.000575252) -1, which is 0.1559 = 15.59%

Annualized standard deviation = 0.013% × √ (252)

We get 0.2063%.

8-2b Coefficient of Variation (Risk/Return Ratio)

Another useful measure for evaluating risky investments is the **coefficient of variation (CV)**, which is the standard deviation divided by the expected return (Equation 8.5):

The coefficient of variation shows the risk per unit of return. It provides a more meaningful basis for comparison when the expected returns and the risk associated with two investments differ. Because both U.S. Electric and Martin Products have

8.5

$$\text{Coefficient of variation} = \text{CV} = \frac{\text{Risk}}{\text{Return}} = \frac{\sigma}{\hat{r}}$$

the same expected return, it is not necessary to compute the coefficient of variation to compare the two investments. In this case, most people would prefer to invest in U.S. Electric, because it offers the same expected return with lower risk.

The coefficient of variation is more useful when we consider investments that have different expected rates of return *and* different levels of risk. For example, Biobotics Corporation is a biological research and development firm that, according to stock analysts, offers investors an expected rate of return equal to 35 percent with a standard deviation of 7.5 percent. Biobotics offers a higher expected return than U.S. Electric, but it is also riskier. If we calculate the coefficient of variation for Biobotics, we find that it is 0.21 = 7.5%/35%, which is slightly less than U.S. Electric's coefficient of variation of 0.24 = 3.6%/15%. Thus, Biobotics actually has less risk per unit of return than U.S. Electric, even though its standard deviation is much higher. In this case, the additional return offered by Biobotics is more than sufficient to compensate investors for taking on the additional risk.

Because the coefficient of variation captures the effects of both risk and return, it is a better measure than the standard deviation for evaluating total (stand-alone) risk in situations where investments differ with respect to both their amounts of total risk and their expected returns.

coefficient of variation (CV) A standardized measure of the risk per unit of return. It is calculated by dividing the standard deviation by the expected return.

8-2c Risk Aversion and Required Returns

Suppose you have worked hard and saved ₹1 million, which you now plan to invest. You can buy a 7 percent Bank deposit, and at the end of one year you will have a sure ₹1.07 million, that is, your original investment plus ₹100,000 in interest. Alternatively, you can buy stock in a risky company - R&D Enterprises. If R&D's research programs are successful, the value of your stock will increase to ₹2.14 million. Conversely, if the firm's programs fail, the value of your stock will go to zero, and you will be penniless. You regard R&D's chances of success or failure as being 50:50, so the expected value of the stock investment is ₹107000 = 0.5(₹0) + 0.5(₹214000). Subtracting the ₹1 million cost of the stock leaves an expected profit of ₹70000, or an expected (but risky) 7 percent rate of return; that is, $\hat{r}$ = ₹700000/₹1,000,000 = 0.07 = 7%.

In this case, you have a choice between a sure ₹70000 profit (representing a 7 percent rate of return) on the Bank depositing and a risky expected ₹70000 profit (also representing a 7 percent expected rate of return) on the R&D Enterprises stock. Which one would you choose? Because most investors are risk averse, they would choose the less risky investment—that is, the Bank deposit—in this situation.

What does it mean to be risk averse? Simply stated, a risk-averse person requires positive rewards to take on risks, and higher risks require higher rewards. When this concept is applied to investments, other things held constant, the higher a security's risk, the higher the return investors demand, and thus the less they are willing to pay for the investment. To see how **risk aversion** affects security prices, we can analyze the situation with two hypothetical companies - Manoharmohan Electric (ME) and Ramanakshatra Fabrics (RF). Suppose each stock sells for ₹100 per share and each has an expected rate of return of 15 percent. Further let us assume that ME is almost risk free whereas RF suffers from uncertainties. To simplify our discussion, let's assume both firms pay a perpetual dividend equal to ₹15 per share. In this case, rational risk-averse investors would prefer ME because there is less variability in its payoffs (less risk , and at the same time the price is the same which signifies that the return is the same for both the stocks. Naturally, any rational investor will prefer the stock with less risk when the return is identical with the other stock). People with money to invest would bid for ME stock rather than RF stock, and RF's stockholders would start selling their stock and using the money to buy ME stock. Buying pressure would drive up the price of ME's stock, and selling pressure would simultaneously cause RF's price to decline. These price changes, in turn, would alter the expected rates of return on the two securities. Suppose, for example, that the price of ME stock was bid up from ₹100 to ₹125, whereas the price of RF stock declined from ₹100 to ₹75. This development would cause ME's expected return to fall to 12 percent, whereas RF's expected return would rise to 20 percent. The difference in returns, 8% = 20% − 12%, is a **risk premium** that represents the compensation investors require for assuming the *additional* risk of buying RF.

risk aversion Risk-averse investors require higher rates of return to invest in higher-risk securities.

risk premium (RP) The portion of the expected return that can be attributed to the additional risk of an investment. It is the difference between the expected rate of return on a given risky asset and the expected rate of return on a less risky asset.

This example demonstrates a very important principle: In a market dominated by risk-averse investors, *riskier securities must have higher expected returns,* as estimated by the average investor, than less risky securities. If this situation does not hold, investors will buy and sell investments, and prices will continue to change until the higher-risk investments have higher expected returns than the lower-risk investments. Figure 8.2 illustrates this relationship. We will consider the question of how much higher the returns on risky securities should be later in the chapter, after we examine how diversification affects the way risk should be measured.

8-3 Portfolio Risk—Holding Combinations of Investments

To this point, we have considered the riskiness of an investment that is held in isolation; that is, the *total* risk of an investment if it is held by itself, which we call *stand-alone* risk. Now we analyze the riskiness of an investment when it is combined with other investments and held in a portfolio.[4] As we shall see, holding an investment—whether it is a stock, bond, or other asset—as part of a portfolio generally is less risky than holding the same investment all by itself, because some of the total, or stand-alone, risk that is associated with the individual security can be spread to the other investments in the portfolio. For this reason, most financial assets are held in portfolios. From an average investor's standpoint, then, the fact that the price of a particular stock goes up or down is not very important. What is important is the return on his or her portfolio and the overall risk of the portfolio. As a result, *the risk and return characteristics of an investment should not be evaluated in isolation;*

[4]A *portfolio* is a collection of investment securities or assets. If you owned some General Motors stock, some ExxonMobil stock, and some IBM stock, you would be holding a three-stock portfolio. For the reasons set forth in this section, the majority of all stocks are held as parts of portfolios.

FIGURE 8.2 Risk/Return Relationship

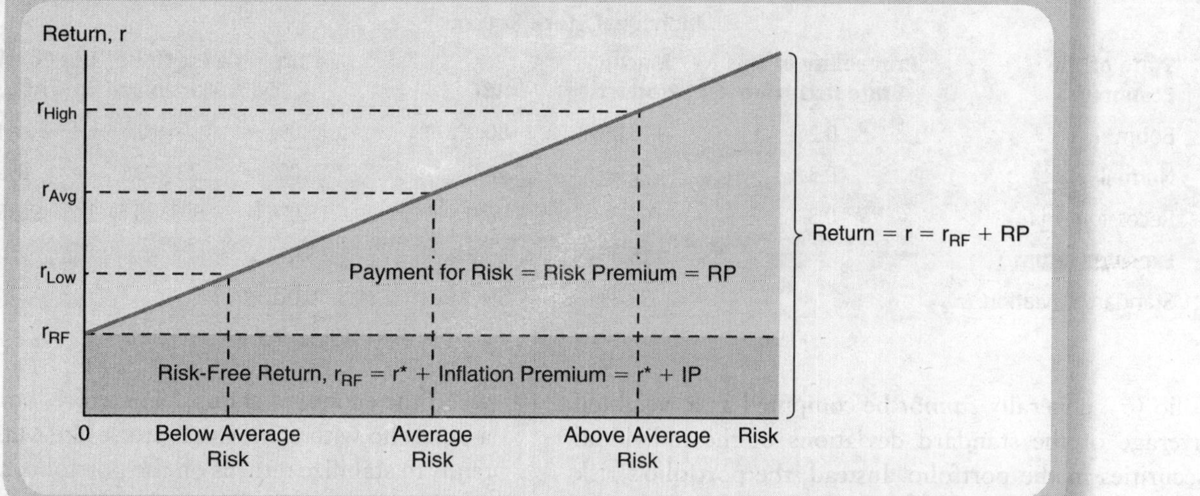

instead, the risk and return of an individual security should be analyzed in terms of how the security affects the risk and return of the portfolio in which it is held.

Portfolio Returns. The **expected return on a portfolio,** $\hat{r}_p$, is simply the weighted average of the expected returns on the individual stocks that are held in the portfolio, with each weight being the proportion of the total funds invested in each stock (Equation 8.6):

8.6

$$\text{Portfolio return} = \hat{r}_p = w_1\hat{r}_1 + w_2\hat{r}_2 + \cdots + w_N\hat{r}_N = \sum_{j=1}^{N} w_j\hat{r}_j$$

Here $\hat{r}_j$ represents the expected return on Stock j, w_j is the weight that represents the proportion of the total funds that is invested in Stock j, and the portfolio includes N stocks (investments). Note two points: (1) w_j is equal to the value of the investment in Stock j divided by the total value of the portfolio and (2) the w_js must sum to 1.0.

To illustrate, suppose securities analysts estimate the following expected returns on four large companies:

Company	Expected Return, $\hat{r}$
Citigroup	6%
General Electric	14
Johnson & Johnson	8
Microsoft	16

If we formed a ₹100,000 portfolio by investing ₹25,000 in each of these four stocks, the expected portfolio return of this portfolio would be 11.0 percent:

$$\begin{aligned}\hat{r}_p &= w_{Citi}\,\hat{r}_{Citi} + w_{GE}\hat{r}_{GE} + w_{JNJ}\hat{r}_{JNJ} + w_{Micro}\hat{r}_{Micro}\\ &= 0.25(6\%) + 0.25(14\%) + 0.25(8\%) + 0.25(16\%)\\ &= 11.0\%\end{aligned}$$

Of course, after the fact and one year later, the actual **realized rate of return,** $\ddot{r}$, on each stock will almost certainly differ from its expected value, so $\ddot{r}_p$ will be somewhat different from $\hat{r}_p = 11\%$. For example, Microsoft's stock might double in price and provide a return of + 100 percent, whereas Citigroup's stock price might fall sharply and provide a return of −75 percent. Note, however, that those two events would offset each other somewhat, so the portfolio's realized return might still be close to its expected return, even though the individual stocks' actual returns turned out to differ significantly from their expected returns.

Portfolio Risk. Although the expected return of a portfolio is a weighted average of the expected returns of the individual stocks in the portfolio, the risk of a port-

expected return on a portfolio, $\hat{r}_p$ The weighted average of the expected returns on stocks held in a portfolio.

realized rate of return, $\ddot{r}$ The return that is actually earned. The actual return ($\ddot{r}$) usually differs from the expected return ($\hat{r}$).

TABLE 8.2 Probability Distributions for Martin Products, American Business Collections (ABC), and a Portfolio Consisting of Both Stocks ($\rho = -1.0$)

		Individual Stock Returns		
State of the Economy	**Probability of This State Occurring**	**Martin Products**	**ABC**	**Return on a Portfolio That Consists of 50% Martin and 50% ABC**
Boom	0.2	110.0%	−80.0%	15.0% = 110%(0.5) + (−80%)(0.5)
Normal	0.5	22.0	8.0	15.0% = 22%(0.5) + 8%(0.5)
Recession	0.3	−60.0	90.0	15.0% = (−60%)(0.5) + 90%(0.5)
Expected return, $\hat{r}$		15.0%	15.0%	15.0%
Standard deviation, σ		59.3%	59.3%	0.0%

folio (σ_P) generally *cannot* be computed as a weighted average of the standard deviations of the individual securities in the portfolio. Instead, the portfolio's risk usually is *smaller* than the weighted average of the individual stocks' standard deviations. In fact, it is theoretically possible to combine two stocks that by themselves are quite risky, as measured by their standard deviations, and form a completely riskless portfolio—that is, the portfolio has $\sigma_P = 0$.

To illustrate the effect of combining securities, suppose that you have ₹5,000 invested in the stock of Martin Products (introduced earlier) and you are considering investing an equal amount in the stock of American Business Collections (ABC), a company that collects delinquent accounts receivables for manufacturing firms. The probability distributions for these two stocks and a portfolio that consists of 50 percent Martin and 50 percent ABC are shown in Table 8.2. The information provided in the table shows that $\hat{r} = 15\%$ for both stocks as well as for the portfolio. Note that both stocks have a fair amount of stand-alone risk, because $\sigma_{Martin} = \sigma_{ABC} = 59.3\%$. However, the risk associated with a portfolio that includes equal amounts invested in each stock is zero; that is, $\sigma_P = 0.0\%$.

The stocks of Martin Products and ABC can be combined to form a riskless portfolio because their returns tend to move in opposite directions; when Martin's returns are low, American's returns are high, and vice versa. In statistical terms, we state that the relationship between the returns of these two stocks is negative. This relationship exists because ABC's stock price rises during recessions when its collection business is booming, whereas the prices of other stocks, such as Martin's, tend to decline when the economy slumps. Therefore, holding ABC in a portfolio with a "normal" stock like Martin Products tends to stabilize returns on the portfolio, and thus lowers the effect of ABC's stand-alone risk on a person's investment funds. The concept of reducing the stand-alone risk of an individual investment by combining it with other investments to form a portfolio is called **diversification.**

diversification Reduction of stand-alone risk of an individual investment by combining it with other investments in a portfolio.

correlation coefficient, ρ A measure of the degree of relationship between two variables.

The relationship between two variables, such as the return on Martin's stock and the return on ABC's stock, is called *correlation,* and it is determined by computing the **correlation coefficient, ρ,** which measures both the direction and the strength of the relationship between two variables,[5] If we compute the correlation coefficient for the returns on Martin's stock and ABC's stock, we would find that $\rho = -1.0$, which means that they are perfectly negatively related. Variables that are perfectly negatively correlated exhibit the same relative movement, but in opposite directions.

The opposite of perfect negative correlation ($\rho = -1.0$) is perfect positive correlation ($\rho = +1.0$). Returns on two perfectly positively correlated stocks exhibit the same relative movement in the same direction. A portfolio consisting of two such stocks would be exactly as risky as the individual stocks, because the stocks would seem like identical twins with respect to the variability of their returns. In this case, there is no diversification effect—that is, *risk is not reduced if the portfolio contains perfectly positively correlated stocks.*

From our discussion, we know that (1) two stocks that are perfectly negatively correlated can be combined to form a portfolio that has no risk which means $\sigma_P = 0$; and (2) when two perfectly positively correlated stocks

[5]The *correlation coefficient*, ρ, can range from +1.0 (denoting that the two variables move in the same direction with exactly the same degree of synchronization every time movement occurs) to −1.0 (denoting that the variables always move with the same degree of synchronization, but in opposite directions). A correlation coefficient of zero suggests that the two variables are not related to each other—that is, changes in one variable occur *independently* of changes in the other variable.

TABLE 8.3 Probability Distributions for Martin Products, Anderson Mechanical, and a Portfolio Consisting of Both Stocks ($\rho = +0.21$)

State of the Economy	Probability of This State Occurring	Individual Stock Returns: Martin Products	Individual Stock Returns: Anderson Mechanical	Return on a Portfolio That Consists of 50% Martin and 50% Anderson
Boom	0.2	110.0%	104.0%	107.0% = 110%(0.5) + 104%(0.5)
Normal	0.5	22.0	−41.0	−9.5% = 22%(0.5) + (−41%)(0.5)
Recession	0.3	−60.0	49.0	−5.5% = (−60%)(0.5) + 49%(0.5)
Expected return, $\hat{r}$		15.0%	15.0%	15.0%
Standard deviation, σ		59.3%	59.2%	46.0%

$$\sigma_p = \sqrt{0.2(107.0\% - 15.0\%)^2 + 0.5(-9.5\% - 15.0\%)^2 + 0.3(-5.5\% - 15.0\%)^2} = \sqrt{2{,}119} = 46.0\%$$

with the same risk are combined, the portfolio risk is equal to the risk associated with the individual stocks which means $\sigma_P = \sigma_{Stock1} = \sigma_{Stock2}$. In reality, however, the correlation coefficient (ρ) for the returns on two randomly selected stocks generally lies in the range from +0.3 to +0.6. However, as we will show, even though it cannot be completely eliminated, risk is reduced when positively related stocks are combined to form portfolios as long as $\rho \neq +1.0$.

Suppose you are considering investing equal amounts in the stock of Martin Products and in the stock of Anderson Mechanical, a company that manufactures water meters, calibrators, and other measuring devices. The probability distribution of returns that is given in Table 8.3 shows that the expected return on Anderson's stock is 15 percent and it has about the same risk as Martin's stock ($\sigma_{Martin} = 59.3\%$ and $\sigma_{Anderson} = 59.2\%$). The correlation coefficient for the returns on these two stocks is +0.21, which means that there exists a less than perfectly positive relationship between the stocks' returns. As Table 8.3 shows, however, when a portfolio is formed by investing equal amounts in both stocks, the portfolio's return is 15 percent, but its standard deviation is only 46 percent. This example shows that the stocks have less risk when held in a portfolio than when either is held all by itself.

We can conclude from our discussion that risk can be completely eliminated in one extreme case ($\rho = -1.0$), whereas diversification does no good in the other extreme case ($\rho = +1.0$). In between these extremes, combining two stocks into a portfolio reduces, but does not eliminate, the riskiness inherent in the individual stocks. The weaker (lower) the positive correlation *or* the stronger (higher) the negative correlation two stocks exhibit, the more risk can be reduced when they are combined in a portfolio—that is, the greater the diversification effect.

8-3a Firm-Specific Risk Versus Market Risk

From our discussion of portfolio risk, you should have concluded that an individual stock (or other investment) generally is less risky when it is held in a portfolio that includes other investments than when it is held by itself. In other words, some of the risk that is associated with a stock can be eliminated by combining it with other investments to form a diversified portfolio. But we know that most stocks are positively correlated, because most companies, and thus their stocks, tend to do well when the economy is strong and to do poorly when it is weak.[6] So, how do investors eliminate some of a stock's risk by combining a bunch of positively correlated investments?

To see more precisely how diversification works, consider Figure 8.3. This figure shows how portfolio risk is affected by forming ever larger portfolios of randomly selected stocks listed on the National Stock Exchange (NSE). Standard deviations are plotted for an average one-stock portfolio, for a two-stock portfolio, and so on, up to a portfolio consisting of all common stocks listed on the NSE. As the graph illustrates, the riskiness of a portfolio consisting of average NSE stocks generally tends to decline and to approach some minimum limit as the size of the portfolio increases. The figure shows that almost half of the riskiness inherent in an average individual stock can be eliminated if the stock is held as part of a reasonably well-diversified portfolio—namely, a portfolio containing 40 or more stocks. Some risk always remains, so it is virtually

[6]It is not too difficult to find a few stocks that happened to rise because of a particular set of circumstances in the past while most other stocks were declining. It is much more difficult to find stocks that could logically be *expected* to go up in the future when other stocks are falling. American Business Collections, the collection agency discussed earlier, is one of those rare exceptions.

FIGURE 8.3 Effects of Portfolio Size on Portfolio Risk for Average Stocks

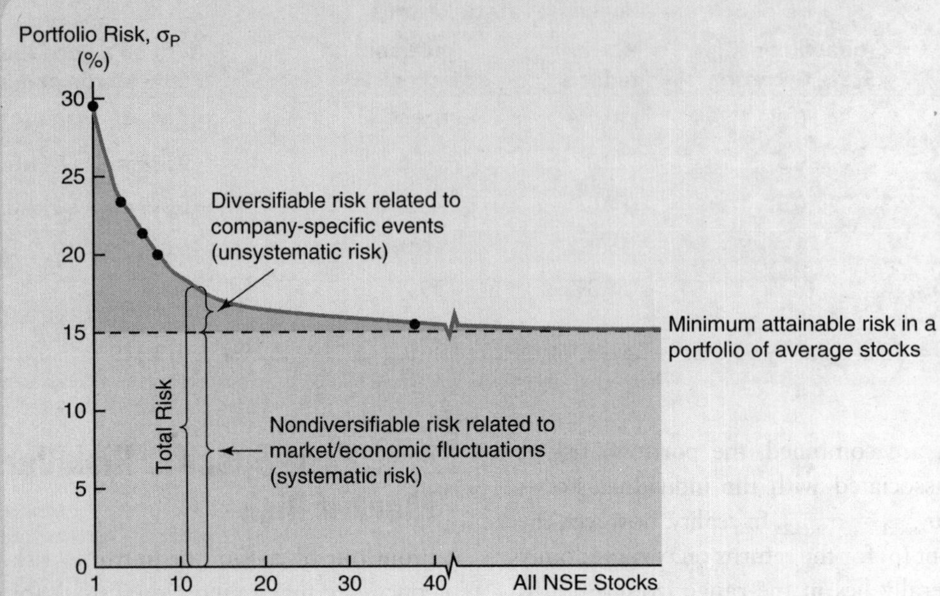

impossible to diversify away the effects of broad stock market (economic) movements that affect all stocks.

That part of the risk of a stock that can be eliminated generally is called *diversifiable risk, firm-specific risk,* or *unsystematic risk,* whereas the part that cannot be eliminated is called *nondiversifiable risk, market risk,* or *systematic risk*. Although the name given to the risk is not especially important, the fact that a large portion of the riskiness of any individual stock can be eliminated through portfolio diversification is vitally important.

Firm-specific, or **diversifiable, risk** is caused by such things as lawsuits, loss of key personnel, strikes, the winning and losing of major contracts, and other events that are unique to a particular firm. Because the actual outcomes of these events are generally unpredictable (fairly random), their effects on a portfolio can be eliminated by diversification; that is, bad events in one firm will be offset by good events in another. **Market**, or **nondiversifiable, risk**, on the other hand, stems from factors that *systematically* affect all firms, such as war, inflation, recessions, and high interest rates. Because all companies, and thus their stocks, are somehow affected by economic, or market, events, such *systematic risk* cannot be eliminated by portfolio diversification.

firm-specific (diversifiable) risk That part of a security's risk associated with random outcomes generated by events or behaviors, specific to the firm. It *can* be eliminated by proper diversification.

market (nondiversifiable) risk The part of a security's risk associated with economic, or market, factors that systematically affect all firms to some extent. It *cannot* be eliminated by diversification.

relevant risk The portion of a security's risk that cannot be diversified away; the security's market risk. It reflects the security's contribution to the risk of a portfolio.

We know that investors demand a premium for bearing risk. That is, the riskier a security, the higher the expected return required to induce investors to buy (or to hold) it, which is the relationship that is given in Figure 8.1. However, if investors really are primarily concerned with *portfolio risk* rather than the risk of the individual securities in the portfolio, how should we measure the riskiness of an individual stock? The answer is this: *The relevant riskiness of an individual stock is its contribution to the riskiness of a well-diversified portfolio.* In other words, the riskiness of General Electric's stock to a doctor who has a portfolio of 40 stocks, or to a trust officer managing a 150-stock portfolio, is the contribution that the GE stock makes to the entire portfolio's riskiness. A stock might be quite risky if held by itself, but if much of this total (stand-alone) risk can be eliminated through diversification, then its **relevant risk**—that is, its *contribution to the portfolio's risk*—is much smaller than its total risk.

A simple example will help clarify this point. Suppose you are offered the chance to flip a coin once. If a head comes up, you win ₹20,000; if the coin comes up tails, you lose ₹16,000. This proposition is a good bet: The expected return is ₹2,000 = 0.5(₹20,000) + 0.5(−₹16,000). It is a highly risky proposition, however, because you have a 50 percent chance of losing ₹16,000. For this reason, you might refuse to make the bet. Alternatively, suppose you were offered the chance to flip a coin 100 times. You would win ₹200 for each head but lose ₹160 for each tail. It is possible that you would flip all heads and win ₹20,000. It is also possible that you would flip all tails and lose ₹16,000. The chances are very high, however, that you would actually flip about 50 heads and 50 tails, winning a net of about ₹2,000. Although each individual flip is a risky bet, collectively this scenario is a low-risk proposition because most of the stand-alone risk that is associated with each flip has been diversified away. This concept underlies the practice of holding portfolios of stocks rather than just one stock.

© iStockphoto.com / PeskyMonkey

8-3b The Concept of Beta[7]

Are all stocks equally risky in the sense that adding them to a well-diversified portfolio would have the same effect on the portfolio's riskiness? The answer is no. Because not all companies are affected in the same way by such economic factors as levels of interest rates and consumer prices, different stocks will affect the portfolio differently, which means that different securities have different degrees of relevant (systematic) risk. How can we measure the relevant risk of an individual stock? As we have seen, all risk except that related to broad market (economic) movements can, and presumably will, be diversified away. After all, why accept risk that we can easily eliminate? The risk that remains after diversifying is called *market risk* because it is the risk that remains in a portfolio that consists of all investments available in both the financial markets and the markets for real assets.

Suppose that you are able to purchase every investment that exists in the financial markets. Because you would have an extremely well-diversified portfolio, the overall return that you earn on your portfolio of investments should be affected by movements in general economic factors that affect all companies (e.g., inflation and interest rates) rather than movements caused by factors that affect only specific companies (e.g., company labor problems or poor marketing campaigns). Thus, such a portfolio should be affected only by systematic, or market, risk, not by unsystematic, or firm-specific, risk. As a result, we should be able to measure the systematic, or market, risk that is associated with an individual stock by observing its tendency to move with the market or with an average stock that has the same characteristics as the market. The measure of a stock's sensitivity to market fluctuations is called its **beta coefficient**, designated with the Greek letter **β**.

An *average-risk stock* is defined as one that tends to move up and down in step with the general market as measured by some index, such as the Dow Jones Industrial Average (DJIA) or the Standard & Poor's 500 Index (S&P 500). Because such a stock mirrors the market, *by definition* its beta (β) is 1.0. This value indicates that, in general, if the market moves up by 10 percent, the average stock price will also increase by 10 percent; if the market falls by 10 percent, the average stock price will decline by 10 percent. If β = 0.5, the stock's systematic risk is only half as volatile as the market, which means that a change in return associated with risk will be only half as much as the average stock. If β = 2.0, the stock's relevant risk is twice as volatile as the market portfolio, so it is considered twice as risky as an average stock.

Because the beta coefficient measures a stock's volatility relative to an average stock (or the market), which has β = 1.0, we can calculate a stock's beta by comparing its returns to the market's returns over some time period. This comparison can be examined by plotting a line like the one shown in Figure 8.4. The slope of the line shows how the stock's returns move in response to movements in the general market; thus, the slope represents the stock's beta coefficient.[8] Betas for literally thousands

[7] Although we refer to the beta coefficient (β) as a measure of a stock's systematic risk in this section, the concept of beta applies to any investment, including bonds.

[8] A stock's beta coefficient generally is computed by performing simple regression analysis, where the dependent variable is the return on the stock and the independent variable is the return on the market.

beta coefficient, β A measure of the extent to which the returns on a given stock move with the stock market.

FIGURE 8.4 Volatility of a Stock's Returns Relative to Volatility of the Market's Returns, β

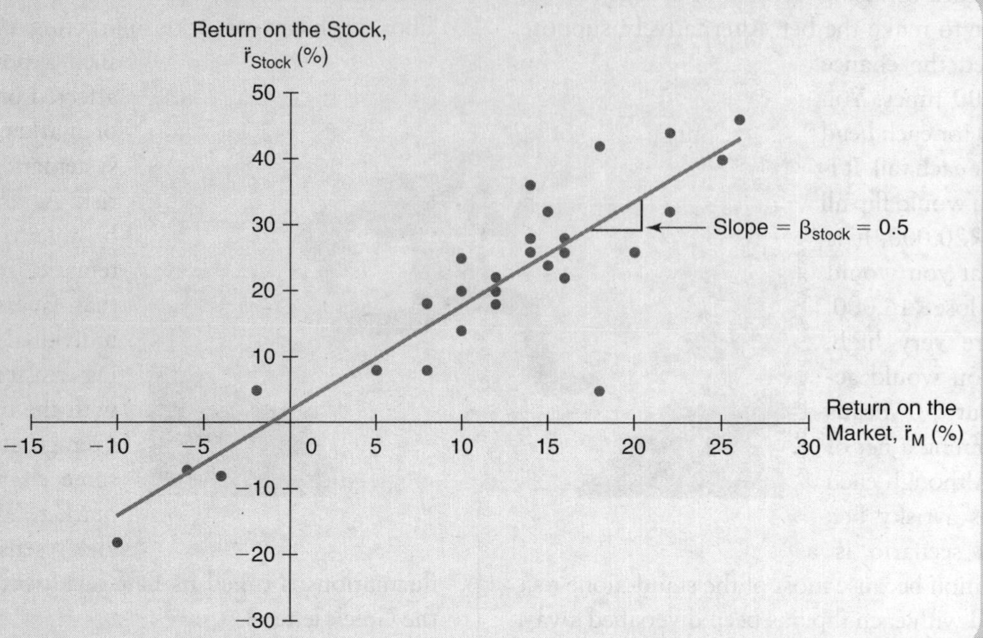

of companies are calculated and published by Bank of America Merrill Lynch, Value Line, Inc., and numerous other organizations. For example, the October 5, 2013, issue of *Standard & Poor's Stock Report* indicates that E*TRADE (β = 2.27), an online investment service, and Las Vegas Sands (β = 3.59), a company that manages casinos, have betas greater than 1.0; Columbia Sportswear (β = 1.05), a sports company, and Texas Instruments (β = 1.08), an information technology manufacturer, have betas approximately equal to 1.0, which is the average for all stocks; and Campbell Soup (β = 0.33), General Mills (β = 0.18), and PepsiCo (β = 0.49) have betas less than 1.0.[9]

If we add a higher-than-average-beta stock ($\beta_{Stock} > 1.0$) to an average-beta portfolio ($\beta_{Portfolio} = 1.0$), then the beta and consequently the riskiness, of the portfolio will increase. Conversely, if we add a lower-than-average-beta stock ($\beta_{Stock} < 1.0$) to an average-risk portfolio, the portfolio's beta and risk will decline. *Thus, because a stock's beta measures its contribution to the riskiness of a well-diversified portfolio, theoretically beta is the correct measure of the stock's riskiness.*

[9]In theory, betas can be negative. For example, if a stock's returns tend to rise when those of other stocks decline, and vice versa, then the regression line in a graph such as Figure 8.3 will have a downward slope, and the beta will be negative. Note, however, that few stocks have negative betas. American Business Collections, the fictitious collection agency introduced earlier, probably would have a negative beta.

We can summarize our discussion to this point as follows:

1. A stock's risk consists of two components: *market risk* and *firm-specific risk*.
2. *Firm-specific risk* can be eliminated through diversification. Most investors do diversify, either by holding large portfolios or by purchasing shares in mutual funds. We are left, then, with *market, or economic, risk,* which is caused by general economic movements that are reflected in the stock market. *Market risk is the only risk that is relevant to a rational, diversified investor because it cannot be eliminated (or reduced).*
3. Investors must be compensated for bearing risk. That is, the greater the riskiness of an investment, the higher its required return. Such *compensation is required only for risk that cannot be eliminated by diversification.* If risk premiums existed on investments with high diversifiable risk, well-diversified investors would start buying these securities and bidding up their prices, and their final (equilibrium) expected returns would eventually reflect only nondiversifiable market (systematic) risk.

An example might help clarify this point. Suppose half of Stock A's risk is market risk (it occurs because

Stock A moves in tandem with the market), and the other half of Stock A's risk is diversifiable. You hold only Stock A, so you are exposed to all of its risk—that is, its stand-alone (total) risk. As compensation for bearing so much risk, *you want* a risk premium that is 8 percent higher than the 5 percent Treasury bond rate; that is, you demand a return of 13 percent (= 5% + 8%) on this investment. But suppose other investors, including your professor, are well diversified: They also hold Stock A, but they have eliminated its diversifiable risk and thus are exposed to only half as much risk as you are. Consequently, their risk premium will be only half as large as yours, and they will *require* a return of only 9 percent (=5% + 4%) to invest in the stock.

If the stock actually yielded more than 9 percent in the market, other investors, including your professor, would buy it. If it yielded the 13 percent you demand, you would be willing to buy the stock, but well diversified investors would compete with you for its acquisition. They would bid its price up and its yield down, which would keep you from getting the stock at the return you need (want) to compensate you for taking on its *total risk*. In the end, you would have to accept a 9 percent return or else keep your money in the bank. Thus, risk premiums in a market populated with *rational* investors—that is, those who diversify—will reflect only market risk.

4. The systematic (nondiversifiable) risk of a stock is measured by its *beta coefficient*, which is an index of the stock's relative volatility compared with that of the entire market because a portfolio that includes all available investments—that is, a market portfolio—is perfectly diversified and thus exhibits systematic risk *only*. The benchmark is the market beta, which is 1.0. Firms with greater systematic risk volatilities than the market have betas that are greater than 1.0 (i.e., $\beta > 1.0$), and firms with smaller systematic risk volatilities than the market have betas that are less than 1.0 (i.e., $\beta < 1.0$).
5. *Because a stock's beta coefficient determines how the stock affects the riskiness of a diversified portfolio, beta (β) is a better measure of a stock's relevant risk than is standard deviation (σ), which measures total, or stand-alone, risk.*

8-3c Portfolio Beta Coefficients

A portfolio consisting of low-beta securities will itself have a low beta, because the beta of any set of securities is a weighted average of the individual securities' betas, as shown in Equation 8.7:

8.7

$$\text{Portfolio beta} = \beta_p = w_1\beta_1 + \cdots + w_N\beta_N = \sum_{j=1}^{N} w_j\beta_j$$

Here β_P, the beta of the portfolio, reflects how volatile the portfolio is in relation to the market; w_j is the fraction of the portfolio invested in the *j*th stock; and β_j is the beta coefficient of the *j*th stock. For example, if an investor holds a ₹105,000 portfolio consisting of ₹35,000 invested in each of three stocks, and each of the stocks has a beta of 0.7, then the portfolio's beta will be $\beta_{P1} = 0.7$:

$$\beta_{P1} = (1/3)(0.7) + (1/3)(0.7) + (1/3)(0.7) = 0.7$$

Such a portfolio will be less risky than the market, which means it should experience narrower price swings and demonstrate smaller rate-of-return fluctuations than the market. When graphed in a fashion similar to Figure 8.3, the slope of its regression line would be 0.7, which is less than that of a portfolio of average stocks.

Now suppose one of the existing stocks is sold and replaced by a stock with $\beta_j = 2.5$. This action will increase the riskiness of the portfolio from $\beta_{P1} = 0.7$ to $\beta_{P2} = 1.3$:

$$\beta_{P2} = (1/3)(0.7) + (1/3)(0.7) + (1/3)(2.5) = 1.3$$

Had a stock with $\beta_j = 0.4$ been added, the portfolio beta would have declined from 0.7 to 0.6. Adding a low-beta stock, therefore, would reduce the riskiness of the portfolio.

8-4 The Relationship between Risk and Rates of Return: The CAPM[10]

Now that we know beta is the appropriate measure of a stock's relevant risk, we must specify the relationship between relevant risk and return. To determine an investment's *required rate of return*, we use a theoretical

[10]This concept is discussed in more detail in investment textbooks. Some of the assumptions of the CAPM theory are unrealistic. As a consequence, the theory does not hold exactly.

model called the **capital asset pricing model (CAPM)**. The CAPM shows how the relevant risk of an investment, as measured by its beta coefficient, is used to determine the investment's appropriate required rate of return.

First, note from Figure 8.1 that the risk premium for any investment is the return that is generated in excess of the risk-free rate of return. Thus, for Stock j the required risk premium, RP_j, is the required rate of return on Stock j minus the risk-free rate, r_{RF}—that is, $RP_j = r_j - r_{RF}$. Using this same logic, we can state the market risk premium as $RP_M = r_M - r_{RF}$. This risk premium represents the additional return above the risk-free rate that is required to compensate investors for taking on the *average amount of risk* that is associated with the market portfolio, or average-risk stock, that has $\beta = 1.0$. Because the market portfolio contains only systematic, or market, risk, RP_M represents the return that investors require to be compensated for taking an average amount of relevant, or systematic, risk. It follows then that if the systematic (relevant) risk of a stock is twice as risky (volatile) as the market, or average systematic risk, the stock's *risk premium* should be twice as high as the market's risk premium, and vice versa. Furthermore, because we can measure a stock's relevant risk by computing its beta coefficient, β_j, we should be able to determine its appropriate risk premium by multiplying the market risk premium by the stock's beta, as shown in Equation 8.8:

8.8

$$\text{Risk premium for Stock j} = RP_j = RP_M \times \beta_j$$
$$= (rM - r_{RF})\beta_j$$

For example, if $\beta_j = 0.5$ and $RP_M = 6\%$, then $RP_j = 3.0\% = 6\% \times 0.5$.

As Figure 8.1 shows, the required return for any investment can be expressed in general terms as shown in Equation 8.9:

8.9

$$\underset{r_j}{\text{Required return}} = \underset{r_{RF}}{\text{Risk-free return}} + \underset{RP_j}{\text{Premium for risk}}$$

If we substitute the definition of RP_j given in Equation 8.8 into Equation 8.9, we have Equation 8.10, which is the equilibrium pricing equation for the CAPM:

8.10

$$r_j = r_{RF} + (RP_M)\beta_j$$
$$= r_{RF} + (r_M - r_{RF})\beta_j$$

To illustrate the application of the CAPM, suppose that the market's required rate of return is 11 percent, the risk-free rate of return is 5 percent, and Stock L has a beta coefficient equal to 0.5. Applying Equation 8.10, the stock's required rate of return would be

$$r_L = 5\% + (11\% - 5\%)(0.5) = 5\% + 6\%(0.5) = 8\%$$

If Stock H had $\beta_H = 2.0$, then its required rate of return would be 17 percent:

$$r_H = 5\% + (6\%)2.0 = 17\%$$

In addition, an average stock, with $\beta = 1.0$, would have a required return of 11 percent, the same as the market return:

$$r_A = 5\% + (6\%)1.0 = 11\% = r_M$$

Equation 8.10 is often expressed in graph form. The line that represents the required rate of return is called the **security market line (SML)**. Figure 8.5 shows the SML when $r_{RF} = 5\%$ and $r_M = 11\%$. Note the following points:

1. *Required rates of return* are shown on the vertical axis, and risk as measured by beta is shown on the horizontal axis.
2. Riskless securities have $\beta_j = 0$; therefore, $r_{RF} = 5\%$ appears as the vertical axis intercept in Figure 8.5.
3. The slope of the SML reflects the degree of *risk aversion* in the economy. The greater the average investor's aversion to risk, (a) the steeper the slope of the line, (b) the greater the risk premium for any stock, and (c) the higher the required rate of return on stocks.[11]
4. The values we worked out for stocks with $\beta_L = 0.5$, $\beta_A = 1.0$, and $\beta_H = 2.0$ agree with the values shown on the graph for r_{Low}, r_{Avg}, and r_{High}.

[11]Students sometimes confuse beta with the slope of the SML. This is a mistake. The slope of any line is equal to the "rise" divided by the "run," or $(Y_1 - Y_0)/(X_1 - X_0)$. Consider Figure 8.5 *on the next page*. If we let Y = r and X = β, and we go from the origin to β = 1.0, we see that the slope is $(r_M - r_{RF})/(\beta_M - \beta_{RF}) = (11\% - 5\%)/(1 - 0) = 6\%$. Thus the slope of the SML is equal to $(r_M - r_{RF})$, the market risk premium. In Figure 8.5, $r_j = 5\% + (6\%)\beta_j$, so a doubling of beta (for example, from 1.0 to 2.0) would produce a six-percentage point increase in r_j.

capital asset pricing model (CAPM) A model used to determine the required return on an asset, which is based on the proposition that an asset's return should be equal to the risk-free return plus a risk premium that reflects the asset's nondiversifiable risk.

security market line (SML) The line that shows the relationship between risk as measured by beta and the required rate of return for individual securities.

FIGURE 8.5 The Security Market Line (SML)

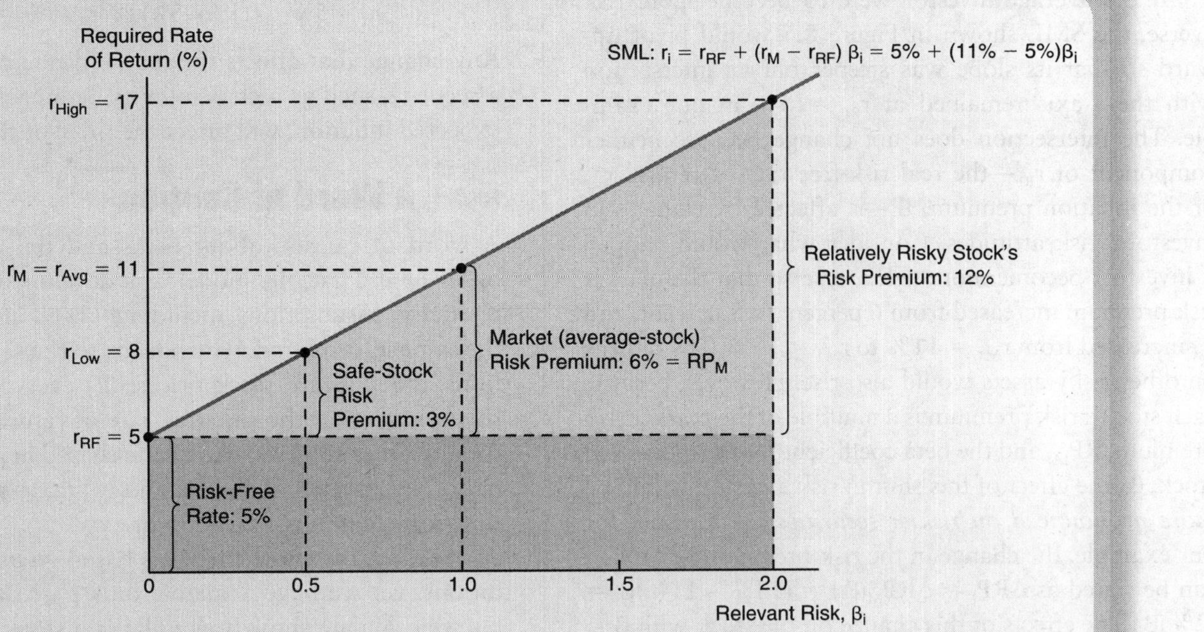

Both the SML and a company's position on it change over time because of changes in interest rates, investors' risk aversion, and individual companies' betas. Such changes are discussed in the following sections.

8-4a **The Impact of Inflation**

As we learned in Chapter 5, the risk-free rate of return, r_{RF}, is the price of money to a riskless borrower. We also learned in Chapter 5 that r_{RF} as measured by the rate on U.S. Treasury securities is called the *nominal,* or *quoted,* rate, and it consists of two elements: (1) a *real inflation-free rate of return, r**, and (2) *an inflation premium, IP,* equal to the anticipated rate of inflation.[12] Thus, $r_{RF} = r^* + IP$.

If the expected rate of inflation rose by 2 percent, r_{RF} would also increase by 2 percent. In this case, the SML shown in Figure 8.5 would shift upward so that it is parallel to the existing line, which indicates that the 2 percent increase in expected inflation causes r_{RF} to increase by 2 percent.[13] Because the inflation premium is built into the required rates of return of both riskless and risky assets, the increase in expected inflation would cause an *equal increase in the rates of return on all risky assets.* Suppose r_{RF} increases from 5 percent to 7 percent. Because inflation affects r_{RF}, the market risk premium will not change; thus, $RP_M = 6\%$. Therefore, the effect on the returns on a stock with $\beta = 1.0$ and a stock with $\beta = 2.0$ would be

Investment	RP_M	$r_{RF} + (RP_M)\beta = r$	
Stock A, $\beta_A = 1.0$	6%	5% + (6%)1.0 = 11%	$\Delta = 2\%$
	6%	7% + (6%)1.0 = 13%	
Stock H, $\beta_H = 2.0$	6%	5% + (6%)2.0 = 17%	$\Delta = 2\%$
	6%	7% + (6%)2.0 = 19%	

Thus, all securities' returns increase by 2 percentage points.

8-4b **Changes in Risk Aversion**

The **market risk premium (RP_M)** depends on the degree of aversion that investors on average have to risk, which is reflected in the slope of the security market line (SML). The steeper the slope of the line, the greater the average investor's risk aversion, and thus the greater the return investors require as compensation

market risk premium (RP_M) The additional return over the risk-free rate needed to compensate investors for assuming an average amount of risk.

[12]Long-term Treasury bonds also contain a maturity risk premium (MRP). Here we consider short-term T-bills; thus, MRP = 0.

[13]Note that r_{RF} in a CAPM analysis can be proxied by either a long-term rate (the T-bond rate) or a short-term rate (the T-bill rate). We use the T-bill rate here.

for risk. *As risk aversion increases, so does the risk premium,* and, therefore, so does the slope of the SML.[14]

If the average investor were to become more risk averse, the SML shown in Figure 8.5 would pivot upward so that its slope was steeper but its intersection with the y-axis remained at r_{RF} = 5% in our example. The intersection does not change because neither component of r_{RF}—the real risk-free rate of return, r*, or the inflation premium, IP—is affected by changes in investors' risk attitudes. Consider what would happen if investors become more risk averse so that the market risk premium increased from 6 percent to 8 percent, and r_M increased from r_{M1} = 11% to r_{M2} = 13%. The returns on other risky assets would also rise. However, because each stock's risk premium is a multiple of the market risk premium, RP_M, and the beta coefficient for the individual stock, β_j, the effect of this shift in risk aversion would be *more pronounced on riskier securities*. As a result, for our example, the change in the risk premium for Stock j can be stated as $\Delta RP_j = \Delta RP_M(\beta_j) = (13\% - 11\%)\beta_j = (2\%)\beta_j$. The effects of this change on the stock with β = 1.0 and the stock with β = 2.0 in Figure 8.5 would be

Investment	RP_M	$r_{RF} + (RP_M)\beta = r$	
Stock A, $\beta_A = 1.0$	6%	5% + (6%)1.0 = 11%	Δ = 2%
	8%	5% + (8%)1.0 = 13%	
Stock H, $\beta_H = 2.0$	6%	5% + (6%)2.0 = 17%	Δ = 4%
	8%	5% + (8%)2.0 = 21%	

As you can see, the securities' returns increased by $\Delta RP_M(\beta_j)$. Because Stock H's beta coefficient is two times Stock A's beta coefficient, the effect of the risk premium change was twice as much for Stock H. Thus, *when the average investor's aversion to risk changes, investments with higher beta coefficients experience greater changes in their required rates of return than investments with lower betas.*

8-4c **Changes in a Stock's Beta Coefficient**

As we will see later in this book, a firm can affect its beta risk by changing the composition of its assets and by modifying its use of debt financing. External factors, such as increased competition within a firm's industry or the expiration of basic patents, can also alter a company's beta. When such changes occur, the required rate of return, r, changes as well. Suppose some action occurred that caused Stock L's beta to increase from 0.5 to 0.8. Stock L's required rate of return would increase from r_{L1} = 8% to

$$r_{L2} = 5\% + (11\% - 5\%)0.8 = 9.8\%$$

Any change that affects the required rate of return on a security, such as a change in its beta coefficient or in expected inflation, will affect the price of the security.

8-4d **A Word of Caution**

A word of caution about betas and the CAPM is in order here. First, the model was developed under very restrictive assumptions, including: (1) all investors have the same information, which leads to the same expectations about future stock prices; (2) everyone can borrow and lend at the risk-free rate of return; (3) stocks (or any other security) can be purchased in any denomination or fraction of shares; and (4) taxes and transaction costs (commissions) do not exist.

Second, the entire theory is based on *expected* conditions, yet we have available only *past* data. The betas we calculate show how volatile a stock has been in the past, but future conditions could certainly change. The stock's *future volatility,* which is the item of real concern to investors, might therefore differ quite dramatically from its past volatility. For this reason, many investors and analysts use the CAPM and the concept of β to provide "ballpark" figures for further analysis. The concept that investors should be rewarded only for taking relevant risk makes sense. Moreover, the CAPM provides an easy way to get a "rough" estimate of the relevant risk and the appropriate required rate of return of an investment (or a portfolio of investments).

8-5 **Stock Market Equilibrium**

Suppose the risk-free return is 5 percent, the market *risk premium* is 6 percent, and Stock Q has a beta of 1.5 (β_Q = 1.5). In this case, an average investor will require a return on Stock Q of r_Q = 5% + 6%(1.5) = 14%. The average investor will want to buy Stock Q if the *expected rate of return*, $\hat{r}_Q$, exceeds 14 percent, will want to sell it if $\hat{r}_Q < 14\%$, and will be indifferent (and therefore will hold but not buy or sell Stock Q) if $\hat{r}_Q = 14\%$. Now suppose the investor's portfolio contains Stock Q, and he or she analyzes the stock's prospects and concludes that its earnings, dividends, and price can be expected to grow at a constant rate of 4 percent per year forever. The last dividend paid was D_0 = ₹3, so the next expected dividend is $\hat{D}_1$ = ₹3.00(1.04) = ₹3.12. Our *average* (marginal)

[14]If investors were *indifferent* to risk, and if r_{RF} was 5 percent, then risky assets would also provide an expected return of 5 percent. If there were no risk aversion, there would be no risk premium, so the SML would be horizontal.

investor observes that the present price of the stock, P_0, is ₹34.67. Should he or she purchase more of Stock Q, sell the present holdings or maintain the present position?

Recall from Chapter 7 that we can calculate Stock Q's *expected rate of return* using Equation 7.3:

$$\hat{r}_Q = \frac{\hat{D}_1}{P_0} + g = \frac{₹3.12}{₹34.67} + 0.04$$
$$= 0.09 + 0.04 = 0.13 = 13\%$$

Because the expected rate of return, $\hat{r}_Q = 13\%$, is less than the required return, $r_Q = 14\%$, this marginal investor would want to sell the stock, as would other stockholders. Because few people would want to buy at the ₹34.67 price, the present owners would be unable to find buyers unless they cut the price of the stock. The price would therefore decline, and this decline would continue until the stock's price reached ₹31.20. At that point, the market for this security would be in **equilibrium** because the expected rate of return, 14 percent, would be equal to the required rate of return:

Comstock/Jupiter Images

$$\hat{r}_Q = \frac{₹3.12}{₹31.20} + 0.04 = 0.10 + 0.04 = 0.14 = 14\% = r_Q$$

Had the stock initially sold for less than ₹31.20—say, ₹28.36—events would have been reversed. Investors would have wanted to buy the stock because its expected rate of return ($\hat{r} = 15\%$) would have exceeded its required rate of return, and buy orders would have driven the stock's price up to ₹31.20.

To summarize, two conditions must hold in equilibrium:

1. The expected rate of return, $\hat{r}_j$, as seen by the marginal investor must equal the required rate of return, r_j; that is, $\hat{r}_j = r_j$.
2. The actual market price of the stock, P_0, must equal its intrinsic value, $\hat{P}_0$, as estimated by the marginal (average) investor; that is, $P_0 = \hat{P}_0$.

Of course, some individual investors might believe that $\hat{r}_j > r_j$ and $P_0 < \hat{P}_0$; hence they would invest most of their funds in the stock. Other investors might ascribe to the opposite view and sell all of their shares. Nevertheless, it is the marginal investor who establishes the actual market price. For this investor, $\hat{r}_j = r_j$ and $P_0 = \hat{P}_0$. If these conditions do not hold, trading will occur until they do hold.

8-6 Different Types of Risk

In Chapter 5, we introduced the concept of risk in our discussion of interest rates. However, we did not discuss risk evaluation in detail; rather, we described some of the factors that determine the total risk associated with debt, such as default risk (DRP), liquidity risk (LP), and maturity risk (MRP). In reality, these risks also affect other types of investments, including equity. Equity does not represent a legal contract that requires the firm to pay defined amounts of dividends at particular times or to "act" in specific ways. There is, however, an expectation that positive returns will be generated through future distributions of cash because dividends will be paid, capital gains will be generated through growth, or both events will occur. Investors also expect the firm to behave "appropriately." If these expectations are not met, investors generally consider the firm to be in "default" of their expectations. In such cases, as long as no laws have been broken, stockholders generally do not have legal recourse, as would be the case for a default on debt. As a result, investors penalize the firm by selling their stock, which causes the value of the firm's stock to decline.

In this chapter, we build on the general concept that was introduced in Chapter 5 by showing how the risk premium associated with any investment should be determined (at least in theory). The basis of our discussion is Equation 5.2, which we develop further in this chapter as follows:

$$r_j = \text{Risk-free rate} + \text{Risk premium}$$
$$= r_{RF} + (r_M - r_{RF})\beta_j = \text{CAPM}$$

According to the CAPM, investors should not expect to be rewarded for all of the risk associated with an individual investment—that is, its total, or stand-alone, risk—because some risk can be eliminated through diversification.

equilibrium The condition under which the expected return on a security is just equal to its required return, $\hat{r} = r$, and the price is stable.

The *relevant risk*, and thus the risk for which investors should be compensated, is that portion of the total risk that cannot be diversified away. Thus, in this chapter we showed the following:

Total risk = σ =	Market (systematic) Risk +	Firm-specific (unsystematic) risk
=	Nondiversifiable risk +	Diversifiable risk
Relevant risk =	Nondiversifiable (systematic) risk	

Systematic risk is represented by an investment's beta coefficient, β, in Equation 8.10.

The specific types and sources of risk to which a firm or an investor is exposed are numerous, and vary considerably depending on the situation. A detailed discussion of all the different types of risks and the techniques used to evaluate risks is beyond the scope of this book. However, you should recognize that risk is an important factor in the determination of the required rate of return (r), which, according to the following equation, is one of the two variables we need to determine the value of an asset:

$$\text{Value} = \frac{\widehat{CF}_1}{(1+r)^1} + \cdots + \frac{\widehat{CF}_n}{(1+r)^n} = \sum_{t=1}^{n} \frac{\widehat{CF}_t}{(1+r)^t}$$

According to this equation, the value of an asset, which could be a stock or a bond, is based on the cash flows that the asset is expected to generate during its life, $\widehat{CF}_t$, and the rate of return, r, that investors require to "put up" their money to purchase the investment. In this chapter, we provide you with an indication as to how r should be determined, and we show that investors demand higher rates of return to compensate them for taking greater amounts of "relevant" risk.

Because it is an important concept and has a direct effect on value, we continue to discuss risk in the remainder of the book. Table 8.4 shows the risks that are discussed in this book and indicates whether each risk is considered a component of systematic (nondiversifiable) risk or of unsystematic (diversifiable) risk. Note that (1) this table oversimplifies risk analysis, because some risks are not easily classified as either systematic or unsystematic; and (2) some of the risks included in the table will be discussed later in the book. Even so, this table should show you the relationships among the different risks discussed in the book.

TABLE 8.4 Different Types (Sources) of Risk

General Type of Risk	Name of Risk	Brief Description
I. Systematic risks (nondiversifiable risk; market risk; relevant risk)	Interest rate risk	When interest rates change, (1) the values of investments change (in opposite directions) and (2) the rate at which funds can be reinvested also changes (in the same direction).
	Inflation risk	The primary reason interest rates change is because investors change their expectations about future inflation.
	Maturity risk	Long-term investments experience greater price reactions to interest rate changes than do short-term investments.
	Liquidity risk	Reflects the fact that some investments are more easily converted into cash on a short notice at a "reasonable price" than are other securities.
	Exchange rate risk	Multinational firms deal with different currencies; the rate at which the currency of one country can be *exchanged* into the currency of another country—that is, the exchange rate—changes as market conditions change.
	Political risk	Any action by a government that reduces the value of an investment.
II. Unsystematic risks (diversifiable risk; firm-specific risk)	Business risk	Risk that would be inherent in the firm's operations if it used no debt—factors such as labor conditions, product safety, quality of management, competitive conditions, and so forth, affect firm-specific risk.
	Financial risk	Risk associated with how the firm is financed; that is, its credit risk.

(continued)

TABLE 8.4 Different Types (Sources) of Risk (*Continued*)

General Type of Risk	Name of Risk	Brief Description
	Default risk	Part of financial risk, the chance that the firm will not be able to service its existing debt.
III. *Combined risks* (some systematic risk and some unsystematic risk)	Total risk (Stand-alone risk)	The combination of systematic risk and unsystematic risk; also referred to as stand-alone risk, because this is the risk an investor takes if he or she purchases only one investment, which is tantamount to "putting all your eggs into one basket."
	Corporate risk	The riskiness of the firm without considering the effect of stockholder diversification; based on the combination of assets held by the firm (inventory, accounts receivable, plant and equipment, and so forth). Some diversification exists because the firm's assets represent a portfolio of investments in real assets.

KEY RISK AND RETURN CONCEPTS

To conclude this chapter, we summarize some risk/return concepts that were discussed.

- In finance, we define risk as the chance that you will not receive the return that you expect, regardless of whether the actual outcome is better than expected or worse than expected.
- Riskier investments must have higher expected returns than less risky investments; otherwise, people will not purchase investments with higher risks.
- The total risk of any investment can be divided into two components: diversifiable risk and nondiversifiable risk. Diversifiable risk is not important to informed investors, because they will eliminate its effects through diversification. Thus, the relevant risk is nondiversifiable risk, because it cannot be eliminated, even in a perfectly diversified portfolio.
- The effects of nondiversifiable risk, which is also labeled systematic risk or market risk, can be determined by computing the beta coefficient (β) of an investment. The beta coefficient measures the volatility of an investment relative to the volatility of the market, which, in theory, is perfectly diversified and thus is affected only by systematic risk.
- According to the capital asset pricing model (CAPM), an investment's required rate of return can be computed as $r_i = r_{RF} + (r_{RF} - r_M)\beta_i = r_{RF} + (RP_M)\beta_i$.

MULTIPLE CHOICE QUESTIONS

1. Expected return is based on

a. Market returns

b. Beta

c. Probability distributions

d. None of the above

2. Risk aversion refers to

a. Investors not taking above average risk

b. Investors taking only very minimum risk

c. Market risk being high

d. Market risk being low

3. For measuring risk,

a. The standard deviation is the best

b. The standard deviation is the only measure

c. The standard deviation calculates both favorable and unfavorable risk

d. Both a and c

4. Systematic and unsystematic risks are different from each other in that

   a. Systematic risk is specific to the company and unsystematic risk is related to macroeconomic conditions

   b. Systematic risk is specific to the company and unsystematic risk is not measurable

   c. Unsystematic risk is specific to the company and systematic risk is related to macroeconomic conditions

   d. Systematic risk is lower than unsystematic risk

5. The effects of non-diversifiable risk can be

   a. Measured by Beta

   b. Cannot be measured

   c. Can be measured by risk free return

   d. Can be measured as market return

6. Calculation of return involves probabilities,

   a. If the return has to be calculated over a past period

   b. If the return has to be calculated over a period just concluded

   c. If the return has to be calculated over a future period

   d. None of the above

7. The expected return in future will be

   a. A function of the probabilities of flows

   b. A function of the quantum of flows

   c. A function of both quantum and probability of flows

   d. A function of the certainty of flows

8. Volatility signifies

   a. Variation from the mean in a negative way

   b. Variation from the mean in both positive and negative ways

   c. Variation from the square of the mean

   d. All of the above

9. Beta measures

   a. The volatility of the market

   b. The volatility of the individual portfolio in relation to the volatility of the market

   c. The return of the market

   d. The return of the individual portfolio in relation to the return of the market

10. Diversifiable risk

   a. Is very important for investors

   b. Is not important for investors

   c. Is important if combined with risk-free return

   d. Cannot be measured in isolation

Answers:

1.	(c)	2.	(b)	3.	(d)	4.	(c)	5.	(a)
6.	(c)	7.	(c)	8.	(b)	9.	(b)	10.	(d)

PROBLEMS

For more problems, login to CourseMate for CFIN at CengageBrain.com

8-1 What are the (a) expected return, (b) standard deviation, and (c) coefficient of variation for an investment with the following probability distribution?

Probability	Payoff
0.2	19.0%
0.7	9.0
0.1	4.0

8-2 Calculate the (a) expected return, (b) standard deviation, and (c) coefficient of variation for an investment with the following probability distribution:

Probability	Payoff
0.45	32.0%
0.35	−4.0
0.20	−20.0

8-3 Compute the (a) expected return, (b) standard deviation, and (c) coefficient of variation for investments with the following probability distributions:

Probability	r_A	r_B
0.3	30.0%	5.0%
0.2	10.0	15.0
0.5	−2.0	25.0

8-4 Suppose you are an average risk-averse investor who can purchase only one of the following stocks. Which should you purchase? Explain your reasoning.

Investment	Expected Return, $\hat{r}$	Standard Deviation, σ
Stock M	6.0%	4.0%
Stock N	18.0	12.0
Stock O	12.0	7.0

8-5 Which of the following investments has the greater *relative* risk?

Investment	Expected Return, $\hat{r}$	Standard Deviation, σ
F	16.0%	7.0%
G	27.0	13.0

8-6 Ramya invested ₹9,000 in a stock that has an expected return equal to 18 percent and ₹21,000 in a stock with an 8 percent expected return. What is the portfolio's expected return?

8-7 What is the expected return of the following portfolio of investments, $\hat{r}_P$:

Investment	$\hat{r}$	Amount Invested
DEF	4%	₹30,000
JKL	24	25,000
TUV	14	45,000

8-8 Currently, the risk-free return is 3 percent, and the expected market rate of return is 9 percent. What is the expected return of the following three-stock portfolio?

Amount Invested	Beta
₹350,000	1.0
250,000	0.2
400,000	2.5

8-9 Compute the (a) expected return and (b) standard deviation of the following investments:

Probability	r_{ABC}	r_{RST}
0.1	22.0%	−2.0%
0.6	12.0	12.0
0.3	2.0	30.0

(c) Suppose you form a portfolio that consists of 60 percent Investment ABC and 40 percent Investment RST. Compute the expected return and standard deviation of the portfolio. (d) Compare the portfolio's standard deviation with the individual investments' standard deviations.

8-10 Of the ₹60,000 invested in a two-stock portfolio, 40 percent is invested in Stock S and 60 percent is invested in Stock X. If Stock S has a beta coefficient equal to 1.5 and the beta of the portfolio is 2.1, what is the beta of Stock X?

8-11 Pradeep's investment portfolio contains five stocks that have a total value equal to ₹40,000. The beta coefficient of this portfolio is 1.2. Pradeep wants to invest an additional ₹10,000 in a stock that has beta equal to 2.2. After he adds this stock, what will be the portfolio's new beta?

8-12 Wajralal currently has ₹120,000 invested in a four-stock portfolio with a beta coefficient equal to 0.8. Wajralal plans to sell one of the stocks in his portfolio for ₹48,000, which will increase the portfolio's beta to 1.0. What is the beta coefficient of the stock Wajralal plans to sell?

8-13 Shilpa's portfolio, which is valued at ₹200,000, contains six stocks and has a beta coefficient equal to 1.5. Later today, Shilpa is going to sell one of the stocks in her portfolio for ₹40,000.

After the sale, the portfolio's beta will be 1.3. What is the beta coefficient of the stock that Shilpa plans to sell?

8–14 The current risk-free rate of return, r_{RF}, is 3 percent and the market *risk premium*, RP_M, is 6 percent. If the beta coefficient associated with a firm's stock is 1.5, what should be the stock's required rate of return?

8–15 Suppose the risk-free rate of return, r_{RF}, is 4 percent, and the market return, r_M, is expected to be 12 percent. What is the required rate of return for a stock with a beta coefficient, β, equal to 2.5?

8–16 ZR Corporation's stock has a beta coefficient equal to 0.8 and a required rate of return equal to 11 percent. If the expected return on the market is 12.5 percent, what is the risk-free rate of return, r_{RF}?

8–17 Stock V has a beta coefficient of 2.0, and Stock W has a beta of 0.5. The expected rate of return on an average stock is 11 percent, and the risk-free rate of return is 5 percent. By how much does the required return on the riskier stock exceed the required return on the less risky stock?

8–18 Recently, Kamini determined that the required rate of return for Stock Q is 11 percent. In her analysis, she determined that the risk-free rate of return, r_{RF}, is 4 percent and that the required return on the market portfolio, r_M, is 9 percent. Today, however, Kamini received new information that indicates the market risk premium, RP_M, is actually 1 percent higher than she estimated in her original analysis. Based on this new information, what should be the required rate of return for Stock Q?

8–19 Suppose the risk-free rate of return is 3.5 percent and the market *risk premium* is 7 percent. Stock U, which has a beta coefficient equal to 0.9, is currently selling for ₹28 per share. The company is expected to grow at a 4 percent rate forever, and the most recent dividend paid to stockholders was ₹1.75 per share. Is Stock U correctly priced? Explain.

8–20 High Energy (HE) Company recently paid a ₹2 per share dividend, which is expected to grow at a constant rate forever. HE's stock, which has a beta coefficient equal to 1.1, is selling for ₹37.50 per share. Currently, the risk-free rate of return is 4 percent, and the return on an average stock is 10 percent. If HE's stock is selling at its equilibrium price, what is its growth rate?

Risk and Rates of Return

Learning Outcomes

LO.1 Explain what it means to take risk when investing.

- Risk is defined as the possibility that you will not earn the return you expect when investing. Stated differently, risk exists when an investment has more than one possible outcome. Some risk can be considered "good" because greater returns than expected are possible, whereas some risk is "bad" because lower returns than expected are possible.

LO.2 Compute the risk and return of an investment, and explain how the risk and return of an investment are related.

- The risk associated with an investment is determined by measuring the variability of returns, or average deviation from the expected return. The standard deviation (σ) measures the scatter, or variability, of the possible outcomes for an investment; σ is a measure of the investment's total, or stand-alone, risk, which is the risk an investor takes when holding an investment by itself.
- The expected return on an investment is the weighted average return that investors will earn over a long period of time if the probability distribution that is associated with the investment is correctly specified.
- Generally, investments with greater risk earn higher rates of return because their risk premiums are higher.

LO.3 Identify relevant and irrelevant risk, and explain how irrelevant risk can be reduced.

- The total risk of an investment consists of (1) firm-specific (unsystematic) risk, which is caused by events that are unique to a particular firm and can be reduced or eliminated through diversification, and (2) market (systematic) risk, which stems from factors that affect the general economy and thus cannot be reduced through diversification. Relevant risk refers to the risk that investors must take; thus, the relevant risk for an investment is its systematic, or market, risk because it cannot be eliminated.

LO.4 Describe how to determine the appropriate reward—that is, risk premium—that investors should earn for purchasing a risky investment.

- Investors should be rewarded for relevant risk only (the investment's systematic risk). Because the market as a whole is considered perfectly diversified, its variability (risk) is related to systematic risk only, and thus the market can be used as a benchmark for measuring the systematic risk of any investment. Thus, the systematic risk associated with an individual investment can be determined by computing the relationship between the investment's variability and the variability of the market. This relationship, which is called the beta coefficient (β), indicates whether the investment's relevant risk is higher than ($\beta > 1.0$), lower than ($\beta < 1.0$), or equal to ($\beta = 1.0$) that of the market. Thus, the risk premium that investors should earn on an investment can be stated as a function of the market risk premium, RP_M. That is, the risk premium for an individual stock should be $RP_{Stock} = RP_M(\beta_{Stock})$, which means that (1) $RP_{Stock} > RP_M$ when $\beta_{Stock} > 1.0$, (2) $RP_{Stock} < RP_M$ when $\beta_{Stock} < 1.0$, and (3) $RP_{Stock} = RP_M$ when $\beta_{Stock} = 1.0$.

LO.5 Describe actions that investors take when the return they require to purchase an investment is different from the return they expect the investment to produce.

- If investors require a return that exceeds the return they expect an investment to generate, they will not purchase the investment, or they will sell the investment if they already own it. Such activity will tend to lower the price of the investment, and thus increase its expected return. Investors' reaction would be opposite if the expected return was greater than their required return.

CHAPTER 8 REVIEW

LO.6 Identify different types of risk and classify each as relevant or irrelevant with respect to determining an investment's required rate of return.

- Risks that are unique to a particular firm are classified as firm-specific risks, which are considered irrelevant when determining an investment's required return. Risks that affect all firms, generally through the economy, are considered relevant because they cannot be eliminated through diversification. These systematic factors represent the risks for which investors should be rewarded.

Chapter 8 Key Risk Concepts

- In finance, we define risk as the chance that you will not receive the return that you expect, regardless of whether the actual outcome is better than expected or worse than expected.
- Riskier investments must have higher expected returns than less-risky investments; otherwise, people will not purchase investments with higher risks.
- The total risk of any investment can be divided into two components: diversifiable risk and nondiversifiable risk. Diversifiable risk is not important to informed investors, because they will eliminate its effects through diversification. Thus, the relevant risk is nondiversifiable risk, because it cannot be eliminated, even in a perfectly diversified portfolio.
- The effects of nondiversifiable risk, which is also called systematic risk or market risk, can be determined by computing the beta coefficient (β) of an investment. The beta coefficient measures the volatility of an investment relative to the volatility of the market, which is considered to be nearly perfectly diversified, and thus is affected only by systematic risk.
- According to the capital asset pricing model (CAPM), an investment's required rate of return can be computed as

$$r_i = r_{RF} + (r_{RF} - r_M)\beta_i = r_{RF} + (RP_M)\beta_i$$

Key Terms

LO.1

risk The chance that an outcome other than the expected one will occur. *p. 126*

probability distribution A listing of all possible outcomes or events, with a probability (chance of occurrence) assigned to each outcome. *p. 126*

LO.2

expected rate of return, $\hat{r}$ The rate of return expected to be realized from an investment, which is the mean value of the probability distribution of possible results. *p. 126*

standard deviation, σ A measure of the tightness, or variability, of a set of outcomes. *p. 127*

coefficient of variation (CV) A standardized measure of the risk per unit of return. It is calculated by dividing the standard deviation by the expected return. *p. 128*

risk aversion Risk-averse investors require higher rates of return to invest in higher-risk securities. *p. 129*

risk premium (RP) The portion of the expected return that can be attributed to the additional risk of an investment. It is the difference between the expected rate of return on a given risky asset and the expected rate of return on a less risky asset. *p. 129*

LO.3

expected return on a portfolio, $\hat{r}_P$ The weighted average of the expected returns on stocks held in a portfolio. *p. 130*

realized rate of return, $\bar{r}$ The return that is actually earned. The actual return ($\bar{r}$) usually differs from the expected return ($\hat{r}$). *p. 130*

diversification Reduction of stand-alone risk of an individual investment by combining it with other investments in a portfolio. *p. 131*

correlation coefficient, ρ A measure of the degree of relationship between two variables. *p. 131*

firm-specific (diversifiable) risk That part of a security's risk associated with random outcomes generated by events or behaviors, specific to the firm. It *can* be eliminated by proper diversification. *p. 133*

market (nondiversifiable) risk The part of a security's risk associated with economic, or market, factors that systematically affect all firms to some extent. It *cannot* be eliminated by diversification. *p. 133*

relevant risk The portion of a security's risk that cannot be diversified away; the security's market risk. It reflects the security's contribution to the risk of a portfolio. *p. 133*

beta coefficient, β A measure of the extent to which the returns on a given stock move with the stock market. *p. 134*

LO.4

capital asset pricing model (CAPM) A model used to determine the required return on an asset, which is based on the proposition that an asset's return should be equal to the risk-free return plus a risk premium that reflects the asset's nondiversifiable risk. *p. 137*

security market line (SML) The line that shows the relationship between risk as measured by beta and the required rate of return for individual securities. *p. 137*

market risk premium (RP_M) The additional return over the risk-free rate needed to compensate investors for assuming an average amount of risk. *p. 138*

LO.5

equilibrium The condition under which the expected return on a security is just equal to its required return, $\hat{r} = r$, and the price is stable. *p. 140*

PART 4

Valuation—Real Assets (Capital Budgeting)

CHAPTER 9

Capital Budgeting Techniques

Learning Outcomes

LO.1 Describe the importance of capital budgeting decisions and the general process that is followed when making investment (capital budgeting) decisions about fixed assets.

LO.2 Describe how the net present value (NPV) technique and the internal rate of return (IRR) technique are used to make investment (capital budgeting) decisions.

LO.3 Compare the NPV technique with the IRR technique, and discuss why the two techniques might not always lead to the same investment decisions.

LO.4 Describe how conflicts that might arise when using the NPV and IRR techniques can be resolved by using the modified internal rate of return (MIRR) technique.

LO.5 Describe other capital budgeting techniques used by businesses to make investment decisions and which techniques are used most often in practice.

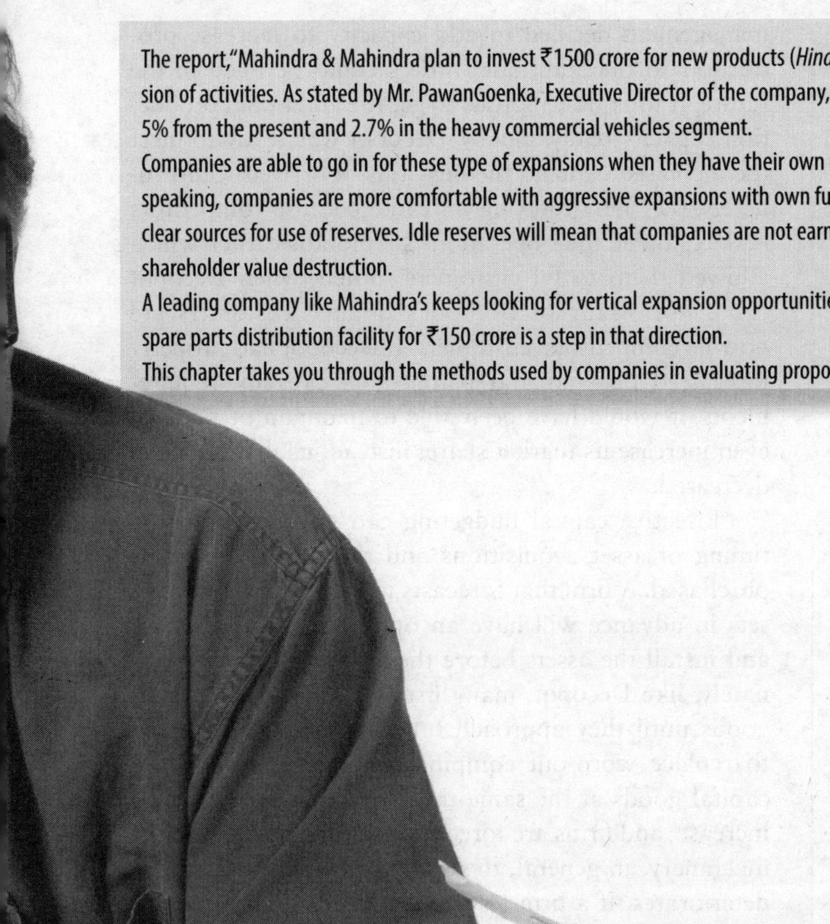

The report,"Mahindra & Mahindra plan to invest ₹1500 crore for new products (*Hindu Business Line*, October 15, 2015)," suggests an aggressive plan for expansion of activities. As stated by Mr. PawanGoenka, Executive Director of the company, the plan seeks to increase the market share of the company to more than 5% from the present and 2.7% in the heavy commercial vehicles segment.

Companies are able to go in for these type of expansions when they have their own reserves of surplus funds or are able to access cheap credit. Generally speaking, companies are more comfortable with aggressive expansions with own funds. This is, in part, a necessity, since there is a constant need to find out clear sources for use of reserves. Idle reserves will mean that companies are not earning enough tofor meeting the cost of capital and this will tantamount to shareholder value destruction.

A leading company like Mahindra's keeps looking for vertical expansion opportunities so that existing strengths can be consolidated. The plan to set up a new spare parts distribution facility for ₹150 crore is a step in that direction.

This chapter takes you through the methods used by companies in evaluating proposals.

In the previous three chapters, we showed how financial assets are valued and how required rates of return are determined. Now we apply these concepts to investment decisions involving the fixed assets of a firm, or *capital budgeting*. Here the term *capital* refers to fixed (long-term) assets used in production, whereas a *budget* is a plan that details projected cash inflows and cash outflows during some future period. Thus, the capital budget is an outline of planned expenditures on fixed assets,

Study Tools

Problems are found at the end of this chapter

+

Login to **CourseMate** for **CFIN** at **CengageBrain.com** for additional problems and other study tools!

and **capital budgeting** is the process of analyzing projects and deciding (1) which are acceptable investments and (2) which should actually be purchased.

Our treatment of capital budgeting is divided into two chapters. First, in this chapter we give an overview and explain the basic techniques used in capital budgeting analysis. In Chapter 10, we show how the cash flows associated with capital budgeting projects are estimated and how risk is considered in capital budgeting decisions.

9-1 Importance of Capital Budgeting

A number of factors combine to make capital budgeting decisions among the most important ones that financial managers must make. First, the impact of capital budgeting is long term; thus, the firm loses some decision-making flexibility when capital projects are purchased. For example, when a firm invests in an asset with a 10-year economic life, its operations are affected for 10 years—that is, the firm is "locked in" by the capital budgeting decision. Further, because asset expansion is fundamentally related to expected future sales, a decision to buy a fixed asset that is expected to last 10 years involves an implicit 10-year sales forecast. An error in the forecast of asset requirements can have serious consequences. If the firm invests too much in fixed assets, it will incur unnecessarily heavy expenses. But if it does not spend enough on fixed assets, it might find that inefficient production and inadequate capacity lead to lost sales that are difficult, if not impossible, to recover.

Timing is also important in capital budgeting. Capital assets must be ready to come on line when they are needed; otherwise, opportunities might be lost. For example, consider what happened to Decopot, a decorative tile manufacturer with no formal capital budgeting process. Decopot attempted to operate at full capacity as often as possible. This was not a bad idea, because demand for Decopot's products and services was relatively stable. A few years ago, however, Decopot began to experience intermittent spurts of additional demand for its products. Decopot could not satisfy the additional demand because it did not have the capacity to produce any more products, and customers had to be turned away. The spurts in demand continued, so senior management decided to add capacity to increase production so the additional orders could be filled in the future. It took nine months to get the additional production capacity ready. Finally, Decopot was ready to meet the increased demand the next time it arrived. Unfortunately, the "next time" never came because competitors had expanded their operations six months earlier, which allowed them to fill customers' orders when Decopot could not. Many of Decopot's original customers are now its competitors' customers. If Decopot had properly forecasted demand and planned its capacity requirements, it would have been able to maintain or perhaps even increase its market share; instead, its market share decreased.

capital budgeting The process of planning and evaluating expenditures on assets whose cash flows are expected to extend beyond one year.

Effective capital budgeting can improve both the timing of asset acquisitions and the quality of assets purchased. A firm that forecasts its needs for capital assets in advance will have an opportunity to purchase and install the assets before they are needed. Unfortunately, like Decopot, many firms do not order capital goods until they approach full capacity or are forced to replace worn-out equipment. If many firms order capital goods at the same time, backlogs result, prices increase, and firms are forced to wait for the delivery of machinery; in general, the quality of the capital goods deteriorates. If a firm foresees its needs and purchases capital assets early, it can avoid these problems.

Finally, capital budgeting is important because the acquisition of fixed assets typically involves substantial expenditures, and before a firm can spend a large amount of money, it must have the funds available. Large amounts of money are not available automatically. Therefore, a firm contemplating a major capital expenditure program must arrange its financing well in advance to ensure that the required funds are available.

9-1a Generating Ideas for Capital Projects

The same general concepts that we developed for valuing financial assets are involved in capital budgeting. However, whereas a set of stocks and bonds already exists in the financial markets and investors select from this set, capital budgeting projects are created by the firm. For example, a sales representative might report that customers frequently ask for a particular product that the company does not currently produce. The sales manager then discusses the idea with the marketing research group to determine the size of the market for the proposed product. If it appears likely that a significant market does exist, cost accountants and engineers will be asked to estimate production costs. If those estimates show the product can be produced and sold at a sufficient profit, the project will be undertaken.

A firm's growth, and even its ability to remain competitive and to survive, depends on a constant flow of ideas for new products, ways to make existing products better, and ways to produce output at lower costs. Accordingly, a well-managed firm will go to great lengths to develop good capital budgeting proposals. Some firms even provide incentives to employees to encourage suggestions that lead to beneficial investment proposals. If a firm has capable and imaginative executives and employees and its incentive system works properly, many ideas for capital investment will be advanced.

9-1b Project Classifications

Capital budgeting decisions generally are termed either *replacement decisions* or *expansion decisions*. **Replacement decisions** involve determining whether capital projects should be purchased to take the place of existing assets that might be worn out, damaged, or obsolete. Usually the replacement projects are necessary to maintain or improve profitable operations using the *existing* production levels. On the other hand, an **expansion decision** is made when a firm determines whether it should add assets either to produce more of its existing products or to offer entirely new products.

In general, relatively simple calculations, and only a few supporting documents, are required for replacement decisions, especially maintenance-type investments in profitable plants. Analysis that is more detailed is required for cost-reduction replacements, for expansion of existing product lines, and especially for investments in new products or areas. In addition, within each category, projects are broken down by their rupee costs: Larger investments require both analysis that is more detailed and approval at a higher level within the firm.

Some of the capital budgeting decisions involve *independent projects*, while others involve *mutually exclusive* projects. **Independent projects** are projects whose cash flows are not affected by one another, so the acceptance of one project does not affect the acceptance of the other project(s). *All independent projects can be purchased if they all are acceptable.* For example, if South-Western Cengage Learning, which publishes this book, decides to purchase the ABC television network, it still could publish new textbooks. Conversely, if a capital budgeting decision involves **mutually exclusive projects**, then when one project is taken on, the others must be rejected. In other words, *only one mutually exclusive project can be purchased, even if they all are acceptable.* For example, suppose Global Sports and Entertainment Ltd. has a parcel of land on which it wants to build either a children's amusement park or a domed baseball stadium. Because the land is not large enough for both alternatives, if Global chooses to build the amusement park, it cannot build the stadium, and vice versa.

9-1c The Post-Audit

An important aspect of the capital budgeting process is the **post-audit**, which involves (1) comparing actual results with those predicted by the project's sponsors and (2) explaining why any differences occurred.

The post-audit has two main purposes:

To Improve Forecasts. When decision makers are forced to compare their projections to actual outcomes, there is a tendency for estimates to improve, conscious or unconscious biases to be observed and eliminated, and new forecasting methods to be sought as the need for them becomes apparent. People simply tend to do everything better, including forecasting, if they know that their actions are being monitored.

To Improve Operations. Businesses are run by people, and people can perform at higher or lower levels of efficiency. When a divisional team has made a forecast about an investment, its members are, in a sense, putting their reputations on the line. If costs are above predicted levels, sales are below expectations, and so on, executives in production, marketing, and other areas will strive to improve operations and to bring results in line with forecasts.

The post-audit is not a simple process; a number of factors can cause complications. First, we must recognize that each element of the cash flow forecast is subject to uncertainty, so a percentage of all projects undertaken by any reasonably venturesome firm will necessarily go awry. This fact must be considered when appraising the performances of the operating executives who submit capital expenditure requests.

replacement decisions Decisions whether to purchase capital assets to take the place of existing assets to maintain or improve existing operations.

expansion decisions Decisions whether to purchase capital projects and add them to existing assets to increase existing operations.

independent projects Projects whose cash flows are not affected by decisions made about other projects.

mutually exclusive projects A set of projects in which the acceptance of one project means the others cannot be accepted.

post-audit A comparison of the actual and expected results for a given capital project.

Second, projects sometimes fail to meet expectations for reasons beyond the control of the operating executives and for reasons that no one could realistically be expected to anticipate. Third, it is often difficult to separate the operating results of one investment from those of a larger system. Although some projects stand alone and permit ready identification of costs and revenues, the actual cost savings that result from a new computer system, for example, might be hard to measure. Fourth, it is often hard to hand out blame or praise, because the executives who were actually responsible for a given decision might have moved on by the time the results of a long-term investment are known.

Because of these difficulties, some firms tend to downplay the importance of the post-audit. However, observations of both businesses and governmental units suggest that the best run and most successful organizations are the ones that put the greatest emphasis on post-audits. Accordingly, we regard the post-audit as being an extremely important element in a good capital budgeting system.

9-2 Evaluating Capital Budgeting Projects

To make capital budgeting decisions, we must value the assets, or projects, that are being evaluated. Not surprisingly, then, capital budgeting involves the same steps used in general asset valuation that were described in the last few chapters:

1. Estimate the cash flows expected to be generated by the asset during its life. (We discuss this topic in Chapter 10.) This is similar to estimating the future dividends that a stock will generate.
2. Evaluate the riskiness of the projected cash flows to determine the appropriate rate of return to use for computing the present value of the estimated cash flows. (We discuss this topic further in Chapter 10.)
3. Compute the present value of the expected cash flows—that is, compute the investment's value. This is equivalent to finding the present value of a stock's expected future dividends. For a real asset, such as a machine, we can solve the following equation:

$$\text{PV of CF} = \frac{\widehat{CF}_1}{(1+r)^1} + \frac{\widehat{CF}_2}{(1+r)^2} + \cdots + \frac{\widehat{CF}_n}{(1+r)^n} = \sum_{t=1}^{n} \frac{\widehat{CF}_t}{(1+r)^t}$$

4. Compare the present value of the future expected cash flows with the initial investment, or cost, required to acquire the asset. Alternatively, the expected rate of return on the project can be calculated and compared with the rate of return that is considered appropriate (required) for the project. *If a firm identifies (or creates) an investment opportunity with a present value (the value of the investment to the firm) that is greater than its cost, the value of the firm will increase if the investment is purchased.* Thus, there is a direct link between capital budgeting and stock values: The more effective the firm's capital budgeting procedures, the higher the price of its stock.

Because some investment projects will be good and others will not, procedures must be established for evaluating the worth of such projects to the firm. Our topic in the remainder of this chapter is the evaluation of the acceptability of capital projects.

9-2a Net Present Value (NPV)

Following the steps outlined in the previous section, to determine the acceptability of a capital budgeting project, we must determine its value and then compare this value to the project's purchase price. Remember from our previous discussions that the value of an asset can be determined by computing the present value of the cash flows it is expected to generate during its life. If we subtract the purchase price of the asset from the present value of its expected future cash flows, the result is the net rupee value, or the net benefit that accrues to the firm if the asset is purchased. This net benefit is called the asset's **net present value (NPV)**. We use Equation 9.1 to compute NPV:

9.1

$$\text{NPV} = \widehat{CF}_0 + \frac{\widehat{CF}_1}{(1+r)^1} + \frac{\widehat{CF}_2}{(1+r)^2} + \cdots + \frac{\widehat{CF}_n}{(1+r)^n} = \sum_{t=0}^{n} \frac{\widehat{CF}_t}{(1+r)^t}$$

Here $\widehat{CF}_t$ is the expected net cash flow in Period t, and r is the rate of return required by the firm to invest in

net present value (NPV)
The present value of an asset's future cash flows minus its purchase price (initial investment).

FIGURE 9.1 Net Cash Flows for Project S and Project L

Year (t)	Expected After-Tax Net cash flows, $\hat{CF}_t$ Project S	Project L
0	₹(3,000)	₹(3,000)
1	1,500	400
2	1,200	900
3	800	1,300
4	300	1,500

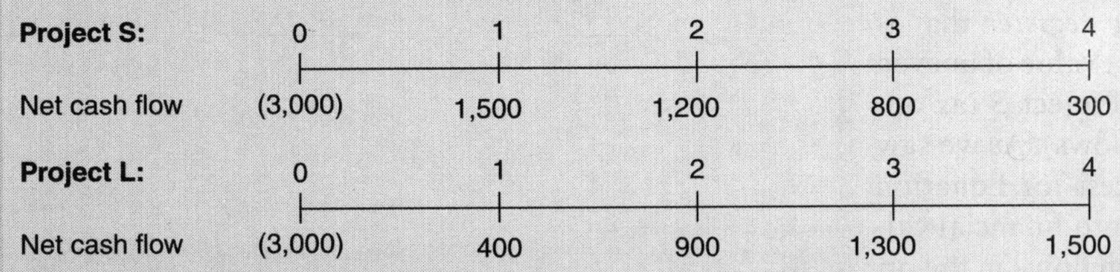

this project.[1] Cash outflows (expenditures on the project, such as the cost of buying equipment or building factories) are treated as negative cash flows. $\widehat{CF}_0$ generally is a negative cash flow because it represents the initial investment in the project, which normally is a cash outflow when the product is purchased (Period 0).[2]

The NPV shows by how much a firm's value, and thus stockholders' wealth, will increase if a capital budgeting project is purchased. *If the net benefit computed on a present value basis—that is, NPV—is positive, then the asset (project) is considered an acceptable investment.* In other words, to determine whether a project is acceptable using the NPV technique, we apply the following decision rule:

NPV Decision Rule: A project is acceptable if NPV > ₹0.

To illustrate the application of the NPV method and the other capital budgeting techniques discussed in this chapter, we use the cash flow data shown in Figure 9.1 for Project S and Project L. Throughout this chapter we assume that these projects are equally risky and that their expected cash flows are known with certainty. In the next chapter, we discuss how these cash flows are determined and how risk should be considered in capital budgeting analyses. The expected cash flows, $\widehat{CF}_t$, shown in Figure 9.1 are the "bottom-line," after-tax cash flows, which we assume occur at the end of the designated year. For Project S and Project L, only $\widehat{CF}_0$ is negative, but for many large projects, such as the Alaska Pipeline or an electric generating plant, outflows occur for several years before operations begin and cash flows turn positive. Incidentally, the *S* stands for "short" and the *L* for "long": Project S is a short-term project in the sense that its cash inflows tend to come in sooner than those of Project L. We use these two illustrative projects to simplify our presentations.

At a 10 percent required rate of return, Project S's net present value, NPV_S, is ₹161.33:

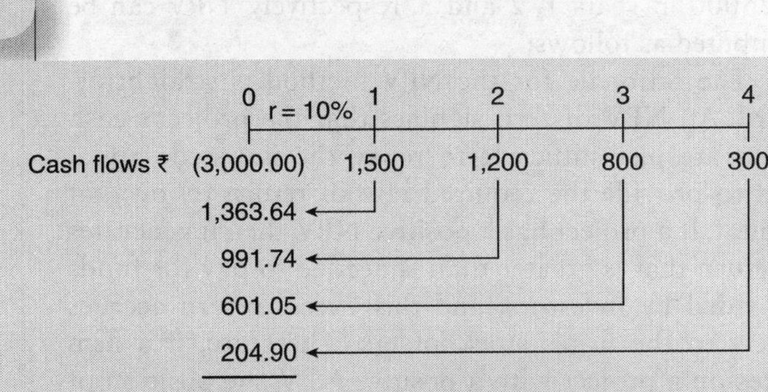

As this cash flow timeline shows, to find the NPV, we compute the present value of each cash flow, including $\widehat{CF}_0$, and sum the results. Using Equation 9.1, the numerical solution for NPV_S is:

[1]The rate of return required by the firm generally is termed the firm's *cost of capital*, because it is the average rate the firm must pay for the funds used to purchase capital projects. The concept of cost of capital is discussed in Chapter 11.

[2]We describe how the cash flows that are associated with a capital budgeting project are determined in Chapter 10.

$$NPV_S = (3{,}000) + \frac{1{,}500}{(1.10)^1} + \frac{1{,}200}{(1.10)^2} + \frac{800}{(1.10)^3} + \frac{300}{(1.10)^4}$$

$$= (3{,}000) + 1{,}363.64 + 991.74 + 601.05 + 204.90$$

$$= 161.33$$

It is not difficult to calculate the NPV using Equation 9.1 and a regular calculator, as we did here. Nevertheless, the most efficient way to find the NPV is by using a financial calculator. Although all financial calculators are not set up identically, they all have a section of memory called the *cash flow register* that is used for computing the present value of uneven cash flows such as those in Project S (as opposed to equal annuity cash flows). As we saw in Chapter 4, a solution process for Equation 9.1 is literally programmed into financial calculators. Simply input the cash flows in the order in which they occur (being sure to observe the signs), along with the value of I/Y = r. For Project S, enter $CF_0 = -3{,}000$, $CF_1 = 1{,}500$, $CF_2 = 1{,}200$, $CF_3 = 800$, $CF_4 = 300$, and I/Y = r = 10%. At this point, you have entered in your calculator the cash flows and the interest rate displayed on the timeline shown in Figure 9.1 for Project S, and you have provided the calculator with the values that are needed to solve Equation 9.1 for the project. There is one unknown, NPV. Now you simply ask the calculator to solve the equation for you; the answer, 161.33, will appear on the screen.[3] Using this same process for Project L, we find NPV_L = ₹108.67. On this basis, both projects should be accepted if they are *independent*, but Project S should be the one chosen if they are *mutually exclusive*, because NPV_S = ₹161.33 > NPV_L = ₹108.67.

Using MS Excel, this can be computed as shown below. Let us take an investment of ₹500000 which is expected to give inflows of ₹150000, ₹300000 and ₹125000 in years 1, 2 and 3, respectively. NPV can be computed as follows:

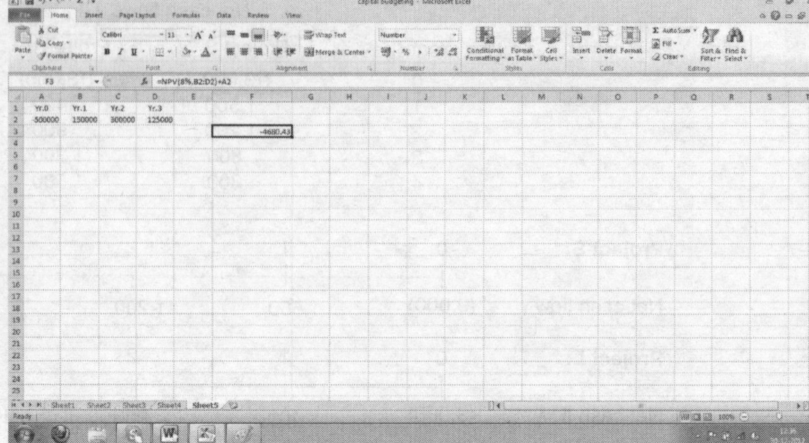

The rationale for the NPV method is straightforward. An NPV of zero signifies that the project's cash flows are just sufficient to repay the invested capital and to provide the required rate of return (r) on that capital. If a project has a positive NPV, then it generates a return that is greater than is needed to pay for funds provided by investors, and this excess return accrues solely to the firm's stockholders. Therefore, if a firm takes on a project with a positive NPV, the position of the stockholders is improved because the firm's value increases. In our example, shareholders' wealth will increase by ₹161.33 if the firm takes on Project S, but by only ₹108.67 if it takes on Project L. Viewed in this manner, it is easy to see why Project S is preferred to Project L, and it is also easy to see the logic of the NPV approach. If the two projects are independent, both should be accepted, because shareholders' wealth would increase by ₹270.00 = ₹161.33 + ₹108.67.[4]

9-2b Internal Rate of Return (IRR)

In Chapter 6, we presented procedures for finding the yield to maturity (YTM), or rate of return, on a bond. Recall that if you invest in a bond and hold it to maturity, the average return you can expect to earn on the money you invest is the YTM. Exactly the same concept is employed in capital budgeting to determine the **internal rate of return (IRR)**, which is the rate of return the firm expects to earn if a project is purchased and held for its useful life (maturity). The IRR is defined as the discount rate that equates the present value of a project's expected future cash flows to the initial amount invested. *As long as the project's IRR, which is the average return it is expected to generate each year of its life, is greater than the rate of return required by the firm for such an investment, the project is acceptable.* In other words, to determine whether a project is acceptable using the IRR technique, we apply the following decision rule:

IRR Decision Rule: A project is acceptable if IRR > r

where r is the firm's required rate of return.

We can use Equation 9.2 to solve for a project's IRR:

internal rate of return (IRR) The discount rate that forces the PV of a project's expected cash flows to equal its initial cost; IRR is similar to the YTM on a bond.

[3]Refer to the manual that came with your calculator to determine how the CF function is used.

[4]This description of the process is somewhat oversimplified. Both analysts and investors anticipate that firms will identify and accept positive NPV projects, and current stock prices reflect these expectations. Thus, stock prices react to announcements of new capital projects only to the extent that such projects were not already expected. In this sense, we can think of a firm's value as consisting of two parts: (1) the value of its existing assets and (2) the value of its growth opportunities, or projects with positive NPVs.

9.2

$$NPV = \widehat{CF}_0 + \frac{\widehat{CF}_1}{(1+IRP)^1} + \cdots + \frac{\widehat{CF}_n}{(1+IRP)^n} = 0$$

or

$$\widehat{CF}_0 = \frac{\widehat{CF}_1}{(1+IRP)^1} + \cdots + \frac{\widehat{CF}_n}{(1+IRP)^n}$$

For Project S, the cash flow timeline for the IRR computation is as follows:

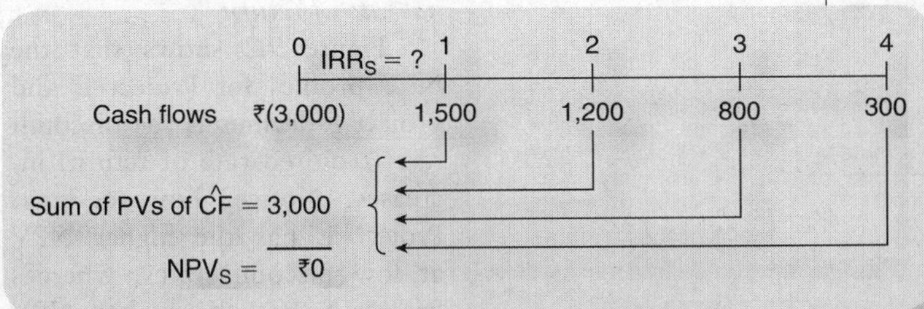

Using Equation 9.2, here is the setup for computing IRR_S:

$$₹(3{,}000) + \frac{1{,}500}{(1+IRR)_1} + \frac{1{,}200}{(1+IRR)_2} + \frac{800}{(1+IRR)_3} + \frac{300}{(1+IRR)_4} = 0$$

Although it is fairly easy to find the NPV without a financial calculator, the same is *not* true of the IRR. Without a financial calculator, you must solve Equation 9.2 by trial and error; that is, you must try different discount rates until you find the one that forces NPV to equal zero. This discount rate is the IRR. For a project with a fairly long life, the trial-and-error approach is a tedious, time-consuming task. Fortunately, it is easy to find IRRs with a financial calculator.

To solve for IRR using a financial calculator, follow the steps used to find the NPV. First, enter the cash flows as shown on the preceding cash flow timeline into the calculator's cash flow register. For Project S, enter $CF_0 = -3{,}000$, $CF_1 = 1{,}500$, $CF_2 = 1{,}200$, $CF_3 = 800$, and $CF_4 = 300$. In effect, you have entered the cash flows into the equation shown on the cash flow timeline (Equation 9.2). You now have one unknown, IRR, or the discount rate that forces NPV to equal zero. The calculator has been programmed to solve for the IRR, and you activate this program by pressing the key labeled "IRR." Following are the IRRs for Project S and Project L, found using a financial calculator:

$$IRR_S = 13.1\%$$

$$IRR_L = 11.4\%$$

A project is acceptable if its IRR is greater than the firm's **required rate of return,** *or* **hurdle rate.** For example, if the hurdle rate required by the firm is 10 percent, then both Project S and Project L are acceptable. If they are mutually exclusive, then Project S is more acceptable than Project L because $IRR_S > IRR_L$. On the other hand, if the firm's required rate of return is 12 percent, only Project S is acceptable; and, if r = 15%, neither project is acceptable.

Notice from Equation 9.2 that *you do not need to know the firm's required rate of return (r) to solve for IRR*. However, you need the required rate of return to make a decision as to whether a project is acceptable once its IRR has been computed. Also, note that (1) the IRR is the rate of return that will be earned by *anyone* who purchases the project and (2) the IRR is dependent on the project's cash flow characteristics (that is, the amounts and the timing of the cash flows), not the firm's required rate of return. As a result, *the IRR of a particular project is the same for all firms, regardless of their particular required rates of return.* A project might be acceptable to some firms (Project S would be acceptable to firms with required rates of return less than 13.1 percent), but not acceptable to other firms (Project S is not acceptable to firms with required rates of return greater than 13.1 percent).

Why is a project acceptable if its IRR is greater than its required rate of return? Because the IRR on a project is the rate of return that the project is expected to generate, and if this return exceeds the cost of the funds used to finance the project, a surplus remains after paying for the funds. This surplus accrues to the firm's stockholders. Therefore, *taking on a project whose IRR exceeds the firm's required rate of return (cost of funds) increases shareholders' wealth*. On the other hand, if the IRR is less than the cost of funds, then taking on the project imposes a cost on current stockholders that decreases wealth. For example, consider what would happen if you borrowed funds at a 10 percent interest rate to invest in the stock market. The 10 percent interest is your *cost of funds*, which is the rate that you must earn on your investments to break even. You would lose money if you earned less than 10 percent, and you would gain money if you earned more than 10 percent. This break-even characteristic makes the IRR useful in evaluating capital projects.

required rate of return (hurdle rate)
The discount rate (cost of funds) that the IRR must exceed for a project to be considered acceptable.

Using MS Excel, the computation can be as shown below. Suppose an investment of ₹80000 is needed in a project, which is expected to result in inflows of ₹30000, ₹35000 and ₹40000, respectively, in the next 3 years. IRR can be calculated with MS Excel as follows:

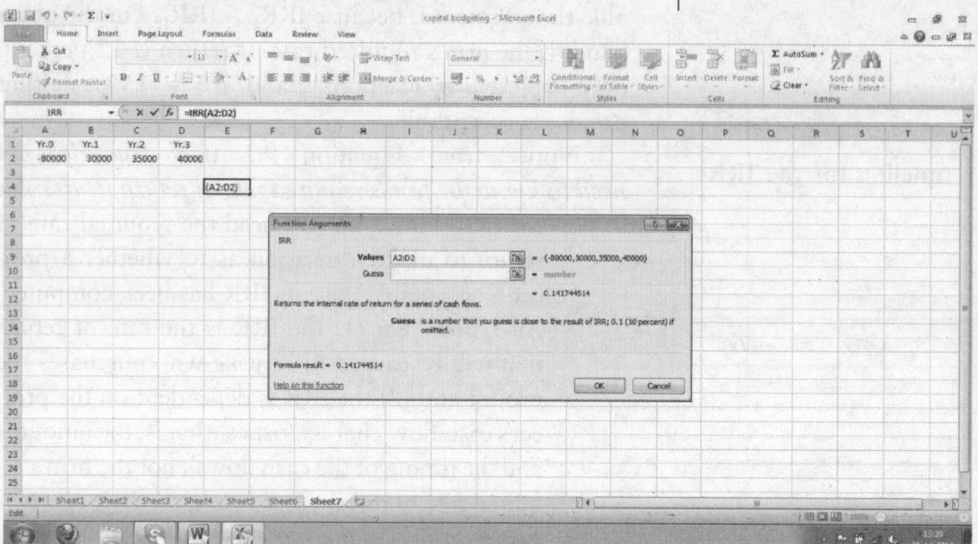

9-3 Comparison of the NPV and IRR Methods

We found that the NPV for Project S is ₹161.33, which means that the firm's value will increase by ₹161.33 if the project is purchased. The IRR for Project S is 13.1 percent, which means that the firm will earn a 13.1 percent rate of return on its investment if it purchases Project S. We generally measure wealth in rupees, so the NPV method should be used to accomplish the goal of maximizing shareholders' wealth. In reality, using the IRR method could lead to investment decisions that increase wealth, but do not maximize it. We choose to discuss the IRR method and compare it to the NPV method because many corporate executives are familiar with the meaning of IRR, it is entrenched in the corporate world, and it does have some virtues. For these reasons, it is important to understand the IRR method and be prepared to explain why a project with *a lower IRR might sometimes be preferable to one with a higher IRR* (discussed later in the chapter).

9-3a NPVs and Required Rates of Return—NPV Profiles

net present value (NPV) profile A graph that shows the NPVs for a project at various discount rates (required rates of return).

A graph that shows a project's NPV at various discount rates (required rates of return) is termed the project's **net present value (NPV) profile.** Figure 9.2 shows the NPV profiles for Project L and Project S. To construct the profiles, we calculate the projects' NPVs at various discount rates—say, 0, 5, 10, and 15 percent—and then plot these values. The points plotted on our graph for each project are shown at the bottom of Figure 9.2.[5] Because the IRR is defined as the discount rate at which a project's NPV equals zero, the point where its *NPV profile crosses the X-axis indicates a project's internal rate of return.*

Figure 9.2 shows that the NPV profiles for Project L and Project S decline as the discount rate (required rate of return) increases. Notice, however, that Project L has the higher NPV at low discount rates, whereas Project S has the higher NPV at high discount rates. According to the graph, $NPV_S = NPV_L =$ ₹268 when the discount rate equals 8.1 percent. We call this point the *crossover rate* because, below this rate, $NPV_S < NPV_L$, and above this rate, $NPV_S > NPV_L$; however, the NPVs are equal and thus the two NPV profile line intersect at 8.1 percent.[6]

Figure 9.2 also indicates that Project L's NPV is more sensitive to changes in the discount rate than is Project S's NPV. That is, Project L's NPV profile has the steeper slope, indicating that a given change in r has a larger effect on NPV_L than on NPV_S. Project L is more sensitive to changes in r because the cash flows from Project L are received later in its life than those from Project S. As a general rule, the impact of a change in the discount rate is much greater on distant cash flows than on near-term cash flows. To illustrate, consider the present value of ₹100 to be received in one year versus ₹100 to be received in 10 years. The present values of each ₹100, discounted at 10 percent and at 15 percent, are as follows:

Future Value	Year Received	PV @ 10%	PV @ 15%	Percent Difference
₹100	1	₹90.91	₹86.96	−4.3%
100	10	38.55	24.72	−35.9

[5]Note that the NPV profiles are curved; they are *not* straight lines. Also, the NPVs approach the cost of the project as the discount rate increases without limit. The reason is that, at an infinitely high discount rate, the PV of the future cash flows would be zero, so NPV at $r = \infty$ is CF_0, which in our example is −₹3,000.

[6]The crossover rate is easy to calculate. Simply go back to Figure 9.1, where we first show the two projects' cash flows. Now calculate the difference in the cash flows for Project S and Project L in each year. The differences are computed as $\hat{CF}_S - \hat{CF}_L$. Thus, the cash flow differences for Projects S and L are $CF_0 =$ ₹0, $CF_1 = +$₹1,100, $CF_2 = +$₹300, $CF_3 = -$₹500, and $CF_4 = -$₹1,200, respectively. To compute the crossover rate using a financial calculator, enter these numbers in the order given here into the cash flow register, and then ask the calculator to compute the IRR. You should find IRR = 8.11%.

FIGURE 9.2 NPV Profiles for Project S and Project L

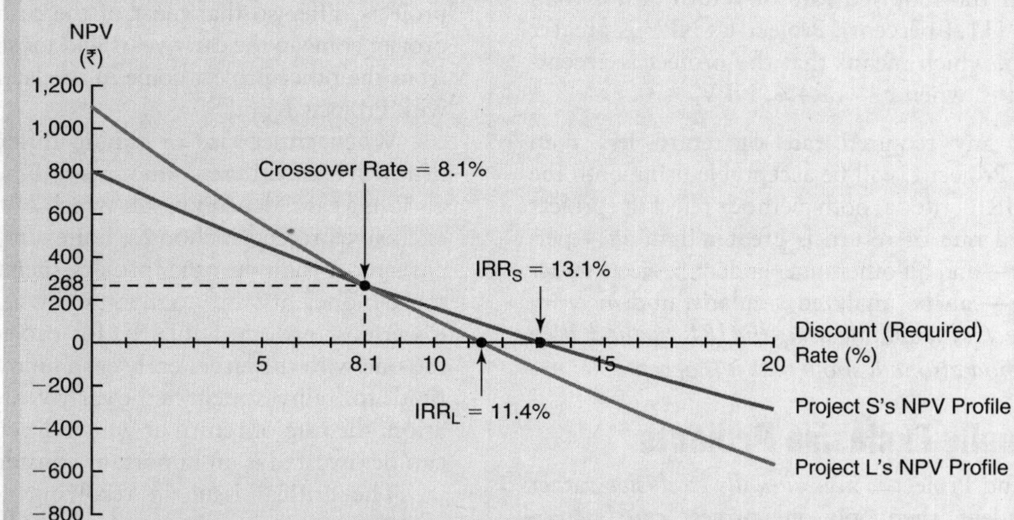

Discount Rate (%)	NPV_S	NPV_L
0%	₹800.00	₹1,100.00
5	454.89	554.32
8.1	268.00	268.00
10	161.33	108.67
15	(90.74)	(259.24)
20	(309.03)	(565.97)

We can conclude from this discussion that if a project has most of its cash flows coming in the early years, its NPV will not be lowered as much if the required rate of return increases as the NPV of a project whose cash flows come later in its life. Accordingly, Project L, which has its largest cash flows in the later years, is hurt badly when the required rate of return is high, whereas Project S, which has relatively rapid cash flows, is affected less by high discount rates.

9-3b Independent Projects

Note that the IRR formula, Equation 9.2, is simply the NPV formula, Equation 9.1, solved for the particular discount rate that forces the NPV to equal zero. Thus, the same basic equation is used for both methods. Mathematically, the NPV and IRR methods will *always* lead to the same accept/reject decisions for independent projects. In other words, *if a project's NPV is positive, its IRR will exceed r; if NPV is negative, r will exceed the IRR*. To see why this is so, look back at Figure 9.2, focus on Project L's profile, and note that

- The IRR criterion for acceptance is that the required rate of return must be less than (or to the left of) the IRR$_L$ (11.4 percent). In other words, if

Rubberball/Jupiter Images

$r < IRR_L = 11.4\%$, Project L is acceptable; otherwise, it is not.

- Whenever the required rate of return is less than the IRR_L (11.4 percent), Project L's NPV is greater than zero, which means that the project is acceptable; that is, when $r < 11.4\%$, $NPV_L > 0$.

Thus, at any required rate of return less than 11.4 percent, Project L will be acceptable using both the NPV and the IRR criteria; both methods reject the project if the required rate of return is greater than 11.4 percent. Project S—and all other independent projects under consideration—can be analyzed similarly, and *in every case, if a project is acceptable using the IRR method, then the NPV method also will show that it is acceptable.*

9-3c Mutually Exclusive Projects

If Project S and Project L are *mutually exclusive* rather than independent, then only one project can be *purchased*. If you use IRR to make the decision as to which project is better, you would choose Project S because $IRR_S = 13.1\% > IRR_L = 11.4\%$. If you use NPV to make the decision, you might reach a different conclusion depending on the firm's required rate of return. Note from Figure 9.2 that if the required rate of return is less than the crossover rate of 8.1 percent, $NPV_L > NPV_S$, but $NPV_L < NPV_S$ if the required rate of return is greater than 8.1 percent. As a result, using the NPV technique, Project L is preferred if the firm's required rate of return is less than 8.1 percent, but Project S is preferred if the firm's required rate of return is greater than 8.1 percent.

As long as the firm's required rate of return is greater than 8.1 percent, using either NPV or IRR will result in the same decision—that is, Project S should be purchased—because $NPV_S > NPV_L$ and $IRR_S > IRR_L$. But, if the firm's required rate of return is less than 8.1 percent, a person who uses NPV will reach a different conclusion as to which mutually exclusive project should be purchased: he or she will choose Project L because $NPV_L > NPV_S$. For example, the table in Figure 9.2 shows that NPV_L = ₹554 > ₹455 = NPV_S when r = 5 percent. In this situation—that is, the required rate of return is less than 8.1 percent—*a conflict exists* because NPV says to choose Project L over Project S, whereas IRR says just the opposite. Which answer is correct? Logic suggests that the NPV method is better because it selects the project that adds more value to shareholder wealth.

Two basic conditions can cause NPV profiles to cross, and thus lead to conflicts between NPV and IRR: (1) when *project size (or scale) differences* exist, meaning that the cost of one project is much larger than that of the other; and (2) when *timing differences* exist, meaning that the timings of cash flows from the two projects differ so that most of the cash flows from one project come in the early years and most of the cash flows from the other project come in the later years, as occurs with Projects L and S.[7]

reinvestment rate assumption The assumption that cash flows from a project can be reinvested (1) at the cost of capital, if using the NPV method or (2) at the internal rate of return, if using the IRR method.

When either size or timing differences occur, the firm will have different amounts of funds to invest in the various years, depending on which of the two mutually exclusive projects it chooses. For example, if one project costs more than the other project, then the firm will have more money at t = 0 to invest elsewhere if it selects the lower-cost project. Similarly, for projects of equal size, the one with the larger early cash inflows provides more funds for reinvestment in the early years. Given this situation, the rate of return at which differential cash flows can be invested is an important consideration.

The critical issue in resolving conflicts between mutually exclusive projects is this: How useful is it to generate cash flows earlier rather than later? The value of early cash flows depends on the rate at which we can reinvest these cash flows. *The NPV method implicitly assumes that the rate at which cash flows can be reinvested is the firm's required rate of return, r, whereas the IRR method implies that the firm has the opportunity to reinvest at the project's IRR*. These assumptions are inherent in the mathematics of the discounting process.

Which is the better assumption: that cash flows can be reinvested at the required rate of return or that they can be reinvested at the project's IRR? To reinvest at the IRR associated with a capital project, the firm must be able to reinvest the project's cash flows in another project with an identical IRR. Such projects generally do not continue to exist, or it is not feasible to reinvest in such projects because competition in the investment markets drives their prices up and their IRRs down. On the other hand, at the very least, a firm could repurchase the bonds and the stock it has issued to raise capital budgeting funds and thus repay some of its investors, which would be the same as investing at its required rate of return. Thus, we conclude that the *more realistic* **reinvestment rate assumption** *is the required rate of return, which is implicit in the NPV method*. This, in turn, leads us to prefer the NPV method, at least for firms willing and able to obtain new funds at a cost reasonably close to their current cost of funds.

Remember that when projects are independent, the NPV and IRR methods provide the same accept/reject decision. As a result, when evaluating independent projects, it doesn't matter whether the NPV technique or the IRR technique is used to make the investment decision, because the firm only wants to know whether the

[7]Of course, it is possible for mutually exclusive projects to differ with respect to both scale and timing. Also, if mutually exclusive projects have different lives (as opposed to different cash flow patterns over a common life), this introduces further complications, and for meaningful comparisons, some mutually exclusive projects must be evaluated over a common life.

projects are acceptable (value increasing) or unacceptable (value decreasing). In this case, it is not necessary to determine which project is most acceptable, because all acceptable projects should be purchased. However, when evaluating mutually exclusive projects, especially those that differ in scale or timing, the NPV method should be used to determine which project should be purchased. In this case, because only one project can be purchased, the firm must determine which project is most acceptable; that is, which project adds the greatest value to the firm.

9-3d Cash Flow Patterns and Multiple IRRs

A project has a *conventional* cash flow pattern if it has cash outflows (costs) in one or more consecutive periods at the beginning of its life, followed by a series of cash inflows. If, however, a project has a large cash outflow at the beginning of its life, and then has another cash outflow either at some time during its life or at the end of it, then it has an *unconventional* cash flow pattern. Projects with unconventional cash flow patterns present unique difficulties when the IRR method is used, including the possibility of **multiple IRRs.**[8] Following are examples of conventional and unconventional cash flow patterns:

Conventional cash flow patterns:	(1) − + + + + + + (2) − − − + + + +
Unconventional cash flow patterns:	(1) − + + − + + + (2) − − + + + − −

There exists an IRR solution for each time the *direction* of the cash flows associated with a project is interrupted, that is, each time outflows change to inflows. For example, each of the conventional cash-flow patterns shown here has only one change in the signs (direction) of the cash flows from negative (outflow) to positive (inflow); thus, there is only one IRR solution. On the other hand, each of the unconventional cash flow patterns shown here has two interruptions, and thus two IRR solutions.

Figure 9.3 illustrates the multiple-IRR problem with a strip-mining project that costs ₹1.6 million. The mine will produce a cash inflow of ₹10 million at the end of Year 1, but ₹10 million must be spent at the end of Year 2 to restore the land to its original condition. Two IRRs exist for this project: 25 percent and 400 percent. The NPV profile for the mine shows that the project would have a positive NPV, and thus be acceptable, if the firm's required rate of return is between 25 percent and 400 percent.

[8]Multiple IRRs result from the manner in which Equation 9.2 must be solved to arrive at a project's IRR. The mathematical rationale and the solution to multiple IRRs will not be discussed here. Instead, we want you to be aware that multiple IRRs can exist because this possibility complicates capital budgeting evaluation using the IRR method.

9-4 Modified Internal Rate of Return

Despite a strong academic preference for NPV, surveys indicate that many business executives prefer IRR. It seems that many managers find it intuitively more appealing to analyze investments in terms of percentage rates of return (IRR) rather than rupees (NPV). However, remember from our earlier discussion that the IRR method assumes the cash flows from the project are reinvested at a rate of return equal to the IRR, which we generally view as unrealistic. Given this fact, can we devise a rate of return measure that is better than the regular IRR? The answer is yes: We can modify the IRR and make it a better indicator of relative profitability, hence better for use in capital budgeting. This "modified" return is called the **modified IRR**, or **MIRR**, and it is defined as follows:

9.3

$$\text{PV of cash outflows} = \frac{TV}{(1+MIRR)^n}$$

$$\sum_{t=0}^{n}\frac{COF_t}{(1+r)^t} = \frac{\sum_{t=0}^{n} CIF_t(1+r)^{n-t}}{(1+MIRR)^n}$$

Here COF refers to the cash outflows (all negative numbers), and CIF refers to the cash inflows (all positive numbers) associated with a project. The term on the left

multiple IRRs The situation in which a project has two or more IRRs.

modified IRR (MIRR) The discount rate at which the present value of a project's cash outflows is equal to the present value of its terminal value, where the terminal value is found as the sum of the future values of the cash inflows compounded at the firm's required rate of return and the present value of the cash outflows is found using the same required rate of return.

FIGURE 9.3 NPV Profile for Project M

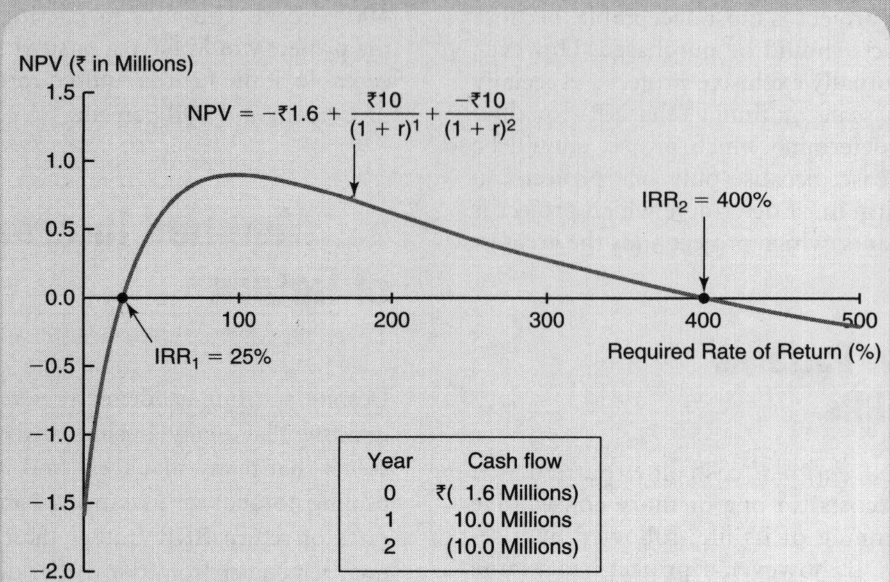

side of the equals sign is simply the present value (PV) of the investment outlays (cash *outflows*) when discounted at the firm's required rate of return, r, and the numerator of the term on the right side of the equals sign is the future value of the cash *inflows*, assuming that these inflows are reinvested at the firm's required rate of return. The future value of the cash inflows is also called the *terminal value*, or TV. The discount rate that forces the PV of the TV to equal the PV of the costs is defined as the MIRR.[9]

We can illustrate the calculation of MIRR with Project S:

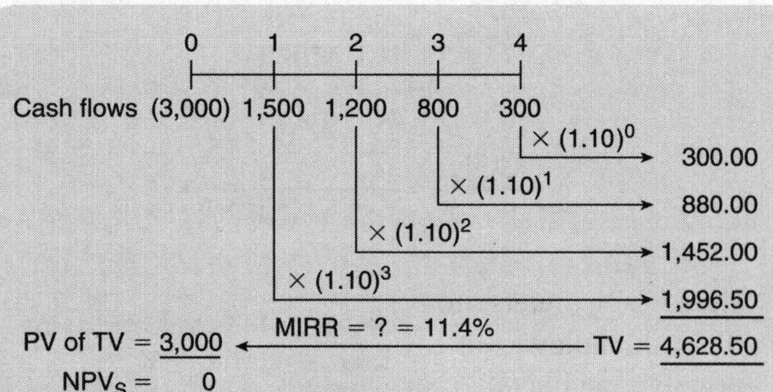

[9]There are several alternative definitions for the MIRR. The differences relate primarily to whether negative cash flows that occur after positive cash flows begin should be compounded and treated as part of the TV, or discounted and treated as a cost. Our definition (which treats all negative cash flows as investments and thus discounts them) generally is the most appropriate procedure. For a complete discussion, see William R. McDaniel, Daniel E. McCarty, and Kenneth A. Jessell, "Discounted Cash Flow with Explicit Reinvestment Rates: Tutorial and Extension," *The Financial Review*, August 1988, 369–385.

Using the cash flows as set out on the cash flow timeline, first find the terminal value by compounding each cash inflow at the 10 percent required rate of return. Then, enter into your calculator PV = −3,000, which is the present value of the project's cash outflows, FV = 4,628.50, which is the future value of the project's cash inflows, and N = 4; compute I/Y = 11.4% = $MIRR_S$. Using the same process, we find $MIRR_L$ = 11.0%.

MIRR Decision Rule: A project is acceptable if MIRR > r.

To determine whether a project is acceptable using the MIRR technique, we apply the following decision rule:

The modified IRR has a significant advantage over the traditional IRR measure. MIRR assumes that cash flows are reinvested at the required rate of return, whereas the traditional IRR measure assumes that cash flows are reinvested at the firm's project's own IRR. Because reinvestment at the required rate of return generally is more correct, the MIRR is a better indicator of a project's true profitability. MIRR also solves the multiple-IRR problem. To illustrate, using a required rate of return equal to 10 percent, the strip mine project described earlier has an MIRR equal to 5.6 percent, so it should be rejected. This is consistent with the decision based on the NPV method, because at r = 10%, NPV = –₹0.77 million.

Is MIRR as good as NPV for choosing between mutually exclusive projects? If two projects are of equal size and have the same life, then NPV and MIRR will always lead to the same project selection decision. Thus, for any projects like Projects S and L, if $NPV_S > NPV_L$, then $MIRR_S > MIRR_L$, and the kinds of conflicts we encountered between NPV and the traditional IRR will not occur. Furthermore, if the projects are of equal size, but have different lives, the MIRR will always lead to the same decision as the NPV if the MIRRs for both projects are calculated using the terminal year of the project with the longer life. (Just fill in zeros for the shorter project's missing cash flows.) However, if the projects differ in size, conflicts can still occur. For example, if we were choosing between a large project and a small, mutually exclusive one, we might find $NPV_{Large} > NPV_{Small}$ and $MIRR_{Large} < MIRR_{Small}$.

FIGURE 9.4 Traditional Payback Period (PB) for Project S and Project L

Project S: ($PB_S = 2.4$)

	0	1	2	3	4
Net cash flow	(3,000)	1,500	1,200	800	300
Cumulative net cash flow	(3,000)	(1,500)	(300)	500	800

$$\text{Payback, } PB_S = 2 + \frac{300}{800} = 2.4 \text{ years}$$

Project L: ($PB_L = 3.3$)

	0	1	2	3	4
Net cash flow	(3,000)	400	900	1,300	1,500
Cumulative net cash flow	(3,000)	(2,600)	(1,700)	(400)	1,100

$$\text{Payback, } PB_L = 3 + \frac{400}{1,500} = 3.3 \text{ years}$$

Taking the reinvestment rate to be 10%, an investment of ₹50000 which has a 3-year annual inflow of ₹25000 will have a MIRR as per computation shown below :

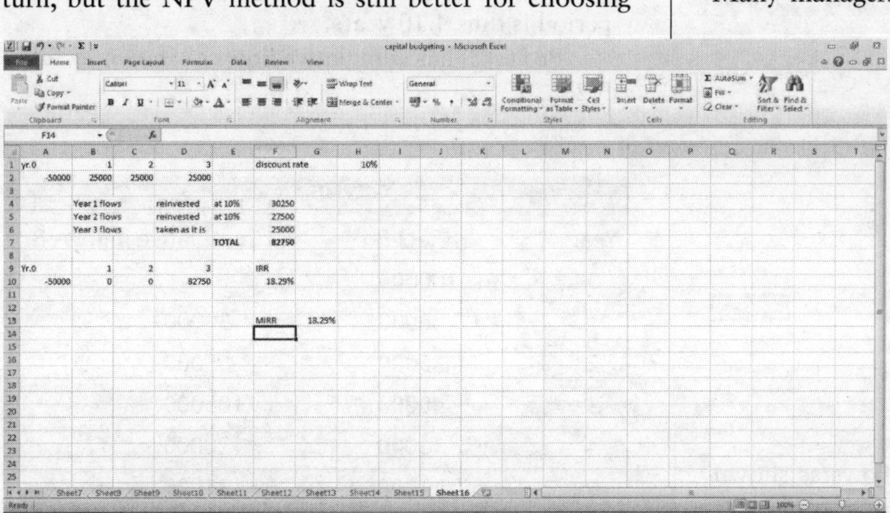

	A	B	C	D	E	F	G	H
1	yr.0	1	2	3		discount rate		10%
2	-50000	25000	25000	25000				
3								
4		Year 1 flows		reinvested	at 10%	30250		
5		Year 2 flows		reinvested	at 10%	27500		
6		Year 3 flows		taken as it is		25000		
7					TOTAL	82750		
8								
9	Yr.0	1	2	3		IRR		
10	-50000	0	0	82750		18.29%		
11								
12								
13						MIRR	18.29%	

Our conclusion is that the MIRR is superior to the regular (traditional) IRR as an indicator of a project's "true" rate of return, or expected long-term rate of return, but the NPV method is still better for choosing among mutually exclusive projects that differ in size because it provides a better indicator of the extent to which each project will increase the value of the firm; thus, NPV is still the recommended approach.

9-5 Use of Capital Budgeting Techniques in Practice

In this section, we describe two additional techniques that firms use when making capital budgeting decisions. And, then we discuss the information that is provided by all of the capital budgeting techniques covered in this chapter and indicate which techniques are most often used in practice.

9-5a Payback Period: Traditional (Nondiscounted) and Discounted

Many managers like to know how long it will take a project to repay its initial investment (cost) from the cash flows it is expected to generate in the future. Thus, many firms compute a project's **traditional payback period (PB)**, which is defined as the expected number of years required to recover the original investment (the cost of the asset). Payback is the simplest and, as far as we know, the oldest *formal* method used to evaluate capital budgeting projects. To compute a project's payback period, simply add up the expected cash flows for each year until the cumulative value equals

traditional payback period (PB) The length of time it takes to recover the original cost of an investment from its unadjusted (raw) expected cash flows.

9.4

$$\text{Payback period} = \left(\begin{array}{c}\text{The year } \textit{just prior} \\ \text{full recovery} \\ \text{of initial investment}\end{array}\right) + \left(\frac{\begin{array}{c}\text{Amount of initial investment that is} \\ \textit{unrecovered} \text{ at the start of the recovery year}\end{array}}{\begin{array}{c}\text{Total cash flow generated} \\ \text{during the recovery year}\end{array}}\right)$$

the amount that is initially invested. The total amount of time, including the fraction of a year if appropriate, that it takes to recapture the original amount invested is the payback period. Figure 9.4 shows the process for computing the payback periods for both Project S and Project L.

The exact payback period can be found using Equation 9.4:

As Figure 9.4 shows, the payback period for Project S is between two years and three years. Using Equation 9.4, the exact payback period for Project S is computed as follows:

$$PB_S = 2 + \frac{300}{800} = 2.4 \text{ years}$$

Applying the same procedure to Project L, we find PB_L = 3.3 years.

The number of years it takes for the investment to be recouped is called the payback period.

Let us consider two projects with flows as indicated below:

EXHIBIT 9.1

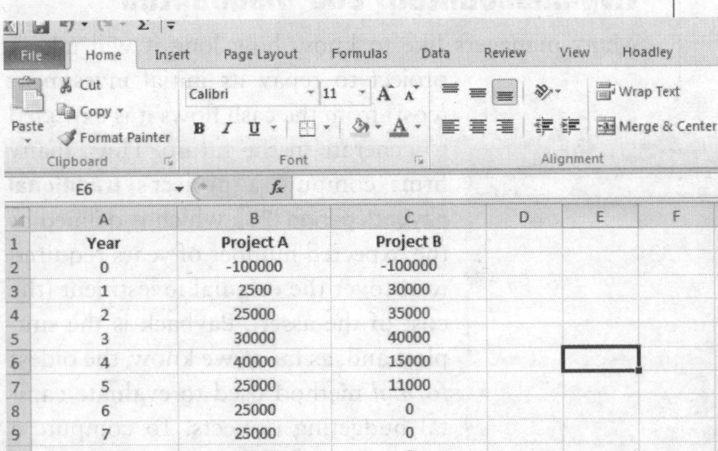

	A	B	C	D	E	F
1	Year	Project A	Project B			
2	0	-100000	-100000			
3	1	2500	30000			
4	2	25000	35000			
5	3	30000	40000			
6	4	40000	15000			
7	5	25000	11000			
8	6	25000	0			
9	7	25000	0			
10	8	25000	0			

Projects A and B have cumulative flows as shown in Exhibit 9.1. From the cumulative flows, it is possible to ascertain the number of years it takes for the investment outlay to be recouped.

TABLE 9.1

Year	Project A	Cumulative inflows A
0	−100000	
1	2500	2500
2	25000	27500
3	30000	57500
4	40000	97500
5	25000	122500
6	25000	147500
7	25000	172500
8	25000	197500

As shown in Table 9.1, in respect of Project A, after four years the inflows cumulate to ₹97,500. This leaves ₹2,500 more to be recouped for meeting the original investment of ₹1,00,000. In the fifth year, an inflow of ₹25,000 is there. Thus, it takes a fraction of the fifth year to get the investment back. This fraction is the amount still to be recouped of ₹2500 divided by the total inflows in the fifth year of ₹25,000, which comes to 0.10. So in all, it takes four years and 0.10 of the fifth year for the payback to be complete. The payback period is thus 4.10 years.

Project B has cumulative flows as shown in Table 9.2.

TABLE 9.2

Year	Project B	Cumulative inflows B
0	−100000	
1	30000	30000
2	35000	65000
3	40000	105000
4	15000	120000
5	11000	131000
6	0	131000
7	0	131000
8	0	131000

After two years, the cumulative flows come to ₹65,000. That leaves ₹35,000 to be recouped to reach the investment outlay of ₹1,00,000. In the third year, the projected inflow is ₹40,000. It means that it takes a portion of (35,000 / 45,000) of the third year to complete the payback. The payback period is thus 2.78 years.

Now, if the company has a benchmark of three as the acceptable level of payback, Project B will pass the test and Project A will not. In case the acceptable level of payback is, say, five years, both the projects can be accepted.

Advantages

- The payback method is easy to understand.
- The calculation and logic are easy to convey to all decision makers.
- The method gives the decision maker a feeling of comfort that the risk taken is not very heavy.

Disadvantages

The method does not take into account the time value of money. Inflows received after one year or four years are treated on an equal platform. While this enables easier computation, the procedure is technically wrong. As we have seen in Chapter 4, money received later has lesser value and this aspect is not reckoned in the payback method.

Further, inflows received after paybacks are not considered at all. Thus, in the above example, though Project B has a smaller payback, Project A keeps giving inflows for a few more years. This aspect is not taken into account in the method.

Using payback to make capital budgeting decisions is based on the concept that it is better to recover the cost of (investment in) a project sooner rather than later. Therefore, Project S is considered better than Project L because it has a shorter payback period. *As a general rule, a project is considered acceptable if its payback period is less than the maximum cost-recovery time established by the firm.* In other words, when we use the traditional payback period method, we apply the following decision rule:

PB Decision Rule: A project is acceptable if PB < n*

where n* is the recovery period that the firm has determined is appropriate. For example, if the firm requires projects to have a payback of three years or less, Project S will be acceptable but Project L will not.

The payback method is simple, which explains why payback traditionally has been one of the most popular capital budgeting techniques. However, because the traditional payback period computation ignores the time value of money, relying solely on this method can lead to incorrect decisions, at least if our goal is to maximize value. If a project has a payback of three years, we know how quickly the initial investment will be covered by the expected cash flows, but this information does not provide any indication of whether the return on the project is sufficient to

Edyta Pawlowska/Shutterstock.com

cover the cost of the funds invested. In addition, when payback is used, the cash flows beyond the payback period are ignored. For example, even if Project L had a fifth year of cash flows equal to ₹50,000, its payback would remain 3.3 years, which is less desirable than the payback of 2.4 years for Project S. However, with the additional ₹50,000 cash flow, Project L most likely would be preferred.

To correct for the fact that the traditional payback method does not consider the time value of money, we can compute the **discounted payback period (DPB)** for Project S, which is the length of time it takes for the project's *discounted* cash flows to recapture the cost of the investment. Applying

discounted payback period (DPB) The length of time it takes for a project's discounted cash flows to repay the cost of the investment.

the general payback concept, we can easily compute how long it takes to recapture the initial outlay of ₹3,000 using the *discounted* (present value of the) cash flows given in the cash flow timeline shown in Figure 9.5. The sum of the present values of the cash flows for the first three years is ₹2,956.43 = ₹1,363.64 + ₹991.74 + ₹601.05, so all of the ₹3,000 cost is not recovered until 3.2 years = 3 years + [(₹3,000 – ₹2,956.43)/₹204.90] years. Therefore, on a *present value basis*, it takes 3.2 years for Project S to recover, or pay back, its original cost. DPB = 3.9 years for Project L; so Project S is more acceptable. Figure 9.5 shows the DPB computations for Projects S and L.

Unlike the traditional payback computation, the discounted payback period computation considers the time value of money. If you look at the cash flow timeline that shows the NPV computation for Project S, you can see that the reason it has a positive NPV is because the initial investment of ₹3,000 is recovered on a present value basis prior to the end of the project's useful life. Thus, using the discounted payback method, a project should be accepted when its DPB is less than its useful life.

DPB Decision Rule: A project is acceptable if DPB < Project's useful life.

As Figure 9.5 shows, when a project's discounted payback is less than its useful life, the present value of the future cash flows that the project is expected to generate exceeds the initial cost of the asset—that is, NPV > 0. Note that the final value given in the row labeled "Cumulative Net Cash Flow" is simply the project's NPV, because it is the result of summing the present values of all of the cash flows, including the initial cost, that are associated with the project.

Discounted Payback

The method

The fact that the time value of money is not considered would act as the principal disadvantage of the payback method. Otherwise, there are a lot of supporters for this method given its simplicity and intuitive risk reduction.

To overcome this disadvantage, a method involving discounting of the flows and then finding the payback has been developed. This is called the discounted payback method.

Continuing the above example, the flows will first be discounted at a known discount rate (assumed to be 10%), and then the cumulative flows will be calculated. After this, payback will be calculated as before. This is illustrated in Table 9.3.

TABLE 9.3 (Amount in ₹)

Year	Project A	Discounted flows	Cumulative discounted flows
0	–100000		
1	2500	2272.73	2272.73
2	25000	20661.16	22933.88

FIGURE 9.5 Discounted Payback Period (DPB) for Project S and Project L

Project S: (r = 10%; $DPB_S = 3.2$)

	0	1	2	3	4
Net cash flow	₹(3,000)	1,500.00	1,200.00	800.00	300.00
Discounted cash flow, DCF	(3,000)	1,363.64	991.74	601.05	204.90
Cumulative net cash flow	(3,000)	(1,636.36)	(644.62)	(43.57)	161.33

Discounted payback, $DPB_S = 3 + \frac{43.57}{204.90} = 3.2$ years

Project L: (r = 10%; $DPB_L = 3.9$)

	0	1	2	3	4
Net cash flow	(3,000)	400.00	900.00	1,300.00	1,500.00
Discounted cash flow, DCF	(3,000)	363.64	743.80	976.71	1,024.52
Cumulative net cash flow	(3,000)	(2,636.36)	(1,892.56)	(915.85)	108.67

Discounted payback, $DPB_L = 3 + \frac{915.85}{1,024.52} = 3.9$ years

3	30000	22539.44	45473.33
4	40000	27320.54	72793.87
5	25000	15523.03	88316.90
6	25000	14111.85	102428.75
7	25000	12828.95	115257.70
8	25000	11662.68	126920.39

Using the approach that we followed for the payback method, we find that the cumulative discounted flows for Project A are ₹88,316.90 after five years, indicating that ₹11,683.10 has to be covered. The discounted flows in Year 6 amount to ₹14,111.85 and so we require (11683.10 / 14111.85) portion of the sixth year to have the payback completed. The discounted payback is thus 5.83 years.

In respect of Project B, the position is as shown in Table 9.4.

TABLE 9.4 (Amount in ₹)

Year	Project B	Discounted flows	Cumulative discounted flows
0	-100000		
1	30000	27272.73	27272.73
2	35000	28925.62	56198.35
3	40000	30052.59	86250.94
4	15000	10245.20	96496.14
5	11000	6830.13	103326.28
6	0	0.00	103326.28
7	0	0.00	103326.28
8	0	0.00	103326.28

Note: The Excel Template for the above illustration is available online (Example 7.1)

Here, after four years the cumulative discounted flows are ₹96,496.14, leaving ₹3,503.86 to be covered. The discounted flows in Year 5 are ₹6,830.15, which means that the discounted payback is 4.51 years.

Advantages

The discounted payback method overcomes the principal disadvantage of the payback method.

The investor gets reassured about the risk involved in the project.

Disadvantages

The computations involved in the method are not that easy.

Like the payback method, this method does not take into account the flows after the payback has been achieved

9-5b Conclusions on the Capital Budgeting Decision Methods

Earlier in this chapter, we compared the NPV and IRR methods to highlight their relative strengths and weaknesses for evaluating capital projects, and in the process we probably created the impression that "sophisticated" firms should use only one method in the decision process—NPV. However, virtually all capital budgeting decisions are analyzed by computer, so it is easy to calculate and list all the decision measures we discussed: traditional payback (PB), discounted payback (DPB), NPV, IRR, and MIRR. In making the accept/reject decision, most large, sophisticated firms, such as IBM, General Electric, and General Motors, calculate and consider multiple measures because each provides decision makers with a somewhat different piece of relevant information.

Traditional payback and discounted payback provide information about both the risk and the *liquidity* of a project. A long payback means that (1) the investment rupees will be locked up for many years, hence the project is relatively illiquid; and (2) the project's cash flows must be forecast far out into the future, hence the project is probably quite risky.[10] A good analogy for this is the bond valuation process. An investor should never compare the yields to maturity on two bonds without considering their terms to maturity, because a bond's riskiness is influenced by its maturity.

NPV is important because it gives a direct measure of the rupee benefit (on a present value basis) to the firm's shareholders, so we regard NPV as the best single measure of *profitability*. IRR also measures profitability, but here it is expressed as a percentage rate of return, which many decision makers, especially nonfinancial managers, seem to prefer. Further, IRR contains information concerning a project's "safety margin," which is not inherent in NPV. To illustrate, consider the following two projects: Project T costs ₹10,000 at t = 0 and is expected to return ₹16,500 at the end of one year, while Project B costs ₹100,000 and has an expected payoff of ₹115,500 after one year. At a 10 percent required rate of return, both projects have an NPV of ₹5,000, so by the NPV rule we should be indifferent between the two. However, Project T actually provides

[10]We generally define *liquidity* as the ability to convert an asset into cash quickly while maintaining the original investment. Thus, in most cases, short-term assets are considered more liquid than long-term assets. We discuss liquidity in greater detail later in the book.

a much larger margin for error. Even if its realized cash inflow turns out to be almost 40 percent below the ₹16,500 forecast, the firm will still recover its ₹10,000 investment. On the other hand, if Project B's inflow falls by only 14 percent from the forecasted ₹115,500, the firm will not recover its investment. Further, if no inflows are generated at all, the firm will lose only ₹10,000 with Project T but will lose ₹100,000 if it takes on Project B.

The NPV contains no information about either the safety margin inherent in a project's cash flow forecasts or the amount of capital at risk, but the IRR does provide "safety margin" information: Project T's IRR is a whopping 65 percent, whereas Project B's IRR is only 15.5 percent. As a result, the realized return could fall substantially for Project T, and it would still make money. Note, however, that the IRR method has a reinvestment assumption that probably is unrealistic, and that it is possible for projects to have multiple IRRs. Both of these problems can be corrected using the MIRR calculation.

In summary, the different methods provide different types of information. Because it is easy to calculate them, all should be considered in the decision process. For any specific decision, more weight might be given to one method than another method, but it would be foolish to ignore the information provided by any of the methods.

In addition, you should have discovered from our discussion that *all capital budgeting methods that consider the time value of money provide the same accept/reject decisions*, but there could be ranking conflicts, which might lead to different investment (purchase) decisions when projects are mutually exclusive depending on which capital budgeting technique is used.

At this point, we should note that multinational corporations use essentially the same capital budgeting techniques described in this chapter. However, foreign governments, international regulatory environments, and financial and product markets in other countries pose certain challenges to Indian companies that must make capital budgeting decisions for their foreign operations. We will wait to discuss some of these challenges/differences until the next chapter.

9-5c Capital Budgeting Methods Used in Practice

Many surveys have been conducted over the years to determine which techniques firms rely on when making capital budgeting decisions. The results consistently show that firms rely on each of the methods discussed in this chapter to some extent to help them make final decisions about the acceptability of capital budgeting projects. As technology has advanced, firms have shifted to using the more sophisticated techniques, such as NPV and IRR. The following table shows to what extent this shift has occurred since the 1970s. The results given in the table were compiled from surveys conducted during each decade.[11] The numbers represent the average percentage of respondents who indicated that their firms use the particular capital budgeting technique "always" or "almost always." In most cases, those who were surveyed were not asked to indicate the primary and secondary methods that were used.

Period	Traditional Payback Period	NPV	IRR
1970s	85%	65%	80%
1980s	78	75	88
1990s	60	80	79
2000s	53	85	77

As the data show, the use of the traditional payback period and IRR methods has declined, whereas the use of the NPV method has increased. Prior to the 1970s, many firms relied heavily on the payback period to make capital budgeting decisions. As technology and understanding of the discounting techniques improved, both NPV and IRR became more popular. It appears that, for the most part, financial managers recognize that these techniques provide correct decisions with respect to value maximization.

[11]Studies that were examined include Lawrence J. Gitman and John R. Forrester, Jr., "A Survey of Capital Budgeting Techniques Used by Major U.S. Firms," *Financial Management*, Fall 1977, 66–71; David J. Oblak and Roy J. Helm, Jr., "Survey and Analysis of Capital Budgeting Methods Used by Multinationals," *Financial Management*, Winter 1980, 37–41; Marjorie T. Stanley and Stanley B. Block, "A Survey of Multinational Capital Budgeting," *Financial Review*, March 1984, 36–51; Glenn H. Petry and James Sprow, "The Theory of Finance in the 1990s," *The Quarterly Review of Economics and Finance*, Winter 1993, 359–381; Erika Gilbert and Alan Reichert, "The Practice of Financial Management among Large United States Corporations," *Financial Practice and Education*, Spring/Summer 1995, 16–23; Patricia. Chadwell-Hatfield, Bernard Goitein, Philip Horvath, and Allen Webster, "Financial Criteria, Capital Budgeting Techniques, and Risk Analysis of Manufacturing Firms," *Journal of Applied Business Research*, Winter 1996/1997, 95–104; John R. Graham and Campbell R. Harvey, "The Theory and Practice of Corporate Finance: Evidence from the Field," *Journal of Financial Economics*, Vol. 60, No. 2–3, May/June 2001,197–243; Patricia A. Ryan and Glenn P. Ryan "Capital Budgeting Practices of the Fortune 1000: How Have Things Changed?" *Journal of Business and Management*, Fall 2002, 335–364; John Graham and Campbell Harvey, "How Do CFOs Make Capital Budgeting and Capital Structure Decisions," *Journal of Applied Corporate Finance*, Vol. 15, No. 1, Spring 2002, 8–23

For the most part, studies have shown that companies (1) use more sophisticated capital budgeting techniques today than in previous times and (2) do not rely on a single evaluation method to make decisions about investing in capital projects. Clearly, firms still use payback period in their capital budgeting analyses. However, even firms that previously relied on the traditional payback period seem to have switched to the discounted payback period. Thus, indications are that firms do use the methods we profess in finance courses.

KEY CAPITAL BUDGETING CONCEPTS

To conclude this chapter, we summarize some of the capital budgeting concepts (rules) that were discussed.

- Capital budgeting decisions are important because they involve long-term assets; thus, the firm loses some financial flexibility when such assets are purchased.
- The process of valuing a capital budgeting project (investment) to determine whether it should be purchased is the same process that is used to value financial assets, such as stocks and bonds: (1) Compute the present value of the cash flows the asset is expected to generate during its useful life, and (2) compare the present value of the asset to its purchase price (cost). If the present value of the project's cash flows is greater than its cost, the asset should be purchased.
- When making capital budgeting decisions, we generally compute an asset's net present value (NPV). NPV equals the present value of the cash flows the asset is expected to generate during its useful life minus the cost of the asset. Thus, the NPV indicates by how much the firm's value will change if the capital budgeting project is purchased. A project should be purchased if its NPV is positive.
- A project's internal rate of return (IRR) represents the average rate of return that a company will earn if the project is purchased and held until the end of its useful life. The IRR is the same for all companies that purchase a particular project. A project should be purchased if its IRR is greater than the firm's required rate of return.
- A ranking conflict might occur when evaluating two mutually exclusive projects using the NPV technique and the IRR technique; that is, the NPV technique might favor one project whereas the IRR technique might favor the other project. This conflict, which results from the reinvestment assumptions associated with each of these capital budgeting techniques, generally can be resolved by using the modified internal rate of return (MIRR) technique rather than the traditional IRR technique.
- All capital budgeting techniques that consider the time value of money will provide the same accept–reject decisions; that is, for a particular project, if NPV > 0, then we know that IRR > r, MIRR > r, and DPB < Project's useful life, all of which indicate that the project is acceptable. However, ranking conflicts could exist, depending on which techniques are used, when mutually exclusive projects are evaluated. Such conflicts are not a concern when independent projects are evaluated, because all acceptable independent projects should be purchased regardless of their rankings.

MULTIPLE CHOICE QUESTIONS

1. The PV has the following relationship with the interest rate.

a. Higher the interest rate, higher the PV

b. Higher the interest rate, lower the PV

c. Lower the interest rate, lower the PV

d. Both a and c

2. The PV of an annuity due will be

a. Higher than the PV of a regular annuity

b. Lower than the PV of a regular annuity

c. Equal to the PV of a regular annuity

d. Having no relationship with the PV of a regular annuity

3. If the interest rate is higher,

a. The number of years it takes for money to double will come down

b. The number of years it takes for money to double will go up

c. This will have no impact on the number of years it takes to double the money

d. Unless tenure is given, no conclusion can be drawn

4. A timeline assumes

a. That all receipts and payments occur at the start of the year

b. That receipts occur at the start of the year and payments at the end of the year

c. That both receipts and payments occur at the end of the year

d. That receipts occur at the end of the year and payments at the start of the year

5. If I require an amount after five years,

a. It is better to put in small amounts every year to make them grow to the target amount at the end of five years

b. It is better to put in a lump sum amount to make it grow to the target amount at the end of five years

c. Either a or b

d. b will be better than a

6. If I take a three-year loan and it has to be rapid in three equated annual installments,

a. The instalment amount will have a high interest in the beginning and a low repayment of principal

b. The instalment amount will have a low interest in the beginning and a high repayment of principal

c. The instalment amount will carry a principal repayment element which is equal across the years

d. Both a and c

7. I have a choice of repaying a loan in ten instalments or fifteen instalments. If I choose to repay in fifteen instalments,

a. I will end up paying lesser instalment amount

b. I will end up paying lesser interest overall

c. I will end up paying higher interest overall

d. Both a and c

8. If I have a target amount in mind to be accumulated after six years,

a. The equated amount will be like an annuity which will grow to the target

b. The equated amount will be like a series of lump sums that will grow to the target

c. Both a and b

d. None of the above

9. When a loan is taken, the total amount repaid with interest will be

a. Higher when the period of the loan is long

b. Lower when the period of the loan is long

c. The same regardless of the period

d. We need figures to get a correct answer

10. After an EMI has been determined for a housing loan, the borrower pays a lump sum amount in partial repayment. Now the EMI will

a. Come down if the period of the loan remains the same

b. Need to be recomputed by considering the new outstanding amount and balance period available

c. Be higher or lower depending on whether the loan is a fixed rate or a floating rate loan

d. Depend on the interest rate now prevailing in the market

Answers:

1.	(b)	2.	(a)	3.	(a)	4.	(c)	5.	(c)
6.	(c)	7.	(a)	8.	(c)	9.	(a)	10.	(a)

PROBLEMS

For more problems, login to CourseMate for CFIN at CengageBrain.com

9-1 Wagle RV is evaluating a capital budgeting project that is expected to generate ₹36,950 per year during its six-year life. If its required rate of return is 10 percent, what is the value of the project to Wagle RV?

9-2 Zamindar Fashions is evaluating a capital budgeting project that should generate ₹104,400 per year for four years. (a) If its required rate of return is 16 percent, what is the value of the project to Zamindar? (b) If Zamindar Fashions evaluates the same project with its required rate of return of 12 percent, what will it determine the value of the project to be?

9-3 Calcutta Corporation is evaluating a capital budgeting project that will generate ₹600,000 per year for the next 10 years. The project costs ₹3.6 million, and Calcutta's required rate of return is 11 percent. Should the project be purchased?

9-4 The CFO of Bal Stylists is evaluating a project that costs ₹42,000. The project will generate ₹11,000 each of the next five years. If Bal's required rate of return is 9 percent, should the project be purchased?

9-5 What is the internal rate of return (IRR) of a project that costs ₹20,070 if it is expected to generate ₹8,500 per year for three years?

9-6 What is the internal rate of return (IRR) of a project that costs ₹74,000 if it is expected to generate ₹16,500 per year for six years?

9-7 Paraji Hot Food Services (PHFS) is evaluating a capital budgeting project that costs ₹75,000. The project is expected to generate after-tax cash flows equal to ₹26,000 per year for four years. PHFS's required rate of return is 14 percent. Compute the project's (a) net present value (NPV) and (b) internal rate of return (IRR). (c) Should the project be purchased?

9-8 Keshav Furniture Corporation (KFC) is evaluating a capital budgeting project that costs ₹34,000 and is expected to generate after-tax cash flows equal to ₹14,150 per year for three years. KFC's required rate of return is 12 percent. Compute the project's (a) net present value (NPV) and (b) internal rate of return (IRR). (c) Should the project be purchased?

9-9 Construct an NPV profile for a capital budgeting project that costs ₹64,000 and is expected to generate ₹18,200 per year for five years. Using the NPV profile, determine the project's internal rate of return (IRR) and its net present value (NPV) at required rates of return equal to 10 percent, 13 percent, and 15 percent.

9-10 Using a required rate of return equal to 12 percent, compute the modified internal rate of return (MIRR) for a project that costs ₹82,000 and is expected to generate ₹35,000, ₹70,000, and –₹10,450, respectively, during the next three years. Should the project be purchased?

9-11 What is the internal rate of return (IRR) for a project that costs ₹5,500 and is expected to generate ₹1,800 per year for the next four years? If the firm's required rate of return is 8 percent, what is the project's modified internal rate of return (MIRR)? Should the firm purchase the project?

9-12 Ramva Clothing is evaluating a new weaving machine that costs ₹90,000. It is expected that the machine will generate after-tax cash flows equal to ₹54,000 per year for two years. Ramva's required rate of return is 9 percent. Compute the project's (a) internal rate of return (IRR) and (b) modified internal rate of return (MIRR). (c) Should the project be purchased?

9-13 Compute both the traditional payback period (PB) and the discounted payback period (DPB) for a project that costs ₹270,000 if it is expected to generate ₹75,000 per year for five years? The firm's required rate of return is 11 percent. Should the project be purchased?

9-14 Compute the traditional payback period (PB) for a project that costs ₹64,000 if it is expected to generate ₹16,000 per year for six years? If the firm's required rate of return is 12 percent, what is the project's discounted payback period (DPB)? Should the project be purchased?

9-15 Kishan Karz is evaluating a project that costs ₹365,000 and is expected to generate ₹260,000 and ₹175,000, respectively, during the next two years. If Kishan's required rate of return is 13 percent, what is the project's (a) net present value, (b) internal rate of return (IRR), and (c) modified internal rate of return (MIRR)?

9-16 Compute the (a) net present value, (b) internal rate of return (IRR), and (c) discounted payback period (DPB) for each of the following projects. The firm's required rate of return is 14 percent.

Year	Project Alpha	Project Beta
0	₹(270,000)	₹(300,000)
1	120,000	0
2	120,000	(80,000)
3	120,000	555,000

Which project(s) should be purchased if they are independent? Which project(s) should be purchased it they are mutually exclusive?

9-17 Compute the (a) net present value, (b) internal rate of return (IRR), (c) modified internal rate of return (MIRR), and (d) discounted payback period (DPB) for each of the following projects. The firm's required rate of return is 13 percent.

Year	Project AB	Project LM	Project UV
0	₹(90,000)	₹(100,000)	₹ (96,500)
1	39,000	0	(55,000)
2	39,000	0	100,000
3	39,000	147,500	100,000

Which project(s) should be purchased if they are independent? Which project(s) should be purchased it they are mutually exclusive?

9-18 Following are the estimated after-tax cash flows for two *mutually exclusive* projects:

Year	Project S	Project T
0	(₹16,000)	(₹15,000)
1	14,000	2,000
2	6,000	18,600

The company's required rate of return is 16 percent. What is the internal rate of return (IRR) of the project(s) the company should purchase?

9-19 Following is information about two *independent* projects that a company is evaluating:

Capital Budgeting Technique	Project X	Project Y
Net present value	₹5,000	₹4,950
Internal rate of return	15.5%	17.0%
Discounted payback period	5.1 years	4.6 years

(a) Which project(s) should be chosen? Explain why. (b) What can be concluded about the company's required rate of return, r?

9-20 The CFO of Hasi Hotels gave three college interns three different *independent* projects to evaluate. Following are the results of their analyses:

Intern's Name	Project's Life	NPV	IRR	Discounted Payback	Decision
Asha	7 years	₹5,300	12.0%	6.8 years	Accept
Joseph	6	(1,800)	8.0	5.8	Reject
Khan	10	4,500	10.0	9.6	Accept

The CFO agrees with the final accept/reject decision that each intern made. But she spotted an error in the numbers reported by one of the interns. (a) Which intern's report has the error? (b) Does the information given here provide an indication of the firm's required rate of return? Explain your answers.

Capital Budgeting Techniques

Learning Outcomes

LO.1 Describe the importance of capital budgeting decisions and the general process that is followed when making investment (capital budgeting) decisions.

- Because capital budgeting decisions deal with funds that will be tied up for a long period of time, such decisions are among the most important ones that financial managers make.
- Making a capital budgeting decision is similar to making other financial decisions. Once the cash flows associated with a capital budgeting project are forecast, their present values must be computed. The sum of the present values, which represents the value of the project to the firm, is then compared to the cost (initial investment) of the project. If the project's cost is less than the present value of its expected future cash flows, the investment should be made.

LO.2 Describe how (a) the net present value (NPV) technique and (b) the internal rate of return (IRR) technique are used to make investment (capital budgeting) decisions.

- Net present value (NPV) is computed by subtracting the cost of a project from the present value of the cash flows the project is expected to generate during its useful life. NPV shows by how much the value of the firm will change if a project is purchased. Thus, if NPV > 0, the project should be purchased; the project should be rejected if NPV < 0.
- Internal rate of return (IRR) represents the return any firm will earn if an asset is purchased and held for its useful life. A project is considered acceptable if its IRR is greater than the firm's required rate of return (r). When IRR $> r$, the firm will earn a higher return than it is paying for funds that are used to invest in assets, which means that the value of the firm will increase if the project is purchased.

LO.3 Compare the NPV technique with the IRR technique and discuss why the two techniques might not always lead to the same investment decisions.

- NPV measures the rupee change in the value of the firm that would occur if a capital budgeting project is purchased; IRR measures the percentage return that the firm would earn if it purchased the same capital budgeting project. Thus, the NPV and IRR techniques provide the same accept/reject decisions when a capital budgeting project is evaluated. In other words, if a project is acceptable using the NPV technique, it is also acceptable using the IRR technique. However, when evaluating two mutually exclusive projects, the NPV technique might suggest that one project is preferred, whereas the IRR technique might suggest that the other project is preferred. If the projects are independent, this conflict does not matter, because both projects should be purchased.

LO.4 Describe how conflicts that might arise between NPV and IRR can be resolved using the modified internal rate of return (MIRR) technique.

- NPV assumes that cash flows produced by the project can be reinvested at the firm's required rate of return, whereas IRR assumes that the cash flows can be reinvested in projects with the same IRR. These differing assumptions can result in different rankings of mutually exclusive projects. MIRR helps resolve the ranking conflict by assuming that all cash flows can be invested at the firm's required rate of return. To compute a project's MIRR, compute the rate of return that equates the future value (FV) of the project's cash inflows to the present value (PV) of its cash outflows, where the FV and the PV are determined using the firm's required rate of return. If MIRR $> r$, the project is acceptable.

LO.5 Describe other capital budgeting techniques that are used by businesses to make investment decisions and which techniques are used most often in practice.

- Traditional payback (PB) period and discounted payback (DPB) period are two popular capital budgeting techniques that are used in addition to NPV and IRR. Both payback techniques determine the time it takes to recover the cost of a project from its expected future cash flows.

CHAPTER 9 REVIEW

Chapter 9 Key Capital Budgeting Concepts

- Capital budgeting decisions are important because they involve long-term assets; thus, the firm loses some financial flexibility when such assets are purchased.
- The process of valuing a capital budgeting project (investment) to determine whether it should be purchased is the same process that is used to value financial assets, such as stocks and bonds: (1) compute the present value of the cash flows the asset is expected to generate during its useful life and (2) compare the present value of the asset to its purchase price (cost). If the present value of the project's cash flows is greater than its cost, the asset should be purchased.
- When making capital budgeting decisions, we generally compute an asset's net present value (NPV). NPV equals the present value of the cash flows the asset is expected to generate during its useful life minus the cost of the asset. Thus, the NPV indicates by how much the firm's value will change if the capital budgeting project is purchased. A project should be purchased if its NPV is positive.
- A project's internal rate of return (IRR) represents the average rate of return that a company will earn if the project is purchased and held until the end of its useful life. The IRR is the same for all companies that purchase a particular project. A project should be purchased if its IRR is greater than the firm's required rate of return (r).
- If a project has a positive NPV (i.e., NPV > 0), its IRR must be greater than the firm's required rate of return (i.e., IRR > r).
- A ranking conflict might occur when evaluating two mutually exclusive projects using the NPV technique and the IRR technique—that is, the NPV technique might favor one project whereas the IRR technique might favor the other project. This conflict, which results from the reinvestment assumptions associated with each of these capital budgeting techniques, generally can be resolved by using the modified internal rate of return (MIRR) technique rather than the traditional IRR technique.
- All capital budgeting techniques that consider the time value of money will provide the same accept–reject decisions—that is, for a particular project, if NPV > 0, then we know that IRR > r, MIRR > r, and DPB < Project's useful life, all of which indicate that the project is acceptable. However, ranking conflicts could exist, depending on which techniques are used, when mutually exclusive projects are evaluated. Such conflicts are not a concern when independent projects are evaluated, because all acceptable independent projects should be purchased regardless of their rankings.

Key Terms

capital budgeting The process of planning and evaluating expenditures on assets whose cash flows are expected to extend beyond one year. *p. 145*

LO.1

replacement decisions Decisions whether to purchase capital assets to take the place of existing assets to maintain or improve existing operations. *p. 146*

expansion decisions Decisions whether to purchase capital projects and add them to existing assets to increase existing operations. *p. 146*

independent projects Projects whose cash flows are not affected by decisions made about other projects. *p. 146*

mutually exclusive projects A set of projects in which the acceptance of one project means the others cannot be accepted. *p. 146*

post-audit A comparison of the actual and expected results for a given capital project. *p. 146*

LO.2

net present value (NPV) The present value of an asset's future cash flows minus its purchase price (initial investment). *p. 147*

internal rate of return (IRR) The discount rate that forces the PV of a project's expected cash flows to equal its initial cost; IRR is similar to the YTM on a bond. *p. 149*

required rate of return (hurdle rate) The discount rate (cost of funds) that the IRR must exceed for a project to be considered acceptable. *p. 150*

LO.3

net present value (NPV) profile A graph that shows the NPVs for a project at various discount rates (required rates of return). *p. 151*

reinvestment rate assumption The assumption that cash flows from a project can be reinvested (1) at the cost of capital, if using the NPV method or (2) at the internal rate of return, if using the IRR method. *p. 153*

multiple IRRs The situation in which a project has two or more IRRs. *p. 154*

LO.4

modified IRR (MIRR) The discount rate at which the present value of a project's cost is equal to the present value of its terminal value, where the terminal value is found as the sum of the future values of the cash inflows compounded at the firm's required rate of return and the present value of the cash outflows is found using the same required rate of return. *p. 155*

LO.5

traditional payback period (PB) The length of time it takes to recover the original cost of an investment from its expected cash flows. *p. 156*

discounted payback period (DPB) The length of time it takes for a project's discounted cash flows to repay the cost of the investment. *p. 157*

CHAPTER 10

Project Cash Flows and Risk

Learning Outcomes

LO.1 Describe the relevant cash flows that must be forecast to make informed capital budgeting decisions.

LO.2 Identify the relevant cash flows and perform a capital budgeting analysis for (a) an expansion project and (b) a replacement project.

LO.3 Describe how the riskiness of a capital budgeting project is evaluated and how the results are incorporated in capital budgeting decisions.

LO.4 Describe how capital budgeting decisions differ for firms that have foreign operations and for firms that only have domestic operations.

Tata Power Company Ltd. (₹ in Millions)			
Year	Mar 15	Mar 16	Mar 17
Cash Flow Summary			
Cash and Cash Equivalents at Beginning of the year	553	2658.5	−1151
Net Cash from Operating Activities	16,879.00	29,472.50	21,060.40
Net Cash Used in Investing Activities	−16,254.10	−16,274.90	−55,784.90
Net Cash Used in Financing Activities	1480.6	−17,007.10	37,288.30
Net Inc/(Dec) in Cash and Cash Equivalent	2105.5	−3809.5	2563.8
Cash and Cash Equivalents at End of the year	2658.5	−1151	1412.8

SOURCE: http://www.capitaline.com

The above statement shows the cash flow analysis. When companies embark upon capital budgeting, they draw up cash flow projections to enable a full evaluation. This chapter deals with the principles behind drawing up of cash flows for project evaluation.

The basic principles of capital budgeting and the methods used to evaluate capital budgeting projects were covered in Chapter 9. In this chapter, we examine some additional issues, including cash flow estimation and incorporating risk into capital budgeting decisions. In addition, we present some of the challenges multinational firms face when making capital budgeting decisions.

Study Tools

Problems are found at the end of this chapter

+

Login to **CourseMate** for **CFIN** at **CengageBrain.com** for additional problems and other study tools!

10-1 Cash Flow Estimation

The most important, and also the most difficult, step in the analysis of a capital project is estimating its cash flows. The relevant cash flows include the investment outlays needed to purchase the project and the net cash flows (both inflows and outflows) the project is expected to generate after it is purchased. Many variables are involved in cash flow estimation, and many individuals and departments participate in the process. For example, the forecasts of unit sales and sales prices normally are made by the marketing group based on its knowledge of advertising effects, the state of the economy, competitors' reactions, and trends in consumers' tastes. Similarly, the capital outlays associated with a new product generally are determined by the engineering and product-development staffs, while operating costs are estimated by cost accountants, production experts, personnel specialists, purchasing agents, and so forth. As difficult as plant and equipment costs are to estimate, sales revenues and operating costs over the life of the project generally are even more uncertain.

The financial staff's role in the forecasting process includes (1) coordinating the efforts of the other departments, such as engineering and marketing; (2) ensuring that everyone involved with the forecast uses a consistent set of economic assumptions; and (3) making sure that no biases are inherent in the forecasts. This last point is extremely important because division managers often become emotionally involved with pet projects or develop empire-building complexes (egos), both of which can lead to cash flow forecasting biases that make bad projects look good on paper.

Although substantial difficulties can be encountered when forecasting cash flows for capital budgeting projects, it is all but impossible to overstate the importance of these forecasts. If cash flows fail to meet the forecasted levels, the company might lose hundreds of millions of rupees. Companies recognize that if cash flow estimates are not reasonably accurate, any analytical technique, no matter how sophisticated, can lead to poor decisions and hence to operating losses and lower stock prices. In this chapter, we give you a sense of some of the inputs that are involved in forecasting the cash flows associated with a capital project and in minimizing forecasting errors.

relevant cash flows The specific cash flows that should be considered in a capital budgeting decision.

10-1a Relevant Cash Flows

One important element in cash flow estimation is the determination of **relevant cash flows**, which are defined as the specific set of cash flows that should be considered in the capital budgeting decision. This process can be rather difficult, but two important rules should be followed:

- Capital budgeting decisions must be based on *cash flows after taxes,* not accounting income.
- Only *incremental cash flows*—that is, cash flows that change if the project is purchased—are relevant to the accept/reject decision.

Cash Flow Versus Accounting Income. In capital budgeting analysis, *after-tax cash flows, not accounting profits,* are used, because cash, not profits, pays the bills, and cash can be invested in capital projects. Cash flows and accounting profits can be very different. To illustrate, consider Table 10.1, which shows how accounting profits and cash flows are related. We assume that for XYZ Textiles, sales and all costs, except depreciation, represent actual cash flows and are projected to be constant over time; and that the division will use accelerated depreciation, which will cause its reported depreciation charges to decline with the passage of time.[1]

The top section of Table 10.1 shows the situation in the first year of operations, 2016. Accounting profits are ₹7 million, but the division's net cash flow—money that is available to XYZ—is ₹22 million. The ₹7 million profit is the *return on the funds* originally invested, while the ₹15 million of depreciation is a *return of part of the funds* originally invested, so the ₹22 million cash flow consists of both a return *on* and a return *of* part of the invested capital.

The bottom part of the table shows the situation projected for 2021. Here, reported profits have doubled because of the decline in depreciation, but net cash flow is down sharply because taxes, which require cash payments (outflows), have doubled. The amount of money received by the firm is represented by the cash flow figure, not the net income figure. Although accounting profits are important for some

[1]Depreciation procedures are discussed in detail in accounting courses, but we provide a summary and review in Appendix 10A at the end of this chapter. In some instances, we simplify the depreciation assumptions to reduce the arithmetic. Because Congress changes depreciation procedures fairly frequently, it is always necessary to consult the latest tax regulations before developing actual capital budgeting cash flows.

TABLE 10.1 XYZ's Accounting Profits versus Net Cash Flows (₹ in Thousands)

	Accounting Profits	Cash Flows
I. 2016 Situation		
Sales	₹50,000	₹50,000
Costs except depreciation	(25,000)	(25,000)
Depreciation	(15,000)	
Net operating income or cash flow	₹10,000	₹25,000
Taxes based on operating income (30%)	(3,000)	(3,000)
Net income or net cash flow	₹ 7,000	₹22,000
Net cash flow = Net income + Depreciation = ₹7,000 + ₹15,000 = ₹22,000		
II. 2021 Situation		
Sales	₹50,000	₹50,000
Costs except depreciation	(25,000)	(25,000)
Depreciation	(5,000)	
Net operating income or cash flow	₹20,000	₹25,000
Taxes based on operating income (30%)	(6,000)	(6,000)
Net income or net cash flow	₹14,000	₹19,000
Net cash flow = Net income + Depreciation = ₹14,000 + ₹5,000 = ₹19,000		

purposes, only cash flows are relevant for the purposes of determining the value of a project. Cash flows can be reinvested to create value; profits cannot. Therefore, in capital budgeting, we are interested in net cash flows, not in accounting profits per se.[2] In most cases, we can estimate an asset's operating cash flows as

Operating Cash Flow = Net Income + Depreciation
= Return *on* Capital + Return *of* Capital

10-1b Incremental (Marginal) Cash Flows

In evaluating a capital project, we are concerned only with those cash flows that result directly from the decision to accept the project. These cash flows, called **incremental (marginal) cash flows**, represent the changes in the firm's total cash flows that occur as a direct result of purchasing the project. Thus, to determine whether a specific cash flow is considered relevant, we need to determine whether it is affected by the purchase of the project. Cash flows that change if the project is purchased are *incremental cash flows* that must be included in the capital budgeting evaluation; they are relevant cash flows. Cash flows that are not affected by the purchase of the project are *not* relevant to the capital budgeting decision, thus they should not be included in the evaluation. Unfortunately, identifying the relevant cash flows for a project is not always as simple as it seems. Some special problems in determining incremental cash flows are discussed next.

Sunk Costs. A **sunk cost** is an outlay that the firm has already committed or that has already occurred, and hence is not affected by the accept/reject decision under consideration. As a result, sunk costs should not be included in the analysis. To illustrate, in 2014 XYZ Textiles considered building a distribution center in New England in an effort to increase sales in that area of the country. To help with its evaluation, XYZ hired a consulting firm to perform a site analysis and to provide a feasibility study for the project; the study's cost was ₹100,000,

incremental (marginal) cash flow The change in a firm's net cash flow attributable to an investment project.

sunk cost A cash outlay that has already been incurred and that cannot be recovered regardless of whether the project is accepted or rejected.

[2]Actually, operating cash flow should be adjusted to reflect all noncash charges, not just depreciation. However, for most projects, depreciation is by far the largest noncash charge. Also, note that Table 10.1 ignores interest charges, which would be present if the firm used debt. Most firms do use debt, and hence finance part of their capital budgets with debt. Therefore, the question has been raised as to whether interest charges should be reflected in capital budgeting cash flow analysis. The consensus is that interest charges should not be dealt with explicitly in capital budgeting; rather, the effects of debt financing are reflected in the cost of funds, or required rate of return, which is used to discount the cash flows. If interest is subtracted and cash flows are then discounted, we would be double-counting the cost of debt.

and this amount was expensed for tax purposes in 2014. This expense is *not* a relevant cost that should be included in the capital budgeting evaluation of the prospective distribution center because XYZ cannot recover this money, regardless of whether the new distribution center is built. Therefore, the ₹100,000 is a sunk cost because it will not change no matter what decision XYZ makes.

Opportunity Costs. The second potential problem relates to **opportunity costs**, which are defined as the cash flows that could be generated from assets the firm *already owns* if they are not used for the project in question. To illustrate, XYZ already owns a piece of land that is suitable for the proposed New England distribution center. When evaluating the prospective center, should the cost of the land be disregarded because no additional cash outlay would be required? The answer is no, because there is an opportunity cost inherent in the use of the property. In this case, the land could be sold to yield ₹750,000 after taxes. Use of the site for the distribution center would require forgoing this inflow, so the ₹750,000 must be charged as an opportunity cost against the project. Note that the proper land cost in this example is the ₹750,000 market-determined current value (after taxes), irrespective of whether XYZ originally paid ₹50,000 or ₹1 million for the property. (What XYZ paid would, of course, have an effect on taxes, and hence on the after-tax opportunity cost.) The ₹750,000 opportunity cost must be included as part of the distribution center's overall investment cost.

Externalities: Effects on Other Parts of the Firm. The third potential problem involves the effects of a project on existing cash flows in other parts of the firm or on the environment in which the firm operates. Economists call these effects **externalities**. For example, XYZ currently has customers in New England who would use the new distribution center because its location would be more convenient than the North Carolina distribution center they have been using. The sales, and hence the cash flows, generated by these customers would not be new to XYZ; rather, they would represent a transfer of existing sales from one distribution center to another. Thus, the net revenues produced by these customers should not be treated as new (incremental) cash flows in the capital budgeting decision. Although they often are difficult to quantify, *externalities* such as these must be identified because they might *not* represent new revenues or relevant cash flows, in which case they should *not* be included in the analysis of the new capital budgeting project.

opportunity cost The return on the best alternative use of an asset; the highest return that will not be earned if funds are invested in a particular project.

externalities The effect accepting a project will have on the cash flows in other parts (areas) of the firm.

Shipping and Installation Costs. When a firm acquires fixed assets, it often incurs substantial costs for shipping and installing the assets. These charges are added to the invoice price of the assets when the total cost of the project is determined. In addition, for depreciation purposes, the *depreciable basis* of an asset, which is the total amount that can be depreciated during the asset's life, includes the purchase price and any additional expenditures required to make the asset operational, including shipping and installation. Therefore, the full cost of the asset, including shipping and installation costs, is used to determine annual depreciation expenses.

Keep in mind that *depreciation is a noncash expense, so there is not a cash outflow associated with the recognition of depreciation expense each year*. Nevertheless, because depreciation is a tax-deductible expense, *it affects the taxable income of a firm, and thus the amount of taxes paid by the firm, which is a cash flow.*

Inflation. Inflation is a fact of life, and it should be recognized in capital budgeting decisions. If expected inflation is not built into the determination of expected cash flows, then the calculated net present value and internal rate of return will be incorrect: both will be artificially low. It is easy to avoid inflation bias; simply build inflationary expectations into the cash flows used in the capital budgeting analysis. Expected inflation should be reflected in the revenue and cost figures, and thus in the annual net cash flow forecasts. The required rate of return does not need to be adjusted for inflation expectations, because investors include such expectations when establishing the rate at which they are willing to allow the firm to use their funds. (We discussed this concept in Chapter 5.)

10-1c Identifying Incremental Cash Flows

Generally, when we identify the incremental cash flows associated with a capital project, we separate them according to when they occur during the life of the project. In most cases, we classify a project's incremental cash flows into one of these three categories:

- Cash flows that occur *only at the start* of the project's life (Period 0) are part of the *initial investment outlay.*

- Cash flows that *continue throughout* the project's life (Periods 1 through n) are part of the *supplemental operating cash flows.*
- Cash flows that occur *only at the end* of the project's life (Period n) and that are associated with the disposal, or termination, of the project are part of the *terminal cash flow.*

We discuss these three incremental cash flow classifications and identify some of the relevant cash flows next. Keep in mind, however, that when identifying the relevant cash flows for capital budgeting, the primary question is which cash flows will be affected by purchasing the project. *If a cash flow does not change, it is not relevant to the capital budgeting analysis.*

Initial Investment Outlay. The **initial investment outlay,** which we designate $\hat{CF}_0$, refers to the incremental cash flows that *occur only at the start of a project's life.* $\hat{CF}_0$ includes such cash flows as the purchase price of the new project and shipping and installation costs. If the capital budgeting decision is a *replacement decision,* then the initial investment must also take into account the cash flows associated with the disposal of the old, or replaced, asset. This amount includes any cash received or paid to scrap the old asset and any tax effects associated with its disposal.

In many cases, the addition or replacement of a capital asset also affects the firm's short-term assets and liabilities, which are known as its *working capital accounts.* For example, additional inventories might be required to support a new operation, and increased inventory purchases will increase accounts payable. The difference between current assets and current liabilities is called *net working capital.* Thus, the difference between the required change in current assets and the spontaneous change in current liabilities is the change in net working capital. If this change is positive, as it generally is for expansion projects, then additional financing, over and above the cost of the project, is needed to fund the increase.[3] *The change in net working capital that results from the acceptance of a project is an incremental cash flow that must be considered in the capital budgeting analysis.* Because the change in net working capital requirements occurs at the start of the project's life, this cash flow impact is an incremental cash flow that is included as a part of the initial investment outlay.

[3]We should note that there are instances in which the change in net working capital associated with a capital project actually results in a decrease in the firm's current funding requirements, which frees up cash flows for investment. Usually this occurs if the project being considered is much more efficient than the existing asset(s).

Supplemental Operating Cash Flows. **Supplemental operating cash flows** are the changes in day-to-day operating cash flows that result from the purchase of a capital project. These changes occur throughout the life of the project; thus, they continue to affect the firm's cash flows until the firm disposes of the asset.

In most cases, the *supplemental operating cash flows* for each year can be computed directly by using Equation 10.1:

10.1

Supplemental operating

$$= \Delta\text{Cash revenues}_t - \Delta\text{Cash expenses}_t - \Delta\text{Taxes}_t$$
$$= \Delta\text{NOI}_t \times (1 - T) + \Delta\text{Depr}_t$$
$$= (\Delta\text{NOI}_t + \Delta\text{Depr}_t) \times (1 - T) + T\Delta\text{Depr}_t$$

The symbols in Equation 10.1 are defined as follows:

Δ = the Greek letter *delta,* which indicates the change in something.

$\boldsymbol{\Delta\text{NOI}_t}$ = $\text{NOI}_{t,\text{ accept}} - \text{NOI}_{t,\text{ reject}}$ = the change in net operating income in Period t that results from accepting the capital project; the subscript *accept* indicates the firm's operations that would exist if the project is accepted and the subscript *reject* indicates the level of operations that would exist if the project is rejected (the existing situation without the project).

$\boldsymbol{\Delta\text{Depr}_t}$ = $\text{Depr}_{t,\text{ accept}} - \text{Depr}_{t,\text{ reject}}$ = the change in depreciation expense in Period t that results from accepting the project.

T = marginal tax rate.

We have emphasized that depreciation is a *noncash* expense. So why is the change in depreciation expense included in the computation of supplemental operating cash flow shown in Equation 10.1? The change in depreciation expense must be computed because when depreciation changes, taxable income changes, and so does the amount of income taxes paid; the amount of taxes paid is a cash flow.

initial investment outlay The incremental cash flows associated with a project that will *occur only at the start of a project's life.*

supplemental operating cash flows The changes in day-to-day cash flows that result from the purchase of a capital project and continue until the firm disposes of the asset.

Terminal Cash Flow. The **terminal cash flow** occurs at the end of the life of the project. It is associated with (1) the final disposal of the project, including any tax effects, and (2) the return of the firm's operations to where they were before the project was purchased. Consequently, the terminal cash flow includes (1) the salvage, or disposal, value, which can be either positive (selling the asset) or negative (paying for removal) and (2) the tax impact associated with the disposal of the project. Also, (3) because we assume the firm will return to the operating level that existed prior to the acceptance of the project, any changes in net working capital that occurred at the beginning of the project's life will be *reversed* at the end of its life. For example, as an expansion project approaches the end of its useful life, inventories will be sold off and not replaced. In this case, the firm will receive an end-of-project cash inflow equal to the net working capital requirement that was incurred when the project was begun.

10-2 Capital Budgeting Project Evaluation

To this point, we have discussed several important aspects of cash flow analysis. Now we illustrate cash flow estimation for (1) an expansion project and (2) a replacement project.

10-2a Expansion Projects

Remember from Chapter 9 that an **expansion project** is one that calls for the firm to invest in new assets to *increase* sales. We illustrate expansion project analysis with a project that is being considered by Household Energy Products (HEP), a Lucknow-based technology company. HEP's research and development department has created a computerized home appliance-control device that will increase a home's energy efficiency by simultaneously controlling all household appliances and electronic devices. At this point, HEP wants to decide whether it should proceed with full-scale production of the appliance-control device.

terminal cash flow The *net* cash flow that occurs at the end of the life of a project, including the cash flows associated with (1) the final disposal of the project and (2) returning the firm's operations to where they were before the project was accepted.

expansion project A project that is intended to increase sales.

HEP's marketing department plans to target sales of the appliance control devise to the owners of larger homes, because the devise is cost-effective only in homes with 4,000 or more square feet of living space. The marketing vice president believes that annual sales will be 15,000 units if each unit is priced at ₹2,000; thus, annual sales are estimated at ₹30 million. The engineering department has determined the firm would need no additional manufacturing or storage space; it would just need the equipment to manufacture the devices. The necessary equipment would be purchased and installed late in 2015. The invoice cost is ₹9.5 million, which does not include the ₹500,000 that would have to be paid for shipping and installation. The equipment would fall under WDV depreciaton of 20%

The project will require an initial increase in net working capital equal to ₹4 million, primarily because the raw materials required to produce the devices will significantly increase the amount of inventory HEP currently holds. The investment necessary to increase net working capital will be made on December 31, 2015, when the decision to manufacture the appliance-control device occurs. The project's estimated economic life is four years. At the end of that time, the equipment is expected to have a market value of ₹2 million and a book value of ₹1.7 million. The production department has estimated that variable manufacturing costs will total 60 percent of sales and fixed overhead costs, excluding depreciation, will be ₹5 million per year. Depreciation expenses will vary from year to year in accordance with the WDV rates. HEP's marginal tax rate is 40 percent; its cost of funds, or required rate of return, is 15 percent; and, for capital budgeting purposes, the company's policy is to assume that operating cash flows occur at the end of each year. If it is determined to be an acceptable investment, manufacture of the new product will begin on January 2, 2016, and the first *supplemental operating cash flows* will occur on December 31, 2016. Table 10.2 shows the computations for the three categories of cash flows for the appliance-control device: initial investment outlay, supplemental operating cash flows, and terminal cash flow.

Analysis of the Cash Flows. The first step in the analysis is to summarize the initial investment outlay required for the project; this is done in the 2015 column of Table 10.2. For HEP's appliance-control device project, the initial cash flows consist of the purchase price of

TABLE 10.2 HEP Expansion Project Net Cash Flows, 2015–2019 (₹ in Thousands)

	2015	2016	2017	2018	2019
I. Initial Investment Outlay					
Cost of new asset	₹(9,500)				
Shipping and installation	(500)				
Increase in net working capital	(4,000)				
Initial investment	₹(14,000)				
II. Supplemental Operating Cash Flow[a]					
Sales revenues		₹30,000	₹30,000	₹30,000	₹30,000
Variable costs (60% of sales)		(18,000)	(18,000)	(18,000)	(18,000)
Fixed costs		(5,000)	(5,000)	(5,000)	(5,000)
Depreciation on new equipment[b]		(2,000)	(1600)	(1280)	(1024)
Earnings before taxes (EBT)		5,000	5400	5720	5976
Taxes (40%)		(2,000)	(2160)	(2288)	(2390)
Net income		3,000	3240	3432	3586
Add back depreciation		2,000	1600	1280	1024
Supplemental operating cash flows		₹ 5,000	₹ 4840	₹ 4712	₹ 4610
III. Terminal Cash Flow					
Return of net working capital					₹ 4,000
Net salvage value (see Table 10.3)					2000
Terminal cash flow					₹ 6000

[b]Depreciation for the new equipment was calculated using WDV (see Appendix 10A at the end of this chapter):

Year	2016	2017	2018	2019
Depreciated	20%	20%	20%	20%

These percentages are multiplied by the depreciable basis of ₹10,000 = ₹9,500 + ₹500 for the first year, and the written down values in the subsequent years, to get the depreciation expense each year.

the needed equipment, the cost of shipping and installation, and the required investment in net working capital (NWC). Notice that these cash flows do not carry over in the years 2016 through 2019; they occur only at the start of the project. Thus, the *initial investment* outlay is a cash outflow equal to ₹14 million.

Having estimated the investment requirements, we must now estimate the cash flows that will occur once production begins and will continue throughout the project's life. These are set forth in the 2016 through 2019 columns of Table 10.2. The supplemental operating cash flow estimates are based on information provided by HEP's various departments. The depreciation amounts were obtained by multiplying the depreciable basis, ₹10 million (₹9.5 million purchase price plus ₹0.5 million shipping and installation), by the WDV rate of 20%. As you can see from the computations given in footnote a in the table, the supplemental operating cash flow differs each year only because the depreciation expense, and thus the impact depreciation has on taxes, differs each year.

The final cash flow component we need to compute is the terminal cash flow. For this computation, remember that the ₹4 million investment in net working capital will be recovered in 2019. In addition, we need an estimate of the net cash flows from the disposal of the equipment in 2019. Table 10.3 shows the calculation of the net salvage value for the equipment. It is expected that the equipment will be sold for less than its book value, which means the company will not have to pay taxes on the capital gain because, in essence, the equipment has not been depreciated adequatly. The book value is calculated as the depreciable basis (purchase price plus shipping and installation) minus the accumulated depreciation. The net cash flow from salvage is merely the sum of the salvage value and the tax impact resulting from the sale of the equipment, ₹20 lakh in this

TABLE 10.3 HEP Expansion Project Net Salvage Value, 2019 (₹ in Thousands)

I. Book Value of HEP's Project, 2019	
Cost of new asset, 2015	₹ 9,500
Shipping and installation	500
Depreciable basis of asset	₹10,000
Depreciation, 2016–2019	(5904)
Book value, 2019	₹ 4096
II. Tax Effect of the Sale of HEP's Project, 2019	
Selling price of asset, 2019	₹ 2,000
Book value of asset, 2019	(4096)
Gain (loss) on sale of asset	₹(2096)
Taxes (40%)	₹ 0
III. Net Salvage Value, TCF, 2019	
Cash flow from sale of project	₹ 2,000
Tax effect of sale	0
Net cash flow from salvage	₹ 2000

case. Thus, the *terminal cash flow* totals ₹6 million: the ₹2 million net cash flow from salvage plus the ₹4 million cash flow from the return of the investment in net working capital.

Notice that the *total* net cash flow for 2019 is the sum of the supplemental operating cash flow for the year and the terminal cash flow. Thus, in the final year of a project's useful (economic) life, the firm incurs two types of cash flows: (1) the last supplemental operating cash flow attributed to the project's normal operation in the final year of its life and (2) the terminal cash flow associated with the disposal of the project.

Making the Decision. A summary of the data and the computation of the project's NPV are provided with the cash flow timeline that follows. The amounts are in thousands of rupees, just like in Table 10.2. The project appears to be acceptable using the NPV and IRR methods. Note, however, that the analysis thus far has been based on the assumption that the project has the same degree of risk as the company's average project. If the project were judged to be riskier than an average project, it would be necessary to increase the required rate of return used to compute the NPV. Later in this chapter, we will extend the evaluation of this project to include a risk analysis.

(₹ in Thousands)

	2015	2016	2017	2018	2019
Initial flows	−14000				
Operating flows		5000	4840	4712	4610
Terminal flows					6000
Net flows	−14000	5000	4840	4712	10610
NPV (15%)	− 3,172.08				
IRR	24.49%				

replacement analysis An analysis involving the decision as to whether to replace an existing asset with a new asset.

10-2b Replacement Analysis

All companies make *replacement decisions* to determine when older, worn assets should be replaced with newer assets to continue normal operations. The analysis relating to replacements is the same as that for expansion projects: Identify the relevant cash flows, and then find the net present value of the project. However, identifying the *incremental* cash flows associated with a replacement project is more complicated than for an expansion project because the cash flows from the new asset *and* from the old asset must be considered. We illustrate **replacement analysis** with another HEP example.

HEP has a lathe for trimming molded plastics that was purchased 10 years ago at a cost of ₹7,900. The machine had an expected life of 15 years at the time it was purchased, and management originally estimated, and still believes, that the salvage value will be ₹400 at the end of its 15-year life (in five more years). The machine has been depreciated on a straight-line basis; therefore, its annual cash depreciation charge is ₹500 = (₹7,900 − ₹400)/15, and its present book value is ₹2,900 = ₹7,900 − 10(₹500).

HEP is considering the purchase of a new special-purpose machine to replace the lathe. The new machine, which can be purchased for ₹12,000 (this price includes shipping and installation), will reduce labor and raw materials usage sufficiently to cut annual cash operating costs from ₹8,000 to ₹4,500.

It is estimated that the new machine will have a useful life of five years, after which it can be sold for ₹2,000. The old machine's *current* market value is ₹1,600, which is below its ₹2,900 book value. If the new machine is purchased, the old lathe will be sold to another company rather than exchanged for the new machine.

Net working capital requirements will increase by ₹1,400 if the old lathe is replaced with the new machine; this increase will occur at the time of replacement. The new machine falls into the WDV 25% class. Because the risk associated with the new machine is considered average for HEP, the project's required rate of return is 15 percent. Should the replacement be made?

Table 10.4 shows the worksheet format HEP uses to analyze replacement projects. Determining the relevant cash flows for a replacement decision is more involved than for an expansion decision because we need to consider the fact that the cash flows associated with the replaced asset will not continue after the new asset is purchased; that is, *the cash flows associated with the new asset will take the place of the cash flows associated with the old asset.* Because we want to evaluate how the acceptance of a capital budgeting project *changes* cash flows, we must compute the increase or decrease (change) in cash flows that results from the replacement of the old asset with the new asset.

Analysis of Cash Flows. The initial investment outlay of ₹11,280 includes the cash flows associated with the cost of the new asset and the change in net working capital. However, when a replacement asset is purchased, the asset being replaced generally can be sold to another firm or to a scrap dealer. If the firm disposes of the old asset at a value different from its book value (its purchase price less accumulated depreciation), there will be a tax effect. In our example, the *old* asset has a current book value equal to ₹2,900, but it can be sold for only ₹1,600. Consequently, the disposal of the old asset will generate a positive cash flow equal to ₹1600. As a result, disposal of the lathe effectively reduces the amount of cash required to purchase the new machine, and thus reduces the initial investment outlay. Any cash flows associated with disposing of the old asset must be included in the computation of the initial investment because they affect the net amount of cash required to purchase the asset.[4]

Next, we need to compute the annual supplemental operating cash flows. Section II of Table 10.4 shows these computations. The procedure is the same as before: determine how operating cash flows will change if the new machine is purchased to replace the lathe. Remember, the lathe is expected to decrease cash operating costs from ₹8,000 to ₹4,500, and thus increase cash operating profits by ₹3,500; that is, less cash will have to be spent to operate the new machine. Had the replacement resulted in an increase in sales in addition to the reduction in costs, this amount would also be reported. Also, note that the ₹3,500 cost savings is constant over the years 2016–2020. Had the annual savings been expected to change over time, this fact would have to be built into the analysis.

The change in depreciation expense must be computed to determine the impact such a change will have on the taxes paid by the firm because taxes require cash payments. If the new machine is purchased, the ₹500 depreciation expense of the lathe (old asset) no longer will be relevant for tax purposes; instead, the depreciation expense for the new machine will be used. For example, in 2016, the depreciation expense for the new machine will be ₹3000 because, according to WDV depreciation, 25 percent of the cost of the new asset can be depreciated in the year it is purchased. Because HEP will dispose of the lathe if it buys the new machine, in 2016 it will replace the ₹500 depreciation expense associated with the lathe with the depreciation expense associated with the new machine; thus the depreciation expense will

[4]If you think about it, the computation of the initial investment outlay for replacement decisions is similar to determining the amount you would need to purchase a new automobile to replace your old one. If the purchase price of the new car is ₹450000 and the dealer is willing to give you ₹100000 for your old car as a trade-in, then the amount you need is only ₹350000. However, if you need to pay someone to take your old car out of the garage because that is where you are going to keep the new car at night, the total amount you need to purchase the new car is, in fact, greater than ₹450000.

TABLE 10.4 HEP Replacement Project Net Cash Flows, 2015–2020 (₹ in Thousands)

	2015	2016	2017	2018	2019	2020
I. Initial Investment Outlay						
Cost of new asset	₹(12,000)					
Change in net working capital	(1,400)					
Net cash flow from sale of old asset[a]	1600					
Initial investment	₹(11,880)					
II. Supplemental Operating Cash Flows						
Δ Operating costs = ₹8,000 – ₹4,500		₹3,500	₹3,500	3,500	₹3,500	₹3,500
Δ Depreciation[b]		(2500)	(1750)	(1188)	(766)	449
Δ Operating income before taxes (EBT)		1000	1750	2313	2734	3051
Δ Taxes (40%)		(400)	700	(925)	(1094)	(1220)
Δ Net operating income		600	(1050)	1388	766	1830
Add back Δ depreciation		2500	1750	1188	766	(449)
Supplemental operating cash flows		₹3100	₹2800	₹2575	₹2406	₹2280
III. Terminal Cash Flow						
Return of net working capital						₹1,400
Net salvage value of *new* asset[c]						2000
Net salvage value of *old* asset[d]						(400)
Terminal cash flow						₹3000
IV. Incremental Cash Flows						
Total net cash flow per period	₹(11,280)	₹3300	₹3000	₹2775	₹2606	₹5480

[a]The net cash flow from the sale of the old (replaced) asset is computed as follows:

Selling price (market value)	₹1,600
Subtract book value	(2,900)
Gain (loss) on sale of asset	(1,300)
Tax	

Net cash flow from the sale of asset = ₹1,600

[b]The change in depreciation expense is computed by comparing the depreciation of the new asset with the depreciation that would have existed if the old asset was not replaced. The old asset has been depreciated on a straight-line basis, with five years of ₹500 annual depreciation remaining. The new asset will be depreciated at WDV method taking the rate as 25%. The change in annual depreciation would be

Year	New Asset Depreciation		Old Asset Depreciation		Change in Depreciation
2016	₹12,000 × 0.25 = ₹ 3000	–	₹500	=	2500
2017	9000 × 0.25 = 2250	–	500	=	1750
2018	6750 × 0.25 = 1688	–	500	=	1188
2019	5063 × 0.25 = 1266	–	500	=	766
2020	= 949	–	500	=	449
Accumulated depreciation =	9152				

[c]The book value of the new asset in 2020 will be 2848. The net salvage value of the new asset in 2020 is computed as follows:

Selling price (market value)	₹2,000
Subtract book value	(2848)
Gain (loss) on sale of asset	(848)
Tax impact of sale of asset (40%)	0

Net salvage value of the new asset in 2020 = ₹2,000 – ₹800 = ₹2000

[d]If the old lathe is not replaced, HEP could sell it for ₹400 in 2020. If HEP purchases the new machine, it will not receive this cash flow in 2020. Because the old lathe would have a book value of ₹400 in 2020, there would be no tax effect from the sale.

increase by ₹2500 = ₹3,000 – ₹500. The computations for the remaining years are the same.

The terminal cash flow includes ₹1,400 for the return of net working capital, because we assume the firm's normal net working capital level, which is the level that existed before buying the new machine, is restored at the end of the new machine's life. Any additional accounts receivables created by the purchase of the new machine will be collected, and any additional inventories required by the new machine will be drawn down and not replaced. The net salvage value of the *new* machine is ₹2000; it is expected that the new machine can be sold in 2020 for ₹2,000, but since the book value is higher there is no tax implication. We must also recognize that if the new machine is purchased, the firm no longer will have the *opportunity* to sell the *old* machine for its estimated salvage value in 2020, which is ₹400. In other words, if the new machine is purchased, the firm will dispose of the old machine in 2015 rather than in 2020. Although we recognized the financial effects of the disposal of the old machine in the initial investment outlay in 2015, we must now recognize the fact that the firm will no longer be able to sell the old machine in 2020 for its estimated ₹400 salvage value. Because it is estimated that the old machine could be sold at its book value in 2020, there would be no tax effect (i.e., the gain on the sale would be ₹0), and the net salvage value of the old machine would be ₹400. This amount appears as a negative cash flow, or an outflow, because the firm will not receive the ₹400 from the sale of the lathe in 2020 if the new machine is purchased. Thus, the total terminal cash flow is ₹2,200 = ₹1,400 + ₹1,200 – ₹400.

Making the Decision. A summary of the data and the computation of the project's NPV are provided with the following cash flow timeline:

(₹ in Thousands)	2015	2016	2017	2018	2019
Initial flows	–14000				
Operating flows		5000	4840	4712	4610
Terminal flows					6000
Net flows	–14000	5000	4840	4712	10610
NPV (15%)	– 3,172.08				
IRR	24.49%				

According to the NPV and IRR methods, HEP should not replace the lathe with the new machine. Before we leave our discussion of replacement decisions, we should note that a replacement decision involves comparing two mutually exclusive projects: (1) retaining the old asset and (2) buying a new asset. To simplify matters, in our replacement example we assumed that the new machine had a life equal to the remaining life of the old machine. If, however, we were choosing between two mutually exclusive alternatives with significantly different lives, an adjustment would be necessary to make the results of the capital budgeting analysis for the two projects comparable. We mention the unequal-life problem here to make you aware that the evaluation of mutually exclusive projects with significantly different lives requires a slightly different analysis to ensure that a correct decision is made. Techniques that are used to adjust for unequal lives are included in more advanced finance textbooks.

10-3 Incorporating Risk in Capital Budgeting Analysis

To this point, we have assumed that the projects being examined have the same risk as the projects the firm currently possesses—that is, the investment risk associated with the projects is considered average, or normal—so that we could use the firm's *average* required rate of return to evaluate the acceptability of the investments. However, three types of risk, which we discuss in this section, must be examined to determine whether it is appropriate to use the firm's average required rate of return to evaluate a project. Although more difficult, evaluating the risk associated with a capital budgeting project is similar to evaluating the risk of a financial asset such as a stock. Therefore, much of our discussion in this section relies on the concepts introduced in Chapter 8.

10-3a Stand-Alone Risk

A project's **stand-alone risk** is the risk that it exhibits when evaluated alone rath-

stand-alone risk The risk an asset would have if it were a firm's only asset. It is measured by the variability of the asset's expected returns.

Comstock/Getty Images/Jupiterimages

er than as part of a combination, or *portfolio*, of assets. As we discovered in Chapter 8, at least in theory stand-alone risk should be of little or no concern, because diversification can eliminate some of this type of risk. However, it is of great importance in capital budgeting decisions because stand-alone risk is easier to estimate than either of the other two risks we discuss in this section, and, in most cases, all three types of risk are highly correlated. As a result, management knows that it can get a good idea of a project's riskiness by determining its stand-alone risk.

The starting point for analyzing a project's stand-alone risk involves determining the uncertainty inherent in the project's cash flows. This analysis can be handled in a number of ways, ranging from informal judgments to complex economic and statistical analyses involving large-scale computer models. We will illustrate what is involved using Household Energy Products' appliance-control computer project, which we discussed earlier. Many of the individual cash flows that were shown in Table 10.2 are subject to uncertainty. For example, although sales for each year were projected at 15,000 units to be sold at a net price of ₹2,000 per unit, actual sales almost certainly would be somewhat higher or lower than 15,000, and the sales price might turn out to be different from the projected ₹2,000 per unit. In effect, estimates of the sales quantity and the sales price are expected values taken from probability distributions, as are many of the other values shown in Table 10.2. The distributions could be relatively "tight," reflecting small standard deviations and low risk, or they could be "wide," denoting a great deal of uncertainty about the final value of the variable in question and hence a high degree of stand-alone risk.

sensitivity analysis A risk analysis technique in which key variables are changed and the resulting changes in the NPV and the IRR are observed.

scenario analysis A risk analysis technique in which "bad" and "good" sets of financial circumstances are compared with a most likely, or base case, situation.

The nature of the individual cash flow distributions, and their correlations with one another, determine the nature of the NPV distribution and, thus, the project's stand-alone risk. Three techniques that are used for assessing a project's stand-alone risk include sensitivity analysis, scenario analysis and Monte Carlo Simulation.

Sensitivity Analysis. Because the cash flows used to determine the acceptability of a project result from forecasts of uncertain events, such as economic conditions in the future and expected demand for a product, we know the cash flow amounts used to determine the NPV of a project might be significantly different from what actually happens in the future. We also know that if a key input variable, such as units sold, changes, the project's NPV will also change. We can use a technique called **sensitivity analysis** to show exactly how much the NPV will change in response to a given change in an input variable, other things held constant. In a sensitivity analysis, we begin with the base-case situation that was developed using the expected values for each input; next, each variable is changed by specific percentage points above and below the expected value, holding other things constant; then a new NPV is calculated for each of these values; and, finally, the set of NPVs is plotted against the variable that was changed.

If we were comparing two projects, the one with the steeper sensitivity lines would be regarded as riskier, because, for that project, a relatively small error in estimating an extremely sensitive variable would produce a large error in the project's expected NPV. Thus, sensitivity analysis can provide useful insights into the riskiness of a project.

Scenario Analysis. In general, a project's stand-alone risk depends on both (1) the sensitivity of its NPV to changes in key variables and (2) the range of likely values of these variables, as reflected in their probability distributions. Sensitivity analysis considers only the first factor. **Scenario analysis** is a risk-analysis technique that considers both factors. In a scenario analysis, the financial analyst asks operating managers to pick a "bad" set of circumstances (low unit sales, low sales price, high variable cost per unit, high construction cost, and so on) and a "good" set of circumstances. The NPVs under the bad and good conditions are then calculated and compared to the expected, or *base case*, NPV.

To carry out the scenario analysis, we use the worst-case variable values to obtain the worst-case NPV and the best-case variable values to obtain the best-case NPV.[5] We then use the results of the scenario analysis to determine the *expected* NPV, the standard deviation of NPV, and the coefficient of variation. To complete these computations, we need estimates of the probabilities of occurrence of the three scenarios, the Pr_i values. Suppose management estimates that there is a 20 percent probability of the worst-case scenario, a 60 percent probability of the base case, and a 20 percent probability of the best case. The scenario probabilities and NPVs constitute a probability distribution of returns just like those we dealt with in Chapter 8, except that the returns are measured in rupees instead of percentages, or rates of return.

The computation of sensitivity analysis and scenario analysis through MS Excel is demonstrated by the following example:

A company intends to make a new investment in a project. The initial outlay will be ₹50 lakh. The project has a life of five years, at the end of which no terminal flows are expected. During the five years, 50,000 units of a product will be sold by the company at a sale price of ₹50 per unit. The variable cost is expected to be ₹20 per unit. There will be no other expenditure or any further tax implication. Find the base case NPV if the discount rate is 11%.

The project team feels that the sales units can vary from 45,000 to 55,000 units. Whatever units are sold in the first year will continue to be sold in the remaining years. Similarly, the sales price per unit can vary from ₹48 per unit to ₹52 per unit and the variable cost can vary from ₹18 per unit to ₹22 per unit. Again, the sale price and the variable cost per unit that occurs in the first year will remain the same for the other years as well.

The solution to this problem involves several steps. First we have to draw up the key parameters into a spreadsheet, as shown in Exhibit 10.2.

EXHIBIT 10.2

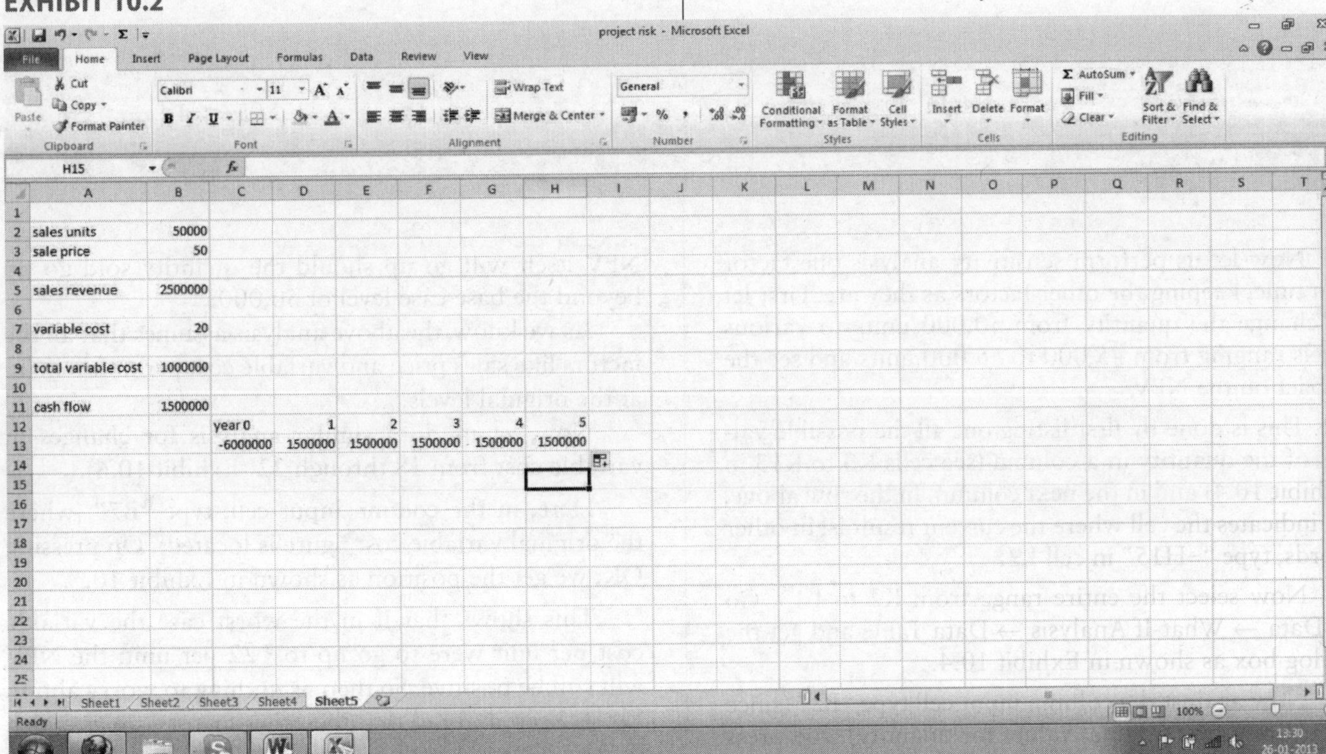

Notice that the spreadsheet has several formulae in it. The sales turnover is shown as a product of the sales quantity and sales price (the product of B2 and B3 is shown as a formula in B5). The total variable cost is a product of the variable cost per unit and the sales quantity (in cell B9, this is shown as formula of

[5]We could have included worst- and best-case values for fixed and variable costs, income tax rates, salvage values, and so on. For illustrative purposes, we limited the changes to only two variables. Also, note that we are treating sales price and quantity as independent variables; that is, a low sales price could occur when unit sales were low, and a high sales price could be coupled with high unit sales, or vice versa. As we discuss in the next section, it is relatively easy to vary these assumptions if the facts of the situation suggest a different set of conditions.

B2 multiplied by B9). In the cash flow timeline, the net cash flow arrived at in B11 is shown as cash inflow by referring to B11.

Now let us find the NPV by using the usual formula and equation, as shown in Exhibit 10.3.

EXHIBIT 10.3

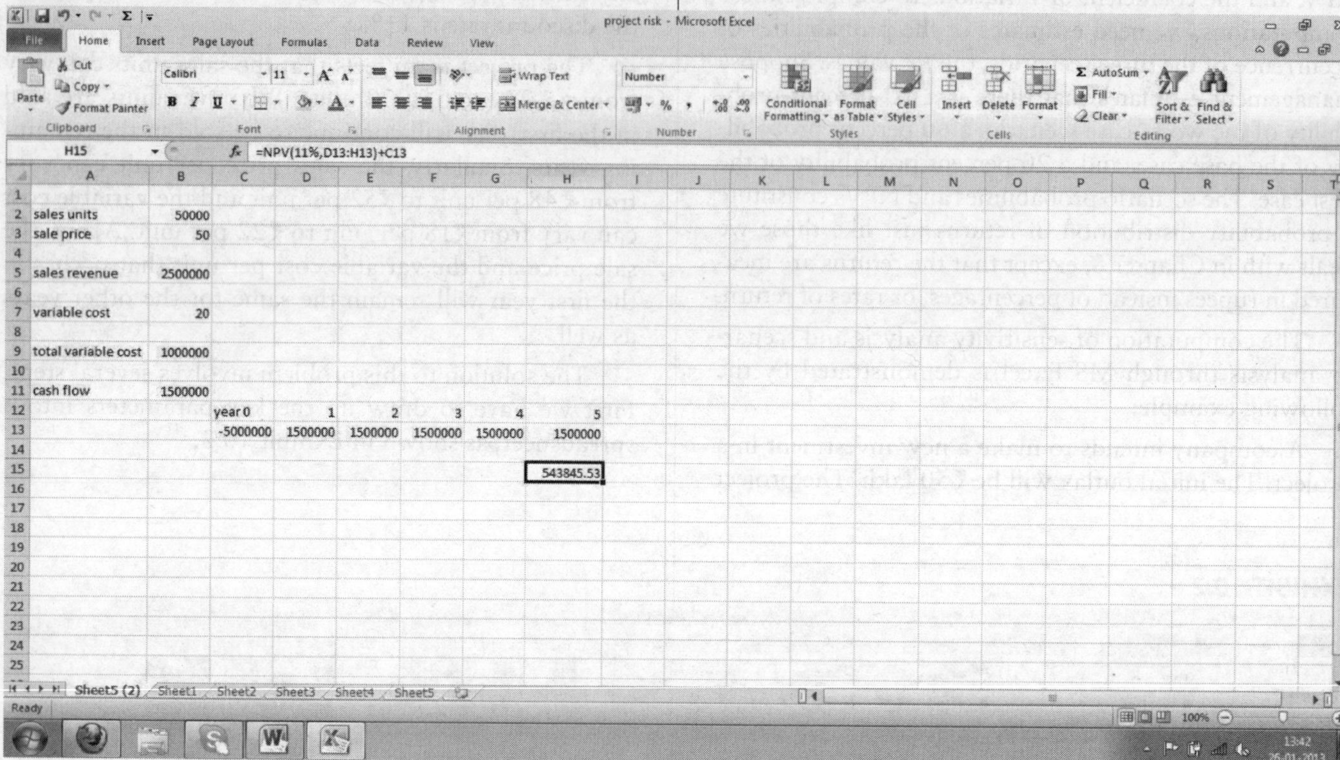

Now let us perform sensitivity analysis one factor at a time, keeping the other factors as they are. First let us change the quantity from 50,000 units to various levels ranging from 45,000 to 55,000 units and see the impact on the NPV.

This is done by first listing out all the possible values of the quantity in a column (see cells K3 to K13 in Exhibit 10.4) and in the next column. In the row above, L2 indicates the cell where the current result is. In other words, type "=H15" in cell L2.

Now select the entire range from K2 to L13. Go to Data → What-If Analysis → Data Table and get the dialog box as shown in Exhibit 10.4.

Now against the column input cell type "B2" (since B2 contains the original values for quantity), and press OK to get the output shown in Exhibit 10.5.

What this shows is that if the quantity were to drop to 45,000 units, the NPV will be negative. Also, the positive NPV in the base case will come down with fall in units below 50,000, as indicated. As per intuition, the NPV itself will go up should the quantity sold go up beyond the base case level of 50,000.

As we know, the above analysis assumes that all the factors like sales price and variable cost per unit remain at the original levels.

Now, let us do a similar analysis for changes in variable cost from 18 through 22 (Exhibit 10.6).

Here, in the column input cell, type "B7" (where the original variable cost figure is located). On pressing OK, we get the position as shown in Exhibit 10.7.

This shows that if in the worst case the variable cost per unit were to go up to ₹22 per unit, the NPV will still be positive. So there is nothing to worry about. Let us keep in mind that the other factors are assumed to remain at the original level.

A similar analysis for changes in sales price from ₹48 ₹52 is shown in Exhibit 10.8.

EXHIBIT 10.4

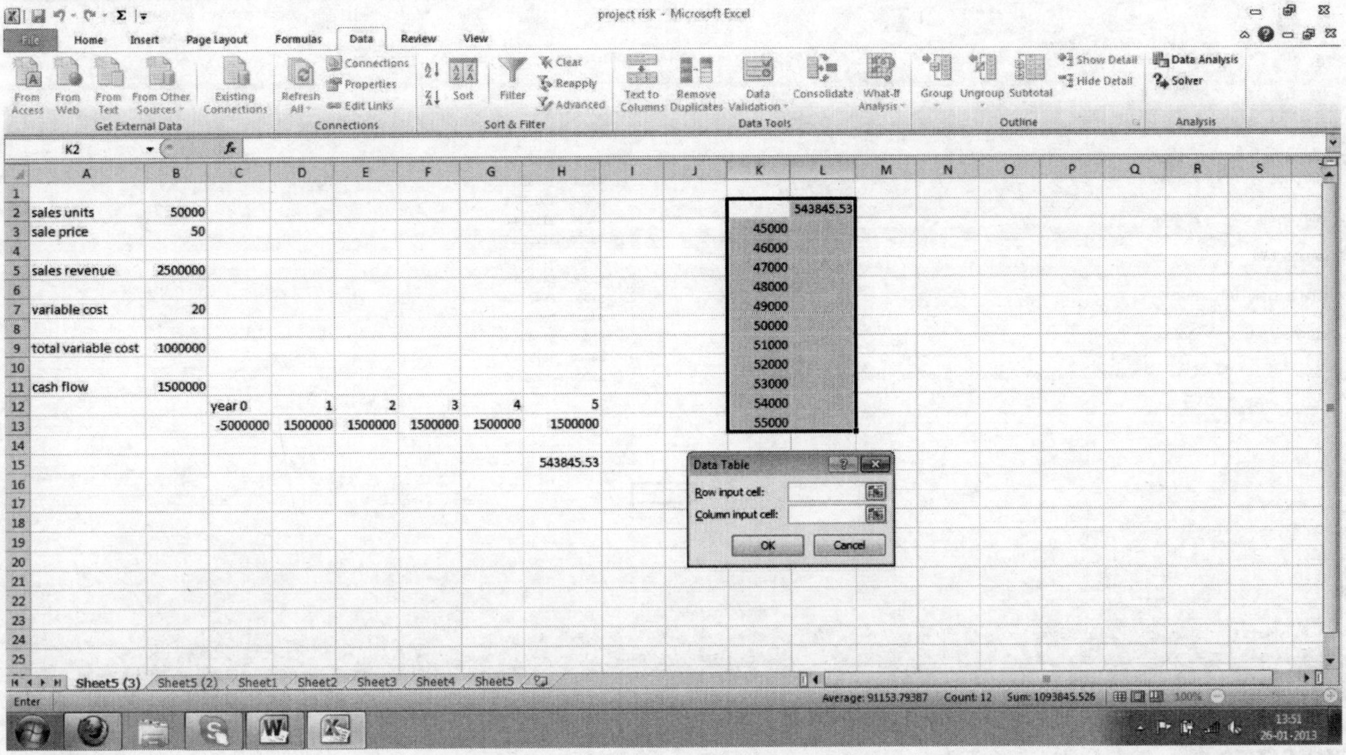

EXHIBIT 10.5

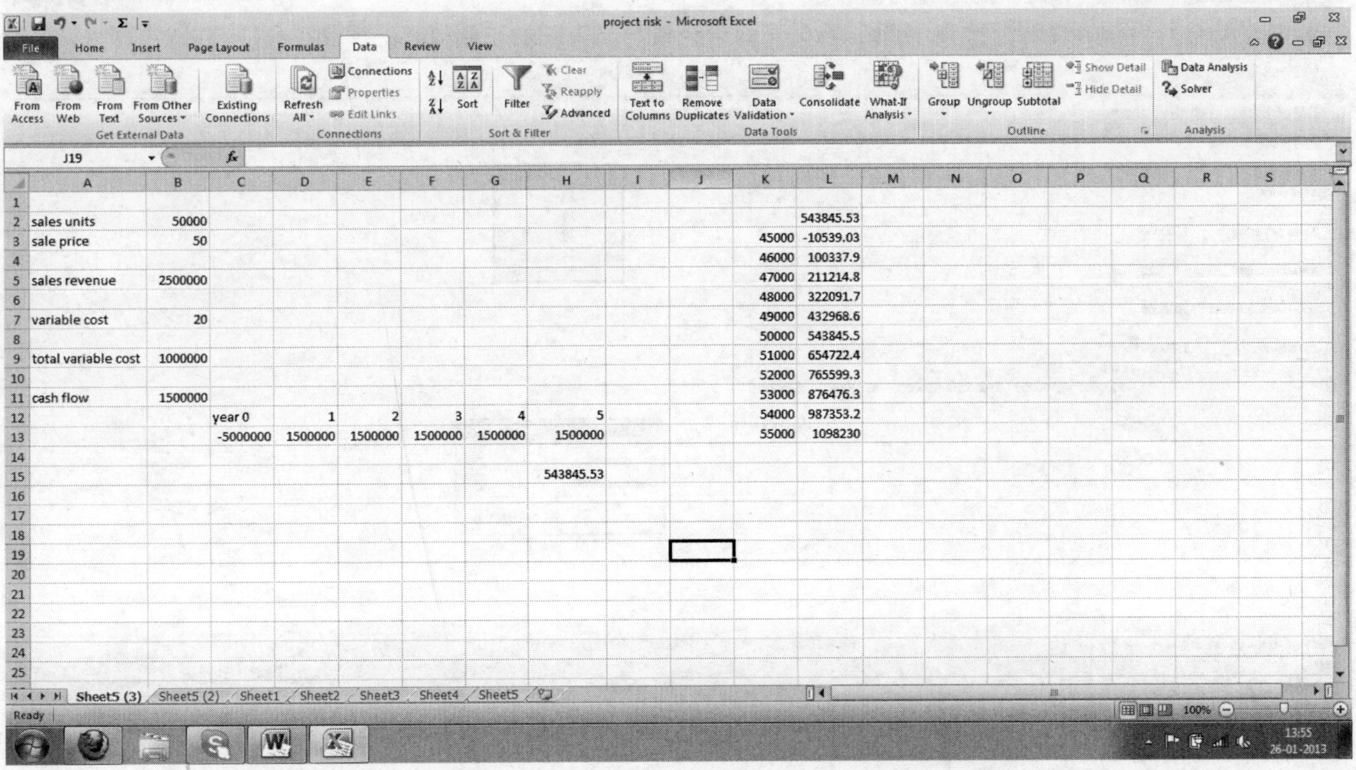

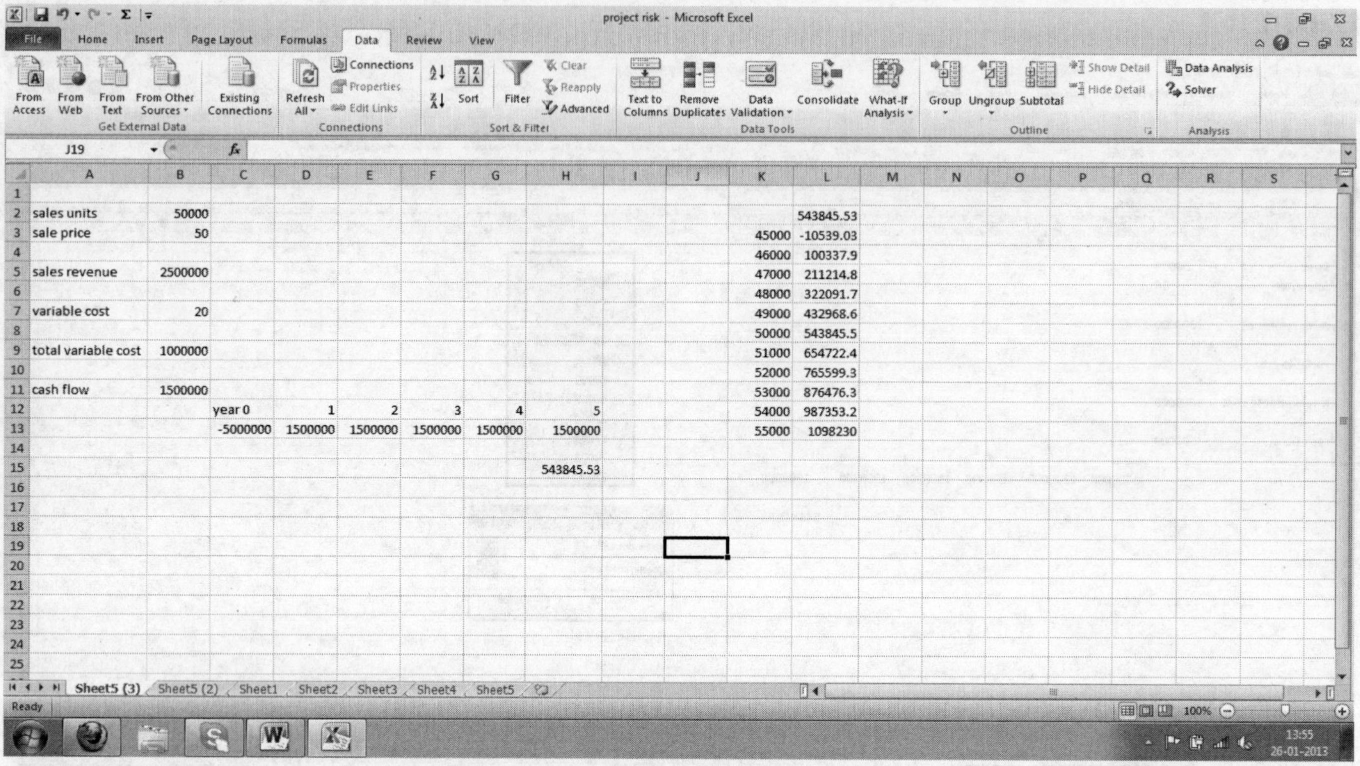
project risk - Microsoft Excel
sales units 50000
sale price 50
sales revenue 2500000
variable cost 20
total variable cost 1000000
cash flow 1500000
year 0 1 2 3 4 5
-5000000 1500000 1500000 1500000 1500000 1500000
543845.53
543845.53
45000 -10539.03
46000 100337.9
47000 211214.8
48000 322091.7
49000 432968.6
50000 543845.5
51000 654722.4
52000 765599.3
53000 876476.3
54000 987353.2
55000 1098230

EXHIBIT 10.6

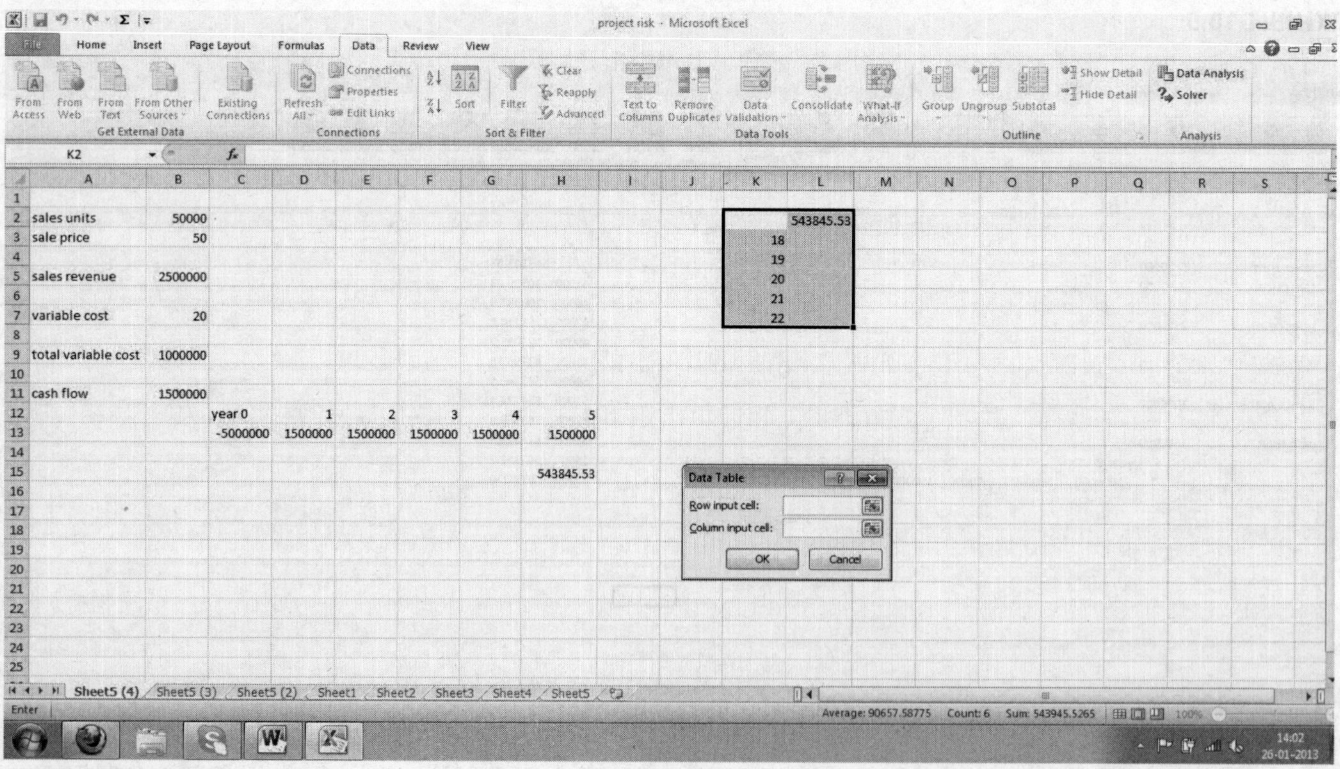
project risk - Microsoft Excel
sales units 50000
sale price 50
sales revenue 2500000
variable cost 20
total variable cost 1000000
cash flow 1500000
year 0 1 2 3 4 5
-5000000 1500000 1500000 1500000 1500000 1500000
543845.53
543845.53
18
19
20
21
22
Data Table
Row input cell:
Column input cell:
OK
Cancel

EXHIBIT 10.7

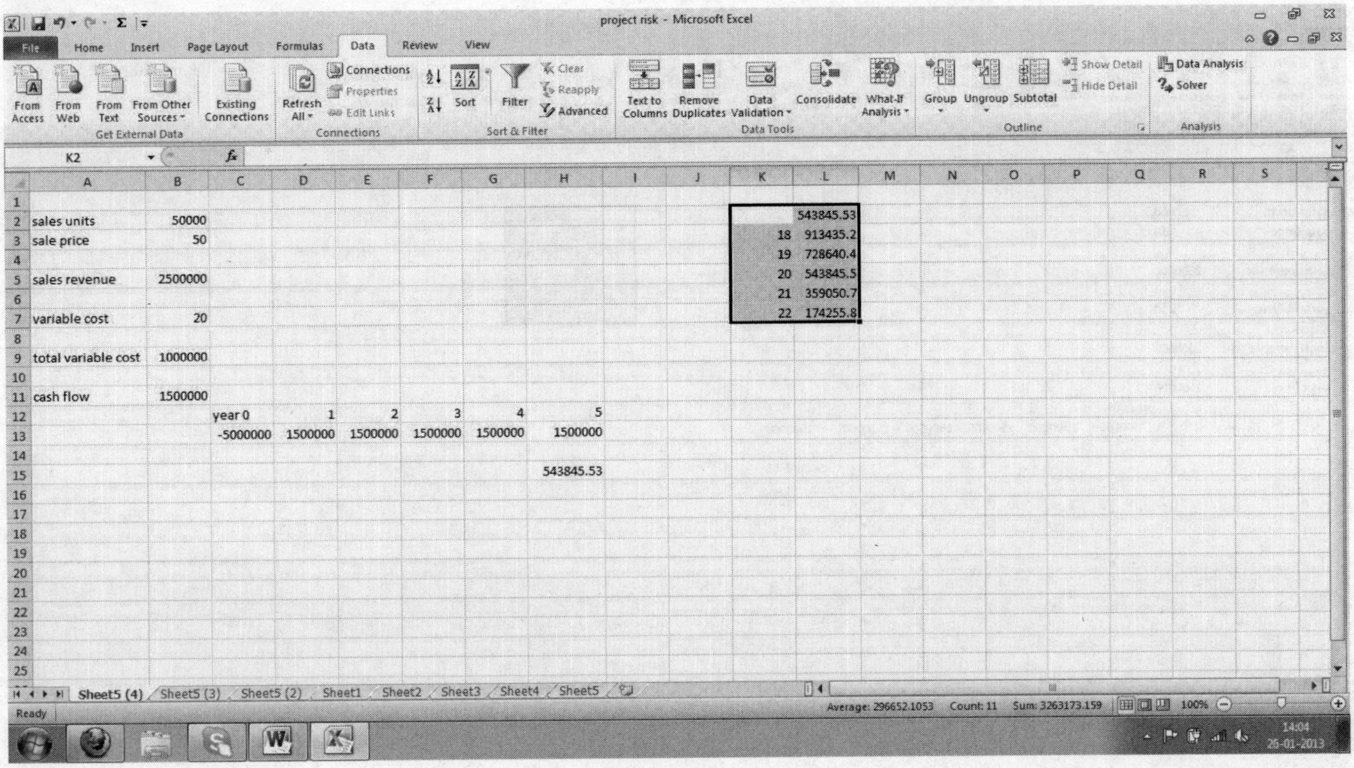

EXHIBIT 10.8

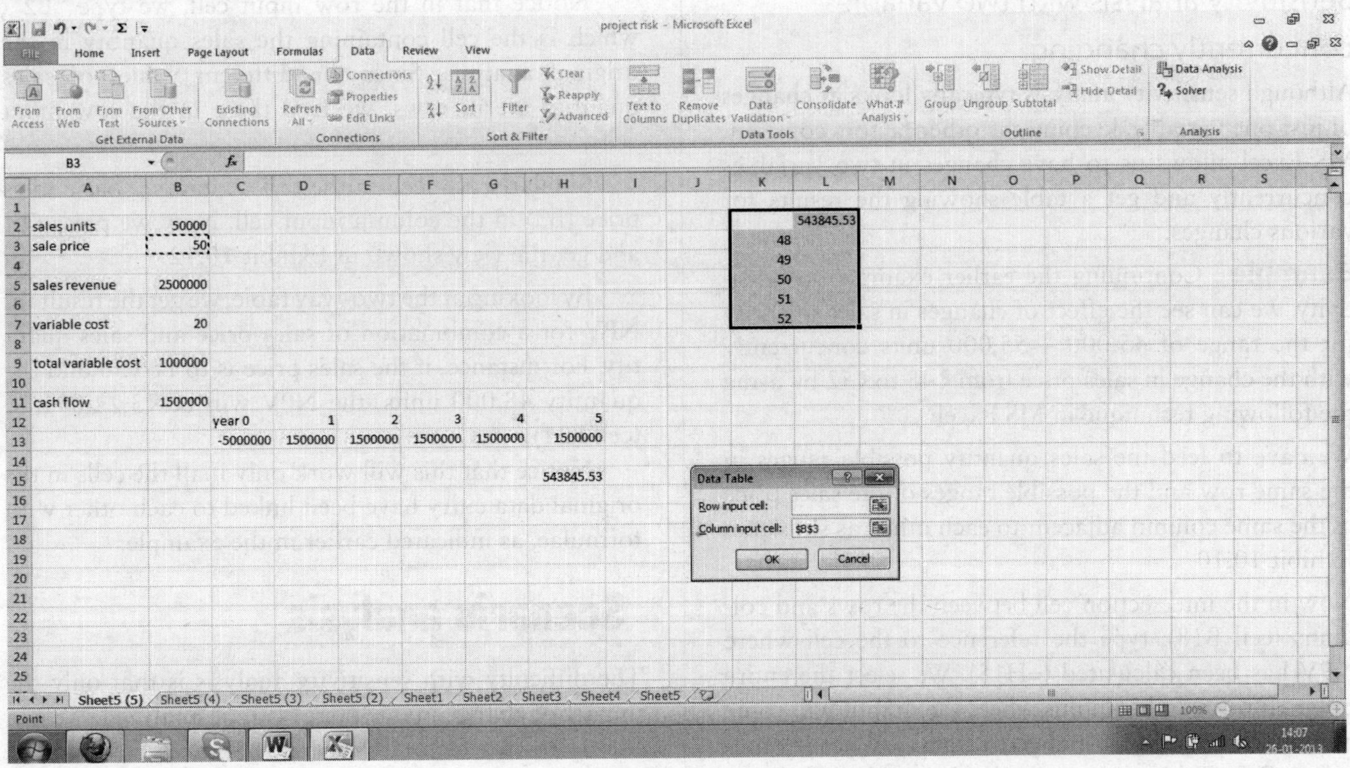

EXHIBIT 10.9

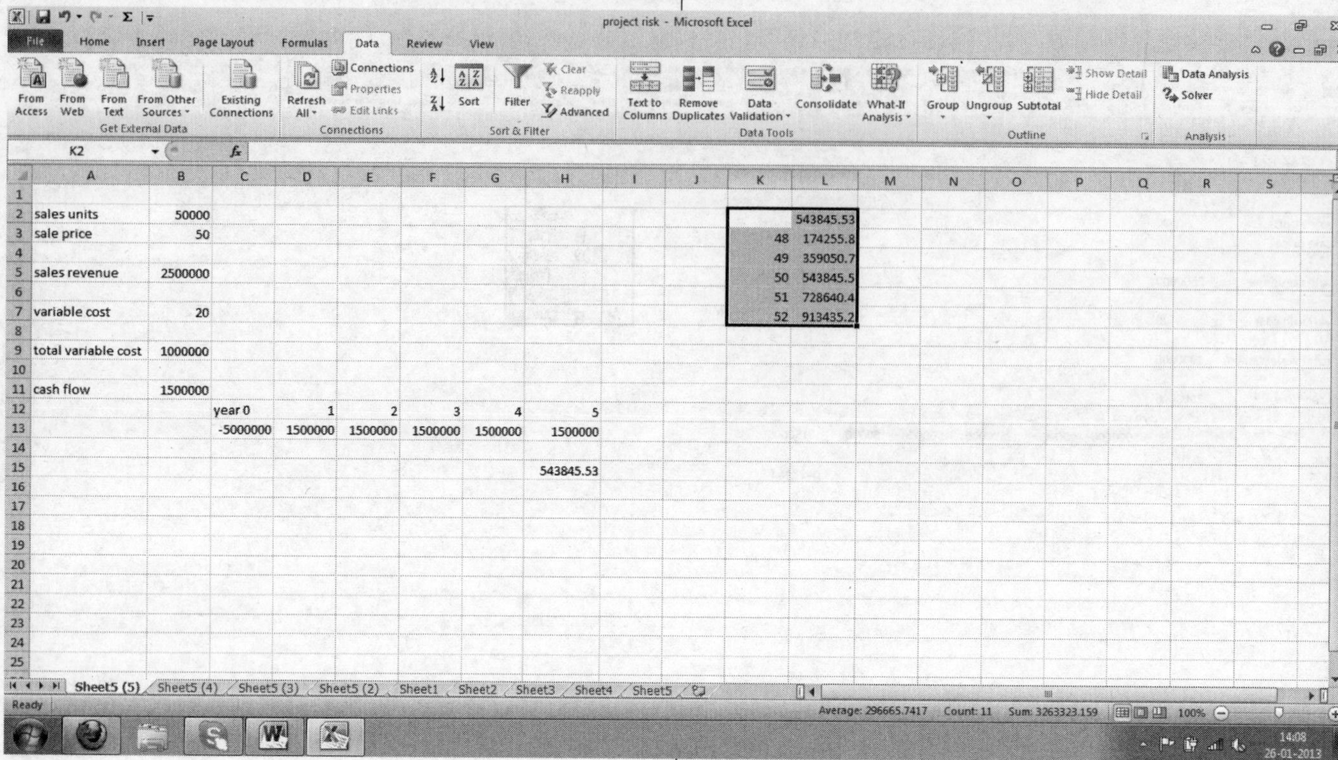

Sensitivity analysis with two variables concurrently changing

Although sensitivity analysis typically looks at changes of just one variable, keeping the other factors constant, MS Excel allows us to have changes in two variables concurrently and get a table showing the results for various changes.

Example Continuing the earlier example on sensitivity, we can see the effect of changes in sales quantity for the range of 45,000 – 55,000 units concurrently with the change in sales price from ₹48 to ₹52 by using the following technique in MS Excel:

We have to feed the sales quantity possible ranges in the same row and the possible ranges of the sales price in the same column adjacent to each other, as shown in Exhibit 10.10.

Now in the intersection cell between the rows and columns (cell B18), type the reference to the cell where NPV has been calculated (=H15). We select the entire range of rows and columns where the output will come about (cells B18:M23) and go to Data -> What-If Analysis -> Data Table and type in the date table dialog box as shown in Exhibit 10.11.

Notice that in the row input cell, we type "B2", which is the cell containing the sales quantity in the original analysis. Since the different values of sales quantity are in rows, we feed these in the row input cells.

Similarly, we feed in the cell containing basic sales price (B3) in the column input cell. Now we press OK and get the view shown in Exhibit 10.12.

By looking at the two-way table, we get the resultant NPV for a combination of sales price and sales quantity. For instance, if the sales price is to be ₹50 and the quantity 48,000 units, the NPV will be ₹3,22,091.71 (cell F21).

Notice that this will work only if all the cells in the original data entry have been linked to each other with formulae, as indicated earlier in the example.

Scenario analysis

The difficulty with sensitivity analysis is that only the impact of change in one factor can be analyzed. We can use up to two factors by using MS Excel, as discussed above. But sometimes we are confronted with the issue of several factors all moving together favorably or

EXHIBIT 10.10

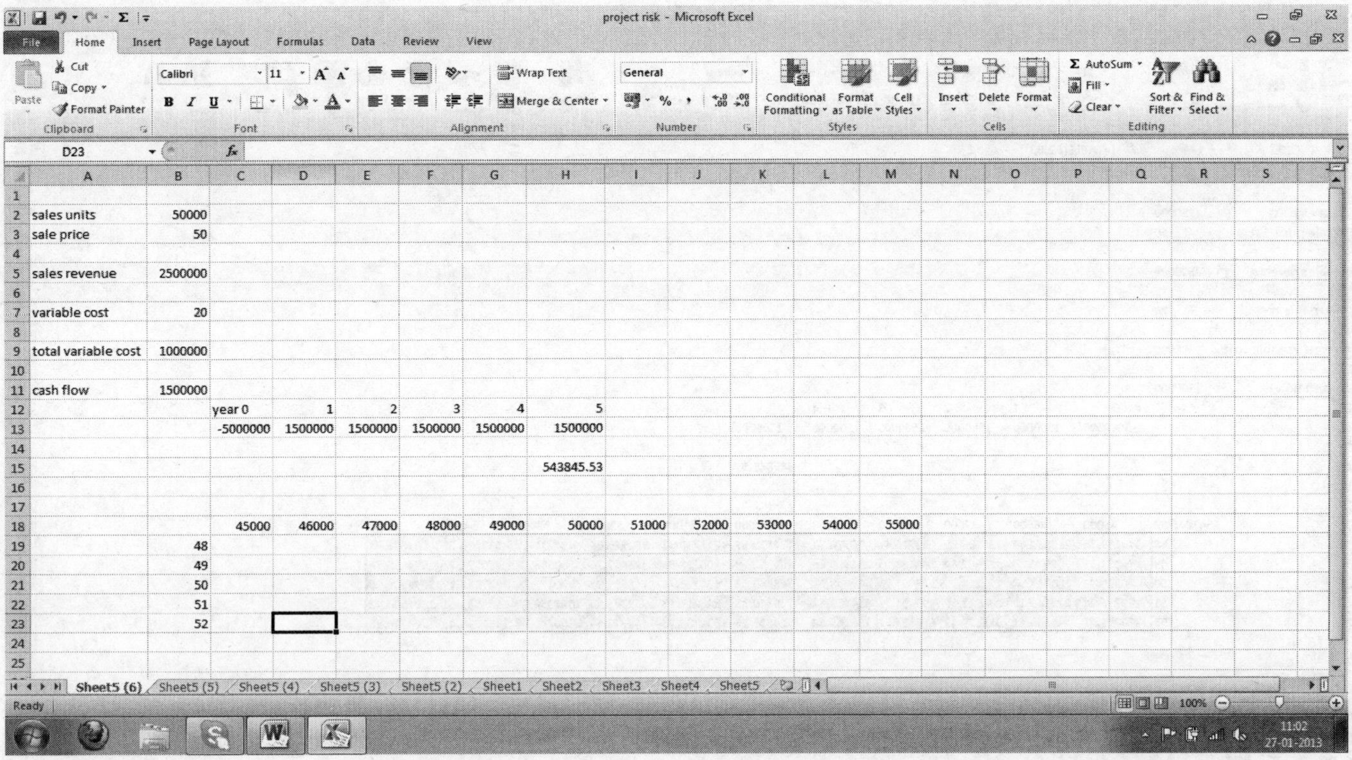

EXHIBIT 10.11

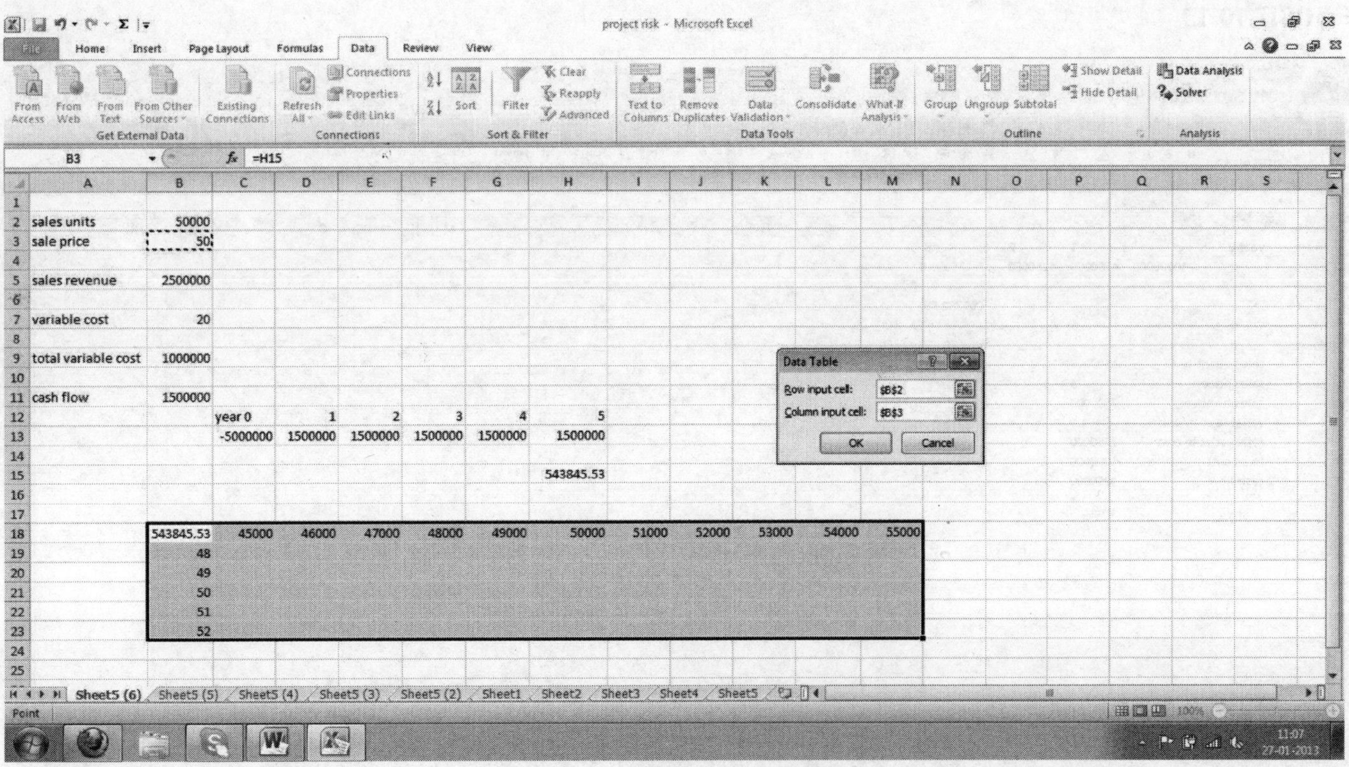

EXHIBIT 10.12

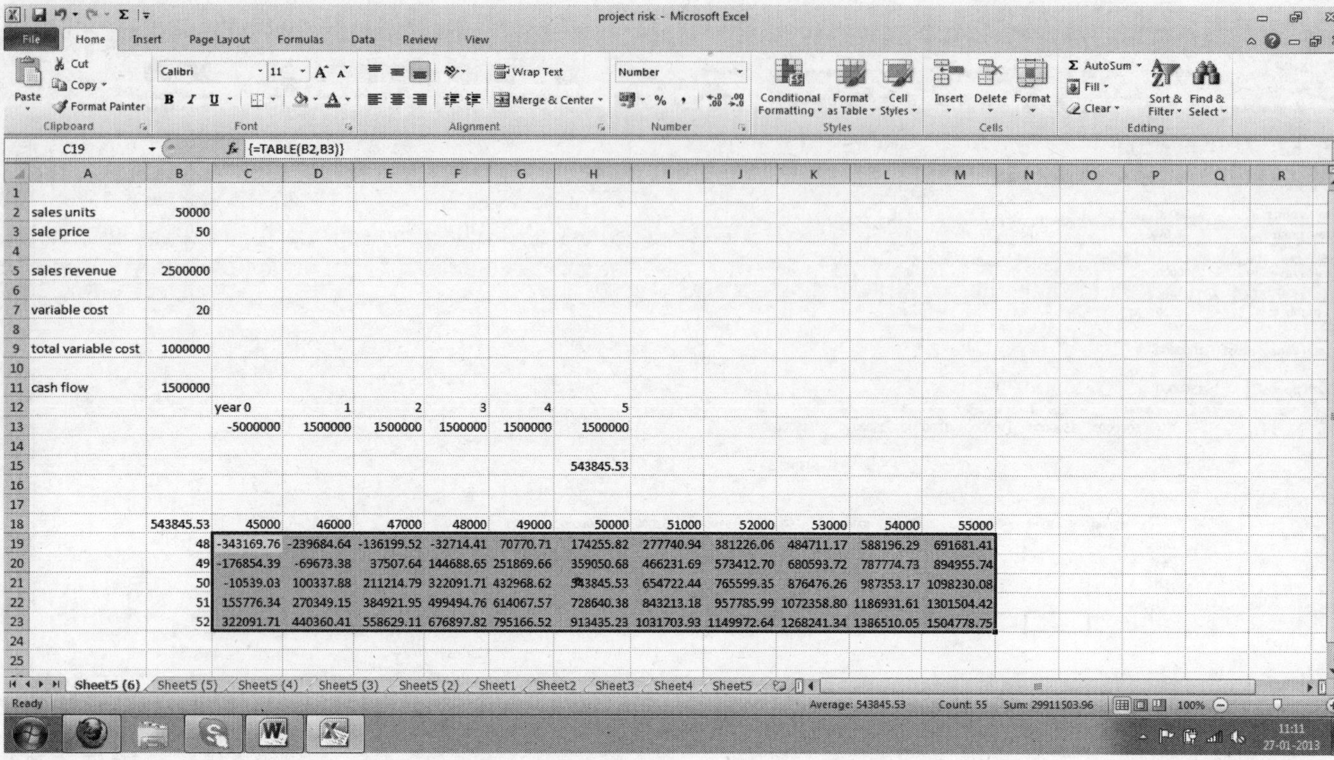

C19: {=TABLE(B2,B3)}

	A	B	C	D	E	F	G	H	I	J	K	L	M
2	sales units	50000											
3	sale price	50											
5	sales revenue	2500000											
7	variable cost	20											
9	total variable cost	1000000											
11	cash flow	1500000											
12			year 0	1	2	3	4	5					
13			-5000000	1500000	1500000	1500000	1500000	1500000					
15								543845.53					
18		543845.53	45000	46000	47000	48000	49000	50000	51000	52000	53000	54000	55000
19		48	-343169.76	-239684.64	-136199.52	-32714.41	70770.71	174255.82	277740.94	381226.06	484711.17	588196.29	691681.41
20		49	-176854.39	-69673.38	37507.64	144688.65	251869.66	359050.68	466231.69	573412.70	680593.72	787774.73	894955.74
21		50	-10539.03	100337.88	211214.79	322091.71	432968.62	543845.53	654722.44	765599.35	876476.26	987353.17	1098230.08
22		51	155776.34	270349.15	384921.95	499494.76	614067.57	728640.38	843213.18	957785.99	1072358.80	1186931.61	1301504.42
23		52	322091.71	440360.41	558629.11	676897.82	795166.52	913435.23	1031703.93	1149972.64	1268241.34	1386510.05	1504778.75

Note: The Excel Template for the above illustration is available online (Example 10.3)

EXHIBIT 10.13

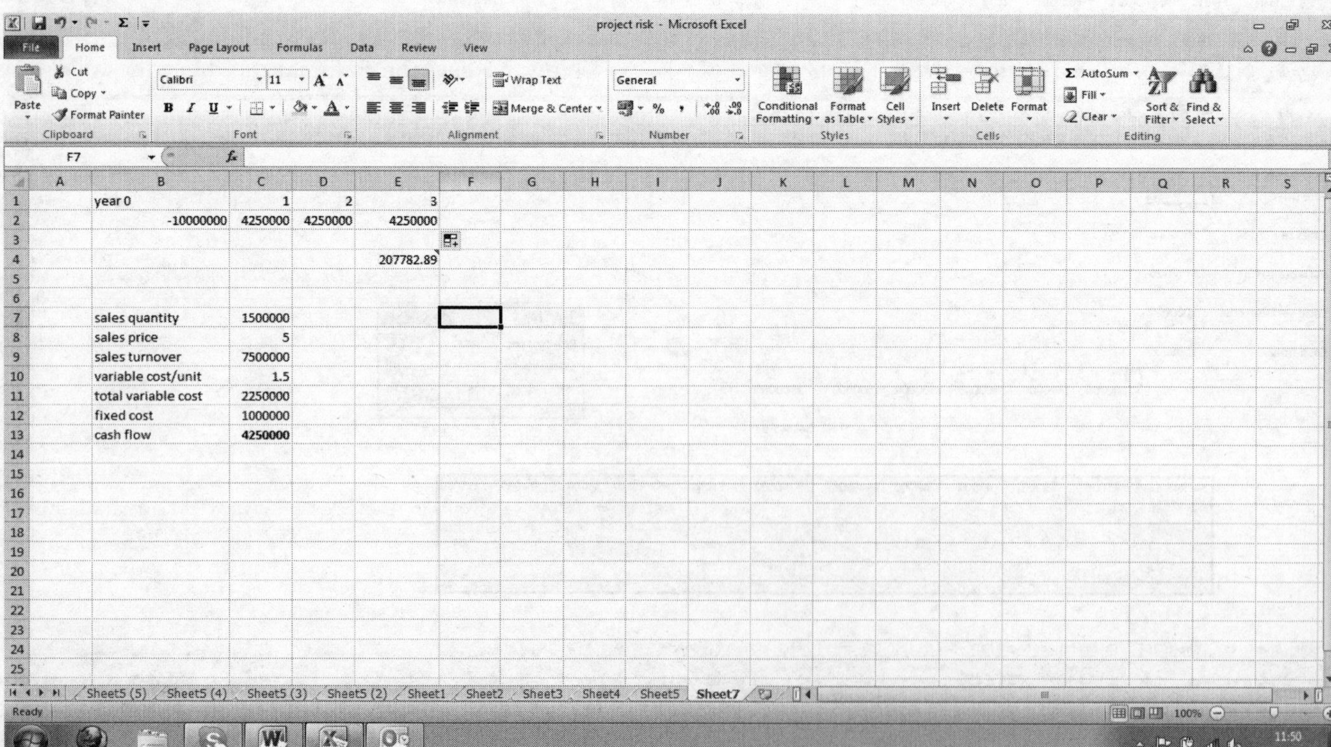

	A	B	C	D	E
1		year 0	1	2	3
2		-10000000	4250000	4250000	4250000
4					207782.89
7		sales quantity	1500000		
8		sales price	5		
9		sales turnover	7500000		
10		variable cost/unit	1.5		
11		total variable cost	2250000		
12		fixed cost	1000000		
13		cash flow	4250000		

Note: The Excel Template for the above illustration is available online (Example 10.4)

unfavorably. Thus, if the economy is growing, we may have sales prices going up, variable costs remaining steady or coming down and the sales quantity going up too. But when the economy itself is not doing well, we can have sales price and sales quantity going down and variable costs going up. In other words, more than one factor will move favorably, or sometimes unfavorably.

If the company is able to foresee scenarios in which factors will have different prices, we can then analyze the impact on NPV through the scenario analysis. Of course, the setting up of the scenarios is subjective or based on an independent study the company makes on possible conditions.

Example A company is considering a project with an outlay of ₹100 lakh. The project has a three-year life. Every year the sales quantity, sales price, variable cost, and fixed cost will be as per the table given below.

Scenario	Sales quantity	Sales price per unit	Variable cost per unit	Fixed cost
		Amount in ₹		
Optimistic	15,00,000	5	1.50	10,00,000
Good	12,00,000	4.50	1.60	10,00,000
Fair	10,00,000	4.00	1.75	10,00,000
Pessimistic	8,00,000	3.75	1.90	10,00,000

Let us assume that any given scenario that occurs in year 1 will continue for the entire horizon of three years. The discount rate applicable is 12%. Analyze the project.

Our first task is to put one of the scenarios into an MS Excel sheet. Normally, the most likely scenario or the "expected" scenario is used for this purpose. In this example, let us take the optimistic scenario as the value for the first input. We should take care to link the variables with formulae and we get the MS Excel sheet in Exhibit 10.13.

Notice that the sales turnover in C9 is given as a formula (product of C7 and C8). Total variable cost in C11 is a formula with the product of C2 and C10. Cash flow in C13 is a formula (C9-C11-C12). Now the cash flows in the timeline C2, C3 and C4 are all referred from C13 (=C13). Unless we put in formula as shown above, further analysis will not be possible.

Now we call for Data → What-If Analysis → Scenario Manager and we get the dialog box in Exhibit 10.14.

We click on Add in the dialog box, and in the resultant dialog box, we type the name of the scenario as "OPTIMISTIC" and indicate that cells C7, C8 and C10 are the changing cells (Exhibit 10.15). These cells are where the three changing variables—sales quantity, sales price and variable cost—had been originally entered. Notice that we do not have to enter the cell containing fixed cost, since it does not change with changes in scenarios.

We press OK and get the dialog box for entering the values of the changing cells (Exhibit 10.16). By default, the values come in as were originally entered. Since we are using the optimistic scenario as the first scenario, and since the values are correct now, we can proceed.

We proceed by clicking on Add. We are taken back to the first dialog box in the scenarios manager, and we fill the name of the scenario now as "GOOD" (Exhibit 10.17).

We fill in the details and click on Add again (Exhibit 10.18).

We now type "FAIR" in the scenario name and press OK (Exhibit 10.19).

We now feed in the details pertaining to the FAIR scenario and after that press Add (Exhibit 10.20).

We repeat the same procedure for the "PESSIMISTIC" scenario (Exhibit 10.21).

The details are fed in as before. We come to the dialog box as shown in Exhibit 10.22.

Now that when all the scenarios have been fed in, we press OK. If any data have to be edited, it can be done at this stage (Exhibit 10.23).

Now we click on Summary and get the following dialog box (Exhibit 10.24).

Notice that we feed in the result cell as E4, where the original NPV computation is housed. We now press OK and get the scenario summary of Exhibit 10.25 in a separate sheet of the same workbook.

Notice that the changing cells have been indicated by full names (sales quantity, sales price and variable cost unit) and the resultant cell has been shown as "NPV." This is possible only if we name the cells accordingly to begin with. We know what cells will change and what the resultant cell is going to be. We should then name these cells by going to the cell and right clicking and pressing Define Name. A default name for the cell will spring up, which can be accepted in most cases.

The Scenario Summary above enables us to make decisions regarding the project. We notice that except the optimistic scenario, we end up with negative NPV in all other cases. This means that unless conditions prevail for the optimistic scenario to happen, the project is not good enough.

EXHIBIT 10.14

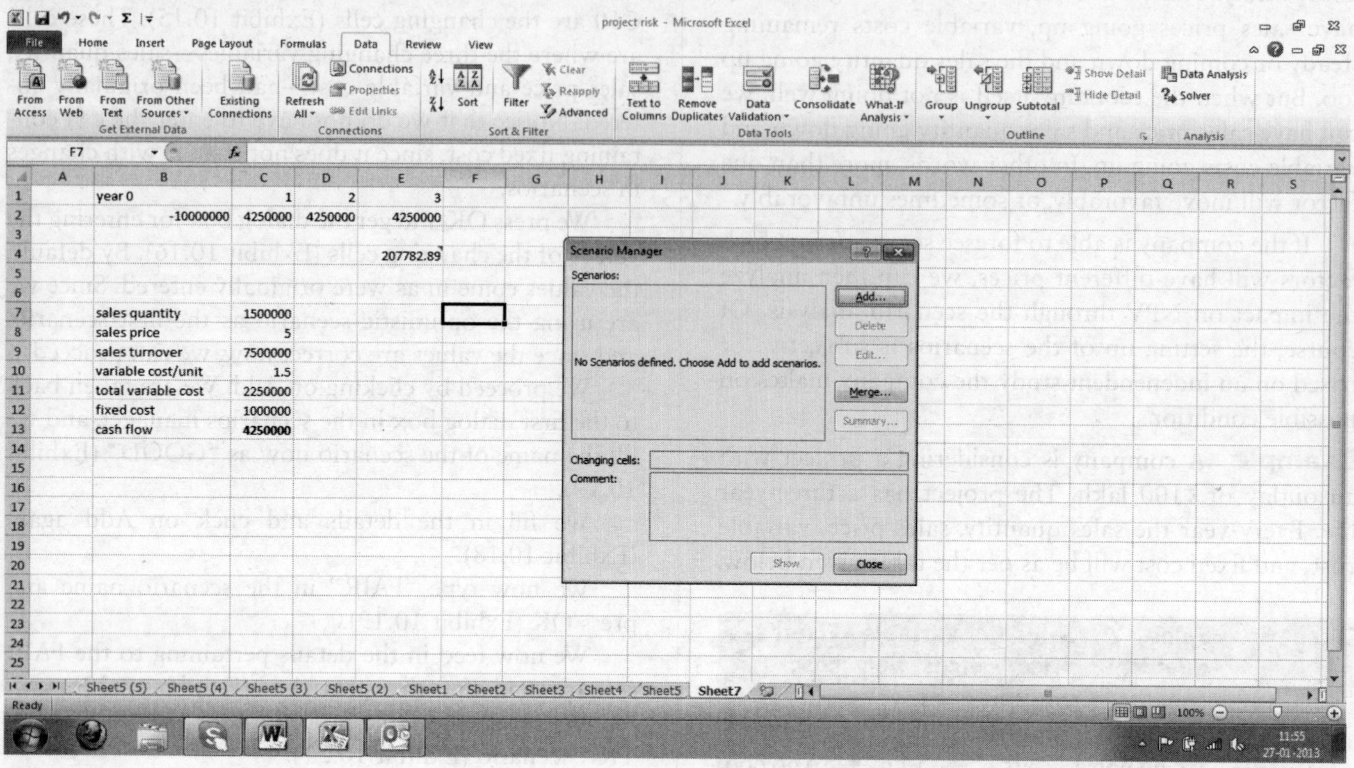

EXHIBIT 10.15

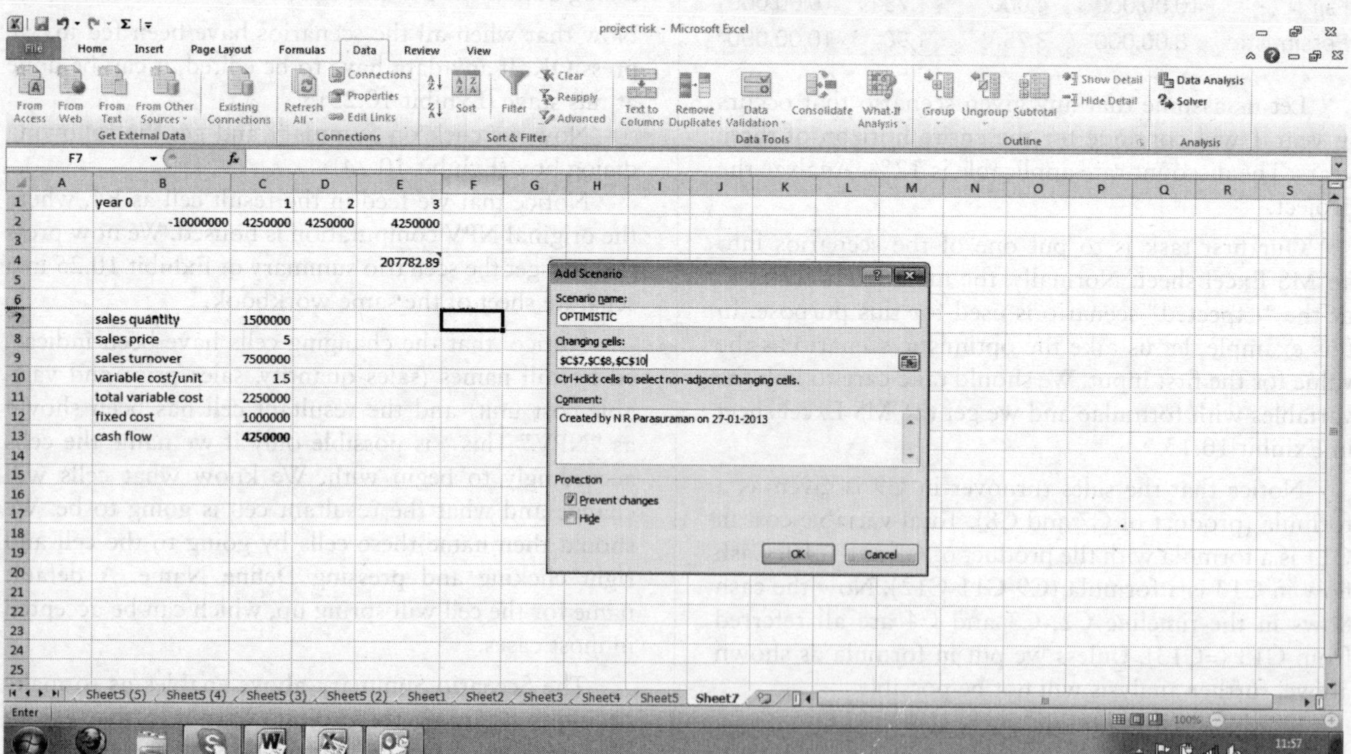

EXHIBIT 10.16

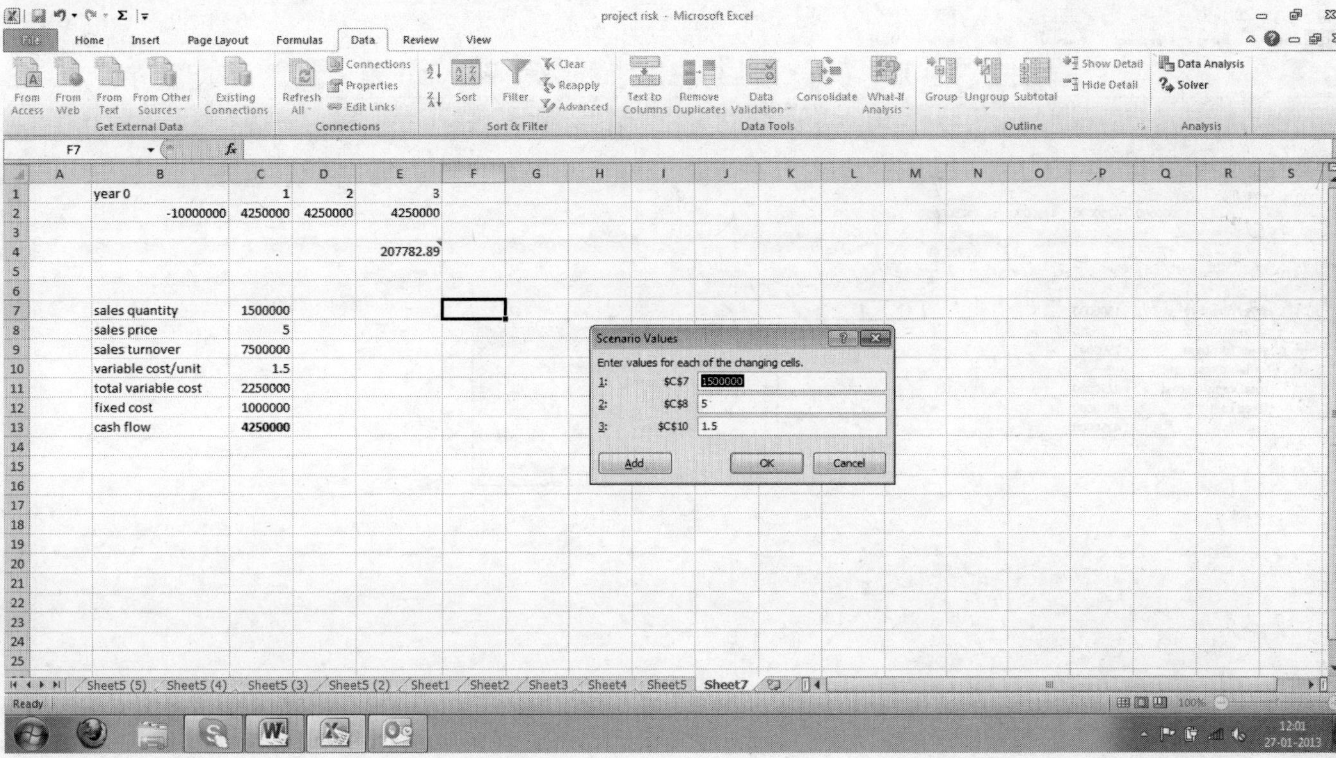

EXHIBIT 10.17

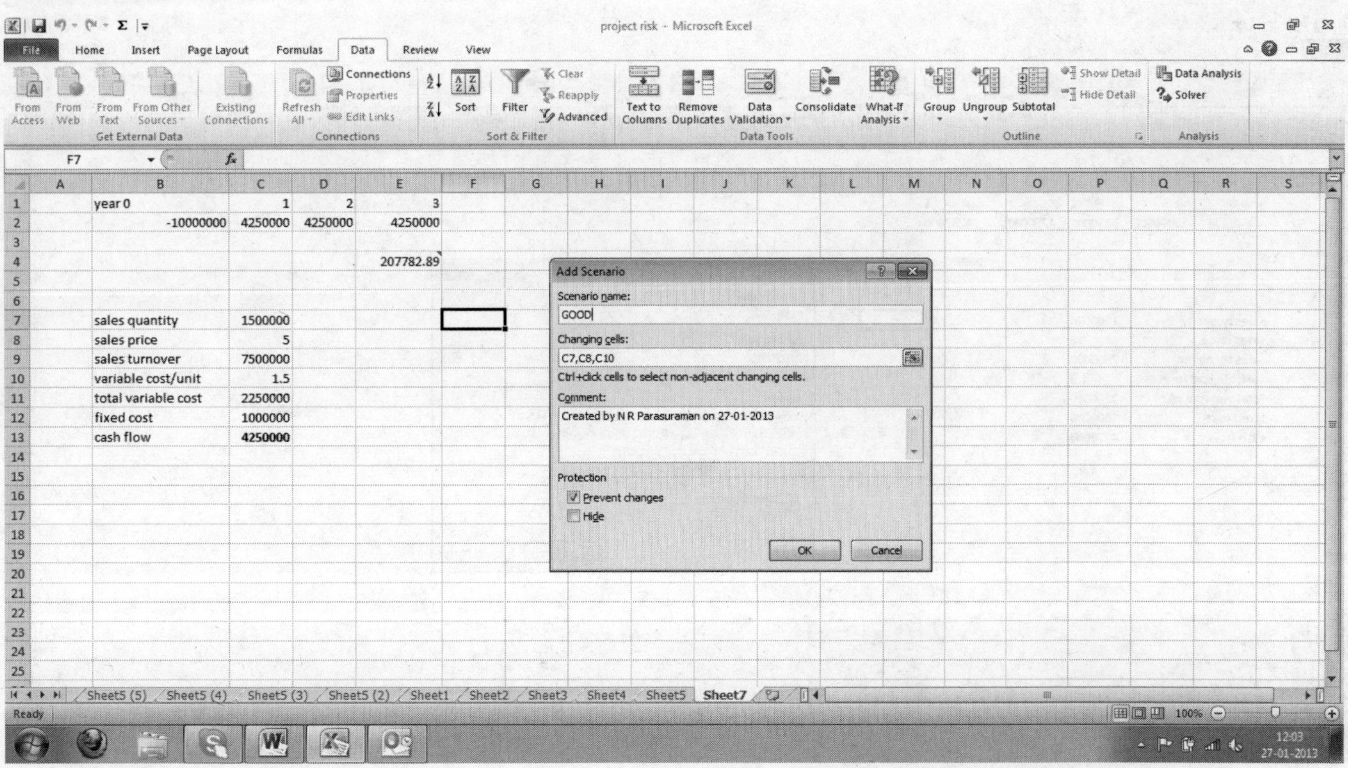

EXHIBIT 10.18

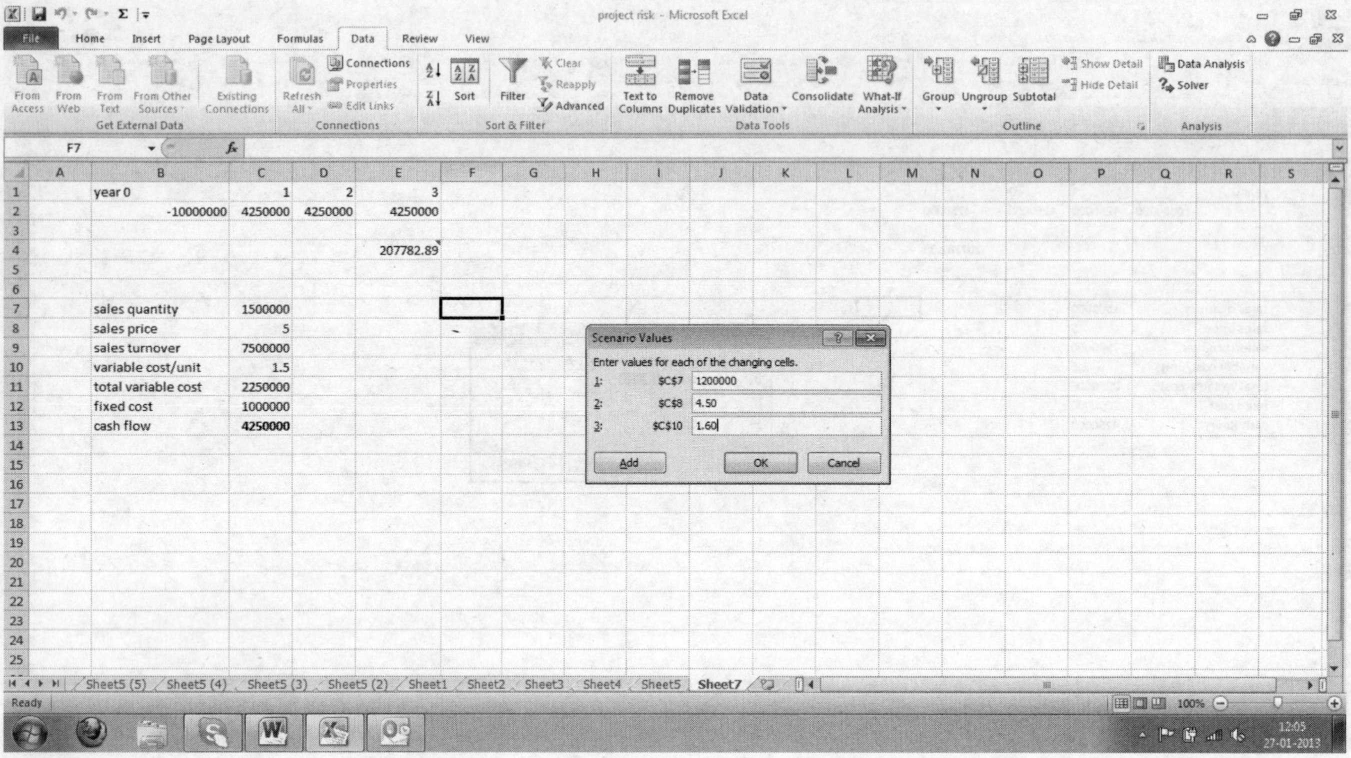

EXHIBIT 10.19

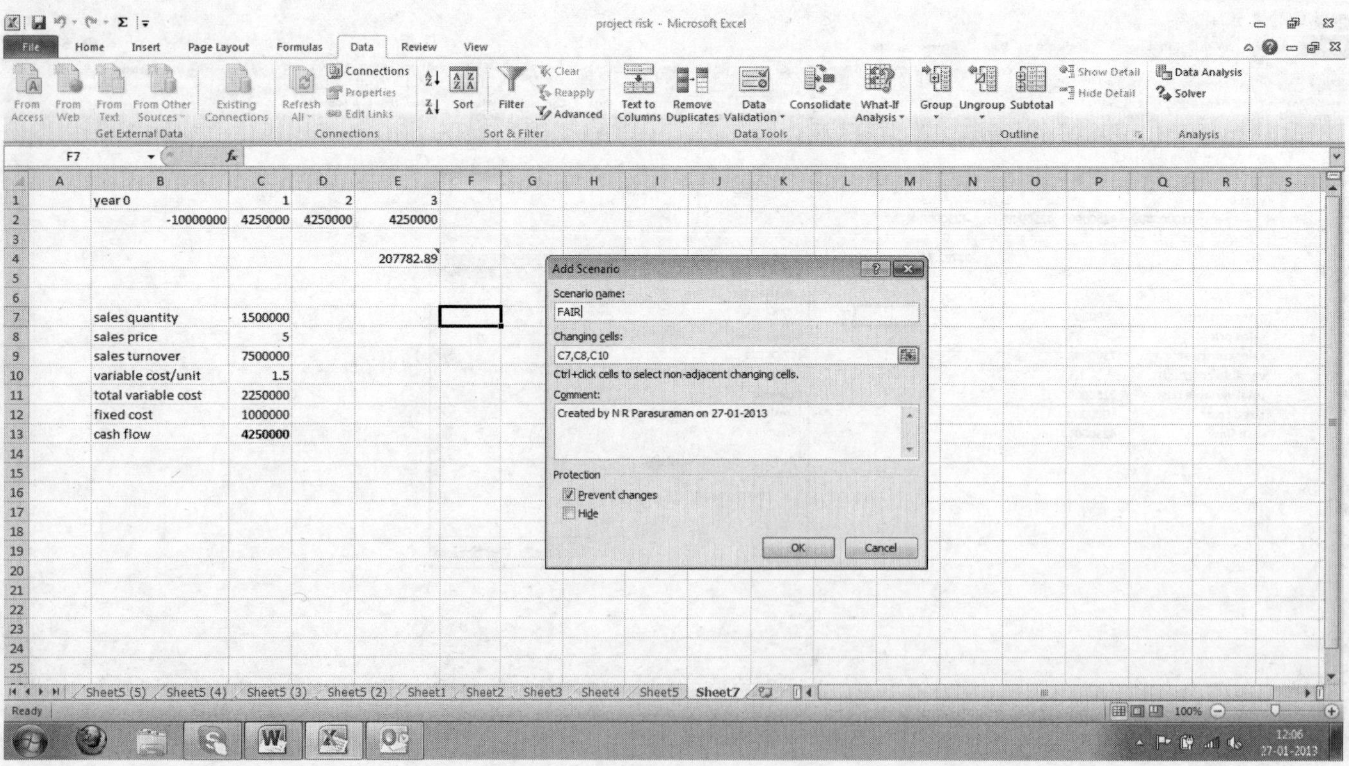

EXHIBIT 10.20

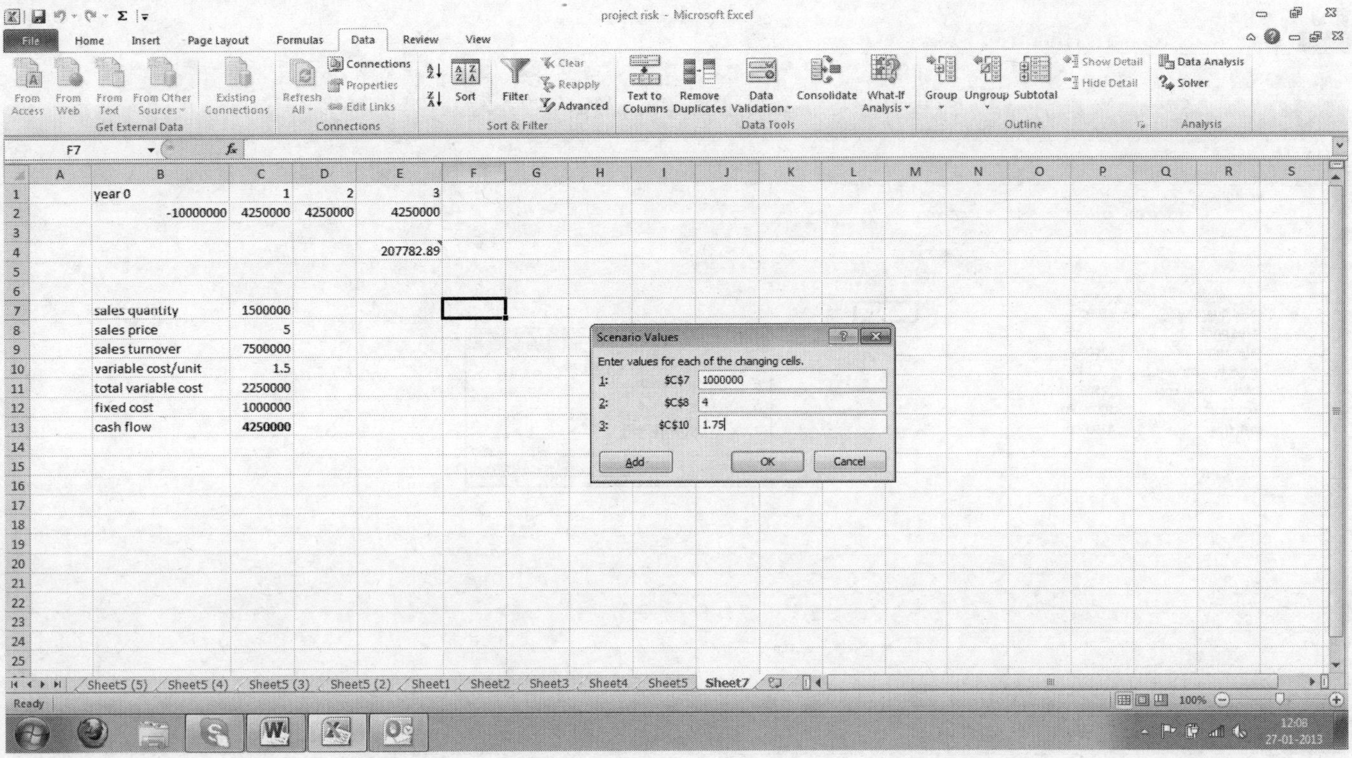

EXHIBIT 10.21

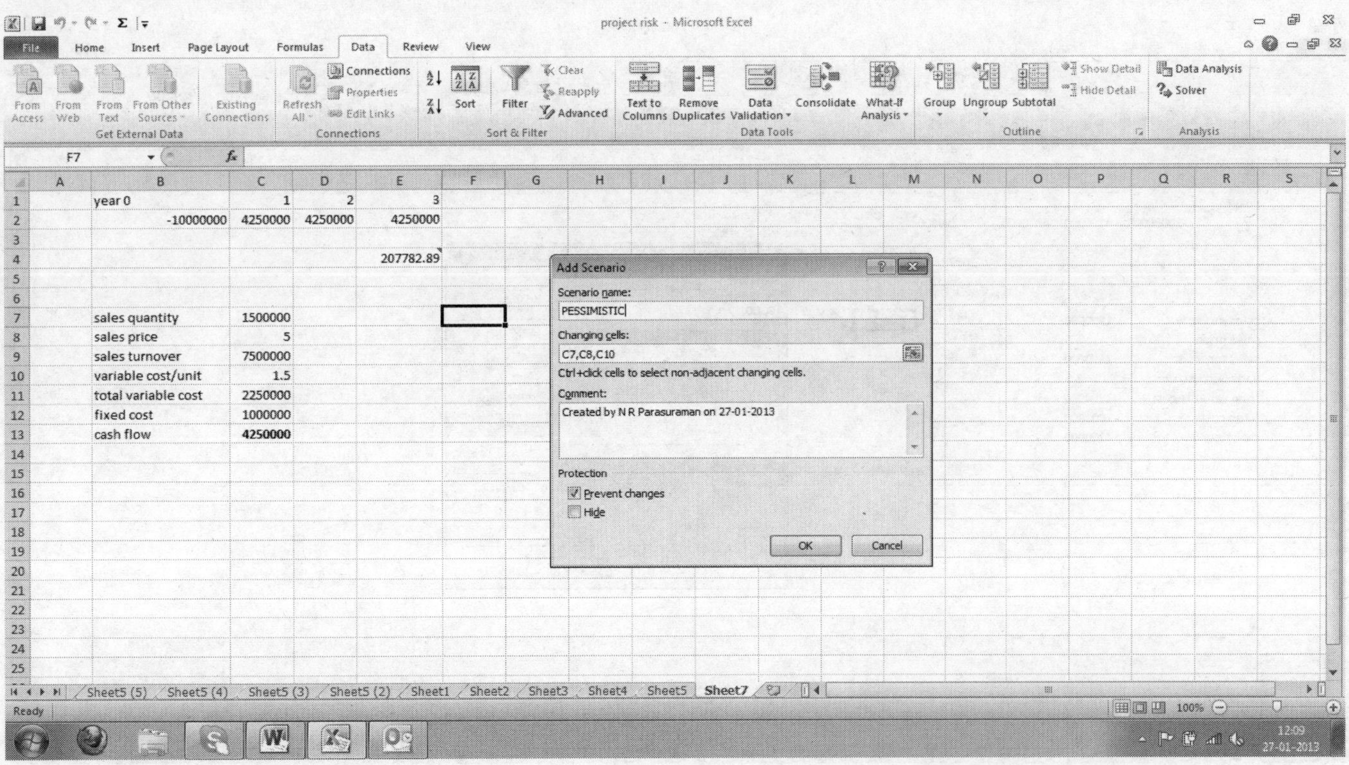

EXHIBIT 10.22

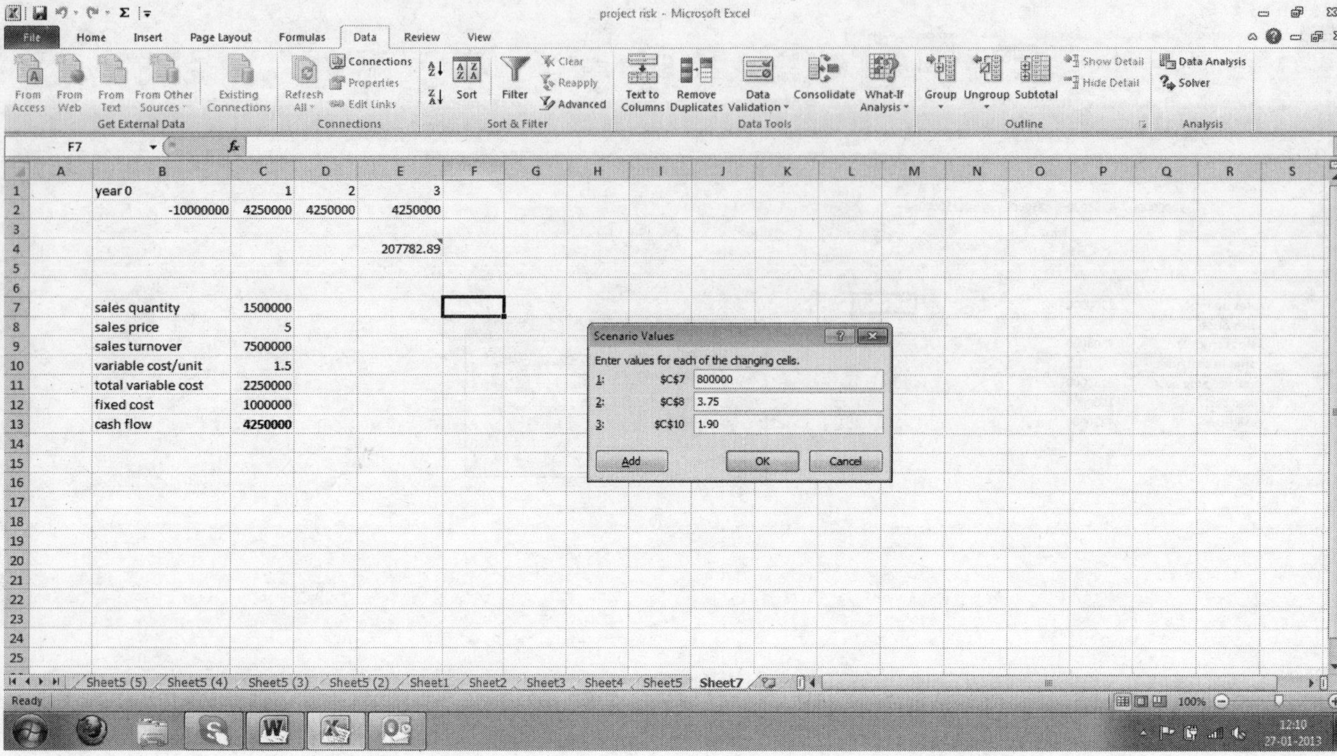

EXHIBIT 10.23

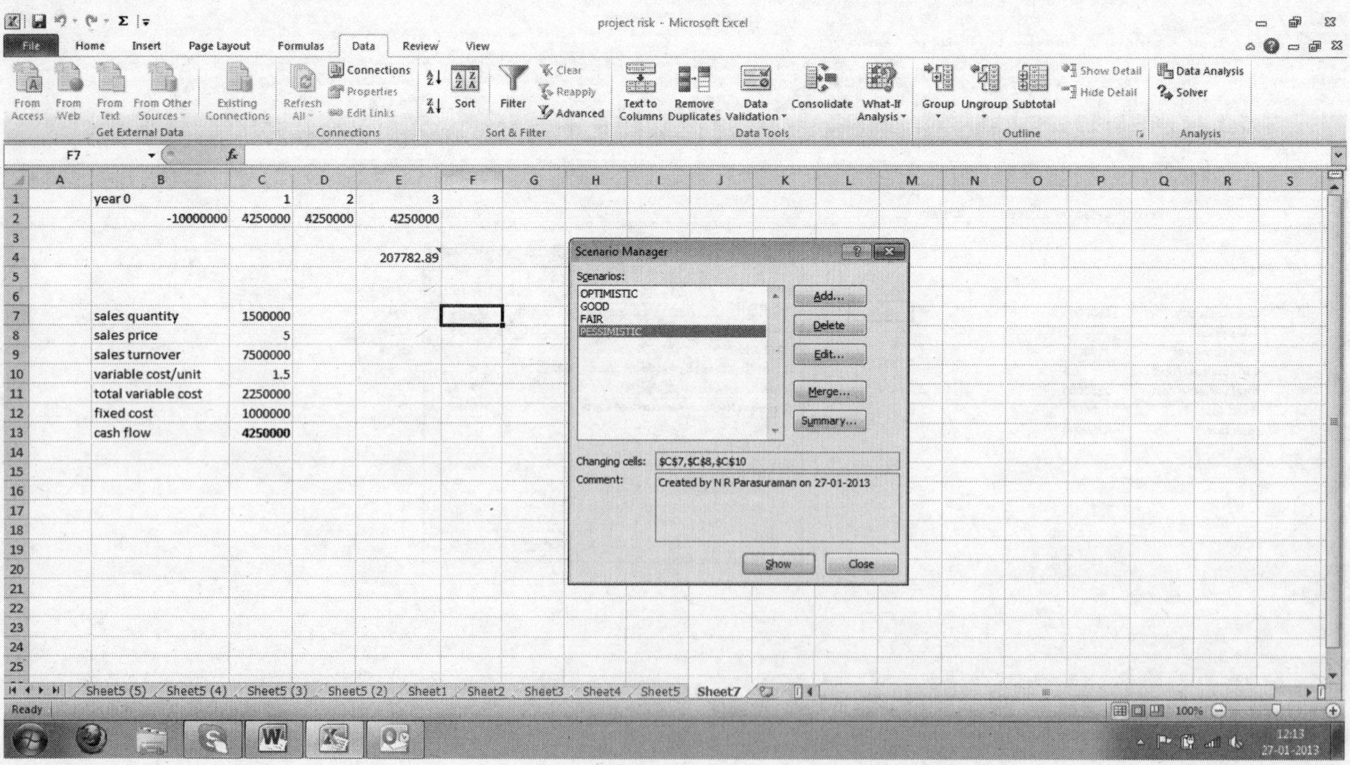

EXHIBIT 10.24

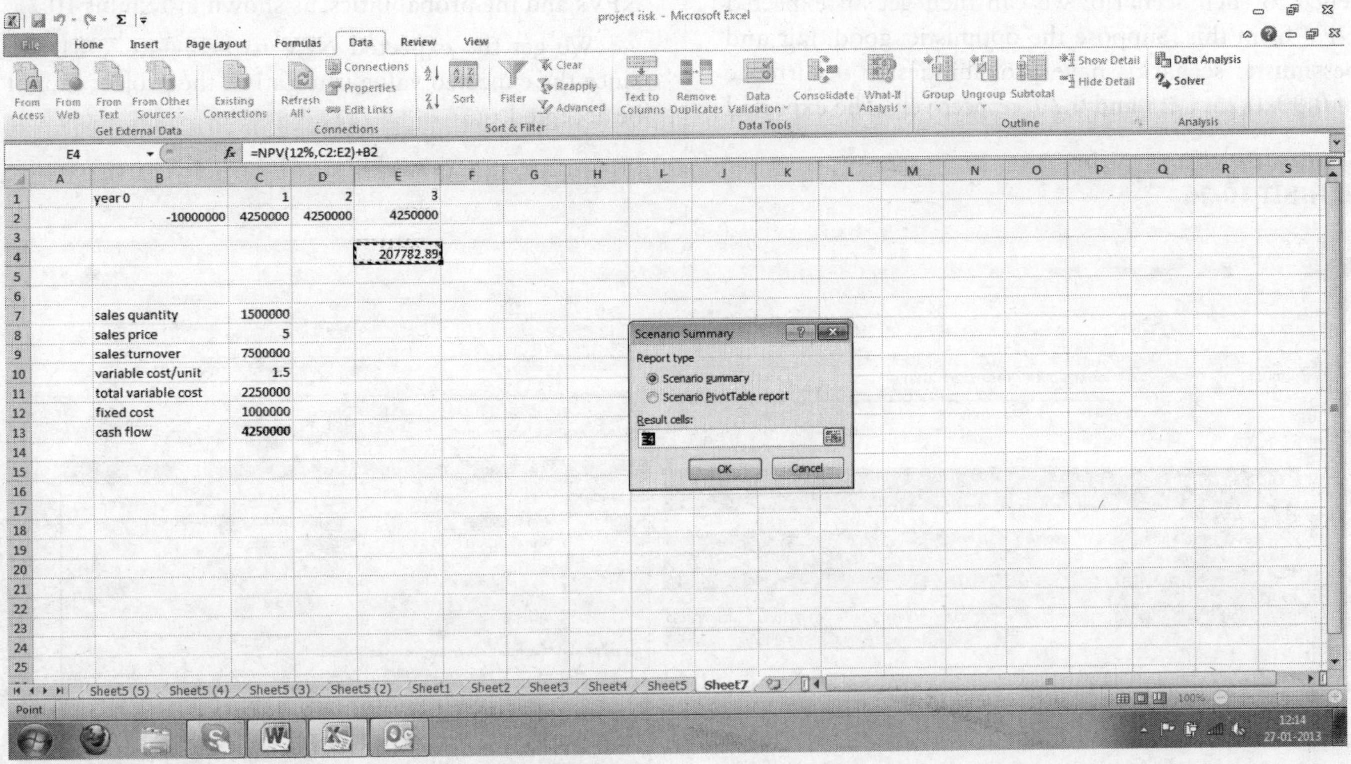

EXHIBIT 10.25

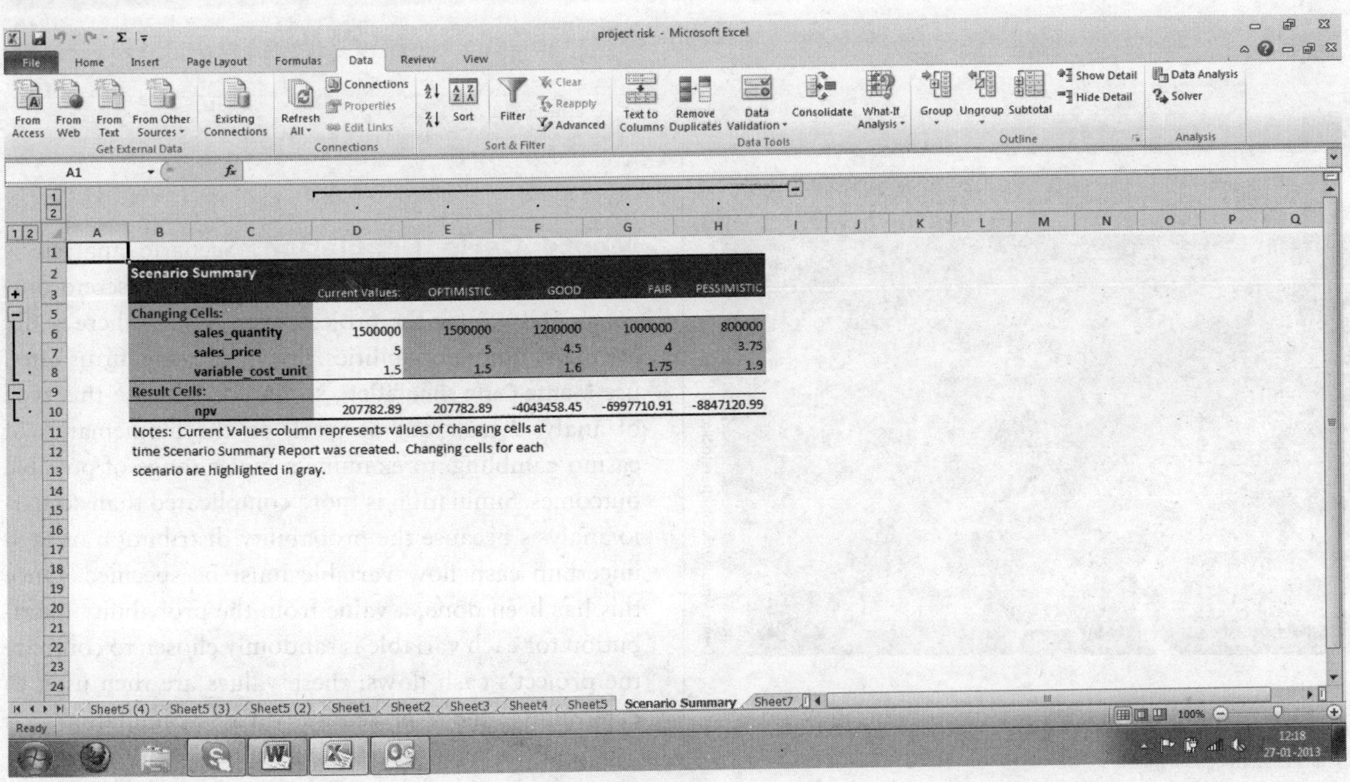

If we are able to attribute probabilities of occurrence to each scenario, we can then get an expected NPV from this. Suppose the optimistic, good, fair and pessimistic scenarios have probabilities of occurrence of 0.30, 0.25, 0.25 and 0.20, respectively. The expected NPV will then be a SUMPRODUCT of the individual NPVs and the probabilities, as shown in Exhibit 10.26.

We get the expected NPV to be (-44,67,381.67). Since the expected value is negative, the project cannot be accepted.

EXHIBIT 10.26

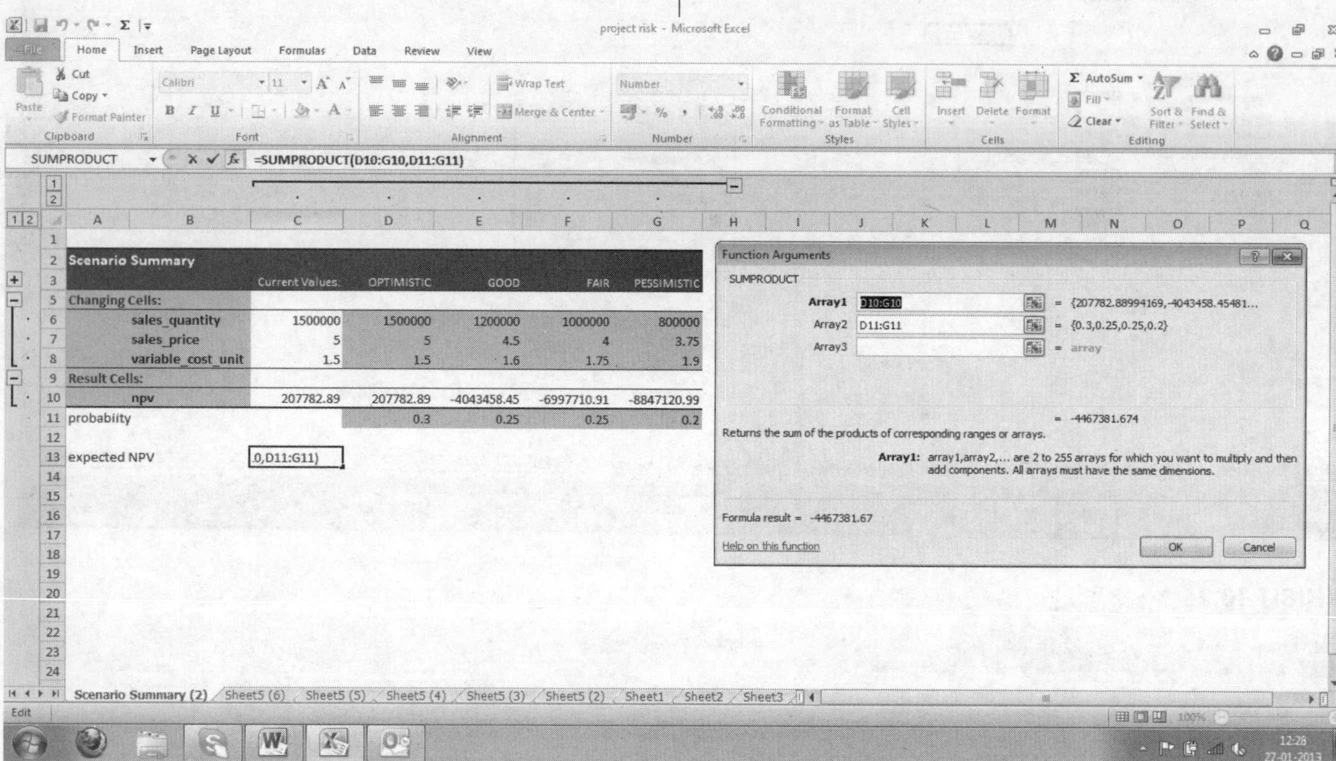

Denis Vrublevski/Shutterstock.com

Monte Carlo simulation A risk analysis technique in which probable future events are simulated on a computer, generating a probability distribution that indicates the most likely outcomes.

Monte Carlo Simulation. Scenario analysis is limited because it only considers a few discrete outcomes (NPVs) for the project, even though there really are many more possibilities. For this reason, firms often use **Monte Carlo simulation**, so named because this type of analysis grew out of work on the mathematics of casino gambling, to examine a wider range of possible outcomes. Simulation is more complicated than scenario analysis because the probability distribution of each uncertain cash flow variable must be specified. Once this has been done, a value from the probability distribution for each variable is randomly chosen to compute the project's cash flows; these values are then used to determine the project's NPV. Simulation is usually completed using a computer because the process just described is repeated again and again—say, 500 times—which results in 500 NPVs and a probability distribution for the project's NPV values. Thus, the output produced by simulation is a probability distribution that can be used to determine the most likely range of outcomes expected from a project. This provides the decision maker with a better idea of the various outcomes that are possible than is available from a single point estimate of the NPV.

10-3b Corporate (Within-Firm) Risk

Corporate, or **within-firm, risk** is the effect a project has on the total, or overall, riskiness of the company, without considering whether adding the project to existing assets affects the firm's systematic or unsystematic risk. To measure corporate, or within-firm, risk, we need to determine how the capital budgeting project is related to the firm's existing assets. Remember from our discussion in Chapter 8 that two assets can be combined to reduce risk if their payoffs move in opposite directions, that is, when the payoffs from the assets are negatively related. In reality, it is not easy to find assets with payoffs that move opposite each other. However, we also discovered in Chapter 8 that as long as assets are *not* perfectly positively related (i.e., $\rho \neq +1.0$), some diversification, or risk- reduction, can still be achieved. Many firms use this principle to reduce the risk associated with their operations by adding new projects that are not highly related to existing assets.

Corporate risk is important for three primary reasons:

1. Undiversified stockholders, including the owners of small businesses, are primarily concerned about the diversification that is associated with a particular firm (i.e., its corporate risk).
2. Empirical studies of the determinants of required rates of return generally find that investors, even those who are well diversified, give some consideration to corporate risk when they establish required returns.
3. The firm's stability is important to its managers, workers, customers, suppliers, and creditors, as well as to the community in which it operates. Firms that are in serious danger of bankruptcy, or even of suffering low profits and reduced output, have difficulty attracting and retaining good managers and workers. In addition, both suppliers and customers are reluctant to depend on weak firms, and such firms have difficulty borrowing money at reasonable interest rates. These factors tend to reduce risky firms' profitability and hence the prices of their stocks; thus they also make corporate risk significant.

From this discussion, it is clear that corporate risk is important even if a firm's stockholders are well diversified.

10-3c Beta (Market) Risk

The types of risk analysis discussed to this point provide insights into a project's risk and thus help managers make better capital budgeting decisions. However, these risk measures do not take account of **beta, or market, risk**, which is project risk assessed from the standpoint of a stockholder who holds a well-diversified portfolio. Thus, in this section, we show how the capital asset pricing model (CAPM), which was introduced in Chapter 8, can be used to evaluate portfolio risk as well as to specify the rates of return that should be used to evaluate projects that have substantially different risks.

In Chapter 8, we developed the concept of beta, β, as a measure of the systematic risk for an individual stock. From our discussion, we concluded that systematic risk is the relevant risk of a stock because unsystematic, or firm-specific, risk can be reduced significantly, or eliminated, through diversification. This same concept can be applied to capital budgeting projects because the firm can be thought of as a composite of all the projects it has undertaken. Thus, the relevant risk of a project can be viewed as the impact it has on the firm's systematic risk (its portfolio of assets). This line of reasoning leads to the conclusion that if the beta coefficient for a project, β_{proj}, can be determined, then the **project required rate of return, r_{proj}**, can be found using the following form of the CAPM equation:

$$r_{proj} = r_{RF} + (r_M - r_{RF})\beta_{proj}$$

As an example, consider the case of Esha Steel Company, an integrated steel producer operating in the Madhya Pradesh region. For simplicity, let's assume that Esha is financed with all equity (stock), so that the *average* required rate of return it needs to earn on capital budgeting projects is based solely on the average return demanded

corporate (within-firm) risk Risk that does not take into consideration the effects of stockholders' diversification; it is measured by a project's effect on the firm's earnings variability

beta (market) risk That part of a project's risk that cannot be eliminated by diversification; it is measured by the project's beta coefficient..

project required rate of return, r_{proj} The risk-adjusted required rate of return for an individual project.

by stockholders; that is, there is no debt that might require a different return. Esha's existing beta = $\beta_{Existing}$ = 1.1; r_{RF} = 8%; and r_M = 12%. Thus, Esha's required rate of return is 12.4% = r_{Erie} = 8% + (12% – 8%)1.1, which suggests that investors should be willing to give Esha money to invest in average-risk projects if the company expects to earn 12.4 percent or more on this money.[6] Here again, by *average-risk projects* we mean projects with risk similar to the firm's existing assets.

Suppose, however, that taking on a particular project will cause a change in Esha's beta coefficient and hence change the company's required rate of return. For example, suppose Esha is considering the construction of a fleet of barges to haul iron ore, and barge operations have betas of 2.1 rather than 1.1. Because the firm itself can be regarded as a "portfolio of assets," Esha's beta, just like the beta of a portfolio of stocks, is a weighted average of the betas of its individual assets. Thus, taking on the barge project will cause the overall corporate beta to rise. If 80 percent of Esha's total funds end up in basic steel operations with a beta of 1.1 and 20 percent in the barge operations with a beta of 2.1, the new corporate beta will increase to 1.3 = 0.8(1.1) + 0.2(2.1). Thus, taking on the new project will cause the *overall* corporate required rate of return to rise from the original 12.4 percent to 13.2 percent; $r_{Erie,New}$ = 8% + (12% − 8%)1.3. This higher average rate can be earned only if the new project generates a return higher than the existing assets are providing. Because Esha's overall return is based on its portfolio of assets, the return required from the barge project must be sufficiently high so that, in combination with returns of the other assets, the firm's average return is 13.2 percent. Because its beta is higher, the barge project, with β_{Barge} = 2.1, should be evaluated at a 16.4 percent required rate of return—that is, r_{Barge} = 8% + (4%)2.1 = 16.4%. On the other hand, a low-risk project such as a new steel distribution center that has a beta of only 0.5 would have a required rate of return of 10 percent.

In Chapter 8, we discussed the estimation of betas for stocks, and we indicated that it is difficult to estimate *true* future betas. The estimation of project betas is even more difficult and more fraught with uncertainty. One way a firm can try to measure the systematic risk of a project is to find *single-product* companies in the same line of business as the project being evaluated and then use the betas of those companies to determine the required rate of return for the project being evaluated. This technique is termed the **pure play method**, and the single-product companies that are used for comparisons are called *pure play firms.* For example, if Esha could find some existing firms that only operate barges, it could use the average of the betas of those firms as a proxy for the barge project's beta.

pure play method An approach used for estimating the beta of a project in which a firm identifies companies whose only business is the product in question, determines the beta for each firm, and then averages the betas to find an approximation of its own project's beta.

10-3d Project Risk Conclusions

We have discussed the three types of risk normally considered in capital budgeting analysis—stand-alone risk, within-firm (or corporate) risk, and beta (or market) risk—and we have discussed ways of assessing each. However, two important questions remain: (1) Should a firm be concerned with stand-alone risk and corporate risk in its capital budgeting decisions? (2) What do we do when the stand-alone or within-firm risk assessments and the beta risk assessment lead to different conclusions?

These questions do not have easy answers. From a theoretical standpoint, well-diversified investors should be concerned only with beta risk, managers should be concerned only with stock price maximization, and these two factors should lead to the conclusion that beta risk should be given virtually all the weight in capital budgeting decisions. However, if investors are not well diversified, if the CAPM does not operate exactly as theory says it should, or if measurement problems keep managers from having confidence in the CAPM approach in capital budgeting, it might be appropriate to give stand-alone and corporate risk more weight than financial theorists suggest. Note also that the CAPM ignores bankruptcy costs, even though such costs can be substantial, and that the probability of bankruptcy depends on a firm's corporate risk, not on its beta risk. Therefore, one can easily conclude that even well-diversified investors should want a firm's management to give at least some consideration to a project's corporate risk instead of concentrating entirely on beta risk.

Although it would be desirable to reconcile these problems and to measure project risk on some absolute scale, the best we can do in practice is to determine project risk in a somewhat nebulous, relative sense. For example, we can generally say with a fair degree of confidence that a particular project has more or less stand-alone risk than the firm's average project. Then,

[6]To simplify things somewhat, we assume at this point that the firm uses only equity capital. If debt is used, the required rate of return used must be a weighted average of the costs of debt and equity. This point is discussed at length in Chapter 11.

assuming that stand-alone risk and corporate risk are highly correlated (which is typical), the project's stand-alone risk will be a good measure of its corporate risk. Finally, assuming that beta risk and corporate risk are highly correlated (as is true for most companies), a project with more corporate risk than average will also have more beta risk, and vice versa, for projects with low corporate risk.

10-3e How Project Risk Is Considered in Capital Budgeting Decisions

From our discussion to this point, you should conclude that it is difficult to develop a really good measure of project risk. As a result, most firms incorporate project risk in capital budgeting decisions using the **risk-adjusted discount rate** approach. With this approach, the appropriate required rate of return at which the expected cash flows are discounted is adjusted if the project's risk is substantially different from the average risk associated with the firm's existing assets. Following this logic, average-risk projects would be discounted at the rate of return required of projects that are considered average, or normal, for the firm; above-average-risk projects would be discounted at a higher-than-average rate; and below-average-risk projects would be discounted at a rate below the firm's average rate of return. Unfortunately, because risk cannot be measured precisely, there is no accurate way of specifying exactly how much higher or lower these discount rates should be. Given the present state of the art, *risk adjustments are necessarily judgmental and somewhat arbitrary.*

Although the process is not exact, many companies use a two-step procedure to develop risk-adjusted discount rates for use in capital budgeting analysis. First, the overall required rate of return is established for the firm's existing assets. This process is completed on a division-by-division basis for very large firms, perhaps using the CAPM. Second, each project might be classified into one of three categories: high risk, average risk, and low risk. Then, the firm or division uses the average required rate of return as the discount rate for average-risk projects, reduces the average rate by 1 to 3 percentage points when evaluating low-risk projects, and raises the average rate by several percentage points for high-risk projects. For example, if a firm's basic required rate of return is estimated to be 12 percent, an 18 percent discount rate might be used for a high-risk project and a 9 percent rate for a low-risk project. Average-risk projects, which constitute about 80 percent of most capital budgets, would be evaluated at the 12 percent rate of return. *If project risk is not considered in capital budgeting analysis, incorrect decisions are possible*: a high-risk project might be accepted when it actually should be rejected, or a low-risk project might be rejected when it should be accepted.

Although the risk-adjusted discount rate approach is far from precise, it does at least recognize that projects with different risks should be evaluated using different required rates of return.

10-4 Multinational Capital Budgeting

Although the basic principles of capital budgeting analysis are the same for both domestic and foreign operations, some key differences need to be mentioned. First, cash flow estimation generally is much more complex for overseas investments. Most multinational firms set up a separate subsidiary in each foreign country in which they operate, and the relevant cash flows for these subsidiaries are the earnings and dividends that can be *repatriated,* or returned, to the parent company (**repatriation of earnings**). Second, these cash flows must be converted into the currency of the parent company, and thus are subject to future exchange rate changes. Third, earnings and dividends normally are taxed by both foreign and home-country governments. Fourth, a foreign government might restrict the amount of cash that can be repatriated to the parent company, perhaps to force multinational firms to reinvest earnings in the host country or to prevent large currency outflows that might affect the exchange rate. Whatever the host country's motivation, the result is that the parent corporation cannot use cash flows blocked in the foreign country to pay current dividends to its shareholders, nor does it have the flexibility to reinvest cash flows elsewhere in the world. Therefore, from the perspective of the parent organization, *the cash flows relevant to the analysis of a foreign investment are the cash flows that the subsidiary legally can send back*

risk-adjusted discount rate The discount rate (required rate of return) that applies to a particular risky stream of income; it is equal to the risk-free rate of interest plus a risk premium appropriate to the level of risk associated with a particular project's income stream.

repatriation of earnings The process of sending cash flows from a foreign subsidiary back to the parent company.

to the parent.

In addition to the complexities of the cash flow analysis, *the rate of return required for a foreign project might be different from that of an equivalent domestic project because foreign projects might be either riskier or less risky.* A higher risk could arise from two primary sources—exchange rate risk and political risk—while a lower risk could result from international diversification.

Exchange rate risk reflects the inherent uncertainty a company has about the value of cash flows that will be sent back to the parent at some date in the future, because the cash has to be converted from the foreign country's currency into the home country's currency. In other words, foreign projects have an added risk element that relates to what the basic cash flows will be worth in the parent company's home currency. The foreign currency cash flows that are to be turned over to the parent must be converted into Indian Rupees by translating them at *expected* future exchange rates. Actual exchange rates might differ substantially from expectations.

exchange rate risk The uncertainty associated with the price at which the currency from one country can be converted into the currency of another country.

political risk The risk of expropriation (seizure) of a foreign subsidiary's assets by the host country or of unanticipated restrictions on cash flows to the parent company.

Political risk refers to any action (or the chance of such action) by a host government that reduces the value of a company's investment. It includes at one extreme the *expropriation* (seizure) without compensation of the subsidiary's assets. However, it also includes less drastic actions that reduce the value of the parent firm's investment in the foreign subsidiary, such as higher taxes, tighter repatriation or currency controls, and restrictions on prices charged. The risk of expropriation of U.S. assets abroad is low in traditionally friendly and stable countries such as the United Kingdom or Switzerland. However, in Latin America and the Middle East, for example, the risk might be substantial.

Generally, political risk premiums are not added to the required rate of return to adjust for this risk. If a company's management has a serious concern that a given country might expropriate foreign assets, it simply will not make significant investments in that country. Expropriation is viewed as a catastrophic or ruinous event, and managers have been shown to be extraordinarily risk averse when faced with ruinous loss possibilities. However, companies can take steps to reduce the potential loss from expropriation in three major ways: (1) by financing the subsidiary with capital raised in the country in which the asset is located, (2) by structuring operations so that the subsidiary has value only as a part of the integrated corporate system, and (3) by obtaining insurance against economic losses from expropriation from a source such as the Overseas Private Investment Corporation (OPIC). In the last case, insurance premiums would have to be added to the project's cost.

KEY CONCEPTS ABOUT PROJECT CASH FLOWS AND RISK

To conclude this chapter, we summarize some project cash flows and risk concepts (rules) that were discussed.

- In capital budgeting analysis, "relevant" cash flows include only those cash flows that are affected by the decision to purchase the project. If a cash flow does not change as a result of the purchase, it is not relevant.
- The relevant, or incremental, cash flows can be categorized as (1) the initial investment outlay, which includes cash flows that occur only at the beginning of the project's life; (2) supplemental operating cash flows, which include changes in the day-to-day operating cash flows during the life of the project; and (3) the terminal cash flow, which includes cash flows that occur only at the end of the project's life.
- Identifying the relevant cash flows for a replacement project is somewhat more complicated than for an expansion project, because the cash flows that will be generated if the new project (the replacement asset) is purchased, as well as the cash flows that will be generated if the old project (the replaced asset) is retained, must be considered.
- If the risk associated with a capital budgeting project differs substantially from the average risk of the firm's existing assets, some adjustment should be made to the firm's required rate of return when evaluating the project. If the project has substantially higher risk, a higher-than-average required rate of return should be used in the capital budgeting evaluation. If the project's risk is lower than average, a lower required rate of return should be used.
- Although the same basic principles should be applied when conducting capital budgeting analysis for multinational operations, application of these principles often is more complicated when dealing with foreign subsidiaries.

MULTIPLE CHOICE QUESTIONS

1. In sensitivity analysis,

a. All variables are changed at the same time

b. Variables together change upwards or downwards

c. Only one or two variables can be changed, keeping others constant

d. None of the above

2. In scenario analysis,

a. All variables are changed at the same time

b. Variables together change upwards or downwards

c. Only one or two variables can be changed, keeping others constant

d. None of the above

3. In Monte Carlo simulation,

a. All variables are changed at the same time

b. Variables together change upwards or downwards

c. Only one or two variables can be changed, keeping others constant

d. None of the above

4. The expected NPV based on scenario analysis

a. Will be greater than the original NPV

b. Will be lesser than the original NPV

c. Will be equal to the original NPV

d. Has an independent calculation and has no relation with the original NPV

5. By using sensitivity analysis,

a. We know the extent to which the NPV can go down if a key variable moves in an adverse direction

b. We know the extent to which the NPV can go down if a key variable moves in a favorable direction

c. We know the extent to which the NPV can go up if a key variable moves in an adverse direction

d. None of the above

6. In scenario analysis,

a. All variables move together favorably or unfavorably

b. Variables can move in opposite directions

c. Some variables need not change at all

d. Both a and c

7. In Monte Carlo simulation,

a. The variables have to be changed more than 100 times to get a reliable solution

b. The variables need to be changed only once for a reliable decision

c. The variables can be changed as many times as we want, depending on the complexity of the issue

d. None of the above

8. The results of the NPV under simulation

a. Will be more reliable than the original NPV

b. Can be used only when the risk is high

c. Can be used when the risk is low

d. Both a and c

9. A lender will

a. Want sensitivity analysis with variables changing adversely

b. Want sensitivity analysis with variables changing both adversely and favorably

c. Want sensitivity analysis with variables changing favorably

d. None of the above

10. In scenario analysis,

a. There is a need for at least five different scenarios

b. The results are more reliable than those in sensitivity analysis

c. The expected NPV will be lower than the original NPV

d. None of the above

Answers:

1.	(c)	2.	(b)	3.	(a)	4.	(d)	5.	(a)
6.	(d)	7.	(c)	8.	(a)	9.	(a)	10.	(d)

PROBLEMS For more problems, login to CourseMate for CFIN at CengageBrain.com

10-1 Nagpur Wilderness Company (NWC) just bought a machine that is expected to generate ₹25,000 in operating income before depreciation expenses each year. The machine, which has a depreciable basis equal to ₹60,000, falls into 15% straight line class. What will be NWC's (a) after-tax operating income and (b) operating cash flow for both this year (Year 1) and three years from now (Year 3)? Assume that all sales and operating expenses, except depreciation, are cash. NWC's marginal tax rate is 40 percent.

10-2 Dinesh Dare Devils (3D) expects to generate ₹92,000 in sales in the long term. 3D's operating costs, excluding depreciation, are 75 percent of sales. The company has only one asset, a machine that was just purchased for ₹150,000. The machine will be depreciated according to the WDV method at 22%. 3D's marginal tax rate is 35 percent, and it has no debt. Compute the company's (a) net income and (b) after-tax operating cash for the next four years.

10-3 Utpal Swimwear recently purchased a new machine for ₹350,000. It cost ₹20,000 to ship the machine to Utpal's facility, and it cost another ₹50,000 to get it installed. Purchase of the new machine will require Utpal to increase its working capital by ₹25,000. If the new machine falls into the WDV depreciation class at 20%, what amount will the firm be able to depreciate during the next five years?

10-4 Xavier Corporation plans to purchase a new machine to replace an older machine on its assembly line. The new machine's purchase price is ₹500,000, and it will cost ₹75,000 to have the new machine shipped and installed. The old machine, which is fully depreciated, can be sold to another company for ₹45,000. The new machine falls into the WDV 24% depreciation class. Compute the depreciation expense associated with the new machine for the next five years?

10-5 Wadi Textiles is trying to determine whether to purchase a new weaving machine that costs ₹214,000. It would cost another ₹26,000 to install the machine. Wadi plans to use the machine for four years and then sell it for ₹80,000. The machine falls into the WDV 25% depreciation class. (a) What will be the depreciation associated with the machine each year Wadi uses it? (b) If its marginal tax rate is 40 percent, what after-tax net cash flow will Wadi's receive when the machine is sold in four years?

10-6 Chogle Campers is evaluating a project that will not affect revenues, but it will save the firm ₹110,000 per year in before-tax operating costs, excluding depreciation. The project's depreciable basis is ₹840,000, and it will be depreciated on a straight-line basis to a book value equal to zero (₹0) over its 10-year life. If the firm's marginal tax rate is 34 percent, what are the annual supplemental operating cash flows?

10-7 Garware Bicycles just bought a new break calibration machine that is expected to generate ₹30,000 in new revenues each of the next four years without increasing cash operating costs. The machine falls in the WDV 30% depreciation class, and its depreciable basis is ₹120,000. If Garware's marginal tax rate is 35 percent, what are the annual supplemental operating cash flows attributed to the machine?

10-8 Chandigarh Cool Cabinets (CCC) is evaluating whether to replace its aging lathe. The existing lathe is being depreciated at ₹40,000 per year, whereas the depreciation for a new lathe is expected to be ₹35,000 per year. CCC's operating income, excluding depreciation, is expected to be ₹90,000 no matter which lathe is used. The firm's marginal tax rate is 40 percent. If the new lathe is purchased, what effect will the change in depreciation have on the firm's (a) net income and (b) supplemental operating cash flows. CCC has no debt.

10-9 Tavare Elevator Company plans to sell one of its machines to another company for ₹102,000. The book value of the machine is ₹90,000. Compute (a) the gain (loss) on the sale of the machine and (b) the net cash flow that will be generated from the sale of the machine. Tavare's marginal tax rate is 40 percent.

10-10 Four years ago Parameshwar Products purchased a machine for ₹250,000. The machine's current book value is ₹60,000. Later today, Parameshwar plans to sell the machine for ₹40,000. The company's marginal tax rate is 35 percent. (a) Compute the tax effect of selling the machine and (b) the net cash flow that will be generated from selling the machine.

10-11 Ravi Railway is determining whether to purchase a new rail setter, which has a base price of ₹432,000 and would cost another ₹52,000 to install. The setter falls into the WDV 25% depreciation class, and it would be sold after three years for ₹220,000. Using the setter requires a ₹22,000 increase in net working capital. Although it would have no effect on revenues, the setter should save the firm ₹185,000 per year in before-tax operating costs (excluding depreciation). Ravi's marginal tax rate is 40 percent, and its required rate of return is 14 percent. Should the setter be purchased?

10-12 Aravind Adobes is considering growing its business by adding a paint machine that costs ₹90,000. The machine will generate an additional ₹29,800 in before-tax operating income (excluding depreciation) for the next five years. At the end of five years, the machine can be sold for ₹8,000. The machine falls into the WDV 24% depreciation class. Aravind's marginal tax rate is 34 percent, and its required rate of return is 15 percent. Should Aravind purchase the machine?

10-13 Eshara Cosmetics is considering whether to replace one of its manufacturing machines with a new one that will increase operating income (excluding depreciation) by ₹143,000 per year for the next three years. The new machine costs ₹375,000, and it falls in the WDV 20% depreciation class. If the new machine is purchased, the old machine, which has a current book value equal to ₹83,000, will be sold for ₹50,000. If the old machine is kept, it will continue to be depreciated on a straight-line basis at ₹23,000 per year, and then it will be sold in three years for ₹20,000. If the new machine is purchased, Eshara plans to sell it in three years for ₹60,000. The firm's marginal tax rate is 40, and its required rate of return is 11 percent. Should the old machine be replaced?

10-14 Omprakash Outside Gear must decide whether to replace a 10 year-old packing machine with a new one that costs ₹153,800. Replacing the old machine will increase net operating income (excluding depreciation) from ₹70,000 to ₹110,000 and it will decrease net working capital by ₹18,000. The new machine falls in the WDV 22% depreciation class. If the new machine is purchased, it will be sold in six years for ₹25,000; whereas, if the old machine is kept, it will have no salvage value in six years. The old machine has a current market value of ₹10,860, and although its current book value is ₹8,000, in one year the old machine's book value will be zero (₹0). The firm's marginal tax rate is 40 percent, and its required rate of return is 12 percent. Should the new packing machine be purchased?

10-15 Quasim Quilts is considering adding another division that requires a cash outlay of ₹295,000, and is expected to generate ₹62,500 in after-tax cash flows each year for seven years. The CFO has determined the new division's beta coefficient is 0.8. The market return is expected to be 11 percent and the risk-free rate of return is 4 percent. Should Quasim add the new division?

10-16 Leelavati Legal Leverage (LLL) is evaluating a project that has a beta coefficient equal to 1.3. The risk-free rate is 3 percent and the market *risk premium* is 6 percent. The project, which requires an investment of ₹405,000, will generate ₹165,000 after-tax operating cash flows for the next three years. Should LLL purchase the project?

10-17 Quadir evaluated a project using scenario analysis. His results indicate that the project normally will generate a net present value (NPV) equal to ₹19,800, which will occur 70 percent of the time. But, he also discovered that 10 percent of the time the NPV will be −₹20,100, and 20 percent of the time the NPV will be ₹31,500. The firm's policy is not to invest in projects that have coefficients of variation greater than 0.8. Should Quadir recommend that the project be purchased?

10-18 After completing a scenario analysis for a prospective investment, the CFO of a company reported to the CEO that there is a 60 percent chance the investment will provide the firm with a net present value (NPV) equal to ₹128,300, there is a 25 percent chance the investment's NPV will be ₹185,400, and there is a 15 percent chance the NPV will be −₹77,600. The CEO will not purchase investments that have coefficients of variation greater than 0.70. Should the CEO purchase the investment?

10-19 Following are three *independent* projects Peanut/Pecan Processing (PPP) is evaluating:

Project	IRR	Risk
P	10.0%	Low
Q	12.0	Average
R	14.5	High

PPP generally considers risk when examining projects by adjusting its average required rate of return, r, which equals 11 percent. A 4 percent adjustment is made for high-risk projects, and a 2 percent adjustment is made for low-risk projects. Which project(s) should PPP purchase?

10-20 The CFO of Bachulal Golf has been given the following information about two *mutually exclusive* investments:

Project	IRR	Risk
X	14.0%	Average
Y	19.0	High

The CFO normally uses a risk-adjusted required rate of return to evaluate such investments. The firm's average required rate of return, which is 15 percent, is adjusted by 5 percent for high-risk projects, and it is adjusted by 3 percent for low-risk projects. Which project(s) should Bachulal purchase?

APPENDIX 10A DEPRECIATION

Remember from your accounting course(s) that depreciation recognizes the annual effect of wear and tear, or reduction in value, for a long-term asset that is used to generate revenues over a number of years. The concept of depreciation is covered in detail in accounting courses, so in this appendix we simply summarize basic information that will help you conduct capital budgeting analysis.

1. Companies often calculate depreciation in one way when figuring taxes and in another way when reporting income to investors: many use the *straight-line* method for stockholder reporting (or book purposes), but they use the fastest rate permitted by law for tax purposes. Because we are concerned with the effect of depreciation on cash flows, not on net income, we use the same depreciation method that firms use when determining their taxes. This is the Written Down Value (WDV) method.
2. According to tax provisions involving WDV method, each depreciable asset is classified into one of several "classes of life" according to its characteristics. The asset's depreciable basis can be written off according to the depreciation rates as given in tax statutes.
3. An asset's depreciable basis, which is the total amount that can be written off under tax laws, is equal to the purchase price of the asset plus any shipping and installation costs. The depreciable basis is not adjusted for salvage value when applying the rates.
4. If a depreciable asset is sold, the sale price (salvage value) minus the then existing undepreciated book value is added to operating income and taxed at the firm's marginal tax rate. For example, suppose a firm buys an asset for ₹100,000 and sells it at the end of the fourth year for ₹25,000. The asset's book value is say ₹17,000 after providing for the applicable depreciation. Therefore, ₹25,000 – ₹17,000 = ₹8,000 is added to the firm's operating income and is taxed. If this difference were negative, the firm would effectively receive a tax deduction, which would be recognized as a cash inflow.

Project Cash Flows and Risk

Learning Outcomes

LO.1 Describe the relevant cash flows that must be forecast to make informed capital budgeting decisions.

- When identifying relevant cash flows for capital budgeting decisions, two rules should be followed: (1) after-tax cash flows should be used and (2) only cash flows that are affected by the capital budgeting decision are relevant to the analysis.
- Relevant cash flows can be classified into one of three categories: (1) initial investment outlays, which occur only at the start of the project's life, (2) supplemental operating cash flows, which occur throughout the life of the project, and (3) terminal cash flows, which occur only at the end (termination) of the project's life.

LO.2 Identify the relevant cash flows and perform a capital budgeting analysis for (a) an expansion project and (b) a replacement project.

- Evaluation of an expansion project generally is easier than evaluation of a replacement project. The relevant cash flows that must be evaluated for an expansion project consist of any costs or savings the project will generate, whereas the relevant cash flows that must be evaluated for a replacement project consist of the *change* in cash flows that will occur as a result of replacing an existing asset with a new asset. In other words, both the cash flows that are generated by the existing asset and the cash flows that will be generated by the new asset must be considered to determine how the cash flows will change when the existing asset is replaced by the new asset. Whether an expansion project or a replacement project, once the relevant cash flows are determined, capital budgeting techniques such as net present value (NPV) and internal rate of return (IRR) should be used to make a final decision as to whether to invest in the project.

LO.3 Describe how the riskiness of a capital budgeting project is evaluated and how the results are incorporated in capital budgeting decisions.

- The firm's required rate of return should be used when evaluating capital budgeting projects that have the same risk as the firm's existing assets (i.e., average risk). When evaluating either an above-average-risk project or a below-average-risk project, a risk-adjusted required rate of return should be used. A higher-than-average required rate of return should be used to evaluate an above-average-risk project, and vice versa.

LO.4 Describe how capital budgeting decisions differ for firms that have foreign operations and for firms that only have domestic operations.

- Factors that make capital budgeting decision making more complex in an international setting include: (1) the amount of cash that can be returned to the parent company (repatriation of earnings), (2) the risk that the foreign government will seize assets or impose tariffs or taxes (political risk), and (3) the risk that value will be lost due to currency fluctuations (exchange-rate risk).

Chapter 10 Key Concepts about Capital Budgeting Cash Flows and Risk

- In capital budgeting analysis, "relevant" cash flows include only those cash flows that are affected by the decision to purchase the project. If a cash flow does not change, it is not relevant.
- The relevant, or incremental, cash flows can be categorized as (1) the initial investment outlay, which includes cash flows that occur only at the beginning of the project's life; (2) supplemental operating cash

- flows, which include changes in the day-to-day operating cash flows during the life of the project; and (3) the terminal cash flow, which includes cash flows that occur only at the end of the project's life.
- Identifying the relevant cash flows for a replacement project is somewhat more complicated than for an expansion project, because the cash flows that will be generated if the new project (the replacement asset) is purchased, as well as the cash flows that will be generated if the old project (the replaced asset) is retained, must be considered.
- If the risk associated with a capital budgeting project differs substantially from the "average" risk of the firm's existing assets, some adjustment should be made to the firm's required rate of return when evaluating the project. If the project has substantially higher risk, a higher-than-average required rate of return should be used in the capital budgeting evaluation. If the project's risk is lower than average, a lower required rate of return should be used.
- Although the same basic principles should be applied when conducting capital budgeting analysis for multinational operations, application of these principles often is more complicated when dealing with foreign subsidiaries.

Key Terms

LO.1

relevant cash flows The specific cash flows that should be considered in a capital budgeting decision. *p. 164*

incremental (marginal) cash flow The change in a firm's net cash flow attributable to an investment project. *p. 165*

sunk cost A cash outlay that has already been incurred and that cannot be recovered regardless of whether the project is accepted or rejected. *p. 165*

opportunity cost The return on the best alternative use of an asset; the highest return that will not be earned if funds are invested in a particular project. *p. 166*

externalities The effect accepting a project will have on the cash flows in other parts (areas) of the firm. *p. 166*

initial investment outlay The incremental cash flows associated with a project that will *occur only at the start of a project's life*. *p. 167*

supplemental operating cash flows The changes in day-to-day cash flows that result from the purchase of a capital project and continue until the firm disposes of the asset. *p. 167*

terminal cash flow The *net* cash flow that occurs at the end of the life of a project, including the cash flows associated with (1) the final disposal of the project and (2) returning the firm's operations to where they were before the project was accepted. *p. 168*

LO.2

expansion project A project that is intended to increase sales. *p. 168*

replacement analysis An analysis involving the decision as to whether to replace an existing asset with a new asset. *p. 171*

LO.3

stand-alone risk The risk an asset would have if it were a firm's only asset; it is measured by the variability of the asset's expected returns. *p. 174*

sensitivity analysis A risk analysis technique in which key variables are changed and the resulting changes in the NPV and the IRR are observed. *p. 175*

scenario analysis A risk analysis technique in which "bad" and "good" sets of financial circumstances are compared with a most likely, or base case, situation. *p. 175*

worst-case scenario An analysis in which all of the input variables are set at their worst reasonably forecasted values. *p. 176*

best-case scenario An analysis in which all of the input variables are set at their best reasonably forecasted values. *p. 176*

base (most likely) case An analysis in which all the input variables are set at their most likely values. *p. 176*

Monte Carlo simulation A risk analysis technique in which probable future events are simulated on a computer, generating a probability distribution that indicates the most likely outcomes. *p. 176*

corporate (within-firm) risk Risk that does not take into consideration the effects of stockholders' diversification; it is measured by a project's effect on the firm's earnings variability. *p. 177*

beta (market) risk The part of a project's risk that cannot be eliminated by diversification; it is measured by the project's beta coefficient. *p. 178*

project required rate of return, r_{proj} The risk-adjusted required rate of return for an individual project. *p. 178*

pure play method An approach used for estimating the beta of a project in which a firm identifies companies whose only business is the product in question, determines the beta for each firm, and then averages the betas to find an approximation of its own project's beta. *p. 178*

risk-adjusted discount rate The discount rate (required rate of return) that applies to a particular risky stream of income; it is equal to the risk-free rate of interest plus a risk premium appropriate to the level of risk associated with a particular project's income stream. *p. 179*

LO.4

repatriation of earnings The process of sending cash flows from a foreign subsidiary back to the parent company. *p. 180*

exchange rate risk The uncertainty associated with the price at which the currency from one country can be converted into the currency of another country. *p. 180*

political risk The risk of expropriation (seizure) of a foreign subsidiary's assets by the host country or of unanticipated restrictions on cash flows to the parent company. *p. 180*

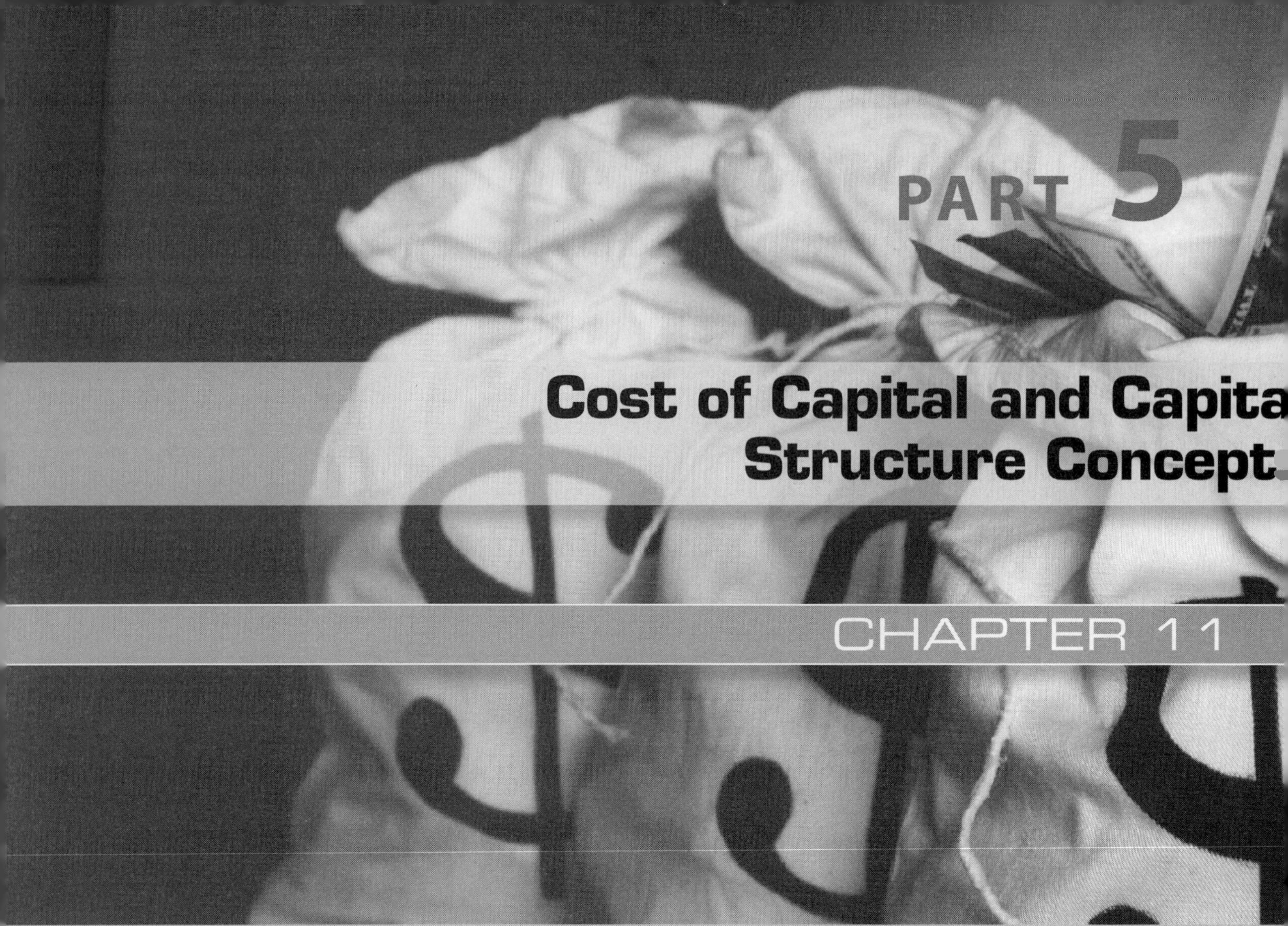

PART 5

Cost of Capital and Capita Structure Concept

CHAPTER 11

The Cost of Capital

Learning Outcomes

LO.1 Compute the component cost of capital for (a) debt, (b) preferred stock, (c) retained earnings, and (d) new common equity.

LO.2 Describe the weighted average cost of capital (WACC), and discuss the logic of using WACC to make informed financial decisions.

LO.3 Describe how the marginal cost of capital (MCC) is used to make capital budgeting decisions.

LO.4 Discuss the relationship between the firm's weighted average cost of capital (WACC) and investors' required rates of return.

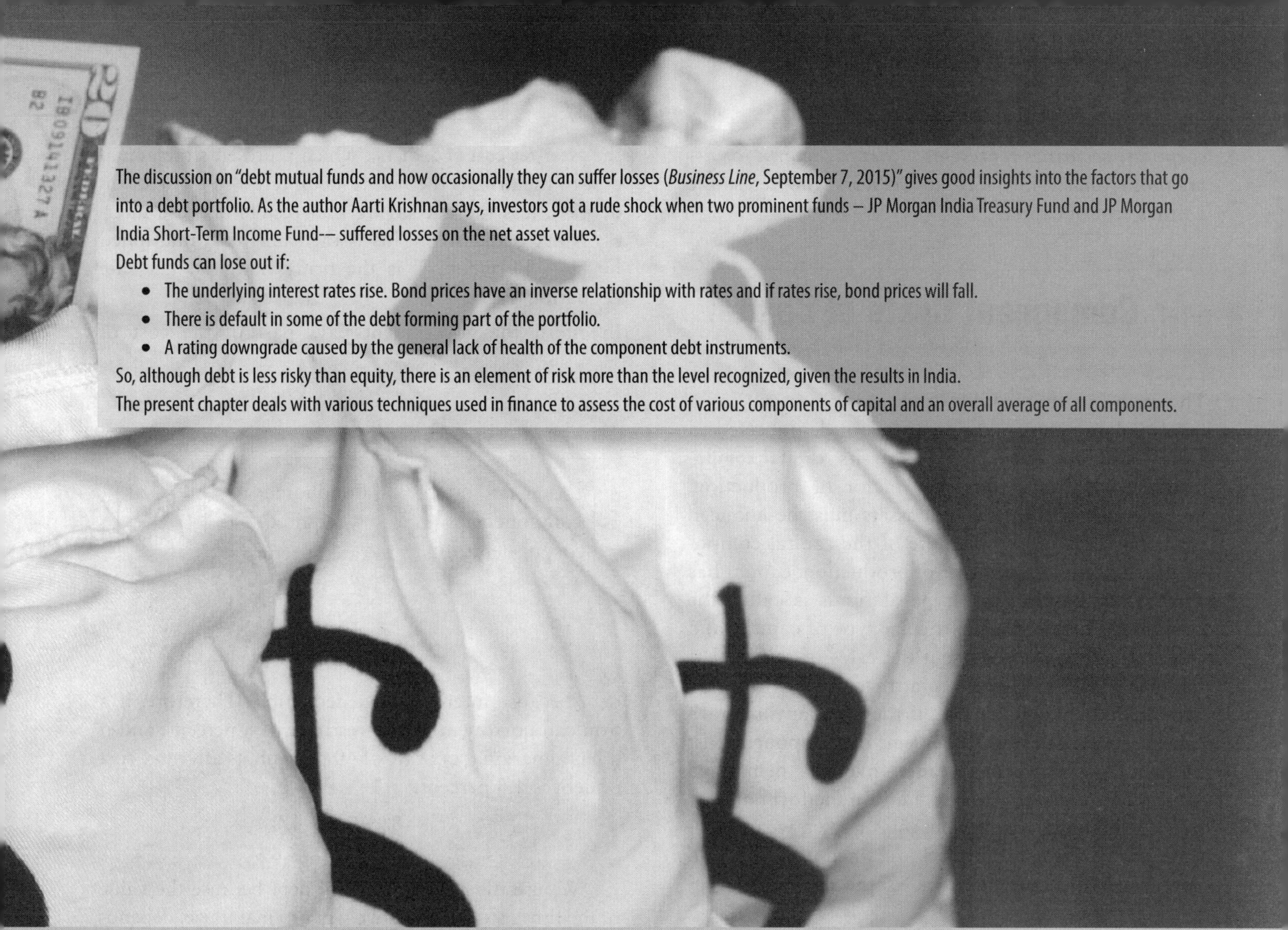

© iStockphoto.com/Lise Gagne

The discussion on "debt mutual funds and how occasionally they can suffer losses (*Business Line*, September 7, 2015)" gives good insights into the factors that go into a debt portfolio. As the author Aarti Krishnan says, investors got a rude shock when two prominent funds – JP Morgan India Treasury Fund and JP Morgan India Short-Term Income Fund-– suffered losses on the net asset values.

Debt funds can lose out if:

- The underlying interest rates rise. Bond prices have an inverse relationship with rates and if rates rise, bond prices will fall.
- There is default in some of the debt forming part of the portfolio.
- A rating downgrade caused by the general lack of health of the component debt instruments.

So, although debt is less risky than equity, there is an element of risk more than the level recognized, given the results in India.

The present chapter deals with various techniques used in finance to assess the cost of various components of capital and an overall average of all components.

It is vitally important that a firm knows how much it pays for the funds used to purchase assets, because the firm's **required rate of return** is determined by its average cost of funds, which is more commonly called the **cost of capital**. The firm's cost of capital represents the minimum rate of return that must be earned from investments, such as capital budgeting projects, to ensure the value of the firm does not decrease.

In this chapter, we discuss the concept of cost of capital, how the average cost of capital is determined, and how the cost of capital is used in financial decision making. Because a firm's cost of funds is based on the return demanded by investors, most of the models and formulas used in this chapter are the same ones we developed in Chapters 6–8, where we described how stocks and bonds are valued by investors and how investors' required rates of return are determined. To attract their funds, a firm must offer (pay) the returns investors want (require), which means *the average rate of return that investors require on*

Study Tools

Problems are found at the end of this chapter

+

Login to **CourseMate** for **CFIN** at **CengageBrain.com** for additional problems and other study tools!

corporate securities represents a cost to the firm for using those funds. Thus, it is the investors who determine a firm's cost of capital.

11-1 Component Costs of Capital

The items in the liability and equity sections of a firm's balance sheet—various types of debt, preferred stock, and common equity—are its **capital components.** *Capital* is a necessary factor of production, because any increase in total assets must be financed by an increase in one or more of the capital components. Like any other factor of production, capital has a cost. The cost of each type of funds is called the *component cost* of that particular type of capital, and the *costs of capital* represent the rates of return that the firm pays to investors to attract various forms of capital funds. For example, if the company Bharath can borrow money at 10 percent, its component cost of debt is 10 percent because investors demand a 10 percent return to provide funds in the form of debt to the company.[1] Throughout this chapter, we concentrate on debt, preferred stock, retained earnings, and new issues of common stock as the capital components for Bharath.

11-1a Cost of Debt, r_{dT}

In Chapter 6, we showed that yield to maturity (YTM) on a bond is the average rate of return that *investors require* to provide funds to the firm in the form of debt. This yield, which we designated r_d, is a cost to the firm for using investors' funds; thus we refer to the YTM, or r_d, on the firm's bonds as its *cost of debt*. However, because interest on debt is a tax-deductible expense to the firm, r_d does not represent the true cost of debt funds to the firm. To determine the actual cost of debt, we must adjust r_d to account for the tax savings associated with interest payments. Thus, the **after-tax cost of debt, r_{dT},** which represents the actual cost to the firm, is the before-tax interest rate (yield) on debt, r_d, less the tax saving that results because interest is tax deductible. This is the same as r_d multiplied by (1 − T), where T is the firm's marginal tax rate (Equation 11.1):

required rate of return The return that must be earned on invested funds to cover the cost of financing such investments; also called the *opportunity cost rate*.

cost of capital The firm's average cost of funds, which is the average return required by the firm's investors—what the firm must pay to attract funds.

capital components The particular types of capital used by the firm—that is, its debt, preferred stock, and common equity.

after-tax cost of debt, r_{dT} The relevant cost of new debt, taking into account the tax deductibility of interest.

11.1

$$\begin{pmatrix}\text{After-tax}\\ \text{component}\\ \text{cost of debt}\end{pmatrix} = r_{DT} = \begin{pmatrix}\text{Bondholders'}\\ \text{required}\\ \text{rate of return}\end{pmatrix} - \begin{pmatrix}\text{Tax}\\ \text{savings}\end{pmatrix}$$
$$= r_d - r_d \times T$$
$$= r_d - (1 - T)$$

In effect, the government pays part of the cost of debt because interest is tax deductible. Therefore, if a firm can borrow at an interest rate of 8 percent, and if it has a marginal tax rate of 40 percent, its after-tax cost of debt is 4.8 percent:

$$r_{dT} = 8.0\%(1.0 - 0.4)$$
$$= 8.0\%(0.6) = 4.8\%$$

We use the after-tax cost of debt because the value of the firm's stock, which we want to maximize, depends on *after-tax* cash flows. It follows that because we are concerned with after-tax cash flows, the after-tax rates of return are appropriate for financial decision making.[2]

Note that the cost of debt is the interest rate on *new* debt, not on already outstanding debt. In other words, we are interested in the *marginal* cost of debt. Our primary concern with the cost of capital is how it is used to make capital budgeting decisions involving investments that generate future cash flows. Thus, the rate at which the firm has borrowed in the past is a sunk cost, and it is irrelevant for cost of capital purposes.

In Chapter 6, we solved the following equation to find r_d, the rate of return, or yield to maturity (YTM), for a bond. Because YTM = r_d = before-tax cost of debt, we can use Equation 11.2 on the next page to determine r_d when interest is paid annually.

[1]We will see shortly that there are both a before-tax cost of debt and an after-tax cost of debt. For now, it is sufficient to know that 10 percent is the before-tax component cost of debt.

[2]The tax rate is *zero* for a firm with losses. Therefore, for a company that does not pay taxes, the cost of debt is not reduced; that is, in Equation 11.1 the tax rate equals zero, so the after-tax cost of debt is equal to the before-tax interest rate.

11.2

$$V_d = \frac{INT}{(1+YTM)^1} + \cdots + \frac{INT+M}{(1+YTM)^N}$$

$$\frac{INT}{(1+r_d)^1} + \cdots + \frac{INT+M}{(1+r_d)^N}$$

where INT is the rupee coupon interest paid per period, M is the face value repaid at maturity, and N is the number of interest payments remaining until maturity.

Assume that Bharath issued a new bond a few years ago. The bond has a face value of ₹1,000, 20 years remaining until maturity, and pays ₹90 interest annually. Bharath is going to issue new bonds in a couple of days that have the same general characteristics as this outstanding bond. If the current market price of the outstanding bond is ₹915, what should the r_d be for the new bond? We would expect that the return investors demand for the new bond should be about the same as that for the outstanding bond, because both bonds have the same characteristics. To determine the before-tax cost of debt, we can solve for r_d in the following equation:

$$₹915 = \frac{₹90}{(1+r_d)^1} + \frac{₹90}{(1+r_d)^2} + \cdots + \frac{₹90 + ₹1{,}000}{(1+r_d)^{20}}$$

Whether you use the trial-and-error method or the time value of money functions on your calculator, you should find $r_d = 10\%$, which is the before-tax cost of debt for this bond.[3] Bharath's marginal tax rate is 40 percent; so its after-tax cost of debt, r_{dT}, is $6.0\% = 10.0\%(1 - 0.40)$.

11-1b Cost of Preferred Stock, r_{ps}

In Chapter 7, we found that the dividend associated with preferred stock, which we designated D_{ps}, is constant, and that preferred stock has no stated maturity. We also discovered that we can determine the rate of return that investors require to provide funds to the firm in the form of preferred stock by solving for r_s in the model that was used to value stock with a constant growth rate equal to 0. (The annual dividend stays the same, which means it does not grow.) That is, we solved for r_s in the constant growth model, and the result was Equation 7.3. To determine the component **cost of preferred stock**, which we designate r_{ps}, we apply Equation 7.3 for a stock with a growth rate equal to 0, but we adjust the current market price to reflect the fact that the firm incurs costs when it issues preferred stock to raise funds. These issuance costs, which are called *flotation costs*, reduce the amount of funds that the firm can use for financing capital budgeting projects, and thus effectively increase the rate that the firm must earn to pay the preferred dividend. In other words, flotation costs require the firm to invest funds provided by preferred stockholders at a higher rate than investors actually demand, because although the firm does not receive the entire amount that investors pay for the stock (due to flotation costs), it still must pay the same preferred dividend to all preferred stockholders.

Thus, r_{ps} is computed by dividing the preferred dividend, D_{ps}, by the net issuing price, NP, or the price the firm receives after deducting the costs of issuing the stock (Equation 11.3):

11.3

$$\text{Component cost of preferred stock} = r_{ps} = \frac{D_{ps}}{P_0 - \text{Flotation costs}}$$

$$= \frac{D_{Ps}}{P_0(1-F)} = \frac{D_{Ps}}{NP_0}$$

Here F is the percentage cost (in decimal form) of issuing preferred stock and P_0 is the current market price of the stock.

To illustrate, although it has no preferred stock at present, Bharath plans to issue preferred stock that pays a ₹12.80 dividend per share and sells for ₹120 per share in the market. It will cost 3 percent, or ₹3.60 per share, to issue the new preferred stock, so Bharath

cost of preferred stock, r_{ps} The rate of return investors require on the firm's preferred stock, r_{ps}; calculated as the preferred dividend, D_{ps}, divided by the preferred stock's net issuing price, NP.

[3]It should also be noted that we have ignored flotation costs (the costs incurred for new issuances) on debt because nearly all debt issued by small and medium-sized firms, as well as that issued by many large firms, is privately placed, and hence has little or no flotation costs. However, if bonds are publicly placed and do involve flotation costs, the solution value of r_d in the following formula is used as the before-tax cost of debt:

$$V_d(1-F) = \sum_{t=1}^{N} \frac{INT}{(1+r_d)^t} + \frac{M}{(1+r_d)^N}$$

Here F is the percentage amount (in decimal form) of the bond flotation, or issuing, cost; N is the number of periods to maturity; INT is the rupees of interest per period; M is the maturity value of the bond; and r_d is the cost of debt adjusted to reflect flotation costs. If we assume that the bond in the example calls for annual payments, that it has a 20-year maturity, and that F = 2%, then the flotation-adjusted, before-tax cost of debt is 10.23 percent (versus 10 percent before the flotation adjustment).

will net ₹116.40 per share. Therefore, Bharath's cost of preferred stock is 11 percent:

$$r_{ps} = \frac{₹12.80}{₹120.00(1-0.03)} = \frac{₹12.80}{₹116.40}$$
$$= 0.11 = 11.0\%$$

No tax adjustments are made when calculating r_{ps} because preferred dividends, unlike interest expense on debt, are not tax deductible, which means there is no tax savings associated with the use of preferred stock.

11-1c Cost of Retained Earnings (Internal Equity), r_s

The costs of debt and preferred stock are based on the returns investors require on these securities. Similarly, the **cost of retained earnings**, which we designate r_s, is the rate of return stockholders require on equity capital the firm "raises" by retaining earnings that otherwise could be distributed to common stockholders as dividends.[4]

The reason we must assign a cost to retained earnings involves the *opportunity cost principle*. Bondholders are compensated by interest payments and preferred stockholders are compensated by preferred dividends, so the earnings that remain after interest and preferred dividends are paid belong to the common stockholders, and these earnings help compensate these stockholders for the use of their capital. Management can either pay out the earnings in the form of dividends or retain earnings and reinvest them in the business. If management decides to retain earnings, there is an opportunity cost involved because common stockholders could have received the earnings as dividends and invested this money for themselves in other stocks, in bonds, in real estate, or in anything else. Thus, the firm should earn a return on earnings it retains that is at least as great as the return stockholders themselves could earn on alternative investments of comparable risk; otherwise, common stockholders will demand that all earnings be paid out as dividends.

What rate of return can stockholders expect to earn on equivalent-risk investments? First, recall from Chapter 8 that stocks normally are in equilibrium, with the expected rate of return, $\hat{r}_s$, equal to the required rate of return, r_s; that is, $\hat{r}_s = r_s$. Therefore, we can assume that Bharath's common stockholders expect to earn a return of r_s on their money. *If the firm cannot invest retained earnings and earn at least r_s, it should pay these funds to its common stockholders and let them invest directly in other assets (investments) that do provide this return.*[5]

cost of retained earnings, r_s
The rate of return required by stockholders on a firm's existing common stock.

Whereas debt and preferred stocks are fixed obligations that have easily determined costs, it is not as easy to measure r_s. However, we can employ the principles developed in Chapters 7 and 8 to produce reasonably good estimates of the cost of retained earnings. To begin, we know that when a stock is in equilibrium (which is the typical situation), its required rate of return, r_s, is equal to its expected rate of return, $\hat{r}_s$. Further, its required return is equal to a risk-free rate, r_{RF}, plus a risk premium, RP, whereas the expected return on a constant growth stock is equal to the stock's dividend yield, $\hat{D}/P_0$, plus its expected growth rate, g. This relationship is shown in Equation 11.4:

11.4

Required rate of return = Expected rate of return

$$r = \hat{r}_s$$

$$r_{RF} + RP_s = \frac{\hat{D}_1}{P_0} + g$$

Because the two must be equal, we can estimate r_s using either the left side or the right side of Equation 11.4.

The CAPM Approach (Required Rate of Return, r_s). The capital asset pricing model (CAPM) we developed in Chapter 8 is stated as Equation 11.5:

11.5

$$r_s = r_{RF} + RP_s = r_{RF} + RP_M\beta_s = r_{RF} + (r_M - r_{RF})\beta_s$$

[4]The term *retained earnings* can be interpreted to mean either the balance sheet item "retained earnings," consisting of all the earnings retained in the business throughout its history, or the income statement item "additions to retained earnings." The income statement item is used in this chapter; for our purpose, *retained earnings* refers to that part of current earnings not paid out in dividends and hence available for reinvestment in the business this year.

[5]In reality, stockholders' preferences are also affected by the tax rates that are applied to dividends and to capital gains. If dividends are taxed at a much higher rate than capital gains, stockholders might prefer for the firm to retain earnings, even if it invests some of these funds at returns that are slightly lower than r_s. We do not consider the effects of investors' taxes on their preferences for dividends versus capital gains in this chapter. Even so, we know that investors prefer for the firm to reinvest any retained earnings at a rate that equals or exceeds r_s.

Equation 11.5 shows that the CAPM estimate of r_s begins with the risk-free rate, r_{RF}, to which is added a risk premium that is based on (1) the stock's relation to the market as measured by its beta coefficient, β_s, and (2) the magnitude of the market risk premium, RP_M, which is the difference between the market return, r_M, and the risk-free rate, r_{RF}.

To illustrate the CAPM approach, assume that $r_{RF} = 6\%$, $r_M = 10.5\%$, and $\beta_s = 1.6$ for Bharath's common stock. Using the CAPM approach, the return required by Bharath's common stockholders and thus its cost of retained earnings, r_s, is calculated as follows:

$$r_s = 6.0\% + (10.5\% - 6.0\%)(1.6)$$
$$= 6.0\% + 7.2\% = 13.2\%$$

Although the CAPM approach appears to yield an accurate, precise estimate of r_s, there actually are several problems with it. First, as we saw in Chapter 8, if a firm's stockholders are not well diversified, they might be concerned with total risk rather than with market risk only (measured by β). In this case, the firm's true investment risk will *not* be measured by its beta, and the CAPM procedure will understate the correct value of r_s. Further, even if the CAPM method is valid, it is difficult to obtain correct estimates of the inputs required to make it operational, because (1) there is controversy about which Treasury yields to use as a measure of r_{RF} and (2) both β_s and r_M should be estimated values, which often are difficult to obtain.

Discounted Cash Flow (DCF) Approach (Expected Rate of Return, $\hat{r}_s$). In Chapter 7, we learned that both the price and the expected rate of return on a share of common stock depend, ultimately, on the dividends the stock is expected to pay. We also discovered that, as long as the firm is growing at a constant rate, the expected rate of return of common stockholders can be determined by applying Equation 7.3. Restating Equation 7.3 in equilibrium form gives Equation 11.6, which we can use to estimate a firm's cost of retained earnings, r_s.

11.6

$$r_{RF} + RP_s = \frac{\hat{D}_1}{P_0} + g$$

Here P_0 is the current price of the stock, $\hat{D}_1$ is the dividend that is *expected* to be paid at the end of the year (Year 1), g is the constant rate at which the firm will grow into perpetuity, and $\hat{r}_s$ is the expected rate of return.

Thus, investors expect to receive a dividend yield, $\hat{D}_1/P_0$, plus a capital gain, g, for a total expected return of $\hat{r}_s$. In equilibrium, this expected return is also equal to the required return, r_s. From this point on, we will assume that equilibrium exists, and we will use the terms r_s and $\hat{r}_s$ interchangeably, so we will drop the hat (^) above r_s.

It is relatively easy to determine the dividend yield, but it is difficult to establish the proper growth rate. If past growth rates in earnings and dividends have been relatively stable, and if investors appear to be projecting a continuation of past trends, then g can be based on the firm's historical growth rate. However, if the company's past growth has been abnormally high or low, either because of its own unique situation or because of general economic fluctuations, historical growth probably should not be used. Securities analysts regularly make earnings and dividend growth forecasts, looking at such factors as projected sales, profit margins, and competitive factors. For example, *Value Line,* which is available in most libraries, provides growth rate forecasts for approximately 1,700 companies, and Bank of America Merrill Lynch, Morgan Stanley Smith Barney, and other investment organizations make similar forecasts. Therefore, someone making a cost of capital estimate can obtain several analysts' forecasts, average them, and use the average as a proxy for the growth expectations, g.[6]

To illustrate the DCF approach, suppose Bharath's common stock currently sells for ₹22 per share; the common stock dividend expected to be paid in 2015 is ₹1.28 per share; and its expected long-term growth rate is 7.5 percent. Bharath's expected and required rate of return on retained earnings is 13.3 percent:

$$r_s = \hat{r}_s = \frac{₹1.28}{₹22.00} + 0.075$$

$$= 0.058 + 0.075 = 0.133 = 13.3\%$$

This 13.3 percent is the minimum rate of return that management must expect to earn to justify retaining earnings and plowing them back into the business rather than paying them out to stockholders as dividends.

[6]Analysts' growth rate forecasts are usually for five years into the future, and the rates provided represent the average growth rate over that five-year horizon. Studies have shown that analysts' forecasts represent the best source of growth rate data for DCF cost of capital estimates. See Robert Harris, "Using Analysts' Growth Rate Forecasts to Estimate Shareholder Required Rates of Return," *Financial Management*, Spring 1986, 58–67.

Bond-Yield-Plus-Risk-Premium Approach. Empirical work suggests that the cost of retained earnings, r_s, can also be estimated by adding a risk premium of 3 to 5 percentage points to the before-tax interest rate on the firm's own long-term debt, r_d. The logic to applying this approach is that firms with risky, low-rated, and consequently high interest rate debt will also have risky, high-cost equity. Although this simplistic method is not likely to produce a precise cost of equity, it can get us into the right "ballpark." For example, Bharath's cost of equity might be estimated as follows:

$$r_s = \text{Bond YTM} + \text{Risk premium}$$
$$= 10.0\% + 4.0\% = 14.0\%$$

Because the 4 percent risk premium is a judgmental estimate, the estimated value of r_s is also judgmental.

We have described three methods to estimate the cost of retained earnings, which should be a single number. To summarize, we found the cost of common equity to be (1) 13.2 percent using the CAPM method, (2) 13.3 percent using the constant growth model (the DCF approach), and (3) 14.0 percent with the bond-yield-plus-risk-premium approach. It is not unusual to get different estimates, because each approach is based on different assumptions. The CAPM assumes investors are well diversified, the constant growth model assumes the firm's dividends and earnings will grow at a constant rate far into the future, and the bond-yield-plus-risk-premium approach assumes the cost of equity is closely related to the firm's cost of debt. Which estimate should be used? Probably all of them. Many analysts use multiple approaches to estimate a single value, then average the results. For Bharath, then, the average of the estimates is $r_s = 13.5\% = (13.2\% + 13.3\% + 14.0\%)/3$.[7]

11-1d Cost of Newly Issued Common Stock (External Equity), r_e

The **cost of new common equity**, or *external equity capital*, which we designate r_e, is similar to the cost of retained earnings, r_s, except it is higher because the firm incurs *flotation costs* when it issues new common stock. As mentioned earlier, the **flotation costs**, which are the expenses associated with issuing new securities (equity or debt), reduce the amount of funds the firm receives, and hence the amount that can be used for investment. Only the amount of funds that is left after paying flotation costs—that is, the *net* amount received by the firm—is available for investment. As a result, *the cost of issuing new common stock (external equity), r_e, is greater than the cost of retained earnings, r_s*, because there are no flotation costs associated with retained earnings (internal equity) financing.

cost of new common equity, r_e The cost of external equity; based on the cost of retained earnings, but increased for flotation costs.

flotation costs The expenses incurred when selling new issues of securities.

In general, the cost of issuing new equity, r_e, can be found by modifying the DCF formula used to compute the cost of retained earnings, r_s. Equation 11.7 shows the modified DCF formula:

11.7

$$r_e = \frac{\hat{D}_1}{NP_0} + g = \frac{\hat{D}_1}{P_0(1 - F)} + g$$

Here F is the percentage flotation cost (in decimal form) incurred in selling the new stock issue, so $P_0(1 - F)$ is the net price per share received by the company, NP_0.

If Bharath can issue new common stock at a flotation cost of 17 percent (remember from our discussion in Chapter 2 that the company's financial position is somewhat precarious), r_e is computed as follows:

$$r_e = \frac{₹1.28}{₹22.00(1-0.17)} + 0.075 = \frac{₹1.28}{₹18.26} + 0.075$$
$$= 0.70 + 0.075 = 0.145 = 14.5\%$$

Using the DCF approach to estimate the cost of retained earnings, we found that investors require a return of $r_s = 13.3\%$ on the stock. However, because of flotation costs, the company must earn more than 13.3 percent on funds obtained by selling stock if it is to provide stockholders a 13.3 percent return. Specifically, if the firm earns 14.5 percent on funds that are raised from issuing new stock, then earnings per share will not fall below previously expected earnings, the firm's expected dividend can be maintained, and, as a result, the price per share will not decline. If the firm earns less than 14.5 percent, then earnings, dividends, and growth

[7]People experienced in estimating equity capital costs recognize that both careful analysis and sound judgment are required. It would be nice to pretend that judgment is unnecessary and to specify an easy, precise way of determining the exact cost of equity capital. Unfortunately, this is not possible; finance is in large part a matter of judgment, and we simply must face that fact.

will fall below expectations, causing the price of the stock to decline. If it earns more than 14.5 percent, the price of the stock will rise.

The reason for the flotation-cost adjustment can be made clear by a simple example. Suppose Weaver Realty Company has ₹100,000 of assets and no debt, it earns a 15 percent return (or ₹15,000) on its assets, and it pays all earnings out as dividends, so its growth rate is zero. The company has 1,000 shares of stock outstanding, so earnings per share (EPS) and dividends per share (DPS) are the same—DPS = ₹15 = ₹15,000/1,000—and P_0 = ₹100 = ₹100,000/1,000. Weaver's cost of equity is thus r_s = ₹15/₹100 + 0 = 15.0%. Now suppose Weaver can get a return of 15 percent on new assets. Should it sell new stock to acquire new assets? If it sold 1,000 new shares of stock to the public for ₹100 per share, but it incurred a 10 percent flotation cost on the issue, it would net ₹100 − 0.10(₹100) = ₹90 per share, or ₹90,000 in total. It would then invest this ₹90,000 and earn 15 percent, or ₹13,500. Its new *total* earnings would be ₹28,500, which would consist of ₹15,000 generated from the old assets plus ₹13,500 from the new assets. However, the ₹28,500 would have to be distributed equally to the 2,000 shares of stock now outstanding. Therefore, Weaver's EPS and DPS would decline from ₹15 to ₹14.25 = ₹28,500/2,000. Because its EPS and DPS would fall, the price of the stock would also fall from P_0 = ₹100 to P_1 = ₹14.25/0.15 = ₹95.00. This result occurs because investors have put up ₹100 per share, but the company received and invested only ₹90 per share. Thus, we see that the ₹90 must earn more than 15 percent to provide investors with a 15 percent return on the ₹100 they put up.

We can use Equation 11.7 to compute the return Weaver must earn on the ₹90,000 of new assets it purchases—that is, the amount it raises with the new issue:

$$r_e = \frac{₹15}{₹100(1-0.10)} + 0.0 = 0.1667 = 16.67\%$$

If Weaver invests the funds from the new common stock issue at 16.67 percent, here is what would happen:

$$\begin{pmatrix}\text{New total}\\ \text{earnings}\end{pmatrix} = \begin{pmatrix}\text{Earnings from}\\ \text{existing assets}\end{pmatrix} + \begin{pmatrix}\text{Earnings from}\\ \text{new assets}\end{pmatrix}$$

$$= ₹15,000 + ₹90,000(0.16667)$$

$$= ₹30,000$$

$$\begin{pmatrix}\text{New EPS}\\ \text{and DPS}\end{pmatrix} = \frac{₹30,000}{2,000} = ₹15$$

$$\text{New price} = \frac{₹15}{0.15} = ₹100$$

Thus, if the return on the new assets is equal to r_e as calculated by Equation 11.7, then EPS, DPS, and the stock price will all remain constant. If the return on the new assets exceeds r_e, then EPS, DPS, and P_0 will rise. Because of flotation costs, the cost of external equity exceeds the cost of equity raised internally from retained earnings—that is, $r_e > r_s$. If F = 0 (which is unlikely), however, then $r_e = r_s$.

11-2 Weighted Average Cost of Capital (WACC)

It is possible to finance a firm entirely with equity funds by issuing only common stock. In that case, the cost of capital used to analyze capital budgeting decisions should be the company's required return on common equity. However, most firms raise a substantial portion of their funds as long-term debt, and some also use preferred stock. For these firms, their cost of capital must reflect the average cost of the various sources of long-term funds used, not just the firms' costs of common equity.

© iStockphoto.com/Sergey Ilin

Suppose that a firm has an 8 percent cost of debt and a 12 percent cost of equity. Further, assume that the company has decided to finance next year's projects by selling debt only. The argument is sometimes made that the cost of capital for these projects is 8 percent because only debt will be used to finance them. However, this position is incorrect. If the company finances a particular set of projects with debt only, the firm will be using up some of its potential for obtaining new debt in the future. As expansion occurs in subsequent years, the company will at some point find it necessary to raise additional equity to prevent the proportion of debt from becoming too large. For example, consider what would happen if the company borrows heavily at 8 percent during 2014, using up its debt capacity in the process, to finance projects yielding 10 percent. If it has new projects available in 2015 that yield 11.5 percent, which is above the return on 2014 projects, it cannot accept them because they would have to be financed with 12 percent equity funds. To avoid this problem, the company should be viewed as an ongoing operation, and *the cost of capital used in capital budgeting should be calculated as a weighted average, or combination, of the various types of funds generally used, regardless of the specific financing used to fund a particular project.*

11-2a Determining WACC

Each firm has an optimal capital structure—a mix of debt, preferred stock, and common equity that causes its stock price to be maximized. Therefore, a rational, value-maximizing firm will establish a **target (optimal) capital structure** and then raise new capital in a manner that will keep the actual capital structure on target over time. In this chapter, we assume that the firm has identified its optimal capital structure, it uses this optimum as the target, and it raises funds so it constantly remains on target. How the target is established will be examined in Chapter 12.

The target proportions of debt, preferred stock, and common equity, along with the component costs of capital, are used to calculate the firm's **weighted average cost of capital (WACC)**. The WACC simply represents the average cost of each rupee of financing, no matter its source, that the firm uses to purchase assets. That is, *WACC represents the minimum rate of return the firm must earn on its investments (assets) to maintain its current level of wealth.*

target (optimal) capital structure The combination (percentages) of debt, preferred stock, and common equity that will maximize the price of the firm's stock.

weighted average cost of capital (WACC) A weighted average of the component costs of debt, preferred stock, and common equity.

To illustrate, suppose Bharath Textiles has determined that in the future it will raise new capital according to the following proportions: 45 percent debt, 5 percent preferred stock, and 50 percent common equity (retained earnings plus new common stock). In the preceding sections, we found that its before-tax cost of debt, r_d, is 10 percent, so its *after-tax* cost of debt, r_{dT}, is 6 percent; its cost of preferred stock, r_{ps}, is 11 percent; and its cost of common equity, r_s, is 13.5 percent if all of its common equity financing comes from retained earnings. Now we can calculate The company's weighted average cost of capital (WACC) using Equation 11.8:

11.8

$$\text{WACC} = w_d(r_{dT}) + w_{ps}(r_{ps}) + w_s(r_s)$$

Here w_d, w_{ps}, and w_s represent the proportions (weights) of debt, preferred stock, and common equity, respectively, that make up the firm's target capital structure; and, as previously described, r_{dT} is the after-tax cost of debt, r_{ps} is the cost of preferred stock, and r_s is the cost of common equity (cost of retained earnings or cost of new equity).

Every rupee of new capital that Bharath obtains consists of ₹0.45 of debt with an after-tax cost of 6 percent, ₹0.05 of preferred stock with a cost of 11 percent, and ₹0.50 of common equity with a cost of 13.5 percent (if all of the common equity funds come from additions to retained earnings). Bharath's WACC is calculated as follows:

$$\text{WACC} = 0.45(6.0\%) + 0.05(11.0\%) + 0.50(13.5\%) = 10.0\%$$

The average cost of each whole rupee, WACC, is 10 percent as long as these conditions continue. If the component costs of capital change when new funds are raised in the future, then WACC changes. We discuss changes in the component costs of capital in the next section.

Determining a firm's WACC is more complicated than simply plugging numbers into Equation 11.8 and performing the math. Most large firms issue different types of debt as well as different classes of common stock that have different component costs, so that there is neither a single cost of debt nor a single cost of common equity. As a result, in practice, the cost of debt, r_d, that is used to compute the firm's WACC is a weighted average of the costs of the various types of debt the firm has issued. Similarly, when a firm raises capital by issuing new common stock, the total amount of equity capital often includes both the amount of earnings retained during the year and the amount raised with the new common stock issue, which means the cost of common equity should be a weighted average of r_s and r_e. To simplify our discussions and the subsequent computations, however, we assume that (1) the firm issues only one type of bond each time it raises new funds using debt and (2) when new common stock is issued, the average cost to the firm for *all* common equity used to finance new investments is the cost of the new common stock, r_e, even if retained earnings have provided some of the common equity capital.

11-2b The Marginal Cost of Capital (MCC)

The marginal cost of any item is the cost of adding another unit of that item. For example, the marginal cost of labor is the cost of adding one additional worker. The marginal cost of labor might be ₹25 per person if 10 workers are added, but ₹35 per person if the firm tries to hire 100 new workers because it will be harder to find that many people willing and able to do the work. The same concept applies to capital. As the firm tries to attract additional new rupees, at some point the cost of each rupee will increase. Thus, the **marginal cost of capital (MCC)** is defined as *the weighted average cost (WACC) of the last rupee of new capital that the firm raises,* and the marginal cost rises as more and more capital is raised during a given period.

In the preceding section, we computed Bharath's WACC to be 10 percent. As long as Bharath keeps its capital structure on target, and as long as its debt has an after-tax cost of 6 percent, its preferred stock has a cost of 11 percent, and its common equity in the form of retained earnings has a cost of 13.5 percent, its weighted average cost of capital will be 10 percent. Each rupee the firm raises will consist of some long-term debt, some preferred stock, and some common equity, and the cost of the whole rupee will be 10 percent; that is, its marginal cost of capital (MCC) will average 10 percent.

11-2c The MCC Schedule

A graph that shows how the WACC changes as more and more new capital is raised by the firm is called the **MCC (marginal cost of capital) schedule**. Figure 11.1 shows Bharath's MCC schedule if the cost of debt, cost of preferred stock, and cost of common equity *never change.*

FIGURE 11.1 Marginal Cost of Capital (MCC) Schedule for Bharath

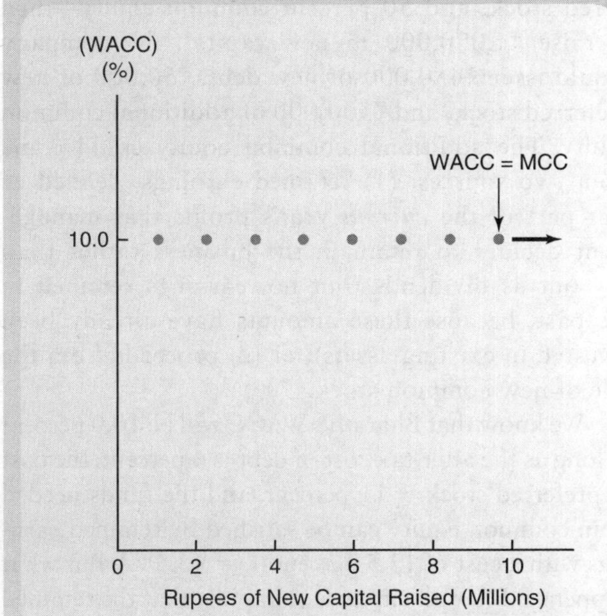

Here the dots represent rupees raised, and because each rupee of new capital will have an average cost equal to 10 percent, the marginal cost of capital (MCC) for Bharath is constant at 10.0 percent under the assumptions we have used to this point.

Do you think Bharath actually could raise an unlimited amount of new capital at the 10 percent cost? Probably not. As a practical matter, as a company raises larger and larger amounts of funds during a given time period, the costs of those funds begin to rise, and as this occurs, the WACC of each new rupee also rises. Thus, companies cannot raise unlimited amounts of capital at a constant cost. At some point, the cost of each new rupee will increase, no matter what its source—debt, preferred stock, or common equity.

How much can Bharath raise before the cost of its funds increases? As a first step in determining the point at which the MCC begins to rise, recognize that although the company's balance sheet shows total long-term capital of ₹715 million at the end of 2014, all of this capital was raised in the past, and these funds have been invested in assets that

marginal cost of capital (MCC) The cost of obtaining another rupee of new capital; the weighted average cost of the last rupee of new capital raised.

MCC (marginal cost of capital) schedule A graph that relates the firm's weighted average cost of each rupee of capital to the total amount of new capital raised.

are now being used in current operations. If Bharath raises new (marginal) capital based on its target capital structure—that is, 45 percent debt, 5 percent preferred stock, and 50 percent common equity—then to raise ₹1,000,000 in new capital, the company should issue ₹450,000 of new debt, ₹50,000 of new preferred stock, and ₹500,000 of additional common equity. The additional common equity could come from two sources: (1) retained earnings, defined as that part of the *current* year's profits that management decides to retain in the business rather than pay out as dividends (but not earnings retained in the past, because these amounts have already been invested in existing assets); or (2) proceeds from the sale of new common stock.

We know that Bharath's WACC will be 10.0 percent as long as the after-tax cost of debt is 6 percent, the cost of preferred stock is 11 percent, and the funds needed from common equity can be satisfied by retained earnings with a cost of 13.5 percent (r_s = 13.5%). But what happens if Bharath expands so rapidly that the retained earnings for the year are not sufficient to meet the common equity needs, forcing the firm to sell new common stock? Earlier, we determined that the cost of issuing new common stock, r_e, will be 14.5 percent, because the flotation costs associated with the new issue will be 17 percent. Because the cost of common equity increases when common stock must be issued, the WACC also increases at that point.

How much new capital can Bharath raise before it exhausts its retained earnings and is forced to sell new common stock? In other words, where will an increase in the MCC schedule occur? Suppose that Bharath's 2015 net income will be ₹61 million and that ₹30.5 million will be paid out as dividends so that ₹30.5 million will be added to retained earnings (the payout ratio is 50 percent). In this case, Bharath can invest in capital projects to the point where the *common equity needs* equal ₹30.5 million before new common stock must be issued. Remember, though, that when Bharath needs new funds, the target capital structure indicates that only 50 percent of the total should be common equity; the remainder of the funds should come from issues of bonds (45 percent) and preferred stock (5 percent). Thus, we know that

$$\text{Common equity} = 0.50 \times \text{Total new capital raised}$$

We can use this relationship to determine how much *total new capital*—that is, the combination of debt, preferred stock, and retained earnings—can be raised before the ₹30.5 million of retained earnings is exhausted and Bharath is forced to sell new common stock. Simply solve the following relationship:

$$\begin{array}{c}\text{Retained} \\ \text{earnings}\end{array} = ₹30.5 \text{ million} = 0.50\begin{pmatrix}\text{Total new} \\ \text{capital raised}\end{pmatrix}$$

$$\begin{pmatrix}\text{Total new} \\ \text{capital raised}\end{pmatrix} = \frac{₹30.5 \text{ million}}{0.50} = ₹61.0 \text{ million}$$

Thus, Bharath can raise a *total* of ₹61 million before it has to sell new common stock to finance its capital projects.

If Bharath needs exactly ₹61 million in new capital, the breakdown of the amount that would come from each source of capital would be as follows:

Capital Source	Weight, w	Amount (₹ in Millions)	Component Cost, r
Debt	0.45	₹27.45	6.0%
Preferred stock	0.05	3.05	11.0
Common equity	0.50	30.50	13.5
	1.00	₹61.00	

For this situation, the computation for the weighted average cost of capital (WACC) is:

$$\begin{aligned}\text{WACC} &= 0.45(6.0\%) + 0.05(11.0\%) + 0.50(13.5\%) \\ &= 10.0\%\end{aligned}$$

Therefore, if Bharath needs *exactly* ₹61 million in new capital in 2015, retained earnings will be just enough to satisfy the common equity requirement, which means the firm will not need to sell new common stock and its weighted average cost of capital (WACC) will be 10 percent. But what will happen if Bharath needs more than ₹61 million in new capital? If Bharath needs ₹64 million, for example, the ₹30.5 million of retained earnings will not be sufficient to cover the ₹32 million common equity requirement (50 percent of the total *new* funds), so new common stock will have to be sold. The cost of issuing new common stock, r_e, is greater than the cost of retained earnings, r_s; hence, the WACC will be greater.

Capital Source	Weight, w	Amount (₹ in Millions)	Component Cost, r
Debt	0.45	₹28.80	6.0%
Preferred stock	0.05	3.20	11.0
Common equity	0.50	32.00	14.5
	1.00	₹64.00	

If Bharath raises ₹64 million in new capital, the breakdown of the amount that would come from each source of capital would be as follows:

For this situation, the computation for the weighted average cost of capital (WACC) is:

$$\begin{aligned} \text{WACC} &= 0.45(6.0\%) + 0.05(11.0\%) + 0.50(14.5\%) \\ &= 10.5\% \end{aligned}$$

The WACC will be greater in this situation because Bharath will have to sell new common stock, which has a higher component cost than retained earnings (14.5 percent versus 13.5 percent). Consequently, if Bharath's capital budgeting needs are greater than ₹61 million, new common stock will need to be sold, and its WACC will increase. The ₹61 million in total new capital is defined as the *retained earnings break point,* because above this amount of total capital, a break, or jump, in Bharath's MCC schedule occurs. In general, a **break point (BP)** is defined as the last rupee of *new total capital* that can be raised *before* an increase in the firm's WACC occurs.

Figure 11.2 graphs Bharath's marginal cost of capital schedule with the retained earnings break point. Because the amount of retained earnings is sufficient to satisfy the common equity portion of total funds as long as financing needs range from ₹1 to ₹61 million, each rupee raised within this range has a weighted average cost of 10.0 percent. However, if Bharath raises one rupee over ₹61 million, each new rupee will contain ₹0.50 of equity *obtained by selling new common stock at a cost of 14.5 percent.* As a result, WACC jumps from 10.0 percent to 10.5 percent, as calculated previously and shown in Table 11.1 on the next page. At this point, we must note two important facts:

- Bharath's cost of equity will not actually jump from 13.5 percent to 14.5 percent when ₹0.50 of new equity is issued. In reality, the cost of common equity would only increase marginally. However, to simplify our discussion and computations, we assume that once Bharath issues common stock, no matter the amount, the cost of equity increases so that the average cost of each rupee of equity is 14.5 percent (even though the common equity financing also includes some retained earnings). For further simplification, we apply this same logic to all types of capital.
- Because we really don't think the MCC jumps by precisely 0.5 percent when we raise ₹1 over ₹61 million, Figure 11.2 should be regarded as an approximation rather than as a precise representation of reality. We will return to this point later in the chapter.

FIGURE 11.2 Marginal Cost of Capital (MCC) Schedule for Bharath Textiles Using Retained Earnings and New Common Stock

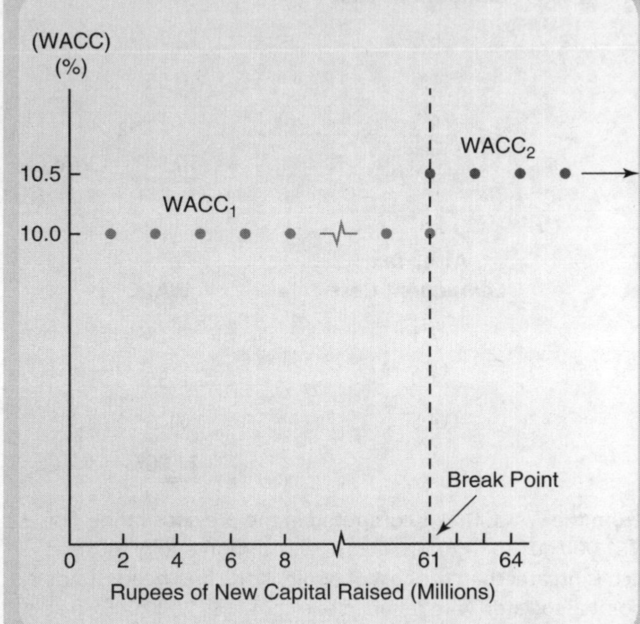

11-2d **Other Breaks in the MCC Schedule**

There is a jump, or break, in Bharath's MCC schedule at ₹61 million of new capital because new common stock must be sold. Could there be other breaks in the schedule? Yes, there could. For example, suppose Bharath could obtain only ₹54 million of debt at a before-tax cost of 10 percent, with any additional debt costing 11.85 percent (before taxes). This would result in a second break point in the MCC schedule, at the point where the ₹54 million of 10 percent debt is exhausted. At what amount of *total financing* would the 10 percent debt be used up? We know that this total financing will amount to ₹54 million of debt plus some amount of preferred stock and common equity. If we let BP_{Debt} represent the total financing

break point (BP) The rupee value of new capital that can be raised before an increase in the firm's weighted average cost of capital occurs.

at this break point for debt, then we know that 45 percent of BP_{Debt} will be debt, so

$$0.45\ (BP_{Debt}) = ₹54 \text{ million}$$

Solving for BP_{Debt}, we have

$$BP_{debt} = \frac{\text{Maximum amount of 10\% debt}}{\text{Proportion of debt}}$$

$$= \frac{₹45 \text{ million}}{0.45} = ₹120 \text{ million}$$

As you can see, in this case, there will be another break in the MCC schedule after Bharath has raised a total of ₹120 million, and this second break will result from an increase in the cost of debt. The higher after-tax cost of debt (r_{dT2} = 11.85%(1 − 0.4) = 7.1% versus r_{dT1} = 10%(1 − 0.4) = 6.0%) will result in a higher WACC. For example, if Bharath raises ₹130 million to fund new capital budgeting projects, the amount of each source of capital that must be issued is:

Capital Source	Weight, w	Amount (₹ in Millions)	Component Cost, r
Debt	0.45	₹ 58.50	7.1%
Preferred stock	0.05	6.50	11.0
Common equity	0.50	65.00	14.5
	1.00	₹130.00	

TABLE 11.1 WACC and Break Points

I. Break Points

1. $BP_{retained\ earnings}$ = ₹30,500,000/0.50 = ₹61,000,000
2. BP_{debt} = ₹54,000,000/0.45 = ₹120,000,000

II. Weighted Average Cost of Capital (WACC)

1. If the firm's new capital needs range from ₹1 to ₹61,000,000

Capital Source	Breakdown of Funds if ₹61,000,000 Is Raised	Weight of Capital	×	After-Tax Component Cost	=	WACC
Debt, r_{dT1}	₹27,450,000	0.45	×	6.0%	=	2.70%
Preferred stock, r_{ps}	3,050,000	0.05	×	11.0	=	0.55
Common equity, r_s	30,500,000	0.50	×	13.5	=	6.75
	₹61,000,000	1.00				10.00% = $WACC_1$

2. If the firm's new capital needs range from ₹61,000,001 to ₹120,000,000

Capital Source	Breakdown of Funds if ₹120,000,000 Is Raised	Weight of Capital	×	After-Tax Component Cost	=	WACC
Debt, r_{dT1}	₹ 54,000,000	0.45	×	6.0%	=	2.70%
Preferred stock, r_{ps}	6,000,000	0.05	×	11.0	=	0.55
Common equity, r_e	60,000,000	0.50	×	14.5	=	7.25
	₹120,000,000	1.00				10.50% = $WACC_2$

3. If the firm's new capital needs are greater than ₹120,000,000

Capital Source	Breakdown of Funds if ₹130,000,000 Is Raised	Weight of Capital	×	After-Tax Component Cost	=	WACC
Debt, r_{dT2}	₹ 58,500,000	0.45	×	7.1%	=	3.20%
Preferred stock, r_{ps}	6,500,000	0.05	×	11.0	=	0.55
Common equity, r_e	65,000,000	0.50	×	14.5	=	7.25
	₹130,000,000	1.00				11.00% = $WACC_3$

NOTE: Each boxed number indicates which component cost differs from the WACC that is computed in the previous range. For example, if the amount of funds that Bharath needs to raise is from ₹61,000,001 to ₹120,000,000, new common equity must be issued, and thus equity will have a cost, r_e, equal to 14.5 percent, which is greater than the cost of equity if the firm needs funds equal to ₹61,000,000 or less (r_s = 13.5%). Remember that the break point associated with retained earnings is ₹61,000,000; so at this point the amount of retained earnings is "used up."

For this situation, the computation for the weighted average cost of capital (WACC) is:

$$WACC = 0.45(7.1\%) + 0.05(11.0\%) + 0.50(14.5\%) = 11.0\%$$

In other words, the next rupee beyond ₹120 million will consist of ₹0.45 of 11.85 percent debt (7.1 percent after taxes), ₹0.05 of 11 percent preferred stock, and ₹0.50 of new common stock at a cost of 14.5 percent (retained earnings were used up much earlier), and this marginal rupee will have a cost of $WACC_3 = 11\%$.

The effect of this second WACC increase is shown in Figure 11.3. Now there are two break points, one caused by using up all the retained earnings and the other caused by using up all the 6 percent debt (after-tax cost). With the two breaks, there are three different WACCs: $WACC_1 = 10.0\%$ for the first ₹61 million of new capital; $WACC_2 = 10.5\%$ in the interval between ₹61 million and ₹120 million; and $WACC_3 = 11.0\%$ for all new capital beyond ₹120 million.

There could, of course, still be more break points; they would occur if the cost of debt continued to increase with more debt, if the cost of preferred stock increased at some level(s), or if the cost of common equity rose as more new common stock was sold.[8] In general, a break point will occur whenever the cost of one (or more) of the capital components increases, and thus a break point can be determined by applying Equation 11.9:

11.9

$$\text{Break point} = \frac{\left(\begin{array}{c}\text{Maximum amount of lower cost}\\ \text{of capital of a given type}\end{array}\right)}{\begin{array}{c}\text{Proportion of the type of capital}\\ \text{in the capital structure}\end{array}}$$

As you can imagine, numerous break points are possible. At the extreme, an MCC schedule might have so many break points that it rises almost continuously beyond some given level of new financing.

The easiest sequence for calculating MCC schedules is as follows:

1. Use Equation 11.9 to determine each point at which a break occurs. A break will occur any time the cost of one of the capital components rises. (It is possible, however, that two capital components could increase at the same point.) After determining the exact break points, make a list of them.
2. Determine the cost of capital for each component in the intervals between breaks.
3. Calculate the weighted averages of these component costs to obtain the WACCs in each interval, as we did in Table 11.1. The WACC is constant within each interval, but it rises at each break point.

FIGURE 11.3 Marginal Cost of Capital (MCC) Schedule for Bharath Textiles Using Retained Earnings, New Common Stock, and Higher-Cost Debt

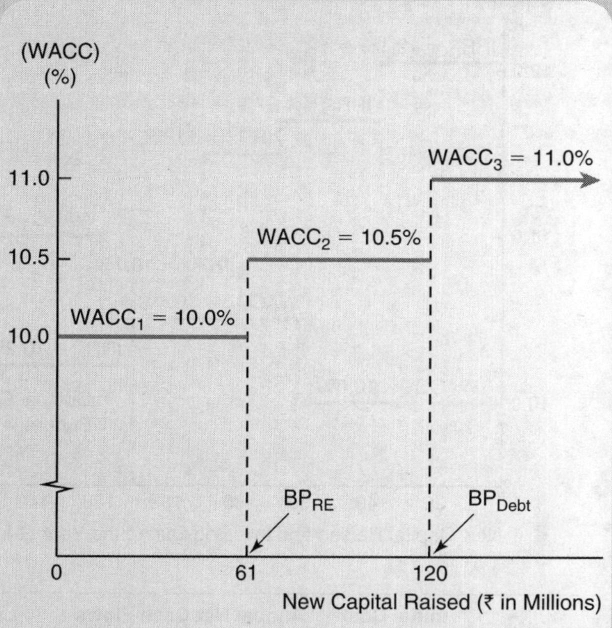

Notice that if there are n separate breaks, there will be n+1 different WACCs. For example, in Figure 11.3 we see two breaks and three different WACCs. We should note again that a different MCC schedule will result if a different capital structure—that is, proportions of debt and equity—is used.

11-3 Combining the MCC and Investment Opportunity Schedules (IOS)

Now that we have calculated the MCC schedule, we can use it to develop a discount rate for use in the capital budgeting process—that is, *we can use the*

[8]The first break point is not necessarily the point at which retained earnings are used up; it is possible for low-cost debt to be exhausted *before* retained earnings have been used up. For example, if Bharath had available only ₹22.5 million of 10 percent debt, BP_{Debt} would occur at ₹50 million:

$$BP_{Debt} = \frac{₹22.5 \text{ million}}{0.45} = ₹50 \text{ million}$$

Thus, the break point for debt would occur before the break point for retained earnings, which occurs at ₹61 million.

FIGURE 11.4 Combining the MCC and IOS Schedules to Determine the Optimal Capital Budget

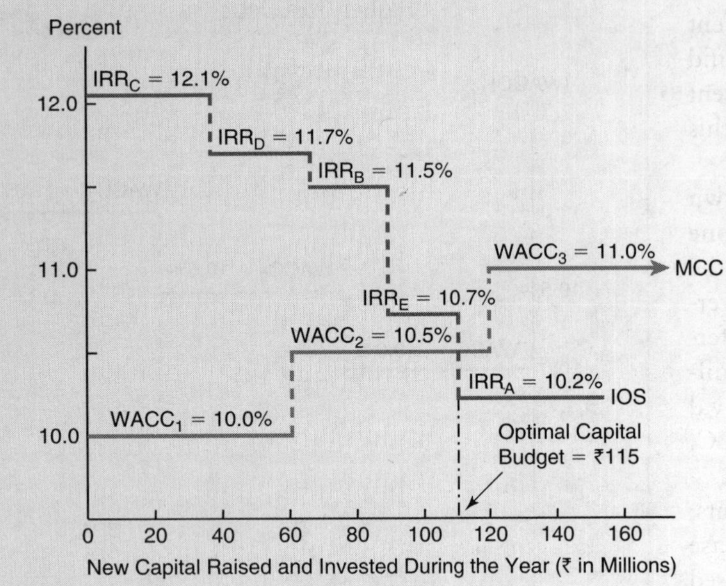

Project	Initial Cost (₹ in Millions)	Annual Net Cash Flows (₹ in Millions)	Life (years)	IRR (%)
A	39	9	6	10.2
B	25	6	6	11.5
C	36	10	5	12.1
D	29	7	6	11.7
E	25	8	4	10.7

MCC schedule to find the appropriate cost of capital for determining projects' net present values (NPVs) as discussed in Chapter 9.

To understand how the MCC schedule is used in capital budgeting, assume that Bharath Textiles has three financial executives: a financial vice president (VP), a treasurer, and a director of capital budgeting (DCB). The financial VP asks the treasurer to develop the firm's MCC schedule, and the treasurer produces the schedule shown in Figure 11.3. At the same time, the financial VP asks the DCB to draw up a list of all projects that are potentially acceptable. The list shows each project's cost, projected annual net cash inflows, life, and internal rate of return (IRR). These data are presented at the bottom of Figure 11.4. For example, Project A has a cost of ₹39 million, it is expected to produce inflows of ₹9 million per year for six years, and, therefore, it has an IRR of 10.2 percent. Similarly, Project C has a cost of ₹36 million, it is expected to produce inflows of ₹10 million per year for five years, and thus it has an IRR of 12.1 percent. (NPVs cannot be shown yet because we do not know the appropriate marginal cost of capital.) For simplicity, we assume now that all projects are independent as opposed to mutually exclusive, that they are equally risky, and that their risks are all equal to those of the firm's average existing assets.

investment opportunity schedule (IOS) A graph of the firm's investment opportunities ranked in order of the projects' internal rates of return.

The DCB then plots the IRR data shown at the bottom of Figure 11.4 as the **investment opportunity schedule (IOS)** shown in the graph. The IOS schedule shows, in rank order, how much money Bharath can invest at different rates of return (IRRs). Figure 11.4 also shows Bharath's MCC schedule as it was developed by the treasurer and plotted in Figure 11.3. Now consider Project C: Its IRR is 12.1 percent, and it can be financed with capital that costs only 10.0 percent. Consequently, it should be accepted. Recall from Chapter 9 that if a project's IRR exceeds its cost of capital, its NPV will be positive; therefore, Project C must also be acceptable by the NPV criterion. Projects B, D, and E can be analyzed similarly. They are all acceptable because IRR > MCC = WACC, and hence NPV > 0. Project A, on the other hand, should be rejected because $IRR_A < MCC$; hence, $NPV_A < 0$.

People sometimes ask this question: "If we took Project A first, it would be acceptable because its 10.2 percent return would exceed the 10.0 percent cost of money used to finance it. Why couldn't we do this?" The answer is that we are seeking, in effect, to maximize the excess of *returns over costs,* or the area that is above the WACC but below the IOS. We accomplish this by graphing (and accepting) the most profitable projects first.

Another question that often arises is this: What would happen if the MCC cut through one of the projects? For example, suppose the second break point in the MCC schedule had occurred at ₹100 million rather than at ₹120 million, causing the MCC schedule to cut through Project E. Should we then accept Project E? If Project E could be accepted in part, we would purchase only the portion that caused the total capital budget to equal ₹100 million, which means we would purchase only ₹10 million of Project E.

The preceding analysis as summarized in Figure 11.4 reveals a very important point: *The cost of capital used in the capital budgeting process, as discussed in Chapters 9 and 10, actually is determined at the intersection of the IOS and MCC schedules. If the cost of capital at the intersection ($WACC_2$ = 10.5% in Figure 11.4) is used, then the firm will make correct accept/reject decisions, and its level of financing and investment will be optimal. If it uses any other rate, its capital budget will not be optimal.*

The WACC intersection as determined in Figure 11.4 should be used to find the NPVs of new projects that are about as risky as the firm's existing assets, but this cost of capital should be adjusted up or down to find NPVs for projects with higher or lower risk than the average project. This point was discussed in Chapter 10 in connection with the Home Energy Products appliance-control computer example.

Timurpix/Shutterstock

11-4 WACC versus Required Rate of Return of Investors

We introduced the concept of risk and rates of return in Chapter 8, where we discovered that investors demand higher rates of return to compensate them for taking higher levels of risk. In Chapters 6 and 7, we discovered that, everything else equal, an asset's value is inversely related to the rate of return investors require to invest in it. The following equation, with which you should be familiar by now, shows this relationship:

$$\text{Value} = \frac{\widehat{CF}_1}{(1+r)^1} + \frac{\widehat{CF}_2}{(1+r)^2} + \cdots + \frac{\widehat{CF}_n}{(1+r)^n} = \sum_{t=1}^{n} \frac{\widehat{CF}_t}{(1+r)^t}$$

This equation shows that the value of any asset—real or financial—is based on (1) the cash flows that the asset is expected to generate during its life, $\widehat{CF}_t$; and (2) the rate of return that investors require to "put up" their money to purchase the investment (asset), r. As a result, we know that investors purchase a firm's stocks and bonds—and thus provide funds to the firm—only if they expect to receive a return that sufficiently compensates them for the risk associated with those stocks and bonds. Consequently, *the investors who purchase a firm's stocks and bonds determine the rates of return, or costs, that the firm must pay to raise funds to invest in capital budgeting projects.*

In Chapters 6 and 7, we discussed valuation from the standpoint of investors. For example, we described r_s as the required rate of return of investors—that is, the rate of return investors demand to purchase the firm's common stock and thus provide funds to the firm. In this chapter, we described r_s as the cost of internal common equity, which represents the return that the firm must earn to satisfy investors' demands when it retains earnings for reinvestment in assets. Which description is correct? They both are. This point can be illustrated with a simple analogy. Assume that Randy borrows money from his credit union to invest in common stocks. The loan agreement requires Randy to repay the amount borrowed plus 10 percent interest at the end of one year. The 10 percent interest rate represents both Randy's cost of borrowing—that is, cost of debt—and his required rate of return (assuming that this is his only debt). If he does not invest the borrowed funds in stocks that earn at least a 10 percent return—that is, have internal rates of return (IRRs) greater than 10 percent—then Randy will lose wealth because he has to pay the credit union 10 percent interest to use the money. The

10 percent interest rate also represents the return the credit union demands to lend money to Randy based on his credit risk; that is, 10 percent is the credit union's required rate of return. Although the situation is much more complex, this same relationship exists for firms that use funds provided by investors. Investors are similar to the credit union in the sense that they provide funds to the firms, whereas firms are similar to Randy in the sense that they use the funds provided by investors and must pay a return that is sufficient to raise (attract) such funds. Moreover, just as the credit union determines the interest rate that Randy must pay for his loan, investors determine the rates that firms must pay to use their funds.

As mentioned in Chapters 6–8, our discussions were presented primarily from the perspective of investors, whereas in this chapter we used the information introduced in these earlier chapters to explain the concept of cost of capital, which was discussed from the perspective of the firm. You should have noticed that the general concepts presented in this chapter are the same as the general concepts presented in Chapters 6–8; that is, determination of required rates of return and of their impact on value. In reality, all of these chapters present the same relationships from two perspectives: the investor's (Chapters 6–8) and the firm's (this chapter). In other words, the rates of return, or component costs of capital, discussed in this

TABLE 11.2 WACC versus Investors' Required Rates of Return

Investor's Required Rate of Return = Firm's Cost of Capital

$$\text{Investor's required rate of return} = r = r_{RF} + \left[\text{Risk premium}\right] = r_d,\ r_{ps},\ \text{or}\ r_s = \text{Firm's component cost of capita}$$

Financial Asset	Financial Asset's Market Value	Return to Investors	Cost to Firms
Debt, r_d	$P_0 = \frac{INT}{(1+YTM)^1} + \cdots + \frac{INT + M}{(1+YTM)^N}$	$YTM = r_d =$ Return investors require to purchase the firm's debt	$r_d = YTM =$ Before-tax cost of debt $r_{dT} = r_d(1-T) =$ After-tax cost of debt
Preferred stock, r_{ps}	$P_0 = \frac{D_{Ps}}{r_{Ps}}$	$r_{Ps} = \frac{D_{Ps}}{P_0} =$ Return investors require to purchase the firm's preferred stock	$r_{Ps} = \frac{D_{Ps}}{P_0(1+F)}$ Cost of preferred stock
Common equity, r_s (internal) or r_e (external)	$P_0 = \frac{\hat{D}_1}{r_s - g}$; (constant growth firm)	$r_s = \frac{\hat{D}_1}{P_0} + g =$ Return investors require to purchase the firm's common stock	$r_s = \frac{\hat{D}_1}{P_0} + g =$ Cost of retained earnings (internal) $r_e = \frac{\hat{D}_1}{P_0(1+F)} + g =$ Cost of new common equity (external)

Variable Definitions:

r_{RF} = nominal risk-free rate of return
P_0 = market value of financial asset
INT = rupee interest payment
M = maturity (face) value of a bond
N = number of remaining interest payments
YTM = yield to maturity = r_d
g = constant growth rate of the firm
T = firm's marginal tax rate
D_{ps} = preferred stock dividend
$\hat{D}$ = next period's dividend
F = cost of issuing new stock (in decimal form)

chapter are the same rates that were introduced in Chapters 6–8. For this reason, we thought it might be a good idea to summarize these rates here. Table 11.2 shows the rates of return discussed in Chapters 6–8 and compares them to the component costs of capital discussed in this chapter. Note that the equations shown in the column labeled "Return to Investors" are the same as those shown in the column labeled "Cost to Firms," except for adjustments for taxes and flotation costs.

KEY COST OF CAPITAL CONCEPTS

To conclude this chapter, we summarize some cost of capital concepts (rules) that were discussed.

- To make appropriate capital budgeting decisions, the firm must know its required rate of return, which is defined as the average rate of return that the firm pays to attract investors' funds. Because the firm pays the average rate of return to investors, the firm's required rate of return is also referred to as its cost of capital.
- To determine its required rate of return, the firm must compute the cost of each source of funds or capital that investors provide; that is, the firm must compute the cost of debt, the cost of preferred stock, the cost of retained earnings, and the cost of new common equity. These costs are then combined by weighting each component by the proportion or weight that it contributes to the total capital of the firm. The result is the weighted average cost of capital, or WACC, which is the required rate of return that the firm should use when making capital budgeting decisions.
- Investors who participate in the financial markets determine firms' WACCs. Investors only provide funds to firms if they expect to earn sufficient returns on their investments; thus, firms must pay investors' demands (required returns) to attract funds.
- When investing in capital budgeting projects, a firm should follow the economics principle that asserts products should continue to be manufactured until marginal costs equal marginal revenues. That is, the firm should invest until the marginal cost of capital (marginal costs) equals the internal rate of return on the last project that is purchased (marginal revenues).

MULTIPLE CHOICE QUESTIONS

1. Cost of debt is

a. Interest percentage payable to the bank

b. Yield to maturity of a bond issue

c. Estimated amount based upon market yield

d. Post-tax cost of servicing debt

2. The cost of debt in relation to the cost of equity

a. Will be higher

b. Can be the same

c. Will always be lower

d. Depends upon the capital structure

3. In a company financed 100% with equity,

a. Cost of debt can be taken as 0%

b. Cost of debt should be estimated

c. Cost of debt will be between the cost of equity and the cost of preference shares

d. None of the above

4. In the Gordon model for calculating the cost of equity,

a. Growth rate has to be constant for all the time to come

b. There need not be a growth rate

c. There can be negative growth rate

d. None of the above

5. In the CAPM approach for calculating the cost of equity,

a. Beta is estimated

b. Beta remains constant for five years

c. There is no need for beta

d. Beta is always taken as one

6. The bond yield plus risk premium approach to calculate cost of equity assumes

a. There will be debt in the structure

b. Substantial portion of the structure is debt financed

c. Risk premium can be estimated

d. None of the above

7. The WACC calculated by book weights

a. Will be lower than the WACC calculated by market weights

b. Will be greater than the WACC calculated by market weights

c. Will be less than the WACC calculated by target weights

d. None of these

8. In calculating the WACC,

a. All component costs can be taken to have equal weights

b. Component costs will have weights based on structure

c. Component weights are taken from the industry

d. None of the above

9. In a company, the cost of equity will be

a. Less than the WACC calculated by market weights

b. Greater than the WACC calculated by target weights

c. Greater than the cost of debt

d. We need figures to determine this

10. Cost of preference shares will be

a. Greater than the cost of equity

b. Less than the cost of debt

c. In between the cost of debt and the cost of equity

d. Cannot be determined without figures

Answers:

1.	(d)	2.	(c)	3.	(a)	4.	(a)	5.	(a)
6.	(c)	7.	(d)	8.	(b)	9.	(c)	10.	(c)

PROBLEMS

For more problems, login to CourseMate for CFIN at CengageBrain.com

11-1 Gwalior Products plans to issue long-term bonds to raise funds to finance its growth. The company has existing bonds outstanding that are similar to the new bonds it expects to issue. The existing bonds have a face value equal to ₹1,000, mature in 10 years, pay ₹60 interest annually, and are currently selling for ₹1,077 each. Gwalior's marginal tax rate is 40 percent. (a) What should be the coupon rate on the new bond issue? (a) What is Gwalior's after-tax cost of debt?

11-2 Natwarlal Nothings plans to issue new bonds with the same yield as its existing bonds. The existing bonds have a coupon rate of interest equal to 5.6 percent (semiannual interest payments), 12 years remaining until maturity, and a ₹1,000 maturity value; they are currently selling for ₹918 each. (a) If Natwarlal issues new bonds today, what will be its before-tax cost of debt? (b) What will be its before-tax cost of debt if the price of its existing bonds is ₹730 when Natwarlal issues the new bonds?

11-3 Bansilal Cruises plans to issue preferred stock with a ₹120 par value and a 5 percent dividend. Even though the current market value of its preferred stock is ₹80 per share, Bansilal expects to net only ₹75 for each share issued. What is its cost of issuing preferred stock? The firm's marginal tax rate is 34 percent.

11-4 Jagarthy Juice's preferred stock pays a constant dividend equal to ₹4.75 per share. The firm's marginal tax rate is 40 percent. Jagarthy Juice incurs a 5 percent flotation cost each time it issues preferred stock. (a) If the firm issues 10,000 shares of preferred stock at ₹50 per share, how much of the total value of the issue will the firm be able to use (receive)? (b) What is Jagarthy Juice's cost of preferred stock?

11-5 Suppose the current risk-free rate of return is 3.5 percent and the expected market return is 9 percent. Falthu Faux-Pas' common stock has a beta coefficient equal to 1.4. Using the CAPM approach, compute the firm's cost of retained earnings.

11-6 Suppose the current risk-free rate of return is 5 percent and the expected market *risk premium* is 7 percent. Using this information, estimate the cost of retained earnings for a company with a beta coefficient equal to 2.0?

11-7 Ekdotheen Engines is trying to estimate its cost of retained earnings. The company has outstanding bonds that pay ₹20 interest every six months. The bonds, which have a ₹1,000 face value and mature in six years, are currently selling for ₹900. Estimate Ekdotheen's cost of retained earnings using the bond-plus-risk-premium approach.

11-8 Thare Thare Hats (TTH) is expected to grow at a 4 percent rate for as long as it is in business. Currently the company's common stock is selling for ₹34 per share. The most recent dividend paid by TTH was ₹4.25 per share. If new common stock is issued, TTH will incur flotation costs equal to 8.5 percent. (a) What is the company's cost of retained earnings? (b) What is its cost of new common equity?

11-9 Chachi's Eatery's common stock, which is currently selling for ₹50 per share, has a beta coefficient equal to 0.75. Chachi's has paid a dividend equal to ₹6 per share since it has been in business, and expectations are that the same dividend will be paid forever. Chachi's investment banker charges 7 percent when new common stock is issued. What is Chachi's (a) cost of retained earnings and (b) cost of new common equity?

11-10 Hari Balloons is expected to grow at 5 percent forever. Its common stock is currently selling for ₹28 per share, and the most recent dividend paid to common stockholders was ₹2.40 per share. If Hari's cost of new common equity is 15 percent, what is the flotation cost charged by its investment banker?

11-11 Bhavani Gold's common stock currently sells for ₹32 per share. Bhavani's investment banker charges 6.5 percent flotation costs when new common stock is issued. The company expects to pay a ₹3.36 per share dividend at the *end of the year*. If Bhavani's cost of retained earnings is 15.5 percent, what is its cost of new common equity?

11-12 Tej Tours is considering an expansion of its operations, which will require the company to issue new debt and equity. Tej's investment banker provided the following information about the cost of issuing new debt:

Amount of Debt Issued	Yield to Maturity, r_d
₹1 – ₹450,000	4.5%
450,001 – 750,000	5.8
Over 750,000	6.5

If Tej's capital structure consists of 60 percent debt, what WACC break points are associated with issuing new debt?

11-13 Wanamnagar Transportation's capital structure consists of 30 percent debt and 70 percent common equity. According to its investment banker, Wanamnagar can issue up to ₹240,000 new debt at a 3.8 percent cost; for any amount of new debt greater than ₹240,000, the cost is 5.5 percent. Wanamnagar expects to generate ₹560,000 in retained earnings this year. Compute the WACC break point(s) associated with raising new funds.

11-14 Damodar Walls Construction (DWC) has determined that the yield to maturity (YTM) on new bonds is 5 percent, its cost of retained earnings is 8 percent, and its cost of new common stock is 11 percent. If DWC's capital structure consists of 40 percent debt and 60 percent common equity, what is its weighted average cost of capital (WACC) if it (a) does not have to issue new stock to raise additional funds and (b) must issue new stock to raise additional funds? DWC's marginal tax rate is 35 percent.

11-15 Karamchand Burgers' capital structure consists of 20 percent debt, 30 percent preferred stock, and 50 percent common stock. If Karamchand raises new capital, its *after-tax* cost of debt will be 3.5 percent, its cost of preferred stock will be 6 percent, its costs of retained earnings will be 10.2 percent, and its cost of new common equity will be 12.4 percent. If Karamchand needs to raise ₹220,000 and it expects to generate ₹100,000 in retained earnings this year, what is its marginal cost of capital to raise the needed funds?

11-16 Falooda Coiffures (FC) needs to raise ₹850,000 to purchase a new machine. FC knows its component costs of capital are r_d = 5%, r_{ps} = 7%, r_s = 11%, and r_e = 13%. FC maintains a capital structure that consists of 60 percent debt, 10 percent preferred stock, and 30 percent common equity. The firm's marginal tax rate is 30 percent. If FC expects to generate ₹260,000 in retained earnings this year, what marginal cost of capital will it incur to raise the needed funds?

11-17 The CFO of Latha Loungers is evaluating the following independent, indivisible projects (₹ in 000s):

Project	Cost	IRR
A	₹10,000	21.0%
B	15,000	20.0
C	25,000	16.0

Latha's weighted average cost of capital (WACC) is 14 percent if the firm does *not* have to issue new common equity; if new common equity is needed, its WACC is 17 percent. Latha's capital structure consists of 40 percent debt. If Latha has no preferred stock and expects to generate ₹24,000 in retained earnings this year, which project(s) should be purchased?

11-18 Over-the-Top Canopies (OTC) is evaluating two independent investments. Project S costs ₹150,000 and has an IRR equal to 12 percent, and Project L costs ₹140,000 and has an IRR equal to 10 percent. OTC's capital structure consists of 20 percent debt and 80 percent common equity, and its component costs of capital are r_{dT} = 4%, r_s = 10%, and r_e = 12.5%. If OTC expects to generate ₹230,000 in retained earnings this year, which project(s) should be purchased?

11-19 Peter Piper's Pies (P^3) is evaluating four independent investments. The cost of each project is ₹214,000. The internal rates of return (IRRs) for the projects are IRR_1 = 19%, IRR_2 = 15%, IRR_3 = 18%, and IRR_4 = 14%. P^3's investment banker has provided the following WACC table:

Total Amount Raised	WACC
₹1–₹520,000	11.0%
520,001– 745,000	12.5
Over 745,000	15.2

Which project(s) should P^3 purchase?

11-20 Tri-Q Supply Company is considering an expansion project to increase sales. The project, which costs ₹2.6 million, has an IRR equal to 9.2 percent. Any portion of the project can be purchased. Tri-Q expects to retain ₹1.3 million of earnings this year. It can raise up to ₹420,000 in new debt with a before-tax cost equal to 5 percent; any additional debt will cost 7 percent before taxes. Tri-Q's cost of retained earnings is 12 percent, and its cost of new common equity is 14 percent. Its target capital structure consists of 35 percent debt and 65 percent common equity. If Tri-Q's marginal tax rate is 40 percent, what is the optimal capital budget?

The Cost of Capital

Learning Outcomes

LO.1 Compute the component cost of capital for (a) debt, (b) preferred stock, (c) retained earnings, and (d) new common equity.

- The before-tax cost of debt, r_d, equals a bond's yield to maturity (YTM), which is determined by computing the rate of return that equates the present value of the bond's future cash flows with its current selling price. The after-tax cost of debt is $r_{dT} = r_d(1 - \text{Tax rate})$.
- The cost of preferred stock is computed as: $r_{ps} = D_{ps}/[P_0(1 - F)]$, where D_{ps} is the preferred dividend, P_0 is the current selling price of the preferred stock, and F is the percentage cost of issuing preferred stock stated as a decimal.
- The earnings retained by the firm has an opportunity cost to the firm, because common stockholders will demand that earnings be paid out as dividends if the firm cannot reinvest those earnings in assets that generate returns that at least compensate investors who provide funds in the form of common stock. The cost of retained earnings, r_s, can be computed using one of the following methods:
  - o $r_s = \hat{D}_1/P_0 + g$, where $\hat{D}_1$ is the dividend that is expected to be paid at the end of the year, P_0 is the current selling price of the common stock, and g is the *constant* rate at which the firm will continue to grow long into the future.
  - o $r_s = r_{RF} + (r_M - r_{RF})\beta_s$, where r_{RF} is the nominal risk-free rate of return, r_M is the return on the market, and β_s is the stock's beta coefficient.
  - o $r_s = r_d + (\text{Risk premium})$, where r_d is the before-tax cost of debt and (Risk premium) is a 3 to 5 percent premium that is added for the additional risk that is associated with common stock compared to debt.
- The cost of new common equity is computed as: $r_e = \hat{D}_1/[P_0(1 - F)] + g$, where the variables are as defined earlier. The cost of new common equity is greater than the cost of retained earnings because the firm incurs flotation (issuing) costs when new equity is issued.

LO.2 Describe the weighted average cost of capital (WACC) and discuss the logic of using WACC to make informed financial decisions.

- The weighted average cost of capital (WACC) represents the average cost of each rupee of financing, regardless of its source. The WACC is determined by first multiplying each component cost of capital by the proportion, or weight, that the source contributes to the firm's total capital, and then summing the results. The WACC is the firm's required rate of return.

LO.3 Describe how the marginal cost of capital (MCC) is used to make capital budgeting decisions.

- Because the MCC is the firm's required rate of return, it represents the minimum rate a capital budgeting project must generate to be considered an acceptable investment. In other words, a project is acceptable if $(MCC = r) > IRR$.

LO.4 Discuss the relationship between the firm's weighted average cost of capital (WACC) and investors' required rate of return.

- Because investors provide the funds that finance a firm's investments (assets), its WACC is essentially determined by the required rates of return that investors demand to purchase the firm's securities (debt, preferred stock, and common equity). That is, WACC = investors' required rate of return = r.

CHAPTER 11 REVIEW

Chapter 11 Key Cost of Capital Concepts

- To make appropriate capital budgeting decisions, the firm must know its required rate of return, which is defined as the average rate of return that the firm pays to attract investors' funds. Because the firm pays this average rate of return to investors, the firm's required rate of return is also referred to as its cost of capital.
- To determine its required rate of return, the firm must compute the cost of each source of funds or capital that investors provide—that is, the firm must compute the cost of debt, the cost of preferred stock, the cost of retained earnings, and the cost of new common equity. These costs are then combined by weighting each component by the proportion or weight that it contributes to the total capital of the firm. The result is the weighted average cost of capital, or WACC, which is the required rate of return, r, that the firm should use when making capital budgeting decisions.
- Investors who participate in the financial markets determine firms' WACCs. Investors only provide funds to firms if they expect to earn sufficient returns on their investments; thus, firms must pay investors' demands to attract funds.
- When investing in capital budgeting projects, a firm should follow the economics principle that asserts products should continue to be manufactured until marginal costs equal marginal revenues. That is, the firm should invest until the marginal cost of capital (marginal costs) equals the internal rate of return on the last project that is purchased (marginal revenues).

Key Terms

required rate of return The return that must be earned on invested funds to cover the cost of financing such investments; also called the *opportunity cost rate*. *p. 186*

cost of capital The firm's average cost of funds, which is the average return required by the firm's investors—what must be paid to attract funds. *p. 186*

LO.1

capital components The particular types of capital used by the firm—that is, its debt, preferred stock, and common equity. *p. 186*

after-tax cost of debt, r_{dT} The relevant cost of new debt, taking into account the tax deductibility of interest. *p. 186*

cost of preferred stock, r_{ps} The rate of return investors require on the firm's preferred stock. r_{ps} is calculated as the preferred dividend, D_{ps}, divided by the preferred stock's net issuing price, NP. *p. 187*

cost of retained earnings, r_s The rate of return required by stockholders on a firm's existing common stock. *p. 188*

cost of new common equity, r_e The cost of external equity; based on the cost of retained earnings, but increased for flotation costs. *p. 190*

flotation costs The expenses incurred when selling new issues of securities. *p. 190*

LO.2

target (optimal) capital structure The combination (percentages) of debt, preferred stock, and common equity that will maximize the price of the firm's stock. *p. 192*

weighted average cost of capital (WACC) A weighted average of the component costs of debt, preferred stock, and common equity. *p. 192*

marginal cost of capital (MCC) The cost of obtaining another rupee of new capital; the weighted average cost of the last rupee of new capital raised. *p. 193*

MCC (marginal cost of capital) schedule A graph that relates the firm's weighted average cost of each rupee of capital to the total amount of new capital raised. *p. 193*

break point (BP) The rupee value of new capital that can be raised before an increase in the firm's weighted average cost of capital occurs. *p. 195*

LO.3

investment opportunity schedule (IOS) A graph of the firm's investment opportunities ranked in order of the projects' internal rates of return. *p. 198*

CHAPTER 12

Capital Structure

Learning Outcomes

LO.1 Describe how business risk and financial risk can affect a firm's capital structure.

LO.2 Describe how businesses determine their optimal capital structures.

LO.3 Describe how leverage can be used to make capital structure decisions, and discuss the effects (a) operating leverage, (b) financial leverage, and (c) total leverage have on risks associated with a firm.

LO.4 Discuss how managers consider liquidity when determining the optimal capital structure for a firm.

LO.5 Discuss the two general theories—(a) trade-off theory and (b) signaling theory—that have been developed to explain what firms' capital structures should be and why firms' capital structures differ.

LO.6 Describe how and why capital structures vary among firms in the United States and around the world.

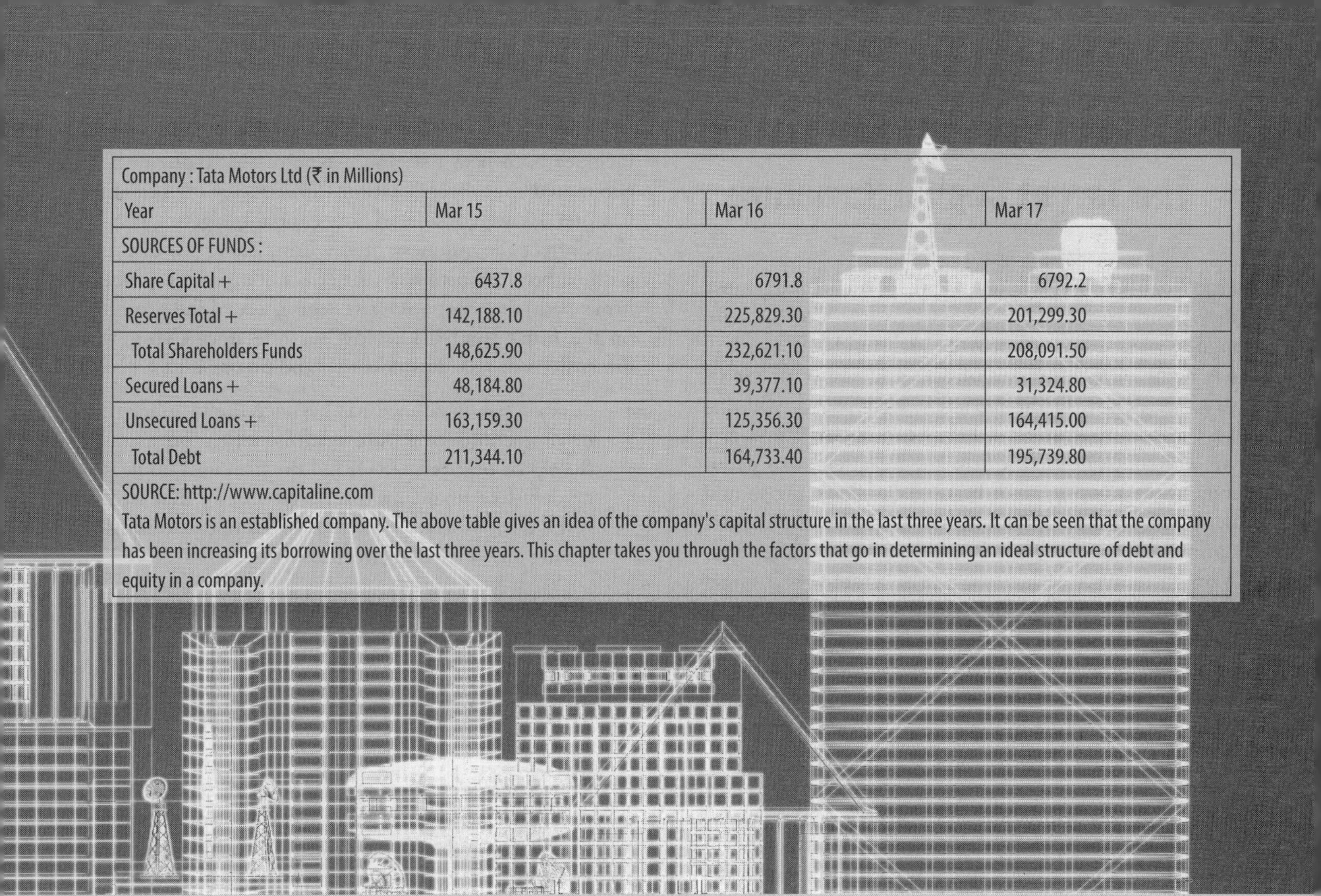

Company : Tata Motors Ltd (₹ in Millions)			
Year	Mar 15	Mar 16	Mar 17
SOURCES OF FUNDS :			
Share Capital +	6437.8	6791.8	6792.2
Reserves Total +	142,188.10	225,829.30	201,299.30
Total Shareholders Funds	148,625.90	232,621.10	208,091.50
Secured Loans +	48,184.80	39,377.10	31,324.80
Unsecured Loans +	163,159.30	125,356.30	164,415.00
Total Debt	211,344.10	164,733.40	195,739.80

SOURCE: http://www.capitaline.com

Tata Motors is an established company. The above table gives an idea of the company's capital structure in the last three years. It can be seen that the company has been increasing its borrowing over the last three years. This chapter takes you through the factors that go in determining an ideal structure of debt and equity in a company.

In Chapter 11, when we calculated the weighted average cost of capital (WACC) for use in capital budgeting, we took the capital structure *weights*, or the mix of securities a firm uses to finance its assets, as a given. However, if the weights are changed, the calculated cost of capital, and thus the set of acceptable capital budgeting projects, will also change. Further, changing the capital structure will affect the riskiness inherent in the firm's common stock, and this will affect both the return demanded by stockholders, r_s, and the stock's price, P_0. Therefore, the choice of a capital structure is an important decision.

Study Tools

Problems are found at the end of this chapter

\+

Login to **CourseMate** for **CFIN** at **CengageBrain.com** for additional problems and other study tools!

Andresr/Shutterstock.com

12-1 The Target Capital Structure

Firms can choose whatever mix of debt and equity they desire to finance their assets, subject to the willingness of investors to provide such funds. As we shall see, many different mixes of debt and equity, or **capital structures**, exist. In the next few sections, we will discuss factors that affect a firm's capital structure, and we will conclude that a firm should attempt to determine what its optimal, or best, mix of financing should be. It will become apparent that determining the exact optimal capital structure is not a science, so after analyzing a number of factors, a firm establishes a **target capital structure** that it believes is optimal and that it uses as guidance for raising funds in the future. This target might change over time as conditions vary, but at any given moment, the firm's management has a specific capital structure in mind, and individual financing decisions should be consistent with this target. If the actual proportion of debt is below the target level, new funds probably will be raised by issuing debt, whereas if the proportion of debt is above the target, stock probably will be sold to bring the firm back in line with the target ratio.

Capital structure policy involves a trade-off between risk and return. Using more debt raises the riskiness of the firm's earnings stream, but a higher proportion of debt generally leads to a higher expected rate of return. From the concepts we discussed in previous chapters, we know that the higher risk associated with greater debt tends to lower the firm's stock price. At the same time, however, the higher expected rate of return makes the stock more attractive to investors, which, in turn, ultimately increases the stock's price. Therefore, *the optimal capital structure is the one that strikes a balance between risk and return to achieve the ultimate goal of maximizing the price of the firm's stock.*

When we examined risk in Chapter 8, we distinguished between *market risk,* which is measured by the firm's beta coefficient, and *total risk,* which includes both beta risk and a type of risk that can be eliminated by diversification *(firm-specific risk).* In Chapter 10, we considered how capital budgeting decisions affect the riskiness of the firm. There we distinguished between *beta risk* (the effect of a project on the firm's beta) and *corporate risk* (the effect of the project on the firm's total risk). Now we introduce two new dimensions of risk: business risk and financial risk.

capital structure The combination of debt and equity used to finance a firm.

target capital structure The mix of debt, preferred stock, and common equity with which the firm plans to finance its investments.

business risk The risk associated with the firm's operations, ignoring any financing effects.

financial risk The portion of stockholders' risk, over and above basic business risk, that results from the manner in which the firm is financed.

1. **Business risk** is defined as the uncertainty inherent in projections of future returns, either on assets (ROA) or on equity (ROE), if the firm uses no debt or debt-like financing (preferred stock); that is, it is the risk associated with the firm's operations, ignoring any financing effects.
2. **Financial risk** is defined as the additional risk, over and above basic business risk, placed on common stockholders that results from using financing alternatives with fixed periodic payments, such as debt and preferred stock—that is, it is the risk associated with the types of funds the firm uses to finance its assets.

Conceptually, the firm has a certain amount of risk inherent in its production and sales operations; this is its business risk. When it uses debt, it partitions this risk and concentrates most of it on one class of investors: the common stockholders. This is its financial risk.[1] Both business risk and financial risk affect the capital structure of a firm.

12-1a Business Risk

Business risk is the single most important determinant of capital structure because it is based on the uncertainty that a company's future operations exhibit. Some companies have fairly stable, and thus somewhat predictable, production and sales patterns, whereas the operations of other companies are very unpredictable. It makes sense that firms with more stable operations generally can more easily take on, or handle, the fixed interest payments that are associated with debt, and therefore they use more debt in their capital structures than firms with less stable operations. In other words, everything else the same, firms with more stable operations have lower business risk than firms with less stable operations, and *firms with less business risk can take on more debt* (fixed financial payments) than firms that have greater business risk.

Business risk varies from one industry to another, and also among firms in a given industry. Further, business risk can change over time. Food processors and grocery

[1]Using preferred stock also adds to financial risk. To simplify matters somewhat, in this chapter we shall consider only debt and common equity.

Bogdan Vasilescu/Shutterstock.com

retailers frequently are cited as examples of industries with low business risk, whereas cyclical manufacturing industries, such as steel and construction, are regarded as having especially high business risk. Smaller companies, especially single-product firms, also have relatively high degrees of business risk.[2]

Business risk depends on a number of factors, the more important of which include the following:

1. ***Sales variability (volume and price)***—The more stable (certain) the unit sales (volume) and prices of a firm's products, the lower its business risk, other things constant.
2. ***Input price variability***—A firm with highly uncertain input prices—labor, product costs, and so forth—is exposed to a high degree of business risk.
3. ***Ability to adjust output prices for changes in input prices***—The greater the ability of the firm to adjust selling prices of its products when input costs change, the lower the degree of business risk. This factor is especially important during periods of high inflation.
4. ***The extent to which costs are fixed: operating leverage***—If a high percentage of a firm's operating costs are fixed and hence do not decline when demand falls off, this increases the company's business risk. This factor is called **operating leverage**; this topic will be discussed in detail later in the chapter.

Each of these factors is determined partly by the firm's industry characteristics, but each is also controllable to some extent by management. For example, most firms can, through their marketing policies, take actions to stabilize both unit sales and sales prices. However, this stabilization might require either large expenditures on advertising or price concessions to induce customers to commit to purchasing fixed quantities at fixed prices in the future. Similarly, some firms can reduce the volatility of future input costs by negotiating long-term labor and materials supply contracts. Of course, they might have to agree to pay prices somewhat above the current price to obtain these contracts.

12-1b Financial Risk

We define *financial risk* as the additional risk, over and above basic business risk, that is placed on common stockholders when the firm uses financing alternatives that require fixed periodic payments. Thus, financial risk results from using **financial leverage**, which exists when a firm uses fixed-income securities, such as

operating leverage The presence of fixed operating costs that do not change when the level of sales changes.

financial leverage The extent to which fixed-income securities (debt and preferred stock) are used in a firm's capital structure.

[2]We have avoided any discussion of market versus company-specific risk in this section. We note now that (1) any action that increases business risk will generally increase a firm's beta coefficient, but (2) a part of business risk as we define it will generally be company-specific and hence is subject to elimination through diversification by the firm's stockholders.

TABLE 12.1 Financial Information for Omkar Company, 2014 (₹ in Thousands, except per-share values)

I. Balance Sheet—12/31/14			
Current assets	₹100.0	Debt	₹0.0
Net fixed assets	100.0	Common equity (10,000 shares)	200.0
Total assets	₹200.0	Total liabilities and equity	₹200.0
II. Income Statement for 2014			
Sales			₹200.0
Variable operating costs (60%)			(120.0)
Gross profit			80.0
Fixed operating costs			(48.0)
Earnings before interest and taxes (EBIT)			32.0
Interest expense			(0.0)
Earnings before taxes (EBT)			32.0
Taxes (40%)			(12.8)
Net income			₹19.2
Common dividend			₹19.2
Addition to retained earnings			₹0.0
III. Per-Share Information			
Earnings per share (EPS) = (₹19,200/10,000 shares) =			₹1.92
Dividends per share (DPS) = (₹19,200/10,000 shares) =			₹1.92
Market price per share (P_0)			₹20.00

debt and preferred stock, to raise capital. When financial leverage is created, a firm intensifies the business risk borne by the common stockholders. To illustrate, suppose 10 people decide to form a corporation to produce operating systems for personal computers. There is a certain amount of business risk in the operation. If the firm is capitalized only with common equity, and if each person buys 10 percent of the stock, then each investor will bear an equal share of the business risk. However, suppose the firm is capitalized with 50 percent debt and 50 percent equity, with five of the investors putting up their capital as debt and the other five putting up their money as equity. In this case, the cash flows received by the debtholders are based on a contractual agreement, so the investors who put up the equity will have to bear essentially all of the business risk, and their position will be twice as risky as it would have been had the firm been financed only with equity. Thus, *the use of debt intensifies the firm's business risk borne by the common stockholders.*

In the next section, we will explain how financial leverage affects a firm's expected earnings per share, the riskiness of those earnings, and, consequently, the price of the firm's stock. The objective of our analysis is to determine the capital structure at which *value is maximized;* this point is then used as the target capital structure.[3]

Debt vs. Equity

A full perspective on debt and equity can be achieved through an example.

Example

Take a company that is considering a project worth ₹100 lakh. Let us assume that banks are prepared to lend up to ₹75 lakh to this project and the rate of interest payable annually is 12%.

Assuming that the company generates a PBIT of ₹16 lakh by utilizing these assets of ₹100 lakh, and if the tax rates are 30%, the position for various levels of borrowing is shown in Exhibit 12.1.

[3]In this chapter, we examine capital structures on a book value (or balance sheet) basis. An alternative approach is to calculate the market values of debt, preferred stock, and common equity, and then to reconstruct the balance sheet on a market value basis. Although the market value approach is more consistent with financial theory, bond rating agencies and most financial executives focus their attention on book values. Moreover, the conversion from book to market values is a complicated process, and because market value capital structures change with stock market fluctuations, they are thought by many to be too unstable to serve as operationally useful targets. Finally, exactly the same insights are gained from the book value and market value analyses. For all these reasons, a market value analysis of capital structure is better suited for advanced finance courses.

EXHIBIT 12.1

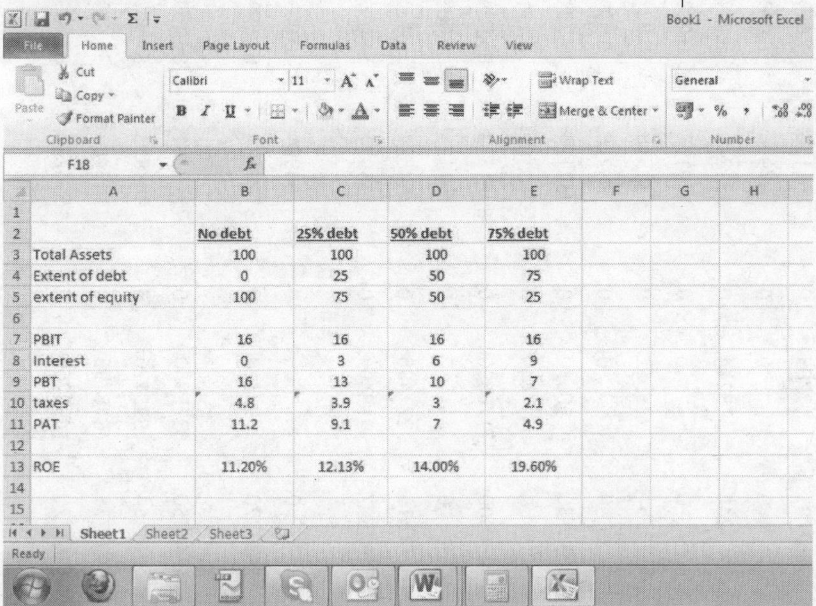

	No debt	25% debt	50% debt	75% debt
Total Assets	100	100	100	100
Extent of debt	0	25	50	75
extent of equity	100	75	50	25
PBIT	16	16	16	16
Interest	0	3	6	9
PBT	16	13	10	7
taxes	4.8	3.9	3	2.1
PAT	11.2	9.1	7	4.9
ROE	11.20%	12.13%	14.00%	19.60%

Note: The Excel template for the above illustration is available online (Example 12.1)

From the above statement, a number of things can be observed:

- When debt is introduced into the structure, there is an additional expense in terms of interest, but there is a tax saving that the interest is a tax-deductible item. This is the same as saying that we pay an amount of interest and then get back a portion of it in terms of tax benefits, thereby effectively paying only interest which is (1 - Tax rate).
- ROE is calculated by taking the net surplus (PAT) as the numerator and equity as the denominator. Since the quantum of equity comes down with additional borrowing, the denominator gets smaller and the ROE goes up with increased levels of debt.
- Since ROE keeps going up with increased borrowing, it might appear that as a general principle it pays to borrow more.
- That is true only if the returns generated by the project (in this case 16%—PBIT of ₹16 lakh divided by the total assets of ₹100 lakh) exceed the interest percentage. If the returns slip down to a level lower than the interest rate, the company will not have enough to service the debt.
- Another factor is the availability of alternative uses for the company's funds. If the company has surplus funds of ₹100 lakh, then by borrowing for this project, the company will end up investing a portion of the surplus funds in other projects. For this, there should be other available projects which generate adequate return on equity. If not, ideally, the company must return the surplus back to the shareholders.
- If the company is unable to service its debt for long periods, the lenders will seek to act against the company and its assets. In any case, there will be restrictions on the way the company operates.
- Based on the risk inherent in the project and availability of debt, it is left to the company to decide on the ideal structure. The discussion on this aspect is continued in the section on financial plans later in the chapter.

Capital structure in India

Like other parts of the world, there has been no clear pattern on capital structure in India. The following points, however merit attention:

Capital structure patterns vary from industry to industry in India. We observe that the Information Technology industry which has been able to generate a lot of reserves and surplus over the years do not have much debt in their structure. Manufacturing companies and fast growing business houses have resorted to debt quite freely. But over the years even companies which had a lot of debt in their structure have targeted to reduce this over time. Recently, we saw some airline industry companies resorting to huge debt to meet their needs for buying aircraft.

12-2 Determining the Optimal Capital Structure

We can illustrate the effects of financial leverage using the data shown in Table 12.1 for a fictional company, which we will call Omkar company (Omkar). As shown in the top section of the table, the company currently has no debt. Should it continue the policy of using no debt, or should it start using financial leverage (debt)? If it does decide to substitute debt for equity, how far should it go? As in all such decisions, the correct answer is that the firm should *choose the combination of debt and equity, or* capital structure, *that will maximize the price of the firm's stock.*

To answer the questions posed here, we examine the effects of changing Omkar's capital structure while

TABLE 12.2 Capital Structure of leading Indian companies (those in NSE 50 Index) (₹ in Millions)

Co_Name	Year Ended	Share Capital	Reserves Total	Total Shareholders Funds	Secured Loans	Unsecured Loans	Total Debt		Debt +Equity	Debt Ratio
Adani Ports & Special Economic Zone Ltd	–201703	4142	162848	168649	72332	123105	195437	0	364086	53.68%
Ambuja Cements Ltd	–201612	3971	186764	190736	236	132	368	0	191104	0.19%
Asian Paints Ltd	–201703	959	68551	69510	124	268	392	0	69902	0.56%
Aurobindo Pharma Ltd	–201703	586	83776	84362	4987	25553	30539	0	114901	26.58%
Axis Bank Ltd	–201703	4790	552835	557625	1050310	4143790	5194100	0	5751725	90.31%
Bajaj Auto Ltd	–201703	2894	167448	170341	0	1199	1199	0	171540	0.70%
Bajaj Finance Ltd	–201703	1094	94909	96003	359679	132818	492497	0	588500	83.69%
Bharat Petroleum Corporation Ltd	–201703	13113	283571	296684	37583	194009	231592	0	528276	43.84%
Bharti Airtel Ltd	–201703	19987	992086	1012070	31	604167	604198	0	1616268	37.38%
Bharti Infratel Ltd	–201703	18496	143875	162371	0	2785	2785	0	165156	1.69%
Bosch Ltd	–201703	305	87691	87996	0	0	0	0	87996	0.00%
Cipla Ltd	–201703	1609	126396	128005	0	3244	3244	0	131249	2.47%
Coal India Ltd	–201703	62074	77124	139198	0	0	0	0	139198	0.00%
Dr Reddys Laboratories Ltd	–201703	829	115177	116006	1	23551	23552	0	139558	16.88%
Eicher Motors Ltd	–201703	272	38954	39226	0	0	0	0	39226	0.00%
GAIL (India) Ltd	–201703	16913	364581	381494	17500	33130	50630	0	432124	11.72%
HCL Technologies Ltd	–201703	2854	256879	259733	449	0	449	0	260182	0.17%
HDFC Bank Ltd	–201703	5125	889498	894623	740289	6436400	7176690	0	8071313	88.92%
Hero MotoCorp Ltd	–201703	399	100714	101113	0	0	0	0	101113	0.00%
Hindalco Industries Ltd	–201703	2227	471098	473326	229883	41615	271498	0	744824	36.45%
Hindustan Petroleum Corporation Ltd	–201703	10163	193311	203474	44900	167597	212497	0	415971	51.08%
Hindustan Unilever Ltd	–201703	2160	62740	64900	0	0	0	0	64900	0.00%
Housing Development Finance Corporation Ltd	–201703	3177	392766	396454	1308600	1488720	2797320	0	3193774	87.59%
ICICI Bank Ltd	–201703	11651	987797	999511	1127200	5248750	6375950	0	7375461	86.45%
Indiabulls Housing Finance Ltd	–201703	848	117841	118693	710956	114164	825120	0	943813	87.42%
Indian Oil Corporation Ltd	–201703	47393	949894	997287	142420	405775	548195	0	1545482	35.47%
IndusInd Bank Ltd	–201703	5982	200328	206461	224537	1265720	1490260	0	1696721	87.83%

Co_Name	Year Ended	Share Capital	Reserves Total	Total Shareholders Funds	Secured Loans	Unsecured Loans	Total Debt		Debt +Equity	Debt Ratio
Infosys Ltd	–201703	11480	668690	680170	0	0	0	0	680170	0.00%
ITC Ltd	–201703	12147	441262	453410	0	258	258	0	453668	0.06%
Kotak Mahindra Bank Ltd	–201703	9205	266956	276179	210955	1574260	1785210	0	2061389	86.60%
Larsen & Toubro Ltd	–201703	1866	458262	460127	8460	97348	105807	0	565934	18.70%
Lupin Ltd	–201703	903	146899	147802	970	4965	5935	0	153737	3.86%
Mahindra & Mahindra Ltd	–201703	2968	253728	256696	83	28073	28156	0	284852	9.88%
Maruti Suzuki India Ltd	–201703	1510	360201	361711	0	4836	4836	0	366547	1.32%
NTPC Ltd	–201703	82455	879858	962312	345160	723242	1068400	0	2030712	52.61%
Oil & Natural Gas Corpn Ltd	–201703	64166	1791220	1855380	0	0	0	0	1855380	0.00%
Power Grid Corporation of India Ltd	–201703	52316	445757	498073	1101690	85286	1186980	0	1685053	70.44%
Reliance Industries Ltd	–201703	32510	2850580	2883130	105940	968520	1074460	0	3957590	27.15%
State Bank of India	–201703	7974	1874890	1882860	3176940	20447500	23624500	0	25507360	92.62%
Sun Pharmaceuticals Industries Ltd	–201703	2399	206316	208715	25328	35138	60466	0	269181	22.46%
Tata Consultancy Services Ltd	–201703	1970	778250	780220	500	2000	2500	0	782720	0.32%
Tata Motors Ltd	–201703	6792	201299	208092	31325	164415	195740	0	403832	48.47%
Tata Steel Ltd	–201703	9714	486876	496590	25518	257329	282846	0	779436	36.29%
Tech Mahindra Ltd	–201703	4868	164015	168902	2625	0	2625	0	171527	1.53%
UltraTech Cement Ltd	–201703	2745	236665	239410	29965	32439	62404	0	301814	20.68%
UPL Ltd	–201703	1830	75670	77500	30	8450	8480	0	85980	9.86%
Vedanta Ltd	–201703	3718	793964	797681	288417	143914	432331	0	1230012	35.15%
Wipro Ltd	–201703	4861	462195	467056	2269	60830	63099	0	530155	11.90%
Yes Bank Ltd	–201703	4565	215976	220541	386067	1428740	1814810	0	2035351	89.16%
Zee Entertainment Enterprises Ltd	–201703	960	43256	44216	15	19077	19092	0	63308	30.16%

Source to be given as http://www.capitalline.com

TABLE 12.3 Cost of Debt, r_d, and Number of Common Shares Outstanding for Omkar Company at Different Capital Structures (₹ in Thousands)

Total Assets	Debt/Assets Ratio	Amount Borrowed[a]	Common Stock	Shares Outstanding[b]	Cost of Debt, r_d
200	0%	₹ 0	₹200	10,000	—
200	10	20	180	9,000	8.0%
200	20	40	160	8,000	8.5
200	30	60	140	7,000	9.0
200	40	80	120	6,000	10.0
200	50	100	100	5,000	12.0
200	60	120	80	4,000	15.0

[a]We assume that the firm must borrow in increments of ₹20,000. We also assume that Omkar cannot borrow more than ₹120,000, or 60 percent of assets because of restrictions in its corporate charter.

[b]We assume that Omkar uses the amount of funds raised by borrowing (issuing debt) to repurchase existing common stock at the current market value, which is ₹20 per share; thus we assume that no commissions or other transaction costs are associated with repurchasing the stock. For example, if Omkar's capital structure contains 40 percent debt, then ₹80,000 of the ₹200,000 total assets is financed with debt. We assume that if Omkar borrows the ₹80,000, it will repurchase 4,000 shares = ₹80,000/₹20 of its existing shares of common stock, so 6,000 shares (10,000 shares − 4,000 shares) remain.

keeping all other factors, such as the level of operations, constant. To keep all other factors constant, we assume that Omkar changes its capital structure by *substituting* debt for equity—that is, as new debt is issued, the proceeds are used to repurchase an equal amount of outstanding stock.

12-2a EPS Analysis of the Effects of Financial Leverage

If a firm changes the percentage of debt used to finance existing assets, we would expect the earnings per share (EPS) and, consequently, the stock price to change as well. To understand the relationship between financial leverage and EPS, we first examine how EPS is affected when our illustrative firm changes its capital structure to include greater relative amounts of debt.

First, to simplify our example, we assume that Omkar's level of operations—that is, production and sales—will not change if its capital structure changes.[4] Table 12.1 shows that Omkar's net operating income (NOI), or earnings before interest and taxes (EBIT), was ₹32,000 in 2014. We expect that its EBIT will remain at this level when economic conditions are normal, but will rise to ₹84,000 when the economy is booming and will fall to −₹6,000 when the economy is in a recession. The probabilities associated with each of these economic states are 0.5, 0.3, and 0.2, respectively. We give the different economic states so that we can see what happens to Omkar's financial risk when its capital structure is changed.

Omkar asked an investment banker to help determine what its before-tax cost of debt, r_d, will be at various levels of debt. The results are shown in Table 12.3. Naturally, we would expect that as a firm increases the percentage of debt it uses, lenders would perceive the debt to be riskier because the chance of financial distress is higher. As a result, lenders (bondholders) will charge higher interest rates to the firm as its percentage of debt increases, which is the pattern shown in the table.

We assume that Omkar does not retain any earnings for reinvestment in the firm; that is, all earnings are paid to shareholders, which currently consist of stockholders only. As long as the firm pays all earnings to shareholders, and no additional funds are raised, growth will equal zero (g = 0), and future production and sales operations will continue as outlined previously; that is, the

[4]In the real world, capital structure *does* at times affect EBIT. First, if debt levels are excessive, the firm probably will not be able to finance at all if its earnings are low at a time when interest rates are high. This could lead to stop–start construction and research and development programs, as well as to the necessity of passing up good investment opportunities. Second, a weak financial condition (i.e. too much debt) could cause a firm to lose sales. For example, prior to the time that its huge debt forced Eastern Airlines into bankruptcy, many people refused to buy Eastern tickets because they were afraid the company would go bankrupt and leave them holding unusable tickets. Third, financially strong companies can bargain hard with unions as well as with their suppliers, whereas weaker ones might have to give in simply because they do not have the financial resources to carry on the fight. Finally, a company with so much debt that bankruptcy is a serious threat will have difficulty attracting and retaining managers and employees, or it will have to pay premium salaries. For all these reasons, it is not entirely correct to say that a firm's financial policy has no effect on its operating income.

TABLE 12.4 Omkar Capital EPS at Different Capital Structures (₹ in Thousands, except per-share values)

	Recession	Normal	Boom
I. Economic States			
Type of economy			
Probability of occurrence	0.2	0.5	0.3
Sales	₹ 105.0	₹200.0	₹330.0
II. Debt/Assets = 0% (current capital structure)			
EBIT	₹(6.0)	₹ 32.0	₹ 84.0
Interest expense	(0.0)	(0.0)	(0.0)
Earnings before taxes (EBT)	(6.0)	32.0	84.0
Taxes (40%)	2.4	(12.8)	(33.6)
Net income (NI)	₹(3.6)	₹ 19.2	₹ 50.4
Earnings per share (EPS) = NI/10,000 shares	₹(0.36)	₹ 1.92	₹ 5.04
Expected EPS		₹ 2.40	
Standard deviation of EPS (σ_{EPS})		₹ 1.93	
Coefficient of variation (CV_{EPS})		0.80	
III. Debt/Assets = 50%			
EBIT	₹(6.0)	₹ 32.0	₹ 84.0
Interest expense = 0.12 × ₹100	(12.0)	(12.0)	(12.0)
Earnings before taxes (EBT)	(18.0)	20.0	72.0
Taxes (40%)	7.2	(8.0)	(28.8)
Net income (NI)	₹(10.8)	₹ 12.0	₹ 43.2
Earnings per share (EPS) = NI/5,000 shares	₹(2.16)	₹2.40	₹ 8.64
Expected EPS		₹3.36	
Standard deviation of EPS (σ_{EPS})		₹ 3.86	
Coefficient of variation (CV_{EPS})		1.15	

size of the firm will remain at its current level. Thus, any changes in EPS that we observe when the proportion of debt is changed will be a direct result of changing the firm's capital structure, not its level of operations.

Table 12.4 compares Omkar's expected EPS at two levels of financial leverage: (1) zero debt, which is the existing capital structure, and (2) 50 percent debt. If Omkar does not change its capital structure, all ₹200,000 of its assets will be financed with stock, so the interest expense will be zero because no debt exists. Section II of Table 12.4 shows that EPS is expected to be ₹2.40 with this capital structure. EPS will be as high as ₹5.04, and as low as –₹0.36, but, on average, it will be ₹2.40. We also calculate the standard deviation of EPS (σ_{EPS}) and the coefficient of variation (CV_{EPS}) as indicators of the firm's risk with this capital structure: σ_{EPS} = ₹1.93 and CV_{EPS} = 0.80.[5]

Section III of Table 12.4 shows the effect on EPS of shifting Omkar's capital structure so that the mix of financing is 50 percent debt and 50 percent equity; that is, when the ₹200,000 in assets are financed with ₹100,000 debt and ₹100,000 equity. To accomplish this shift, Omkar would issue ₹100,000 of debt and repurchase ₹100,000 of its existing equity. If we assume that stock can be repurchased at its current market price and transaction costs are negligible, then, using the information given in Table 12.1, we will find that Omkar can repurchase 5,000 shares = ₹100,000/₹20 per share. Thus, the number of shares outstanding will decrease from 10,000 to 5,000. At the same time, because the firm now has debt, it will have to pay interest, which, according to the schedule given in Table 12.3, will equal ₹12,000 = ₹100,000 × 0.12 per year. The ₹12,000 interest expense is a fixed cost because it is the same regardless of Omkar's level of sales.

[5]See Chapter 8 for a review of procedures for calculating standard deviations and coefficients of variation. Recall that the advantage of the coefficient of variation is that it permits better comparisons when the expected values of EPS vary, as they do here for the two capital structures.

FIGURE 12.1 Omkar: Relationships among Expected EPS, Risk, and Financial Leverage

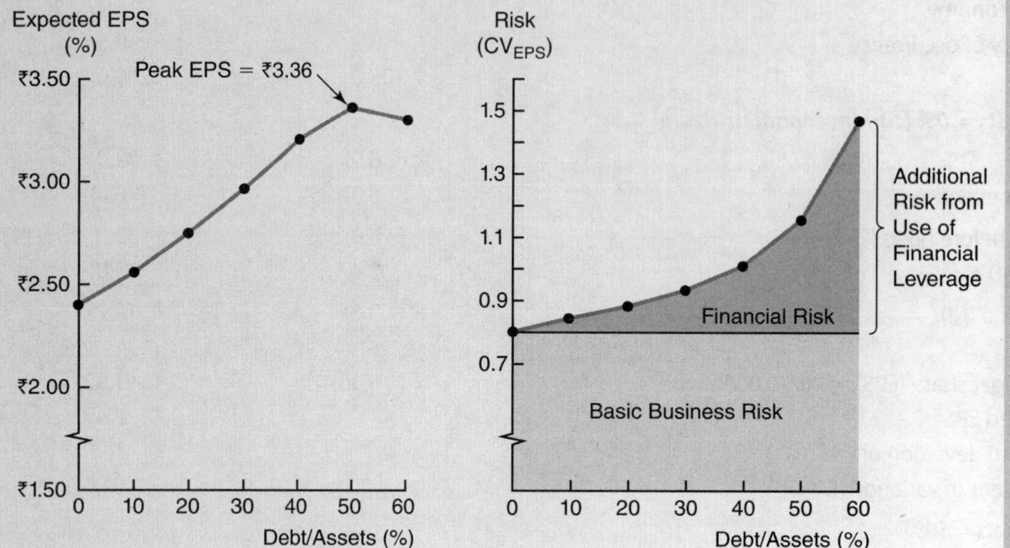

Debt Ratio = Debt/Assets	Expected EPS	Standard Deviation $= \sigma_{EPS}$	Coefficient of Variation $= CV_{EPS}$
0%	₹2.40	₹1.93	0.80
10	2.56	2.15	0.84
20	2.75	2.41	0.88
30	2.97	2.76	0.93
40	3.20	3.22	1.01
50	3.36	3.86	1.15
60	3.30	4.83	1.46

With a debt/assets ratio of 50 percent, the expected EPS is ₹3.36, which is ₹0.96 higher than if the firm uses no debt. The EPS range is also greater; EPS can be as low as –₹2.16 when the economy is poor or as high as ₹8.64 when the economy is booming. Thus, EPS has greater variability, which suggests that this capital structure is riskier than the capital structure of 100 percent equity financing. The standard deviation of EPS and the coefficient of variation computed for the capital structure with 50 percent debt are σ_{EPS} = ₹3.86 and $CV_{EPS} = 1.15$. As you can see, these computations support our suspicion that this capital structure is riskier than the capital structure that consists of equity only.

Figure 12.1 shows the relationships among expected EPS, risk, and financial leverage for Omkar for the all-equity capital structure and the various capital structures given in the lower section of the figure. The tabular data given in Figure 12.1 were calculated in the manner set forth in Table 12.3, and the graphs plot these data. In the left panel of Figure 12.1, we see that expected EPS rises until the firm is financed with 50 percent debt. Interest charges rise (Table 12.3), but this effect is more than offset by the decline in the number of shares outstanding as debt is substituted for equity. Beyond 50 percent debt, however, the interest rate rises so rapidly that EPS declines despite the smaller number of shares outstanding.

The right panel of Figure 12.1 shows that risk, as measured by the coefficient of variation of EPS, rises continuously and at an increasing rate as debt is substituted for equity. We see, then, that using leverage has both good and bad effects. Higher leverage increases expected EPS (in this example, until the firm is financed

FIGURE 12.2 Omkar's Earnings per Share (EPS) for 100 Percent Stock Financing and for 50 Percent Debt Financing

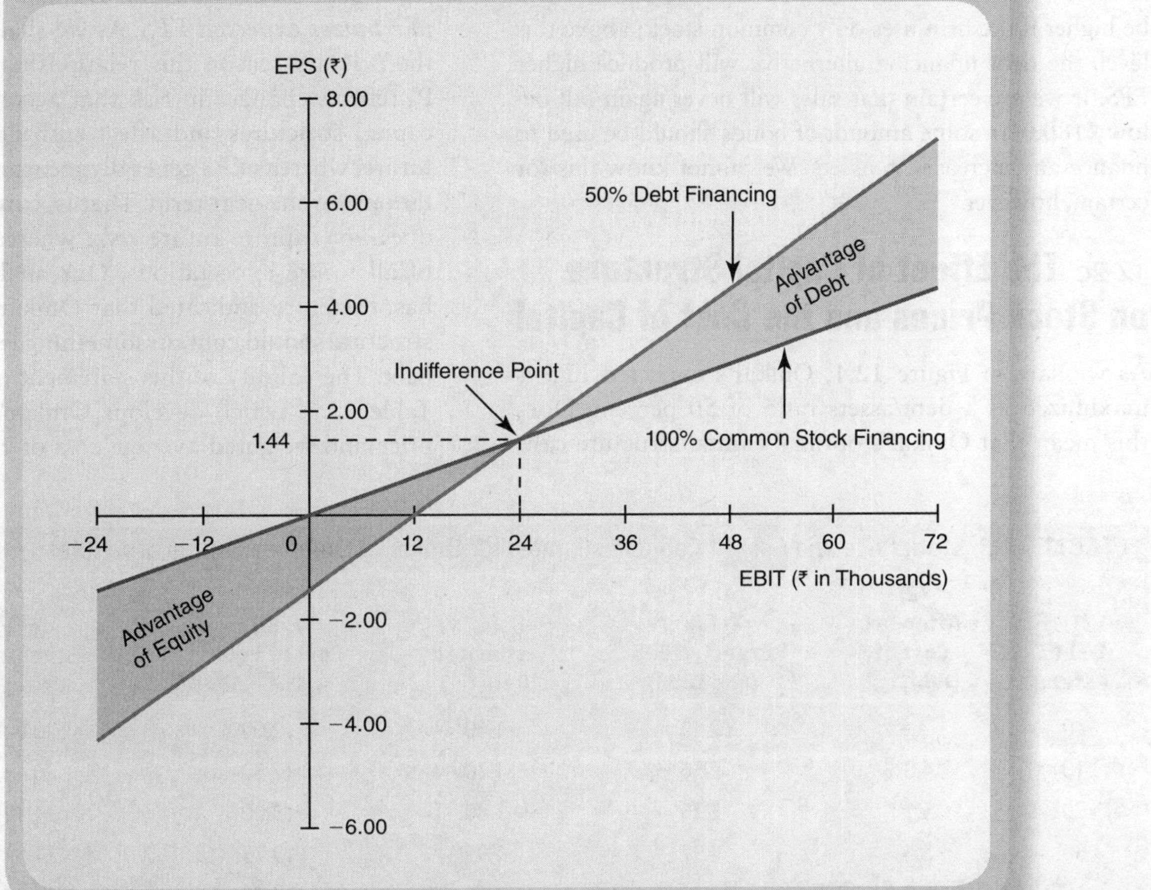

with 50 percent debt), but it also increases the firm's risk. Clearly, for Omkar, the debt/assets ratio should not exceed 50 percent. But where in the range of 0 to 50 percent is the best debt/assets ratio for Omkar? This issue is discussed in the following sections.

12-2b EBIT/EPS Examination of Financial Leverage

In the previous section, we assumed that Omkar's EBIT had to be one of three possible values: –₹6,000, ₹32,000, or ₹84,000. Another way of evaluating alternative financing methods is to plot the EPS of each capital structure at many different levels of EBIT. Figure 12.2 shows such a graph for the two capital structures we considered for Omkar in Table 12.3; that is, (1) 100 percent stock and (2) 50 percent stock and 50 percent debt. Notice that at low levels of EBIT, and hence low levels of sales, EPS is higher if Omkar's capital structure includes only stock. At high levels of EBIT, however, EPS is higher with the capital structure that includes debt. Notice also that the 50% Debt line has a steeper slope than the 100% Common Stock line, showing that earnings per share will increase more rapidly with increases in EBIT, and hence sales, if the firm uses debt. This relationship exists because the firm has a greater degree of financial leverage with the capital structure that includes 50 percent debt. In this case, the benefits of *additional sales need not be shared with debt holders because debt payments are fixed*; rather, any profits that remain after debt holders are paid "belong" to stockholders.

The point on the graph where the two lines intersect is called the **EPS indifference point,** and it is the level of EBIT

EPS indifference point The level of sales at which EPS will be the same whether the firm uses debt or common stock financing.

(sales) where EPS is the same no matter which capital structure Omkar uses. In Figure 12.2, the two lines cross where EBIT is equal to ₹24,000, which equates to sales of ₹180,000. If sales are below ₹180,000, EPS will be higher if the firm uses only common stock; above this level, the debt financing alternative will produce higher EPS. If we are certain that sales will never again fall below ₹180,000, some amount of bonds should be used to finance any increases in assets. We cannot know this for certain, however.

12-2c The Effect of Capital Structure on Stock Prices and the Cost of Capital

As we saw in Figure 12.1, Omkar's expected EPS is maximized at a debt/assets ratio of 50 percent. Does this mean that Omkar's optimal capital structure calls for 50 percent debt? The answer is a resounding no. *The optimal capital structure is the one that maximizes the price of the firm's stock, and this always calls for a debt/assets ratio that is lower than the one that maximizes expected EPS.* As we shall discover shortly, the primary reason this relationship exists is because P_0 reflects changes in risk that accompany changes in capital structures and affect cash flows long into the future, whereas EPS generally measures only the expectations for the near term. That is, current EPS generally does not capture future risk, whereas P_0 is indicative of all future expectations. Our analysis to this point has, therefore, indicated that Omkar's optimal capital structure should contain something less than 50 percent debt. The validity of this statement is demonstrated in Table 12.5, which develops Omkar's estimated stock price and weighted average cost of capital (WACC) at

TABLE 12.5 Stock Price and Cost of Capital Estimates for Omkar at Different Capital Structures

(1) Debt/ Assets	(2) After-Tax Cost of Debt, r_{dT}[a]	(3) Expected EPS (and DPS[b])	(4) Estimated Beta (β_s)	(5) Cost of Equity[c] $r_s = 4\% + 5\%(\beta_s)$	(6) Estimated Price[d]	(7) WACC[e]
0	—	₹2.40	1.60	12.00%	₹20.00	12.00%
10	4.8%	2.56	1.70	12.50	20.48	11.73
20	5.1	2.75	1.80	13.00	21.12	11.42
30	5.4	2.97	1.95	13.75	21.57	11.25
40	6.0	3.20	2.10	14.50	22.07	11.10
50	7.2	3.36	2.30	15.50	21.68	11.35
60	9.0	3.30	2.60	17.00	19.41	12.20

[a]The after-tax cost of debt, r_{dT}, is the before-tax cost of debt, r_d, given in Table 12.3 adjusted for the taxes: $r_{dT} = r_d(1 - T)$. For example, at a capital structure of 40 percent debt, $r_{dT} = 10.0\%(1 - 0.4) = 6.0\%$.

[b]Omkar pays out all earnings as dividends, so DPS = EPS. Although the values in this column are rounded to the nearest penny, the values shown in Column 6 are computed based on DPS figures carried to four decimal places.

[c]We assume that $r_{RF} = 4\%$ and $r_M = 9\%$, so $r_{PM} = 9\% - 4\% = 5\%$, and, at debt/assets equal to 40 percent, $r_s = 4\% + (5\% \times 2.10) = 14.5\%$. Other values of r_s are calculated similarly.

[d]Because all earnings are paid out as dividends, no retained earnings are available to be reinvested in the firm, which means growth in EPS and DPS will be zero (g = 0). Therefore, we use the constant growth model, where g = 0, developed in Chapter 7 to compute the estimated stock price. To illustrate, at debt/assets equal to 40 percent, we have

$$\hat{P}_0 = \frac{\widehat{DPS}}{r_s} = \frac{₹3.20}{0.1450} = ₹22.07$$

Other prices were computed similarly.

[e]The WACC, or weighted average cost of capital, is computed using Equation 11.8, which was developed in Chapter 11. At a capital structure that has 40 percent debt, the computation is

$$WACC = w_d[r_d(1-T)] + w_s r_s = (0.40)\,6.00\% + (1 - 0.40)\,14.50\% = 11.10\%$$

The WACCs for the other capital structures were computed similarly.

FIGURE 12.3 Omkar's Cost of Equity, r_s at Different Capital Structures

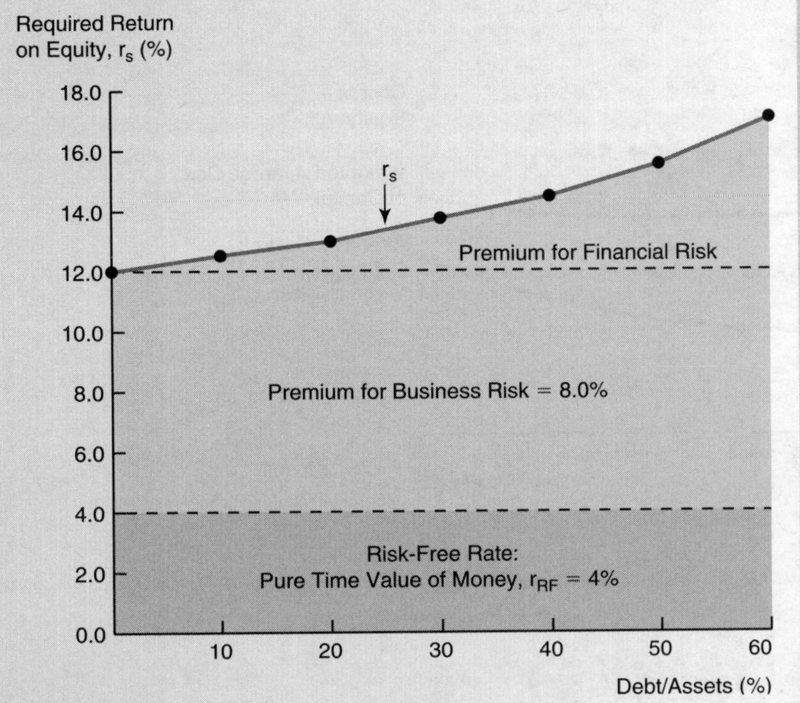

different debt/assets ratios. The debt costs and EPS data in Columns 2 and 3 were taken from Table 12.3 and Figure 12.1. The beta coefficients shown in Column 4 were estimated. Recall from Chapter 8 that a stock's beta measures its relative volatility compared with the volatility of an average stock. It has been demonstrated both theoretically and empirically that a firm's beta increases with its degree of financial leverage. The exact nature of this relationship for a given firm is difficult to estimate, but the values given in Column 4 show the approximate nature of the relationship for Omkar.

If we assume that the risk-free rate of return, r_{RF}, is 4 percent and the required return on an average stock, r_M, is 9 percent, we can use the CAPM equation to develop estimates of the required rates of return on equity, r_s, for Omkar as shown in Column 5. Here we see that $r_s = 12\% = 4\% + (9\% - 4\%)1.6$ if no financial leverage is used, but $r_s = 17\% = 4\% + (9\% - 4\%)2.6$ if the company finances with 60 percent debt, the maximum permitted by its corporate charter.

Figure 12.3 graphs Omkar's required rate of return on equity at different debt levels. The figure also shows the composition of Omkar's required return, including the risk-free rate of 4 percent and the premiums for both business and financial risk. As you can see from the graph, the business risk premium does not depend on the debt level. Instead, it remains constant at 8 percent at all debt levels, which is the difference between the 12 percent WACC when the firm is financed with 100 percent equity and the risk-free rate of 4 percent (i.e., 8% = 12% – 4%). However, the financial risk premium varies depending on the debt level; the higher the debt level, the greater the premium for financial risk.

The zero growth stock valuation model developed in Chapter 7 is used, along with the Column 3 values of dividends per share (DPS) and the Column 5 values of r_s, to develop the estimated stock prices shown in Column 6 in Table 12.5. Here we see that the expected stock price initially rises with additional financial leverage, hits a peak of ₹22.07 at a debt/assets ratio of 40 percent, and then begins to decline. Thus, Omkar's optimal capital structure calls for 40 percent debt.

Finally, Column 7 shows Omkar's weighted average cost of capital (WACC), calculated as described in Chapter 11, at the different capital structures. If the company uses zero debt, its capital is all equity, so WACC = r_s = 12%. As the firm begins to use lower-cost debt, its WACC declines. However, as the debt/assets ratio increases, the costs of both debt and equity rise, and the increasing costs of the two components begin to offset the fact that larger amounts of the lower-cost debt are being used. At 40 percent debt, WACC hits a minimum at 11.10 percent, and then it begins rising as the debt/assets ratio is increased.

The cost of capital and stock price data shown in Table 12.5 are plotted in Figure 12.4 on the next page. As the graph shows, the expected stock price is maximized, and the cost of capital is minimized, at a 40 percent debt/assets ratio. Thus, *Omkar's optimal capital structure calls for 40 percent debt and 60 percent equity. Management should set its target capital structure at these ratios, and if the existing ratios are off target, it should move toward the target when new securities offerings are made.*

FIGURE 12.4 Relationship among Omkar's Capital Structure, Cost of Capital, and Stock Price

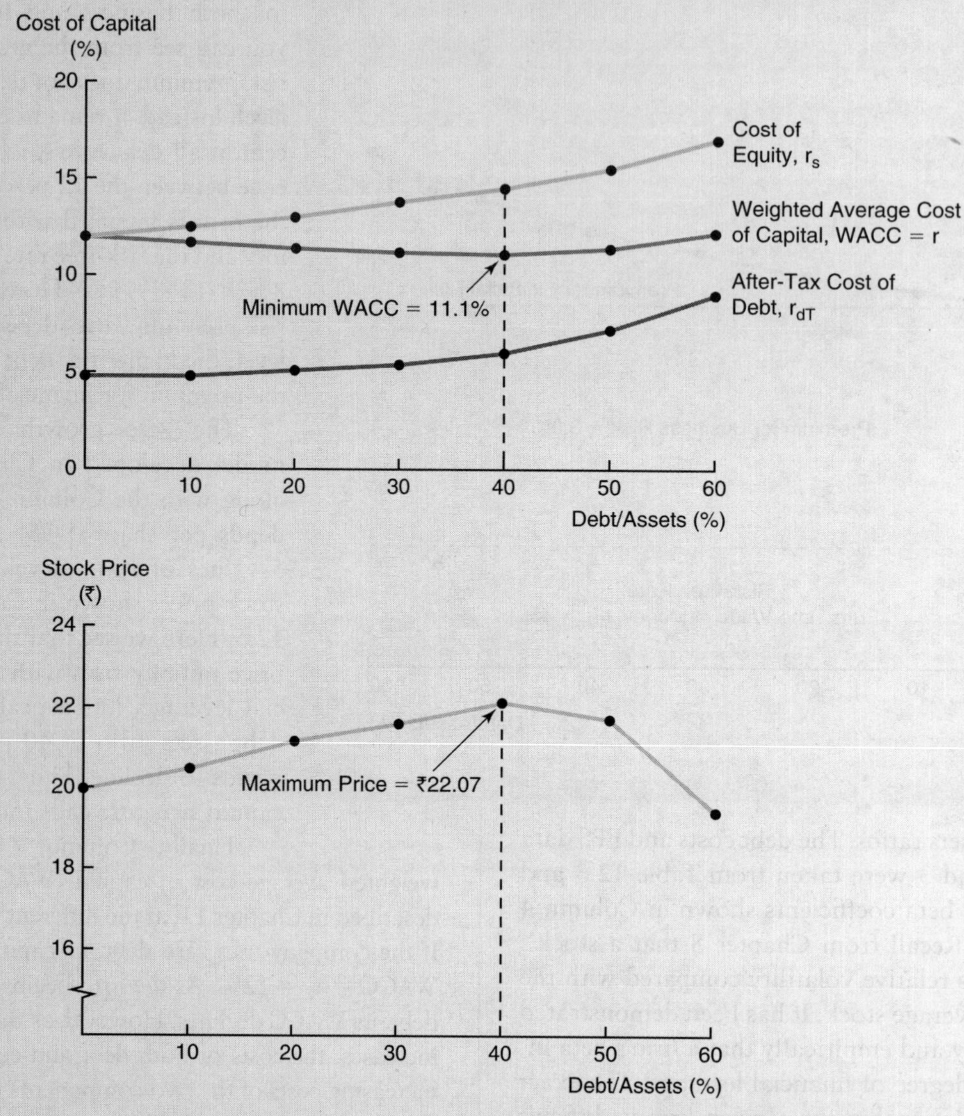

12-3 Degree of Leverage[7]

Leverage, whether operating or financial, is created when a firm has *fixed costs* associated either with its sales and production operations or with the types of financing it uses. These two types of leverage—operating and financial—are interrelated. If Omkar can *reduce* its operating leverage, its optimal capital structure probably would call for *more* debt, and vice versa. In this section we show, through an analysis of the degree of leverage concept, how operating and financial leverage interact, which shows how business risk and financial risk affect a firm's projected income.

[7]A more detailed discussion of leverage is presented in Chapter 17, and the derivations of the equations contained in this section are included in the footnotes in that chapter.

12-3a Degree of Operating Leverage (DOL)

The **degree of operating leverage (DOL)** is defined as the percentage change in net operating income (NOI)—that is, earnings before interest and taxes, or EBIT—associated with a given percentage change in sales. Thus, the degree of operating leverage is computed as in Equation 12.1:

12.1

$$\text{Degree of operating leverage} = \text{DOL} = \frac{\%\Delta \text{ in NOI}}{\%\Delta \text{ in sales}} = \frac{\left(\frac{\Delta \text{ EBIT}}{\text{EBIT}}\right)}{\left(\frac{\Delta \text{Sales}}{\text{Sales}}\right)}$$

Here the Greek symbol Δ indicates change.

According to Equation 12.1, the DOL is an index that measures the effect of a change in sales on EBIT (operating income).

The DOL for a particular level of production and sales can be computed using Equation 12.2:

12.2

$$\text{DOL} = \frac{Q(P - V)}{Q(P - V) - F} = \frac{S - VC}{S - VC - F}$$

$$= \frac{\text{Gross profit}}{\text{EBIT}}$$

Here, Q is the intial units of output, P is the average sales price per unit of output, V is the variable cost per unit, F is fixed operating costs, S is initial sales in rupees, and VC is total variable costs in rupees.

Applying Equation 12.2 to data for Omkar at a sales level of ₹200,000, as shown in Table 12.1, we find its degree of operating leverage to be 2.5:

$$\text{DOL}_{₹200,000} = \frac{₹200,000 - ₹120,000}{₹200,000 - ₹120,000 - ₹48,000}$$

$$= \frac{₹80,000}{₹32,000} = 2.5\%$$

Thus, for every 1 percent change (increase; decrease) in sales there will be a 2.5 percent change (increase; decrease) in EBIT. This situation is confirmed by examining Section II of Table 12.3, where we see that a 65 percent increase in sales, from ₹200,000 to ₹330,000, causes EBIT to increase by 162.5 percent (= 65% × 2.5), from ₹32,000 to ₹84,000. Note, however, that if sales decrease by 65 percent, then EBIT will decrease by 162.5 percent. Also, note that the DOL is specific to a particular sales level; thus, if we evaluated Omkar from a sales base of ₹330,000, DOL would be different:

$$\text{DOL}_{₹330,000} = \frac{₹330,000 - ₹330,000(0.6)}{₹330,000 - ₹330,000(0.6) - ₹48,000}$$

$$= \frac{₹132,000}{₹84,000} = 1.57\times$$

Based on these examples, we conclude that when a firm's operations are closer to the breakeven level (at sales = ₹120,000, EBIT = ₹0), its degree of operating leverage will be higher, but DOL will decline the higher the base level of sales is above breakeven sales. (For example, at sales = ₹200,000, DOL = 2.5 times, whereas at sales = ₹330,000, DOL = 1.57 times.) Remember that in Chapter 8 we used the word "variability" to define risk. Thus, we can conclude that, all else equal, *a lower (higher) DOL suggests that lower (higher) risk is associated with the firm's normal operating activities*, because there will be lower (higher) variability in EBIT as a result of a change in sales.

12-3b Degree of Financial Leverage (DFL)

Operating leverage affects earnings *before* interest and taxes (EBIT), whereas financial leverage affects earnings *after* interest and taxes, or the earnings that are available to pay common stock dividends. In terms of Table 12.1, operating leverage affects the section of the income statement from sales to EBIT, which shows the results of the firm's normal operations and is termed the *operating section* of the income statement, whereas financial leverage affects the section from EBIT to net income, which shows the effects of the firm's financing arrangements on net income and is termed the *financing section* of the income statement. Thus, financial leverage takes over where operating leverage leaves off, further magnifying the effects on earnings per share (EPS) of changes in sales.

The **degree of financial leverage (DFL)** is defined as the percentage change in EPS that results from a given percentage change in EBIT, and is calculated as shown in Equation 12.3 (when there is no preferred stock):[8]

degree of financial leverage (DFL) The percentage change in earnings per share (EPS) associated with a given percentage change in earnings before interest and taxes (EBIT).

12.3

$$\text{Degree of financial leverage} = \text{DEL} = \frac{\%\Delta \text{ in EPS}}{\%\Delta \text{ in EBIT}} = \frac{\left(\frac{\Delta\text{EPS}}{\text{EPS}}\right)}{\left(\frac{\Delta\text{EBIT}}{\text{EBIT}}\right)}$$

$$= \frac{\text{EBIT}}{\text{EBIT} - 1}$$

At sales of ₹200,000 and EBIT of ₹32,000, the degree of financial leverage when Omkar has a 50 percent debt/assets ratio (Section III, Table 12.3) is

$$\text{DFL}_{₹200{,}000, \text{Debt/TA} = 50\%} = \frac{₹32{,}000}{₹32{,}000 - ₹12{,}000}$$

$$= \frac{₹32{,}000}{₹20{,}000} = 1.6\times$$

This index indicates that every 1 percent change in EBIT will result in a 1.6 percent change in net income and EPS. Therefore, the previous 162.5 percent change (increase) in EBIT would result in a 260% = 162.5% × 1.6 change (increase) in earnings per share. This can be confirmed by referring to Section III of Table 12.3, where we see that a 162.5 percent increase in EBIT, from ₹32,000 to ₹84,000, produces a 260 percent increase in EPS:

$$\%\Delta\text{EPS} = \frac{\Delta\text{EPS}}{\text{EPS}_0} = \frac{₹8.64 - ₹2.40}{₹2.40} = \frac{₹6.24}{₹2.40}$$

$$= 2.60 = 260\%$$

If no debt were used, by definition, the degree of financial leverage would be 1.0, so a 162.5 percent increase in EBIT would produce exactly a 162.5 percent increase in EPS. This can be confirmed from the data in Section II of Table 12.3 (i.e., %ΔEPS = (₹5.04 − ₹1.92)/₹1.92 = 1.625 = 162.5%). We can conclude that, all else equal, *a lower (higher) DFL suggests that lower (higher) risk is associated with the firm's mix of debt and equity financing.*

degree of total leverage (DTL) The percentage change in EPS that results from a given percentage change in sales; DTL shows the effects of both operating leverage and financial leverage.

12-3c Degree of Total Leverage (DTL)

We have seen that (1) the greater the degree of operating leverage (fixed operating costs), the more sensitive EBIT will be to a change in sales and (2) the greater the degree of financial leverage (fixed financial costs), the more sensitive EPS will be to a change in EBIT. Therefore, we can conclude that when a firm uses a considerable amount of both operating and financial leverage, even small changes in sales will lead to wide fluctuations in EPS.

Equation 12.2, which we use to compute DOL, can be combined with Equation 12.3, which we use to compute DFL, to produce an equation to compute **degree of total leverage (DTL)**, which shows how a given change in sales will affect earnings per share. Equation 12.4 gives equivalent equations for computing DTL (assuming no preferred stock exists):

12.4

$$\text{Degree of total leverage} = \text{DTL} = \frac{\%\Delta \text{ in EPS}}{\%\Delta \text{ in sales}}$$

$$= \text{DOL} \times \text{DFL}$$

$$= \frac{\text{Grossprofit}}{\text{EBIT}} \times \frac{\text{EBIT}}{\text{EBIT} - \text{I}}$$

$$= \frac{\text{Q(P} - \text{V)}}{\text{Q(P} - \text{V)} - \text{F} - \text{I}}$$

$$= \frac{\text{S} - \text{VC}}{\text{S} - \text{VC} - \text{F} - \text{I}}$$

For Omkar, at sales of ₹200,000 we can substitute data from Tables 12.1 and 12.3 into Equation 12.4 to find the degree of total leverage if the debt ratio is 50 percent:

$$\text{DFL}_{₹200{,}000, \text{Debt/TA} = 50\%} = \frac{₹200{,}000 - ₹120{,}000}{₹200{,}000 - ₹120{,}000 - ₹48{,}000 - ₹12{,}000}$$

$$\text{DPS}_1 = \frac{₹500{,}000 - ₹300{,}000}{250{,}000} = \frac{₹200{,}000}{250{,}000} = ₹0.80$$

$$= \text{DOL} \times \text{DFL} = 2.5 \times 1.6 = 4.0 \text{ times}$$

[8]We illustrate DFL at 50 percent debt rather than at OptiCap's optimal capital structure of 40 percent debt to save space. Because EPS figures are available in Table 12.3, they do not have to be computed for our illustration.

We can use the degree of total leverage (DTL) to find the new earnings per share (EPS_1) for any given percentage change in sales, proceeding as shown in Equation 12.5:

12.5

$$EPS_1 = EPS_0 + EPS_0(\Delta TL \times \%\Delta Sales)$$
$$= EPS_0[1 + (DTL \times \% \Delta Sales)]$$

For example, a 65 percent increase in sales, from ₹200,000 to ₹330,000, would cause EPS_0 (₹2.40 as shown in Section III of Table 12.3) to increase to ₹8.64:

$$EPS_1 = ₹2.40[1.0 + (4)(0.65)] = ₹2.40(3.60) = ₹8.64.$$

This figure agrees with the one for EPS shown in Table 12.3. All else being equal, *a lower (higher) DTL suggests that lower (higher) risk is associated with both the firm's business risk and its financial risk*, which in combination represent total risk.

The degree of leverage concept is useful primarily for the insights it provides regarding the joint effects of operating and financial leverage on earnings per share. The concept can be used to show management the effect of financing the firm with debt versus common stock. For example, management might find that the current capital structure is such that a 10 percent decline in sales would produce a 50 percent decline in earnings, whereas with a different financing package, and thus a different degree of total leverage, a 10 percent sales decline might cause earnings to decline by only 20 percent. Having the alternatives stated in this manner gives decision makers a better idea of the ramifications of alternative financing plans, and hence of different capital structures.[9]

12-4 Liquidity and Capital Structure

Some practical difficulties are associated with the type of analysis described in the previous section, including the following:

1. It is difficult to determine exactly how either P/E ratios or equity capitalization rates (r_s values) are affected by different DFLs.
2. A firm's managers might be more or less conservative than the average stockholder, so management might set a somewhat different target capital structure than the one that would maximize the stock price. Managers of a publicly owned firm never would admit this, because they might be removed from office if they did.
3. Managers of large firms, especially those that provide vital services such as electricity or phones, have a responsibility to provide continuous service. Therefore, they must refrain from using leverage to the point where the firm's long-run survival is endangered. Long-run viability might conflict with short-run stock price maximization and capital cost minimization.[10]

For all these reasons, managers are concerned about the effects of financial leverage on the risk of bankruptcy, and an analysis of this factor is therefore an important input in all capital structure decisions. Accordingly, managers give considerable weight to financial strength indicators such as the **times-interest-earned (TIE) ratio**, which is computed by dividing EBIT by interest expense. The TIE ratio provides an indication of how well the firm can cover its interest payments with operating income (EBIT): the lower this ratio, the higher the probability that a firm will default on its debt and be forced into bankruptcy.

times-interest-earned (TIE) ratio A ratio that measures the firm's ability to meet its annual interest obligations; calculated by dividing earnings before interest and taxes (EBIT) by interest charges.

[9]The degree of leverage concept is also useful for investors. If firms in an industry are classified as to their degrees of total leverage, an investor who is optimistic about prospects for the industry might favor those firms with high leverage, and vice versa if he or she expected industry sales to decline. However, it is very difficult to separate fixed from variable costs. Accounting statements generally do not contain this breakdown, so the analyst must make the separation in a judgmental manner. Note that costs really are fixed, variable, and semivariable, for if times get tough enough, firms will sell off depreciable assets and thus reduce depreciation charges (a fixed cost), lay off "permanent" employees, reduce salaries of the remaining personnel, and so on. For this reason, the degree of leverage concept generally is more useful in explaining the general nature of the relationship than in developing precise numbers, and any numbers developed should be thought of as approximations rather than as exact specifications.

[10]Recognizing this fact, most public service commissions that regulate utilities require them to obtain the commission's approval before issuing long-term securities, and Congress has empowered the SEC to supervise the capital structures of public utility holding companies. However, in addition to concern over the firms' safety, which suggests low debt ratios, both managers and regulators recognize a need to keep all costs as low as possible, including the cost of capital. Because a firm's capital structure affects its cost of capital, regulatory commissions and utility managers try to select capital structures that will minimize the cost of capital, subject to the constraint that the firm's financial flexibility not be endangered.

Following are expected TIE ratios that Omkar would experience at the different debt/assets ratios we examined.

Debt/Assets Ratio	Expected TIE
10%	25.0×
20	11.8
30	7.4
40	5.0
50	3.3
60	2.2

As you can see, if the debt/assets ratio is only 10 percent, the expected TIE is very high at 25×, but the interest coverage ratio would decline rapidly if the debt/assets ratio is increased. Note, however, that these coverages are expected values at different debt/assets ratios; the actual TIE for any debt/assets ratio will be higher if sales exceed the expected level, but lower if sales fall below this level. In general, we know that with less debt, there is a much lower probability of a TIE of less than 1.0, the level at which the firm is not earning enough to meet its required interest payments and thus is seriously exposed to the threat of bankruptcy.[11]

12-5 Capital Structure Theory

Over the years, researchers have proposed numerous theories to explain what firms' capital structures should be and why firms have different capital structures. The general theories of capital structure have been developed along two main lines: (1) tax benefit/bankruptcy cost trade-off theory and (2) signaling theory. These two theories are discussed in this section.

12-5a Trade-Off Theory

Modern capital structure theory began in 1958, when Professors Franco Modigliani and Merton Miller (hereafter MM) published what is considered by many to be the most influential finance article ever written.[12] MM proved—under a very restrictive set of assumptions, including that such financial costs as personal income taxes, brokerage costs, and bankruptcy do not exist—that due to the tax deductibility of interest on corporate debt, a firm's value rises continuously as more debt is used, and hence its value will be maximized by financing almost entirely with debt.

Because several of the assumptions outlined by MM obviously were, and still are, unrealistic, MM's position was only the beginning of capital structure research. Subsequent researchers, and MM themselves, extended the basic theory by relaxing the assumptions. Other researchers attempted to test the various theoretical models with actual data to see exactly how stock prices and capital costs are affected by capital structure. Both the theoretical and the empirical results have added to our understanding of capital structure, but none of these studies has produced results that can be used to precisely identify a firm's optimal capital structure. A summary of the theoretical and empirical research to date is expressed graphically in Figure 12.5.

Here are the key points in the figure:

1. The fact that interest is a tax-deductible expense makes corporate debt less expensive than common stock or preferred stock. In effect, the government pays, or subsidizes, part of the cost of debt capital; thus, using debt causes more of the firm's operating income (EBIT) to flow through to investors. Accordingly, the more debt a company uses, the higher its value.

2. A firm pays higher interest rates as it uses greater amounts of debt. In addition, expected tax rates fall at high debt levels, which further reduces the expected value of the debt tax shelter. Further, as the firm uses more debt, the probability of bankruptcy, which brings with it lawyers' fees and other costs, increases.

3. There is some threshold level of debt, labeled D/A_1 in Figure 12.5, below which the effects noted in point 2 are immaterial. Beyond D/A_1, however, the bankruptcy-related costs, especially higher interest rates on new debt, become increasingly important, and they reduce the tax benefits of debt at an increasing rate. In the range from D/A_1 to D/A_2, bankruptcy-related costs reduce but do not completely offset the tax benefits of debt, so the firm's stock price rises (but at a decreasing rate) as the debt/assets ratio increases.

[11]Note that cash flows can be sufficient to cover required interest payments even though the TIE is less than 1.0. Thus, at least for a while, a firm might be able to avoid bankruptcy even though its operating income is less than its interest charges. However, most debt contracts stipulate that firms must maintain the TIE ratio above some minimum level, say, 2.0 or 2.5, or else they cannot borrow any additional funds, which can severely constrain operations. Such potential constraints, as much as the threat of actual bankruptcy, limit the use of debt.

[12]Franco Modigliani and Merton H. Miller, "The Cost of Capital, Corporation Finance, and the Theory of Investment," *American Economic Review*, June 1958, 261–297, and "Corporate Income Taxes and the Cost of Capital," *American Economic Review*, June 1963, 433–443. Modigliani and Miller both won Nobel Prizes for their work.

FIGURE 12.5 Effect of Leverage on the Value of Omkar's Stock

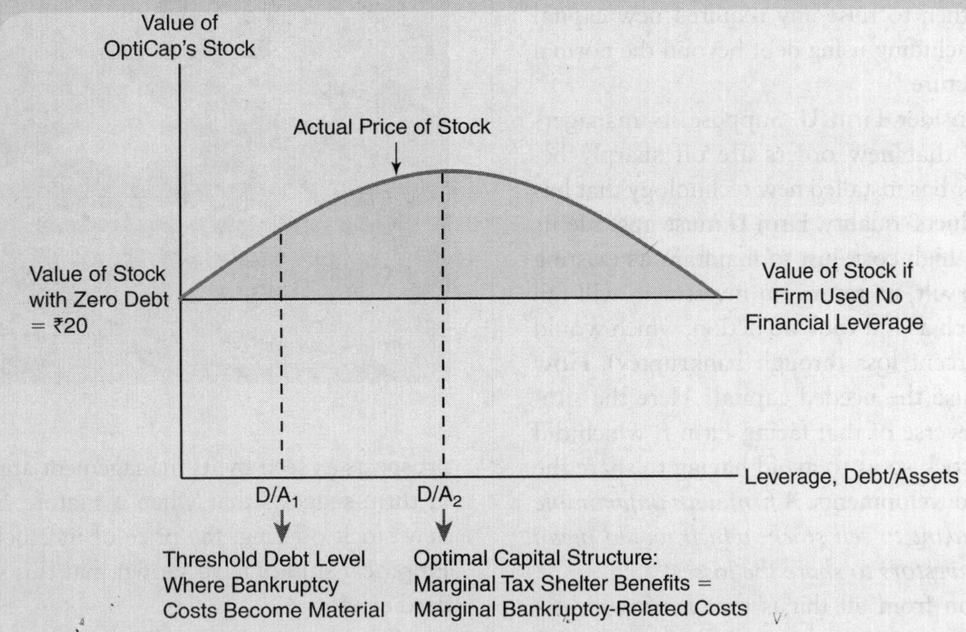

However, beyond D/A_2, bankruptcy-related costs exceed the tax benefits, so from this point on increasing the debt/assets ratio lowers the value of the stock. Therefore, D/A_2 is the optimal capital structure.

4. Although both theory and empirical evidence support the preceding discussion, researchers have not been able to identify points D/A_1 and D/A_2 precisely. As a result, the graphs shown in Figures 12.4 and 12.5 must be taken as approximations, not as precisely defined functions.

Another disturbing aspect of capital structure theory as expressed in Figure 12.5 is the fact that many large, successful firms, such as Microsoft, use far less debt than the theory suggests. This point led to the development of signaling theory, which is discussed next.

12-5b **Signaling Theory**

MM assumed that investors have the same information about a firm's prospects as its managers. This is called **symmetric information**, because both those who are inside the firm (managers and employees) and those who are outside the firm (investors) have identical information. However, in reality, we know that managers have substantially more and better information about their firms than do outside investors. This is called **asymmetric information**, and it has an important effect on decisions to use either debt or equity to finance capital projects. To see why, consider two situations, one in which the company's managers know that its prospects are extremely favorable (Firm F) and one in which the managers know that the future looks very unfavorable (Firm U).

Suppose, for example, that Firm F's research and development labs have just discovered a cure for the common cold, but the product is not patentable. Firm F's managers want to keep the new product a secret for as long as possible to delay competitors' entry into the market. New plants and distribution facilities must be built to exploit the new product, so capital must be raised. How should Firm F's management raise the needed capital? If the firm sells stock, when profits from the new product start flowing in, the price of the stock will rise sharply and the purchasers of the new stock will have made a bonanza. The current stockholders (including the managers) also will do well, but not as well as they would have if the company had not sold stock before the price increased, because then they would not have had to share the benefits of the new product

symmetric information The situation in which investors and managers have identical information about the firm's prospects.

asymmetric information The situation in which managers have different (better) information about their firm's prospects than do outside investors.

with the new stockholders. Therefore, *one would expect a firm with very favorable prospects to try to avoid selling stock* and, rather, to raise any required new capital by other means, including using debt beyond the normal target capital structure.[13]

Now let's consider Firm U. Suppose its managers have information that new orders are off sharply because a competitor has installed new technology that has improved its products' quality. Firm U must upgrade its own facilities at a high cost, just to maintain its existing sales level. As a result, its return on investment will fall (but not by as much as if it took no action, which would lead to a 100 percent loss through bankruptcy). How should Firm U raise the needed capital? Here the situation is just the reverse of that facing Firm F, which did not want to sell stock so as to avoid having to share the benefits of future developments. *A firm with unfavorable prospects would want to sell stock, which would mean bringing in new investors to share the losses!*[14]

The conclusion from all this is that firms with extremely bright prospects prefer not to finance through new stock offerings, whereas firms with poor prospects do like to finance with outside equity. How would you, as an investor, react to this conclusion? You ought to say, "If I see that a company plans to issue new stock, this should worry me because I know that management would not want to issue stock if future prospects looked good, but it *would* want to issue stock if things looked bad. Therefore, I should lower my estimate of the firm's value, other things constant, if I read an announcement of a new stock offering." Of course, the negative reaction would be stronger if the stock sale were by a large, established company such as Reliance or TCS, which surely would have many financing options, than if it were by a small company. For a small company, a stock sale might mean truly extraordinary investment opportunities that are so large they just could not be financed without a stock sale.

If you gave the preceding answer, your views are consistent with those of many sophisticated portfolio managers. Simply stated, the announcement of a stock offering by a mature firm that seems to have multiple financing alternatives is taken as a **signal** that the firm's prospects as seen by its management are not bright. This, in turn, suggests that when a mature firm announces a new stock offering, the price of its stock should decline. Empirical studies have shown that this situation does indeed exist.

signal An action taken by a firm's management that provides clues to investors about how management views the firm's prospects.

reserve borrowing capacity The ability to borrow money at a reasonable cost when good investment opportunities arise; firms often use less debt than specified by the optimal capital structure to ensure that they can obtain debt capital later if necessary.

Photolibrary/Jupiter Images

What are the implications of all this for capital structure decisions? The answer is that firms should, in normal times, maintain a **reserve borrowing capacity** that can be used in the event that some especially good investment opportunities come along. This means that firms should generally use less debt than would be suggested by the tax benefit/bankruptcy cost trade-off expressed in Figure 12.5.

Signaling and asymmetric information concepts also have implications for the marginal cost of capital (MCC) curve discussed in Chapter 11. There we saw that the weighted average cost of capital (WACC) increased when retained earnings were exhausted and the firm was forced to sell new common stock to raise equity. The jump in the WACC, or the break in the MCC schedule, was attributed only to flotation costs. However, if the announcement of a stock sale causes a decline in the price of the stock, then r_e as measured by $r_e = \hat{D}_1/P_0(1 - F) + g$ will increase more because of the decline in P_0. This factor magnifies the effects of flotation costs, and perhaps it is an even more important explanation for the jump in the MCC schedule at the point at which new stock must be issued.

[13]It would be illegal for Firm F's managers to purchase more shares on the basis of their inside knowledge of the new product. They could be sent to jail if they did.

[14]Of course, Firm U would have to make certain disclosures when it offered new shares to the public, but it might be able to meet the legal requirements without fully disclosing management's worst fears.

12-6 Variations in Capital Structures among Firms

As might be expected, wide variations in the use of financial leverage occur both across industries and among the individual firms in each industry. For example, drug and biotechnology companies generally do not use much debt (their common equity ratios are high), because the production of successful pharmaceuticals or biotech products is unpredictable. The uncertainties inherent in industries such as these as well as those that are cyclical, oriented toward research, or subject to huge product liability suits normally render the heavy use of debt unwise. On the other hand, utilities traditionally use large amounts of debt, particularly long-term debt. Their fixed assets make good security for mortgage bonds, and their relatively stable sales make it safe for them to carry more debt than would be true for firms with more business risk.

Wide variations in capital structures also exist among firms in particular industries. For example, although the average pharmaceutical firm had a capital structure consisting of approximately 25 percent debt in 2012, Pfizer had approximately 50 percent debt in its capital structure whereas GlaxoSmithKline had greater than 75 percent debt in its capital structure. Thus, we can conclude that factors unique to individual firms, including managerial attitudes, play an important role in setting target capital structures.

12-6a Capital Structures around the World[15]

As you might expect, when we examine the capital structures of companies around the world, we also find wide variations. Companies in Italy and Japan use greater proportions of debt (65 to 80 percent) than do companies in the United States and Canada (45 to 55 percent), and companies in the United Kingdom use the lowest proportion of debt of industrialized countries (30 to 35 percent). Of course, different countries use somewhat different accounting conventions, which make comparisons difficult. Still, even after adjusting for accounting differences, researchers find that Italian and Japanese firms use considerably more financial leverage than U.S. and Canadian companies.

It seems reasonable to attribute differences in firms' capital structures among countries to dissimilar tax structures. Although the interest on corporate debt is deductible in most countries, and individuals must pay taxes on interest received, both dividends and capital gains are taxed differently around the world. The tax codes in most developed countries encourage personal investing and savings more than the U.S. tax code does. For example, Germany, Italy, and many other European countries do not tax capital gains, and in most other developed countries, including Japan, France, and Canada, capital gains are not taxed unless they exceed some minimum amount. Further, in Germany and Italy, dividends are not taxed as income, and in most other countries, some amount of dividends is tax exempt. From these observations, we can make the following general conclusions: (1) From a tax standpoint, corporations should be equally inclined to use debt in most developed countries. (2) In countries where capital gains are not taxed, investors should show a preference for stocks compared to investors in countries that have capital gains taxes. (3) Investor preferences should lead to relatively low equity capital costs in those countries that do not tax capital gains, and this, in turn, should cause firms in those countries to use significantly more equity capital than their U.S. counterparts. For the most part, however, this is exactly the opposite of the actual capital structures we observe, so differences in tax laws cannot explain the observed capital structure differences.

If tax rates cannot explain the different capital structures, perhaps risks, such as the risk of bankruptcy, can. Actual bankruptcy, and even the threat of potential bankruptcy, imposes a costly burden on firms with large amounts of debt. In the United States, *equity* monitoring costs are comparatively low because corporations produce quarterly reports and must comply with relatively stringent audit requirements, which are less prevalent in other countries. On the other hand, costs associated with monitoring debt probably are lower in such countries as Germany and Japan than in the United States, because most of the corporate debt in those countries consists of bank loans as opposed to publicly issued bonds. More importantly, though, the banks in many European and developed Asian countries are closely linked to the corporations that borrow from them, often holding major equity positions in, and having substantial influence over, the management of the debtor firms. Given these close relationships, the banks in Germany and Japan are much more directly

[15]The information provided in this section was obtained primarily from *OECD Financial Statistics, Part 3: Non-Financial Enterprises Financial Statement, 1996.*

involved than U.S. banks are with debtor firms' affairs, and as a result, they also are more accommodating than are U.S. bondholders in the event of financial distress. This, in turn, suggests that any given amount of debt gives rise to a lower threat of bankruptcy for a firm in Germany and Japan than for a U.S. firm with the same amount of business risk. Thus, an analysis of both bankruptcy costs and equity monitoring costs leads to the conclusion that U.S. firms should have more equity and less debt than do firms in countries such as Japan and Germany, which is what we typically observe.

We cannot state that one financial system is better than another one in the sense of making the firms in one country more efficient than those in another. However, as U.S. firms become increasingly involved in worldwide operations, they must become increasingly aware of worldwide conditions, and they must be prepared to adapt to conditions in the various countries in which they do business.

KEY CAPITAL STRUCTURE CONCEPTS

To conclude this chapter, we summarize some capital structure concepts that were discussed. Basic factors that influence capital structure decisions include the following:

- The greater the firm's *business risk*, or the riskiness that would be inherent in the firm's operations if it used no debt, the lower the amount of debt that is optimal.
- *Financial risk* is the risk common stockholders must take when the firm uses financing alternatives that require fixed periodic payments (e.g., debt and preferred stock).
- Firms that maintain *financial flexibility*, or the ability to raise capital on reasonable terms under adverse conditions, are less risky and find it easier to raise funds when money is tight than firms that don't have financial flexibility.
- Some managers are more aggressive than others when using debt; hence, managerial attitude (conservatism or aggressiveness) influences the amount of debt a firm takes on. This factor does not affect the optimal, or value-maximizing, capital structure.
- Leverage, which is the presence of fixed costs (both operating and financial), magnifies the effects of changes in sales on operating income and net income. Everything else the same, more leverage generally indicates more risk. Thus, leverage should be considered when making capital structure decisions.
- Even though scientific models have not been developed to determine the optimal capital structure of a firm, it is important for a company to evaluate the effects of leverage on its value (as outlined in this chapter) to establish a target capital structure that can be followed when raising funds.

MULTIPLE CHOICE QUESTIONS

1. What will constitute equity in deciding the debt to equity ratio of a company?

a. The share capital of the company

b. All the assets of the company

c. Past accumulated and undistributed profits of the company

d. Both a and c

2. When debt goes up,

a. WACC comes down

b. WACC goes up

c. There is no impact on the WACC

d. There is no relationship between the two

3. Cost of debt is taken into WACC

a. Always post-tax

b. Always pre-tax

c. Depends on the circumstances

d. Cost of debt is not taken into WACC

4. A firm's WACC will be

a. Higher under the book value method than under the market value method

b. Lower under the book value method than under the market value method

c. Most of the time the two methods will return the same WACC

d. No generalization is possible

5. Under the Modigliani-Miller propositions,

a. Value of a firm will not change with capital structure

b. Value of a firm will keep going up with increased debt when there is no tax shield on interest on debt

c. Value of a firm will keep going up with increased debt when there is tax shield on interest on debt

d. Value of a firm will be lower with increased debt

6. The ROE of a firm,

a. Keeps going up with increased debt

b. Remains the same at all debt levels

c. ROE is not a function of the debt level

d. ROE will go up only if ROA goes up

7. The target capital structure refers to

a. A structure that is ideal but not expected to be achieved

b. A structure that the company plans to achieve over a short period of time

c. An average of the structure under book weights and market weights

d. None of the above

8. Homemade leverage

a. Is a theoretical concept that cannot be practiced easily

b. Shows why leverage is not important

c. Both a and b

d. None of the above

9. A pro forma balance sheet and income statement is

a. Balance sheet and income statement without details

b. An estimated statement for the ensuing year

c. More like a target and a budget

d. Both b and c

10. The degree of operating leverage is

a. A figure that shows the extent to which profits will change with change in scale of operations

b. A figure that shows the extent to which variable costs will change with change in scale of operations

c. A figure that shows the extent to which total costs will change with change in scale of operations

d. Both b and c

Answers:

1.	(d)	2.	(a)	3.	(a)	4.	(d)	5.	(b)
6.	(d)	7.	(b)	8.	(a)	9.	(a)	10.	(d)

PROBLEMS

For more problems, login to CourseMate for CFIN at CengageBrain.com

In all of the following problems, it is assumed that the firm's capital structure consists of debt and common equity only; preferred stock is not used to finance the firm.

12–1 Using the information provided in Tables 12.1 and 12.2, compute the company's EPS when sales are ₹200,000 and the debt-to-total-assets ratio (D/TA) is 20 percent.

12–2 Lonavala Gardens (LG) has ₹6 million in assets, ₹700,000 EBIT, 80,000 shares of stock outstanding, and a marginal tax rate equal to 40 percent. If LG's debt-to-total-assets ratio (D/TA) is 70 percent, it pays 12 percent interest on debt, whereas if the D/TA ratio is 40 percent, interest is 9 percent. Calculate LG's EPS and ROE (ROE = Net income/Equity) for each capital structure. Which capital structure is better?

12–3 Firm AB and Firm YZ are identical except for their debt-to-total-assets ratios (D/TAs) and interest rates on debt. Each has ₹200,000 in assets, ₹40,000 EBIT, and a 40 percent marginal tax rate. Firm AB has a D/TA ratio of 40 percent and pays 7.5 percent interest on its debt, whereas YZ has a 60 percent D/TA ratio and pays 10 percent interest on debt. Each firm has 5,000 shares of common stock outstanding. Calculate each firm's EPS and ROE (ROE = Net income/Equity). Discuss your results.

12-4 Firm LM's debt-to-total-assets ratio (D/TA) is 25 percent, whereas Firm QR's D/TA ratio is 50 percent. LM has ₹800,000 in assets, ₹60,000 EBIT, and 15,000 shares of stock outstanding, and it pays 8 percent interest. QR has ₹400,000 in assets, ₹70,000 EBIT, and 25,000 shares of stock outstanding, and it pays 10 percent interest. The marginal tax rate for both firms is 40 percent. Calculate each firm's EPS and ROE (ROE = Net income/Equity). Discuss your results.

12-5 Senior management of Neha's Nooks (NN) has determined that there is a 20 percent chance EPS will be ₹4.50 next year, there is a 70 percent chance EPS will be 1.50, and there is a 20 percent chance EPS will be –₹1.80. Calculate the expected value, standard deviation, and coefficient of variation for NN's forecasted EPS.

12-6 Given the following information, calculate the expected value, standard deviation, and coefficient of variation of the EPS for both firms.

	Probability		
	0.3	0.6	0.1
Firm 1: EPS_1	₹2.00	₹1.30	(₹1.20)
Firm 2: EPS_2	₹3.00	1.80	(2.20)

12-7 The CFO of Ink Imagination (II) wants to calculate next year's EPS using different leverage ratios. II's total assets are ₹5 million, and its marginal tax rate is 40 percent. The company has estimated next year's EBIT for three possible economic states: ₹1.2 million with a 0.2 probability, ₹800,000 with a 0.5 probability, and ₹500,000 with a 0.3 probability. Calculate II's expected EPS, standard deviation, and coefficient of variation for each of the following capital structures. Which capital structure do you recommend?

Leverage (Debt/Assets)	Interest Rate	Shares of Stock Outstanding
20%	6%	300,000
50	10	200,000

12-8 Anantha Corporation currently has ₹50 million in liabilities and common equity in combination. The firm has no preferred stock. After careful evaluation, the CFO constructed the following table to show the CEO the effect of changing the firm's capital structure:

Amount of Debt in the Capital Structure	Earnings per Share (EPS)	Market Price per Share (P_0)
₹10,000,000	₹5.00	₹125.50
20,000,000	5.50	130.75
30,000,000	5.70	130.00

According to this information, what is Anantha's optimal capital structure? Explain your answer.

12-9 Using the following information for Harsh Hardware, determine the capital structure that results in the lowest weighted average cost of capital (WACC) for the firm. Explain your answer.

Proportion of Debt	Earnings per Share (EPS)	Stock Price, P_0
10%	₹3.85	₹95.40
30	3.98	97.25
50	4.10	96.80

12-10 Following is the latest income statement for Surfside Airlines:

Sales	₹150,000
Variable operating costs	(105,000)
Gross profit	45,000
Fixed operating costs	(20,000)
Net operating income	25,000
Interest	(15,000)
Earnings before taxes	10,000
Taxes (40%)	(4,000)
Net income	₹ 6,000

Compute Surfside's degree of operating leverage (DOL), degree of financial leverage (DFL), and degree of total leverage (DTL).

12-11 Deepak Recovery Systems (DRS) has a degree of operating leverage (DOL) equal to 3.2× and a degree of total leverage (DTL) equal to 8×. DRS forecasts that this year's sales will be ₹300,000 and that EBIT will be ₹180,000. If sales actually turn out to be ₹313,500, what will DRS's EBIT be?

12-12 The CFO of Janardhan Jibs (JJ) expects this year's sales to be ₹2.5 million. EBIT is expected to be ₹1 million. The CFO knows that if sales actually turn out to be ₹2.3 million, JJ's EBIT will be ₹880,000. What is JJ's degree of operating leverage (DOL)?

12-13 The CFO of The Chetan Shop has determined that the company's degree of operating leverage (DOL) is 2.5× and that its degree of financial leverage (DFL) is 3.0×. According to this information, how will the firm's EPS be affected if its amount of EBIT turns out to be 5 percent higher than expected?

12-14 Ekalavya Energy has forecasted that its EPS will be ₹4 per share this year. If the firm's degree of operating leverage (DOL) is 3.0× and its degree of financial leverage (DFL) is 2.0×, what will its EPS be if sales turn out to be 10 percent lower than expected?

12-15 Maragad Murphy's degree of financial leverage (DFL) is 4×. The company knows that if sales are 6 percent higher than forecasted, its EPS will increase by 36 percent. What is Maragad Murphy's degree of operating leverage (DOL)?

12-16 Leela Leisure's forecasted EBIT is ₹750,000. This year, Leela will pay ₹250,000 interest on its debt and ₹320,000 dividends to its common stockholders. If its marginal tax rate is 40 percent, what is Leela's degree of financial leverage (DFL)?

12-17 A firm has determined that its degree of operating leverage (DOL) is 5× and that its degree of financial leverage (DFL) is 2×. As a result, what will be the change in its expected EPS if sales are 7 percent lower than expected?

12-18 Smita Bottling Company (SBC) expects this year's sales to be ₹560,000. SBC's variable operating costs are 75 percent of sales and its fixed operating costs are ₹90,000. SBC pays interest on its debt equal to ₹30,000 per year and its marginal tax rate is 35 percent. (a) Compute at SBC's DOL, DFL, and DTL. (b) If sales turn out to be ₹588,000 rather than ₹560,000, what will be SBC's EBIT and net income?

12-19 The CFO determined that the firm's degree of operating leverage (DOL) is 3× at sales equal to ₹900,000. She also determined that, if sales are actually ₹945,000, EPS will be ₹2.60 rather than the forecasted value of ₹2.00. What is the firm's degree of financial leverage (DFL)?

12-20 Excellent Analysts Resources (EAR) has provided you with the following information about three companies you are currently evaluating:

Company	Degree of Operating Leverage (DOL)	Degree of Financial Leverage (DFL)
Acme	1.5×	6.0×
Apex	3.0×	4.0×
Alps	5.0×	2.0×

Which firm would be considered riskiest? Explain your answer.

Capital Structure

Learning Outcomes

LO.1 Describe how business risk and financial risk affect a firm's capital structure.

- Business risk refers to the risk of a firm's normal operations, ignoring how it is financed. Financial risk refers to the risk that is associated with how the firm is financed. Firms that have greater business risk generally use less debt in their capital structures, because such firms normally generate cash flows that are less stable than firms that have less business risk. Firms that have greater financial risk generally either find it difficult to borrow additional funds or must borrow at higher rates than firms that have less financial risk.

LO.2 Describe how businesses determine their optimal capital structures.

- The primary objective of the firm is to maximize its value. As a result, when determining the optimal capital structure, a firm evaluates how changes in its capital structure will affect the value of its common stock. The optimal capital structure is the mixture of debt and equity that maximizes the value of the firm (minimizes its cost of capital).

LO.3 Describe how leverage can be used to make capital structure decisions, and discuss the effects (a) operating leverage, (b) financial leverage, and (c) total leverage have on risks associated with a firm.

- Leverage refers to fixed costs, whether those costs are associated with the firm's operations or its financing structure. Leverage magnifies the effects changes in sales and operating income have on the firm's net income; the possibility of greater changes implies greater risk.
- Operating leverage refers to fixed operating costs, which include expenses that do not change if there are changes in the level of production. The degree of operating leverage (DOL) indicates by what percentage operating income will change if sales turn out to be 1 percent different than expected.
- Financial leverage refers to fixed financing costs, which generally include interest payments and preferred stock dividends. The degree of financial leverage (DFL) indicates by what percentage net income will change if net operating income (EBIT) turns out to be 1 percent different than expected.
- Total leverage is the combination of operating leverage and financial leverage. The degree of total leverage can be computed as: $DTL = DOL \times DFL$. DTL indicates by what percentage net income will change if sales turn out to be 1 percent different than expected.

LO.4 Discuss how managers consider liquidity when determining the optimal capital structure for a firm.

- Managers want to maintain a level of liquidity that will keep the firm operating. As a result, firms generally try to maintain a particular value for their times-interest-earned (TIE) ratios. In addition, debt covenants (restrictions) often require firms to maintain specific TIE values to ensure that interest payments can be covered with operating income.

LO.5 Discuss the two general theories—that is, (a) trade-off theory and (b) signaling theory—that have been developed to explain what firms' capital structures should be and why firms' capital structures differ.

- The trade-off theory suggests that a firm should issue debt as long as the tax deductibility of the interest payments is advantageous (i.e., lowers the overall cost of capital). Although interest is tax deductible, interest rates increase as more debt is used, because the chances that the firm will go bankrupt also increase (the trade-off).
- According to the signaling theory, firms might issue debt when funds are needed to invest in growth and value increasing projects so that existing stockholders do not have to share the firm's future success

with new stockholders. On the other hand, stockholders don't mind sharing when prospects are poor.

LO.6 Describe how and why capital structures vary among firms in the United States and around the world.

- Generally, firms that have more stable operations are able to take on more debt than firms with less stable operations. Internationally, whichever form of funding (debt or equity) is easier to monitor generally is more prevalent in firms' capital structures.

Chapter 12 Key Capital Structure Concepts

- The greater the firm's *business risk*, or the riskiness that would be inherent in the firm's operations if it used no debt, the lower the amount of debt that is optimal.
- Because interest on debt is tax deductible, everything else equal, the effective after-tax cost of debt is lower for firms with high tax rates than for firms with low tax rates.
- Firms that maintain *financial flexibility*, or the ability to raise capital on reasonable terms under adverse conditions, are less risky and find it easier to raise funds when money is tight than firms that don't have financial flexibility.
- Some managers are more aggressive than others when using debt; hence, managerial attitude (conservatism or aggressiveness) influences the amount of debt a firm takes on. This factor does not affect the optimal, or value-maximizing, capital structure.
- Leverage, which is the presence of fixed costs (both operating and financial), magnifies the effects of changes in sales on operating income, net income, or both of these income levels. Everything else the same, more leverage generally indicates more risk. Thus, leverage should be considered when making capital structure decisions.
- Even though scientific models have not been developed to determine the optimal capital structure of a firm, it is important for a company to evaluate the effects of leverage on its value (as outlined in this chapter) to establish a target capital structure that can be followed when raising funds.

Key Terms

LO.1

capital structure The combination of debt and equity used to finance a firm. *p. 205*

target capital structure The mix of debt, preferred stock, and common equity with which the firm plans to finance its investments. *p. 205*

business risk The risk associated with the firm's operations, ignoring any financing effects. *p. 205*

financial risk The portion of stockholders' risk, over and above basic business risk that results from the manner in which the firm is financed. *p. 205*

operating leverage The presence of fixed operating costs that do not change when the level of sales changes. *p. 206*

financial leverage The extent to which fixed-income securities (debt and preferred stock) are used in a firm's capital structure. *p. 206*

LO.2

EPS indifference point The level of sales at which EPS will be the same whether the firm uses debt or common stock financing. *p. 211*

LO.3

degree of operating leverage (DOL) The percentage change in operating income (EBIT) associated with a given percentage change in sales. *p. 214*

degree of financial leverage (DFL) The percentage change in earnings per share (EPS) associated with a given percentage change in earnings before interest and taxes (EBIT). *p. 215*

degree of total leverage (DTL) The percentage change in EPS that results from a given percentage change in sales; DTL shows the effects of both operating leverage and financial leverage. *p. 216*

LO.4

times-interest-earned (TIE) ratio A ratio that measures the firm's ability to meet its annual interest obligations; calculated by dividing earnings before interest and taxes (EBIT) by interest charges. *p. 217*

LO.5

symmetric information The situation in which investors and managers have identical information about the firm's prospects. *p. 219*

asymmetric information The situation in which managers have different (better) information about their firm's prospects than do outside investors. *p. 219*

signal An action taken by a firm's management that provides clues to investors about how management views the firm's prospects. *p. 220*

reserve borrowing capacity The ability to borrow money at a reasonable cost when good investment opportunities arise; firms often use less debt than specified by the optimal capital structure to ensure that they can obtain debt capital later if necessary. *p. 220*

CHAPTER 13

Distribution of Retained Earnings: Dividends and Stock Repurchases

Learning Outcomes

LO.1 Describe the views that have been proposed to explain why firms follow particular dividend policies and why investors react when firms change dividend policies.

LO.2 Discuss (a) the types of dividend payments and (b) payment procedures that firms follow in practice.

LO.3 Discuss factors that firms consider when making dividend policy decisions.

LO.4 Describe stock dividends and stock splits, and discuss how stock prices are affected by these activities.

LO.5 Describe stock repurchases and discuss reasons firms use repurchases.

LO.6 Discuss differences in dividend polices around the world.

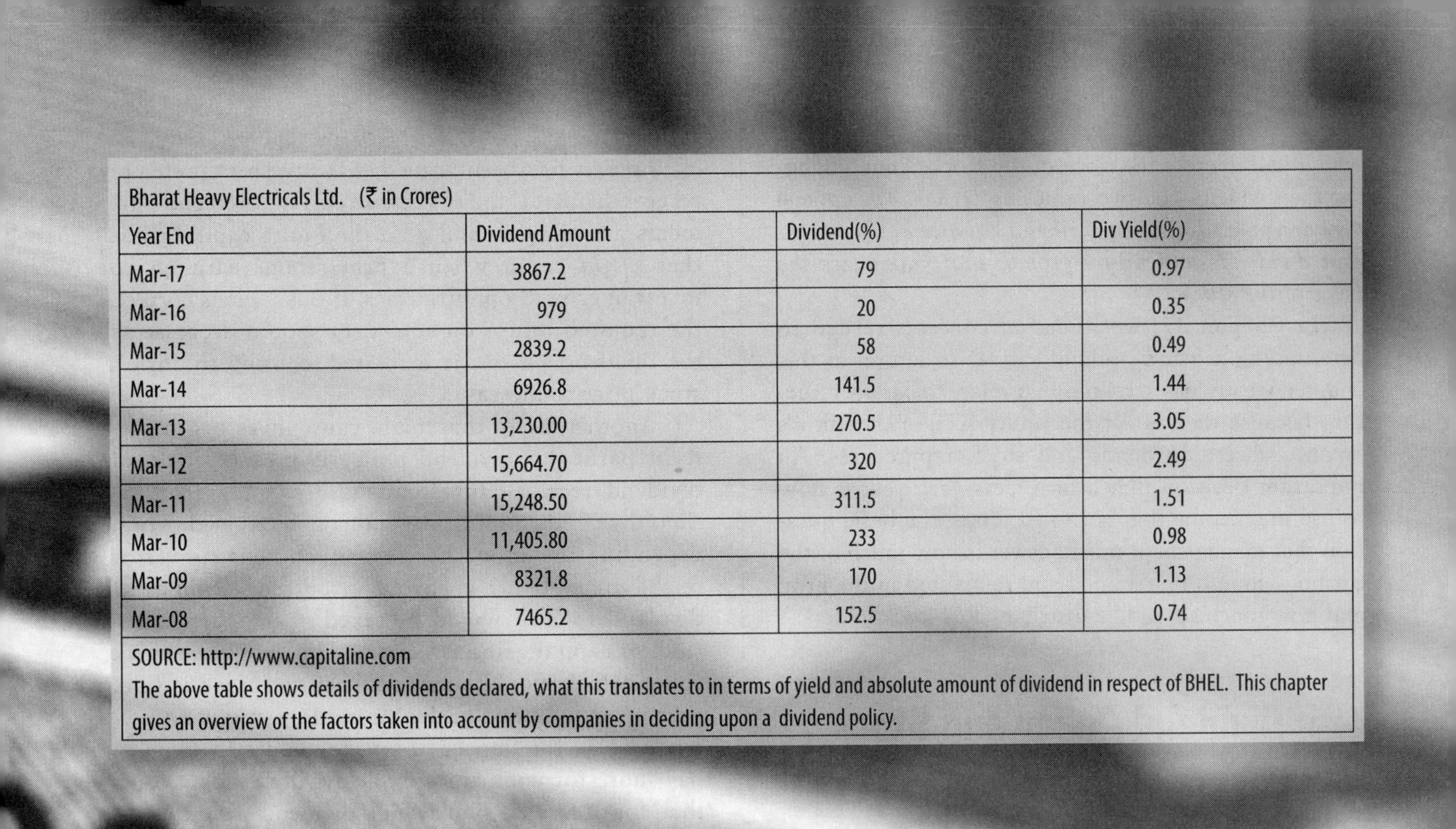

Bharat Heavy Electricals Ltd. (₹ in Crores)			
Year End	Dividend Amount	Dividend(%)	Div Yield(%)
Mar-17	3867.2	79	0.97
Mar-16	979	20	0.35
Mar-15	2839.2	58	0.49
Mar-14	6926.8	141.5	1.44
Mar-13	13,230.00	270.5	3.05
Mar-12	15,664.70	320	2.49
Mar-11	15,248.50	311.5	1.51
Mar-10	11,405.80	233	0.98
Mar-09	8321.8	170	1.13
Mar-08	7465.2	152.5	0.74

SOURCE: http://www.capitaline.com

The above table shows details of dividends declared, what this translates to in terms of yield and absolute amount of dividend in respect of BHEL. This chapter gives an overview of the factors taken into account by companies in deciding upon a dividend policy.

A firm's *dividend policy* involves the decision whether to pay out earnings or to retain them for reinvestment in the firm. Remember that, according to the constant dividend growth model introduced in Chapter 7, the value of common stock can be computed as $\hat{D}_1/(r_s - g)$. This equation shows that if the firm adopts a policy of paying out more in cash dividends, $\hat{D}_1$ rises, which tends to increase the price of the stock. However, everything else equal, if cash dividends are increased, less money is available for reinvestment in the firm and the expected future growth rate, g, will be lowered,

Study Tools

Problems are found at the end of this chapter

+

Login to **CourseMate** for **CFIN** at **CengageBrain.com** for additional problems and other study tools!

which will depress the price of the stock. Thus, changing the dividend has two opposing effects. *The* **optimal dividend policy** *for a firm strikes a balance between current dividends and future growth that maximizes the price of the stock.*

In Chapter 12, we discussed concepts related to determining a firm's optimal capital structure. In this chapter, we discuss activities that relate to capital structure because they affect the equity section of a firm's balance sheet: dividends and stock repurchases. An important decision that a firm faces each year is how to use the income that is earned. Thus, the basic question that management must answer is how much of the earnings should be retained and reinvested in the firm, and how much should be distributed to stockholders.

13-1 Dividend Policy and Stock Value

How do dividend policy decisions affect a firm's stock price? Academic researchers have studied this question extensively for many years, and they have yet to reach definitive conclusions. On the one hand, there are those who suggest that dividend policy is *irrelevant* because they argue that a firm's value should be determined by the basic earning power and business risk of the firm, in which case value depends only on the income (cash) produced, not on how the income is split between dividends and retained earnings (and hence growth). Proponents of this line of reasoning, called the **dividend irrelevance theory,** would contend that investors care only about the *total returns* they receive, not whether they receive those returns in the form of dividends, capital gains, or both. Thus, *if the dividend irrelevance theory is correct, there exists no optimal dividend policy, because dividend policy does not affect the value of the firm.*[1]

On the other hand, it is quite possible that investors do prefer one dividend policy to another; if so, a firm's dividend policy is *relevant*. For example, it has been argued that investors prefer to receive dividends today because current dividend payments are more certain than the future capital gains that *might* result when a firm retains earnings to invest in growth opportunities. If this logic is correct, the required return on equity, r_s, should decrease as the dividend payout is increased, causing the firm's stock price to increase.[2]

Another factor that might cause investors to prefer a particular dividend policy is the tax effect of dividend receipts. Investors must pay taxes at the time dividends and capital gains are received. Thus, depending on his or her tax situation, an investor might prefer either a payout of current earnings as dividends, which would be taxed in the current period, or capital gains associated with growth in stock value, which would be taxed when the stock is sold, perhaps many years in the future. Investors who prefer to delay the impact of taxes would be willing to pay more for companies with low dividend payouts than for otherwise similar high dividend-payout companies, and vice versa.

Those who believe that the firm's dividend policy is relevant are proponents of the **dividend relevance theory,** which asserts that dividend policy can affect the value of a firm through investors' preferences.

Although academic researchers have studied the dividend policy issue extensively, they cannot tell corporate decision makers exactly how dividend policy affects stock prices and capital costs. However, the research has provided some views concerning investors' reactions to dividend policy changes as well as why firms have particular dividend policies. Three of these views are discussed in this section.

13-1a Information Content, or Signaling

If investors expect a company's dividend to increase by 5 percent per year, and the dividend actually increases by 5 percent, the stock price generally will not change significantly on the day the dividend increase is announced. In Wall Street parlance, the announcement of such a dividend increase would be *discounted*, or anticipated, by

optimal dividend policy The dividend policy that strikes a balance between current dividends and future growth, and maximizes the firm's stock price.

dividend irrelevance theory The theory that a firm's dividend policy has no effect on either its value or its cost of capital.

dividend relevance theory The value of a firm is affected by its dividend policy— the optimal dividend policy is the one that maximizes the firm's value.

[1]The principal proponents of the *dividend irrelevance theory* are Miller and Modigliani (MM), who outlined their theory in "Dividend Policy, Growth, and the Valuation of Shares," *Journal of Business*, October 1961, 411–433. The assumptions MM made to develop their dividend irrelevance theory are similar to those they introduced in their capital structure theory mentioned in Chapter 12, which include no personal taxes, no brokerage costs, no bankruptcy, and so forth. Such assumptions are made to afford them the ability to develop a manageable theory.

[2]Myron J. Gordon, "Optimal Investment and Financing Policy," *Journal of Finance*, May 1963, 264–272, and John Lintner, "Dividends, Earnings, Leverage, Stock Prices, and the Supply of Capital to Corporations," *Review of Economics and Statistics*, August 1962, 243–269.

the market, so it would not be considered newsworthy. However, if investors expect a 5 percent increase but the company actually increases the dividend by 25 percent—say, from ₹2.00 to ₹2.50—this generally will be considered good, unanticipated news that should be accompanied by an increase in the price of the stock. Conversely, a lower-than-expected dividend increase, or an unexpected reduction, generally would result in a price decline.

It is a well-known fact that corporations are extremely reluctant to cut dividends, and therefore *managers do not raise dividends unless they anticipate higher, or at least stable, earnings in the future to sustain the higher dividends.* This means that a larger-than-expected dividend increase is taken by investors as a signal that the firm's management forecasts improved future earnings, whereas a dividend reduction signals a forecast of poor earnings. Thus, it can be argued that investors' reactions to changes in dividend payments do not show that investors prefer dividends to retained earnings; rather, stock price changes simply indicate that important information is contained in dividend announcements, because, in effect, such announcements provide investors with information previously known only to management. This theory is referred to as the **information content,** or **signaling, hypothesis.**

13-1b Clientele Effect

It also has been shown that it is certainly possible for a firm to set a particular dividend payout policy, which then attracts a *clientele* consisting of those investors who like the firm's dividend policy. For example, some stockholders, such as retired individuals, prefer current income to future capital gains, so they invest in firms that pay out higher percentages of their earnings as dividends. Other stockholders have no need for current investment income, so they favor low dividend-payout ratios. If investors could not invest in companies with different dividend policies, it might be very expensive for them to achieve their investment goals. For example, investors who prefer capital gains can reinvest any dividends they receive, but they first will have to pay taxes on the income. In essence, then, a **clientele effect** might exist if investors are attracted to certain companies because they have particular dividend policies. In reality, those investors who desire current investment income can purchase shares in high dividend-payout firms, whereas those who do not need current income can invest in low-payout firms. Consequently, we would expect the stock price of a firm to change if the firm changes its dividend policy, because investors will adjust their portfolios to include firms with the desired dividend policy.

13-1c Free Cash Flow Hypothesis

If it is the intent of the financial manager to maximize the value of the firm, then investors should prefer that the firm pay dividends only if acceptable capital budgeting opportunities do not exist. We know that acceptable capital budgeting projects increase the value of the firm. We also know that, because flotation costs are incurred when new stock is issued, it costs a firm more to raise funds using new common equity than it does to use retained earnings. To maximize value, therefore, wherever possible a firm should use retained earnings rather than issue new common stock to finance capital budgeting projects. Proponents of this line of reasoning argue that dividends should be paid only when *free cash flows* in excess of capital budgeting needs exist; if management does otherwise, the firm's value will not be maximized. According to the **free cash flow hypothesis,** the firm should distribute any earnings that cannot be reinvested at a rate that is at least as great as the investors' required rate of return, which is the same as the cost of retained earnings that was discussed in Chapter 11. In other words, free cash flows should be paid out as dividends. Everything else being equal, *firms that retain free cash flows have lower values than firms that distribute free cash flows,* because such firms decrease investors' wealth by investing in projects with IRRs $< r_s$.

The free cash flow hypothesis might help to explain why investors react differently to identical dividend changes made by similar firms. For example, a firm's stock price should not change dramatically, and it might even increase, if dividends are reduced for the purposes of investing in capital budgeting projects with positive NPVs. On the other hand, a company that reduces its dividend simply to increase free cash flows should experience a significant decline in the market value of its stock, because the dividend reduction is not in the best interests of the stockholders.

information content (signaling) hypothesis The theory that investors regard dividend changes as signals of management's earnings forecasts.

clientele effect The tendency of a firm to attract the type of investor who likes its dividend policy.

free cash flow hypothesis All else equal, firms that pay dividends from cash flows that cannot be reinvested in positive net present value projects (*free cash flows*) have higher values than firms that retain free cash flows.

(In this case, an agency problem exists.) Thus, the free cash flow hypothesis suggests that a firm's dividend policy can provide information about management's behavior with respect to wealth maximization.

13-2 Dividend Payments in Practice

Although no one has been able to develop a formula that can be used to tell management specifically how a given dividend policy will affect a firm's stock price, management still must establish a dividend policy that specifies how much the annual dividend payment should be as well as when and how the payment should be made. In this section, we discuss dividend payout policies that are generally observed in practice.

13-2a Residual Dividend Policy

In practice, dividend policy is very much influenced by investment opportunities and by the availability of funds with which to finance new investments. This fact has led to the development of a **residual dividend policy,** which states that a firm should follow these steps when deciding how much should be paid out as dividends each year: (1) Determine the optimal capital budget for the year. (2) To the extent possible, use retained earnings to provide the equity component of the total funds that are needed to finance the projects. (3) Pay dividends only if more earnings are generated than are needed to support the optimal capital budget. The word *residual* means "leftover," and the residual policy implies that dividends should be paid only out of *leftover earnings, which are the earnings that remain after capital budgeting funding requirements are satisfied.*

The basis of the residual policy is the fact that investors prefer to have the firm retain and reinvest earnings rather than pay them out in dividends *if the rate of return the firm can earn on reinvested earnings exceeds the rate investors, on average, can themselves earn on other investments of comparable risk.* For example, if the corporation can reinvest retained earnings at a 12 percent rate of return, whereas the best rate the average stockholder can obtain if the earnings are passed on in the form of dividends is 11 percent, stockholders should prefer to have the firm retain the profits.

residual dividend policy A policy in which the dividend paid is set to equal the actual earnings minus the amount of retained earnings necessary to finance the firm's optimal capital budget.

To continue, we saw in Chapter 11 that the cost of retained earnings is an *opportunity cost* that reflects rates of return available to equity investors. If a firm's stockholders can buy other stocks of equal risk and obtain an 11 percent return, then 11 percent is the firm's cost of retained earnings. The cost of new outside equity raised by selling common stock will be higher than 11 percent due to the costs associated with issuing the new stock (flotation costs).

From our discussion in Chapter 12, we know that most firms have target capital structures that call for at least some debt, so new financing is done partly with debt and partly with equity. As long as the firm finances with the optimal mix of debt and equity, and as long as it uses only internally generated equity (retained earnings), its marginal cost of each new rupee of capital will be less than if new equity financing is used. Internally generated equity is available for financing a certain amount of new investment, so beyond that amount the firm must turn to new common stock, which is more expensive. At the point where new stock must be sold, the cost of equity, and consequently the marginal cost of capital, rises.

These concepts are illustrated in Figure 13.1 with data from the Tarun and Wadibhai (T&W) Transport Company. T&W has a marginal cost of capital (MCC) equal to 10 percent. However, this rate assumes that all additional equity comes from retained earnings. Therefore, MCC = 10% as long as retained earnings are available, but the MCC begins to rise at the point where new stock must be sold.

T&W has ₹60 million of net income and a 40 percent debt ratio at its optimal capital structure. If it does not pay cash dividends, T&W can make investments equal to ₹100 million, consisting of ₹60 million from retained earnings plus ₹40 million of new debt, at a 10 percent marginal cost of capital. Therefore, its MCC is constant at 10 percent up to ₹100 million of capital, beyond which the MCC rises as the firm begins to use more expensive new common stock.

Suppose T&W's director of capital budgeting has determined that the optimal capital budget requires a total investment equal to ₹70 million. The ₹70 million will be financed using ₹28 million debt (= ₹70 million × 0.40) and ₹42 million in common equity (= ₹70 million × 0.60). The ₹60 million retained earnings will be more than sufficient to cover the common equity financing requirement, so the *residual earnings*

FIGURE 13.1 Tarun and Wadibhai Transport Company; Marginal Cost of Capital (MCC)

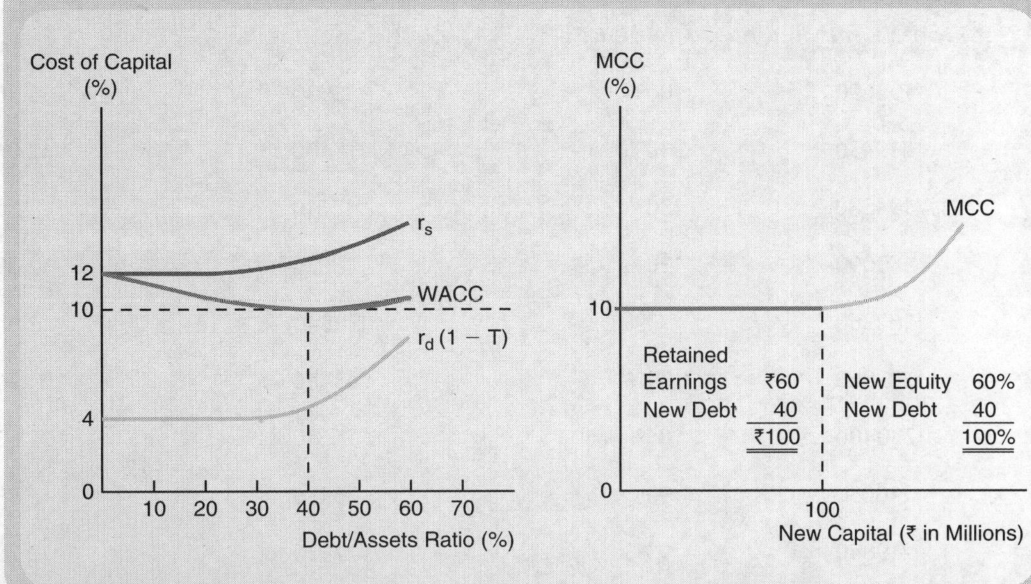

of ₹18 million (= ₹60 million – ₹42 million) can be paid out as dividends to stockholders.

Now suppose T&W's optimal capital budget is ₹150 million. Should dividends be paid? Not if T&W follows the residual dividend policy. Its ₹150 million capital budgeting needs will be financed with ₹60 million debt (= ₹150 million × 0.40) and ₹90 million common equity (= ₹150 million × 0.60). The common equity financing requirement of ₹90 million exceeds the ₹60 million of available retained earnings, so ₹30 million of new common equity will have to be issued. The new, or *external,* common equity will have a higher cost than retained earnings, so the marginal cost of capital for T&W will be higher than 10 percent. Under these conditions, T&W should not pay dividends to its stockholders. If the company pays part of its earnings in dividends, the marginal cost of capital will be even higher because more common stock will have to be issued to account for the amount of retained earnings paid out as dividends. For example, if T&W pays stockholders ₹20 million in dividends, it still needs ₹90 million of common equity to satisfy the capital budgeting requirements. In this case, ₹50 million of external equity will be required [= ₹90 million – (₹60 million – ₹20 million)], which means T&W's marginal cost of capital will increase sooner because new common equity will have to be issued when ₹40 million rather than ₹60 million of retained earnings are used. To maximize value, T&W should retain all of its earnings for capital budgeting needs in this case. Consequently, *according to the residual dividend policy, a firm that has to issue new common stock to finance capital budgeting projects does not have residual earnings, and thus should not pay dividends.*

Because both the earnings level and the capital budgeting needs of a firm generally vary from year to year, *strict adherence to the residual dividend policy would result in dividend variability.* One year the firm might declare zero dividends because investment opportunities are good, but the next year it might have a large dividend payout because investment opportunities are poor. Similarly, fluctuating earnings would also lead to variable dividends even if investment opportunities were stable over time. Thus, *following the residual dividend policy would be optimal only if investors were not bothered by fluctuating dividends.* If investors prefer stable, dependable dividends, r_s will be higher, and the stock price lower, if the firm follows the residual theory in a strict sense rather than attempting to stabilize its dividends over time.

13-2b Stable, Predictable Dividends

In the past, many firms set a specific annual rupee dividend per share and then maintained it, increasing the dividend only if it seemed clear that future earnings would be sufficient to maintain the new dividend. A corollary of this policy was the following rule: *Never reduce the annual dividend.*

Table 13.1 illustrates a fairly typical dividend policy, that of Reliance Industries Limited (RIL). As you can see, RIL's earnings fluctuated fairly from 2005-06

TABLE 13.1 Reliance Industries Limited Dividend payout over the years				
Year	**Net Profit in ₹ in Millions**	**Dividend%**	**Dividend amount in ₹ in Millions**	**Payout ratio**
2005-06	90690	100%	13930	15.36%
2006-07	119430	110%	14400	12.06%
2007-08	194580	130%	16310	8.38%
2008-09	153090	130%	18970	12.39%
2009-10	162360	70%	20840	12.84%
2010-11	202860	80%	23850	11.76%
2011-12	200400	85%	25310	12.63%
2012-13	210030	90%	26430	12.58%
2013-14	219840	95%	27930	12.70%
2014-15	227190	100%	29440	12.96%

Source Annual report of Reliance Industries Ltd. 2014-15

through 2014-15 and its dividends remained more or less steady throughout the period. RIL follows the **stable, predictable dividend policy;** for a long time now.

There are two good reasons for paying stable, predictable dividends rather than following the residual dividend policy. First, given the existence of the information content (signaling) concept, a fluctuating payment policy would lead to greater uncertainty—and hence to a higher r_s and a lower stock price—than would exist under a stable policy. Second, many stockholders use dividends for current consumption, and they would be put to trouble and expense if they had to sell part of their shares to obtain cash if the company cut the dividend.

As a rule, everything else the same, *stable, predictable dividends imply more certainty than do variable dividends, and thus a lower r_s and a higher firm value*. Accordingly, most firms follow this dividend policy because they want investors to perceive stability (more certainty) in dividend payments.

stable, predictable dividend policy Payment of a specific rupee dividend each year, or periodically increasing the dividend at a constant rate, so that the annual rupee dividend is relatively predictable by investors.

constant payout ratio Payment of a constant *percentage* of earnings as dividends each year.

13-2c Constant Payout Ratio

It would be possible for a firm to pay out a constant *percentage* of its earnings each year, but because earnings surely would fluctuate, this policy would mean that the rupee amount of dividends would also vary each year. We can conclude that *with the* **constant payout ratio** *dividend policy, if earnings fluctuate, investors have much greater uncertainty concerning the expected dividends each year, and chances are that r_s will also be greater; hence, the firm's stock price will be lower*.

© iStockphoto.com/Ollo

13-2d **Low Regular Dividend Plus Extras**

A policy of paying a low regular dividend plus a year-end extra payment in good years represents a compromise between a stable, predictable dividend and a constant payout ratio. Such a policy gives the firm flexibility, yet investors can count on receiving at least a minimum dividend. Therefore, if a firm's earnings and cash flows are quite volatile, this policy might be a good choice. The board of directors can set a relatively *low regular dividend*—low enough so that it can be maintained even in low-profit years or in years when a considerable amount of retained earnings are needed to fund capital budgeting projects—and then supplement it with an **extra dividend** in years when excess funds are available.

Indian rules regarding dividends

The following rules regarding Dividend as given in the Companies Act are relevant (Refer to Table 7.1):

1. Dividends are recommended by the Board of Directors and approved at the same rate or lesser rate by the general meetings.
2. Additionally, interim dividends can be declared by the Board of Directors based on excess profits made in any year. Separate rules have been formulated as to the factors that the Board has to take into account before declaring interim dividend.
3. Dividends can be paid only out of profits of the company. Profits have to necessarily take into account provisions for depreciation.
4. Preference shareholders have to be paid dividend before this is paid to equity shareholders. In the case of interim dividend, the Board has to make sure that amount needed for preference shares is set aside before declaring such dividend.

13-2e **Application of the Different Types of Dividend Payments: An Illustration**

Table 13.2 illustrates the application of the four different types of dividend payments we described previously. Panel I in the table provides general information about each of the four dividend policies, Panel II gives financial information for a fictitious firm, and Panel III shows the dividends that this firm would pay over a four-year period if it followed each of the payout procedures. For reference, Panel IV shows how the dividend is determined in Year 1 for each of the policies for which a computation is required. Note that the annual dividend would vary under each type of payment except the stable, predictable dividend policy. This illustration shows that *firms with incomes and capital budgets that vary each year will pay fairly constant dividends only if they follow the stable, predictable dividend policy*. Therefore, as we mentioned earlier, because investors perceive more certainty with stable, predictable dividend payments, most firms try to follow this dividend policy in practice.

13-2f **Payment Procedures**

Dividends normally are paid semiannually or quarterly, and an announcement, or declaration, of the dividend is made prior to its payment. The three dates mentioned in this announcement are important to current stockholders. These dates, as well as the ex-dividend date, are defined as follows:

1. *Declaration date.* On the **declaration date** the board of directors meets and declares the dividend. For accounting purposes, the declared dividend becomes an actual liability on the declaration date. In the books of the company declaring dividend, the dividend per share multiplied by the number of shares outstanding would appear as a current liability, and retained earnings would be reduced by a like amount, because dividends are paid out of earnings that were retained in the current year and from previous years.
2. *Holder-of-record date.* At the close of business on the **holder-of-record date,** or **date of record,** the company closes its stock transfer books and produces a list of shareholders as of that date; these are the stockholders who will receive the next dividend payment.
3. *Ex-dividend date.* The securities industry has established a convention of declaring that the right to the dividend remains with the stock until two *business days* prior to the holder-of-record date. This policy is meant to ensure the company is notified of an ownership transfer in time to record the new owner's information and thus pay the

extra dividend A supplemental dividend paid in years when the firm does well, and excess funds are available for distribution.

declaration date The date on which the board of directors declares the amount and the specifics of the next dividend payment.

holder-of-record date (date of record) The date on which the company opens the ownership books to determine who will receive the next dividend; the stockholders of record on this date receive the dividend.

TABLE 13.2 Application of Different Types of Dividend Payments: Illustration

I. Dividend Policies

A. Residual dividend—pay dividends if earnings are "left over" after financing capital budgeting needs.

B. Stable, predictable dividend—pay ₹1 dividend each year.

C. Constant payout ratio—pay 60 percent of earnings each year.

D. Low regular dividend plus extras—pay a minimum dividend equal to ₹0.75, plus 40 percent of earnings greater than ₹400,000.

II. Financial Information

	Year 1	Year 2	Year 3	Year 4
Net income	₹500,000	₹300,000	₹800,000	₹150,000
Capital budget	₹300,000	₹350,000	₹200,000	₹140,000
Number of shares outstanding	250,000	250,000	250,000	250,000

III. Dividend Payments (Per Share)

	Year 1	Year 2	Year 3	Year 4
A. Residual dividend	₹0.80	—	₹2.40	₹0.04
B. Stable, predictable dividend	₹1.00	₹1.00	₹1.00	₹1.00
C. Constant payout ratio (60%)	₹1.20	₹0.72	₹1.92	₹0.36
D. Low regular dividend plus extras	₹0.91	₹0.75	₹1.39	₹0.75

IV. Computations of Year 1 Dividend Payments for the Policies

A. Residual dividend

$$DPS_1 = \frac{₹500,000 - ₹300,000}{250,000} = \frac{₹200,000}{250,000} = ₹0.80$$

C. Constant payout ratio

$$DPS_1 = \frac{₹500,000\ (0.60)}{250,000} = \frac{₹200,000}{250,000} = ₹1.20$$

D. Low regular (minimum) dividend

$$DPS_1 = ₹0.75 + \frac{(₹500,000 - ₹400,000)0.40}{250,000} = ₹0.75 + \frac{₹40,000}{250,000} = ₹0.9$$

next dividend to him or her. The date when the right to receive the *next* dividend payment no longer goes with the stock—that is, when new purchasers will not receive the next dividend—is called the **ex-dividend date.** In the case of UPS, the ex-dividend date was Thursday, August 15, 2013, because the holder-of-record date was on Monday August 19. As a result, any investor who purchased the stock on or after August 15 did not receive the ₹0.62 dividend payment associated with the stock. All else equal, we would expect the price of the company's stock to drop on the ex-dividend date by approximately the amount of the next dividend.

ex-dividend date The date on which the right to the next dividend no longer accompanies a stock; it usually is two working days prior to the holder-of-record date.

Payment date The date on which a firm actually makes a dividend payment

4. *Payment date.* The company would pay dividends to shareholders appearing in the register of members on the record date. Today most firms pay dividends electronically.

13-3 Factors Influencing Dividend Policy

In addition to management's beliefs concerning which dividend theory is most correct, a number of other factors are considered when a particular dividend policy is chosen. The factors firms take into account can be grouped into these five broad categories:

1. **Constraints on dividend payments**—The amount of dividends a firm can pay might be limited due to (a) debt contract restrictions, which often stipulate

that no dividends can be paid unless certain financial measures exceed stated minimums; (b) the fact that dividend payments cannot exceed the balance sheet item "Retained earnings" (this is known as the *impairment of capital rule*, which is designed to protect creditors by prohibiting the company from distributing assets to stockholders before debt holders are paid); (c) cash availability, because cash dividends can be paid only with cash; and (d) restrictions imposed by the Internal Revenue Service (IRS) on improperly accumulated retained earnings. If the IRS can demonstrate that a firm's dividend payout ratio is being held down deliberately to help its stockholders avoid personal taxes, the firm is subject to tax penalties. However, this factor generally is relevant only to privately owned firms.

2. **Investment opportunities**—Firms that have large numbers of acceptable capital budgeting projects generally have low dividend-payout ratios, and vice versa. However, if a firm can accelerate or postpone projects (i.e., has flexibility), then it can adhere more closely to a target dividend policy.
3. **Alternative sources of capital**—When a firm needs to finance a given level of investments and flotation costs are high, the cost of external equity, r_e, will be well above the cost of internal equity, r_s, making it better to set a low payout ratio and to finance by retaining earnings rather than through the sale of new common stock. In addition, if the firm can adjust its debt/assets ratio without raising capital costs sharply, it can maintain a stable rupee dividend, even if earnings fluctuate, by using a variable debt/assets ratio.
4. **Ownership dilution**—If management is concerned about maintaining control, it might be reluctant to sell new stock; hence, the company might retain more earnings than it otherwise would to finance capital budgeting projects.
5. **Effects of dividend policy on r_s**— The effects of dividend policy on the cost of common equity, r_s, might be considered in terms of four factors: (a) stockholders' desire for current versus future income; (b) the perceived riskiness of dividends versus capital gains; (c) any tax differences that apply to capital gains versus dividends; and (d) the information content of dividends (signaling). Because we discussed each of these factors earlier, we need only note here that the importance of each factor in terms of its effect on r_s varies from firm to firm depending on the make-up of its current and possible future stockholders.

It should be apparent from our discussions that dividend policy decisions truly are exercises in informed judgment, not decisions that can be quantified precisely. Even so, to make rational dividend decisions, financial managers must consider all the points discussed in the preceding sections.

13-4 Bonus shares and Stock Splits

Although little empirical evidence exists to support the contention, there is widespread belief that an *optimal, or psychological, price range* exists for stocks. *Optimal* means that if the price is within this range, the value of the firm will be maximized. A firm that follows this way of thinking might use a stock dividend or a stock split to adjust the market price of its stock when it moves outside the optimal price range.

The rationale for stock dividends and stock splits can best be explained through an example. We will use Porter Electronic Controls Inc., a ₹700 million electronic components manufacturer, for this purpose. Since its inception, Porter's markets have been expanding, and the company has enjoyed growth in sales and earnings. Some of its earnings have been paid out in dividends, but some have been retained each year, causing earnings per share and market price per share to grow. The company began its life with only a few thousand shares outstanding, and after some years of growth, Porter's stock had very high earnings per share (EPS) and dividends per share (DPS). When a normal price/earnings (P/E) ratio was applied, the derived market price was so high that Porter's management felt demand for the stock was restricted, which kept the total market value of the firm below what it could have been if more shares, at a lower price, had been outstanding. To correct this situation, Porter might "split" its stock, as described next.

13-4a Stock Splits

If Porter believes that the best price range for its stock is from ₹40 to ₹80, then management probably will declare a 2-for-1 **stock split** when the price of the stock rises to greater than ₹80 per share. With a 2-for-1 split, each share of stock that currently exists is replaced with two *new* shares. In this way, the number of shares outstanding is

stock split An action taken by a firm to decrease the per-share price of its stock.

doubled, and all per-share values—including EPS, DPS, and market value—are halved. All else equal, after a stock split each stockholder would have more shares, but each share would be worth less than the pre-split per-share value. For example, suppose that Porter declared a 2-for-1 split when the market value of its stock reached ₹90 per share. If the post-split price settles at ₹45 per share, stockholders will be *exactly as well off* after the split as they were before the split, because they will have twice as many shares at half the price as before the split. If the price of the stock stabilizes above ₹45, however, stockholders will be better off.

Stock splits can be of any size. For example, the stock could be split 2-for-1, 5-for-1, or in any other way. For example, on January 20, 2010, Berkshire Hathaway initiated a 50-for-1 split for its Class B common stock. The split was intended to lower the price of the stock, which was selling for ₹3,475 per share prior to the split, so that the stock would become more affordable to a greater number of investors. Reverse splits, which *reduce* the shares outstanding, can also be used. For instance, a company whose stock sells for ₹5 might employ a 1-for-5 reverse split, exchanging one new share for five old ones and raising the value of the shares to about ₹25, which might be considered to be within the stock's optimal range. For example, on June 16, 2003, Priceline.com initiated a 1-for-6 reverse split to avoid being delisted from NASDAQ. During the first six months of 2009, quite a few companies considered using reverse splits to increase the per-share values of their stocks, which were depressed as a result of a significant downturn in the financial markets.

13-4b Bonus Shares

Bonus Shares are similar to stock splits in that they divide the pie into smaller slices without affecting the fundamental wealth position of the current stockholders. When a stock dividend is "paid," existing stockholders receive additional shares of stock rather than a cash payment. For example, on a 5 percent stock dividend, the holder of 100 shares would receive an additional 5 shares (without cost); on a 20 percent stock dividend, the same holder would receive 20 new shares; and so on. As in a stock split, the total number of shares is increased, so EPS, DPS, and price per share all decline proportionately. Because all stockholders receive the same proportion of additional shares, "payment" of a stock dividend neither affects the ownership structure of the firm nor the *total* value of the stock that is outstanding.

Bonus Shares A dividend paid in the form of additional shares of stock rather than cash.

13-4c Price Effects of Stock Splits and Bonus Shares

If a firm wants to reduce the price of its stock, should it use a stock split or a stock dividend? Stock splits generally are used after a sharp price run-up to produce a large price reduction. Stock dividends typically are used on a regular annual basis to keep the stock price more or less constrained. For example, if a firm's earnings and dividends were growing at about 10 percent per year, its stock price would tend to go up at about that same rate, and it would soon be outside the desired trading range. A 10 percent annual stock dividend would maintain the stock price within the optimal trading range.

Stock splits and stock dividends have the same *economic* effect—none. In other words, these actions simply cut the pie into more slices in the sense that investors are neither better off nor worse off after a stock dividend is paid or a stock split is initiated. Investors own the same proportion of the company, just with more shares of stock than they owned before these actions were taken. To determine whether this reasoning is correct, several empirical studies have examined the effects of stock splits and stock dividends on stock prices. These studies suggest that investors see stock splits and stock dividends for what they are—*simply additional pieces of paper.* The studies show that investors bid up the price of the stock only if stock dividends and splits are accompanied by higher earnings and cash dividends. When stock dividends are not accompanied by increases in earnings and cash dividends, however, the dilution of earnings and dividends per share causes the price of the stock to drop by the same percentage as the stock dividend (or stock split). Because the fundamental determinants of price are the underlying earnings and cash dividends per share, stock splits and stock dividends merely cut the same pie into smaller slices.

13-4d Balance Sheet Effects of Stock Splits and Bonus Shares

Although the economic effects of stock splits and stock dividends are virtually identical, accountants treat them somewhat differently. On a 2-for-1 split, the shares outstanding are doubled and the stock's par value is halved in the equity section of the balance sheet. This treatment is shown for

Paradeep Electronic Controls in Section II of Table 13.3 on the next page, using a pro forma 2015 balance sheet.

Section III of Table 13.3 shows the effect of a 20 percent stock dividend. With a stock dividend, the stock's par value is not changed, but an accounting entry is made to transfer funds from the Retained earnings account to the Common stock and Additional paid-in capital accounts. In essence, the payment of a stock dividend is treated as two simultaneous accounting events: the payment of a dividend and the sale of stock for an equal amount. The transfer from retained earnings is calculated using Equation 13.1:

13.1

$$\text{Loan amount} = \left(\begin{array}{c}\text{Payment owed}\\\text{to suppliers}\end{array}\right) + \left(\begin{array}{c}\text{Wages owed}\\\text{employees}\end{array}\right) - \left(\begin{array}{c}\text{Cash}\\\text{receipts}\end{array}\right)$$

Here "Transfer from RE" represents the rupee amount that must be taken out of Retained earnings and redistributed to the Common stock and Additional paid-in capital accounts, "Shrs" is the number of shares of common stock that is outstanding prior to the stock dividend, "% stock dividend" is the percentage of the stock dividend stated in decimal form, and P_0 is the current market price of the firm's common stock.

Paradeep has five million shares outstanding (Section I of Table 13.3), and each share currently sells for ₹90, so a 20 percent stock dividend would require the transfer of ₹90 million:

$$\text{Rupees transferred} = [(5{,}000{,}000)(0.2)](₹90)$$
$$= ₹90{,}000{,}000$$

As shown in the table, ₹1 million (= ₹1 par value × 1 million shares) of this ₹90 million is added to the Common stock account and the remaining ₹89 million is added to the Additional paid-in capital account. The Retained earnings account is reduced from ₹285 million to ₹195 million (₹195 million = ₹285 million – ₹90 million).[3]

[3]Note that Porter could not pay a stock dividend that exceeded 71.25 percent; a stock dividend of that percentage would exhaust the retained earnings. Thus, a firm's ability to declare stock dividends is constrained by the amount of its retained earnings. Of course, if Porter had wanted to pay a 50 percent stock dividend, it could have just switched to a 1½-for-1 stock split and accomplished the same thing in terms of the number of shares owned by stockholders.

[4]See Amy K. Dittmar, "Why Do Firms Repurchase Stock?" *The Journal of Business*, Vol. 73, No. 3 (July 2000), 331–355, for an excellent discussion of this topic.

13-5 Stock Repurchases

Rather than paying regular cash dividends, firms sometimes distribute earnings by repurchasing shares of their own stock in the financial markets. The primary reasons that are given for repurchasing stock are as follows:[4]

1. **To distribute excess funds to stockholders**—Firms sometimes use stock repurchases to distribute funds that exceed capital budgeting needs in a particular year, especially when the price of the stock is considered low (undervalued). A firm might repurchase stock to distribute excess funds because, unlike regular dividend payments, a **stock repurchase** generally is not expected to continue in the future. Further, a repurchase has different tax implications than a cash dividend. With a repurchase, because investors sell their stock to the company, any gains they realize generally are taxed at the capital gains rate, which might be lower than the ordinary tax rate at which dividends are taxed.

2. **To adjust the firm's capital structure**—When a firm has more equity than its target capital structure suggests, it might issue debt and use the proceeds to repurchase shares of stock to bring the mix of debt and equity in line with the target.

3. **To acquire shares needed for employee options or compensation**—If a firm knows that many of the stock options that have been "paid" to employees as bonuses or incentives will be exercised soon, it might buy back shares in the financial markets to ensure sufficient shares are available when the options are exercised. Such repurchases also help support the price of the stock by reducing the dilution effect that occurs when employee stock options are exercised; that is, a repurchase reduces the impact on the market value of the stock that otherwise occurs if the number of shares of stock is increased by the number of exercised options.

4. **To protect against a takeover attempt**—A stock repurchase can be used to fend off a hostile takeover attempt because (a) repurchasing stock increases demand in the stock markets, which increases the value of the stock and thus the purchase price associated with the acquisition of the firm and (b) managers

stock repurchase Distribution of earnings by a firm to stockholders by repurchasing shares of its stock in the financial markets.

TABLE 13.3 Paradeep Electronic Controls, Ltd.: Stockholders' Equity Accounts, Pro Forma, December 31, 2015 (₹ in Millions, except per-share values)

I. Before a Stock Split or Stock Dividend	
Common stock (5 million shares outstanding, ₹1 par value)	₹5.0
Paid-in capital	10.0
Retained earnings	285.0
Total common stockholders' equity	₹300.0
Book value per share = ₹300/5	₹60.0
II. After a 2-for-1 Stock Split	
Common stock (10 million shares outstanding, ₹0.50 par value)	₹5.0
Paid-in capital	10.0
Retained earnings	285.0
Total common stockholders' equity	₹300.0
Book value per share = ₹300/10	₹ 30.0
III. After a 20 Percent Stock Dividend	
Common stock (6 million shares outstanding, ₹1 par value)[a]	₹ 6.0
Additional paid-in capital[b]	99.0
Retained earnings[b]	195.0
Total common stockholders' equity	₹300.0
Book value per share = ₹300/6	₹50.0

[a]Shares outstanding are increased by 20 percent, from 5 million to 6 million.

[b]A transfer equal to the market value of the new shares is made from the Retained earnings account to the Additional paid-in capital and common stock accounts:

Transfer = [(5,000,000 shares)(.020)]₹90 = ₹90,000,000

Of this ₹90 million, ₹1,000,000 = (₹1 par)(1,000,000 shares) goes in the Common stock account and the remaining ₹89 million goes in the Additional paid-in capital account.

and other interested parties who hold their stock rather than selling back to the firm will have more concentrated ownership of the firm after the repurchase is complete, which might provide such groups with enough control to block the takeover.

Shares of stock that are repurchased are placed in the firm's treasury of stock, and thus are part of the *treasury stock* that can be reissued at some later date if funds are needed to support capital investments or for other purposes. Because a stock repurchase decreases the number of outstanding shares that are held by stockholders, as long as investors believe that the firm's basic earning power will not change or will improve following the repurchase, both earnings per share and the stock's market price per share should increase as a result of the repurchase.

13-5a Advantages and Disadvantages of Stock Repurchases

The principal advantages of repurchases include the following:

1. A company can use a stock repurchase to distribute excess cash (free cash flows) without increasing the amount of the dividends that might otherwise be paid during the year. As mentioned earlier, most firms are reluctant to increase dividend payments unless management is confident that future operations can sustain the increase. Firms generally follow this strategy because management is extremely reluctant to decrease dividends even when there is good reason to do so; investors often interpret a dividend decrease as a bad signal with respect to the firm's future financial position. As a result, dividends generally are increased only when man-

agement believes that the higher dividend can be maintained in future years. A stock repurchase allows the firm to distribute earnings to stockholders without changing the amount of regular cash dividends.

2. A repurchase is an effective method to immediately change the firm's capital structure when the proportion of equity is substantially higher than the target capital structure prescribes. For example, if a firm issues debt and uses the proceeds to repurchase its stock, the capital structure will include a greater proportion of debt and a lower proportion of equity as soon as the process is completed.
3. When a firm expects managers and other employees to exercise stock options that have been paid to them as compensation in previous years, a repurchase can be used to minimize the dilution effect associated with exercising the options. That is, if the firm repurchases the number of shares needed to cover the stock options that it expects will be exercised, it will not have to issue new shares of stock, and the number of shares outstanding after the options are exercised will be the same as before the exercise. If a firm can predict the number of shares that will be needed to cover the exercise of the options and repurchase these shares in the stock markets, the effect of the exercise on the stock price and earnings per share should be minimal.
4. Stockholders do not have to sell their shares to the company during a repurchase period. Thus, those investors who need cash and don't mind paying the taxes associated with selling their stock will participate in the repurchase program; other stockholders will not. If the firm pays a cash dividend, all investors must pay taxes on the dividends they receive.
5. Many investors believe that a stock repurchase program is a signal from management that the firm's stock is undervalued in the financial markets, and thus it is a bargain to purchase. Empirical studies seem to support this belief. Hence, often when a firm initiates a stock repurchase, many investors who don't sell their shares to the company actually purchase additional shares in the stock markets.

The principal disadvantages of stock repurchases include the following:

1. The company might pay too much for stock that is repurchased. A firm that buys back substantial amounts of its stock will bid up the per-share price of the stock that remains outstanding, perhaps to an artificially high level. When this happens, the stock price will fall after the repurchase program ends, and this will harm new investors who purchased the company's stock during the repurchase period.
2. The interval between one stock repurchase and another one generally is irregular, which means that participating investors cannot rely on the cash that they receive from stock repurchases. As a result of the irregularity of stock repurchases, some investors might prefer to receive cash through regular dividend payments rather than through repurchases.

In recent years, the number of firms that have repurchased stock in the financial markets has increased dramatically; at the same time, the proportion of firms that pay regular dividends has decreased. In fact, currently more firms participate in stock repurchases than pay regular dividends to distribute earnings.[5]

13-6 Dividend Policies Around the World

The dividend policies of companies around the world vary considerably. Research indicates that the dividend payout ratios of companies range from 10.5 percent in the Philippines to nearly 70 percent in Taiwan.[6] The dividend payout ratios of companies in Canada, France, and the United States range from about 20 percent to 25 percent, in Spain and the United Kingdom the range is from 30 percent to 40 percent, in Germany and Mexico the rate is between 40 percent and 50 percent, and it is greater than 50 percent for companies in Japan and Southeast Asia. A study of firms in developing countries, such as Zimbabwe and Pakistan, shows that emerging market firms have average payout ratios that range from approximately 30 percent to 60 percent.[7]

[5]See: Eugene F. Fama and Kenneth R. French, "Disappearing Dividends: Changing Firm Characteristics or Lower Propensity to Pay?," *Journal of Financial Economics*, Vol. 60, No. 1, (April 2001), 3–43; Malcolm Baker and Jeffrey Wurgler, "Appearing and Disappearing Dividends: The Link to Catering Incentives," *Journal of Financial Economics*, Vol. 73, No. 2, (August 2004), 271–288; Douglas J. Skinner, "The Evolving Relation between Earnings, Dividends, and Stock Repurchases," *Journal of Financial Economics*, Vol. 87, No. 3, (March 2008), 582–609; and Jim Hsieh and Qinghai Wang, "Stock Repurchases: Theory and Evidence," *Blackwell Companion to Dividends and Dividend Policy*, edited by H. Kent Baker (Blackwell Publishing: New York, 2009).

[6]Rafael La Porta, Florencio Lopez-de-Silanes, Andrei .Shleifer, and Robert W. Vishny, "Agency Problems and Dividend Policies Around the World," *Journal of Finance*, February 2000, 1–34.

[7]Varouj Aivazian, Laurence Booth, and Sean Cleary, "Do Emerging Market Firms Follow Different Dividend Policies from U.S. Firms?" *Journal of Financial Research*, Fall 2003, 371–387.

Why do dividend payment policies differ so much around the world? As we mentioned in Chapter 12, it seems logical to attribute the differences to dissimilar tax structures, because both dividends and capital gains are taxed differently around the world. The tax codes in most developed countries encourage personal investing and savings more than the U.S. tax code does. For example, Germany, Italy, and many other European countries do not tax capital gains, and in most other developed countries, including Japan, France, and Canada, capital gains are not taxed unless they exceed some minimum amount. Furthermore, in Germany and Italy, dividends are not taxed as income, and in most other countries, some amount of dividends is tax exempt. The general conclusion we can draw, then, is that in countries where capital gains are not taxed, investors should show a preference for companies that retain earnings over those that pay dividends.

It has been found that differences in taxes do not fully explain the differences in dividend payout ratios among countries. A study by Rafael La Porta, Florencio Lopez-de-Silanes, Andrei Shleifer, and Robert W. Vishny offers some additional insight into the dividend policy differences that exist around the world.[12] They suggest that, all else equal, companies pay out greater amounts of earnings as dividends in countries that have measures that help protect the rights of minority stockholders. In such countries, however, firms with many growth opportunities tend to pay lower dividends, which is to be expected because the funds are needed to finance the growth, and shareholders are willing to forgo current income in hopes of greater future benefits. On the other hand, in countries where shareholders' rights are not well protected, investors are more likely to accept whatever dividends are offered, even if companies have numerous good investment opportunities, because great uncertainty exists about whether management will use earnings for self-gratification rather than to benefit stockholders; investors prefer a "bird in hand." Some countries where minority shareholders have few, if any, protected rights, including Brazil, Chile, Colombia, and Venezuela, have regulations requiring firms to pay dividends.

Tateos/Shutterstock.com

In summary, it appears the most important factor that determines whether stockholders prefer earnings to be retained or paid out as dividends is the level of risk associated with future expected dividends, which is mitigated to some degree by regulations that protect minority shareholders' rights.

KEY DISTRIBUTION OF RETAINED EARNINGS CONCEPTS

To conclude this chapter, we summarize some of the concepts that were discussed.

- Because the firm's goal is to maximize shareholders' wealth, the optimal dividend policy is the one that maximizes the value of the firm. When a firm pays dividends, it decreases the amount of earnings that can be used to invest in acceptable capital budgeting projects. As a result, firms that have many acceptable capital budgeting projects generally pay few or no dividends because earnings are retained to reinvest in the firm. On the other hand, firms with few acceptable capital budgeting projects generally pay out most of their earnings as dividends because not as much internal financing is needed.
- Of the different types of dividend payments discussed in the chapter, most firms follow the stable, predictable dividend policy. Everything else the same, it is believed that a stable, predictable pattern of dividend payments provides investors with a perception that there is less risk associated with the firm, and a perception of less risk often leads to a lower cost of capital. To maximize value, however, it might be better for a firm to follow the residual dividend policy so that cheaper funds (retained earnings rather than new equity) can be used to finance capital budgeting needs.
- Factors that influence a firm's dividend policy decisions include constraints on payments, investment opportunities, ownership dilution, and the effect on the firm's cost of capital. In some instances, these factors might prevent the firm from following either the optimal dividend policy or the policy it prefers.
- Both a stock split and a stock dividend increase the number of shares of outstanding stock. Neither action requires stockholders to invest any additional funds. Thus, although both actions reduce the per-share value of the firm's stock, neither action *by itself* changes the *total* market value of the firm's stock.
- Firms use stock repurchases as an alternative to temporary changes in regular annual dividends when distributing earnings to stockholders. Recently, the use of repurchases has increased while the proportion of dividend-paying companies has decreased. In fact, currently a greater percentage of publicly traded firms engage in repurchase activities than pay regular dividends.

MULTIPLE CHOICE QUESTIONS

1. A dividend of 20% means

a. A dividend of ₹2 per ₹10 share

b. A dividend of 20% of the total profits of the company

c. a and b are equal

d. None of the above

2. The bird-in-hand theory says,

a. It does not matter what dividend we pay

b. A dividend payment reassures the shareholders that they are in the right investment

c. Dividends can be paid only if there are no expansion projects

d. None of the above

3. A decision as to the extent of dividend to be paid depends on

a. Profits generated in the current year

b. Past record of dividends

c. Fear of adverse reaction from the market

d. All of the above

4. A growing company

a. Will pay a high dividend

b. Will retain a substantial portion of profits for growth

c. Will pay greater than previous year's dividend

d. None of the above

5. Dividends are also influenced by

a. Tax liability of person receiving the dividend

b. Tax liability of company

c. Tax paid by the company in the previous year

d. Taxes do not matter

6. Growth and dividends are connected to each other in that

a. High growth shares pay high dividends

b. Growth is a function of the retention of profits

c. Growth is possible only if we do not pay dividends

d. None of the above

7. Residual dividend payout theory says,

a. Dividends do not matter

b. Dividends are to be paid only if there is no growth opportunity

c. Dividends are to be paid after earmarking funds for growth opportunity

d. Dividends are to be paid from what is left over after paying debt holders

8. A target dividend payout ratio

a. Is a fixed dividend rate year after year

b. Is an increasing dividend rate year after year

c. Is dependent on growth opportunities

d. Is dependent on growth, past practices and signalling implications

9. Stock repurchase is done

a. To help minority shareholders to get their capital back

b. To reduce the quantum of equity so that the ROE in future can grow

c. Due to regulatory compulsions

d. Could be on account of any of the above reasons

10. Dividend irrelevant theory assumes that

a. Markets take into account the amount of profits made and do not deem it necessary that profits be paid off as dividends

b. Markets are not sensitive enough to take profits and dividend payouts into account

c. Value of the firm is same whether dividends are paid or not

d. Both a and c

Answers:

1.	(a)	2.	(b)	3.	(d)	4.	(b)	5.	(a)
6.	(b)	7.	(c)	8.	(d)	9.	(d)	10.	(d)

PROBLEMS

For more problems, login to CourseMate for CFIN at CengageBrain.com

13–1 Divya A/C plans to invest ₹50 million to expand operations. The firm wants to maintain a 60 percent debt/assets ratio in its capital structure. If net income is expected to be ₹25 million this year and Divya follows the residual dividend policy, what amount of dividends will be paid this year?

13–2 Oppanakara Door Manufacturer earned ₹100,000 this year. The company follows the residual dividend policy when paying dividends. Oppanakara Door has determined that it needs a total of ₹120,000 for investment in capital budgeting projects this year. If the company's debt-to-asset ratio is 50 percent, what will its dividend payout ratio be this year?

13–3 The Harini Corporation expects this year's net income to be ₹12 million. The firm's target debt/assets ratio is 30 percent. This year, Harini has ₹20 million profitable investment opportunities. According to the residual dividend policy, what should be Harini dividend payout ratio this year?

13–4 In 2015, Sangeetha Company's earnings are expected to be ₹14.4 million, and the firm expects to have profitable investment opportunities of ₹8.4 million. Last year, the company paid dividends equal to ₹9 million. It is predicted that Sangeetha will grow at a constant 5 percent in the future. What will be Sangeetha's total dividends for 2015 if it follows (a) a policy that requires dividends to grow at the long-run growth rate in earnings and (b) a pure residual dividend policy. Sangeetha's target debt/assets ratio is 40 percent.

13–5 Bava Island Tours (BIT) expects to grow at a constant rate of 4 percent forever. Its target debt/assets ratio is 40 percent, and it expects to have profitable investments of ₹1.3 million this year. BIT plans to continue paying the same dividend that has been paid the past 10 years, ₹2.25 per share, long into the future. The firm has 500,000 shares of stock outstanding. If net income is expected to be ₹2 million, what should be BIT's dividend payout ratio this year?

13-6 Deena's Dry Cleaning has been growing at a constant 6 percent rate for more than 20 years, and this growth is epxected to continue forever. Last year, Deena's paid a dividend equal to ₹3.50 per share. If dividends grow at the same rate as the company's growth rate, what should be the per share dividend that Deena's pays this year?

13-7 Trivandrum Tea's dividend policy calls for the dividend to be increased each year by the same rate. Last year, the company paid a dividend equal to ₹2.50 per share. This year, after the company initiates a 5-for-1 stock split, Trivandrum Tea expects to pay a dividend equal to ₹0.54 per share. At what rate does Trivandrum Tea increse its dividend each year?

13-8 Last year, the Chotta Artists retained ₹100,000 of the ₹250,000 net income it generated. This year, Chotta generated net income equal to ₹275,000. If Chotta follows the constant dividend payout ratio dividend policy, how much should be paid in dividends this year?

13-9 Last year, Harish News Corporation paid ₹600,000 in dividends and retained ₹360,000 of the earnings it generated. The company follows a constant payout ratio dividend policy. If Harish News generates ₹1.25 millon in income this year, how much will be paid in dividends?

13-10 Raman Auto Transport (RAT) follows a constant payout ratio dividend policy, which requires the company to pay out 30 percent of income as dividends each year. If it wants to pay ₹840,000 in dividends next year, how much must RAT earn?

13-11 Orissa Office Products and Supplies (OOPS) follows the constant payout ratio dividend policy by paying out 40 percent of earnings each year. This year, OOPS expects the dividend payment to be 7 percent higher than last year's payment, which was ₹130,000. (a) What is the amount of net income that OOPS expects to generate this year? (b) If its target capital structure calls for 50 percent common equity, what will be the total funds the company can invest in capital budgeting projects this year before new common stock must be issued to raise new funds?

13-12 Ullasnagar Utilities (U2) applies the low regular dividend plus extras policy when determining how much of its income will be paid out as dividends each year. U2's policy states that the minimum dividend that will be paid each year is ₹0.50 per share. But, when net income is greater than ₹600,000, the total dividend will be increased by 25 percent of the amount that exceeds ₹600,000. The firm currently has 100,000 shares of stock outstanding. What will be the dividend per share if U2 earns (a) ₹760,000 and (b) ₹580,000?

13-13 Last year, Alkananda Zero Freezers paid a dividend equal to ₹0.95 per share. Alaknanda follows the low-regular-dividend-plus-extras policy to determine its annual dividend. The policy requires the minimum dividend to be increased by 30 percent of the amount of earnings that is exceeds ₹30,000. Last year's earnings were ₹50,000. If Alkananda has 40,000 shares outstanding, how much is the minimum (low regular) dividend that the firm pays each year?

13-14 Davesh Grooming's optimal capital structure calls for 40 percent debt and 60 percent common equity. The company's weighted average cost of capital (WACC) is 10 percent if the amount of retained earnings generated during the year is sufficient to fund the equity portion of its capital budgeting requirements, whereas its WACC is 14 percent if new common stock must be issued. Davesh has the following independent investment opportunities:

If Davesh expects to generate net income of ₹720,000 and it pays dividends according to the residual policy, what will its dividend payout ratio be?

Project A: Cost = ₹684,000; IRR = 16%
Project B: Cost = ₹640,000; IRR = 13%
Project C: Cost = ₹660,000; IRR = 9%

13-15 Anu Bhen's Barbeque (ABB) has two independent investment opportunities this year: Project S costs ₹45,000, and it has an IRR equal to 11 percent; Project T costs ₹52,000 and its IRR is 8 percent. The firm's weighted average cost of capital (WACC) is 9 percent as long as new common stock is not needed to finance capital budgeting projects, but its WACC is 12 percent if new common stock must be issued. ABB's target capital structure is 70 percent debt and 30 percent common equity. The firm expects to generate net income of ₹39,000 this year. ABB follows stable, predictable dividend policy by increasing its dividend payment by 5 percent each year. If ABB paid ₹20,000 in dividends last year, and it continues to follow the stable, predictable dividend policy, which capital budgeting project(s) should it purchase?

13-16 BKP plans to initiate a 10-for-1 stock split. BKP's stock currently sells for ₹225 per share. What will be the stock price immediately after the split takes place?

13-17 CCC Fishery is considering a 1-for-4 reverse stock split. Its stock is currently selling for ₹15 per share. CCC plans to pay a dividend equal to ₹0.15 per share after the split. But it would like to pay an equivalent dividend per share even if the split does not take place. (a) What will the price of the stock be immediately after the stock split? (b) What should the per share dividend be if CCC doesn't split the stock?

13–18 One week after Dada's Kitchen split its stock 3-for-1, it paid a dividend of ₹0.55 per new share. The dividend payment was 10 percent greater than last year's presplit dividend. What was last year's dividend per share?

13–19 Kitty Hawk Airlines recently declared a 10 percent stock dividend. Prior to the stock dividend, the equity section on Kitty Hawk's balance sheet was:

Common stock (12,000 shares outstanding, ₹2 par value)	₹24,000
Additional paid-in capital	16,000
Retained earnings	10,000
Total common shareholders' equity	₹50,000

Kitty Hawk's stock currently sells for ₹5 per share. Show what the equity section of the balance sheet will look like after the stock dividend is initiated.

13–20 Suppose that Kitty Hawk Airlines (see Problem 13–19) decided to initiate a 5-for-1 stock split rather than the stock dividend described in the problem. Show what the equity section of the balance sheet will look like after the stock split takes place.

Distribution of Retained Earnings: Dividends and Stock Repurchases

Learning Outcomes

LO.1 Describe the views that have been proposed to explain why firms follow particular dividend policies and why investors react when firms change dividend policies.

- Firms follow particular dividend polices based on three primary factors: (1) information content, or signaling, which suggests that current dividends and any changes in future dividends signal information to investors; when investors interpret signals as good news, the price of the firm's stock increases, and vice versa; (2) clientele effect, which suggests that some investors purchase the stock of particular companies because of their dividend policies; and (3) the free cash-flow hypothesis, which suggests that firms should pay dividends only when earnings exceed the amounts needed to invest in value-increasing projects.

LO.2 Discuss (a) the types of dividend payments and (b) payment procedures that firms follow in practice.

- The primary types of dividend payments that firms follow include (1) residual dividend policy, which permits payment of dividends only after all capital budgeting needs have been supported by current earnings; (2) stable, predictable dividends, which require the firm to maintain a fairly predictable rupee dividend payment; (3) constant payout ratio, which requires the firm to apply the same dividend payout ratio (percentage of EPS paid out) when determining the annual dividend payment; and (4) low regular plus extras, which calls for a minimum dividend that is supplemented in the years when excess earnings are available.
- On the declaration date, the firm's board of directors announces the amount of dividends to be paid on the payment date. Stockholders who will receive the dividend payments are identified on the holder-of-record date. The ex-dividend date, which is two working days prior to the holder-of-record date, is important because those who purchase the stock on this day or later will not receive the next dividend payment. Thus, on the ex-dividend date, the market value of the stock should decrease by the present value of the next dividend payment.

LO.3 Discuss factors that firms consider when making dividend policy decisions.

- Factors that influence a firm's dividend policy include: (1) constraints placed on dividend payments by debt contracts or the firm's liquidity position, (2) whether the firm has investment opportunities that must be funded with earnings, (3) whether the firm can raise capital using sources other than earnings, (4) concern for dilution of ownership if additional shares of stock must be issued because dividends were paid, and (5) how dividend payments affect the cost of equity, r_s.

LO.4 Describe stock dividends and stock splits, and discuss how stock prices are affected by these activities.

- Stock dividends and stock splits are used to adjust the market value of a firm's stock. If the per-share stock price is considered too high, everything else equal, it can be reduced by increasing the number of shares outstanding through either a stock split or a stock dividend. Neither action by itself should affect the total value of the firm. After a stock split or stock dividend, there exist more shares at a lower per-share price, but the total value of all outstanding shares is the same.

LO.5 Describe stock repurchases and discuss reasons firms use repurchases.

- A firm might repurchase its stock to (1) distribute excess funds to stockholders, (2) adjust its capital structure, (3) acquire shares needed for employees' stock options or compensation plans, or (4) protect against a takeover attempt.

LO.6 Discuss differences in dividend policies around the world.

- Dividend policies differ substantially around the world. In countries where future payouts are extremely uncertain or little regulation exists, investors prefer companies that pay current dividends rather than those that retain earnings, and vice versa.

Chapter 13 Key Distribution of Retained Earnings Concepts

- Because the firm's goal is to maximize shareholders' wealth, the optimal dividend policy is the one that maximizes the value of the firm. When a firm pays dividends, it decreases the amount of earnings that can be used to invest in acceptable capital budgeting projects. As a result, firms that have many acceptable capital budgeting projects generally pay few or no dividends because earnings are retained to reinvest in the firm. On the other hand, firms with few acceptable capital budgeting projects generally pay out most of their earnings as dividends because not as much internal financing is needed.
- Of the different types of dividend payments discussed in the chapter, most firms follow the stable, predictable dividend policy. Everything else the same, it is believed that a stable, predictable pattern of dividend payments provides investors with a perception that there is less risk associated with the firm, and a perception of less risk often leads to a lower cost of capital. To maximize value, however, it might be better for a firm to follow the residual dividend policy so that cheaper funds (retained earnings rather than new equity) can be used to finance capital budgeting needs.
- Factors that influence a firm's dividend policy decisions include constraints on dividend payments, investment opportunities, ownership dilution, and the effect on the firm's cost of capital. In some instances, these factors might prevent the firm from following either the optimal dividend policy or the policy it prefers.
- Both a stock split and a stock dividend increase the number of shares of outstanding stock. Neither action requires stockholders to invest any additional funds. Thus, although both actions reduce the per share value of the firm's stock, neither action *by itself* changes the *total* market value of the firm's stock.
- Firms use stock repurchases as an alternative to temporary changes in annual dividends when distributing earnings to stockholders. Recently, the use of repurchases has increased while the proportion of dividend-paying companies has decreased. In fact, currently a greater percentage of publicly traded firms engage in repurchase activities than pay regular dividends.

Key Terms

optimal dividend policy The dividend policy that strikes a balance between current dividends and future growth, and maximizes the firm's stock price. *p. 226*

LO.1

dividend irrelevance theory The theory that a firm's dividend policy has no effect on either its value or its cost of capital. *p. 226*

dividend relevance theory The value of a firm is affected by its dividend policy—the optimal dividend policy is the one that maximizes the firm's value. *p. 226*

information content (signaling) hypothesis The theory that investors regard dividend changes as signals of management's earnings forecasts. *p. 227*

clientele effect The tendency of a firm to attract the type of investor who likes its dividend policy. *p. 227*

free cash flow hypothesis All else equal, firms that pay dividends from cash flows that cannot be reinvested in positive net present value projects (*free cash flows*) have higher values than firms that retain free cash flows. *p. 227*

LO.2

residual dividend policy A policy in which the dividend paid is set equal to the actual earnings minus the amount of retained earnings necessary to finance the firm's optimal capital budget. *p. 228*

stable, predictable dividend policy Payment of a specific rupee dividend each year, or periodically increasing the dividend at a constant rate, so that the annual rupee dividend is relatively predictable by investors. *p. 230*

constant payout ratio Payment of a constant *percentage* of earnings as dividends each year. *p. 231*

extra dividend A supplemental dividend paid in years when the firm does well, and excess funds are available for distribution. *p. 231*

declaration date The date on which the board of directors declares the amount and the specifics of the next dividend payment. *p. 231*

holder-of-record date (date of record) The date on which the company opens the ownership books to determine who will receive the next dividend; the stockholders of record on this date receive the dividend. *p. 232*

ex-dividend date The date on which the right to the next dividend no longer accompanies a stock; it usually is two working days prior to the holder-of-record date. *p. 232*

payment date The date on which a firm actually makes the dividend payment. *p. 233*

dividend reinvestment plans (DRIPs) Plans that enable stockholders to automatically reinvest dividends received in the stocks of the paying firms. *p. 233*

LO.4

stock split An action taken by a firm to decrease the per-share price of its stock. *p. 234*

stock dividend A dividend paid in the form of additional shares of stock rather than cash. *p. 235*

LO.5

stock repurchase Distribution of earnings by a firm to stockholders by repurchasing shares of its stock in the financial markets. *p. 237*

PART 6

Working Capital Management

CHAPTER 14

Working Capital Policy

Learning Outcomes

LO.1 Discuss why working capital is needed and how working capital accounts are related.

LO.2 Describe the cash conversion cycle and how it can be used to better manage working capital activities.

LO.3 Describe the policies that a firm might follow (a) when investing in current assets and (b) when financing current assets.

LO.4 Discuss the advantages and disadvantages of using short-term financing rather than long-term financing.

LO.5 Describe how working capital management in multinational firms differs from working capital management in purely domestic firms.

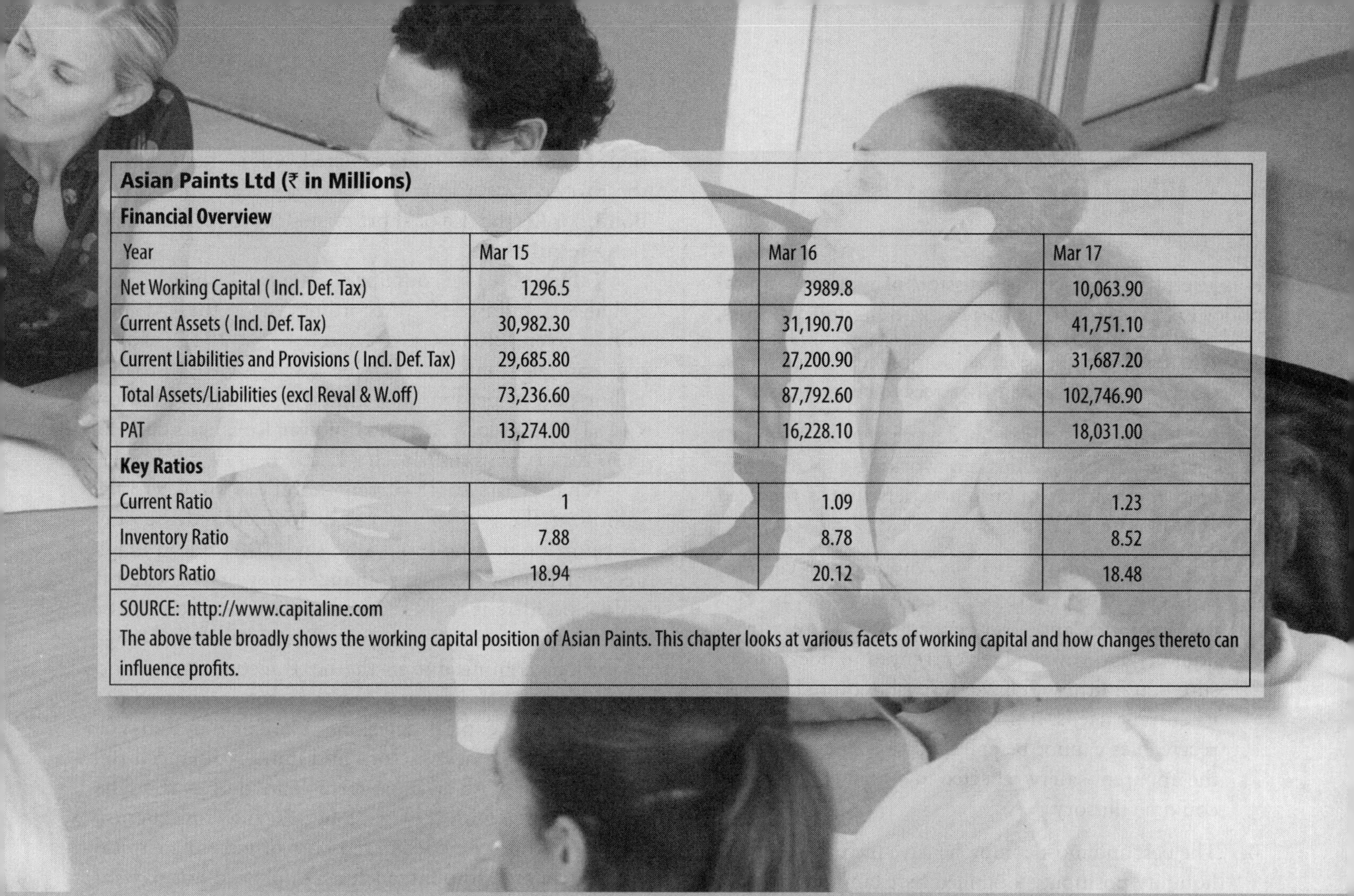

Monkey Business Images/Shutterstock.com

Asian Paints Ltd (₹ in Millions)			
Financial Overview			
Year	Mar 15	Mar 16	Mar 17
Net Working Capital (Incl. Def. Tax)	1296.5	3989.8	10,063.90
Current Assets (Incl. Def. Tax)	30,982.30	31,190.70	41,751.10
Current Liabilities and Provisions (Incl. Def. Tax)	29,685.80	27,200.90	31,687.20
Total Assets/Liabilities (excl Reval & W.off)	73,236.60	87,792.60	102,746.90
PAT	13,274.00	16,228.10	18,031.00
Key Ratios			
Current Ratio	1	1.09	1.23
Inventory Ratio	7.88	8.78	8.52
Debtors Ratio	18.94	20.12	18.48

SOURCE: http://www.capitaline.com

The above table broadly shows the working capital position of Asian Paints. This chapter looks at various facets of working capital and how changes thereto can influence profits.

Generally, we divide financial management decisions into the management of assets (investments) and liabilities (sources of financing) in (1) the *long term* and (2) the *short term*. We discussed long-term decisions and analyses in previous chapters. In this and the next two chapters, we discuss *short-term financial management*, also termed **working capital management**, which involves management of the current assets and the current liabilities of a firm. As you read this chapter, you will realize that a firm's value cannot be maximized in the long run unless it survives the short run. In fact, the principal reason firms fail is because they are unable to meet their working capital needs. Thus, *sound working capital management is a requisite for firm survival.*

Study Tools

Problems are found at the end of this chapter

+

Login to **CourseMate** for **CFIN** at **CengageBrain.com** for additional problems and other study tools!

14-1 Working Capital[1]

It is useful to begin the discussion of working capital policy by reviewing some basic definitions and concepts.

1. The term **working capital**, sometimes called *gross working capital,* generally refers to current assets.
2. **Net working capital** is defined as current assets minus current liabilities. Thus, net working capital represents the amount of current assets that is financed with long-term funds.
3. The *current ratio,* which was discussed in Chapter 2, is calculated by dividing current assets by current liabilities, and it is intended to measure a firm's liquidity. However, a high current ratio does not ensure that a firm will have the cash required to meet its current needs. If inventories cannot be sold or if receivables cannot be collected in a timely manner, the apparent safety reflected in a high current ratio could be illusory.
4. The best and most comprehensive picture of a firm's liquidity position is obtained by examining its *cash budget.* The cash budget, which forecasts cash inflows and outflows, focuses on what really counts: the firm's ability to generate sufficient cash inflows to meet its required cash outflows. Cash budgeting is discussed in Chapter 15.
5. **Working capital policy** refers to the firm's basic policies regarding (a) target levels for each category of current assets and (b) how current assets will be financed.

We must distinguish between those current liabilities that are specifically used to finance current assets and those current liabilities that result from long-term decisions. Such "long-term" current liabilities include (1) current maturities of long-term debt; (2) financing associated with a construction program that, after the project is completed, will be funded with the proceeds of a long-term security issue (perhaps a bond); or (3) the use of short-term debt to finance fixed (long-term) assets.

working capital management The management of short-term assets (investments) and liabilities (financing sources).

working capital A firm's investment in short-term assets—cash, marketable securities, inventory, and accounts receivable.

net working capital Current assets minus current liabilities—the amount of current assets financed by long-term liabilities.

working capital policy Decisions regarding (1) the target levels for each current asset account and (2) how current assets will be financed.

Table 14.1 contains balance sheets for Reliance Industries. According to the definitions given, Reliance's March 31, 2015 working capital—that is, current assets—was ₹116152 billion and its net working capital was ₹248.51 billion ₹1161.52 biliion − ₹913.01 biliion. Reliance's current ratio was 1.27 as on March 31, 2015.

What if the total current liabilities of ₹ 913.01 biliion at the end of March, 2015 included the current portion of long-term debt, say ₹100 million? This account is unaffected by changes in working capital policy because it is a function of past long-term debt financing decisions. Thus, even though we define long-term debt coming due in the next accounting period as a current liability, it is not a factor in current period working capital decisions. Similarly, if Reliance were building a new factory and initially financed the construction with a short-term loan that was to be replaced later with mortgage bonds, the construction loan would not be considered part of working capital management. Although such accounts are not part of Reliance's working capital decision process, they cannot be ignored. Because these obligations are *due* in the current period, they must be taken into account when Reliance's managers construct the cash budget and assess the firm's ability to meet its current obligations (its liquidity position).

14-1a The Requirement for External Working Capital Financing

Let us suppose Reliance's operations and the sale of textile products are seasonal, typically peaking in September and October. In that case, at the end of September Reliance's inventories will be significantly higher than they are at the end of the calendar year. Reliance would then offer significant sales incentives to wholesalers during August and September in an effort to move inventories out of its warehouses and into

[1]The term *working capital* originated with the old Yankee peddler, who would load up his wagon with goods and then go off on his route to peddle his wares. The merchandise was called *working capital* because it was what he actually sold, or turned over, to produce his profits. The wagon and horse were his fixed assets. He generally owned the horse and wagon, so they were fifnanced with "equity" capital. However, to buy the merchandise, he borrowed funds through *working capital* loans, which had to be repaid after each trip to demonstrate to the bank that the credit was sound. If the peddler was able to repay the loan, then the bank would make another loan, and banks that followed this procedure were said to be employing sound banking practices.

TABLE 14.1 Balance Sheet of Reliance Industries Limited (₹ in Millions)

	Mar 15	Mar 14
Sources Of Funds		
Share capital	32360	32320
Reserves	2129230	1938420
Share application pending allotment	170	0
Long-term borrowings	762270	627080
Defered tax liabilities	126770	122150
Long-term provisions	14040	0
Short-term borrowings	129140	227700
Accounts payables	544700	578620
Other Current liabilities	190630	107670
Short-term provisions	48540	41670
Total Liabilities	3977850	3675630
Application Of Funds		
Fixed Assets:	1903160	1511220
Non-current investments	620580	526920
Long-term advances	292590	284360
Current investments	505150	333700
Inventories	365510	429320
Accounts Receivable	46610	106640
Cash and Bank Balance	115710	366240
Short-term advances	123070	112770
Other current assets	5470	4660
Total Assets	3977850	3675830

those of its customers; otherwise, inventories would end up higher.

Let us hypothesise what would happen to Reliance's current assets and current liabilities from end March to end September. Suppose the working capital (current assets-current liabilities) is expected to go up by ₹ 200 billion. Because increases on the asset side of the balance sheet must be financed by identical increases on the liabilities and equity side, the firm must raise ₹ 200 billion to meet the expected increase in working capital over the period. However, the higher volume of purchases, plus labor expenditures associated with increased production, will cause accounts payable and accruals to increase *spontaneously*. This leaves current asset financing requirement only for the difference amount. This occurs because most, but not all, of the funds invested incurrent assets are expected to come from current liabilities.[2]

Fluctuations in working capital position can result from seasonal variations. Similar fluctuations in working capital requirements, and hence in financing needs, also occur during business cycles. Working capital needs typically decline during recessions but increase during booms. For some companies, such as those involved with agricultural products, seasonal fluctuations are much greater than business cycle fluctuations, but for other companies, such as appliance or automobile

[2]Mathematically, when both the numerator and the denominator of a ratio that has a value greater than 1.0 increase by the same amount (magnitude), the value of the ratio decreases. If the ratio's value is less than 1.0, its value will increase when both the numerator and denominator are increased by the same magnitude.

manufacturers, cyclical fluctuations are larger. In the following sections, we look in more detail at the requirement for working capital financing, and we examine some alternative working capital policies.

14-1b **The Relationships among Working Capital Accounts**

It is important that you understand how the various working capital accounts are related. To illustrate the process of producing and selling inventory and the relationships between current assets and current liabilities. Let's call a new business Ghatkopar Cloth Products (GCP). Under normal conditions, the new plant is expected to produce and sell 50,000 units of handkerchiefs each day. Each unit, which will be sold for ₹14, has a direct production cost equal to ₹11. For simplicity, we will assume that the ₹11 unit cost can be broken into two components—the cost of raw materials purchased from suppliers (cotton, dye, etc.), which is ₹6.50, and the cost of labor, which is ₹4.50—and that there are no other costs associated with the manufacture and sale of the product. GCP will purchase materials from its suppliers for credit, with cash payment due 15 days after the purchase. Likewise, GCP will allow its customers to purchase for credit, and it will require cash payment 15 days after the sale. In our illustration, we assume that all GCP customers will pay for their purchases 15 days after the sales, and that GCP will pay its suppliers 15 days after purchasing raw materials. In addition, employees will be paid every 15 days (twice per month).[3] Therefore, all the cash flows associated with the production and sales functions will occur 15 days after the purchase, manufacture, and sale of GCP's products. To simplify the illustration, we assume that all cash flows occur at the beginning of the day, before daily purchasing, producing, and selling activities begin. Thus, at the beginning of Day 16, (1) inventory purchases that were made on the first day of business are paid, (2) the firm collects for the products sold on the first day of business, and (3) the employees are paid for their first 15 days of work.

GCP will use ₹300,000 in common stock to finance the new processing plant facilities, and the raw materials purchases will be made daily and financed in the short term with accounts payable (owed to suppliers), wages payable (owed to employees), and notes payable (short-term bank loans). Each day, the raw materials that are purchased will be converted into finished goods and sold before the close of business.

On the first day of operations, just *prior to selling any products,* GCP will have 50,000 units in inventory at a cost of ₹11 per unit, so the inventory balance will be ₹550,000 = 50,000 × ₹11. The inventory cost consists of the raw materials, which amounts to ₹325,000 = 50,000 × ₹6.50 owed to suppliers, and the cost of labor, which is ₹225,000 = 50,000 × ₹4.50 owed to employees. At this point, then, the balance sheet for GCP's processing plant would be as follows:

Cash	₹ 0	Accounts payable	₹325,000
Accounts receivable	0	Accrued wages	225,000
Inventory	550,000	Notes payable	0
Current assets	₹550,000	Current liabilities	₹550,000
Fixed assets	300,000	Common equity	300,000
		Retained earnings	0
Total assets	₹850,000	Total liabilities and equity	₹850,000

On the first day of business, all of the 50,000 units in inventory will be sold for ₹14 each, so the first day's sales will be ₹700,000 = 50,000 × ₹14. After the first day's sales are complete—that is, at the end of Day 1—GCP's balance sheet will be as follows:

Cash	₹ 0	Accounts payable	₹ 325,000
Accounts receivable	700,000	Accrued wages	225,000
Inventory	0	Notes payable	0
Current assets	₹ 700,000	Current liabilities	₹ 550,000
Fixed assets	300,000	Common equity	300,000
		Retained earnings	150,000
Total assets	₹1,000,000	Total liabilities and equity	₹1,000,000

Notice that the ₹150,000 profit on the first day's sales, which is the difference between the inventory cost of ₹550,000 and the first day's sales of ₹700,000, is recognized via retained earnings.[4] This shows that not all of the ₹700,000 in accounts receivable has to be financed because ₹150,000 represents the profit on the sales.

[3]The 15-day period is used for simplicity because there are two 15-day periods in a 30-day month and 24 15-day periods in a 360-day year. If a 14-day period were used, the illustration would become more cumbersome.

At the start of the second day, *after inventories are replenished but before daily sales begin,* the inventory balance again will be ₹550,000 and the balances in accounts payable and accrued wages will *increase* by ₹325,000 and ₹225,000, respectively. Thus, the balance sheet will be as follows:

Cash	₹ 0	Accounts payable	₹ 650,000
Accounts receivable	700,000	Accrued wages	450,000
Inventory	550,000	Notes payable	0
Current assets	₹1,250,000	Current liabilities	₹1,100,000
Fixed assets	300,000	Common equity	300,000
		Retained earnings	150,000
Total assets	₹1,550,000	Total liabilities and equity	₹1,550,000

When the products are sold on the second day, accounts receivable again will increase by ₹700,000. In fact, the balances in accounts receivable, accounts payable, wages payable, and retained earnings will continue to increase (accumulate) until cash flows affect these accounts' balances. Therefore, the balances in receivables, payables, and accrued wages will increase for a total of 15 days, while the balance in retained earnings will continue to increase until dividends are paid or losses are incurred.

GCP neither receives nor disburses any cash until 15 days after the first day of business. At that time, GCP will have to pay for both the raw materials purchased on the first day of business and the wages owed to employees for the first 15 days of work. In addition, GCP will receive payment from those customers who purchased its products on the first day of business. Accordingly, for the first 15 days of business, the balances in receivables, payables, accruals, and retained earnings will continue to increase, reflecting the purchasing and selling activities of GCP prior to the receipt or payment of any cash flows. At the *end* of Day 15, therefore, the balance in each of these accounts would be as follows:

Accounts receivable	= ₹700,000 × 15 days = ₹10,500,000
Accounts payable	= ₹325,000 × 15 days = ₹ 4,875,000
Accrued wages	= ₹225,000 × 15 days = ₹ 3,375,000
Retained earnings	= ₹150,000 × 15 days = ₹ 2,250,000

The balance sheet at the *end* of Day 15 would be as follows:

Cash	₹ 0	Accounts payable	₹ 4,875,000
Accounts receivable	10,500,000	Accrued wages	3,375,000
Inventory	0	Notes payable	0
Current assets	₹10,500,000	Current liabilities	₹ 8,250,000
Fixed assets	300,000	Common equity	300,000
		Retained earnings	2,250,000
Total assets	₹10,800,000	Total liabilities and equity	₹10,800,000

At the *beginning* of Day 16, GCP must pay its employees ₹3,375,000 for the first 15 days of work, and it also must pay ₹325,000 to the suppliers for the raw materials purchased on the *first* day of business. However, at the same time, GCP will be paid ₹700,000 for the products that were sold on the first day of business. This cash receipt can be used to pay the ₹325,000 now due to the suppliers, which leaves only ₹375,000 to help pay employees' salaries. This means GCP must borrow to meet its cash obligations. If GCP uses the entire ₹375,000 to help pay employees' salaries, the amount that needs to be borrowed to pay the remaining wages is:

$$\text{Loan amount} = \left(\begin{array}{c}\text{Payment owed}\\ \text{to suppliers}\end{array}\right) + \left(\begin{array}{c}\text{Wages owed}\\ \text{employees}\end{array}\right) - \left(\begin{array}{c}\text{Cash}\\ \text{receipts}\end{array}\right)$$

$$= (₹\ 325{,}000 + ₹3{,}375{,}000) - ₹700{,}000$$

$$= ₹3{,}700{,}000 - ₹\ 700{,}000 = ₹\ 3{,}000.000$$

If GCP borrows the funds needed from a local bank, consider what the balance sheet would look like if all of the cash flow activity occurred at the very beginning of Day 16, *prior to the daily materials purchases, inventory production, and product sales.* At this point, GCP would have (1) paid *all* of the ₹3,375,000 wages owed its employees, so the balance of accrued wages would equal zero; (2) paid ₹325,000 to its suppliers, so the balance of accounts payable would decrease by ₹325,000; (3) received a ₹700,000 payment from its customers, so the balance of accounts receivable would decrease by ₹700,000; and (4) borrowed ₹3,000,000 from a local bank to pay employees, so the balance of notes payable would increase by ₹3,000,000. Thus, the balance sheet would be as follows:

[4]In reality, profits are not posted to retained earnings each day; rather, the recognition of profits (income) occurs at the end of the fiscal period via the income summary account. We recognize the daily profits in this manner for illustrative purposes only.

Cash	₹ 0	Accounts payable	₹ 4,550,000
Accounts receivable	9,800,000	Accrued wages	0
Inventory	0	Notes payable	3,000,000
Current assets	₹ 9,800,000	Current liabilities	₹ 7,550,000
Fixed assets	300,000	Common equity	300,000
		Retained earnings	2,250,000
Total assets	₹10,100,000	Total liabilities and equity	₹10,100,000

However, on Day 16, GCP must also conduct its normal daily business. Raw materials must be purchased and finished goods must be manufactured and sold. Because no additional cash flows will occur on this day, the purchase of raw materials will increase accounts payable by ₹325,000, the use of employees to manufacture finished goods will increase accrued wages by ₹225,000, and credit sales will increase accounts receivable by ₹700,000. The profit on the day's sales will also increase retained earnings by ₹150,000. Consequently, at the *end* of Day 16, the balance sheet will be as follows:

Cash	₹ 0	Accounts payable	₹ 4,875,000
Accounts receivable	10,500,000	Accrued wages	225,000
Inventory	0	Notes payable	3,000,000
Current assets	₹10,500,000	Current liabilities	₹ 8,100,000
Fixed assets	300,000	Common equity	300,000
		Retained earnings	2,400,000
Total assets	₹10,800,000	Total liabilities and equity	₹10,800,000

At this point, the accounts payable and accounts receivable balances reflect 15 days' worth of credit activities associated with the production and sales operations that took place from Day 2 through Day 16. On the other hand, because at the beginning of the day the employees were paid the wages due to them for the first 15 days of business, accrued wages include only the amount owed to employees for their work to produce inventory on Day 16. And because there have not been any cash disbursements to stockholders, the balance in retained earnings represents the profits from the products sold for all 16 days GCP has been in business: ₹2,400,000 = ₹150,000 × 16 days.

At the beginning of Day 17, GCP will pay for the materials it purchased on Day 2. It will also receive payment for the products that were sold on Day 2. This process will continue as long as the purchasing and payment patterns of both GCP and its customers do not change. As a result, GCP will pay out ₹325,000 every day to pay for materials purchased 15 days earlier (a decrease in payables), but the payables balance will remain the same from this point forward because GCP will also purchase on credit raw materials valued at ₹325,000 (an increase in payables) every day to produce the product needed for that day's sales. Therefore, the accounts payable balance will remain constant at ₹4,875,000. Similarly, the balance in accounts receivable will remain at ₹10,500,000, because each day, once this steady state has been reached (after Day 15), GCP will receive cash payments from customers totaling ₹700,000 (a decrease in receivables) at the same time ₹700,000 worth of products are sold for credit (an increase in receivables).

Now consider the cash flow position of GCP. Beginning on Day 16, each day GCP will receive cash payments from its customers that total ₹700,000, and it will make cash payments to its suppliers that total ₹325,000. However, the employees are paid every 15 days, not every day. Therefore, GCP can accumulate ₹375,000 = ₹700,000 − ₹325,000 in cash each day until employees' salaries must be paid again. The next time employees' salaries are paid is at the beginning of Day 31, so the cash account balance will increase by ₹375,000 for 15 days. Accordingly, on Day 31, after all cash flows except accrued wages are recognized, GCP will have a cash balance equal to ₹5,625,000 = ₹375,000 × 15 days. Accrued wages will equal ₹3,375,000 = ₹225,000 × 15 days, so, after paying its employees, GCP will still have a cash balance equal to ₹2,250,000. This amount represents the *total cash profit* GCP has generated during the previous 15 days of business. This amount can be used to pay off a portion of the bank loan, or it can be used to expand operations. In any event, once the balances in receivables and payables have stabilized because the daily adjustments to those accounts offset one another, GCP actually will realize a *cash* profit of ₹150,000 per day.

This illustration shows that, in general, once GCP's operations have stabilized so that the credit sales and credit purchasing patterns and the collection and payment activities stay the same day after day, the balances in accounts receivable and accounts payable will remain constant; that is, the daily increase associated with each account will be offset by the daily decrease associated with the account. Therefore, once the firm's operations have stabilized and cash collections from credit sales and cash payments for credit purchases have begun, the balances in accounts receivable and accounts payable can be computed using Equation 14.1:

14.1

$$\text{Account balance} = \left(\text{Amount of daily activity}\right) \times \left(\text{Average life of the account}\right)$$

For accounts receivable, the balance would be the daily credit sales times the length of time each account remains outstanding, or ₹700,000 × 15 days = ₹10,500,000.

The preceding scenario will occur only if GCP's expectations, including forecasted sales, become reality. But what happens if GCP's forecasts are too optimistic? If GCP finds it cannot sell 50,000 units each day, its cash collections will decrease, its inventory probably will build up, and notes payable also might increase. If this pattern continues, GCP eventually could find itself in financial difficulty.

Although the illustration we used here is oversimplified, it should give you an indication of the interrelationships among the working capital accounts. It should be apparent that a decision affecting one working capital account—for example, inventory—will have an impact on other working capital accounts—for example, receivables and payables.

14-2 The Cash Conversion Cycle

The concept of working capital management originated with the old Yankee peddler, who would borrow to buy inventory, sell the inventory to pay off the bank loan, and then repeat the cycle. The previous section illustrates the impact of such activity on the working capital accounts of the firm. That general concept has been applied to businesses that are more complex, and it is useful when analyzing the effectiveness of a firm's working capital management process.

The working capital management process that a company faces is similar to the process we described in the previous section for GCP. It can be summarized as follows:

1. The company orders and then receives the materials it needs to produce the textile products its sells. The company purchases from its suppliers on credit, so an account payable is created for credit purchases. Such purchases have no immediate cash flow effect because payment is not made until some later date, perhaps 20 to 30 days after purchase.
2. Labor is used to convert the materials (cotton and wool) into finished goods (cloth products, thread, etc.). However, wages are not fully paid at the time the work is done, so accrued wages build up, maybe for a period of one or two weeks.
3. The finished products are sold, but on credit. The credit sales create receivables, not immediate cash inflows.
4. At some point during the cycle, the company must pay off its accounts payable and accrued wages. If these payments are made before the company collects cash from its receivables, a net cash outflow occurs, and this outflow must be financed.
5. The cycle is completed when the company's receivables are collected, perhaps 30 to 40 days after the original sale. At that time, the company is in a position to pay off the credit that was used to finance production of the product, and it can then repeat the cycle.

The preceding steps are formalized with the cash conversion cycle model, which focuses on the length of time between when the company makes payments, or invests in the manufacture of inventory, and when it receives cash inflows, or realizes a cash return from its investment in production.[5] The following terms are used in the model:

1. The **inventory conversion period** is the average length of time required to convert materials into finished goods and then to sell those goods; it is the amount of time the product remains in inventory in various stages of completion. The inventory conversion period, which is equivalent to the average age of the firm's inventory, is calculated by dividing inventory by the cost of goods sold per day.
2. The **receivables collection period** is the average length of time required to convert the firm's receivables into cash—that is, the time it takes to collect cash following a sale. The receivables collection period is also called the days sales outstanding (DSO), and it is calculated by dividing accounts receivable by the average credit sales per day.

inventory conversion period The amount of time a product remains in inventory in various stages of completion.

receivables collection period The time it takes to collect cash following a sale; also known as days sales outstanding (DSO).

[5]See Verlyn Richards and Eugene Laughlin, "A Cash Conversion Cycle Approach to Liquidity Analysis," *Financial Management*, Spring 1980, 32–38.

© Monty Rakusen/Digital Vision/Getty Images

3. The **payables deferral period** is the average length of time between the purchase of raw materials and labor and the payment of cash for them. It is computed by dividing accounts payable by the daily credit purchases.
4. The **cash conversion cycle** computation nets out the three periods just defined, resulting in a value that equals the length of time between when the firm pays cash for (invests in) productive resources (materials and labor) and cash is received from the sale of products. In other words, the cash conversion cycle represents the length of time between paying for labor and materials and collecting on receivables. The cash conversion cycle thus equals the average length of time a rupee is tied up, or invested, in current assets.

   We can now use these definitions to analyze company's cash conversion cycle. The concept, which is diagrammed in Figure 14.1, can be expressed by Equation 14.5.

In Equation 14.5, ICP, DSO, and DPO represent the inventory conversion period, days sales outstanding, and days payables outstanding as defined in Equations 14.2, 14.3, and 14.4, respectively.

Given its cash conversion cycle, a

14.2

$$\text{Inventory conversion periodsICP} = \frac{\text{Inventory}}{\text{Cost of good sold per day}} = \frac{\text{Inventory}}{\left(\dfrac{\text{Cost of good sold}}{360\text{ days}}\right)} = \frac{360\text{ day}}{\left(\dfrac{\text{Cost of good sold}}{\text{Inventory}}\right)} = \frac{360\text{ day}}{\text{Inventory turnover}}$$

14.3

$$\text{Receivables collection periods(DSO)} = \frac{\text{Receivebles}}{\text{Daily credit sales}} = \frac{\text{Receivables}}{\left(\dfrac{\text{Annual credit sales}}{360}\right)} = \frac{360\text{ days}}{\left(\dfrac{\text{Annual credit sales}}{\text{Receivables}}\right)} = \frac{360\text{ days}}{\text{Receivables turnover}}$$

14.4

$$\text{Payables deferral periods(DPO)} = \frac{\text{Accounts payable}}{\text{Credit purchases per day}} = \frac{\text{Accounts payable}}{\left(\dfrac{\text{Cost of goods sold}}{360}\right)} = \frac{360\text{ days}}{\left(\dfrac{\text{Cost of goods sold}}{\text{Accounts payable}}\right)} = \frac{360\text{ days}}{\text{Payables turnover}}$$

payables deferral period The average length of time between the purchase of raw materials and labor and the payment of cash for them; also known as days payables outstanding (DPO).

cash conversion cycle The length of time from the payment for the purchase of raw materials to manufacture a product until the collection of accounts receivable associated with the sale of the product.

FIGURE 14.1 The Cash Conversion Cycle for the Company

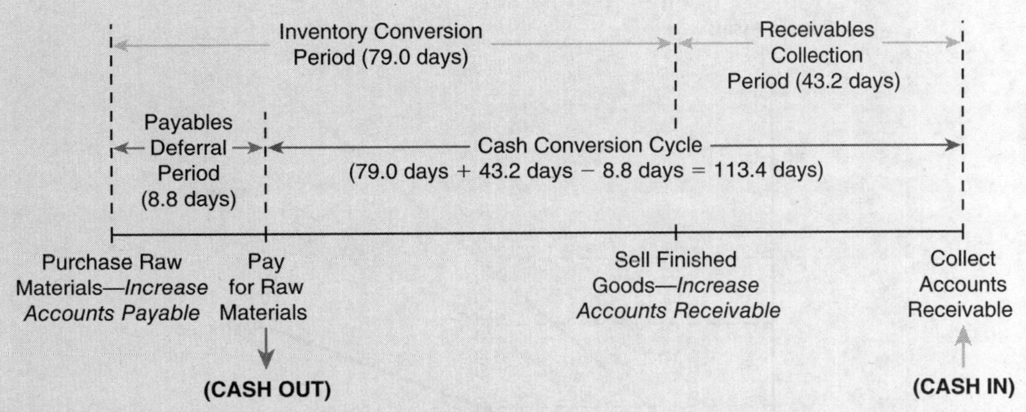

14.5

$$\text{Cash conversion cycle} = \text{ICP} + \text{DSO} - \text{DPO}$$

company knows that it will have to finance the manufacturing and other operating costs associated with the production and sale of its products for a given period. The firm's goal should be to shorten its cash conversion cycle as much as possible without harming operations. This would improve profits, because the longer the cash conversion cycle, the greater the need for external, or nonspontaneous, financing (e.g., bank loans), which is more costly than internal financing (e.g., accruals).

The cash conversion cycle can be shortened by (1) reducing the inventory conversion period by processing and selling goods more quickly (efficiently); (2) reducing the receivables collection period by speeding up collections; or (3) lengthening the payables deferral period by slowing down payments to suppliers (and employees). To the extent that these actions can be taken *without harming the return* associated with the management of these accounts, they should be carried out. Thus, when taking actions to reduce the inventory conversion period, a firm should be careful to *avoid inventory shortages* that could cause good customers to buy from competitors; when taking actions to speed up the collection of receivables, a firm should be careful to *maintain appropriate relations with its good credit customers*; and when taking actions to lengthen the payables deferral period, a firm should be careful *not to harm its own credit reputation.*

14-3 Working Capital Investment and Financing Policies

Working capital policy involves two basic questions: (1) What is the appropriate level for current assets, both in total and by specific accounts? (2) How should current assets be financed?

14-3a Alternative Current Asset Investment Policies

Figure 14.2 shows three alternative policies regarding the total amount of current assets carried. Essentially, these policies differ in that different amounts of current assets are carried to support any given level of sales. The line with the steepest slope represents a **relaxed** (or "fat-cat") **current asset investment policy** under which relatively large amounts of cash and marketable securities and inventories, and a correspondingly high level of receivables, are carried, and sales are stimulated by the use of a credit policy that provides liberal financing to customers. Conversely, with the **restricted current asset investment** (or "lean-and-mean") **policy,**

relaxed current asset investment policy A policy under which relatively large amounts of cash and marketable securities and inventories are carried, and under which sales are stimulated by a liberal credit policy that results in a high level of receivables.

restricted current asset investment policy A policy under which holdings of cash and marketable securities, inventories, and receivables are minimized.

FIGURE 14.2 Alternative Current Asset Investment Policies (₹ in Millions)

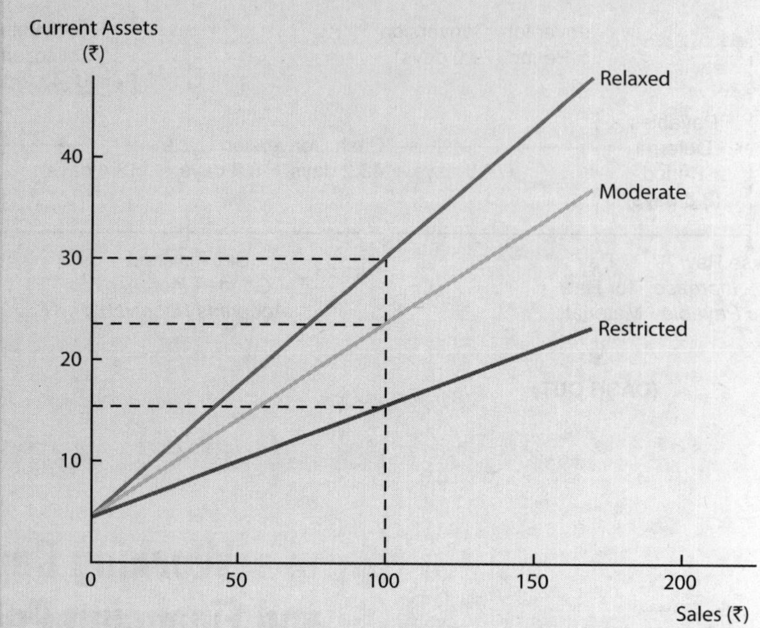

the firm's holings of cash and marketable securities, inventories, and receivables are minimized. The **moderate current asset investment policy** is between the two extremes.

Under conditions of certainty—when sales, costs, lead times, payment periods, and so on, are certain—all firms would hold only minimal levels of current assets. The firm would follow a restricted current asset investment policy. Holding larger amounts would increase the need for external funding without a corresponding increase in profits, whereas smaller holdings would involve late payments to employees and suppliers and lost sales caused by inventory shortages and an overly restrictive credit policy.

However, the picture changes when uncertainty is introduced. Here the firm requires some minimum amount of cash and inventories based on expected payments, expected sales, expected order lead times, and so on, plus additional amounts, or *safety stocks,* that enable it to deal with departures from the expected values. Similarly, accounts receivable levels are determined by credit terms, and the tougher the credit terms, the lower the receivables for any given level of sales. Firms that face greater uncertainty in operations tend to follow a more relaxed current asset investment policy.

moderate current asset investment policy A policy between the relaxed and restrictive policies.

With a restricted current asset investment policy, the firm would hold minimal levels of safety stocks for cash and inventories, and it would have a tight credit policy even though this would mean running the risk of losing sales. A restricted, lean-and-mean current asset investment policy generally provides the highest expected return on investment, but it entails the greatest risk, whereas the reverse is true under a relaxed policy. The moderate policy falls in between the two extremes in terms of both expected risk and return.

In terms of the cash conversion cycle, a restricted investment policy would tend to reduce the inventory conversion and receivables collection periods, which would result in a relatively short cash conversion cycle. Conversely, a relaxed policy would create higher levels of inventories and receivables, longer inventory conversion and receivables collection periods, and a relatively long cash conversion cycle. A moderate policy would produce a cash conversion cycle somewhere between the two extremes.

14-3b **Alternative Current Asset Financing Policies**

Most businesses experience seasonal fluctuations, cyclical fluctuations, or both. For example, construction firms have peaks in the spring and summer, retailers peak around Diwali and the manufacturers who supply construction companies and retailers follow patterns similar to their customers' patterns. Moreover, virtually all businesses must build up current assets when the economy is strong, but they then sell off inventories and have net reductions of receivables when the economy slacks off. Still, current assets rarely drop to zero, and this realization has led to the development of the idea that some current assets should be considered **permanent current assets** because their levels remain stable no matter the seasonal or economic conditions. Temporary current assets are those amounts of current assets that vary with respect to the seasonal or economic conditions of a firm. The manner in which the permanent and temporary current assets are financed is called the firm's *current asset financing policy,* which generally can be classified as one of the three approaches described next.

Maturity Matching, or "Self-Liquidating," Approach. The **maturity matching**, or **"self-liquidating," approach** calls for matching asset and liability maturities as shown in Panel A of Figure 14.3. This strategy minimizes the risk that the firm will be unable to pay off its maturing obligations *if* the liquidations of the assets can be controlled to occur on or before the maturities of the obligations. At the limit, a firm could attempt to match exactly the maturity structure of its assets and liabilities. Inventory expected to be sold in 30 days could be financed with a 30-day bank loan; a machine expected to last for five years could be financed by a five-year loan; a 20-year building could be financed by a 20-year mortgage bond; and so forth. In fact, of course, two factors prevent this exact maturity matching: (1) there is uncertainty about the lives of assets; and (2) some common equity must be used, and common equity has no maturity. To illustrate the uncertainty factor, the company might finance inventories with a 30-day loan, expecting to sell the inventories and to use the cash generated to retire the loan. However, if sales were slow, the cash would not be forthcoming, and the use of short-term credit could end up causing a problem. (For example. look at the cash conversion cycle computed for the company in the previous section.) Still, if the company makes an attempt to match asset and liability maturities, we would define this as a *moderate current asset financing policy*.

Aggressive Approach. Panel B of Figure 14.3 illustrates the **aggressive approach**, used by a firm that (1) finances all of its temporary assets with short-term, nonspontaneous debt; and (2) finances all of its fixed assets and some of its permanent assets with long-term capital, financing the remainder of its permanent current assets with short-term, nonspontaneous credit. Returning to Figure 14.3, note that we used the term *relatively* in the title for Panel B because there can be different *degrees* of aggressiveness. For example, the dashed line in Panel B could have been drawn *below* the line designating fixed assets, indicating that all of the permanent current assets and part of the fixed assets were financed with short-term credit. This would be a highly aggressive, extremely nonconservative position, and the firm would be very much subject to dangers from rising interest rates as well as to loan renewal problems. However, short-term debt often is cheaper than long-term debt, and some firms are willing to sacrifice safety for the chance of higher profits.

Conservative Approach. As shown in Panel C of Figure 14.3, the dashed line could also be drawn *above* the line designating permanent current assets, indicating that permanent capital is being used to finance all permanent asset requirements (both fixed assets and permanent current assets) and also to meet some or all of the seasonal, temporary demands. In the situation depicted in our graph, the firm uses a small amount of short-term, nonspontaneous credit to meet its peak requirements, but it also meets a part of its seasonal needs by storing liquidity in the form of marketable securities during the off-season. The humps above the dashed line represent short-term financing; the troughs below the dashed line represent short-term security holdings. Panel C represents the **conservative approach**, which is a very safe current asset financing policy that generally is not as profitable as the other two approaches because there are times when the firm carries unnecessary liquidity.

permanent current assets Current assets balances that remain stable no matter the seasonal or economic conditions; balances that exist no matter the type of business cycle.

maturity matching ("self-liquidating") approach A financing policy that matches asset and liability maturities. This would be considered a moderate current asset financing policy.

aggressive approach A policy under which all of the fixed assets of a firm are financed with long-term capital, but some of the firm's permanent current assets are financed with short-term nonspontaneous sources of funds.

conservative approach A policy under which all of the fixed assets, all of the permanent current assets, and some of the temporary current assets of a firm are financed with long-term capital.

14-4 Advantages and Disadvantages of Short-Term Financing

The three possible financing policies described in the previous section were distinguished by the relative amounts of short-term debt used under each policy. The aggressive policy calls for the greatest use of short-term debt, whereas the conservative policy requires the least, and maturity matching falls in between. Although using short-term credit generally is riskier than using long-term credit, short-term credit does have some significant advantages. The pros and cons of short-term financing are considered in this section.

14-4a Speed

A short-term loan can be obtained much more quickly than a long-term loan. Lenders will insist on a more thorough financial examination before extending long-term credit, and the loan agreement will have to be spelled out in considerable detail because much can happen during the life of a 10- or 20-year loan. Therefore, if funds are needed in a hurry, a firm generally looks to short-term borrowing sources.

14-4b Flexibility

If the needs for funds are seasonal or cyclical, a firm might not want to commit itself to long-term debt for three reasons. First, the costs associated with issuing long-term debt are significantly greater than the costs of getting short-term credit. Second, some long-term debt carries expensive penalties for prepayment (paying prior to maturity). Accordingly,

FIGURE 14.3 Alternative Current Asset Financing Policies

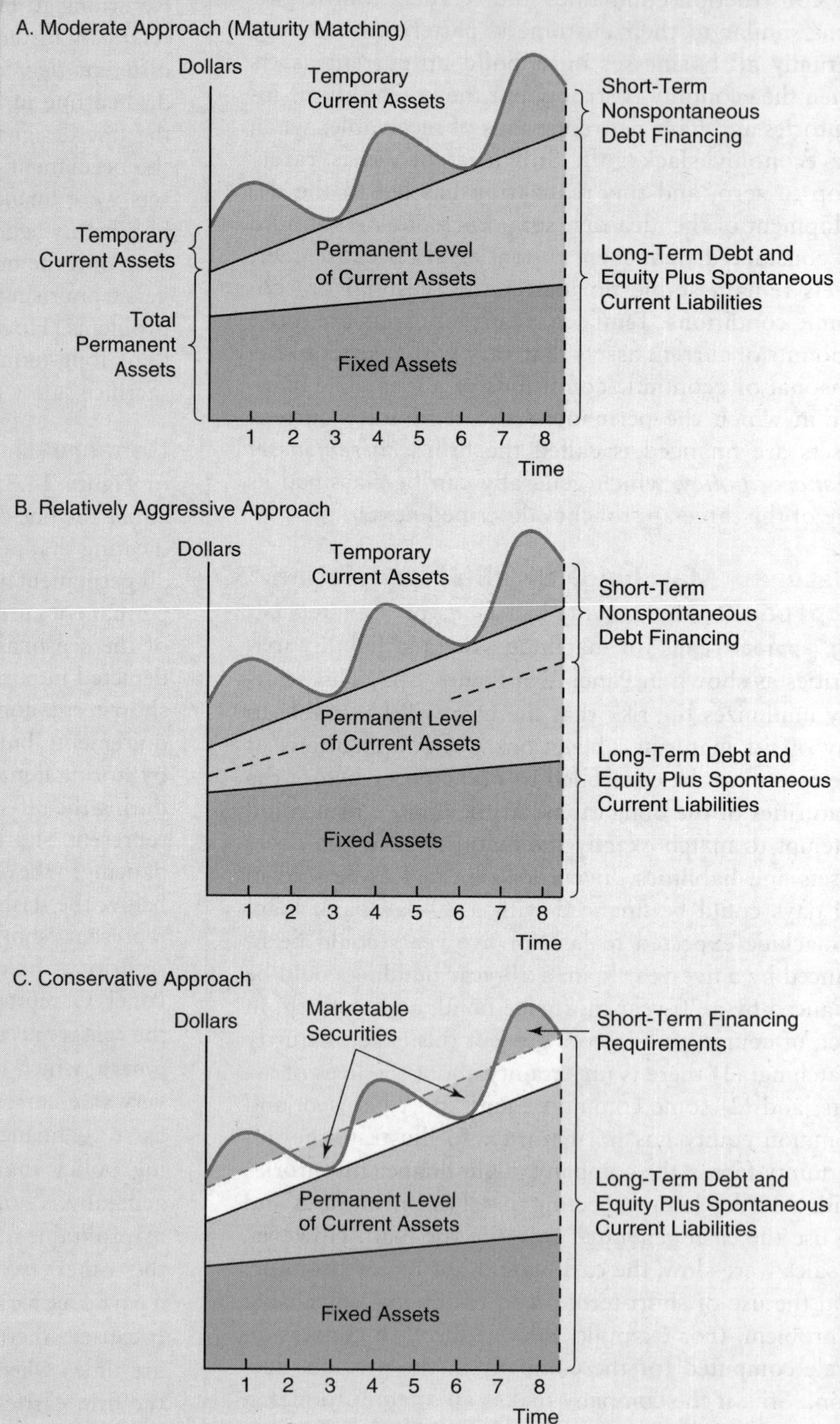

if a firm thinks its need for funds will diminish in the near future, it should choose short-term debt for the flexibility it provides. Third, long-term loan agreements always contain provisions, or *covenants*, that constrain the firm's future actions. Short-term credit agreements generally are much less onerous in this regard.

14-4c Cost of Long-Term versus Short-Term Debt

The yield curve normally is upward sloping, indicating that, at any point in time, interest rates generally are lower on short-term debt than on long-term debt (see Chapter 5). Thus, under normal conditions, interest costs at the time the funds are obtained will be lower if the firm borrows on a short-term basis rather than on a long-term basis.

14-4d Risk of Long-Term versus Short-Term Debt

Even though short-term debt is often less expensive than long-term debt, short-term credit subjects the firm to more risk than does long-term financing. This occurs for two reasons. (1) If a firm borrows on a long-term basis, its interest costs will be relatively stable, perhaps even fixed, over time. But if it uses short-term credit, its interest expense will fluctuate widely, at times reaching quite high levels. For example, short-term rates increased by 4.25 percent from June 2004–July 2006 because the Federal Reserve increased rates nearly every month during this two-year period, which created a significant burden for many firms. (2) If a firm borrows heavily on a short-term basis, it could find itself unable to repay this debt, and it might be in such a weak financial position that the lender will not extend the loan; this could force the firm into bankruptcy.

14-5 Multinational Working Capital Management

For the most part, the techniques used to manage short-term assets and liabilities in multinational corporations are the same as those used in purely domestic corporations. However, multinational corporations face a far more complex task because they operate in many different business cultures, political environments, and economic conditions. In Chapter 1, we described six factors that generally complicate managerial finance in the international business arena: (1) different currency denominations, (2) differences in economic and legal environments, (3) language differences, (4) cultural differences, (5) governmental role, and (6) political risk. Difficulties with each of these factors are more acute when managing working capital internationally, because decisions made in the short run can have significant consequences for the long-run survival of the firm. Such decisions are more difficult to adjust or reverse when rules, regulations, and business cultures differ significantly from one business setting to another.

The results of one study provide some indication of how working capital policies of U.S. firms and European firms differ.[7] First, the average cash conversion cycle of European firms (about 263 days) was more than twice the average cash conversion cycle of U.S. firms (about 116 days). A possible explanation for this disparity is that European firms had much higher growth rates than their U.S. counterparts. Second, it appears that U.S. firms follow much more conservative working capital policies than do European firms. The average current ratio and the average quick ratio proved to be significantly greater for U.S. firms than for European firms, which suggests that corporations in the United States use significantly more long-term financing alternatives than corporations in Europe. Although a more in-depth study is needed to determine why U.S. firms seem to follow more conservative working capital policies than European firms, one possible explanation might be found in the differences that are apparent in the banking systems in Europe and in the United States. In Chapter 3, we mentioned that U.S. financial institutions have traditionally been at a competitive disadvantage in the global arena because they are subject to more restrictions and regulations than banking organizations in other countries. Foreign banks generally can branch with few or no restrictions and are allowed, in many cases, to own corporations to which they also lend funds. For these reasons, European banks often have very close relationships with their debtor corporations; thus, they tend be more willing to provide short-term, risky debt than we observe in U.S. banking organizations.

[7] Chun-Hao Chang, Krishnan Dandapani, and Arun J. Prakish, "Current Assets Policies of European Corporations: A Critical Examination," *Management International Review*, Special Issue 1995/2, 105–117.

KEY WORKING CAPITAL POLICY CONCEPTS

To conclude this chapter, we summarize some concepts that were discussed.

- Working capital refers to the short-term, or current, assets of a firm. Liquidation of working capital accounts produces the cash that is needed to pay current bills. If a firm cannot pay its current bills, it will not survive to see the long term. As a result, poor working capital management generally results in financial distress, and perhaps (often) bankruptcy.
- The working capital management process and the relationships among the working capital accounts can be described as follows: (1) A company orders materials to manufacture the product its sells, during which time inventories and accounts payable increase (assuming a credit purchase). (2) During the production stages accrued wages build up, perhaps for a period of one or two weeks, because employees are not paid at the end of each working day. (3) If the finished product is sold on credit, accounts receivables increase. (4) At some point, the company must pay off its accounts payable and accrued wages. (5) The cycle is completed when the firm collects cash payment for the products that are sold on credit.
- The cash conversion cycle represents the length of time funds are tied up, or invested, in current assets. Often a firm has to pay for the materials and labor that are needed to manufacture and sell its products before customers pay for their purchases. During the period from when the firm invests in the product—that is, pays for materials and labor—until it receives cash payment from the sale of the product, external financing is needed to support operations. If a firm reduces its cash conversion cycle, it reduces its need for external financing.
- More liquid firms are better able to weather financial difficulties, but they also generate lower returns than less liquid firms during prosperous times. Thus, there is a tradeoff between liquidity (risk) and return. As a result, a firm must determine whether it should follow a current asset investment strategy that is a relaxed, or "fat cat," policy; a restricted, or "lean-and-mean" policy; or a moderate policy.

© iStockphoto.com/Chris Rogers

▸▸ Short-term financing generally is riskier but cheaper than long-term financing. Thus, a firm must determine what level of financing risk it can handle. Firms that are able to take on substantial amounts of financial risk are more likely to finance current assets with more short-term debt (i.e., follow the aggressive approach) than firms that are not able to handle as much financial risk (i.e., follow the conservative approach). Most firms follow the maturity matching, or "self-liquidating," approach, a moderate approach that is between the aggressive and conservative approaches.

MULTIPLE CHOICE QUESTIONS

1. If the time taken to produce the end product is longer than it was the previous year,

a. The operating cycle will be longer this year

b. The cash conversion cycle will be longer this year

c. Both a and b

d. None of the above

2. The cash conversion cycle will be equal to the operating cycle when

a. There is no inventory

b. There are no receivables

c. There are no payables

d. None of the above

3. Working capital needs are calculated on the basis of

a. Operating cycle

b. Cash conversion cycle

c. The difference between the operating cycle and the cash conversion cycle

d. The sum of the operating cycle and the cash conversion cycle

4. A cash budget

a. Tells the company the months during which liquidity is poor

b. Tells the company the months during which there is excess liquidity

c. Both a and b

d. None of the above

5. If a proposal from the sales department for extending DSO is accepted

a. Working capital needs will go up

b. Working capital needs will come down if collection is prompt

c. Working capital needs will remain the same

d. We need more information before we can answer this

6. Working capital is financed by

a. Debt

b. Equity

c. Partly debt and equity

d. This matter is left to the company

7. If working capital is financed by equity,

a. Cost will be higher than if it were financed by debt

b. Cost will be the same as if it were financed by debt

c. Cost will be lower than if it were financed by debt

d. Cannot be determined without more information

8. Cost of working capital financing

a. Determines profitability

b. Is an influencing factor in profitability

c. Has no impact on profitability

d. Both a and b

9. Having a scheme of giving discounts for prompt payment seeks to

a. Increase working capital needs

b. Reduce working capital needs

c. There is no impact on the working capital

d. None of the above

10. Having cash sales results in greater profits than corresponding credit sales

a. To the extent of working capital interest for the days of credit

b. To the extent of working capital credit for double the credit days

c. To the extent of the discount given for early payment

d. Both a and c

Answers:

1.	(c)	2.	(c)	3.	(b)	4.	(c)	5.	(a)
6.	(d)	7.	(a)	8.	(b)	9.	(b)	10.	(a)

PROBLEMS

For more problems, login to CourseMate for CFIN at CengageBrain.com

14-1 Rakshit Company's normal daily credit sales are ₹50,000. The average collection period is 30 days. (a) What is the average accounts receivable that is reported on Rakshit's balance sheet? (b) If Rakshit's opportunity cost is 10 percent, how much would the company save if the average collection period can be reduced to 20 days?

14-2 The balance in Ganaras Inn's (GI) accounts payable averages ₹164,000, and its payables deferral period (DPO) is 10 days. (a) How much does GI normally purchase each day from its suppliers. (b) If GI's opportunity cost is 8 percent, how much can the company save if it can increase its DPO by five days?

14-3 Big Bang Fireworks normally purchases ₹120,000 of inventory each day. Each item normally remains in inventory 18 days before it is sold. (a) What is the average amount of inventory that is reported on Big Bang's balance sheet? (b) What is the inventory turnover?

14-4 A+ Airplanes normally sells ₹125,000 of its product on credit each day, and it takes an average of 40 days to collect the credit sales. (a) What is the average accounts receivable that is reported on A+'s balance sheet? (b) What is the company's accounts receivable turnover?

14-5 Chachi Letter Service's (CLS) days sales outstanding (DSO) currently is 50 days. (a) If annual sales are ₹144,000, what is the average balance in accounts receivable? (b) If CLS can reduce its DSO to 45 days, what impact would this change have on its accounts receivable balance?

14-6 Lalitmahal Out Utilities (LOU) purchases ₹150000 in raw materials from its suppliers each day. LOU's accounts payable turnover is 12. (a) What is LOU's payables deferral period (DPO)? (b) What is the average accounts payable balance that is reported on LOU's financial statements?

14-7 The average inventory shown on Dippy's Plumbing's balance sheet is ₹270,000. The inventory conversion period is nine days. (a) What is the inventory turnover? (b) What amount of inventory does Dippy normally purchase each day?

14-8 Beena Auctions carries an average inventory equal to ₹100,000. The company's cost of goods sold averages ₹1.5 million. What are Beena's (a) inventory turnover, and (b) inventory conversion period?

14-9 CEO Manufacturing generally has inventory that equals ₹4800000. If the inventory turnover for the company is 18, what are its (a) inventory conversion period and (b) cost of goods sold?

14-10 Lucknow Landscaping and Lawn Service (3LS) projects net income for this year to be ₹138,000, and that its net profit margin will be 3 percent. Cost of goods sold normally equal 75 percent of sales. If 3LS turns over its inventory 20 times during the year, what is the average amount of inventory that is shown on its balance sheet?

14-11 Rohtak Drilling generally carries an amount of receivables equal to ₹1600000, and its annual credit sales equal ₹3.2 million. What are Roughneck's (a) receivables turnover and (b) receivables collection period (DSO)?

14-12 Ernakulam Eyeware generally has accounts receivables that equal ₹265,000. If the accounts receivables turnover for the company is 6, what are its (a) receivables collection period (DSO) and (b) annual credit sales?

14-13 At any point in time, Tamarind Hospitals owes its suppliers ₹45,000. The company's cost of goods sold averages ₹810,000. What are Tamarind's (a) payables turnover and (b) payables deferral period (DPO)?

14-14 The accounts payables of Aurobindo Publishing generally equal ₹6.4 million. If the turnover of accounts payables is 30, what are its (a) payables deferral period (DPO) and (b) annual credit purchases?

14-15 Balmurugan Payment Financial (BPF) has an inventory conversion period of 45 days, a receivables collection period of 30 days, and a payables deferral period of 20 days. (a) What is the length of the firm's cash conversion cycle? (b) If BPF's annual sales are ₹1,800,000 and all sales are on credit, what is the average balance in accounts receivable? (c) How many times per year does BPF turn over its inventory? (d) What would happen to BPF's cash conversion cycle if, on average, inventories could be turned over 12 times a year?

14–16 The Farmer Corporation is trying to determine the effect of its inventory turnover ratio and days sales outstanding (DSO) on its cash flow cycle. Last year, Farmer's sales (all on credit) were ₹180,000, and its cost of goods sold were 85 percent of sales. Inventory was turned over eight times during the year, and the accounts receivable turnover was 10. Farmer's payables deferral period is 30 days. (a) Calculate Farmer's cash conversion cycle. (b) Compute the average balances in accounts receivable, accounts payable, and inventory.

14–17 Samayapuram Wireless is examining its cash conversion cycle. The company expects its cost of goods sold, which equal 80 percent of sales, to equal ₹480,000 this year. Samayapuram normally turns over inventory 24 times per year, accounts receivable are turned over 15 per year, and the accounts payable turnover is 40. Calculate (a) the cash conversion cycle and (b) the average balances in accounts receivable, accounts payable, and inventory.

14–18 Refer to Table 14.1, which shows the balance sheets for Reliance Industries on three different dates. Assume all sales and all purchases are made on credit. Calculate the length of Reliance's cash conversion cycle on September 30, 2015 and December 31, 2015.

14–19 Go back to the GCP illustration at the beginning of the chapter. Assume the collection and payment patterns of both GCP and its customers do not change. (a) Construct the balance sheet for GCP at the close of business on Day 31. Remember that the employees' salaries will have been paid at the *beginning* of the day for the *previous* 15 days they have worked, so accrued wages will include only one day of salaries (Day 31). (b) How long will it take GCP to pay off the bank loan it took out on Day 16 if the *daily cash profits* are used to repay the loan (ignore any interest costs)?

14–20 Subhash Ox Real Estate (SORE) has been growing at a constant 5 percent rate for many years, and it expects to continue this growth long into the future. On January 1 of this year, which is the slow part of its selling season, SORE's total assets were ₹420 million. At the height of its selling season, which is at the end of June, SORE expects total assets to be ₹480 million. How much of the ₹480 million in assets represents permanent assets, and how much represents temporary current assets?

Working Capital Policy

Learning Outcomes

LO.1 Discuss why working capital is needed and how working capital accounts are related.

- Working capital represents the current assets that a firm liquidates to generate revenues from normal operations. Often a firm purchases raw material on credit, which increases the balances that are shown in accounts payable and inventory. As the raw materials are transformed into finished goods that can be sold to customers, the balance in accrued wages increases. If the finished product is sold on credit to customers, the accounts receivable balance increases and the inventory balance decreases. If the firm needs to arrange financing from its bank to pay suppliers, the balance in notes payable increases. When the firm collects for credit sales and pays the bank, balances in receivables and notes payable decrease.

LO.2 Describe the cash conversion cycle and how it can be used to better manage working capital activities.

- The cash conversion cycle (CCC) represents the length of time from when the firm pays for inventory until it collects for the sale of that inventory; that is, the CCC is the time that funds are tied up, or invested in, inventory and receivables (if the firm sells on credit). Everything else equal, a firm should strive to reduce its CCC so that funds can be freed up to invest in value-increasing projects. The CCC can be decreased by extending the time it takes to pay suppliers (payables deferral period), reducing the amount of time it takes to sell inventory (inventory conversion period), or reducing the amount of time it takes to collect receivables (receivables collection period).

LO.3 Describe the policies that a firm might follow (a) when investing in current assets and (b) when financing current assets.

- A firm generally follows one of three current-asset investment policies: (1) relaxed (fat-cat), which calls for large amounts of current assets; (2) restricted, which calls for minimal amounts of current assets; and (3) moderate, which falls between the relaxed and restricted investing policies.
- A firm generally follows one of three current asset financing approaches: (1) maturity matching (self-liquidating), which calls for matching the maturities of short-term assets and liabilities; (2) aggressive, which calls for financing all temporary assets and some permanent current assets with short-term, nonspontaneous debt and financing the remainder of the assets with long-term funds and spontaneous current liabilities; and (3) conservative, which calls for financing all of the permanent assets and some of the temporary assets with long-term funds plus spontaneous debt, and financing the remainder of the temporary assets with short-term nonspontaneous debt.

LO.4 Discuss the advantages and disadvantages of using short-term financing rather than long-term financing.

- The major advantages of short-term debt are the speed with which a loan can be obtained and the flexibility of the debt arrangement. The major disadvantages of using short-term debt are that the firm might not be able pay off the loan when due, and that it might be difficult for the firm to get additional loans in the future if economic or financial conditions have deteriorated.

LO.5 Describe how working capital management in multinational firms is different from working capital management in purely domestic firms.

- Although the same general concepts apply, such factors as currency differences, cultural differences, political risk, and government intervention make working capital management in multinational firms somewhat more complicated than in purely domestic firms.

CHAPTER 14 REVIEW

Chapter 14 Key Working Capital Management Concepts

- Working capital refers to the short-term, or current, assets of a firm. Liquidation of working capital accounts produces the cash that is needed to pay current bills. If a firm cannot pay its current bills, it will not survive to see the long term. As a result, poor working capital management generally results in financial distress, and perhaps bankruptcy.
- The working capital management process and the relationships among the working capital accounts can be described as follows: (1) A company orders materials to manufacture the product its sells, during which time inventories and accounts payable increase (assuming a credit purchase). (2) During the production stages accrued wages build up, perhaps for a period of one or two weeks, because employees are not paid at the end of each working day. (3) If the finished product is sold on credit, accounts receivables increase. (4) At some point, the company must pay off its accounts payable and accrued wages. (5) The cycle is completed when the firm collects cash payment for the products.
- The cash conversion cycle represents the length of time funds are "tied up," or invested, in current assets. Often a firm has to pay for the materials and labor that are needed to manufacture and sell its products before customers pay for their purchases. During the period from when the firm invests in the product—that is, pays for materials and labor—until it receives cash payment from the sale of the product, external financing is needed to support operations. If a firm reduces its cash conversion cycle, it reduces its need for external financing.
- More liquid firms are better able to weather financial difficulties, but they also generate lower returns than less liquid firms during prosperous times. Thus, there is a tradeoff between liquidity (risk) and return. As a result, a firm must determine whether it should follow a current asset investment strategy that is a relaxed, or "fat cat," policy; a restricted, or "lean-and-mean," policy; or a moderate policy.
- Short-term financing generally is riskier but cheaper than long-term financing. Thus, a firm must determine what level of financing risk it can handle. Firms that are able to take on substantial amounts of financial risk are more likely to finance current assets with more short-term debt (i.e., follow the aggressive approach) than firms that are not able to handle as much financial risk (i.e., follow the conservative approach). Most firms follow the maturity matching, or "self-liquidating," approach, a moderate approach that is between the aggressive and conservative approaches.

Key Terms

working capital management The management of short-term assets (investments) and liabilities (financing sources). *p. 243*

LO.1

working capital A firm's investment in short-term assets—cash, marketable securities, inventory, and accounts receivable. *p. 243*

net working capital Current assets minus current liabilities—the amount of current assets financed by long-term liabilities. *p. 243*

working capital policy Decisions regarding (1) the target levels for each current asset account and (2) how current assets will be financed. *p. 243*

LO.2

inventory conversion period The amount of time a product remains in inventory in various stages of completion. *p. 248*

receivables collection period The time it takes to collect cash following a sale; also known as days sales outstanding (DSO). *p. 249*

payables deferral period The average length of time between the purchase of raw materials and labor and the payment of cash for them; also known as days payables outstanding (DPO). *p. 250*

cash conversion cycle The length of time from the payment for the purchase of raw materials to manufacture a product until the collection of accounts receivable associated with the sale of the product. *p. 250*

LO.3

relaxed current asset investment policy A policy under which relatively large amounts of cash and marketable securities and inventories are carried and under which sales are stimulated by a liberal credit policy that results in a high level of receivables. *p. 252*

restricted current asset investment policy A policy under which holdings of cash and marketable securities, inventories, and receivables are minimized. *p. 252*

moderate current asset investment policy A policy between the relaxed and restrictive policies. *p. 252*

permanent current assets Current assets balances that remain stable no matter the seasonal or economic conditions; balances that exist no matter the type of business cycle. *p. 253*

temporary current assets Current assets that fluctuate with seasonal or cyclical variations in a firm's business. *p. 253*

maturity matching ("self-liquidating") approach A financing policy that matches asset and liability maturities. This would be considered a moderate current asset financing policy. *p. 253*

aggressive approach A policy under which all of the fixed assets of a firm are financed with long-term capital, but *some* of the firm's permanent current assets are financed with short-term nonspontaneous sources of funds. *p. 255*

conservative approach A policy under which all of the fixed assets, all of the permanent current assets, and some of the temporary current assets of a firm are financed with long-term capital. *p. 255*

CHAPTER 15

Managing Short-Term Assets

Learning Outcomes

LO.1 Discuss the goal of effective cash management and how (a) the cash budget, (b) techniques that exist to accelerate cash receipts, and (c) cash disbursement controls should be employed to develop an optimal cash management policy.

LO.2 Explain the rationale for holding marketable securities, and describe the general characteristics of investments that should be included in portfolios of marketable securities.

LO.3 Discuss accounts receivable (credit) management, and describe how a proposed credit policy change should be evaluated.

LO.4 Explain the rationale for holding various forms of inventory, and describe how a firm can determine its optimal level of inventory.

LO.5 Describe how management of current assets differs for multinational firms and for purely domestic firms.

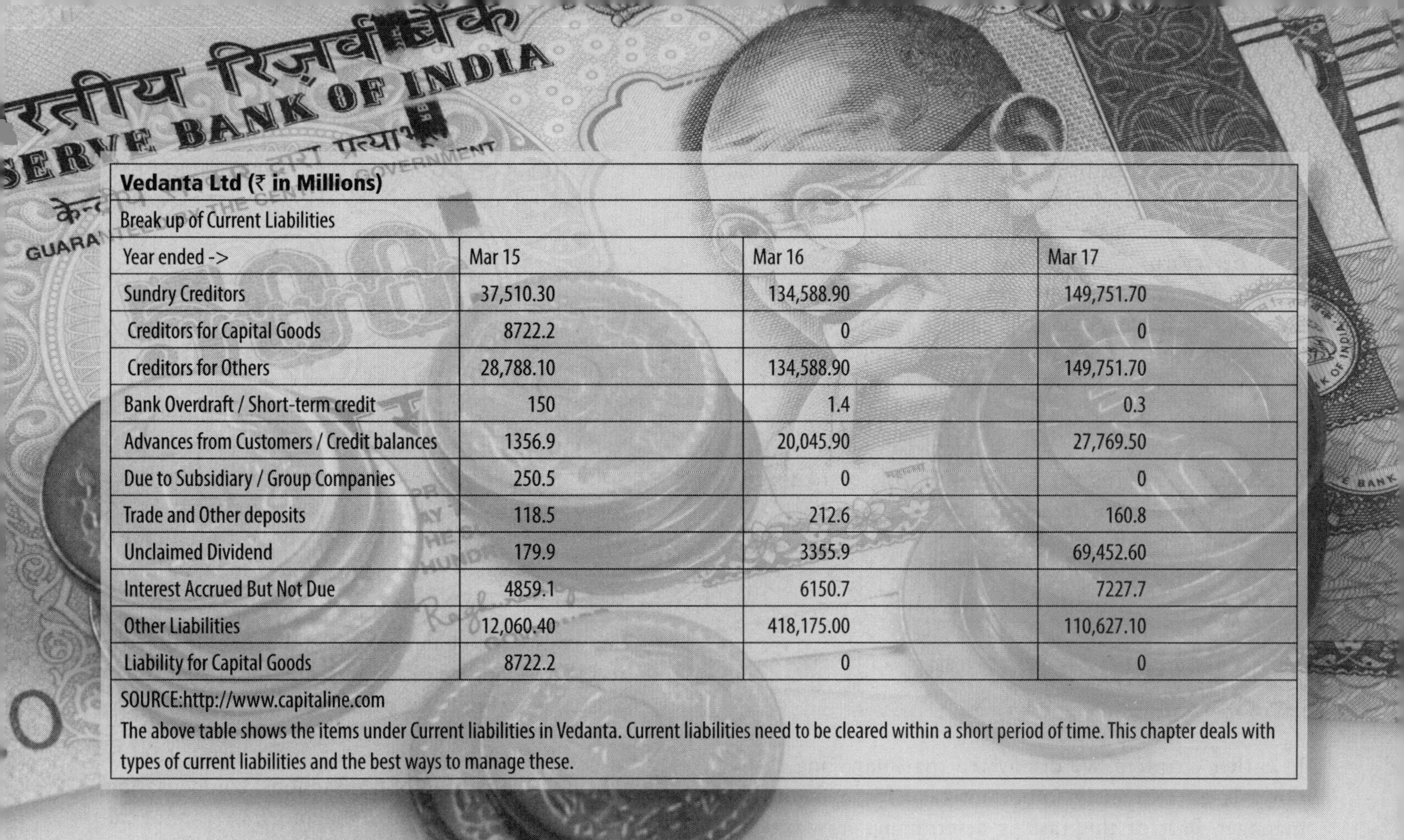

Vedanta Ltd (₹ in Millions)			
Break up of Current Liabilities			
Year ended ->	Mar 15	Mar 16	Mar 17
Sundry Creditors	37,510.30	134,588.90	149,751.70
Creditors for Capital Goods	8722.2	0	0
Creditors for Others	28,788.10	134,588.90	149,751.70
Bank Overdraft / Short-term credit	150	1.4	0.3
Advances from Customers / Credit balances	1356.9	20,045.90	27,769.50
Due to Subsidiary / Group Companies	250.5	0	0
Trade and Other deposits	118.5	212.6	160.8
Unclaimed Dividend	179.9	3355.9	69,452.60
Interest Accrued But Not Due	4859.1	6150.7	7227.7
Other Liabilities	12,060.40	418,175.00	110,627.10
Liability for Capital Goods	8722.2	0	0

SOURCE:http://www.capitaline.com

The above table shows the items under Current liabilities in Vedanta. Current liabilities need to be cleared within a short period of time. This chapter deals with types of current liabilities and the best ways to manage these.

As we discovered in the previous chapter, all else equal, the riskiness of the portfolio of assets held by a firm is based on the combination of its short- and long-term investments (assets). The relative amount invested in short-term assets is a function of decisions that are made concerning the management of cash and marketable securities, accounts receivable, and inventories. Of these three accounts (assets), we generally consider cash and marketable securities to be least risky, or most *liquid*. However, the degree of risk can vary for either accounts receivable or inventories, depending on the general characteristics of the firm's working capital policy.

In this chapter, we discuss working capital management policies with respect to the

Study Tools

Problems are found at the end of this chapter

+

Login to **CourseMate** for **CFIN** at **CengageBrain.com** for additional problems and other study tools!

©: iStock/Thinkstock

short-term assets of the firm. As you read the chapter, keep in mind that, although short-term assets generally are safer than long-term assets, they also earn lower rates of return. Thus, all else equal, firms that hold greater amounts of short-term assets are considered less risky than firms that hold greater amounts of long-term assets; at the same time, however, firms with more short-term assets earn lower returns than are earned by firms with more long-term assets. Consequently, financial managers are faced with a dilemma of whether to forgo higher returns to attain lower risk or to forgo lower risk to achieve higher returns.

15-1 Cash Management

In earlier chapters, we discovered that managing cash flows is an extremely important task for a financial manager. Part of this task is determining how much cash a firm should have on hand at any time to ensure that normal business operations continue uninterrupted. For the purposes of our discussion, the term *cash* refers to the funds a firm holds that can be used for immediate disbursement. This includes the amount a firm holds in its checking account as well as the amount of actual coin and currency it holds. Cash is a *nonearning*, or *idle*, *asset* that is required to pay bills. When possible, cash should be "put to work" by investing in assets that have positive expected returns. Thus, the goal of the cash manager is to minimize the amount of cash the firm must hold for use in conducting its normal business activities, yet, at the same time, to have sufficient cash to (1) pay suppliers, (2) maintain the firm's credit rating, and (3) meet unexpected cash needs.

Firms generally hold cash for the following reasons:

transactions balance
A cash balance necessary for day-to-day operations; the balance associated with routine payments and collections.

compensating balance
A minimum checking account balance that a firm must maintain with a bank to help offset the costs of services such as check clearing and cash management advice.

precautionary balance
A cash balance held in reserve for unforeseen fluctuations in cash flows.

speculative balance
A cash balance held to enable the firm to take advantage of any bargain purchases that might arise.

1. Cash balances associated with routine business payments and collections are known as **transactions balances.**

2. A bank often requires a firm to maintain a **compensating balance** on deposit to help offset the costs of providing services such as check clearing and cash management advice.

3. Because cash inflows and cash outflows are somewhat unpredictable, firms generally hold some cash in reserve for random, unforeseen fluctuations in cash flows. These *safety stocks* are called **precautionary balances.** The less predictable the firm's cash flows, the larger such balances should be.

4. Sometimes cash balances are held to enable the firm to take advantage of bargain purchases that might arise. These funds are called **speculative balances.**

Although the cash accounts of most firms can be thought of as consisting of transactions, compensating, precautionary, and speculative balances, we cannot calculate the amount needed for each purpose, sum them, and produce a total desired cash balance, because the same money often serves more than one purpose. For instance, precautionary and speculative balances can also be used to satisfy compensating balance requirements. In addition, firms that have easy access to borrowed funds are likely to rely on their ability to borrow quickly rather than carrying cash balances. Firms do, however, consider all four factors when establishing their target cash positions.

In addition to these four motives, a firm maintains cash balances to preserve its credit rating by keeping its liquidity position in line with the average liquidity position of other firms in the industry. A strong credit rating enables the firm both to purchase goods from suppliers on favorable terms and to maintain ample short-term credit with its bank.

15-1a The Cash Budget[1]

Perhaps the most critical ingredient of proper cash management is the ability to estimate the cash flows of the firm so that the firm can make plans to borrow when cash is deficient or to invest when cash is in excess

[1]Spreadsheets are particularly well suited for constructing and analyzing cash budgets, especially with respect to the sensitivity of cash flows to changes in sales levels, collection periods, and the like. We could change any assumption—for example, the projected monthly sales or the average collection period—and the cash budget would automatically and instantly be recalculated. We used a spreadsheet to generate the cash budget discussed in this section.

of what is needed. Without a doubt, financial managers will agree that the most important tool for managing cash is the cash budget (forecast).

The firm estimates its general needs for cash as a part of its overall budgeting, or forecasting, process. First, the firm forecasts its operating activities, such as expenses and revenues, for the period in question. Then, the financing and investment activities necessary to attain that level of operations must be forecast. Such forecasts entail the construction of pro forma financial statements, which are discussed in Chapter 17. The information from the pro forma balance sheet and income statement is combined with projections about the delay in collecting accounts receivable, the delay in paying suppliers and employees, tax payment dates, dividend and interest payment dates, and so on. All of this information is summarized in the **cash budget**, which shows the firm's projected cash inflows and cash outflows over some specified period.

The cash budget provides information concerning a firm's future cash flows that is much more detailed than the information provided in forecasted financial statements. For example, when we develop the forecasted financial statements for U.P. Textiles in Chapter 17, we project net sales in 2015 to be ₹1,650 million and net income to be ₹61 million. Based on the forecasted financial statements, we can determine that U.P. expects to generate a ₹50 million cash inflow through normal production and sales operations. Much of this ₹50 million will be used to satisfy the financing and investment activities of the firm. Even after these activities are considered, U.P's cash account is projected to increase by ₹1.5 million in 2015. Does this mean that U.P. will not have to worry about cash shortages during 2015? To answer this question, we must construct U.P's cash budget for 2015.

To simplify the construction of U.P.'s cash budget, we will consider only the latter half of 2015 (July through December). Further, we will not list every cash flow that is expected to occur, but instead will focus on the operating cash flows. Remember that U.P.'s sales peak is in September and October. All sales are made on credit with terms that allow a 2 percent cash discount for payments made within 10 days of the billing period, and if the discount is not taken, the full amount is due in 30 days. However, like most companies, U.P finds that some of its customers delay payment for more than 90 days. Experience has shown that payment on 20 percent of U.P.'s *rupee* sales is made during the month in which the sales are made; these are the discount sales. On 70 percent of sales, payments are made during the month immediately following the month of sale, and payments are made on 10 percent of sales two months or more after the initial sale. To simplify the cash budget, however, we will assume the last 10 percent of sales is collected two months after the sales.

The costs to U.P. for cotton, wool, and other cloth-related materials average 60 percent of the sales prices of the finished products. These purchases generally are made one month before the firm expects to sell the finished products. In 2015, U.P.'s suppliers have agreed to allow payment for materials to be delayed for 30 days after the purchase. Accordingly, if July sales are forecast at ₹150 million, then purchases during June will amount to ₹90 million (= ₹150 million × 0.6), and this amount actually will be paid in July.

Other cash expenses, such as wages and rent, also are built into the cash budget, and U.P. must make estimated tax payments of ₹16 million on September 15 and ₹10 million on December 15; in addition, a ₹20 million payment for a new plant must be made in October. Assuming that U.P.'s **target**, or **minimum**, **cash balance** is ₹5 million and that it projects ₹8 million to be on hand on July 1, 2015, what will the firm's monthly cash surpluses or shortfalls be for the period from July through December?

U.P.'s 2015 cash budget for July through December is presented in Table 15.1. The approach used to construct this cash budget is termed the **disbursements and receipts method** (also referred to as **scheduling**) because the cash disbursements and cash receipts are estimated to determine the net cash flow that is expected to be generated each month. The format used in Table 15.1 is quite simple; it is much like balancing a checkbook. The cash receipts are lumped into one category and the cash disbursements are lumped into another category to determine the net effect monthly cash flows have on the cash position of the firm. Other formats also can be used, depending on how the firm prefers to present the cash budget information.

The first line of Table 15.1 gives the sales forecast for the period from May through December. These estimates are necessary to determine collections for July through December.

cash budget A schedule showing cash receipts, cash disbursements, and cash balances for a firm over a specified time period.

target (minimum) cash balance The minimum cash balance a firm desires to maintain in order to conduct business.

disbursements and receipts method (scheduling) Method of determining net cash flow by estimating the cash disbursements and the cash receipts expected to be generated each period.

TABLE 15.1 U.P Textiles: 2015 Cash Budget (₹ in Millions)

	May	June	July	Aug	Sept	Oct	Nov	Dec
Credit sales	₹100.0	₹125.0	₹150.0	₹200.0	₹250.0	₹180.0	₹130.0	₹100.0
Credit purchases = 60% of next month's sales		90.0	120.0	150.0	108.0	78.0	60.0	
	May	**June**	**July**	**Aug**	**Sept**	**Oct**	**Nov**	**Dec**
Cash Receipts								
Collections of sales from:								
Current month = 0.2 × 0.98 × (current month's sales)			₹ 29.4	₹ 39.2	₹ 49.0	₹ 35.3	₹ 25.5	₹ 19.6
Previous month = 0.7 × (previous month's sales)			87.5	105.0	140.0	175.0	126.0	91.0
Two months previously = 0.1 × (sales two months ago)			10.0	12.5	15.0	20.0	25.0	18.0
Total cash receipts			₹126.9	₹156.7	₹204.0	₹230.3	₹176.5	₹128.6
Cash Disbursements								
Payments for credit purchases (1-month lag)			90.0	120.0	150.0	108.0	78.0	60.0
Wages and salaries (22% of monthly sales)			33.0	44.0	55.0	39.6	28.6	22.0
Rent			9.0	9.0	9.0	9.0	9.0	9.0
Other expenses			7.0	8.0	11.0	10.0	5.0	4.0
Taxes					16.0			10.0
Payment for plant construction						20.0		
Total cash disbursements			₹139.0	₹181.0	₹241.0	₹186.6	₹120.6	₹105.0
Net Cash Flow (Receipts − Disbursements)			(₹ 12.1)	(₹ 24.3)	(₹ 37.0)	₹ 43.7	₹ 55.9	₹ 23.6
Beginning Cash Balance			8.0	(4.1)	(28.4)	(65.4)	(21.7)	34.2
Ending Cash Balance			(4.1)	(28.4)	(65.4)	(21.7)	34.2	57.8
Target (Minimum) Cash Balance			5.0	5.0	5.0	5.0	5.0	5.0
Surplus (Shortfall) Cash			(₹ 9.1)	(₹ 33.4)	(₹ 70.4)	(₹ 26.7)	₹ 29.2	₹ 52.8

Similarly, the second line of the table gives the credit purchases expected in each month based on the sales forecasts, so the monthly payments for credit purchases can be determined.

The Cash Receipts category shows cash collections based on credit sales originating in three different months—the current month and the previous two months. Take a look at the collections expected in July. Remember that U.P. expects 20 percent of the rupee sales to be collected in the month of the sales, and thus to be affected by the 2 percent cash discount that is offered, 70 percent of the sales will be collected one month after the sales occur, and the remaining 10 percent of the sales will be collected two months after the sales occur. (It is assumed that there are no bad debts.) So in July, ₹29.4 million = 0.20 × (1 − 0.02) × ₹150 million collections will result from sales in July; ₹87.5 million = 0.70 × ₹125 million will be collected from sales that occurred in June; and, ₹10.0 million = 0.10 × ₹100 million will be collected from sales that took place in May. Thus, the total collections expected in July equal ₹126.9 million (= ₹29.4 million + ₹87.5 million + ₹10.0 million).

The Cash Disbursements category shows payments for raw materials, wages, rent, and so forth. Raw materials are purchased on credit one month before the finished goods are expected to be sold, but payments for the materials are not made until the month of the expected sales (that is, one month after the credit purchase). The cost of the raw materials is expected to be 60 percent of sales. July sales are forecast at ₹150 million, so U.P. will purchase ₹90 million of materials in June and pay for these purchases in July. Additional monthly cash disbursements include employees' salaries, which equal 22 percent of monthly sales; rent, which remains constant; and other operating expenses, which vary with respect to production levels. Cash disbursements that are not expected to occur monthly include taxes (September and December) and payment for the construction of additional facilities (October).

The line labeled Net Cash Flow shows whether U.P.'s operations are expected to generate positive or negative net cash flows each month. However, this is only the beginning of the story. We need to examine the firm's cash position based on the cash balance that exists at the beginning of the month and based on the *target (minimum) cash balance* desired by U.P.. The bottom line provides information as to whether U.P. can expect a monthly cash surplus that can be invested temporarily in marketable securities or a monthly cash shortfall that must be financed with external, nonspontaneous sources of funds.

At the beginning of July, U.P will have cash equal to ₹8 million on hand. During July, U.P. is expected to generate a negative ₹12.1 million net cash flow; thus, July cash disbursements are expected to exceed cash receipts by ₹12.1 million (deficit spending is expected). Because U.P. only has ₹8 million cash to begin July, the cash balance at the end of July is expected to be overdrawn by ₹4.1 million if the firm doesn't find additional funding. To make matters worse, U.P. has a target cash balance equal to ₹5 million, so without any additional financing, its cash balance at the end of July is expected to be ₹9.1 million short of its target. As a result, U.P. must make arrangements to borrow ₹9.1 million in July to bring the cash account balance up to the target balance of ₹5 million. Assuming that this amount is indeed borrowed, loans outstanding will total ₹9.1 million at the end of July. (We assume that U.P. does not have any bank loans outstanding on July 1 because its beginning cash balance exceeds the target balance.)

The cash surplus or required loan balance (shortfall) is given on the bottom line of the cash budget. A positive value indicates a cash surplus, whereas a negative value (in parentheses) indicates a loan requirement. Note that the *bottom line* surplus cash or loan requirement that is shown is a *cumulative amount*. Thus, U.P must borrow ₹9.1 million in July. Because it has a cash shortfall of ₹24.3 million during August as reported on the Net Cash Flow line, U.P.'s total loan requirement at the end of August is ₹33.4 million = ₹9.1 million + ₹24.3 million, as reported on the bottom line for August. U.P's arrangement with the bank permits it to increase its outstanding loans on a daily basis, up to a prearranged maximum, just as you can increase the amount you are permitted to owe on a credit card. U.P. will use any surplus funds it generates to pay off its loans, and because the loans can be paid down at any time, on a daily basis the firm will never have both a cash surplus and an outstanding short-term loan balance. If U.P. actually does have a cash surplus and no short-term loans to repay, these funds will be invested in short-term, temporary investments.

This same procedure is used in the following months. Sales will peak in September, accompanied by increased payments for purchases, wages, and other items. Receipts from sales will also go up, but the firm will still be left with a ₹37 million net cash outflow during the month. The total short-term loan requirement at the end of September will hit a peak of ₹70.4 million, representing the cumulative cash deficits plus the target cash balance.[2]

Sales, purchases, and payments for past purchases will fall sharply in October, but collections will be the highest of any month because they will reflect the high September sales. As a result, U.P. will generate a healthy ₹43.7 million net cash gain during October. This net gain can be used to pay off borrowings, so short-term loans outstanding will decline by ₹43.7 million to ₹26.7 million.

U.P. will generate an even larger cash surplus in November, which will permit the firm to pay off all of its short-term loans. In fact, the company is expected to have ₹29.2 million in surplus cash by the month's end, and another cash surplus in December will swell the excess cash to ₹52.8 million. With such a large amount of unneeded funds, U.P's treasurer certainly will want to invest in interest-bearing securities or to put the funds to use in some other way.

Before concluding our discussion, we must make some additional points that should be considered and could easily be included in our simple cash budget.

1. For simplicity, our illustrative budget for U.P. omitted many important cash flows that are anticipated for 2015, such as dividends, proceeds from stock and bond sales, and investment in additional fixed assets.

2. Even though it could easily be included, our cash budget example does not reflect interest on loans or income from investing surplus cash.

3. If cash inflows and outflows are not uniform during the month, we could seriously understate the firm's peak financing requirements. The data in Table 15.1 show the situation expected on the last day of each month, but on any given day during the month it could be quite different. For example, if all payments had to be made on the fifth of each month, but collections came in uniformly throughout the month, the firm would need to borrow much larger amounts than those shown in the table. In this case, we would have to prepare a cash budget identifying requirements on a daily basis.

4. Because the cash budget represents a forecast, all

[2]This figure is easily calculated as follows:

$$\text{Cash}_{\text{Stept}} = \begin{pmatrix}\text{Beginning cash}\\ \text{balance in July}\end{pmatrix} + \text{Net CF}_{\text{July}} + \text{Net CF}_{\text{Aug}} + \text{Net CF}_{\text{Sep}} - \begin{pmatrix}\text{Target cash}\\ \text{balance}\end{pmatrix}$$

$$= ₹8.0 + (-₹12.1) + (-₹24.3) + (-₹37.0) - ₹5.0 = ₹70.4$$

the values in the table are *expected* values. If the actual results differ from the forecasted levels, the projected cash deficits and surpluses will also differ.

5. Finally, we should note that the target cash balance will probably be adjusted over time, rising and falling with seasonal patterns and with long-term changes in the scale of the firm's operations. Thus, U.P. probably will plan to maintain larger cash balances during August and September than at other times, and as the company grows, so will its required cash balance.[3]

15-1b Cash Management Techniques

Most cash management activities are performed jointly by the firm and its primary bank, but the financial manager ultimately is responsible for the effectiveness of the cash management program. Effective cash management encompasses proper management of both the cash inflows and the cash outflows of a firm, which entails consideration of the factors discussed next.

Cash Flow Synchronization. Companies try to arrange their finances so that cash inflows and cash outflows are matched as closely as possible. Having **synchronized cash flows** enables a firm to reduce its cash balances, decrease its bank loans, lower interest expenses, and boost profits. *The more predictable the timing of the cash flows, the greater the synchronization that can be attained.*

synchronized cash flows A situation in which cash inflows coincide with cash outflows, thereby permitting a firm to hold low transactions balances.

float The difference between the balance shown in a firm's (or individual's) checkbook and the balance shown on the bank's records.

disbursement float The value of the checks that have been written and *disbursed* (paid) but have not yet fully cleared through the banking system, and thus have not been deducted from the account on which they were written.

collections float The amount of checks that have been received and deposited but have not yet been made available to the account in which they were deposited.

net float The difference between disbursement float and collections float; the difference between the balance shown in the checkbook and the balance shown on the bank's books.

Check Clearing and the Use of Float. When a customer writes and mails a paper check, this does *not* mean that the funds are immediately available to the receiving firm. The check must be processed by the receiving firm, deposited at its bank, and cleared through the banking system before the funds are available for use. These activities result in a lag between the time when a firm deposits a check and records the amount on its books and when the funds are available for use. This lag results from factors associated with *float*.

Float is defined as the difference between the balance shown in a firm's (or individual's) checkbook and the balance on the bank's records. Suppose a firm writes, on average, checks for ₹5,000 each day, and it normally takes four days from the time a check is mailed until it is cleared and deducted from the firm's bank account. This will cause the firm's own checkbook to show a balance that is ₹20,000 = ₹5,000 × 4 days smaller than the balance on the bank's records; this difference is called **disbursement float**. Now suppose the firm also receives checks in the amount of ₹6,000 daily, but it loses two days while they are being processed, deposited, and cleared. This will result in ₹12,000 of **collections float**. In total, the firm's **net float**—the difference between the ₹20,000 positive disbursement float and the ₹12,000 negative collections float—will be ₹8,000, which means the balance the bank shows in the firm's checking account will be ₹8,000 greater than the balance the firm shows in its own checkbook.

Delays that create float arise because it takes time for checks (1) to travel through the mail (*mail delay*), (2) to be processed by the receiving firm (*processing delay*), and (3) to clear through the banking system (*clearing, or availability, delay*). Basically, the size of a firm's net float is a function of its ability to speed up collections on checks received and to slow down collections on checks written. Efficient firms go to great lengths to speed up the processing of incoming checks, thus putting the funds to work faster, and, at the same time, they try to delay their own payments for as long as possible.

[3]The firm might even set the target cash balance at zero. This could be done if it carried a portfolio of marketable securities that could be sold to replenish the cash account, or if it had an arrangement with its bank that permitted it to borrow any funds needed on a daily basis. In that event, the target cash balance would simply be equal to zero. Note, though, that most firms would find it difficult to operate with a zero-balance bank account, just as you would, and the costs of such an operation would in most instances offset the costs associated with maintaining a positive cash balance. Therefore, most firms do set positive target cash balances.

15-1c Acceleration of Receipts

A firm cannot use customers' payments until they are received *and* converted into a spendable form. Thus, it would benefit the firm to accelerate the collection of customers' payments and conversion of those payments into cash. Although some of the delays that cause float cannot be controlled directly, the techniques described next can be used to manage collections.

Lockboxes. A **lockbox arrangement** requires customers to send their payments to a post office box located in the area near where they live rather than directly to the firm, which might be located a far distance from many customers. The firm arranges for a local bank to collect the checks from the post office box, perhaps several times a day, and to immediately deposit them into the company's checking account. By having lockboxes close to the customers, a firm can reduce float because, at the very least, (1) the mail delay is less than if the payment had to travel farther and (2) checks are cleared faster because the banks the checks are written on are in the same Federal Reserve district; thus, fewer parties are involved in the clearing process.

Preauthorized Debits. If a firm receives regular, repetitious payments from its customers, it might want to establish a **preauthorized debit system** (sometimes called *preauthorized payments*). With this arrangement, the collecting firm and its customer (paying firm) enter into an agreement whereby the paying firm's bank periodically transfers funds from the paying firm's account to the collecting firm's account, even if that account is located at another bank. Preauthorized debiting accelerates the transfer of funds because the collecting firm's mail and processing delays are completely eliminated, and availability delay is reduced substantially.

Concentration Banking. **Concentration banking** is a cash management arrangement used to mobilize funds from decentralized receiving locations, whether they are lockboxes or decentralized company locations, into one or more central cash pools. The cash manager then uses these pools for short-term investing or reallocation among the firm's various bank accounts. By pooling its cash, the firm is able to take maximum advantage of economies of scale in cash management and investment.

15-1d Disbursement Control

Accelerating collections represents one side of cash management, and controlling funds outflows, or

Geoff Hardy/Shutterstock.com

disbursements, represents the other side. Three methods commonly used to control disbursements include the following:

Payables Concentration. Centralizing the processing of payables permits the financial manager to evaluate the payments coming due for the entire firm and to schedule the availability of funds to meet these needs on a company-wide basis, and it also permits more efficient monitoring of payables and the effects of float. A disadvantage of a centralized disbursement system is that regional offices might not be able to make prompt payment for services received, which can create ill will and raise the company's operating costs.

Zero-Balance Accounts. A **zero-balance account (ZBA)** is a special disbursement account that has a balance equal to zero when there is no disbursement activity. Typically, a firm establishes several ZBAs in its concentration bank and funds them from a master account. As checks are presented to a ZBA for payment, funds are automatically transferred from the master account to ensure the checks are covered.

lockbox arrangement A technique used to reduce float by having payments sent to post office boxes located near customers.

preauthorized debit system A system that allows a customer's bank to periodically transfer funds from its account to a selling firm's bank account for the payment of bills.

concentration banking A technique used to move funds from many bank accounts to a more central cash pool to more effectively manage cash.

zero-balance account (ZBA) A special checking account used for disbursements that has a balance equal to zero when there is no disbursement activity.

Controlled Disbursement Accounts. Whereas ZBAs typically are established at concentration banks, **controlled disbursement accounts (CDA)** can be set up at any bank. Such accounts are not funded until the day's checks are presented against the account. The firm relies on the bank that maintains the CDA to provide information in the morning (generally before 11 A.M. New York time) concerning the total amount of the checks that will be presented for payment that day. This permits the financial manager (1) to transfer funds to the CDA to cover the checks presented for payment or (2) to invest excess cash at midday, when money market trading is at a peak.

Float, both collection and disbursement, has been reduced significantly with the increased use of electronic payment systems. As these systems become more sophisticated and widespread, float will continue to decrease, perhaps to the point where it is virtually nonexistent. Even so, as long as firms can use the postal service to submit payments, mail delay will exist, which means that the effects of float must be considered when making cash management decisions (policy).

15-2 Marketable Securities

Realistically, the management of cash and the management of marketable securities cannot be separated. Management of one implies management of the other, because the amount of marketable securities held by a firm depends on its short-term cash needs.

Marketable securities, or *near-cash* assets, are extremely liquid short-term investments that permit the firm to earn positive returns on cash that is not needed to pay bills immediately but will be needed sometime in the near term, perhaps in a few days, weeks, or months. Although such investments typically provide much lower yields than other assets, nearly every large firm has them. The two basic reasons for owning marketable securities are as follows:

1. Marketable securities serve as a *substitute for cash balances*. Firms often hold portfolios of marketable securities, liquidating part of the portfolio to increase the cash account when cash is needed, because the *marketable securities offer a place to temporarily put cash balances to work earning positive returns*. In such situations, the marketable securities could be used as a substitute for transactions balances, for precautionary balances, for speculative balances, or for all three.
2. Marketable securities are also used as a *temporary investment* (a) to finance seasonal or cyclical operations and (b) to amass funds to meet financial requirements in the near future. For example, if the firm has a conservative financing policy, as we discussed in Chapter 14, its long-term capital will exceed its permanent assets, and marketable securities will be held when inventories and receivables are low.

controlled disbursement accounts (CDA) Checking accounts in which funds are not deposited until checks are presented for payment, usually on a daily basis.

marketable securities Securities that can be sold on short notice without loss of principal or original investment (liquid investments).

Because marketable securities are temporary investments, financial assets that are considered appropriate investments include those that are traded in the money markets. Examples of such short-term securities, which were described in Chapter 6, include Treasury bills, commercial paper, negotiable certificates of deposit, and Eurorupee time deposits. Depending on how long they will be held, the financial manager decides upon a suitable set of securities, and a suitable maturity pattern, to hold as *near-cash reserves* in the form of marketable securities. Long-term securities are not appropriate investments for marketable securities. As we have described in this section, safety, especially maintenance of principal, should be paramount when putting together a marketable securities portfolio.

15-3 Credit Management

Firms would prefer to sell products and services for cash only. So why do firms sell for credit? The primary reason many firms offer credit sales is that their competitors offer credit. Consider what you would do if you had the opportunity to purchase the same product for the same price from two different firms, but one firm required cash payment at the time of the purchase, whereas the other firm allowed you to pay for the product one month after the purchase without any additional cost. From which firm would you purchase? Like you, firms prefer to delay their payments, especially if there are no additional costs associated with the delay.

Effective credit management is extremely important because too much credit is costly in terms of the investment in, and maintenance of, accounts receivable, whereas too little credit could result in the loss of profitable sales. Carrying receivables not only has both direct and indirect costs, but it also has an important benefit: granting credit should increase profits. Thus, to maximize shareholders' wealth, a financial manager needs to understand how to effectively manage the firm's credit activities.

15-3a Credit Policy

The major controllable variables that affect demand for a company's products are sales prices, product quality, advertising, and the firm's **credit policy**. The firm's credit policy, in turn, includes the factors we discuss next.

1. **Credit standards** refer to the strength and creditworthiness a customer must exhibit to qualify for credit. The firm's credit standards are applied to determine which customers qualify for its regular credit terms and how much credit each customer should receive. The major factors that are considered when setting credit standards relate to the likelihood that a given customer will pay slowly or perhaps even end up as a bad debt loss. Determining the credit quality, or creditworthiness, of a customer probably is the most difficult part of credit management. Nevertheless, credit evaluation is a well-established practice and a good credit manager can make reasonably accurate judgments of customers' default probabilities.
2. **Terms of credit** are the conditions of the credit sale, especially with regard to the payment arrangements. Firms need to determine when the **credit period** begins, how long the customer has to pay for credit purchases before the account is considered delinquent, and whether a cash discount for early payment should be offered. A variety of credit terms are offered by firms in the United States, ranging from cash before delivery (CBD) and cash on delivery (COD) to **cash discounts** for early payment. For example, a firm that offers terms of 2/10 net 30 gives its customers a 2 percent discount from the purchase price if the bill is paid on or before Day 10 of the billing cycle; otherwise the entire bill (the net amount) is due by Day 30.
3. **Collection policy** refers to the procedures the firm follows to collect its credit accounts. The firm needs to determine when and how notification of the outstanding bill is conveyed to the buyer. The more quickly a customer receives an invoice, the sooner the bill *can* be paid. In today's world, firms have increasingly turned to the use of electronics to send invoices to customers. Another important collection policy decision is how the past-due accounts should be handled—that is, when past-due notices should be sent, or when an account should be turned over to a collection agency.

15-3b Receivables Monitoring

Once a firm sets its credit policy, it wants to adhere to it. Thus, it is important that a firm periodically examine its receivables to determine whether customers' payment patterns have changed such that credit operations are

© iStockphoto.com/serts

credit policy A set of decisions that includes a firm's credit standards, credit terms, methods used to collect credit accounts, and credit monitoring procedures.

credit standards Standards that indicate the minimum financial strength a customer must have to be granted credit.

terms of credit The payment conditions offered to credit customers; these terms include the length of the credit period and any cash discounts offered.

credit period The length of time for which credit is granted; after that time, the credit account is considered delinquent.

cash discount A reduction in the invoice price of goods offered by the seller to encourage early payment.

collection policy The procedures followed by a firm to collect its accounts receivable.

outside the credit policy limits. **Receivables monitoring** refers to the process of evaluating the credit policy to determine whether a shift in customers' payment patterns has occurred. Traditionally, firms have monitored receivables by using methods that measure the amount of time credit remains outstanding. Two such methods are the *days sales outstanding (DSO)* and the *aging schedule*.

Days Sales Outstanding (DSO). The **days sales outstanding (DSO)**, which is sometimes called the *average collection period*, represents the average time it takes to collect credit accounts. DSO is computed by dividing *annual* credit sales by *daily* credit sales. For example, in the previous chapter (and in Chapter 2), we found the receivables collection period, or DSO, for U.P. Textiles was 43.2 days in 2014. The DSO of 43.2 days can be compared with the credit terms offered by U.P.. If U.P.'s credit terms are 2/10 net 30, then we know there are quite a few customers who are delinquent when paying their accounts. One way to identify delinquent accounts is to use an aging schedule, as described next.

Aging Schedule. An **aging schedule** is a breakdown of a firm's receivables by age of account. Table 15.2 contains the December 31, 2014, aging schedule for U.P Textiles. The standard format for aging schedules generally includes age categories broken down by month, because banks and financial analysts usually want companies to report their receivables' ages in this form. However, more precision, and thus better monitoring information, can be attained by using narrower age categories (for example, one or two weeks).

According to U.P's aging schedule, only 40 percent of its credit sales were collected within the credit period of 30 days; thus, 60 percent of the credit sales collections were delinquent. Some of the payments were delinquent by only a few days, while others were delinquent by three to four times the 30-day credit period.

receivables monitoring The process of evaluating the credit policy to determine whether a shift in the customers' payment patterns has occurred.

days sales outstanding (DSO) The average length of time required to collect accounts receivable; also called the *average collection period*.

aging schedule A report showing how long accounts receivable have been outstanding; the report divides receivables into specified periods, which provides information about the proportion of receivables that is current and the proportion that is past due for given lengths of time.

TABLE 15.2 U.P. Textiles: Receivables Aging Schedule for 2014

Age of Account (days)	Net Amount Outstanding (₹ in Millions)	Percentage of Total Receivables	Average Days
0–30	₹ 72.0	40%	18
31–60	90.0	50	55
61–90	10.8	6	77
Over 90	7.2	4	97
	₹180.0	100%	

DSO = 0.40(18 days) + 0.50(55 days) + 0.06(77 days) + 0.04(97 days) = 43.2 days

Management should constantly monitor the DSO and the aging schedule to detect trends, to see how the firm's collection experience compares with its credit terms, and to see how effectively its credit department is operating in comparison with those of other firms in the industry. If the DSO starts to lengthen, or if the aging schedule begins to show an increasing percentage of past-due accounts, the firm's credit policy might need to be tightened.

We must be careful when interpreting changes in DSO or the aging schedule, however, because if a firm experiences sharp seasonal variations, or if it is growing rapidly, both measures could be distorted. For example, recall that U.P's peak selling season is in the fall. Using the information provided in Chapter 14 (Table 14.1), we would determine that U.P.'s DSO is expected to be 54.9 days on September 30, 2015 but 43.2 days on December 31, 2015. This decline in DSO would not indicate that U.P. had tightened its credit policy or more efficiently collected its receivables, but only that its sales and receivables had fallen due to seasonal factors. Similar problems arise with the aging schedule when sales fluctuate widely. If a firm generally experiences widely fluctuating sales patterns, some type of modified aging schedule should be used to correctly account for these fluctuations.[4] Still, days sales outstanding and the aging schedule are useful tools for evaluating customers' payment patterns.

[4]See Eugene F. Brigham and Phillip R. Daves, *Intermediate Financial Management*, 11th ed. (Cincinnati, OH: South-Western Cengage Learning, 2013), Chapter 21, for a more complete discussion of the problems with the DSO and aging schedule and how to correct them.

15-3c Analyzing Proposed Changes in Credit Policy

The key question when deciding on a proposed credit policy change is this: How will the firm's value be affected? Unless the added benefits expected from a credit policy change exceed the added costs (on a present value basis), the policy change should *not* be made.

To illustrate how to determine whether a proposed change in a firm's credit policy is appropriate, let's examine what will happen if U.P Textiles makes changes to reduce its average collection period. Suppose that U.P's financial manager has proposed this task be accomplished in 2015 by (1) billing customers sooner and exerting more pressure on delinquent customers to pay their bills on time and (2) examining the accounts of existing credit customers and suspending the credit of customers who are considered habitually delinquent. These actions will result in a direct increase in the costs associated with U.P's credit policy. At the same time, even though U.P has an extremely loyal customer base, it is expected that some sales will be lost to competitors because some customers will have their credit decreased or even eliminated. However, because the credit policy changes do not affect the "good" credit customers, the financial manager does not expect there to be a change in the payments of those customers who currently take advantage of the cash discount. If the proposed credit policy changes are approved, the financial manager believes the average collection period, or DSO, for receivables can be reduced from 43.2 days to 34.8 days, which is more in line with the credit terms offered by U.P (2/10 net 30) and is closer to the industry average of 32.1 days. In addition, if the average collection period is reduced, the amount carried in accounts receivable will be reduced, which means less funds will be tied up in receivables.

Table 15.3 provides information relating to U.P's existing credit policy and the financial manager's proposed changes. According to this information, if the company changes its credit policy, its sales will drop by ₹2 million per year. Note that only the amount paid by customers who do not take the cash discount will be affected by this decrease. This group of customers includes the habitually delinquent payers, which is the category of customers the credit policy change is intended to affect. As a result, the amount paid by the *nondiscount* customers will decrease if the proposed credit policy is adopted, but the amount paid by the discount customers will not change.

To determine whether U.P. should adopt the financial manager's proposal, we need to evaluate the effect the proposed changes will have on the value of the firm. Thus, we must compare the net present values (NPVs) of the two credit policies. To complete the analysis, we make two simplifying assumptions: (1) Sales occur evenly throughout the year. (2) Each production/selling cycle is constant; cash inflows and cash outflows occur at the same point in time relative to the credit sale, no matter what time of the year is examined. These assumptions allow us to evaluate the cash inflows and cash outflows associated with the credit sales for only one day to determine whether the proposed credit policy change should be made. Table 15.3 gives specific assumptions concerning the timing of the cash flows, and Figure 15.1 shows the results of the NPV analysis assuming U.P.'s required rate of return is 10 percent annually. According to these results, the NPV for the existing credit policy is ₹725,800 per day, whereas the NPV for the proposed credit policy is ₹732,500 per day. If the company changes its credit policy, the change in the daily NPV shown in Section III of Figure 15.1 is ₹6,700. Given the assumptions we have stated here, as well as the assumptions given in Table 15.3, we would expect this change to have a permanent, or continuing, effect on the firm. Thus, the ₹6,700 change represents a daily perpetuity, which, according to Section III of Figure 15.1, will increase the value of the firm by ₹24.1 million. Clearly, then, the proposed changes should be made.

The analysis in Table 15.3 provides U.P.'s managers with a vehicle for considering the impact of credit policy changes on the firm's value. A great deal of judgment must be applied to the decision, because customers' as well as competitors' responses to credit policy changes are difficult to estimate. Nevertheless, this type of analysis is essential.

15-4 Inventory Management

If it could, a firm would prefer to have no inventory at all because while products are in inventory they do not generate returns and they must be financed. However, most firms find it necessary to maintain inventory in some form because (1) demand cannot be predicted with certainty and (2) it takes time to transform a product into a form that is ready for sale. Moreover, while excessive inventories are costly to the firm, so are insufficient inventories, because customers might purchase from competitors if products are not available when demanded, which could result in lost future business.

Although inventory models are covered in depth in production management courses, it is important to understand the basics of inventory management, because proper management requires coordination among the sales, purchasing, production, and finance departments. Lack of coordination among these departments, poor sales forecasts, or both can lead to financial ruin.

TABLE 15.3 U.P. Textiles: Existing and Proposed Credit Policies, 2015

	Existing Policy	Proposed Policy
I. General Credit Policy Information		
Credit terms	2/10 net 30	2/10 net 30
Days sales outstanding (DSO) for all customers[a]	43.2 days	34.8 days
DSO for customers who take the cash discount (20%)	10.0 days	10.0 days
DSO for customers who forgo the cash discount (80%)	51.5 days	41.0 days
II. Annual Credit Sales and Costs (₹ in Millions)		
Net credit sales[b]	₹1,650.0	₹1,648.0
Amount paid by discount customers[c]	324.7	324.7
Amount paid by nondiscount customers[c]	1,325.3	1,323.3
Variable operating costs (82 percent of *net* sales)[d]	1,353.0	1,351.4
Bad debts	0.0	0.0
Credit evaluation and collection costs[d]	16.0	17.0
III. Daily Credit Sales and Costs (₹ in Thousands)[e]		
Net sales	₹4,583.3	₹4,577.8
Amount paid by discount customers	901.9	901.9
Amount paid by nondiscount customers	3,681.4	3,675.8
Variable operating costs (82 percent of *net* sales)	3,758.3	3,753.9
Bad debts	0.0	0.0
Credit evaluation and collection costs	44.4	47.2

Notes:

[a]With the existing policy, 20 percent of the customers take the cash discount and pay on Day 10, and the remaining customers (80 percent) pay, on average, on Day 51.5; thus, the DSO for all customers is 43.2 days = 0.2(10 days) + 0.8(51.5 days).

[b]In Chapter 17, we determine that U.P.'s 2015 net *forecasted* sales are ₹1,650 million, which represent what the firm expects to collect from credit sales, net of cash discounts. The gross sales, which include cash discounts, can be computed as follows:

$$\text{Net sales} = 0.8(\text{Gross Sales}) + 0.2(1 - 0.02)(\text{Gross sales}) = (\text{Gross sales})[0.8 + 0.2(0.98)] = (\text{Gross sales})(0.996)$$
$$= ₹1{,}650 \text{ million}$$

$$\text{Gross sales} = \frac{₹\,1{,}650 \text{ million}}{0.996} = ₹1{,}656.6 \text{ million}$$

[c]Currently, 20 percent of U.P.'s customers pay on Day 10, taking advantage of the 2 percent cash discount. As a result, the amount expected to be paid by this group of customers is ₹324.7 million = 0.2 × (1.0 − 0.02) × ₹1,656.6 million. Customers who take the discount will not be affected by the credit policy changes that are intended to affect delinquent customers; thus the amount paid by customers who take the discount will be the same under either policy (₹324.7 million). Consequently, the ₹2 million decrease in sales associated with the proposed credit policy will reduce the amount paid by customers who do not take the discount from ₹1,325.3 million (= 0.8 × ₹1,656.6 million) to ₹1,323.3 million (= ₹1,325.3 million − ₹2 million).

[d]The variable operating costs are paid at the time of the credit sale. Fixed operating costs are not included in the analysis because the amount does not change if the credit policy is changed. Expenses related to credit sales (evaluation and collection costs) are also paid at the time of the credit sale. These assumptions are made to simplify the analysis.

[e]Daily figures are required to evaluate whether the proposal should be adopted. See Figure 15.1 on the next page for the actual analysis. For consistency, we use a 360-day year to compute the daily figures.

FIGURE 15.1 U.P. Textiles: NPV Analysis of Credit Policies for 2015 (₹ in Thousands)

I. Existing Credit Policy

0	r = (10%/360) = 0.02778%	10	. . .	51.5 Days
(3,758.3)		901.9		3,681.4
(44.4)				
(3,802.7)				

Cash Flow Timeline

$$NPV_{Existing} = (3{,}802.7) + \frac{901.9}{\left(1+\frac{0.10}{360}\right)^{10}} + \frac{3{,}681.4}{\left(1+\frac{0.10}{360}\right)^{51.5}} = (3{,}802.7) + 899.4 + 3{,}629.1 = 725.8$$

II. Proposed Credit Policy

0	r = (10%/360) = 0.02778%	10	. . .	41 Days
(3,753.9)		901.9		3,675.8
(47.2)				
(3,801.1)				

Cash Flow Timeline

$$NPV_{Proposed} = (3{,}801.1) + \frac{901.9}{\left(1+\frac{0.10}{360}\right)^{10}} + \frac{3{,}675.8}{\left(1+\frac{0.10}{360}\right)^{41}} = (3{,}801.1) + 899.4 + 3{,}634.2 = 732.5$$

III. Effect on Firm's Value if Proposal Is Adopted

$$\Delta NPV \text{ on a daily basis} = ₹732.5 - ₹725.8 = ₹6.7$$

$$\Delta Value = \frac{₹6.7}{\left(\frac{0.10}{360}\right)} = ₹24{,}120.0$$

15-4a Types of Inventory

An inventory item generally is classified into one of three groups:

1. **Raw materials** represent the new inventory items purchased from suppliers; they are the materials a firm purchases to transform into finished products for sale. As long as the firm has an inventory of raw materials, delays in ordering and delivery from suppliers do not affect the production process.
2. **Work-in-process** refers to inventory items that are at various stages in the production process. If a firm has work-in-process at every stage in the production process, it will not have to shut down production if a problem arises at one of the earlier stages.
3. **Finished goods** are the products that are ready for sale. Firms carry finished goods to ensure that orders can be filled when they are received. If there are no finished goods, demand might not be satisfied when it arrives. When a customer arrives and there is no inventory to satisfy that demand, a **stockout** exists, and the firm might lose the demand to competitors, perhaps permanently.

15-4b Optimal Inventory Level

The goal of inventory management is to provide the inventories required to sustain operations at the lowest possible cost. Thus, the first step in determining the optimal inventory level is to identify the costs involved in purchasing and maintaining inventory; then, we need to determine at what point those costs are minimized.

raw materials The inventories purchased from suppliers that ultimately will be transformed into finished goods.

work-in-process Inventory in various stages of completion; some work-in-process is at the very beginning of the production process while some is at the end of the process.

finished goods Inventories that have completed the production process and are ready for sale.

stockout Occurs when a firm runs out of inventory *and* customers arrive to purchase the product.

Inventory Costs. We generally classify inventory costs into three categories: those associated with carrying inventory, those associated with ordering and receiving inventory, and those associated with running short of inventory (stockouts). First, let's look at the two costs that are most directly observable—carrying costs and ordering costs.

1. **Carrying costs** include any expenses associated with having products in inventory, such as rent paid for the warehouse where inventory is stored and insurance on the inventory. These costs generally increase in direct proportion to the average amount of inventory carried.
2. **Ordering costs** are those expenses associated with placing and receiving an order for new inventory, which include the costs of generating memos, fax transmissions, and so forth. For the most part, the total cost associated with each order is fixed regardless of the order size.[5]

If we assume that the firm knows how much total inventory it needs and that sales are distributed evenly during each period, we can use Equation 15.1 to combine the total carrying costs (TCC) and the total ordering costs (TOC) to determine total inventory costs (TIC).

15.1

$$\text{Total inventory costs} = \text{Total carrying costs} + \text{Total ordering costs}$$

$$= \left(\begin{array}{c}\text{Carrying cost}\\ \text{per unit}\end{array}\right) \times \left(\begin{array}{c}\text{Average units}\\ \text{in inventory}\end{array}\right) + \left(\begin{array}{c}\text{Cost per}\\ \text{order}\end{array}\right) \times \left(\begin{array}{c}\text{Number of}\\ \text{orders}\end{array}\right)$$

$$= (C \times PP) \times \left(\frac{Q}{2}\right) + O \times \left(\frac{T}{Q}\right)$$

According to Equation 15.1, the average investment in inventory depends on how frequently orders are placed and the size of each order. If we order every day, average inventory will be much smaller than if we order once per year and inventory carrying costs will be lower, but the number of orders will be larger and inventory ordering costs will be higher. We can reduce ordering costs by ordering greater amounts less often, but then average inventory, and thus the total carrying cost, will be high. This trade-off between carrying costs and ordering costs is shown in Figure 15.2 on the next page. Note from the figure that there is a point where the total inventory cost (TIC) is *minimized*; this is called the **economic (optimum) ordering quantity (EOQ)**.

The Economic Ordering Quantity (EOQ) Model. The EOQ is determined by using calculus to find the point where the slope of the TIC curve in Figure 15.2 is perfectly horizontal; thus, it equals zero. The result is Equation 15.2:

15.2

$$\text{Economic ordering quantity} = EOQ = \sqrt{\frac{2 \times O \times T}{C \times PP}}$$

The variables in the equation are defined as follows:

C	=	carrying costs as a percentage (stated as a decimal) of the purchase price of each inventory item.
PP	=	purchase price, or cost, per unit.
Q	=	number of units purchased with each order.
T	=	total demand, or number of units sold, per period.
O	=	fixed costs per order.

carrying costs The costs associated with having inventory, which include storage costs, insurance, cost of tying up funds, and so on; these costs generally increase in proportion to the average amount of inventory held.

ordering costs The costs of placing an order; the cost of *each* order generally is fixed regardless of the average size of the inventory.

economic (optimum) ordering quantity (EOQ) The optimal quantity that should be ordered; it is this quantity that will minimize the *total inventory costs*.

[5]In reality, both carrying and ordering costs can have variable and fixed cost elements, at least over certain ranges of average inventory. For example, security and utilities charges probably are fixed in the short run over a wide range of inventory levels. On the other hand, labor costs of receiving inventory could be tied to the quantity received, and hence could be variable. To simplify matters, we treat all carrying costs as variable and all ordering costs as fixed.

FIGURE 15.2 Determination of the Economic Ordering Quantity

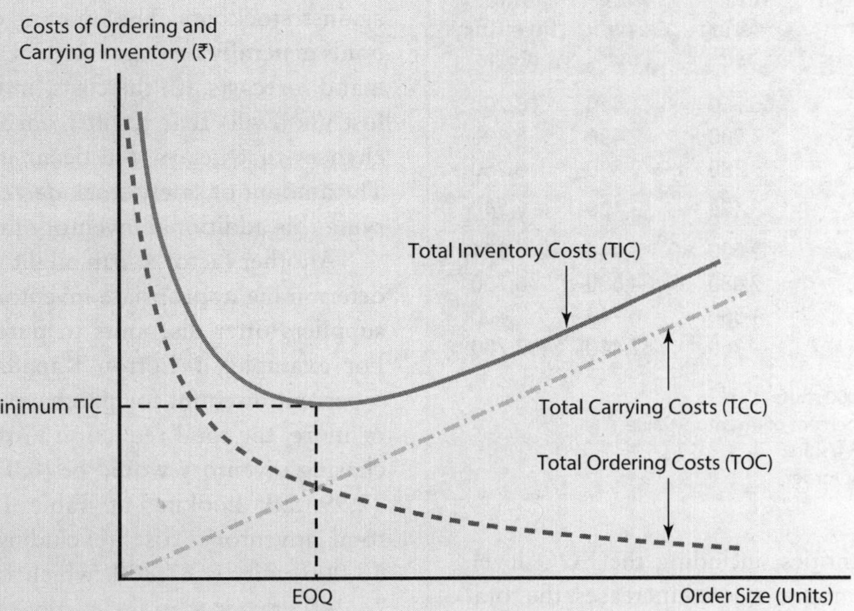

The primary assumptions of the **EOQ model** given by Equation 15.2 are that (1) sales are evenly distributed throughout the period examined and can be forecast precisely, (2) orders are received when expected, and (3) the purchase price (PP) of each item in inventory is the same regardless of the quantity ordered.[6]

To illustrate the EOQ model, consider the following data provided by Cotton Kapada Ltd. a distributor of custom-designed T-shirts that supplies concessionaires at Daisy World:

T	=	78,000 shirts per year.
C	=	25 percent of inventory value.
PP	=	₹3.84 per shirt. (The shirts sell for ₹9, but this is irrelevant for our purposes here.)
O	=	₹260 per order.

Substituting these data into Equation 15.2, we find an EOQ equal to 6,500 units:

$$EOQ = \sqrt{\frac{2 \times ₹260 \times 78{,}000}{0.25 \times ₹3.84}} = \sqrt{42{,}250{,}000}$$
$$= 6{,}500 \text{ units}$$

[6]The EOQ model can also be written as follows:

$$EOQ = \sqrt{\frac{2 \times O \times T}{C^*}}$$

where C^* is the annual carrying cost per unit expressed in rupees.

If Cotton Kapada orders 6,500 shirts each time it needs inventory, it will place 78,000/6,500 = 12 orders per year and carry an average inventory of 6,500/2 = 3,250 shirts. Thus, at the EOQ quantity, Cotton Kapada's total inventory costs would equal ₹6,240:

$$TIC = (C \times PP)\frac{Q}{2} + O\left(\frac{T}{Q}\right)$$
$$= [0.25 \times (₹3.84)]\left[\frac{6{,}500}{2}\right] + (₹260)\left[\frac{78{,}000}{6{,}500}\right]$$
$$= ₹\ 3{,}120 + ₹3.120 = 46{,}240$$

Note these two points: (1) Because we assume the purchase price of each inventory item does not depend on the amount ordered, TIC does *not* include the ₹299,520 = 78,000(₹3.84) annual cost of purchasing the inventory itself. (2) As we see both in Figure 15.2 and in the numbers here, at the EOQ, total carrying cost (TCC) equals total ordering cost (TOC). This property is not unique to our Cotton Kapada's illustration; it always holds.

Table 15.4 contains the total inventory costs that Cotton Kapada would incur

EOQ model A formula for determining the order quantity that will minimize total inventory costs.

TABLE 15.4 Cotton Kapada Ltd.: Total Inventory Costs for Various Order Quantities

	Quantity	Number of Orders	Total Ordering Costs	Total Carrying Costs	Total Inventory Costs
	3,000	26	₹6,760	₹1,440	₹8,200
	5,200	15	3,900	2,496	6,396
	6,000	13	3,380	2,880	6,260
EOQ	**6,500**	**12**	**3,120**	**3,120**	**6,240**
	7,800	10	2,600	3,744	6,344
	9,750	8	2,080	4,680	6,760
	13,000	6	1,560	6,240	7,800
	78,000	1	260	37,440	37,700

T = annual sales = 78,000 shirts
C = carrying cost = 25 percent of inventory value
PP = purchase price = ₹3.84/shirt
O = ordering cost = ₹260/order

at various order quantities, including the EOQ level. Note that (1) as the amount ordered increases, the total carrying costs increase but the total ordering costs decrease, and vice versa; (2) if less than the EOQ amount is ordered, then the higher ordering costs more than offset the lower carrying costs; and (3) if more than the EOQ amount is ordered, the higher carrying costs more than offset the lower ordering costs.

EOQ Model Extensions. It should be obvious that some of the assumptions necessary for the basic EOQ to hold are unrealistic. To make the model more useful, we can apply some simple extensions. First, if there is a delay between the time inventory is ordered and when it is received, the firm must reorder before it runs out of inventory. For example, if it normally takes two weeks to receive orders, then Cotton Kapada should reorder when two weeks of inventory are left. Cotton Kapada sells 78,000/52 = 1,500 shirts per week, so its **reorder point** is when inventory drops to 3,000 shirts. Even if Cotton Kapada orders additional inventory at the appropriate reorder point, unexpected demand might cause it to run out of inventory before the new inventory is delivered. To avoid this, the firm could carry **safety stock**, which represents additional inventory that helps guard against stockouts. The amount of safety stock a firm holds generally *increases* with (1) the uncertainty of demand forecasts, (2) the costs (in terms of lost sales and lost goodwill) that result from stockouts, and (3) the chances that delays will occur in receiving shipments. The amount of safety stock *decreases* as the cost of carrying this additional inventory increases.

reorder point The level of inventory at which an order should be placed.

safety stock Additional inventory carried to guard against unexpected changes in sales rates or production/shipping delays.

quantity discount A discount from the purchase price; offered for inventory ordered in large quantities.

redline method An inventory control procedure where a red line is drawn around the inside of an inventory-stocked bin to indicate the reorder point level.

Another factor a firm might need to consider when determining appropriate inventory levels is whether its suppliers offer discounts to purchase large quantities. For example, if Cotton Kapada's supplier offered a 1 percent discount for purchases equal to 13,000 units or more, the total reduction in the annual cost of purchasing inventory would be [0.01(₹3.84)] × 78,000 = ₹2,995.20. Looking at Table 15.4, we see that the total inventory cost (excluding purchase price) at 13,000 units is ₹7,800, which is ₹1,560 = ₹7,800 − ₹6,240 greater than the cost at the EOQ level of 6,500 units. However, the net benefit of taking advantage of the **quantity discount** is ₹1,435.20 = ₹2,995.20 − ₹1,560.00. Therefore, under these conditions, each time Cotton Kapada orders inventory it will be more beneficial to order 13,000 units rather than the 6,500 units prescribed by the basic EOQ model.

In cases in which it is unrealistic to assume that the demand for the inventory is uniform throughout the year, the EOQ should not be applied on an annual basis. Rather, it would be more appropriate to divide the year into seasons within which sales are relatively constant, say, the summer, the spring and fall, and the winter; then the EOQ model can be applied separately to each period.

Although we did not explicitly incorporate the extensions we mentioned here into the basic EOQ, our discussion should give you an idea of how the EOQ amount should be adjusted to determine the optimal inventory level if any of these conditions exists.

15-4c Inventory Control Systems

The EOQ model can be used to help establish the proper inventory level, but inventory management also involves the establishment of an *inventory control system*. Inventory control systems run the gamut from very simple to extremely complex, depending on the size of the firm and the nature of its inventories. For example, one simple control procedure is the **redline method**. Inventory items are stocked in a bin, a red line is drawn around the inside of the bin at the level of the reorder point, and the inventory clerk places an order when the red line shows. This procedure works well for parts such as bolts in a manufacturing process, and for many items in retail businesses.

Most firms employ some type of **computerized inventory control systems.** Large companies often have fully integrated computerized inventory control systems in which the computer adjusts inventory levels as sales are made, orders inventory when the reorder point is reached, and records the receipt of an order. The computer records are also used to determine whether the usage rates of inventory items change, so that adjustments to reorder amounts can be made. Another approach to inventory control that requires a coordinated effort between the supplier and the buyer is called the **just-in-time system**, which was refined by Japanese firms many years ago. With this system, materials are delivered to the company at about the same time they are needed, perhaps a few hours before they are used. Still another important development related to inventories is **outsourcing**, which is the practice of purchasing components rather than making them in house. Outsourcing often is combined with just-in-time systems to reduce inventory levels.

Inventory control systems require coordination of inventory policy with manufacturing and procurement policies. Companies try to minimize *total production and distribution costs*, and inventory costs are just one part of total costs. Still, they are an important cost, and financial managers should be aware of the determinants of inventory costs and how they can be minimized.

15-5 Multinational Working Capital Management

Although the methods used to manage short-term assets in multinational corporations are essentially the same as those used in purely domestic corporations, there are some differences in business, legal, and economic environments that make application of these methods somewhat more complex.

15-5a Cash Management

Like a purely domestic company, a multinational corporation wants to (1) speed up collections and to slow down disbursements where possible, (2) shift cash as rapidly as possible to those areas where it is needed, and (3) try to put temporary cash balances to work earning positive returns. Multinational companies use the same general procedures for achieving these goals as domestic firms use, but because of longer distances and more serious mail delays, lockbox systems and electronic funds transfers are even more important.

One potential problem a multinational company faces that a purely domestic company does not is the chance that a foreign government will restrict transfers of funds out of the country. Foreign governments often limit the amount of cash that can be taken out of their countries because they want to encourage domestic investment. Even if funds can be transferred without limitation, deteriorating exchange rates might make it unattractive for a multinational firm to move funds to its operations in other countries.

Once it has been determined what funds can be transferred out of the various nations in which a multinational corporation operates, it is important to get those funds to locations where they will earn the highest returns. Whereas domestic corporations tend to think in terms of domestic securities, multinationals are more likely to be aware of investment opportunities all around the world. Most multinational corporations use one or more global concentration banks, located in money centers such as London, New York, Tokyo, Zurich, or Singapore. The corporations' staffs in those cities, working with international bankers, are able to take advantage of the best rates available anywhere in the world.

15-5b Credit Management

Credit policy generally is more important for a multinational corporation than for a purely domestic firm for two reasons. First, much U.S. trade is with poorer, less-developed nations, and in such situations, granting credit generally is a necessary condition for doing business. Second, and in large part as a result of the first point, developed nations whose economic health depends on exports often help their manufacturers compete internationally by granting credit to foreign countries that purchase from these firms.

When granting credit, the multinational firm faces a riskier situation than purely

computerized inventory control system A system of inventory control in which a computer is used to determine reorder points and to adjust inventory balances.

just-in-time system A system of inventory control in which a manufacturer coordinates production with suppliers so that raw materials of components arrive just as they are needed in the production process.

outsourcing The practice of purchasing components rather than making them in-house.

domestic firms because, in addition to the normal risks of default, (1) political and legal environments often make it more difficult to collect defaulted accounts and (2) multinational corporations must worry about exchange rate changes between the time a sale is made and the time a receivable is collected. We know that hedging can reduce this type of risk, but at a cost.

15-5c **Inventory Management**

Inventory management in a multinational setting is more complex than in a purely domestic setting because of logistical problems that arise with handling inventories. For example, should a firm concentrate its inventories in a few strategic centers located worldwide? While such a strategy might minimize the total amount of, and thus the investment in, inventories needed to operate the global business, it might also cause delays in getting goods from central storage locations to user locations all around the world.

Exchange rates can significantly influence inventory policy. For example, if a local currency is expected to increase in value against the rupee, a U.S. company operating in that country will want to increase stocks of local products before the rise in the currency, and vice versa. Another factor that must be considered is the possibility of import or export quotas or tariffs. Quotas restrict the quantities of products firms can bring into a country, while tariffs, like taxes, increase the prices of products that are allowed to be imported. Both quotas and tariffs are designed to restrict the ability of foreign corporations to compete with domestic companies; at the extreme, foreign products are excluded altogether.

Another danger in certain countries is the threat of *expropriation*, or government takeover of the firm's local operations. If the threat of expropriation is large, inventory holdings will be minimized, and goods will be brought in only as needed. Similarly, if the operation involves extraction of raw material, processing plants might be moved offshore rather than located close to the production site.

Taxes also must be considered, because countries often impose property taxes on assets, including inventories. When this is done, the tax is based on holdings as of a specific date. Such rules make it advantageous for a multinational firm (1) to schedule production so that inventories are low on the assessment date and (2) if assessment dates vary among countries in a region, to hold safety stocks in different countries at different times during the year.

KEY CONCEPTS FOR MANAGING SHORT-TERM ASSETS

To conclude this chapter, we summarize some concepts that were discussed.

- Firms prefer not to hold cash, because cash is considered an idle asset that does not earn interest. However, firms find that they must hold some cash to ensure that day-to-day obligations can be paid.

  The firm should construct a cash budget to forecast its cash flows so that funds can be invested when there are cash surpluses, and arrangements can be made to borrow funds when there are cash deficiencies. To efficiently manage cash flows, the firm should try to collect funds owed as quickly as possible and try to delay payments of funds owed for as long as possible. Of course, any actions taken should not be detrimental to the value of the firm.

- Marketable securities are short-term, highly liquid investments that have little investment risk. As a result, the returns on such investments are fairly low. Marketable securities provide the firm with safe instruments where *idle cash* that will be needed in the near term—perhaps in a few days or months—can be invested.

- Firms sell on credit because competitors sell on credit. A firm that sells on credit must have a credit policy that specifies how customers qualify for credit, the maximum amount of credit that customers are allowed, the terms of credit sales to customers, and what actions will be taken if customers do not pay on time. To ensure that the credit policy is being followed and it is achieving the desired objective, a firm's credit policy should be monitored. Moreover, when customers' payment patterns change significantly, the firm should consider changing its credit policy. Proposed credit policy changes should be evaluated using net present value (NPV) to ensure the firm is maximizing its value.

- Firms carry inventory to ensure that demand is met when it arrives. If inventory is not available, then a sale cannot be made when a customer wants to purchase the firm's product, and arriving customers might take their business to competitors. Because carrying inventory is costly, firms do not want to have too much inventory on hand at any time. As a result, a firm determines how much inventory to hold by examining the demand for its product, the costs associated with not having enough inventory, and the costs of carrying sufficient inventory to satisfy demand. The EOQ, or economic ordering quantity, model is used to determine the optimal amount of inventory that a firm should carry.

MULTIPLE CHOICE QUESTIONS

1. The reorder level of inventory will always be

a. Between the minimum and maximum levels

b. Can be less than the minimum level

c. Can be equal to the maximum level

d. Is independent of the minimum and maximum levels

2. The economic order quantity

a. Determines the number of days it takes to get inventory

b. Determines the optimum quantity of inventory to be ordered

c. Determines the maximum quantity of inventory to be ordered

d. None of the above

3. Just-in-time inventory

a. Does away with the need to have EOQ

b. Involves ordering large quantities at a single time

c. Involves ordering small quantities at a single time

d. Involves frequent ordering of inventory

4. In a company having sales that vary based on the season,

a. The working capital needs are different between months

b. A core amount of working capital is decided for use throughout the year

c. a and b are right

d. None of the above

5. If financing of the working capital is done by debt,

a. One need not monitor the working capital closely

b. One needs to monitor the working capital closely to enable reduction of interest

c. Monitoring has to be done in any case

d. b and c are right

6. A commercial paper

a. Is a debt instrument issued by a company repayable over a medium term

b. Is an equity instrument issued by a company

c. Is a debt instrument issued by a company repayable over a long term

d. None of the above

7. An ageing schedule

a. Shows the extent of receivables outstanding for various days

b. Shows the extent of receivables that have been paid after due date

c. Shows only amounts not paid

d. Shows interest on the working capital

8. A cash budget is

a. Prepared with each period as one year

b. Prepared with each period as one quarter

c. Prepared with each period as one month

d. Can be prepared with each period being of any length

9. A revolving credit involves

a. A lump sum debt from the bank

b. Has to be repaid in equal instalments

c. The quantum varies depending upon the actual withdrawal

d. None of the above.

10. A bank overdraft

a. Is a deposit with a bank

b. Is in the nature of a short loan from a bank

c. Does not require any specific sanction from a bank

d. All of the above

Answers:

1.	(a)	2.	(b)	3.	(d)	4.	(c)	5.	(d)
6.	(d)	7.	(d)	8.	(d)	9.	(c)	10.	(b)

PROBLEMS

For more problems, login to CourseMate for CFIN at CengageBrain.com

15-1 Fathuma Clothing has generated ₹130,000 in sales during the past few months, and it is expected that this level of sales will continue for the next year. Based on past experience, 40 percent of the sales will be collected in the month of the sale, and these customers will take the 3 percent cash discount that is offered for early payment. The remaining 60 percent of the sales will be collected one month after the sale. Fathuma normally purchases and pays for raw materials, which cost 70 percent of the sales prices, in the same month the finished goods are sold. Employees' wages represent 15 percent of the sales price, and monthly rent is ₹15,000. The company currently has no cash, but its target cash balance is ₹6,000. Construct Fathuma's cash budget for the next three months.

15-2 Veer Ladder Company (VLC) forecasts that its sales for January through April will be ₹60,000, ₹70,000, ₹90,000, and ₹80,000, respectively. All sales are made on credit, and past experience indicates that 30 percent of the sales will be collected in the month of the sale and that the remaining 70 percent will be collected the following month. Customers who pay in the month of the sale will take the 2 percent cash discount offered by VLC for paying early. VLC normally purchases and pays for raw materials, which cost 55 percent of the sales prices, one month prior to selling the finished products. Employees' wages represent 25 percent of the sales price, and rent is ₹3,000 per month. At the beginning of February, VLC expects to have ₹4,000 in cash, which is ₹1,000 greater than its target cash balance. Using the information provided, construct a cash budget for February, March, and April.

15-3 Sonawala's Chop Shop normally writes checks in the amount of ₹15,000 each day. It takes five days for these checks to clear through the banking system. The firm also receives checks in the amount of ₹12,000 daily but loses four days while they are being deposited and cleared. What is the firm's disbursement float, collections float, and net float?

15-4 On average, Bhanubhai Farms receives checks that amount to ₹420,000 each day, whereas the amount of checks the company writes each day averages ₹380,000. It normally takes three days for incoming checks to clear through the banking system, and outgoing checks generally clear in five days. What is the firm's disbursement float, collections float, and net float?

15-5 Currently, it takes six days for Alleppey Corporation to receive, process, and deposit its customers' payments. If it sets up a lockbox collection system, Alleppey estimates collection float would be reduced to two days. Alleppey receives an average of ₹125,000 in payments per day. If Alleppey has an opportunity cost of 12 percent, what is the maximum monthly charge it should pay for the lockbox system?

15-6 Currently, it takes five days from the time customers mail payments until Sharmila Bhen Rafts (SBR) deposits them. SBR would like to set up a lockbox collection system that would reduce this collection float by three days. If SBR receives an average of ₹2,500 in payments per day and its opportunity cost is 18 percent, how much should SBR be willing to pay each month for the lockbox system?

15-7 Compute the DSO for Baroda Corporation, which has the following aging schedule

Account Age	Amount Outstanding	Average Days
0 – 30 days	₹65,000	23
31 – 60 days	25,000	43
Over 60 days	10,000	63

15-8 Following is the aging schedule for QRM Corporation:

Account Age	Amount Outstanding	Average Days
0 – 30 days	₹100,000	22
31 – 60 days	70,000	40
Over 60 days	30,000	?

If its DSO is 37 days, on average, on what day does QRM collect from customers who take longer than 60 days to pay for their purchases?

15-9 Falgun Company's average collection period (DSO) is 37 days, which is only seven days longer than the net 30 terms the company offers credit customers. Fifty percent of Falgun's customers pay on average on Day 20, and 30 percent pay on Day 40. On what day do the remaining credit customers pay? Assume Falgun has no bad debts.

15-10 Garima Munchies (GM) Corporation has a variable operating cost ratio of 60 percent, its cost of capital is 12 percent, and current sales are ₹100,000. All of its sales are on credit, and it currently sells on terms of net 30. Its accounts receivable balance is ₹20,000. GM is considering a new credit policy with terms of net 45. Under the new policy, sales will increase to ₹120,000, and accounts receivable will rise to ₹30,000. Compute the days sales outstanding (DSO) under the existing policy and the proposed policy.

15-11 Aparna Wells and Excavation (AWE) currently generates ₹72,000 in annual credit sales. AWE sells on terms of net 50, and its accounts receivable balance averages ₹12,000. AWE is considering a new credit policy with terms of net 25. Under the new policy, sales will decrease to ₹68,000, and accounts receivable will average ₹13,600. Compute the days sales outstanding (DSO) under the existing policy and the proposed policy.

15-12 Lekha Lumber is considering changing its credit terms from net 55 to net 30 to bring its terms in line with other firms in the industry. Currently, annual sales are ₹360,000, and the average collection period is 62 days. Lekha estimates that tightening the credit terms would reduce annual sales to ₹355,000, but accounts receivable would drop to 38 days of sales. Lekha's variable cost ratio is 65 percent and its average cost of funds is 12 percent. Should the change in credit terms be made? Assume all operating costs are paid when inventory is sold and that *all* sales are collected at the DSO.

15-13 The CFO of JJ's Jungle Equipment has decided that the company must sell its products on credit. As a result, she is evaluating two credit terms. (1) Net 45, which would generate ₹50,000 in annual sales and have an average collection period equal to 55 days. (2) Net 30, which would generate ₹48,000 in sales and have an average collection period equal to 36 days. The firm's variable cost ratio is 70 percent, and its average cost of funds 14 percent. Which credit terms should the CFO recommend? Assume all operating costs are paid when inventory is sold and *all* sales are collected at the DSO.

15-14 Naya Week's Technology (NWT) is evaluating whether to change its credit terms from 2/10, net 30 to 3/10, net 30. At present, 50 percent of NWT's sales are paid on Day 10, whereas, under the new terms, 60 percent of sales will be paid on Day 10. Regardless of the credit terms, half of the customers *who do not take the discount* are expected to pay on Day 30, whereas the remainder will pay 15 days late (no bad debts exist). But, as a result of the higher cash discount offered with the new terms, sales are expected to increase sales from ₹360,000 to ₹396,000 per year. NWT's variable cost ratio is 80 percent and its cost of funds is 9 percent. All production costs are paid on the day of the sale. Should NWT change its credit terms?

15-15 Manohar's Mechanical sells 6,000 jettison machines annually. Each machine costs Manohar's ₹2,000 to purchase, inventory carrying costs are 30 percent of the purchase price, and the cost of placing an order with its supplier is ₹120. (a) What is the EOQ? (b) What is the total inventory cost at the EOQ level?

15-16 PC Calculators sells calculators that it purchases for ₹15 each. It costs PC ₹60 each time calculators are ordered, and carrying costs are 20 percent of the calculator's purchase price. Annual demand is 100,000 calculators. (a) Compute the EOQ. (b) Compute the inventory costs if PC orders (i) the EOQ amount, (ii) 1,000 calculators, and (iii) 2,500 calculators.

15-17 Media Moguls (M&M) normally sells 240,000 units per year. It costs M&M ₹52 to purchase each unit, the fixed cost of ordering is ₹260, and the carrying costs equal 15 percent of the unit's purchase price. (a) What is the EOQ? (b) How many orders should M&M place each year?

15-18 Refer to the information provided for M&M in Problem 15–17. Suppose that M&M must place orders in increments of 5,000 units and that it takes three days for each order to be delivered. (a) How many orders should M&M place each year? (b) At what inventory level should an order be placed?

15-19 Ramanashree Corporation sells children's safe toy sets that cost ₹160 each to purchase and prepare for sale. Annual sales are 5,000 toy sets, carrying costs are 20 percent of inventory costs, and Ramanashree incurs a cost of ₹32 each time an order is placed. (a) What is the EOQ for the mowers? (b) What will be the total inventory costs if the EOQ amount is ordered?

15-20 Refer to the information provided for Ramanashree Corporation in Problem 15–19. Suppose that Ramanashree's supplier decides to offer a 2 percent cash discount if products are ordered in increments of 1.000. How many mowers should Ramanashree order each time an order is placed to minimize total inventory costs?

Managing Short-Term Assets

Learning Outcomes

LO.1 Discuss the goal of effective cash management and how (a) the cash budget, (b) techniques that exist to accelerate cash receipts, and (c) cash disbursement controls should be employed to develop an optimal cash management policy.

- Proper cash management helps the firm match its cash inflows and cash outflows, and thus minimize its cash holdings.

LO.2 Explain the rationale for holding marketable securities, and describe the general characteristics of investments that should be included in portfolios of marketable securities.

- Marketable securities provide a mechanism for a firm to temporarily "put cash to work." Such investments are short-term and extremely liquid, which means that their risks and returns are low.

LO.3 Discuss accounts receivable (credit) management, and describe how a proposed credit policy change should be evaluated.

- A credit policy should be developed that maximizes the value of the firm. Receivables should be monitored to ensure that the prescribed credit policy is followed. Any proposed policy changes should be evaluated using the NPV technique.

LO.4 Explain the rationale for holding various forms of inventory, and describe how a firm can determine its optimal level of inventory.

- Firms hold inventory because demand for their products cannot be predicted with certainty. At the optimal inventory level, the total cost of holding inventory is minimized.

LO.5 Describe how management of current assets differs for multinational firms and for purely domestic firms.

- Some of the complications that arise in the management of current assets in multinational firms include: (1) difficulty moving cash to other countries; (2) higher risk associated with credit operations; and (3) import quotas, tariffs, and taxes that are imposed on inventory.

Chapter 15 Key Concepts for Managing Short-Term Assets

- Firms prefer not to hold cash, because cash is considered an idle asset that does not earn interest. However, firms find that they must hold some cash to ensure that day-to-day obligations can be paid.

  The firm should construct a cash budget to forecast its cash flows so that funds can be invested when there are cash surpluses, and arrangements can be made to borrow funds when there are cash deficiencies. To efficiently manage cash flows, the firm should try to collect funds owed as quickly as possible and try to delay payments of funds for as long as possible. Of course, any actions taken should not be detrimental to the value of the firm.
- Marketable securities are short-term, highly liquid investments that have little investment risk. As a result, the returns on such investments are fairly low. Marketable securities provide the firm with safe instruments where *idle cash* that is needed in the near term—perhaps in a few days or months—can be invested.
- Firms sell on credit because competitors sell on credit. A firm that sells on credit must have a credit policy that specifies how customers qualify for credit, the maximum amount of credit that customers are allowed, the terms of credit sales to customers, and what actions will be taken if customers do not pay on time. To ensure that the credit policy is being followed and it is achieving the desired objective, a firm's credit policy should be monitored. Moreover, when customers' payment patterns change significantly, the firm should consider changing its credit policy. Proposed credit policy changes should be evaluated using net present value (NPV) to ensure the firm is maximizing its value.
- Firms carry inventory to ensure that demand is met when it arrives. If inventory is not available, then a sale cannot be made when a customer wants to purchase the firm's product, and arriving customers might take their business to competitors. Because carrying inventory is costly, firms do not want to have too much inventory on hand at any time. As a result, a firm determines how much inventory to hold by examining the demand for its product, the costs associated with not having enough inventory, and the costs of carrying sufficient inventory to satisfy demand. The EOQ, or economic ordering quantity, model is used to determine the optimal amount of inventory that a firm should carry.

CHAPTER 15 REVIEW

Key Terms

LO.1

transactions balance A cash balance necessary for day-to-day operations; the balance associated with routine payments and collections. *p. 261*

compensating balance A minimum checking account balance that a firm must maintain with a bank to help offset the costs of services such as check clearing and cash management advice. *p. 261*

precautionary balances A cash balance held in reserve for unforeseen fluctuations in cash flows. *p. 261*

speculative balance A cash balance that is held to enable the firm to take advantage of any bargain purchases that might arise. *p. 261*

cash budget A schedule showing cash receipts, cash disbursements, and cash balances for a firm over a specified time period. *p. 262*

target (minimum) cash balance The minimum cash balance a firm desires to maintain in order to conduct business. *p. 262*

disbursements and receipts method (scheduling) The net cash flow is determined by estimating the cash disbursements and the cash receipts expected to be generated each period. *p. 262*

synchronized cash flows A situation in which cash inflows coincide with cash outflows, thereby permitting a firm to hold low transactions balances. *p. 265*

float The difference between the balance shown in a firm's (or individual's) checkbook and the balance on the bank's records. *p. 265*

disbursement float The value of the checks that have been written and *disbursed* but have not yet fully cleared through the banking system, and thus have not been deducted from the account on which they were written. *p. 265*

collections float The amount of checks that have been *received* and deposited but have not yet been made available to the account in which they were deposited. *p. 265*

net float The difference between disbursement float and collections float; the difference between the balance shown in the checkbook and the balance shown on the bank's books. *p. 265*

lockbox arrangement A technique used to reduce float by having payments sent to post office boxes located near the customers. *p. 266*

preauthorized debit system A system that allows a customer's bank to periodically transfer funds from its account to a selling firm's bank account for the payment of bills. *p. 266*

concentration banking A technique used to move funds from many bank accounts to a more central cash pool to more effectively manage cash. *p. 266*

zero-balance account (ZBA) A special checking account used for disbursements that has a balance equal to zero when there is no disbursement activity. *p. 266*

controlled disbursement accounts (CDA) Checking accounts in which funds are not deposited until checks are presented for payment, usually on a daily basis. *p. 266*

LO.2

marketable securities Securities that can be sold on short notice without loss of principal or original investment (liquid investments). *p. 267*

LO.3

credit policy A set of decisions that includes a firm's credit standards, credit terms, methods used to collect credit accounts, and credit monitoring procedures. *p. 268*

credit standards Standards that indicate the minimum financial strength a customer must have to be granted credit. *p. 268*

terms of credit The payment conditions offered to credit customers; the terms include the length of the credit period and any cash discounts offered. *p. 268*

credit period The length of time for which credit is granted; after that time, the credit account is considered delinquent. *p. 268*

cash discount A reduction in the invoice price of goods offered by the seller to encourage early payment. *p. 268*

collection policy The procedures followed by a firm to collect its accounts receivables. *p. 268*

receivables monitoring The process of evaluating the credit policy to determine if a shift in the customers' payment patterns has occurred *p. 268*

days sales outstanding (DSO) The average length of time required to collect accounts receivable; also called the *average collection period*. *p. 269*

aging schedule A report showing how long accounts receivable have been outstanding; the report divides receivables into specified periods, which provides information about the proportion of receivables that is current and the proportion that is past due for given lengths of time. *p. 269*

LO.4

raw materials The inventories purchased from suppliers that ultimately will be transformed into finished goods. *p. 272*

work-in-process Inventory in various stages of completion; some work-in-process is at the very beginning of the production process while some is at the end of the process. *p. 272*

finished goods Inventories that have completed the production process and are ready for sale. *p. 272*

stockout Occurs when a firm runs out of inventory *and* customers arrive to purchase the product. *p. 272*

carrying costs The costs associated with having inventory, which include storage costs, insurance, cost of tying up funds, depreciation costs, and so on; these costs generally increase in proportion to the average amount of inventory held. *p. 273*

ordering costs The costs of placing an order; the cost of each order generally is fixed regardless of the average size of the inventory. *p. 273*

economic (optimum) ordering quantity (EOQ) The optimal quantity that should be ordered; it is this quantity that will minimize the *total inventory costs*. *p. 273*

EOQ model A formula for determining the order quantity that will minimize total inventory costs. *p. 273*

reorder point The level of inventory at which an order should be placed. *p. 275*

safety stock Additional inventory carried to guard against unexpected changes in sales rates or production/shipping delays. *p. 275*

quantity discount A discount from the purchase price offered for inventory ordered in large quantities. *p. 275*

redline method An inventory control procedure where a *red line* is drawn around the inside of an inventory-stocked bin to indicate the reorder point level. *p. 275*

computerized inventory control system A system of inventory control in which a computer is used to determine reorder points and to adjust inventory balances. *p. 276*

just-in-time system A system of inventory control in which a manufacturer coordinates production with suppliers so that raw materials of components arrive just as they are needed in the production process. *p. 276*

outsourcing The practice of purchasing components rather than making them in-house. *p. 276*

CHAPTER 16

Managing Short-Term Liabilities (Financing)

Learning Outcomes

LO.1 Describe the characteristics of the various sources of short-term credit, including (a) accruals, (b) trade credit, (c) bank loans, and (d) commercial paper.

LO.2 Discuss and compute the cost (both APR and r_{EAR}) of short-term credit.

LO.3 Describe the procedures and benefits of using (a) accounts receivable and (b) inventory to obtain secured short-term loans.

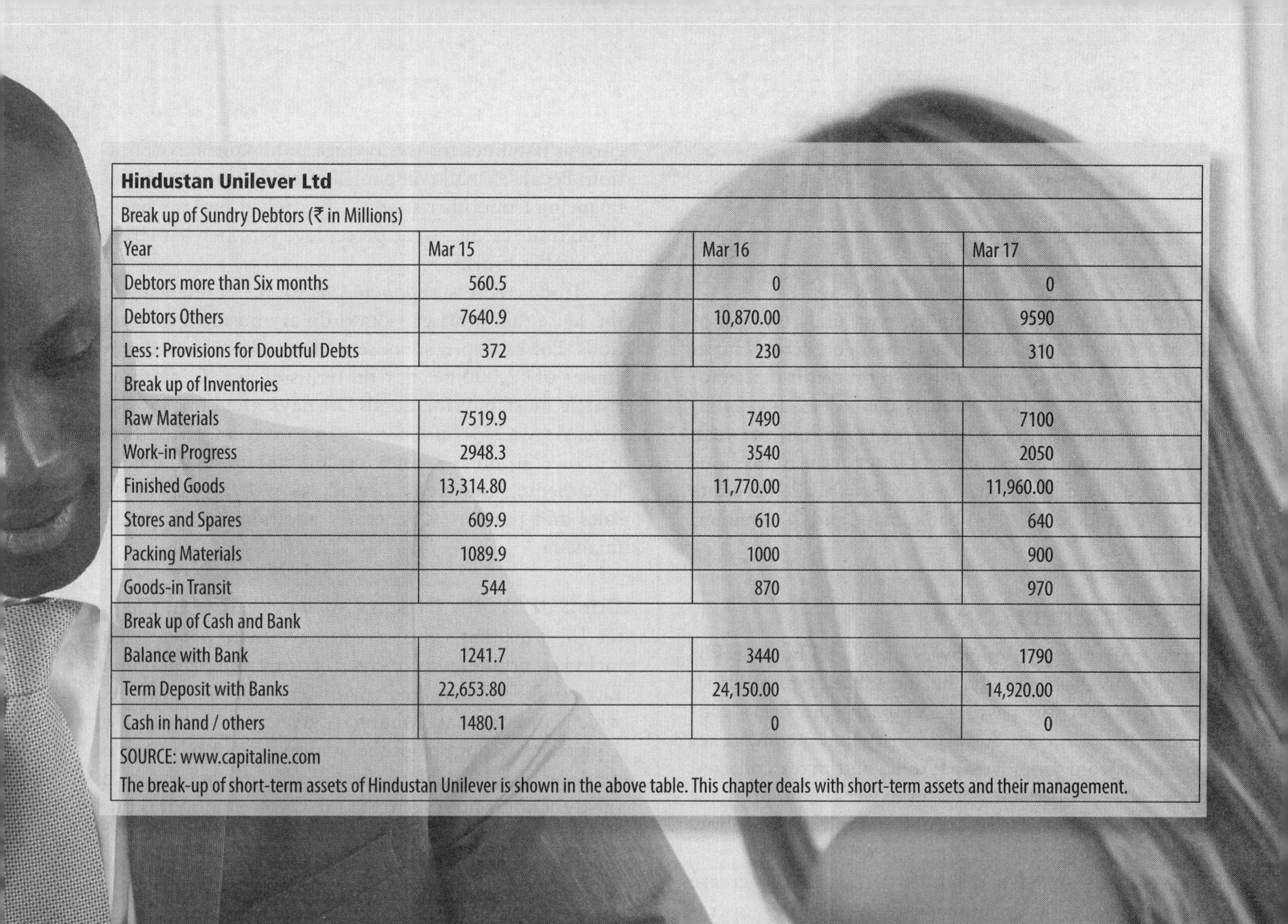

Hindustan Unilever Ltd			
Break up of Sundry Debtors (₹ in Millions)			
Year	Mar 15	Mar 16	Mar 17
Debtors more than Six months	560.5	0	0
Debtors Others	7640.9	10,870.00	9590
Less : Provisions for Doubtful Debts	372	230	310
Break up of Inventories			
Raw Materials	7519.9	7490	7100
Work-in Progress	2948.3	3540	2050
Finished Goods	13,314.80	11,770.00	11,960.00
Stores and Spares	609.9	610	640
Packing Materials	1089.9	1000	900
Goods-in Transit	544	870	970
Break up of Cash and Bank			
Balance with Bank	1241.7	3440	1790
Term Deposit with Banks	22,653.80	24,150.00	14,920.00
Cash in hand / others	1480.1	0	0
SOURCE: www.capitaline.com The break-up of short-term assets of Hindustan Unilever is shown in the above table. This chapter deals with short-term assets and their management.			

Goodluz/Shutterstock.com

In Chapter 14, we discussed the decisions the financial manager must make concerning alternative current asset financing policies. We also showed how debt maturities can affect both risk and expected returns: While short-term debt generally is a riskier source of funds than long-term debt, it generally is also less expensive, and it can be obtained faster and under terms that are more flexible. The primary purpose of this chapter is to examine the different types of short-term credit that are available to the financial manager. We also examine some of the issues the financial manager must consider when selecting among the various types of short-term credit, or current liabilities.

Study Tools

Problems are found at the end of this chapter

+

Login to **CourseMate** for **CFIN** at **CengageBrain.com** for additional problems and other study tools!

16-1 Sources of Short-Term Financing

Statements about the flexibility, cost, and riskiness of short-term debt versus long-term debt depend to a large extent on the type of short-term credit that actually is used. **Short-term credit** is defined as any liability *originally* scheduled for payment within one year. There are numerous sources of short-term funds, four of which we describe here: (1) accruals, (2) accounts payable (trade credit), (3) bank loans, and (4) commercial paper.

16-1a Accruals

Firms generally pay employees on a weekly, biweekly, or monthly basis, so the balance sheet typically will show some accrued wages. Similarly, the firm's estimated income taxes, Social Security and income taxes withheld from employee payrolls, and taxes collected on sales generally are paid on a weekly, monthly, or quarterly basis, so the balance sheet typically will show some taxes in accruals accounts as well.

As we showed in Chapter 14, **accruals** increase automatically, or spontaneously, as a firm's operations expand. Further, this type of debt generally is considered "free" in the sense that no explicit interest is paid on funds generated by accruals. However, a firm ordinarily cannot control its accruals: The timing of wage payments is set by economic forces and industry custom, while tax payment dates are established by law. Thus, firms use all the accruals they can, but they have little control over the levels of these accounts.

16-1b Accounts Payable (Trade Credit)

Firms generally make purchases from other firms (for example, suppliers) on credit, recording these debts as *accounts payable*. This type of financing, which is called **trade credit**, typically is the largest single category of short-term debt, representing about 35–40 percent of the current liabilities for the average nonfinancial corporation. Because small companies often do not qualify for financing from other sources, they rely especially heavily on trade credit, so the percentage is somewhat larger for smaller firms.[1]

short-term credit Any liability originally scheduled for repayment within one year.

accruals Recurring short-term liabilities; liabilities such as wages and taxes that change spontaneously with operations.

trade credit The credit created when one firm buys on credit from another firm.

Trade credit is a *spontaneous* source of financing in the sense that it arises from ordinary business transactions. For example, suppose a firm makes average purchases of ₹2,000 per day on terms of net 30, meaning that it must pay for goods 30 days after the invoice date. As we saw in Chapter 14, on average, the firm will owe 30 times ₹2,000, or ₹60,000, to its suppliers. Lengthening the credit period, as well as expanding sales and purchases, generates additional trade credit financing.

Cost of Trade Credit. As we discussed in Chapter 15, firms that sell on credit have *credit policies* that includes certain *terms of credit*. For example, Manohar Electronics sells on credit with terms of 2/10, net 30, which means that Manohar gives its customers a 2 percent discount from the invoice price if payment is made within 10 days of the billing date; otherwise, if the discount is not taken, the full invoice amount is due within 30 days of the billing date.

Note that the *true* price of the products Manohar offers is the net price, which is 98 percent of the list price, because any customer can purchase an item at a 2 percent "discount" as long as payment is made within 10 days of the billing cycle. Consider Piyush Computer Company (PCC), which buys its memory chips from Manohar. One commonly used memory chip is listed at ₹100, so the true cost to PCC is ₹98. If PCC wants an additional 20 days of credit beyond the 10-day discount period, it will effectively incur a finance charge of ₹2 per chip for that credit. Thus, the ₹100 list price can be thought of as follows:

List price = ₹100 = ₹98 true price + ₹2 finance charge

The question that PCC must ask before it takes the additional 20 days of credit from Microchip is whether the firm could obtain similar credit with better terms from some other lender, say, a bank. In other words, could 20 days of credit be obtained for less than ₹2 per item?

[1]In a credit sale, the seller records the transaction as a receivable, whereas the buyer records the transaction as a payable. We examined accounts receivable as an asset in Chapter 15. Our focus in this chapter is on accounts payable, a liability item. We should also note that if a firm's accounts payable exceed its receivables, it is said to be *receiving net trade credit*, whereas if its receivables exceed its payables, it is *extending net trade credit*. Smaller firms frequently receive net credit; larger firms generally extend it.

To answer the question as to whether PCC should take the cash discount, we must compute the cost of using trade credit to finance the firm. The cost of short-term credit is discussed later in this chapter.

Components of Trade Credit: Free versus Costly. On the basis of the preceding discussion, trade credit can be divided into two components: (1) **"free" trade credit**, which involves credit received during the discount period; and (2) **costly trade credit**, which involves credit in excess of the free trade credit and whose cost is an implicit one based on the forgone discounts.[2] *Financial managers always should use the free component, but they should use the costly component only after analyzing the cost of this source of financing to make sure that it is less than the cost of funds that could be obtained from other sources.* Under the terms of trade found in most industries, the costly component will involve a relatively high percentage cost (usually greater than 25 percent), so stronger firms will take the cash discounts offered and avoid using trade credit as a source of additional financing.

Firms sometimes can and do deviate from the stated credit terms, thus altering the percentage cost figures cited. For example, a Chennai manufacturing firm that buys on terms of 2/10, net 30 makes a practice of paying in 15 days (rather than 10 days), but it still takes discounts. The company's suppliers want its business, so they tolerate this practice. Similarly, a Wisconsin firm that also buys on terms of 2/10, net 30 does not take discounts, but it pays in 60 days rather than in 30 days, thus **stretching** its **accounts payable**. Both practices reduce the cost of trade credit. Neither of these firms is loved by its suppliers, and neither could continue these practices in times when suppliers operate at full capacity and have order backlogs. But, these practices can and do reduce the costs of trade credit to customers during times when suppliers have excess capacity.

16-1c Short-Term Bank Loans

Commercial banks, whose loans generally appear on firms' balance sheets as notes payable, are second in importance to trade credit as a source of short-term financing.[3] The influence of banks actually is greater than it appears from the rupee amounts they lend, because banks provide *nonspontaneous* funds. As a firm's financing needs increase, it specifically requests additional funds from its bank. If the request is denied, the firm might be forced to abandon attractive growth opportunities. The key features of bank loans are discussed in this section.

Maturity. Although banks do make longer-term loans, the *bulk of their commercial lending is on a short-term basis*. Bank loans to businesses frequently are written as 90-day notes, so these loans must be repaid or renewed at the end of 90 days. Of course, if a borrower's financial position has deteriorated, the bank might refuse to renew the loan, which could mean serious trouble for the borrower.

Promissory Note. When a bank loan is approved, the borrower executes the agreement by signing a **promissory note.** The note specifies (1) the amount borrowed; (2) the interest rate; (3) the repayment schedule, which can call for payment either in a lump-sum amount or as a series

© iStockphoto.com/Christopher Futcher/iStockphoto.com

"free" trade credit Credit received during the discount period.

costly trade credit Credit taken in excess of "free" trade credit, whose cost is equal to the discount lost.

stretching accounts payable The practice of deliberately paying accounts payable late.

promissory note A document specifying the terms and conditions of a loan, including the amount, interest rate, and repayment schedule.

[2]There is some question as to whether any credit is really "free," because the supplier will have a cost of carrying receivables, which must be passed on to the customer in the form of higher prices. Still, if suppliers sell on standard credit terms such as 2/10, net 30, and if the base price cannot be negotiated downward for early payment, then the 10 days of trade credit are indeed free.

[3]Although commercial banks remain the primary source of short-term loans, other sources are available. For example, in 2013 General Electric Capital Corporation (GECC) had several billion rupees in commercial loans outstanding. Firms such as GECC, which was initially established to finance consumers' purchases of GE's durable goods, often find business loans to be more profitable than consumer loans.

of installments; (4) any collateral that has to be put up as security for the loan; and (5) any other terms and conditions to which the bank and the borrower have agreed.

Compensating Balance. Banks sometimes require borrowers to maintain an average checking account (demand deposit) balance equal to 10 percent to 20 percent of the amount borrowed. This is called a **compensating balance (CB)**. In effect, the bank charges borrowers for servicing their loans (bookkeeping, maintaining an overdraft, and so on) by requiring compensating balances, and such balances might increase the costs of the loans.[4]

Overdraft An **overdraft** is an agreement between a bank and a borrower indicating the maximum credit the bank will extend to the borrower. For example, on December 31 a bank loan officer might indicate to a financial manager that the bank regards the firm as being "good" for up to ₹200,000 during the forthcoming year. If on January 10 the financial manager signs a 90-day promissory note for ₹60,000, this would be termed *drawing down* ₹60,000 of the total overdraft. This amount would be credited to the firm's checking account at the bank, and before repayment of the ₹60,000, the firm could borrow additional amounts up to a *total* of ₹200,000 outstanding at any one time. Therefore, if the firm has ₹60,000 "drawn" on its overdraft it could borrow an additional ₹140,000 at any time.

When an overdraft is *guaranteed*, it is called a **revolving credit agreement (line)**. A revolving credit agreement is similar to a regular, or general overdraft except that the bank has a *legal obligation* to provide the funds when requested by the borrower. The bank generally charges a **commitment fee** on the unused balance of a revolving credit line (or, sometimes, on the total credit commitment) for guaranteeing the availability of the funds. To illustrate, in 2013 Dynactic Promotions Company (DPC) negotiated a revolving credit agreement for ₹100 million with a group of banks. The banks were formally committed for four years to lend the firm up to ₹100 million *if the funds were needed*. DPC, in turn, paid an annual *commitment fee* of 1/4 of 1 percent on the unused balance of the guaranteed overdraft. Thus, if DPC did not draw down any of the ₹100 million commitment during the year, it would still be required to pay a ₹250,000 annual fee (1/4 of 1 percent of the ₹100 million credit agreement), normally in monthly installments of ₹20,833. If DPC borrowed ₹60 million on the first day of the agreement, the unused portion of the overdraft would fall to ₹40 million, and the annual commitment fee would fall to ₹100,000 = 0.0025 × ₹40 million. Of course, interest also would have to be paid on the money DPC actually borrowed. As a general rule, the rate of interest on "revolvers" is pegged to a benchmark interest rate, such as the prime rate, so the cost of the loan varies over time as interest rates change.[5] DPC's rate was set at the prime rate plus 1/2 percent.

compensating balance (CB) A minimum checking account balance that a firm must maintain with a bank to borrow funds—generally 10 to 20 percent of the amount of loans outstanding.

overdraft An arrangement in which a bank agrees to lend up to a specified maximum amount of funds during a designated period.

revolving credit agreement (line) A formal, committed overdraft extended by a bank or other lending institution.

commitment fee A fee charged on the *unused* balance of a revolving credit agreement to compensate the bank for guaranteeing that the funds will be available when needed by the borrower; the fee normally is about ¼ percent of the unused balance.

prime rate A published rate of interest charged by banks to short-term borrowers (usually large, financially secure corporations) with the best credit; rates on short-term loans sometimes are "pegged" to the prime rate.

Note that an important feature distinguishes a revolving credit agreement from a general overdraft. The bank has a *legal obligation* to honor a revolving credit agreement, and it receives a commitment fee for guaranteeing that the funds will be available when requested by the borrower. Neither the legal obligation nor the fee exists under a general overdraft.

The Cost of Bank Loans. The cost of bank loans varies for different types of borrowers at any given point in time and for all borrowers over time. Interest rates are higher for riskier borrowers, and rates also are higher on smaller loans because of the fixed costs involved in making and servicing such loans. If a firm can qualify as a "prime credit" because of its size and financial strength, it might be able to borrow at the **prime rate**, which traditionally has been the lowest rate banks charge. Rates on other loans generally are scaled up from the prime rate.[6]

[4]Note, however, that the compensating balance might be set as a minimum monthly *average*, and if the firm generally maintains this average anyway, the compensating balance requirement might not raise the effective interest rate. Also, note that these loan compensating balances often are added to any compensating balances that the firm's bank might require for *services performed*, such as clearing checks.

[5]Each bank sets its own prime rate, but because of competitive forces, most banks' prime rates are identical. Further, most banks follow the rate set by the large New York City banks.

[6]In recent years, many banks have been lending to the strongest companies at rates below the prime rate. As we discuss later in this chapter, larger firms have ready access to the commercial paper market, and if banks want to do business with these larger companies, they must match or at least come close to the commercial paper rate. As competition in financial markets increases, as it has been doing because of the deregulation of banks and other financial institutions, "administered" rates such as the prime rate are giving way to flexible, negotiated rates based on market conditions.

Bank rates vary widely over time, depending on economic conditions and Federal Reserve policy. When the economy is weak, loan demand usually is slack, and rates on all types of loans are relatively low. Conversely, when the economy is booming, loan demand typically is strong and the Fed restricts the money supply; the result is high interest rates.

Choosing a Bank. Individuals whose only contact with their bank is through their use of its checking services generally choose a bank for the convenience of its location and the competitive cost of its services. However, a business that borrows from banks must look at other criteria, and a potential borrower seeking a banking relationship should recognize that important differences exist among banks. Some of these differences are considered here.

- **Willingness to Assume Risks.** Banks have different basic policies toward risk. Some banks are inclined to follow relatively conservative lending practices, whereas others engage in what are properly termed "creative banking practices." These policies partly reflect the personalities of officers of the bank and partly reflect the characteristics of the bank's deposit liabilities. Thus, a bank with fluctuating deposit liabilities in a static community will tend to be a conservative lender, whereas a bank whose deposits are growing with little interruption might follow more liberal credit policies. Similarly, a large bank with broad diversification over geographic regions or across industries can obtain the benefit of combining and averaging risks. Thus, marginal credit risks that might be unacceptable to a small bank or a specialized bank can be pooled by a large branch banking system to reduce the overall risk of a group of marginal accounts.
- **Advice and Counsel.** Some bank loan officers are active in providing counsel and in facilitating development loans to firms in their early and formative years. Certain banks have specialized departments that make loans to firms expected to grow, and thus to become more important as customers in the future. The personnel of these departments can provide valuable counseling to customers (borrowers).
- **Loyalty to Customers.** Banks differ in the extent to which they support the activities of borrowers in bad times. This characteristic is referred to as the degree of *loyalty* of the bank. Some banks might put great pressure on a business to liquidate its loans when the firm's outlook becomes clouded, whereas others will stand by the firm and work diligently to help it get back on its feet.
- **Specialization.** Banks differ greatly in their degrees of loan specialization. Larger banks have separate departments that specialize in different kinds of loans—for example, real estate loans, farm loans, and commercial loans. Within these broad categories, there might be a specialization by line of business, such as steel, machinery, cattle, or textiles. The strengths of banks also are likely to reflect the nature of the business and the economic environment in which the banks operate. A sound firm can obtain cooperation that is more creative and support that is more active by going to a bank that has experience and familiarity with its particular type of business. Therefore, a bank that is excellent for one firm might be unsatisfactory for another.
- **Maximum Loan Size.** The size of a bank can be an important factor. Because the maximum loan a bank can make to any one customer generally is limited to 15 percent of the bank's capital accounts (capital stock plus retained earnings), it generally is not appropriate for large firms to develop borrowing relationships with small banks.
- **Other Services.** Many banks also provide cash management services such as those described in Chapter 15, assist with electronic funds transfers, help firms obtain foreign exchange, and the like. The availability of such services should be taken into account by a firm when selecting a bank. In addition, if the firm is a small business whose manager owns most of its stock, the bank's willingness and ability to provide trust and estate services also should be considered.

16-1d Commercial Paper

Commercial paper is a type of unsecured promissory note issued by large, financially strong firms, and it is sold primarily to other businesses, insurance companies, pension funds, money market mutual funds, and banks. This form of financing has grown rapidly in recent years; the amount of commercial paper outstanding currently is about the same as the amount of regular business loans at banks.

Use of Commercial Paper. The use of commercial paper is restricted to a comparatively small number of firms that are

commercial paper Unsecured, short-term promissory notes issued by large, financially sound firms to raise funds.

exceptionally good credit risks. Dealers prefer to handle the "paper" of firms whose net worth is ₹100 million or more and whose annual borrowing exceeds ₹10 million. One potential problem with commercial paper is that a debtor who is in temporary financial difficulty might receive little help, because commercial paper dealings generally are less personal than are bank relationships; thus, a bank generally is more able and willing to help a good customer weather a temporary storm than a commercial paper dealer would be. On the other hand, using commercial paper permits a corporation to tap a wider range of credit sources, including financial institutions outside its own area and industrial corporations across the country, and this can reduce interest costs.

Maturity and Cost. Maturities of commercial paper vary from one to nine months, with an average of about five months.[7] The rate on commercial paper fluctuates with supply and demand conditions; it is determined in the marketplace, varying daily as conditions change. Generally, the rates on commercial paper are lower than the stated prime rate of interest.[8] For example, in September 2013, the average rate on 90-day commercial paper was 0.08 percent, which was 3.17 percent less than the prime rate but 0.06 percent greater than 90-day Treasury bill rates. All rates were at extremely low levels during 2013 because the economy was struggling to recover from an earlier recession, which created a great deal of consumer and business uncertainty with regard to future economic movements.

Commercial paper is called a *discount instrument* because it is sold at a price below its *face*, or maturity, value. The cost of using commercial paper as a source of financing is computed in the same way as the cost of a discount interest loan, which is discussed in the next section.

16-2 Computing the Cost of Short-Term Credit

For short-term financing, the percentage cost of using the funds for a given period, r_{PER}, can be computed as shown in Equation 16.1:

16.1

$$\text{Percentage cost per period} = r_{PER} = \frac{\left(\text{Rupee cost of borrowing}\right)}{\left(\text{Rupee amount of usable funds}\right)}$$

In this equation, the numerator represents the rupee amount that must be paid for using the borrowed funds, which includes the interest paid on the loan, application fees, charges for commitment fees, and so forth. The denominator represents the amount of the loan that actually can be used (spent) by the borrower. This amount is not necessarily the same as the principal amount (amount borrowed) of the loan because discounts, compensating balances, or other costs might reduce the amount of the loan principal that the firm can actually use. In this section, we show that *when loan restrictions prevent the borrower from using the entire amount of the loan, the effective annual rate paid for the loan is higher than the stated (simple) interest rate.*

Using Equation 16.1 and the concepts described in Chapter 4, the effective annual rate (EAR) and the annual percentage rate (APR) for short-term financing can be computed as shown in Equations 16.2 and 16.3

16.2

$$\text{Effective annual rate (EAR)} = r_{EAR} = (1 + r_{PER})^{m} - 1.0$$

16.3

$$\text{Annual percentage rates(APR)} = r_{PER} \times m = r_{SIMPLE}$$

where m is the number of borrowing (interest) periods in one year (that is, if the loan is for one month, m = 12). Recall from our discussion in Chapter 4 that the EAR incorporates interest compounding in the computation, whereas the APR does not. Both computations adjust the percentage cost per period so that it is stated on an annual basis. We annualize the cost to make it easier to compare short-term credit instruments that have different maturities.

Next, we illustrate the application of these equations to compute the cost of three short-term financing alternatives: (1) trade credit, (2) bank loans, and (3) commercial paper.

[7]The maximum maturity without SEC registration is 270 days. In addition, commercial paper can only be sold to sophisticated investors; otherwise, SEC registration would be required even for maturities of 270 days or less.

[8]Generally, the prime rate is higher than the commercial paper rate, because (1) banks have operating costs that are built into the prime rate and (2) only large, financially strong firms are permitted to issue commercial paper, and these are the same firms that would be able to borrow at the prime rate or better.

16-2a **Computing the Cost of Trade Credit (Accounts Payable)**

Consider Microchip's credit terms of 2/10, net 30, which allow its customers, such as Personal Computer Company (PCC), to take a 2 percent discount from the purchase price if payment is made on or before Day 10 of the billing cycle; otherwise, the entire bill is due by Day 30. If the invoice price is ₹100 and the firm does not take the discount, it effectively pays ₹2 to borrow ₹98 for a 20-day period, so the cost of using the funds for the additional 20 days is

$$r_{PER} = \frac{₹2}{₹98}$$
$$= 0.020408 < 2.0408\%$$

Because there are 18 = 360/20 20-day periods in a 360-day year, the APR, or simple interest rate, associated with trade credit with these terms is

$$\text{APR} = 2.0408\% \times 18$$
$$= 36.73\%$$

The effective annual cost (rate), EAR, of using trade credit with these terms as a source of short-term financing is

$$r_{EAR} = (1 + 0.020408)^{18} - 1.0 = 0.4386 = 43.86\%$$

According to this computation, if PCC chooses to pay its bill on Day 30, then it will forgo the 2 percent cash discount, which is equivalent to borrowing funds at a rate of nearly 44 percent per year.[9] PCC should forgo the cash discount to pay on Day 30 only if alternative financing, such as a bank loan, has a cost greater than 43.9 percent.

16-2b **Computing the Cost of Bank Loans**

A bank loan can take the form of a *simple interest loan*, a *discount loan*, or an *installment loan*. Factors such as a compensating balance or application fees can affect the cost of borrowing for each of these types of loans. Here we give some examples of how to compute the cost for each of these loans.

Simple Interest Loan. With a **simple interest loan**, the borrower receives the **face value** of the loan—that is, the amount borrowed, or the principal—and repays both the principal and the interest at maturity. For example, with a simple interest loan of ₹10,000 at 12 percent interest for nine months, the borrower receives the ₹10,000 upon approval of the loan and pays back the ₹10,000 principal plus ₹900 = ₹10,000[0.12 × (9/12)] in interest at maturity. Note that interest is paid only for the portion of the year the loan is outstanding, which is nine months in this case. The 12 percent is the **quoted**, or **simple, interest rate.**

The nine-month interest rate for this loan is

$$r_{PER} = \frac{\text{9-month}}{\text{interest rate}} = \frac{₹10{,}000 \times \left[0.12 \times \left(\frac{9}{12}\right)\right]}{₹10{,}000}$$
$$= \frac{₹900}{₹10{,}000} = 0.09 = 9.0\%$$

The APR for this loan is

$$\text{APR} = 2.0408\% \times 18$$
$$= 36.73\%$$

The EAR is:

$$r_{EAR} = (1.09)^{(12/9)} - 1.0 = 0.1218 = 12.18\%$$

EAR > APR because this is a nine-month loan, which means interest compounding is assumed to occur every nine months.

Discount Interest Loan. With a **discount interest loan**, the interest due is deducted "up front" so that the borrower receives less than the principal amount, or face value, of the loan. Suppose U.P. Textiles receives a nine-month, ₹10,000 discount interest loan with a 12 percent quoted (simple) interest rate. The interest payment on this loan is ₹900 = ₹10,000[0.12 × (9/12)]. Because the interest is paid in advance, U.P. has only ₹9,100 = ₹10,000 − ₹900 of the amount borrowed available to use as it wants. Thus, the nine-month interest rate paid for the loan is

simple interest loan Both the amount borrowed and the interest charged on that amount are paid at the maturity of the loan; there are no payments made before maturity.

face value The amount of the loan, or the amount borrowed; also called the *principal amount* of the loan.

quoted (simple) interest rate The annual percentage rate (APR) that is used to compute the interest rate per period (r_{PER}).

discount interest loan A loan in which the interest, which is calculated on the amount borrowed (principal), is paid at the beginning of the loan period; interest is paid in advance.

[9] We assume that the firm pays its supplier on the last day possible. That is, if it takes the discount, payment is made on Day 10; if it doesn't take the discount, payment is made on Day 30. This is rational business behavior. If, however, the firm does not take the discount, but pays the full invoice price on Day 20 (or any other time before the final due date), then the cost associated with using this source of financing is higher than that computed here. The funds cost more because the firm uses them for a shorter period.

$$r_{EAR} = \frac{\text{9-month}}{\text{interest rate}} = \frac{₹10{,}000 \times \left[0.12 \times \left(\frac{9}{12}\right)\right]}{₹10{,}000 - \left\{₹10{,}000\left[0.12 \times \left(\frac{9}{12}\right)\right]\right\}}$$

$$= \frac{₹900}{₹9{,}100} = 0.0989 = 9.89\%$$

The APR for this loan is

$$\text{APR} = 9.89\% \times \left(\frac{12}{9}\right) = 13.19\%$$

The EAR is

$$r_{EAR} = (1.0989)^{(12/9)} - 1.0 = 0.1340 = 13.40\%$$

What do you think the cost of the loan described here would be if U.P.'s bank charged a ₹50 fee to cover the cost of processing the loan? To answer this question, first take a look at Equation 16.1 and determine whether payment of the fee affects the numerator (that is, the rupee cost of borrowing); the denominator (that is, the amount of usable funds); or both the numerator and the denominator. The general rule is that the numerator is affected by any expense associated with the loan, and the denominator is affected if funds must be put aside (for example, to satisfy a compensating balance requirement) or costs are paid out of the loan proceeds at the beginning of the loan period. Thus, if U.P. uses the proceeds from the loan to pay the ₹50 fee, both the numerator and the denominator are affected, and the nine-month interest rate is

$$r_{PER} = \frac{\text{9-month}}{\text{Interest rate}} = \frac{₹900 + ₹50}{₹9{,}100 - ₹50} = \frac{₹950}{₹9{,}050}$$

$$= 0.1050 = 10.50\%$$

Check to see that the APR and the EAR are now 14.0 percent and 14.2 percent, respectively. (See the computation for the cost of commercial paper later in this section.)

Installment Loan: Add-On Interest. Lenders often charge **add-on interest** on various types of installment loans. The term *add-on* means that the interest is calculated and then added to the amount borrowed to obtain the total rupee amount to be paid back in equal installments. To illustrate, suppose U.P. borrows ₹10,000 on an add-on basis at a simple rate of 12 percent, with the loan to be repaid in nine monthly installments. At a 12 percent add-on rate, U.P. will pay a total interest charge of ₹900 as computed earlier, and a total of ₹10,900 in nine equal payments. The monthly payments would be ₹1,211.11 = ₹10,900/9. Therefore, each month U.P. would pay ₹100 interest (1/9 of the total interest) and ₹1,111.11 principal repayment (1/9 of the ₹10,000 borrowed). Because the loan is paid off in monthly installments, U.P. will have use of the full ₹10,000 only for the first month, and the outstanding balance will decline by ₹1,111.11 each month so that the remaining principal due at the beginning of the last month of the loan will be ₹1,111.11. As a result, the percentage cost of the loan will vary each month.

add-on interest Interest that is calculated and then added to the amount borrowed to obtain the total rupee amount to be paid back in equal installments.

U.P. would pay ₹900 for the use of approximately 50 percent of the loan's face amount, because the average outstanding balance of the loan is only about ₹5,000 = (₹10,000 + ₹0)/2. (The ₹10,000 is paid down evenly over the life of the loan.) With this information, we can *approximate* the rate for the nine-month period as follows:

$$r_{PER} \approx \frac{\text{Approximate rate}}{\text{per period}} = \frac{₹900}{₹5{,}000} = 0.18 = 18.0\%$$

The *approximate* APR would be 24.0% = 18.0% × (12/9).

To determine the EAR, recognize that the ₹1,211.11 payment U.P. makes each month represents an annuity. The cash flow timeline for the loan would be:

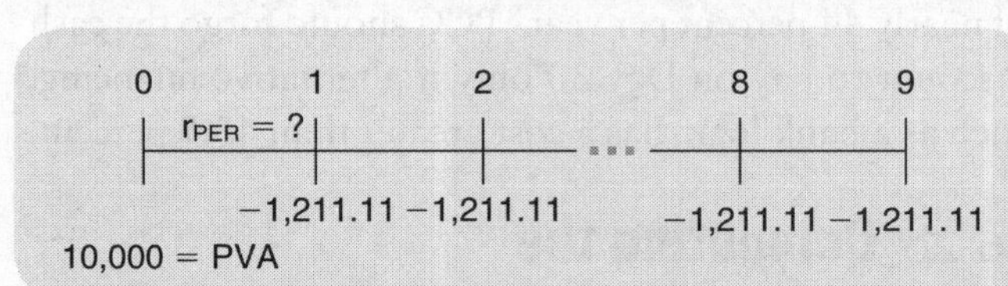

Using a financial calculator, enter N = 9, PV = 10,000, PMT = −1,211.11, and then solve for I. The *monthly* rate equals 1.7591. In this case, we assume monthly compounding, because the installment payments are made each month. When we annualize the monthly rate, the EAR is

$$r_{EAR} = (1.017591)^{12} - 1.0 = 0.2328 = 23.28\%$$

16-2c Computing the Cost of Commercial Paper

Suppose U.P. issues 270-day commercial paper with a face value equal to ₹10,000. The simple annual interest rate on the commercial paper is 12 percent, and the total transactions fee, which includes the cost of a backup overdraft is 1/2 of 1 percent of the amount of the issue. Because commercial paper is a discount instrument similar to a discount loan, U.P. will not be able to use the total ₹10,000 face value. Instead, investors will purchase the commercial paper issue for ₹9,100 = ₹10,000 − ₹10,000[0.12 × (9/12)], and then receive ₹10,000 at maturity. The transaction fee, which equals ₹50 = 0.005 × ₹10,000, is "taken off the top," so U.P. would, in fact, receive only ₹9,050 = ₹9,100 − ₹50 to use from the commercial paper issue. The total rupee cost of borrowing using commercial paper would be ₹950, which includes "interest" equal to ₹900 and the ₹50 transaction fee. As a result, the nine-month cost of the commercial paper would be

$$r_{PER} = \begin{matrix}9\text{-month}\\ \text{Interest rate}\end{matrix} = \frac{₹900 + ₹50}{₹10{,}000 - (₹900 + ₹50)}$$

$$= \frac{₹950}{₹9{,}050} = 0.1050 = 10.50\%$$

The APR for this loan is

$$\text{APR} = 10.50\% \times \left(\frac{12}{9}\right) = 14.00\%$$

The EAR is

$$r_{EAR} = (1.1050)^{(12/9)} - 1.0 = 0.1424 = 14.24\%$$

16-2d Borrowed (Principal) Amount Versus Required (Needed) Amount

Compensating balances can raise the effective rate on a loan. To illustrate, suppose U.P. *needs* ₹10,000 to pay for some equipment it recently purchased. Oriental Bank of Commerce offers to lend U.P. the money for nine months at a 12 percent simple rate, but the company must maintain a *compensating balance (CB)* equal to 20 percent of the loan amount (principal, or face, value). First, note that U.P. must have ₹10,000 to pay for the equipment. If the firm's checking account balance is not sufficient to cover the compensating balance requirement, then the principal amount of the loan must be greater than ₹10,000, because some of the amount borrowed must be put aside to satisfy the compensating balance requirement. In this case, the question is, how much must the firm borrow so that it has ₹10,000 available for use? To answer this question, first we must determine the *usable funds* from the loan (Equation 16.4):

16.4

$$\begin{matrix}\text{Usable}\\ \text{funds}\end{matrix} = \text{Principal} - \left(\begin{matrix}₹\text{ reductions from}\\ \text{principal amount}\end{matrix}\right)$$

Here "Principal" represents the face value of the loan, which is the amount that must be repaid at maturity, and "₹ reductions from principal amount" includes anything that reduces the amount of money that the firm can actually use from the total amount that is borrowed.

If the rupee reductions from the face value of the loan are stated as percentages, Equation 16.4 can be written as Equation 16.4a.

16.4a

$$\begin{matrix}\text{Usable}\\ \text{funds}\end{matrix} = \text{Principal} \times \left[1 - \left(\begin{matrix}\%\text{ reductions from}\\ \text{principal amount}\end{matrix}\right)\right]$$

Here "% reductions from principal amount" Oriental Bank of commerce the items that reduce the amount that the firm can actually use from the borrowed amount stated in decimal form.

If we know how much of the amount borrowed actually is needed as usable funds, Equation 16.4a can be rearranged to solve for the amount that must be borrowed (principal amount) to provide these needed funds. The computation is shown in Equation 16.5.

16.5

$$\begin{matrix}\text{Required loan}\\ \text{(principal) amount}\end{matrix} = \frac{\left(\begin{matrix}\text{Amount of funds}\\ \textit{needed}\text{ for use}\end{matrix}\right)}{1 - \left[\begin{matrix}\text{Reductions from principal}\\ \text{stated as a decimal}\end{matrix}\right]}$$

If it does not have a checking account at Oriental Bank of Commerce, U.P. will have to borrow ₹12,500 to be able to satisfy the 20 percent compensating balance requirement and have ₹10,000 available to pay for the equipment. The computation follows.

$$\begin{matrix}\text{Required loan}\\ \text{(principal) amount}\end{matrix} = \frac{₹10{,}000}{1 - 0.20} = ₹12{,}500$$

Let's check to ensure that this is the amount that the firm must borrow. If the firm borrows ₹12,500, but has nothing deposited in the bank, ₹2,500 = ₹12,500 ×

0.2 must be taken out of the principal amount to satisfy the compensating balance requirement, which leaves the firm with ₹10,000 = ₹12,500 − ₹2,500 available to pay for the equipment.

In this case, the nine-month rate for this loan would be

$$r_{PER} = \frac{\text{9-month}}{\text{interest rate}} = \frac{₹12{,}500 \times \left[0.12 \times \left(\frac{9}{12}\right)\right]}{₹12{,}500 - ₹12{,}500(0.20)}$$

$$= \frac{₹1{,}125}{₹10{,}000} = 0.1125 = 11.25\%$$

The APR and EAR are

$$\text{APR} = 11.25\% \times \left(\frac{12}{9}\right) = 15.00\%$$

$$r_{EAR} = (1.1125)^{(12/9)} - 1.0 = 0.1527 = 15.27\%$$

If a firm normally keeps a positive checking account balance at the lending bank, it needs to borrow less to have a specific amount of funds available for use, which means the effective cost of the loan will be lower.

From the examples presented here, you should recognize that the percentage cost of short-term financing is higher when the rupee expenses, such as those associated with interest, clerical efforts, and loan processing, are higher, when the net proceeds from the loan are less than the principal amount, or when both conditions exist. Thus, in most cases the effective interest rate (cost) of short-term financing is greater than its stated (quoted) interest rate. *The effective interest rate of a loan is equal to the quoted (simple) rate only if (1) the entire principal amount borrowed can be used by the borrower for the entire year and (2) the only rupee cost associated with the loan is the interest charged on the outstanding balance.*

16-3 Use of Secured Short-Term Financing

secured loans Loans backed by collateral; for short-term loans, the collateral often is inventory, receivables, or both.

pledging of receivables Using accounts receivable as collateral for a loan.

recourse The lender can seek payment from the borrowing firm when receivables' accounts used to secure a loan are uncollectible.

Thus far we have not addressed the question of whether loans should be secured. Commercial paper is not secured, but all other types of loans can be secured if this is deemed necessary or desirable. Given a choice, it ordinarily is better to borrow on an unsecured basis because the bookkeeping costs of **secured loans** often are high. However, weak firms might find that they can borrow only if they put up some type of security, or that by using security they can borrow at a lower rate.

Several different kinds of security, or *collateral*, can be employed, including marketable securities, land or buildings, equipment, inventories, and accounts receivable. Marketable securities make excellent collateral, but few firms that need loans also hold such portfolios. Similarly, real property (land and buildings) and equipment are good forms of collateral, but they generally are used as security for long-term loans rather than for working capital loans. Therefore, most secured short-term business borrowing involves the use of accounts receivable and inventories as collateral.

To understand the use of security, consider the case of a Chandigarh hardware dealer who wanted to modernize and expand his store. He requested a ₹200,000 bank loan. After examining his firm's financial statements, the bank indicated that it would lend him a maximum of ₹100,000 and that the interest rate would be 12 percent, discount interest, for an effective rate of 13.6 percent. The owner had a substantial personal portfolio of stocks, and he offered to put up ₹300,000 of high-quality stocks to support the ₹200,000 loan. The bank then granted the full ₹200,000 loan, and at a rate of only 11 percent, simple interest. The store owner also might have used his inventories or receivables as security for the loan, but processing costs would have been high.[10]

16-3a Accounts Receivable Financing

Accounts receivable financing involves either the **pledging of receivables** or the selling of receivables (called *factoring*). The pledging of accounts receivable is characterized by the fact that the lender not only has a claim against the receivables but also has **recourse** to the borrower: If the firm's customer (the receivables account) does not pay, the firm that pledges the account (borrower), rather than the lender, must take the loss. Therefore, the risk of default on the pledged accounts remains with the pledging firm. The customers of the pledging firm ordinarily are not notified about the pledging of their receivables, and the financial institution that

[10]The term *asset-based financing* is often used as a synonym for *secured financing*. In recent years, accounts receivable have been used as security for long-term bonds, and this permits corporations to borrow from lenders such as pension funds rather than being restricted to banks and other traditional short-term lenders.

lends on the security of accounts receivable generally is either a commercial bank or a large finance company.

Factoring, or *selling accounts receivable,* involves the purchase of accounts receivable by the lender (called a *factor*), generally without recourse to the borrower, which means that if an account that is factored cannot be collected, the lender, rather than the seller of the goods (borrowing firm), takes the loss. Under factoring, the borrowing firm's customers generally are notified of the transfer and are asked to make payments directly to the lending institution (the factor). Because the factor assumes the risk of default on bad accounts, it generally carries out the credit investigations of the customers of the borrowing firm. Accordingly, factors provide not only money but also a credit department for the borrower. Incidentally, the same financial institutions that make loans against pledged receivables also serve as factors. Thus, depending on the circumstances and the wishes of the borrower, a financial institution will provide either type of receivables financing.

Procedure for Pledging Accounts Receivable. The financing of accounts receivable is initiated by a legally binding agreement between the seller of the goods (borrower) and the financing institution (lender). The agreement sets forth in detail the procedures to be followed and the legal obligations of both parties. Once the working relationship has been established, the borrowing firm periodically takes a batch of invoices to the financing institution. The lender reviews the invoices and makes credit appraisals of the buyers. Invoices of credit customers who do not meet the lender's credit standards are not accepted for pledging.

The financial institution seeks to protect itself at every phase of the operation. First, selection of sound invoices is one way the lender safeguards itself. Second, if the buyer of the goods does not pay the invoice, the lender still has recourse against the borrowing firm. Third, additional protection is afforded the lender because the loan generally will be for less than 100 percent of the pledged receivables; for example, the lender might advance the borrowing firm only 85 percent of the amount of the pledged invoices. The percent advanced depends on the quality of the accounts pledged.

Procedure for Factoring Accounts Receivable. The procedures used in factoring receivables are somewhat different from those used in pledging. Again, an agreement between the seller and the factor specifies legal obligations and procedural arrangements. When the receivables seller gets an order from a customer, a credit approval slip is written and immediately sent to the factoring company for a credit check. If the factor approves the credit, shipment is made and the invoice is stamped to notify the customer to make payment directly to the factoring company. If the factor does not approve the sale, the receivables seller generally refuses to fill the order; if the firm makes the sale anyway, the factor will not buy the account.

The factor normally performs three functions: (1) credit checking, (2) lending, and (3) risk bearing. Consider a typical factoring situation: The goods are shipped, and even though payment is not due for 30 days, the factor immediately makes funds available to the borrower (the firm selling the goods).

Factoring normally is a continuous process instead of a single cycle. The firm that sells the goods receives an order; it transmits this order to the factor for approval; when it receives approval, the firm ships the goods; the factor advances the invoice amount minus withholdings to the selling firm; the buyer (customer) pays the factor when payment is due; and the factor periodically remits any excess funds to the selling firm. Once a routine has been established, a continuous circular flow of goods and funds takes place between the selling firm, the buyers of the goods, and the factor. Thus, once the factoring agreement is in force, funds from this source are *spontaneous* in the sense that an increase in sales automatically generates additional credit.

Visa and MasterCard represent prime examples of nonrecourse factoring. When you purchase from a retailer such as Wal-Mart using Visa or MasterCard, the retailer is paid only 95 to 97 percent of the invoice by these credit companies. The reason the 3 to 5 percent discount is charged by Visa and MasterCard is that they provide credit-checking services and suffer any losses resulting from customer nonpayment, which means that the retailer does not incur these costs.

Cost of Receivables Financing. Accounts receivable pledging and factoring are convenient and advantageous, but they can be costly. The credit-checking and risk-bearing fee is 1 percent to 5 percent of the amount of invoices accepted by the factor, and it can be even more if the receivables represent poor credit risks. The cost of money is reflected in the interest rate (usually 2 to 3 percentage points over the prime rate) charged on the unpaid balance of the funds advanced by the factor.

factoring The outright sale of receivables.

Evaluation of Receivables Financing. It cannot be said categorically that accounts receivable financing is either a good way or a bad way to raise funds. Among the advantages is, first, the flexibility of this source of financing: As the firm's sales expand, more financing is needed, but a larger volume of invoices, and hence a larger amount of receivables financing, is generated automatically. Second, receivables can be used as security for loans that otherwise would not be granted. Third, factoring can provide the services of a credit department that otherwise might be available only at a higher cost.

Accounts receivable financing also has disadvantages. First, when invoices are numerous and relatively small in rupee amount, the administrative costs be excessive. Second, because receivables represent the firm's most liquid noncash assets, some trade creditors might refuse to sell on credit to a firm that factors or pledges its receivables on the grounds that this practice weakens the firm's financial strength.

Future Use of Receivables Financing. It is easy to make a prediction at this point: In the future, accounts receivable financing will increase in relative importance. Computer technology has advanced to the point where credit records of individuals and firms are kept on electronic media. For example, one device used by retailers consists of a box that, when an individual's magnetic credit card is inserted, gives a signal that the credit is good and that a bank is willing to "buy" the receivable created as soon as the store completes the sale. The cost of handling invoices will be reduced greatly over present-day costs because the new systems will be so electronically sophisticated. This will make it possible to use accounts receivable financing for very small sales, and it will reduce the cost of all receivables financing. The net result will be a marked expansion of accounts receivable financing.

Strategies with Accounts Receivable Often, companies are faced with the situation of having to decide on the question of having a tight policy for receivables, combined with a discount scheme, and also the impact all this will have on the sales, profits and bad debts. The estimations for sales under various schemes will be based on market intelligence and past experience. While there is no guarantee that the estimations will turn out to be correct, one has to have a starting point for taking decisions.

Example

Suppose a company has an existing level of sales of ₹35,00,000. The company is currently making a profit on sales of 9%, which is likely to continue. There is a proposal for a tighter credit policy involving narrowing of the receivables period from the present 36 days to a strict 30 days. In addition, the company proposes to offer a discount of 1% for payment within 10 days, failing which the customers are expected to pay in 30 days (terms 1/10, 30). Currently, the company has a bad-debt level of 2%, which is likely to come down to 1.5% as a result of the changes suggested. The cost of capital relevant for the calculation of interest on accounts receivable investment is 11%, say. Under the new policy, sales are likely to come down to ₹ 33,00,000 overall, with a third of that availing discount. The profit margin is likely to remain the same. Should the company go in for the proposed change on purely financial considerations? See Exhibit 16.3.

EXHIBIT 16.3

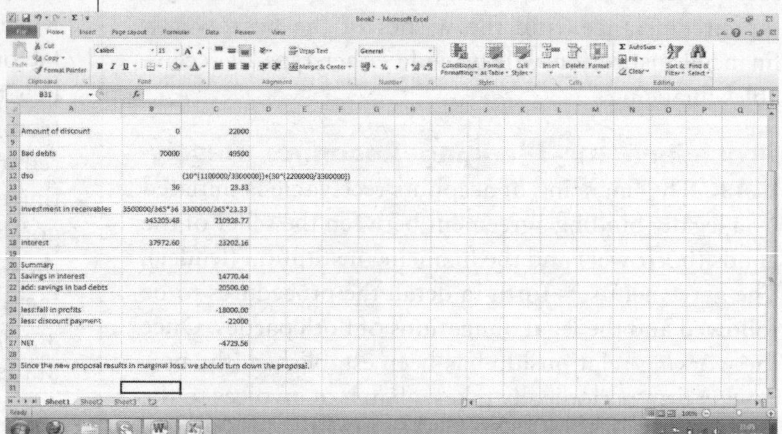

	A	B	C
8	Amount of discount	0	22000
10	Bad debts	70000	49500
12	dso		(10*(1100000/3300000))+(30*(2200000/3300000))
13		36	23.33
15	investment in receivables	3500000/365*36	3300000/365*23.33
16		345205.48	210928.77
18	interest	37972.60	23202.16
20	Summary		
21	Savings in interest		14770.44
22	add: savings in bad debts		20500.00
24	less:fall in profits		-18000.00
25	less: discount payment		-22000
27	NET		-4729.56
29	Since the new proposal results in marginal loss, we should turn down the proposal.		

Note: The Excel template for the above illustration is available online (Example 16.2)

In making the above calculations, certain aspects have been reckoned:

- One third of sales will avail discount. So, ₹ 11,00,000 worth of sales will avail discount. Since discount is paid for payment within ten days, it is assumed that all customers who avail discount will pay on the 10th day.
- The other two-third sales will have a receivable period of 30 days. So the two together will have a DSO of 23.33 days.
- This DSO is then used for calculating average investment in receivables.
- The new proposal results in gains in respect of savings in interest and reduction in bad debts. But the proposed change would also mean a fall in profits and a new expenditure on discounts. On balance, it is not found worthwhile.

16-3b Inventory Financing

A substantial amount of credit is secured by business inventories. If a firm is a relatively good credit risk, the mere existence of the inventory might be a sufficient basis for its receiving an unsecured loan. However, if the firm is a *relatively poor risk*, the lending institution might insist on security in the form of a *lien*, or legal claim, against the inventory. Methods for using inventory as security are discussed in this section.

Blanket Liens. The *inventory blanket lien* gives the lending institution a lien against the borrower's entire inventory. However, the borrower controls the inventory and is free to sell products in the course of its normal operations, which means that the value of the collateral can be reduced below the level that existed when the loan was granted. A blanket lien generally is used when the inventory that is put up as collateral is relatively low priced, fast moving, and difficult to identify individually.

Trust Receipts. Because of the inherent weakness of the blanket lien, another procedure for inventory financing has been developed—the *trust receipt*, which is an instrument acknowledging that the goods are held in trust for the lender. Under this method, the borrowing firm, as a condition for receiving funds from the lender, signs and delivers a trust receipt for the goods. The goods can be stored in a public warehouse or held on the premises of the borrower. The trust receipt states that the goods are held in trust for the lender or are segregated on the borrower's premises on the lender's behalf, and that any proceeds from the sale of the goods must be transmitted to the lender at the end of each day. Automobile dealer financing is a good example of trust receipt financing.

One defect of trust receipt financing is the requirement that a trust receipt be issued for specific goods. For example, if the security is automobiles in a dealer's inventory, the trust receipts must indicate the cars by registration number. To validate its trust receipts, the lending institution must send someone to the borrower's premises periodically to see that the auto numbers are listed correctly, because auto dealers who are in financial difficulty have been known to sell cars backing trust receipts and then use the funds for other operations rather than to repay the bank. Problems are compounded if the borrower has a number of different locations, especially if they are separated geographically from the lender. To offset these inconveniences, *warehousing* has come into wide use as a method of securing loans with inventory.

Warehouse Receipts. Warehouse receipt financing is another way to use inventory as security. A *public warehouse* is an independent third-party operation engaged in the business of storing goods. Items that require aging, such as tobacco and liquor, are often financed and stored in public warehouses. When the inventory products used as collateral are moved to public warehouses, the financing arrangement is termed *terminal warehousing*. Sometimes terminal warehousing is not practical because of the bulkiness of goods and the expense of transporting them to and from the borrower's premises. In such cases, a *field warehouse* might be established on the borrower's grounds. To provide inventory supervision, the lending institution employs a third party in the arrangement, called the *field warehousing company*, which acts as its agent.

Field warehousing can be illustrated by a simple example. Suppose a firm that has iron stacked in an open yard on its premises needs a loan. A field warehousing concern can place a temporary fence around the iron, erect a sign stating, "This is a field warehouse supervised by the Smith Field Warehousing Corporation," and then assign an employee to supervise and control the fenced-in inventory.

This example illustrates the three essential elements for the establishment of a field warehouse: (1) public notification, (2) physical control of the inventory, and (3) supervision by a custodian of the field warehousing concern. When the field warehousing operation is relatively small, the third condition is sometimes violated by hiring an employee of the borrower to supervise the warehoused inventory. This practice is viewed as undesirable by most lenders, because there is no control over the collateral by a person who is independent of the borrowing firm.[11]

- **Acceptable Products.** Products that are relatively nonperishable and are sold in well-developed, organized markets are considered most acceptable for warehousing arrangements. Nonperishability protects the lender if it has to take over the security. For this reason, a bank would not make a field warehousing loan on perishables such as fresh fish. However, frozen fish, which can be stored for a long time, can be field warehoused.
- **Cost of Financing.** The fixed costs of a field warehousing arrangement are relatively high; such financing therefore is not suitable for a very small firm. If a field warehousing company sets up a field warehouse, it typically will set a minimum charge per year, plus about 1 to 2 percent of the amount of credit extended to the borrower. Furthermore, the financing institution will charge an interest rate of 2 to 3 percentage points over the prime rate. An efficient field warehousing operation generally requires a fairly large inventory (often greater than ₹1 million).
- **Evaluation of Inventory Financing.** The use of inventory financing, especially field warehouse financing, as a source of funds has many advantages. First, the amount of funds available is flexible because the financing is tied to the growth of inventories, which in turn is related directly to financing needs. Second, the field warehousing arrangement increases the acceptability of inventory as loan collateral; some inventories simply would not be accepted by a bank as security without such an arrangement. Third, the necessity for inventory control and safekeeping, as well as the use of specialists in warehousing, often results in improved warehouse practices, which in turn save handling costs, insurance charges, theft losses, and so forth. Thus, field warehousing companies often save money for firms despite the costs of financing that we have discussed. The major disadvantages of field warehousing include the paperwork; physical separation requirements; and, for small firms, the fixed-cost element.

KEY CONCEPTS FOR MANAGING SHORT-TERM LIABILITIES

To conclude this chapter, we summarize some concepts that were discussed.

- A variety of sources of short-term credit exist. Examples of short-term debt include accruals, which arise because firms do not pay salaries to employees daily; trade credit, which represents purchases from suppliers; short-term bank loans, which include lines of credit; and commercial paper, which is unsecured debt issued by large, financially strong companies.
- The percentage cost of credit per period, r_{PER}, is based on both the rupee cost associated with the credit and the amount of the borrowed funds that is available for use. Accruals and a portion of trade credit (the portion associated with cash discounts) are considered "free" in the sense that specific interest is not paid for using these types of credit. These are also considered spontaneous in the sense that the amount a firm uses automatically increases and decreases as a result of increases and decreases in normal business operations. Some form of interest is associated with other forms of short-term credit.
- Both accounts receivable and inventory are considered good collateral for short-term loans, because they are liquid operating assets. Accounts receivable represent sales that have been made, but for which the cash has not been collected. Thus, the accounts receivable balance is an indication of the cash that the firm expects to collect (be paid) in the near future. Inventory represents products that the firm expects to sell in the near term. The attractiveness of inventory as collateral depends on its characteristics. Nonperishable inventory that is easy to sell is considered to be better collateral than hard-to-sell inventory that is perishable.

[11]The absence of independent control was the main cause of a breakdown that resulted in more than ₹200 million of losses on loans to the Allied Crude Vegetable Oil Company by Bank of America and other banks. American Express Field Warehousing Company was handling the operation, but it hired men from Allied's own staff as custodians. Their dishonesty was not discovered because of another breakdown—the fact that the American Express touring inspector did not actually take a physical inventory of the warehouses. As a consequence, the swindle was not discovered until losses running into the hundreds of millions of rupees had been suffered.

MULTIPLE CHOICE QUESTIONS

1. As the firm's operations expand,
   - **a.** Accruals go up
   - **b.** Accruals come down
   - **c.** Accruals remain the same
   - **d.** Accruals will have nothing to do with expansion of operations
2. Trade credit
   - **a.** Expands spontaneously with expansion of operation
   - **b.** Remains the same with expansion of operation
   - **c.** Has a more than proportionate increase as operations go up
   - **d.** None of the above
3. An overdraft facility
   - **a.** Is exactly like a loan
   - **b.** Becomes a loan once the company borrows beyond its available balance
   - **c.** No interest is charged on the amount
   - **d.** None of the above
4. Commercial paper
   - **a.** Is an instrument of long term debt
   - **b.** Is an instrument of working capital loan issued by small companies
   - **c.** Is an instrument of working capital loan issued by large companies to a select group of takers
   - **d.** Is an instrument of working capital loan issued by large companies like a public issue of debt
5. The cost of Accounts Payable is
   - **a.** Discount divided by Invoice price
   - **b.** Discount percentage
   - **c.** Discount dividend by (invoice value –discount)
   - **d.** None of the above
6. In a system of add-on interest,
   - **a.** Interest is included in the equal instalments payable
   - **b.** Interest is paid at the beginning
   - **c.** Interest is added to principal
   - **d.** None of the above
7. Interest for bank overdraft is paid
   - **a.** By debiting the account concerned
   - **b.** By separate interest payment
   - **c.** Interest itself is treated as a new loan
   - **d.** None of the above
8. Rupee cost of credit per period is
   - **a.** Based on rupee cost of borrowing available
   - **b.** Based on bank interest rates
   - **c.** Both a and b
   - **d.** None of the above
9. The following is considered as good collateral for short-term loans
   - **a.** Inventory
   - **b.** Fixed assets
   - **c.** Accounts receivable
   - **d.** Both a and c
10. Within the inventory the following is considered as better collateral
    - **a.** Perishable inventory
    - **b.** Long-term inventory
    - **c.** Non-perishable inventory
    - **d.** All of the above

Answers:

1.	(a)	2.	(a)	3.	(b)	4.	(d)	5.	(d)
6.	(a)	7.	(a)	8.	(c)	9.	(c)	10.	(b)

PROBLEMS

For more problems, visit CourseMate for CFIN at www.cengagebrain.com

16-1 If a firm buys on terms of 3/15, net 45, what is the APR of its nonfree trade credit? What is the effective annual rate, r_{EAR}?

16-2 What is the APR and r_{EAR} on the nonfree credit associated with credit terms of (a) 2/15, net 45 and (b) 3/5 net 45?

16-3 Ransco Corporation buys on terms of 2/10, net 30 but pays on Day 12 and still takes the discount. What is the APR of Ransco's nonfree trade credit?

16-4 Calculate the APR and r_{EAR} of nonfree trade credit associated with credit terms of 3/10, net 50 and 2.5/15, net 45 assuming that customers who do not take the discount (a) pay on the last due date and (b) delay payment until 10 days after the last due date.

16-5 Foster Industries sells on terms of 2/10, net 35. Gross sales last year were ₹450,000, and accounts receivable averaged ₹60,000. Half of Foster's customers paid on Day 10 and took discounts. (a) What are Foster's sales net of cash discounts taken? (b) What is the total *rupee* finance charge paid by the non-discount-paying customers? (c) What is the average collection period (DSO) for the nondiscount customers?

16-6 Chandigarh Advanced Technologies (CAT) is planning to get a 30-day, ₹150,000, simple interest loan from its bank. The quoted interest rate on the loan is 10 percent. Calculate the APR and r_{EAR} assuming the loan (a) has no compensating balance requirement and (b) has a 20 percent compensating balance requirement, and CAT currently holds no funds at the lending bank.

16-7 Periyapatnam Air Transportation (PAT) borrowed ₹80,000 for 60 days from its bank. The stated interest rate on the loan is 12 percent. Calculate the APR and r_{EAR} assuming the loan is a simple interest loan with (a) no compensating balance requirement and (b) a 25 percent compensating balance requirement, and CAT currently holds no funds at the lending bank.

16-8 Mohana Allied Products (MAP) must borrow ₹5.1 million to finance its working capital requirements. The bank has offered a 45-day simple interest loan with a quoted interest rate of 8 percent. Calculate the loan's APR and r_{EAR} assuming there is (a) no compensating balance requirement and (b) a 15 percent compensating balance requirement, which MAP must satisfy from the loan proceeds.

16-9 Refer to the information provided in Problem 16–8. To borrow the funds it needs, MAP had to agree to a simple interest loan that required a 15 percent compensating balance. Suppose that MAP needs ₹5.1 million to pay bills that are currently due. (a) If it does not normally maintain a cash balance at the bank, how much must MAP borrow? (b) If it normally maintains a cash ₹500,000 balance at the bank, how much must MAP borrow? In this case, what is the loan's APR and r_{EAR}?

16-10 Aarthi Boats can borrow ₹450,000 from its bank using a 30-day discount interest loan. The loan has a quoted interest of 9 percent and no compensating balance requirement. Compute the loan's APR and r_{EAR}.

16-11 Chowgule Leisure has a 40-day discount interest loan outstanding. The principal amount of the loan is ₹60,000, its quoted interest rate is 12 percent, and there is no compensating balance requirement. Compute the loan's APR and r_{EAR}.

16-12 MR Consulting recently borrowed from its bank using a 45-day discount interest loan that has a quoted interest equal to 10 percent. The loan requires MR to maintain a compensating balance equal to 20 percent of the amount borrowed. Prior to getting the loan, MR tried to maintain a checking account balance close to zero. (a) How much did MR borrow so that it was able pay ₹86,625 in bills that were due at the time the money was borrowed? (b) Compute the loan's APR and r_{EAR}.

16-13 United Sales Association (USA) recently borrowed ₹25,000 from its bank at a simple interest rate of 11 percent. The loan is for one year, and the loan agreement calls for the interest to be added to the amount borrowed and the total amount to be repaid in monthly installments. (a) What are the loan's monthly payments? (b) Compute the loan's APR and r_{EAR}.

16-14 X Xrays (XX) recently issued 180-day commercial paper with a face value of ₹100,000 and a simple interest rate of 7 percent. XX paid a transaction fee equal to 0.3 percent of the issue, which was taken out of the issue amount before the company received any funds. Compute the commercial paper's APR and r_{EAR}.

16-15 Yadav's Yearlings (YY) is able to raise funds by issuing commercial paper with a face value of ₹100,000. If commercial paper is issued, the simple interest rate would be 5 percent, the time to maturity would be 90 days, and YY would have to pay a transaction fee equal to 0.25 percent of the issue, which would be taken out of the issue amount. Compute the commercial paper's APR and r_{EAR}.

16–16 Cochin Corporation must raise ₹50,000 to support operations for the next 12 months. Cochin buys from its suppliers on terms of 2.5/20, net 80, and it normally pays on Day 20 to take the cash discounts, but it could forgo the discounts and pay on Day 90 to get the needed amount in the form of nonfree trade credit. Alternatively, Cochin can borrow form its bank using a one-year discount interest loan that has a 12 percent quoted interest rate and requires a 15 percent compensating balance. Cochin normally maintains a negligible deposit at the bank. What is the EAR of the lower cost source? Assume the face value of the bank loan is ₹50,000.

16–17 PDQ Enterprise can borrow from its bank using a one-year (a) simple interest loan with a 12 percent quoted rate and no compensating balance or (b) discount interest loan with a quoted rate equal to 10 percent that requires a 15 percent compensating balance. What is the EAR of the lower cost loan? PDQ normally tries to keep its checking account balance close to ₹0.

16–18 Refer to the information provided in Problem 16–17. Suppose PDQ needs ₹90,000 today to pay past-due bills. How much must PDQ borrow for each loan so that it has ₹90,000 available to pay the bills? How much of the total amount borrowed PDQ will actually be able to use?

16–19 BoGo Textbooks is evaluating two options for funding its working capital during the next year. Option 1 is borrowing from the bank using a 180-day discount interest loan, which has a quoted interest rate equal to 8 percent and requires a 20 percent compensating balance. BoGo normally maintains an average checking account balance of ₹10,000. Option 2 is to issue 180-day commercial paper, which has an annual interest equal to 9 percent and requires BoGo to pay a transactions fee equal to 0.3 percent. If the amount borrowed with either option is ₹200,000, which one should BoGo choose?

16–20 Refer to the information provided in Problem 16–19. Suppose BoGo actually needs ₹200,000 to finance working capital during the next year. (a) How much must BoGo borrow with each option so that ₹200,000 can be used to pay the bills? (b) Which option is better?

Managing Short-Term Liabilities (Financing)

Learning Outcomes

LO.1 Describe the characteristics of the various sources of short-term credit, including (a) accruals, (b) trade credit, (c) bank loans, and (d) commercial paper.

- Short-term credit includes debt instruments with original maturities equal to one year or less.
- Accruals increase spontaneously with the firm's operations, expanding during the height of the selling season and contracting when sales are slow. The two primary accruals are (1) wages owed to employees and (2) sales and withholding taxes owed to local, state, and national governments.
- Trade credit (accounts payable) represents amounts that are owed to suppliers of inventory or suppliers of other items that are purchased on credit from other firms. Generally, a portion of this type of credit is considered free, because there is no explicit cost to using it.
- Bank loans generally appear on the firm's balance sheets as notes payable. Such loans can be in the form of (1) a specific amount that is borrowed and must be repaid on a particular date; or (2) an overdraft, which represents an agreement with the bank that specifies the maximum amount of credit the firm can have outstanding at any time (much like credit cards for individuals).
- Commercial paper can best be described as an IOU that is issued by a large firm with outstanding credit. Investors in commercial paper do not receive interest payments; thus, they purchase this investment at a discount below the face value of the issue. The rupee return on commercial paper is the difference between its face value and its discounted market price.

LO.2 Discuss and compute the cost (both APR and r_{EAR}) of short-term credit.

- The cost of any type of financing is based on the amount of funds that actually can be used, or spent, by the firm and the total costs (in rupees) associated with such funds. To compute the cost of a short-term credit instrument, we must first determine r_{PER}, which is the percentage cost that the firm pays each period and is computed as: r_{PER} = (₹ cost of borrowing)/(₹ amount of usable funds). r_{PER} then is annualized by computing either the APR or the r_{EAR}. $APR = r_{PER} \times m$; $r_{EAR} = (1 + r_{PER})^m - 1.0$, where m is the number of borrowing periods in one year. APR is the non-compounded cost of credit, whereas r_{EAR} is the effective, or compounded, cost.

LO.3 Describe the procedures and benefits of using (a) accounts receivable and (b) inventory to obtain secured short-term loans.

- Both receivables and inventory are good forms of collateral for short-term financing that requires such security, because these assets are expected to be liquidated, and thus generate cash flows, in the short term.
- Receivables financing involves either pledging or factoring accounts receivable. Pledging receivables refers to the use of particular accounts as collateral for a short-term loan. When receivables are pledged, the lender generally has recourse against the borrower if one of the receivables customers does not pay. Factoring receivables involves selling accounts receivable to an organization called a factor. When receivables are factored, the lending firm often buys the credit accounts without recourse, which means that the factor takes the loss when one of the selling firm's credit customers does not pay.
- Inventory that is non-perishable and is sold in well-developed markets generally is the most acceptable collateral for secured short-term loans. Inventory financing arrangements include: (1) blanket liens, which require the borrowing firm to put up its entire inventory as collateral, but permit the borrower to retain control of the inventory; (2) trust receipts, which require the borrower to identify particular items as collateral and to notify the lender when these items are sold; and (3) warehouse receipts, which require the items that are used as collateral to be physically separated and taken out of the control of the borrower.

CHAPTER 16 REVIEW

Chapter 16 Key Concepts of Managing Short-Term Liabilities

- A variety of sources of short-term credit exist. Examples of short-term debt include accruals, which arise because firms do not pay salaries to employees each day; trade credit, which represents credit purchases from suppliers; short-term bank loans, which include lines of credit; and commercial paper, which is unsecured debt issued by large, financially strong companies.
- The percentage cost of credit per period, r_{PER}, is based on both the rupee cost associated with the credit and the amount of the borrowed funds that is available for use. Accruals and a portion of trade credit (the portion associated with cash discounts) are considered "free" in the sense that specific interest is not paid for using these types of credit. These are also considered spontaneous in the sense that the amount a firm uses automatically increases and decreases as a result of increases and decreases in normal business operations. Some form of interest is associated with most other forms of short-term credit.
- Both accounts receivable and inventory are considered good collateral for short-term loans, because they are liquid operating assets. Accounts receivable represent sales that have been made, but for which the cash has not been collected. Thus, the accounts receivable balance is an indication of the cash that the firm expects to collect (be paid) in the near future. Inventory represents products that the firm expects to sell in the near term. The attractiveness of inventory as collateral depends on its characteristics. Nonperishable inventory that is easy to sell is considered to be better than hard-to-sell inventory that is perishable.

Key Terms

LO.1

short-term credit Any liability originally scheduled for repayment within one year. *p. 281*

accruals Continually recurring short-term liabilities; liabilities such as wages and taxes that change spontaneously with operations. *p. 281*

trade credit The credit created when one firm buys on credit from another firm. *p. 281*

"free" trade credit Credit received during the discount period. *p. 282*

costly trade credit Credit taken in excess of "free" trade credit, whose cost is equal to the discount lost. *p. 282*

stretching accounts payable The practice of deliberately paying accounts payable late. *p. 282*

promissory note A document specifying the terms and conditions of a loan, including the amount, interest rate, and repayment schedule. *p. 282*

compensating balance (CB) A minimum checking account balance that a firm must maintain with a bank to borrow funds—generally 10 to 20 percent of the amount of loans outstanding. *p. 283*

overdraft An arrangement in which a bank agrees to lend up to a specified maximum amount of funds during a designated period. *p. 283*

revolving credit agreement (line) A formal, committed overdraft extended by a bank or other lending institution. *p. 283*

commitment fee A fee charged on the *unused* balance of a revolving credit agreement to compensate the bank for guaranteeing that the funds will be available when needed by the borrower; the fee normally is about 1/4 percent of the unused balance. *p. 283*

prime rate A published rate of interest charged by banks to short-term borrowers (usually large, financially secure corporations) with the best credit; rates on short-term loans sometimes are "pegged" to the prime rate. *p. 283*

commercial paper Unsecured, short-term promissory notes issued by large, financially sound firms to raise funds. *p. 284*

LO.2

simple interest loan Both the amount borrowed and the interest charged on that amount are paid at the maturity of the loan; there are no payments made before maturity. *p. 286*

face value The amount of the loan, or the amount borrowed; also called the *principal amount* of the loan. *p. 286*

quoted, or simple, interest rate The annual percentage rate (APR) that is used to compute the interest rate per period (r_{PER}). *p. 286*

discount interest loan A loan in which the interest, which is calculated on the amount borrowed (principal), is paid at the beginning of the loan period; interest is paid in advance. *p. 286*

add-on interest Interest that is calculated and then added to the amount borrowed to obtain the total rupee amount to be paid back in equal installments. *p. 287*

LO.3

secured loans Loans backed by collateral; for short-term loans, the collateral often is inventory, receivables, or both. *p. 289*

Uniform Commercial Code A system of standards that simplifies procedures for establishing loan security. *p. 289*

pledging receivables Using accounts receivable as collateral for a loan. *p. 290*

recourse The lender can seek payment from the borrowing firm when receivables' accounts used to secure a loan are uncollectible. *p. 290*

factoring The outright sale of receivables. *p. 290*

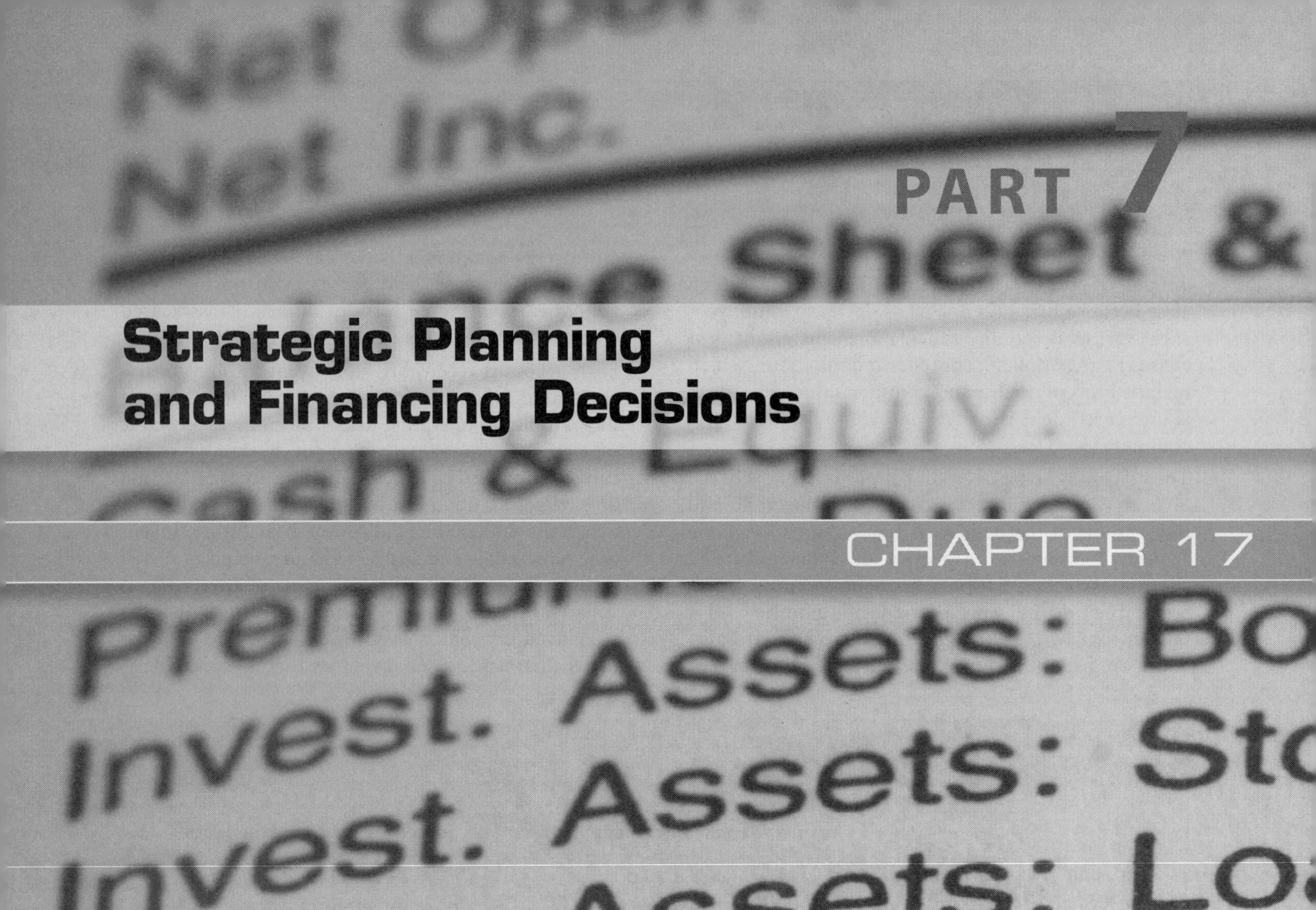

PART 7

Strategic Planning and Financing Decisions

CHAPTER 17

Financial Planning and Control

Learning Outcomes

LO.1 Construct simple pro forma financial statements that can be used to forecast financing and investment needs.

LO.2 Discuss some of the complications that management should consider when constructing pro forma financial statements.

LO.3 Describe and compute (a) operating breakeven and operating leverage, (b) financial breakeven and financial leverage, and (c) total leverage.

LO.4 Discuss how knowledge of leverage is used in the financial forecasting and control process and why financial planning is critical to firm survival.

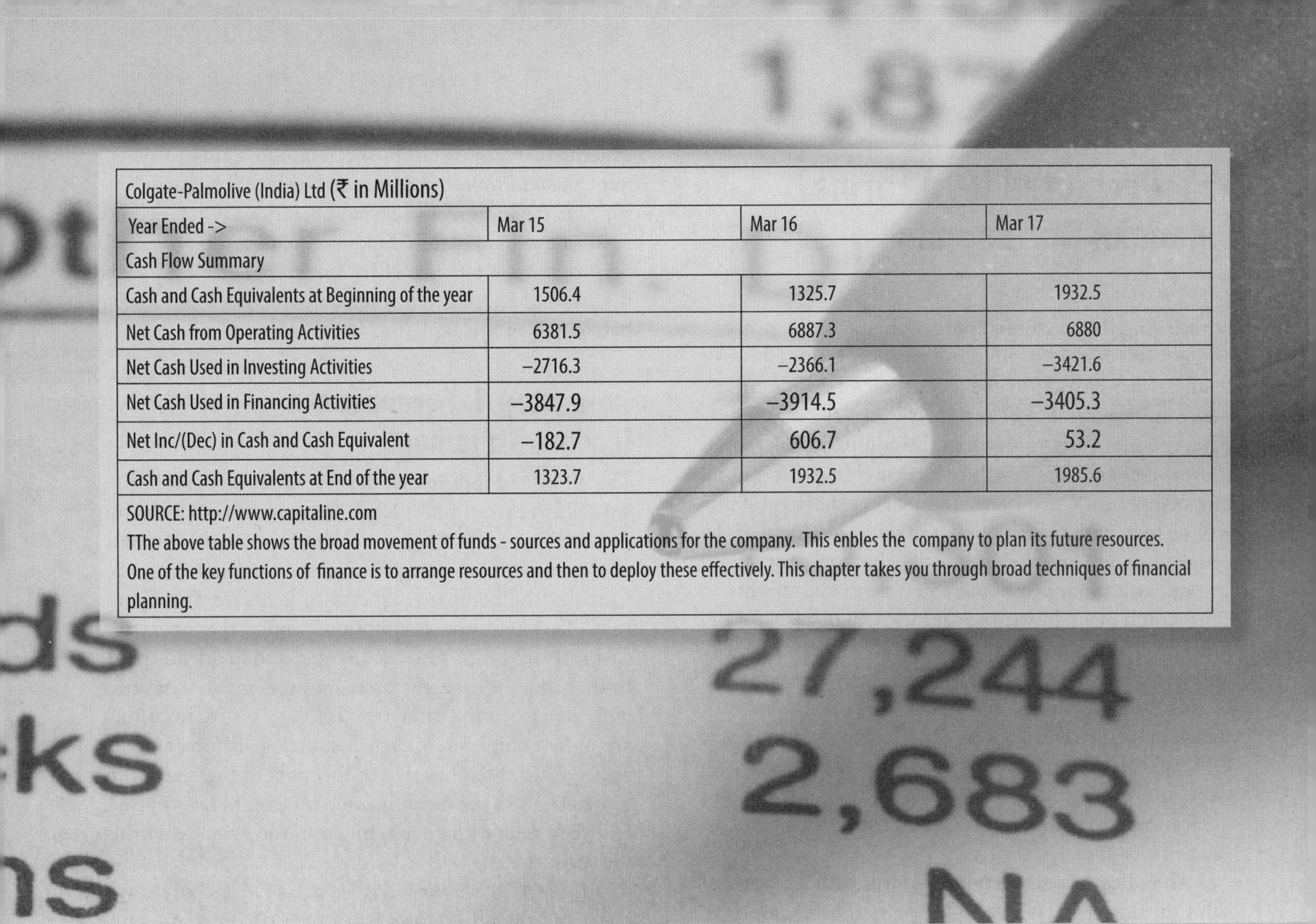

Colgate-Palmolive (India) Ltd (₹ in Millions)			
Year Ended ->	Mar 15	Mar 16	Mar 17
Cash Flow Summary			
Cash and Cash Equivalents at Beginning of the year	1506.4	1325.7	1932.5
Net Cash from Operating Activities	6381.5	6887.3	6880
Net Cash Used in Investing Activities	−2716.3	−2366.1	−3421.6
Net Cash Used in Financing Activities	−3847.9	−3914.5	−3405.3
Net Inc/(Dec) in Cash and Cash Equivalent	−182.7	606.7	53.2
Cash and Cash Equivalents at End of the year	1323.7	1932.5	1985.6

SOURCE: http://www.capitaline.com

TThe above table shows the broad movement of funds - sources and applications for the company. This enbles the company to plan its future resources. One of the key functions of finance is to arrange resources and then to deploy these effectively. This chapter takes you through broad techniques of financial planning.

Daniel Padavona/Shutterstock.com

The **financial planning** process begins with forecasts of financial statements to detemine the firm's future financing and investment needs. Once the base case forecasted financial statements have been prepared, managers want to know (1) how realistic the results are, (2) how to attain the results, and (3) what impact changes in operations would have on the forecasts. At this stage, which is the **financial control** phase, the firm is concerned with implementing the financial plans and dealing with the feedback and adjustment processes that are necessary to ensure the goals of the firm are pursued appropriately. In this chapter, we show how the information obtained through financial statement analysis (discussed in Chapter 2) can be used for financial planning and control of future operations, which are vital to the future success of the firm.

Study Tools

Problems are found at the end of this chapter

+

Login to **CourseMate** for **CFIN** at **CengageBrain.com** for additional problems and other study tools!

17-1 Projected (Pro Forma) Financial Statements

Forecasting is an essential part of the planning process, and a **sales forecast** is the most important ingredient of financial forecasting. If the sales forecast is inaccurate, the consequences can be serious. First, if the market expands significantly more than the company has geared up for, demand likely will not be met, customers will buy competitors' products, and market share probably will be lost, perhaps for good. On the other hand, if the projections are overly optimistic, the company could end up with too much plant, equipment, and inventory. This would mean low turnover ratios, high costs for depreciation and storage, and the likelihood that obsolete and unusable inventory will have to be written off. All of this would result in a low rate of return on equity, which in turn would depress the company's stock price. Of course, if an unnecessary expansion is financed with debt, the firm's problems will be compounded. Thus, an accurate sales forecast is critical to the well-being of the firm.

The sales forecast generally starts with a review of sales during the past five to 10 years. For example, to form its sales forecasts, U.P. Textiles considers projections of economic activity, competitive conditions, and product development and distribution in the markets in which it currently operates, as well as in the markets the company plans to enter in the future. Based on its historical sales trend for the past five years, U.P's planning committee has projected a 10 percent growth rate for sales during 2015.

Any forecast of financial requirements involves (1) determining how much money the firm will need during a given period; (2) determining how much money (funds) the firm will generate internally during the same period; and (3) subtracting the funds generated internally from the required funds to determine the *additional funds needed* (external financing) to support the level of forecasted operations. One method used to estimate external requirements is the *projected, or pro forma, balance sheet method*. The basic steps that should be followed when constructing a pro forma balance sheet are explained in this section.

financial planning The projection of sales, income, and assets, as well as the determination of the resources needed to achieve these projections.

financial control The phase in which financial plans are implemented; control deals with the feedback and adjustment process required to ensure adherence to plans and modification of plans because of unforeseen changes.

sales forecast A forecast of a firm's unit and rupee sales for some future period; generally based on recent sales trends plus forecasts of the economic prospects for the nation, region, industry, and so forth.

projected (pro forma) balance sheet method A method of forecasting financial requirements based on forecasted financial statements.

17-1a Step 1: Forecast the Income Statement

The **projected (pro forma) balance sheet method** begins with a forecast of sales. Next, the income statement for the coming year is forecast to obtain an initial estimate of the amount of retained earnings (internal equity financing) the company expects to generate during the year. This requires assumptions about the operating cost ratio, tax rate, interest charges, and dividends paid. In the simplest case, the assumption is made that costs will increase at the same rate as sales; in situations that are more complicated, each cost change is forecast separately. Still, the objective of this part of the analysis is to determine how much income the company will earn and then retain for reinvestment in the business during the forecast year.

Table 17.1 shows U.P's actual 2014 income statement and the initial forecast of the 2015 income statement if the firm grows at 10 percent. To simplify our analysis, we assume that U.P. currently *operates at full capacity,* which means it will need to expand its plant capacity by 10 percent in 2015 to handle the increase in operations. As a result, in Table 17.1, *all* operating costs, including depreciation, are 10 percent greater than their 2014 levels. The result is that earnings before interest and taxes (EBIT) are forecast to be ₹143 million in 2015, which is 10 percent higher than in 2014 ($EBIT_{2014}$ = ₹130 million).

To complete the initial forecast of 2015 income, we assume no change in the external financing of the firm, because at this point it is not known whether additional financing is needed. Thus, *initially* we keep the 2015 interest expense and dividends the same as they were in 2014; that is, ₹40 million and ₹29 million, respectively. Of course, we know that both of these payments will increase if U.P. determines that it needs to raise additional funds by issuing new bonds and new shares of stock. At this stage of the forecasting process, however, we do not know whether such external financing is needed to support U.P's projected growth in sales.

From the initial forecast, we see that ₹32.8 million rupees are *expected* to be added to retained earnings in

TABLE 17.1 U.P. Textiles: Actual 2014 and Projected 2015 Income Statements (₹ in Millions, except per-share data)

	2014 Actual Results	Forecast Basis[a]	2015 Initial Forecast
Net sales	₹1,500.0	× 1.10	₹1,650.0
Cost of goods sold	(1,230.0)	× 1.10	(1,353.0)
Gross profit	₹270.0		₹297.0
Fixed operating costs except depreciation	(90.0)	× 1.10	(99.0)
Depreciation	(50.0)	× 1.10	(55.0)
Earnings before interest and taxes (EBIT)	₹130.0		₹143.0
Less: Interest	(40.0)	→	(40.0)[b]
Earnings before taxes (EBT)	₹ 90.0		₹103.0
Taxes (40%)	(36.0)		(41.2)
Net income	₹54.0		₹61.8
Common dividends	(29.0)	→	(29.0)[b]
Addition to retained earnings	₹ 25.0		₹32.8
Earnings per share	₹2.16		₹2.47
Dividends per share	₹1.16		₹1.16
Number of common shares (millions)	25.0		25.0

[a]×1.10 indicates "times (1 + g)"; it is used for items that grow proportionally with sales.
[b]Indicates a figure carried over from 2014 for the preliminary forecast. See discussion for explanation.

2015. This addition to retained earnings represents the amount U.P. is expected to invest in itself (i.e., internally generated funds) to support growth in operations in 2015, assuming that no additional (external) financing is used. To determine whether external financing is required, we must evaluate the impact this level of investment will have on U.P.'s forecasted 2015 balance sheet.

17-1b Step 2: Forecast the Balance Sheet

If we assume the 2014 end-of-year asset levels were just sufficient to support 2014 operations (i.e. U.P. operated at full capacity), then if U.P. is to grow its sales in 2015, its assets must also grow. To simplify our analysis, we assume that each asset account, including plant and equipment, must grow at the same rate as sales (i.e., 10 percent).

Further, if U.P.'s assets increase, its liabilities and equity must also increase, because the additional assets must be financed in some manner. Some liabilities will increase *spontaneously* due to normal business relationships. For example, as sales increase, so will U.P's purchases of raw materials, and these larger purchases will spontaneously lead to higher levels of accounts payable. Similarly, a higher level of operations will require more labor, which will increase accruals. In general, current liabilities that change naturally (spontaneously) with changes in sales provide **spontaneously generated funds** that tend to change at the same rate as sales. On the other hand, notes payable, long-term bonds, and common stock will not change spontaneously with sales. Rather, the levels of these accounts depend on conscious financing decisions that are made once U.P. determines how much external financing it needs to support the projected operations. Therefore, until it is determined whether external financing is needed, the account balances for notes payable, long-term debt, and common stock remain unchanged from their 2014 levels.

Table 17.2 contains U.P's 2014 actual balance sheet and an initial forecast of its 2015 balance sheet. The mechanics of the balance sheet forecast are similar to those used to develop the forecasted income statement. First, those balance sheet accounts that are expected to increase directly with sales are multiplied by 1.10 to obtain the initial 2015 forecasts. Because we assume that all assets must grow at the same rate as sales, we multiply each asset account by 1.10. The result—₹929.5 million—represents the total amount U.P. needs to invest in assets to support forecasted 2015 sales.

Next, the spontaneously

spontaneously generated funds Funds that are obtained from routine business transactions.

TABLE 17.2 U.P. Textiles: Actual 2014 and Projected 2015 Balance Sheets (₹ in Millions)

	2014 Actual Results	Forecast Basis[a]	2015 Initial Forecast	Change
Cash	₹15.0	× 1.10	₹16.5	₹1.5
Accounts receivable	180.0	× 1.10	198.0	18.0
Inventory	270.0	× 1.10	297.0	27.0
Total current assets	₹465.0		₹511.5	
Net plant and equipment	380.0	× 1.10	418.0	38.0
Total assets	₹845.0		₹929.5	₹84.5
Accounts payable	₹30.0	× 1.10	₹33.0	3.0
Accruals	60.0	× 1.10	66.0	6.0
Notes payable	40.0	→	40.0[b]	0.0
Total current liabilities	₹130.0		₹139.0	
Long-term bonds	300.0	→	300.0[b]	0.0
Total liabilities	₹430.0		₹439.0	
Common stock (26.27 million shares)	130.0	→	130.0[b]	0.0
Retained earnings	285.0	+₹32.8[c]	317.8	32.8
Total owners' equity	₹415.0		₹447.8	
Total liabilities and equity	₹845.0		₹886.8	₹41.8
Additional funds needed (AFN)			₹42.7[d]	₹42.7

[a]× 1.10 indicates "times (1 + g)"; it is used for items that grow proportionally with sales.
[b]Indicates a figure carried over from 2014 for the initial forecast.
[c]The ₹32.8 million represents the "addition to retained earnings" from the 2015 projected income statement given in Table 17.1.
[d]The additional funds needed (AFN) is computed by subtracting the forecasted amount of total liabilities and equity from the forecasted amount of total assets.

increasing liabilities (accounts payable and accruals) are forecast by increasing each of these accounts by 10 percent. At this stage of the forecast, however, those liability and equity accounts whose values reflect conscious management decisions (notes payable, long-term bonds, and stock) *initially are not changed from* their 2014 levels. Thus, the amount of 2015 notes payable *initially* is set at its 2014 level of ₹40.0 million, the long-term bonds account is forecast at ₹300.0 million, and so forth. The forecasted 2015 level of retained earnings will be the 2014 level plus the forecasted addition to retained earnings, which was computed as ₹32.8 million in the projected income statement that we created in Step 1 (Table 17.1).

Because the forecast of total assets in Table 17.2 is ₹929.5 million, U.P. must add ₹84.5 million of new assets (compared to 2014 assets) to support the higher sales level expected in 2015. However, according to the initial forecast on the 2015 balance sheet, the total liabilities and equity sum to ₹886.8 million, which is an increase of only ₹41.8 million. Therefore, the forecasted amount of total assets exceeds the forecasted amount of liabilities and equity by ₹42.7 million = ₹929.5 million − ₹886.8 million. This indicates that ₹42.7 million of the forecasted increase in total assets will not be financed by liabilities that spontaneously increase with sales (accounts payable and accruals), or by an increase in retained earnings. U.P. can raise the additional ₹42.7 million, which we designate **additional funds needed (AFN)**, by borrowing from the bank (notes payable), by issuing long-term bonds, by selling new common stock, or by some combination of these actions.

additional funds needed (AFN) Funds that a firm must raise externally through new borrowing or by selling new stock.

The initial forecast of U.P.'s financial statements has shown us that (1) higher sales must be supported by higher asset levels; (2) some of the asset increases can be financed by spontaneous increases in accounts payable and accruals as well as by an increased retained earnings; and (3) any shortfall must be financed from external sources, either by borrowing or by selling new stock.

17-1c **Step 3: Raising the Additional Funds Needed**

U.P's financial manager will base the decision of exactly how to raise the ₹42.7 million AFN on several factors, including its ability to handle additional debt, conditions in the financial markets, and restrictions imposed by existing debt agreements. Regardless of how U.P. raises the ₹42.7 million, the initial forecasts of both the income statement and the balance sheet will be affected. If U.P. takes on new debt, its interest expenses will increase; if additional shares of common stock are sold, *total* dividend payments will increase, assuming that the *same dividend per share* is paid to all common stockholders. Each of these changes, which we term *financing feedbacks,* will affect the amount of additional retained earnings that was originally forecast in Step 1, which in turn will affect the amount of AFN that was computed in Step 2.

17-1d **Step 4. Accounting for Financing Feedbacks**

If U.P. raises the ₹42.7 million AFN by issuing new debt and new common stock, it will find that both the interest expense and the total dividend payments are higher than the amounts contained in the forecasted income statement shown in Table 17.1. Consequently, after adjusting for the higher interest and dividend payments, the forecasted addition to retained earnings will be lower than the initial forecast of ₹32.8 million. Because retained earnings will be lower than projected, a financing shortfall will exist even after the original AFN of ₹42.7 million is considered. Thus, U.P. must raise more than ₹42.7 million to account for the **financing feedbacks** that affect the amount of internal financing expected to be generated from the increase in operations. To determine the amount of external financing that is actually needed, we must adjust the initial forecasts of both the income statement (Step 1) and the balance sheet (Step 2) to reflect the impact of raising the additional external financing. This process must be repeated until AFN = 0 in Table 17.2, which means that Steps 1 and 2 might have to be repeated several times to fully account for the financing feedbacks.

Table 17.3 contains the adjusted 2015 preliminary forecasts for the income statement and the balance sheet of U.P. Textiles after all of the financing effects (feedbacks) are considered. To generate the adjusted forecasts, it is assumed that of the total external funds needed, 65 percent will be raised by selling new common stock at ₹23 per share, 15 percent will be borrowed from the bank at an interest rate of 7 percent, and 20 percent will be raised by selling long-term bonds with a coupon interest rate equal to 10 percent. Under these conditions, it can be seen from Table 17.3 that U.P. actually needs ₹45.0 million to support the forecasted increase in operations, not the ₹42.7 million contained in the initial forecast (Table 17.2). The additional ₹2.3 million is needed because the added amounts of debt and common stock will cause interest and dividend payments to increase, which in turn will decrease the contribution to retained earnings by ₹2.3 million compared to the initial forecast.

Equation 17.1 summarizes our discussion and provides a simple way to *estimate* the AFN for a firm that is operating at full capacity.

17.1

$$\text{Estimated AFN} = \begin{array}{c}\text{Forecasted}\\ \text{increase}\\ \text{in assets}\end{array} - \begin{array}{c}\text{Forecasted}\\ \text{increase}\\ \text{in liabilities}\end{array} - \begin{array}{c}\text{Forecasted}\\ \text{increase in}\\ \text{retained earnings}\end{array}$$

$$= [(TA_0 - SL_0) \times g] - [NI_0\,(1 + g) - D]$$

Here TA_0 represents existing assets (in 2014), SL_0 represents existing spontaneous liabilities (which include accounts payable and accruals), g is the forecasted growth in sales in 2015, NI_0 represents existing sales, and D is the amount of dividends expected to be paid out of forecasted earnings. For firms that pay out a constant proportion of earnings as dividends each year, $D = [NI_0\,(1 + g) \times (1 - P/O)]$, where P/O is the dividend payout ratio (P/O = Dividends/NI).

Using Equation 17.1 to estimate U.P's AFN when sales are expected to grow by 10 percent and the firm expects to pay the same dividend in 2015 as it did in 2014, we find

$$\text{Estimated AFN} = [₹845 - (₹30 + ₹60)](0.10) - [₹54(1.10) - ₹29]$$
$$= ₹75.5 - ₹30.4 = ₹45.1 \text{ million}$$

The estimated AFN given here is higher than the *initial* forecast of ₹42.7 million shown in Table 17.2 primarily because the initial forecast of AFN assumes that the firm's interest expense does not change,

financing feedbacks The effects on the income statement and balance sheet of actions taken to finance forecasted increases in assets.

TABLE 17.3 U.P. Textiles: 2015 Adjusted Forecast of Financial Statements (₹ in Millions)

	Initial Forecast	Adjusted Forecast	Financing Adjustment	
Income Statement[a]				
Earnings before interest and taxes (EBIT)	₹143.0	₹143.0		
Less: Interest	(40.0)	(41.4)	₹(1.4)	
Earnings before taxes (EBT)	₹103.0	101.6	(1.4)	
Taxes (40%)	(41.2)	(40.6)	0.6	
Net income	₹61.8	₹61.0	(0.8)	
Common dividends	(29.0)	(30.5)	(1.5)	
Addition to retained earnings	₹32.8	₹30.5	(2.3)[b]	
Earnings per share	₹2.47	₹2.32		
Dividends per share	₹1.16	₹1.16		
Number of common shares (millions)	25.00	26.27		
Balance Sheet[a]				
Total assets	₹929.5	₹929.5		
Accounts payable	₹33.0	₹33.0		
Accruals	66.0	66.0		
Notes payable	40.0	46.8	₹6.8	
Total current liabilities	₹139.0	₹145.8		
Long-term bonds	300.0	309.0	9.0	Total AFN = 45.0[c]
Total liabilities	₹439.0	₹454.8		
Common stock (26.27 million shares)	130.0	159.2	29.2	
Retained earnings	317.8	315.5	(2.3)[b]	
Total owners' equity	₹447.8	₹474.7		
Total liabilities and equity	₹886.8	₹929.5		
Initial amount of additional funds needed (AFN)			₹42.7	

[a]Because the operating section of the income statement and the asset section of the balance sheet are not affected by financing feedbacks, these sections are not shown in the table.

[b]The financing adjustment for the addition to retained earnings in the income statement is the same as the financing adjustment for retained earnings in the balance sheet.

[c]The total AFN (or external financing needs) equals the initial AFN of ₹42.7 million plus the ₹2.3 million decrease in retained earnings from the initial forecast. Thus the total external funds needed equal ₹45.0 million, of which ₹6.8 million will be from new bank notes, ₹9.0 million will come from issuing new bonds, and the remaining ₹29.2 million will be raised by issuing new common stock.

whereas the result produced by Equation 17.1 assumes the interest expense changes proportionally with the change in sales and net income. Note, however, that estimated AFN computation is close to the *final* forecast of AFN given in Table 17.3 (₹45 million).

17-1e **Analysis of the Forecast**

The 2015 forecast as developed here represents a preliminary forecast, because we have completed only the first stage of the entire forecasting process. Next, the projected statements must be analyzed to determine whether the forecast meets the firm's financial targets. If the statements do not meet the targets, then elements of the forecast must be changed.

Table 17.4 shows U.P's 2014 ratios plus the projected 2015 ratios based on the preliminary forecast and the industry average ratios. The firm's financial condition at the close of 2014 was weak, with many ratios being well below the industry averages. The preliminary final forecast for 2015, which assumes that U.P's past practices will continue into the future, shows an improved debt position. Nevertheless, the overall financial position still is somewhat weak, and this condition will persist unless management takes actions to

TABLE 17.4 U.P. Textiles: Key Ratios

	2014	Adjusted Preliminary 2015	Industry Average
Current ratio	3.6×	3.5×	4.1×
Inventory turnover	4.6×	5.6×	7.4×
Days sales outstanding (DSO)	43.2 days	43.2 days	32.1 days
Total assets turnover	1.8×	1.8×	2.1×
Debt ratio	50.9%	48.9%	42.0%
Times interest earned (TIE)	3.3×	3.5×	6.5×
Profit margin	3.6%	3.7%	4.9%
Return on assets (ROA)	6.4%	6.6%	10.3%
Return on equity (ROE)	13.0%	12.8%	17.7%

improve things.

U.P's management actually plans to take steps to improve its financial condition. The plans are to (1) close down certain operations, (2) modify the credit policy to reduce the collection period for receivables, and (3) better manage inventory so that products are turned over more often. These proposed operational changes will affect both the income statement and the balance sheet, so the preliminary forecast will have to be revised again to reflect the impact of such changes. When this process is complete, management will have its final forecast. To keep things simple, we do not show the final forecast here. Instead, for the remaining discussions we assume the preliminary forecast is not substantially different and use it as the final forecast for U.P's 2015 operations.

We have presented a simple method for constructing pro forma financial statements under rather restrictive conditions. In this section, we describe some other conditions that should be considered when creating forecasts.

17-2 Other Considerations in Forecasting

17-2a Excess Capacity

The construction of the 2015 forecasts for U.P. was based on the assumption that the firm's 2014 operations were at full capacity, so any increase in sales would require additional assets, especially plant and equipment. If U.P. did not operate at full capacity in 2014, then plant and equipment would only have to be increased if the additional sales (operations) forecasted in 2015 exceeded the unused capacity of the existing assets. For example, if U.P. actually utilized only 80 percent of its fixed assets' capacity to produce 2014 sales of ₹1,500 million, then

$$₹\ 1{,}500 \text{ million} = 0.80 \times (\text{plant capacity})$$

$$\text{Plant Capacity} = \frac{₹1{,}500 \text{ million}}{0.80} = ₹1{,}875 \text{ million}$$

In this case, U.P. could increase sales to ₹1,875 million, or by 25 percent of 2014 sales, before full capacity—the point where plant and equipment would have to be increased to achieve additional growth—was reached. If U.P. did not have to increase plant and equipment, fixed assets would remain at the 2014 level of ₹380 million, and depreciation and fixed operating costs would stay near ₹140 million. In this case, the AFN would actually be negative, which means that the amount of internally generated funds would be more than sufficient to support (finance) the forecasted 10 percent increase in sales in 2015. If this occurred, U.P. could increase the per-share dividend it pays to stockholders in 2015.

We can compute the sales capacity of the firm using Equation 17.2:

17.2

$$\text{Full capacity sales} = \frac{\text{Existing sales lavel}}{\left(\begin{array}{c}\text{Percent of capacity used}\\ \text{to generate existing sales lavel}\end{array}\right)}$$

In addition to the excess capacity of fixed assets,

the firm could have excesses in other assets that can be used to support increases in operations. For instance, we assume that U.P's inventory level at the end of 2014 probably was greater than it should have been. If this is true, some increase in 2015 forecasted sales could be absorbed by the above-normal inventory, and production would not have to be increased until inventory levels were reduced to normal. This would require no additional financing.

In general, excess capacity means less external financing is required to support increases in operations than would be needed if the firm had previously operated at full capacity.

17-2b **Economies of Scale**

There are economies of scale in the use of many types of assets, and when such economies occur, a firm's variable cost of goods sold ratio is likely to change as the size of the firm changes (either increases or decreases) substantially. Currently, U.P's variable cost ratio is 82 percent of sales; but the ratio might decrease to 80 percent of sales if operations increase significantly. If everything else is the same, changes in the variable cost ratio affect the addition to retained earnings, which in turn affects the amount of AFN.

17-2c **Lumpy Assets**

In many industries, technological considerations dictate that if a firm is to be competitive, it must add fixed assets in large, discrete units. Such assets often are referred to as **lumpy assets**. For example, in the paper industry, there are strong economies of scale in basic paper mill equipment, so when a paper company expands capacity, it must do so in large, lumpy increments. Lumpy assets primarily affect the turnover of fixed assets and, consequently, the financial requirements associated with expanding. For instance, if instead of ₹38 million, U.P. needed an additional ₹50 million in fixed assets to increase operations by 10 percent, the AFN would be much greater (₹57.6 million rather than ₹45.0 million). With lumpy assets, it is possible that a small projected increase in sales would require a significant increase in plant and equipment, which would require a large financial commitment.

werny/Shutterstock.com

17-3 **Financial Control—Budgeting and Leverage**[1]

In the previous section, we focused on financial forecasting, emphasizing how growth in sales requires additional investment in assets, which in turn generally requires the firm to raise new funds externally. In the sections that follow, we consider the planning and control systems used by financial managers when implementing the forecasts. The planning process can be enhanced by examining the effects of changing operations on the firm's profitability, both from the standpoint of profits from operations and from the standpoint of profitability after financing effects are considered. In the next few sections, we will look at some of the areas financial managers evaluate to provide information about the effects of changing operations. To simplify our discussions, we assume that the firm has sufficient excess capacity to support any additional sales that are mentioned in the examples.

17-3a **Operating Breakeven Analysis**

The relationship between sales volume and *operating profitability* is explored in cost-volume-profit planning, or operating breakeven analysis. **Operating breakeven analysis** is a method of determining the point at which sales will just cover *operating costs*; that is, the point at which the firm's operations will break even. It also shows the magnitude of the firm's operating profits or losses if sales exceed or fall

lumpy assets Assets that cannot be acquired in small increments, but instead must be obtained in large, discrete amounts.

operating breakeven analysis An analytical technique for studying the relationship between sales revenues, operating costs, and profits.

[1]Because the numbers generated from the computations contained in the rest of the chapter are not rounded until final result is reported, you might find some slight rounding differences when performing the computations yourself.

TABLE 17.5 U.P. Textiles: 2015 Forecasted Operating Income (₹ in Millions)

Sales (S)	₹1,650.0
Variable cost of goods sold (VC)	(1,353.0)
Gross profit (GP)	₹ 297.0
Fixed operating costs (F)	(154.0)
Net operating income (NOI = EBIT)	₹ 143.0

Notes:

Selling price per unit = ₹15.00.

Sales in units = (₹1,650.0 million)/₹15 = 110 million units.

Variable costs per unit = (₹1,353.0 million)/(110 million units) = ₹12.30 = 0.82(₹15.00)

Fixed operating costs = ₹154 million, which includes ₹55 million depreciation and ₹99 million in other fixed costs, such as rent, insurance, and general office expenses. (See Table 17.1.)

below that point. Breakeven analysis is important in the planning and control process because the cost-volume-profit relationship can be influenced greatly by the proportion of the firm's investment in fixed assets. A sufficient volume of sales must be anticipated and achieved if both fixed and variable costs are to be covered; otherwise, the firm will incur losses from operations.[2]

Operating breakeven analysis deals only with the upper portion of the income statement—the portion from sales to net operating income (NOI).[3] This portion of the income statement generally is referred to as the *operating section,* because it contains only the revenues and expenses that are associated with the *normal production and selling operations* of the firm. Table 17.5 gives the operating section of U.P's forecasted 2015 income statement, which was shown in Table 17.1. For the discussion that follows, we assume that all of U.P's products sell for ₹15.00 each and that the variable cost of goods sold per unit is ₹12.30, which is 82 percent of the selling price.

Operating Breakeven Graph. Table 17.5 shows the net operating income for U.P. if 110 million products are produced and sold during the year. But, what if U.P. doesn't sell 110 million products? Certainly, the firm's net operating income will be something other than ₹143 million. Figure 17.1 shows the total revenues and total operating costs for U.P. at various levels of sales, beginning with zero. According to the information given in Table 17.5, U.P. has fixed costs, which include depreciation, rent, insurance, and so forth, equal to ₹154 million. This amount must be paid even if the firm produces and sells nothing, so the ₹154 million fixed cost is depicted by a horizontal line in Figure 17.1. If U.P. produces and sells nothing, its sales revenues will be zero; but *for each unit sold,* the firm's sales will increase by the selling price of ₹15. Therefore, the total revenue line starts at the origin of the *X*- and *Y*-axes, and it has a slope equal to ₹15 to account for the rupee increase in sales for each additional unit sold. On the other hand, the line that represents the total operating costs intersects the *Y*-axis at ₹154 million, which represents the fixed costs incurred even when no products are sold, and it has a slope equal to the variable cost of goods sold per unit (₹12.30). The point at which the total revenue line intersects the total operating cost line is the **operating breakeven point (Q_{OpBE}** on the *X*-axis **and S_{OpBE}** on the *Y*-axis), because this is where sales revenues just cover the *total operating costs* of the firm. Notice that prior to (to the left of) the breakeven point, the total cost line is above the total revenue line, which indicates that U.P. will suffer operating losses because the total costs cannot be covered by the sales revenues. Beyond (to the right of) the breakeven point, the total revenue line is above the total cost line because revenues are more than sufficient to cover total operating costs; thus, U.P. will realize operating profits in this region.[4]

Operating Breakeven Computation. Figure 17.1 shows that U.P. must sell 57.04 million units to be at its operating breakeven point. Remember, the operating breakeven point is where the revenues generated from sales just cover the total operating costs,

operating breakeven point (Q_{OpBE} and S_{OpBE}) Represents the level of production and sales at which net operating income is zero; it is the point at which revenues from sales just equal total operating costs.

[2]Costs that vary directly with the level of production generally include the labor and materials needed to produce and sell the product, whereas the fixed operating costs generally include costs such as depreciation, rent, and insurance expenses that are incurred regardless of the firm's production level.

[3]Net operating income (NOI) is the same as earnings before interest and taxes (EBIT); that is, NOI = EBIT.

[4]In Figure 17.1, we assume the operating costs can be divided into two distinct groups: fixed costs and variable costs. It should be noted that some costs are considered semivariable (or semifixed). These costs are fixed for a certain range of operations, but change if operations are either higher or lower. For the analysis that follows, we have assumed there are no semivariable costs, so that the operating costs can be separated into either a fixed component or a variable component.

FIGURE 17.1 U.P. Textiles: Operating Breakeven Chart

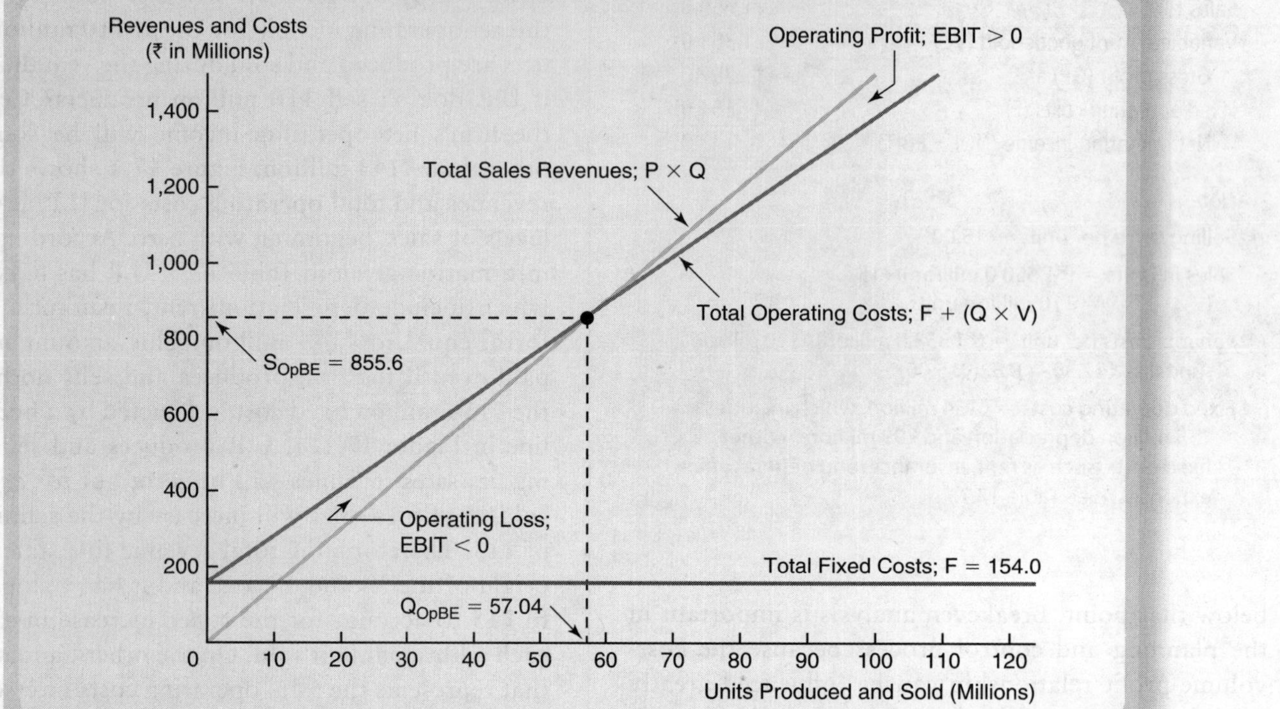

which include both the costs directly attributable to producing each unit (variable costs) and the fixed operating costs that remain constant regardless of the production level. As long as the selling price of each unit (the slope of the total revenue line) is greater than the variable operating cost of each unit (the slope of the total operating cost line), each unit sold will generate revenues that contribute to covering the fixed operating costs. For U.P. this contribution (termed the *contribution margin*) is ₹2.70, which is the difference between the ₹15.00 selling price and the ₹12.30 variable cost per unit. To compute the operating breakeven for U.P. we have to determine how many units must be sold to cover the fixed operating cost of ₹154 million if each unit has a contribution margin equal to ₹2.70. Simply divide the ₹154 million fixed cost by the ₹2.70 contribution margin and you will discover that the breakeven point is 57.04 million units, which equates to ₹855.6 million in sales revenues.

More formally, the operating breakeven point can be found by setting the total revenues equal to the total operating costs so that net operating income (NOI) is zero. In equation form, NOI = 0 if

$$\text{Sales revenues} = \text{Total operating costs} = \text{Total variable costs} + \text{Total fixed costs}$$

$$(P \times Q) = TOC = (V \times Q) + F$$

Here P is the sales price per unit, Q is the number of units produced and sold, V is the variable operating cost per unit, and F is the total fixed operating costs. Solving for the quantity that must be sold, Q, produces Equation 17.3, which can be used to find the operating breakeven point:

17.3

$$Q_{OpBE} = \frac{F}{P - V} = \frac{F}{\text{Contribution margin}}$$

Thus, the operating breakeven point for U.P. is

$$Q_{OpBE} = \frac{₹1540.0 \text{ million}}{₹15.00 - ₹12.30} = \frac{₹154.0 \text{ million}}{₹2.70}$$

$$= 57.04 \text{ million units}$$

The operating breakeven point also can be stated in terms of the total sales. Simply restate the contribution margin as a percent of the sales price per unit (this is called the *gross profit margin*), and then apply Equation 17.4. That is,

Solving Equation 17.4 for U.P. the operating breakeven stated in rupee sales is

17.4

$$S_{OpBE} = \frac{F}{1-\left(\frac{V}{P}\right)} = \frac{F}{\text{Gross profit margin}}$$

$$S_{OpBE} = \frac{₹154.0\text{ million}}{1-\left(\frac{₹12.30}{₹15.00}\right)} = \frac{₹154.0\text{ million}}{1-0.82}$$

$$= \frac{₹154.0\text{ million}}{0.18} = ₹855.6\text{ million}$$

This computation shows that ₹0.18 of every ₹1.00 of sales goes to cover the fixed operating costs, which means nearly ₹856 million worth of the product must be sold for U.P. to break even. (In the remainder of the chapter, for simlicity we omit the word *million* in the computations and include it only in the final answer.)

From Equations 17.3 and 17.4, we can see that a firm's operating breakeven point is lower (higher) if its fixed costs are lower, if the selling price of its product is higher, if its variable operating cost per unit is lower, or if some combination of these states exists.

Using Operating Breakeven Analysis. Operating breakeven analysis can shed light on three important types of business decisions: (1) When making new product decisions, breakeven analysis can help determine how large the sales of a new product must be for the firm to achieve profitability. (2) Breakeven analysis can be used to study the effects of a general expansion in the level of the firm's operations. An expansion would cause the levels of both fixed and variable costs to rise, but it would also increase expected sales. (3) When considering modernization projects where the fixed investment in equipment is increased to lower variable costs, particularly the cost of labor, breakeven analysis can help management analyze the consequences of purchasing these projects.

Care must be taken when using operating breakeven analysis. To apply breakeven analysis as we have discussed here requires that the sales price *per unit*, the variable cost *per unit*, and the *total* fixed operating costs do not change with the level of the firm's production and sales. Within a narrow range of production and sales, this assumption probably is not a major issue. However, if the firm expects either to produce a much greater (fewer) number of products than normal or to expand (reduce) its plant and equipment significantly, these costs will change. Therefore, use of a single breakeven chart like the one presented in Figure 17.1 is impractical. Such a chart provides useful information, but the fact that it cannot deal with changes in the price of the product, changing variable cost rates, and changes in fixed cost levels suggests the need for a more flexible type of analysis. Firms generally perform breakeven analyses that are more complicated using computer simulation and other sophisticated models.

17-3b Operating Leverage

Remember that in Chapter 12 we defined leverage as the existence of fixed costs associated with either normal operations or the financing a firm uses. **Operating leverage** arises because the firm has *fixed operating costs* that must be covered no matter the level of production. The impact of this leverage, however, depends on the actual operating level of the firm. For example, U.P. has ₹154.0 million in fixed operating costs, which are covered rather easily because the firm projects sales of 110 million products, a quantity that is well above its operating breakeven point of 57.04 million units. But what would happen to its operating income if U.P. sold more or less than was forecast? To answer this question we need to determine the **degree of operating leverage (DOL)** associated with U.P's forecasted 2015 operations.

Operating leverage can be defined more precisely in terms of the way a given change in sales volume affects operating income (NOI). To measure the effect of a change in sales volume on NOI, we calculate the DOL, which is defined as the percentage change in NOI (or EBIT) that will result from a given percentage change in sales (Equation 17.5):

The symbol Δ—the

operating leverage The existence of fixed operating costs such that a change in sales will produce a larger change in operating income (EBIT).

degree of operating leverage (DOL) The percentage change in NOI (or EBIT) associated with a given percentage change in sales.

TABLE 17.6 U.P. Textiles: Operating Income at Sales Levels of 110 Million Units and 121 Million Units (₹ in Millions)

	2015 Forecasted Operations	Sales with 10% Increase	Unit Change	Percentage Change
Sales in units (millions) (Q)	110.0	121.0	11.0	+10.0%
Sales revenues (Q × ₹15.00)	₹1,650.0	₹1,815.0	₹165.0	+10.0%
Variable cost of goods sold (Q × ₹12.30)	(1,353.0)	(1,488.3)	(135.3)	+10.0%
Gross profit	₹ 297.0	₹ 326.7	29.7	+10.0%
Fixed operating costs	(154.0)	(154.0)	(0.0)	0.0%
Net operating income (EBIT)	₹ 143.0	₹ 172.7	₹ 29.7	+20.8%

Greek letter for "delta"—means *change*. The term with the asterisk (*) indicates the actual outcome, whereas

17.5

$$\text{Degree of operating leverage} = \text{DOL} = \frac{\%\ \Delta \text{ in NOI}}{\%\ \Delta \text{ in sales}} = \frac{\left(\frac{\Delta \text{NOI}}{\text{NOI}}\right)}{\left(\frac{\Delta \text{Sales}}{\text{Sales}}\right)}$$

$$= \frac{\left(\frac{\text{NOI}^* - \text{NOI}}{\text{NOI}}\right)}{\left(\frac{\text{Sales}^* - \text{Sales}}{\text{Sales}}\right)}$$

the term without the asterisk is the forecasted result.

In effect, the DOL is an index that measures the effect a change in sales has on operating income or EBIT. Table 17.6 shows the EBIT for U.P. (1) if sales turn out to be 110 million units, which the firm has forecast and (2) if sales turn out to be 10 percent higher than expected (121 million units). The far right column of the table shows that EBIT is magnified because fixed operating costs do not change when sales increase. As a result, a 10 percent increase in U.P's forecasted 2015 sales will result in an *additional* 10.8 percent increase in operating income, so that the total increase is 20.8 percent.

Equation 17.5 can be simplified so that the degree of operating leverage at *a particular level of operations* can be calculated using one of the forms shown in Equation 17.6:[5]

To compute DOL using Equation 17.6, we only need information from U.P's forecasted operations; we do not need information about the possible

17.6

$$\text{DOL}_Q = \frac{Q(P - V)}{Q(P - V) - F}$$

$$= \frac{S - VC}{S - VC - F}$$

$$= \frac{\text{Gross profit}}{\text{EBIT}}$$

change in forecasted operations. Thus, Q represents the forecasted 2015 level of production and sales, and S and VC are the sales and variable operating costs, respectively, at that level of operations. For U.P. the solution for DOL at sales equal to 110 million units is

$$\text{DOL}_{Q=110} = \frac{110(₹15.00 - ₹12.30)}{110(₹15.00 - ₹12.30) - ₹154}$$

[5]Equation 17.6 can be derived by restating Equation 17.5 in terms of the variables we have defined previously, and then simplifying the result. Starting with Equation 17.5, we have

$$\text{DOL} = \frac{\%\ \Delta \text{ in NOI}}{\%\ \Delta \text{ in sales}} = \frac{\left(\frac{\Delta \text{NOI}}{\text{NOI}}\right)}{\left(\frac{\Delta \text{Sales}}{\text{Sales}}\right)}$$

NOI can be stated as the gross profit, Q(P – V), minus the fixed operating costs, F. So, if we use Q to indicate the level of operations forecasted for 2015 and Q* to indicate the level of operations that would exist if operations were different, the percent change in NOI is stated as

$$\%\Delta \text{ in NOI} = \frac{[Q^*(P - V) - F] - [Q(P - V) - F]}{Q(P - V) - F} = \frac{(Q^* - Q)(P - V)}{Q(P - V) - F}$$

Substituting into Equation 17.5, restating the denominator, and solving, yields

$$\text{DOL} = \frac{\left[\frac{(Q^* - Q)(P - V)}{Q(P - V) - F}\right]}{\left[\frac{P(Q^* - Q)}{P(Q)}\right]} = \frac{(Q^* - Q)(P - V)}{Q(P\text{-}V) - F} \boxtimes \left(\frac{Q}{Q^* - Q}\right) = \frac{Q(P - V)}{Q(P - V) - F}$$

$$= \frac{₹1{,}650 - ₹1{,}353}{₹1{,}650 - ₹1{,}353 - ₹154}$$

$$= \frac{₹297}{₹143} = 2.08\%$$

The DOL of 2.08× indicates that *each* 1 percent *change* in sales will result in a 2.08 percent *change* in operating income. What would happen if U.P's sales turn out to be 10 percent lower than expected? According to the interpretation of the DOL figure, U.P's operating income would be expected to decrease by 20.8 percent. If you compute U.P's operating income at 99 million units, which is 10 percent less than the forecasted 110 million units, you will find that EBIT equals ₹113.3 million, which is 20.8 percent lower than the forecasted EBIT (₹143 million). Therefore, *the DOL indicates the change (increase or decrease) in operating income that results from a change (increase or decrease) in the level of operations (sales).* It should be apparent that the greater the DOL, the greater the impact of a change in operations on operating income, whether the change is an increase or a decrease. And, as we discussed in Chapter 8, greater change (variability) suggests greater risk. Thus, we generally conclude that firms with higher DOLs have riskier business operations than firms with lower DOLs.

The DOL value found by using Equation 17.6 is the degree of operating leverage for a specific initial sales level. For U.P. that sales level is 110 million units, or ₹1,650 million. The DOL value will differ if the initial (existing) level of operations differs. For example, if U.P's operating cost structure is the same, but only 65 million units are produced and sold, the DOL would be

$$DOL_{Q=65} = \frac{65(₹15.00 - ₹12.30)}{65(₹15.00 - ₹12.30) - ₹154} = \frac{₹175.5}{₹21.5} = 8.16\times$$

The DOL at sales equal to 65 million units is nearly four times greater than the DOL at 110 million units. Thus, from a base sales of 65 million units, a 10 percent increase in sales (from 65 million units to 71.5 million units) would result in an 81.6% = 8.16 × 10% increase in operating income, from ₹21.5 million to ₹39.05 million. This shows that when U.P's operations are closer to its operating breakeven point of 57.04 million units, its degree of operating leverage is higher.

Operating Leverage and Operating Breakeven. In general, given the same operating cost structure, if a firm's level of operations is decreased, its DOL increases. Stated differently, the closer a firm is to its operating breakeven point, the greater is its degree of operating leverage. This occurs because, as Figure 17.1 indicates, the closer a firm is to its operating breakeven point, the more likely it is to incur an operating loss due to a decrease in sales. In other words, the closer its operations are to the operating breakeven point, the smaller the cushion, or buffer that exists for a firm to absorb a decrease in sales and still be able to cover the fixed operating costs. Similarly, at the same level of production and sales, a firm's DOL will be higher if the contribution margin for its products is lower. The lower the contribution margin, the less each product sold is able to help cover the fixed operating costs, and the closer the firm is to its operating breakeven point. Therefore, *it generally can be concluded that the higher the DOL for a particular firm, the closer the firm is to its operating breakeven point*, and the more sensitive its operating income is to a change in sales volume. Greater sensitivity generally implies greater risk; thus, it can be stated that *firms with higher DOLs generally are considered to have riskier operations than firms with lower DOLs.*

17-3c Financial Breakeven Analysis

Operating breakeven analysis deals with evaluation of production and sales to determine the level at which the firm's sales revenues will just cover its operating costs—the point where the operating income is zero. **Financial breakeven analysis** is used to determine the operating income, or EBIT, the firm needs to generate to cover all of its *financing costs* and produce earnings per share equal to zero. Typically, the financing costs involved in financial breakeven analysis consist of the interest payments to bondholders and the dividend payments to preferred stockholders. Usually these financing costs are fixed, and, in every case, they must be paid before dividends can be paid to common stockholders.

Financial breakeven analysis deals with the lower section of the income statement—the portion from operating income (EBIT = NOI) to earnings available to common stockholders. This portion of the income statement generally is referred to as the *financing section* because it contains the costs associated with the financing arrangements of

financial breakeven analysis Determining the operating income (EBIT) the firm needs to just cover all of its financing costs and produce earnings per share equal to zero.

TABLE 17.7 U.P. Textiles: 2015 Forecasted Earnings per Share (₹ in Millions, except per-share data)	
Sales in units (millions) (Q)	110.0
Earnings before interest and taxes (EBIT)	₹ 143.0
Less: Interest	(41.4)
Earnings before taxes (EBT)	₹ 101.6
Taxes (40%)	(40.6)
Net income (NI)	₹ 61.0
Preferred dividends (D_{ps})	0.0
Earnings available to common stockholders (EAC)	₹ 61.0
Earnings per share (EPS) = NI/(26.27 million shares)	₹ 2.32

the firm. The financing section of U.P's forecasted 2015 income statement is shown in Table 17.7.

Financial Breakeven Graph. Figure 17.2 shows the earnings per share (EPS) for U.P. at various levels of EBIT. The point at which EPS equals zero is referred to as the **financial breakeven point ($EBIT_{FinBE}$)**. As the graph indicates, the financial breakeven point for U.P. is where EBIT equals ₹41.4 million. At this EBIT level, the income generated from operations is just sufficient to cover the financing costs and income taxes; thus, EPS equals zero at EBIT equal to ₹41.4 million. To see that this is the case, we can compute the EPS when EBIT is ₹41.4 million:

Earnings before interest and taxes (EBIT)	₹41.4
Interest	(41.4)
Earnings before taxes (EBT)	0.0
Taxes (40%)	(0.0)
Net income	0.0
Preferred stock dividends	0.0
Earnings available to common stockholders (EAC)	₹ 0.0
EPS = ₹0/26.27 =	₹ 0.0

Financial Breakeven Computation. The results shown in Figure 17.2 can be translated algebraically to produce a relatively simple equation that can be used to compute the financial breakeven point of any firm. First, remember that the financial breakeven point is defined as the level of EBIT that generates EPS equal to zero. Equation 17.7, shows the definition of the financial breakeven point.

financial breakeven point ($EBIT_{FinBE}$) The level of EBIT at which EPS equals zero.

Here EBIT is the earnings before interest and taxes, I represents the interest payments on debt, T is the marginal tax rate, D_{ps} is the amount

17.7

$$EPS = \frac{\left(\begin{array}{c}\text{Earning aviable to}\\ \text{common stockholders}\end{array}\right)}{\left(\begin{array}{c}\text{Numbers of common}\\ \text{shares outstanding}\end{array}\right)} = 0$$

$$= \frac{(EBIT - I)(1 - T) - D_{ps}}{Shrs_C} = 0$$

of dividends paid to preferred stockholders, and $Shrs_C$ is the number of shares of common stock outstanding. Notice that EPS equals zero if the numerator in Equation 17.7, which is the earnings available to common stockholders, equals zero. Thus, the financial breakeven point also can be stated as follows:

$$(EBIT - I)(1 - T) - D_{ps} = 0$$

Rearranging this equation to solve for EBIT gives the level of EBIT that is needed to produce EPS equal to zero. Therefore, the computation for a firm's financial breakeven point is as shown in Equation 17.8:

Using Equation 17.8, the financial breakeven point for U.P. Textiles in 2015 is

17.8

$$EBIT_{FinBE} = I + \frac{D_{ps}}{(1 - T)}$$

FIGURE 17.2 U.P. Textiles: Financial Breakeven Chart

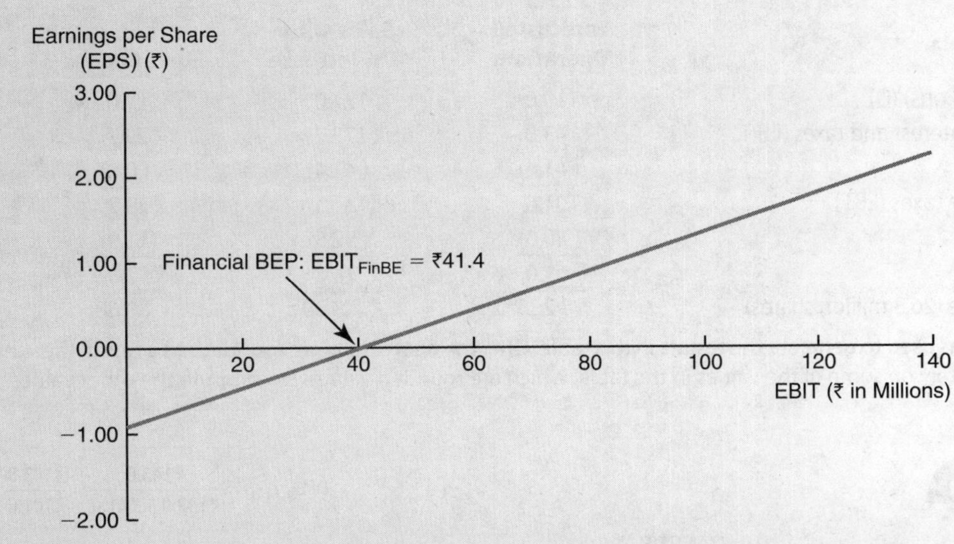

$$\text{EBIT}_{\text{FinBE}} = ₹41.4 + \frac{₹0.0}{(1 - 0.4)} = ₹41.4$$

This is the same result shown in Figure 17.2.

According to Equation 17.8, the amount of preferred stock dividends must be stated on a before-tax basis to determine the financial breakeven point, because we want to determine the before-tax operating income (EBIT) that will result in EPS = 0. However, if it has no preferred stock, the firm only needs to cover its interest payments, so the financial breakeven point simply equals the interest expense. This is the case for U.P. because it has no preferred stock. Because most corporations in the United States do not have preferred stock outstanding, we will not include preferred dividends in the discussions that follow.

Using Financial Breakeven Analysis. Financial breakeven analysis can be used to help determine the impact of the firm's financing mix on EPS.[6] When the financing mix includes financing alternatives that require fixed costs, such as interest, financial leverage exists. *Financial leverage affects the financing section of the income statement like operating leverage affects the operating section.* This point is discussed next.

[6]The effect of financing the firm with various proportions of debt and equity is discussed in greater detail in Chapter 12.

17-3d Financial Leverage

While operating leverage considers how changing sales volume affects operating income, **financial leverage** considers how changing operating income affects EPS, or earnings available to common stockholders (EAC). Operating leverage affects the operating section of the income statement, whereas financial leverage affects the financing section of the income statement. In other words, *financial leverage takes over where operating leverage leaves off, magnifying the effects on EPS of changes in operating income (EBIT).*

Like operating leverage, financial leverage arises because fixed costs exist. However, in this case, the fixed costs are associated with how the firm is financed. The **degree of financial leverage (DFL)** is defined as the percentage change in EPS that results from a given percentage change in EBIT. Thus, DFL is computed as shown in Equation 17.9:

As in our previous discussions, the term with the asterisk (*) indicates the actual outcome, whereas the term without the asterisk is the forecasted result.

Table 17.8 shows

financial leverage The existence of fixed financial costs such as interest and preferred dividends; occurs when a change in EBIT results in a larger change in EPS.

degree of financial leverage (DFL) The percentage change in EPS that results from a given percentage change in EBIT.

TABLE 17.8 U.P. Textiles: Net Income and Earnings per Share at Sales Levels of 110 Million Units and 121 Million Units (₹ in Millions)[a]

	2015 Forecasted Operations	Sales with 10% Increase	Unit Change	Percentage Change
Sales in units (millions) (Q)	110.0	121.0	11.0	+10.0%
Earnings before interest and taxes (EBIT)	₹143.0	₹172.7	₹29.7	+20.8%
Interest (I)	(41.4)	(41.4)	(0.0)	0.0%
Earnings before taxes (EBT)	₹101.6	₹131.3	₹29.7	+29.2%
Taxes (40%)	(40.6)	(52.5)	(11.9)	+29.2%
Net income (NI)	₹ 61.0	₹ 78.8	₹17.8	+29.2%
Earnings per share (26.3 million shares)	₹ 2.32	₹ 3.00	₹0.68	+29.2%

[a]A spreadsheet was used to generate the results in this table. Only the final results are rounded. As a result, there might be rounding differences if you rely on some of the values in the table, which are rounded values, to compute the other values.

17.9

$$\text{Degree of financial leverage} = \text{DFL} = \frac{\%\ \Delta \text{ in EPS}}{\%\ \Delta \text{ in EBIT}} = \frac{\left(\dfrac{\Delta\text{EPS}}{\text{EPS}}\right)}{\left(\dfrac{\Delta\text{EBIT}}{\text{EBIT}}\right)}$$

$$= \frac{\left(\dfrac{\text{EPS}^* - \text{EPS}}{\text{EPS}}\right)}{\left(\dfrac{\text{EBIT}^* - \text{EBIT}}{\text{EBIT}}\right)}$$

the results of increasing U.P.'s EBIT by 20.8 percent. The increase in EPS is 29.2 percent, which is 1.41 times the change in EBIT; thus, the DFL for U.P. equals 1.41.

The degree of financial leverage at a particular level of EBIT can be computed easily by using Equation 17.10:[7] Using Equation 17.10, the DFL for U.P. Textiles at EBIT equal to ₹143.0 million (sales of 110 million units) is

17.10

$$\text{DFL} = \frac{\text{EBIT}}{\text{EBIT - EBIT}_{\text{FinBE}}}$$

$$= \frac{\text{EBIT}}{\text{EBIT} - \text{I}} \qquad \text{when } D_{ps} = 0$$

$$\text{DFL}_{Q=110} = \frac{₹143.0}{₹143.0 - ₹41.4} = \frac{₹143.0}{₹101.6} = 1.41\times$$

The interpretation of the DFL value is the same as for DOL, except that the starting point for evaluating

[7]Equation 17.10 can be derived easily by expanding Equation 17.9, rearranging the terms, and then simplifying the results. If we use EPS and EBIT to indicate the forecasted 2015 EPS and EBIT, respectively, and EPS* and EBIT* to indicate the EPS and EBIT that would exist after a change in sales volume, then

$$\text{DFL} = \frac{\left(\dfrac{\Delta\text{EPS}}{\text{EPS}}\right)}{\left(\dfrac{\Delta\text{EBIT}}{\text{EBIT}}\right)} = \frac{\left(\dfrac{\text{EPS}^* - \text{EPS}}{\text{EPS}}\right)}{\left(\dfrac{\text{EBIT}^* - \text{EBIT}}{\text{EBIT}}\right)}$$

The computation for forecasted earnings per share is

$$\text{EPS} = \frac{(\text{EPIT} - 1)(1 - \text{T})}{\text{Shrs}_\text{C}}$$

where Shrs_C is the number of common shares outstanding. The percent change in EPS can be written and simplified as follows:

$$\Delta\text{EPS} = \frac{\left[\dfrac{(\text{EBIT}^* - 1)(1 - \text{T})}{\text{Shrs}_\text{C}}\right] - \left[\dfrac{(\text{EBIT} - 1)(1 - \text{T})}{\text{Shrs}_\text{C}}\right]}{\left[\dfrac{(\text{EBIT} - 1)(1 - \text{T})}{\text{Shrs}_\text{C}}\right]}$$

$$= \frac{[(\text{EBIT}^* - 1)(1 - \text{T})] - [(\text{EBIT} - 1)(1 - \text{T})]}{(\text{EBIT} - 1)(1 - \text{T})}$$

$$= \frac{\text{EBIT}^* - \text{EBIT}}{\text{EBIT} - 1}$$

Substituting this relationship into the computation of DFL, we have

$$\text{DFL} = \frac{\left(\dfrac{\text{EBIT}^* - \text{EBIT}}{\text{EBIT} - 1}\right)}{\left(\dfrac{\text{EBIT}^* - \text{EBIT}}{\text{EBIT}}\right)} = \frac{\text{EBIT}^* - \text{EBIT}}{\text{EBIT} - 1} \times \frac{\text{EBIT}}{\text{EBIT}^* - \text{EBIT}}$$

$$= \frac{\text{EBIT}}{\text{EBIT} - 1} = \frac{\text{EBIT}}{\text{EBIT} - \text{EBIT}_{\text{FinBE}}}$$

If a firm has preferred stock, the relationship given in Equation 17.8 should be substituted in this equation for the $\text{EBIT}_{\text{FinBE}}$.

financial leverage is EBIT and the ending point is EPS. Because the DFL for U.P. is 1.41×, the company can expect a 1.41 percent change in EPS for every 1 percent change in EBIT; a 20.8 percent increase in EBIT results in an approximately 29.2 percent (20.8 percent × 1.41) increase in EPS. Unfortunately, the opposite also is true—if U.P.'s 2015 EBIT turns out to be 20.8 percent below expectations, its EPS will be 29.2 percent below the forecast of ₹2.32. To prove this result is correct, construct the financing section of U.P.'s income statement when EBIT equals ₹113.3 million = (1 – 0.208) × ₹143.0 million, and you will find EPS = ₹1.64, which is 29.2 percent lower than the forecasted amount of ₹2.32.

The DFL value found using Equation 17.10 pertains to one specific EBIT level. If the level of sales differs, and thus EBIT differs, so does the value computed for DFL. For example, at sales equal to 75 million units, U.P.'s DFL would be

$$DFL_{Q=75} = \frac{75(₹15.00 - ₹12.30) - ₹154}{[75(₹15.00 - ₹12.30) - ₹154] - ₹41.4}$$

$$= \frac{₹48.5}{₹7.1} = 6.83\times$$

Compared to sales equal to 110 million units, at sales equal to 75 million units U.P. would have greater difficulty covering the fixed financing costs, so its DFL is much greater. At EBIT equal to ₹48.5 million, U.P. is close to its financial breakeven point of ₹41.4 million, so its degree of financial leverage is high. Consequently, the more difficulty a firm has covering its fixed financing costs with operating income, the greater its degree of financial leverage. In general then, *the higher the DFL for a particular firm, the closer the firm is to its financial breakeven point*, and the more sensitive its EPS is to a change in operating income. Greater sensitivity implies greater risk; thus, it can be stated that *firms with higher DFLs generally are considered to have greater financial risk than firms with lower DFLs.*

17-3e Combining Operating and Financial Leverage—Degree of Total Leverage (DTL)

Our analysis of operating leverage and financial leverage has shown that *(1) the greater the DOL, or fixed operating costs, for a particular level of operations, the more sensitive EBIT will be to changes in sales volume; and (2) the greater the DFL, or fixed financial costs, for a particular level of operations, the more sensitive EPS will be to changes in EBIT.* Therefore, if a firm has considerable amounts of both operating leverage and financial leverage, even small changes in sales will lead to wide fluctuations in EPS. Look at the impact leverage has on U.P's forecasted 2015 operations. We found that if the sales volume increases by 10 percent, U.P.'s EBIT will increase by 20.8 percent, and if EBIT increases by 20.8 percent, its EPS will increase by 29.2 percent. Thus, a 10 percent increase in sales volume would result in a 29.2 percent increase in EPS. This shows the impact of *total leverage*, which is the combination of both operating leverage and financial leverage, with respect to U.P.'s current operations.

The **degree of total leverage (DTL)** is defined as the percentage change in EPS resulting from a 1 percent change in sales volume. This relationship, which represents the combination of DOL and DFL, can be written as Equation 17.11:

17.11

$$\text{Degree of total leverage} = DTL = DOL \times DFL = \frac{\text{Gross profit}}{\text{EBIT}} \times \frac{\text{EBIT}}{\text{EBIT} - \text{EBIT}_{FinBE}} = \frac{\text{Gross profit}}{\text{EBIT} - \text{EBIT}_{FinBE}} = \left.\frac{S - VC}{\text{EBIT} - 1} = \frac{Q(P - V)}{[Q(P - V) - F] - I}\right\} \text{ when } D_{ps} = 0$$

Using Equation 17.11, the degree of total leverage for U.P. would be

$$DTL_{Q=110} = 2.077 \times 1.407$$

$$= \frac{₹2907.0}{₹143.0} \times \frac{₹143.0}{₹143.0 - ₹41.4}$$

$$= \frac{₹1,650.0 - ₹1,353.0}{₹143.0 - ₹41.4}$$

$$= \frac{110(₹15.00 - ₹12.30)}{[110(₹15.00 - ₹12.30) - ₹154.0] - ₹41.4}$$

$$= \frac{₹297.0}{₹101.6} = 2.92\times$$

This value indicates that for every 1 percent change in sales volume, U.P.'s EPS will change by 2.92 percent; thus, a 10 percent increase in sales will result in a 29.2 percent increase

degree of total leverage (DTL) The percentage change in EPS that results from a 1 percent change in sales.

in EPS. This is exactly the impact expected.

© iStockphoto.com/E_Y_E

The value of DTL can be used to compute the new earnings per share (EPS*) after a change in sales volume. We already know that U.P's EPS will change by 2.92 percent for every 1 percent change in sales. Accordingly, EPS* resulting from a 10 percent increase in sales can be computed as follows:

$$EPS^* = EPS[1 + (.10)(2.92)]$$

$$= ₹2.32 \times (1 + 0.292) = ₹3.00$$

This is the same result given in Table 17.8.

The degree of (total) leverage concept is useful primarily for the insights it provides regarding the joint effects of operating leverage and financial leverage on EPS. For example, the concept can be used to show management that a decision to finance new equipment with debt would result in a situation in which a 10 percent decline in sales would result in a nearly 30 percent decline in earnings, whereas with a different operating and financial package, a 10 percent sales decline would cause earnings to decline by only 15 percent. Having the alternatives stated in this manner gives decision makers a better idea of the ramifications of alternative actions with respect to the firm's level of operations and how those operations are financed.

17-4 Using Leverage and Forecasting for Control

From the discussion in the previous sections, it should be clear what the impact on income would be if the 2015 sales forecast for U.P. Textiles is different from what is expected. If sales are greater than expected, both operating and financial leverage will magnify the "bottom line" effect on EPS (DTL = 2.92). However, the opposite also holds. Consequently, if U.P. does not meet its forecasted sales level, leverage will result in a magnified loss in income compared to what is expected. This will occur because production facilities might be expanded too greatly, inventories might be built up too quickly, and so on, and the end result might be that the firm suffers a significant income loss. This loss will result in a lower than expected addition to retained earnings, which means that plans for additional external funds needed to support the firm's operations will be inadequate. Likewise, if the sales forecast is too low, then, if the firm is at full capacity, it will not be able to meet the additional demand, and sales opportunities will be lost—perhaps forever. In the previous sections, we showed only how changes in operations (2015 forecasts) affect the income generated by the firm; we did not continue the process to show the impact on the balance sheet and the financing needs of the firm. To determine the impact on the financial statements, the financial manager must repeat the steps discussed in the first part of this chapter. At this stage, the financial manager needs to evaluate and act on the feedback received from the forecasting and budgeting processes. In effect, then, the forecasting (planning) and control of the firm is an ongoing activity, a vital function to the long-run survival of any firm.

The forecasting and control functions described in this chapter are important for several reasons. First, if the projected operating results are unsatisfactory, management can "go back to the drawing board," reformulate its plans, and develop targets that are more reasonable for the coming year. Second, it is possible that the funds required to meet the sales forecast simply cannot be obtained. If so, it obviously is better to know this in advance and to scale back the projected level of operations than to suddenly run out of cash and have operations grind to a halt. Third, even if the required funds can be raised, it is desirable to plan for their acquisition well in advance. Finally, any deviation from the projections must be dealt with to improve future forecasts and the predictability of the firm's operations, and therefore to ensure that the goals of the firm are being pursued appropriately.

KEY FINANCIAL PLANNING AND CONTROL CONCEPTS

To conclude this chapter, we summarize some concepts that were discussed.

- Financial planning requires the firm to forecast future operations. A firm forecasts its financial statements (called pro formas) so that arrangements can be made to accommodate expected changes in production, future financing needs, and so forth. A financial plan represents a "road map" for the firm to follow to attain future goals. The process doesn't stop when financial forecasts are completed, because the firm needs to monitor operations as the financial plan is implemented to determine whether modifications are needed.
- A firm evaluates its breakeven points and degrees of leverage to assess the risk associated with its forecasts. In general, a firm with a higher degree of leverage is considered riskier than a similar firm that has a lower degree of leverage. A firm uses the concept of leverage to estimate how fixed costs, both operating and financial, affect its "bottom line" (net) income. Everything else equal, a firm can decrease its risk by decreasing its relative fixed costs, by increasing sales, or by performing both actions. Remember from our discussions in previous chapters that, everything else equal, when a firm reduces its risk, its cost of capital decreases, and thus its value increases.
- Inadequate financial planning is the principal reason businesses fail. As a result, well-run companies generally base their operating plans on a set of well designed forecasted financial statements. Simply stated, forecasting (planning) is an essential part of successful business.

MULTIPLE CHOICE QUESTIONS

1. In drawing up projected financial statements,

a. Income statement is drawn before Balance sheet

b. Balance sheet is drawn before Income statement

c. Either Income statement or Balance sheet can be drawn leading to the other

d. Statement of additional funds required needs to be drawn up first

2. Estimated additional funds needed is a function of

a. Increase in assets

b. Increase in liabilities

c. Increase in retained earnings

d. All of the above

3. In drawing up financial projections,

a. Company is assumed to be working at less than 100% capacity

b. Company is assumed to be working at 100% capacity

c. Company is assumed to be working at more than 100% capacity

d. Can be any of the above

4. Breakeven analysis is needed for

a. Determining maximum losses that can be suffered

b. Determining capacity needed to start making profits

c. Determining maximum profits that can be made

d. None of the above

5. Contribution margin is

a. Sales minus fixed cost

b. Variable plus fixed cost

c. Sales minus variable cost

d. Sales minus total cost

6. Operating leverage measures the

a. Extent to which profits change for a change in sales volume

b. Extent to which expenses change for a change in profits

c. Extent to which borrowings change for a change in profits

d. None of the above

7. Degree of financial leverage measures the

a. Extent of debt for changing levels of equity

b. Extent of equity for changing levels of debt

c. Extent of change in net profits for changes in EBIT, at a level of leverage

d. None of the above

8. Total leverage is useful for

a. Understanding the effect of change in EBIT and PAT

b. Understanding the effect of change in sales and PAT

c. Both a and b

d. Understanding the effect of change in EPS for a small change in sales volume

9. In forecasting,

a. Estimating leverage is more important than estimating sales

b. Estimating income is more important than estimating sales

c. We need to estimate sales, income and leverage for a given asset level

d. None of the above

10. Financial planning involves

a. Working on financial statements projections

b. Looking at leverage options

c. Projections of income statements

d. All of the above

Answers:

1.	(a)	2.	(d)	3.	(d)	4.	(b)	5.	(c)
6.	(a)	7.	(c)	8.	(d)	9.	(c)	10.	(d)

PROBLEMS

For more problems, login to CourseMate for CFIN at CengageBrain.com

17–1 Mohan Wasla Mining (MWM) expects its sales to grow by 20 percent next year. Last year, when the firm was operating at *full capacity*, MWM generated sales equal to ₹250,000 with assets of ₹800,000. MWM's current balance sheet shows that accounts payable and accruals are ₹150,000, notes payable are ₹25,000, long-term debt is ₹100,000, common stock is ₹450,000, and retained earnings are ₹75,000. Next year, MWM's net profit margin is expected to be the same as this past year, 5 percent, and the company plans to continue to pay 60 percent of earnings as dividends. Estimate MWM's additional funds needed (AFN) for next year.

17–2 Ekta's Farm is constructing its pro forma financial statements for this year. At year end, assets were ₹400,000 and accounts payable (the only current liabilities account) were ₹125,000. Last year's sales were ₹500,000. Ekta's expects to grow by 15 percent this year. Assets and accounts payable are expected to grow proportionally to sales. Common stock currently equals ₹140,000, and retained earnings are ₹98,000. Ekta's plans to sell ₹15,000 of new common stock this year. The firm's profit margin on sales is 6 percent, and 40 percent of earnings will be paid out as dividends. How much *new* long-term debt financing will Ekta's need this year to finance its expected growth?

17–3 In its most recent fiscal year, SuriCorp generated ₹810,000 in sales. The firm was operating at 90 percent capacity. How much more sales can SuriCorp generate before it is at full capacity?

17–4 Tushar Industries has been operating at 60 percent capacity the past few years. In each of these years, Tushar generated sales of ₹5.4 million. By what percentage can Tushar increase its sales before full capacity is reached?

17–5 Prema Colors (PC) sells one-litre can of house paint for ₹125 each. The variable cost to produce each can is ₹95, and fixed operating costs are ₹600000. PC normally sells 30,000 litre cans of paint each year, has an interest expense equal to ₹125000, and its marginal tax rate is 30 percent. Given this information, what is PC's operating breakeven point?

17–6 Meghna's Pumps (MP) sells pumps for ₹9500 each. Each pump costs ₹5500 to produce, and MP's fixed operating costs equal ₹65 million. (a) What is MP's operating breakeven point? (b) What is MP's operating income (NOI) when 25000 pumps are sold?

17–7 Feroze Gordon Memory (FGM) sells 64 GB memory cards for ₹1900 per unit memory. Fixed costs are ₹90,00,000 for output up to 200,000 cards. Variable costs are ₹1250 per card. (a) What is

FGM's operating income at sales of 75,000 cards? (b) What is the operating breakeven point?

17-8 Anthim Mouka Gaming manufactures slot machines that are sold to individuals for ₹57500 each. Fixed operating costs are ₹69 lakhs and each machine's variable cost is 70 percent of its selling price. What is the firm's degree of operating leverage at sales equal to (a) 60000 machines, (b) 90000 machines, and (c) 100000 machines?

17-9 Lalit Time Watch (LTW) Company manufactures alarm clocks that are sold for ₹1000 each. Fixed operating costs are ₹25 lakhs and variable costs are ₹680 per clock. (a) What is LTW's operating breakeven point? (b) What is LTW's degree of operating leverage (DOL) at sales of 10,000 units? (c) Everything else equal, what would happen to the operating breakeven point if the selling price is raised to ₹1100?

17-10 Oswal Door Manufacturing (ODM) and Closed Window Industries (CWI) have identical operating cost structures. Both firms incur a fixed operating cost equal to ₹420,000, their variable cost ratio is 80 percent of the unit selling price, and they sell their products for ₹1,400 each. ODM normally sells 2,000 units per year, whereas CWI normally sells 2,500 units each year. (a) Compute the operating breakeven point. (b) Compute the degree of operating leverage (DOL) for each firm at their normal sales levels, and show that ODM is operating closer to the operating breakeven point than CWI.

17-11 Meera Air's debt consists of ₹50,000 in accounts payable, ₹100,000 in 10 percent notes payable, and ₹240,000 in 8 percent bonds. Meera has no preferred stock. If its marginal tax rate is 35 percent, what is Meera's financial breakeven point?

17-12 Jana Jams' balance sheet shows that its outstanding debt consists of ₹15,000 in 9 percent notes payable and ₹48,000 in 6 percent bonds. In addition, Jana has ₹60,000 preferred stock that pays a 5 percent dividend. If its marginal tax rate is 40 percent, what is Jana's financial breakeven point?

17-13 Natwarlal Art has only one type of debt outstanding: a long-term bond with a face value of ₹300,000 and a coupon rate of interest equal to 11 percent. Natwarlal expects this year's EBIT to equal ₹99,000, and its marginal tax rate is 30 percent. (a) If Natwarlal has no preferred stock, what is its degree of financial leverage (DFL)? (b) If Natwarlal has preferred stock that pays an annual dividend equal to ₹18,480, what is its DFL?

17-14 Subramaniam Farm forecasts that its net income will be ₹40 lakhs this year. The firm's marginal tax rate is 35 percent, and it must pay ₹750000 interest on outstanding debt. Subramaniam Farm has no preferred stock. What is the firm's degree of financial leverage (DFL)?

17-15 Deepak Sod Farm (DSF) expects its EBIT to be ₹2250000 this year. DSF's marginal tax rate is 40 percent, it must pay ₹500000 in interest this year, and it has 100000 shares of common stock outstanding. (a) Compute the EPS that DSF expects to generate this year. (b) What is DSF's degree of financial leverage (DFL)?

17-16 Bahadur Treasures has determined that its degree of operating leverage (DOL) is 3.5 and its degree of financial leverage (DFL) is 2.0. (a) What is Bahadur's degree of total leverage (DTL)? (b) What impact will a 5 percent decrease in sales have on Bahadur's (i) EBIT and (ii) net income?

17-17 Ekalavya Insurance has a degree of financial leverage (DFL) equal to 4.0 and a degree of total leverage (DTL) equal to 10.0. Ekalavya expects sales to be ₹600,000 this year, and its net profit margin is 8 percent. (a) What is Ekalavya's degree of operating leverage (DOL)? (b) If Ekalavya's sales turn out to be 7 percent higher than expected, what will its net income be?

17-18 Analysts have evaluated the Wignesh Company and discovered that when sales are ₹400,000, EBIT equals ₹125,000, the company's degree of operating leverage (DOL) is 2.0, its degree of financial leverage (DFL) is 4.0, and EPS equals ₹2.50. According to this information, what will Wignesh's EBIT be if sales actually equal ₹360,000 rather than ₹400,000? What will the EPS be?

17-19 Chandra Corporation's products sell for ₹180 each. The variable cost of each product is ₹135, and fixed operating costs are ₹371,250. Chandra pays ₹61,875 interest on its outstanding debt each year, and its marginal tax rate is 40 percent. If Chandra expects to sell 11,000 units, what is its degree of operating leverage (DOL), the degree of financial leverage (DFL), and the degree of total leverage (DTL)?

17-20 LPM Corporation sells its product for ₹10 each. Fixed operating costs equal ₹100,000, and variable operating costs are 75 percent of the selling price. The firm pays ₹37,500 in interest, and its marginal tax rate is 35 percent. (a) What are LPM's operating breakeven point and financial breakeven point? (b) If LPM expects to sell 65,000 units, what are its degree of operating leverage (DOL), degree of financial leverage (DFL), and degree of total leverage (DTL)?

Financial Planning and Control

Learning Outcomes

LO.1 Construct simple pro forma financial statements that can be used to forecast financing and investment needs.

- Pro forma financial statements are forecasts that are used to help the firm plan for the future. The firm must (1) determine how much money is needed to achieve its goals, (2) determine how much money it expects to generate through normal operations, and (3) make arrangements to finance expected shortfalls and to invest expected surpluses. This process is accomplished in four repetitive steps: (1) Forecast the income statement for the next one or two years to determine the amount of funds that the firm expects to generate through normal operations. (2) Forecast the balance sheet for the next one or two years to determine (a) the amount that must be invested in assets to reach particular goals and (b) the amount of internally generated funds that basic operations are expected to provide during the forecast period. (3) If the amount that is needed for investment in assets exceeds the amount of funds that the firm expects to generate internally, then the firm must determine how the additional funds that are needed (AFN) will be raised externally. (4) Because raising new funds increases interest payments, dividends, or both, the firm must consider the effects of such "financing feedbacks" on the original forecasts. These steps should be continued until AFN = 0.

LO.2 Discuss some of the complications that management should consider when constructing pro forma financial statements.

- Some factors that firms must consider when constructing pro forma financial statements include (1) excess capacity, (2) economies of scale, and (3) lumpy assets.
- If a firm is not operating at full capacity (i.e., if excess capacity exists), existing assets can be used to satisfy some or all of an increase in production that is needed to attain growth goals.
- As a firm grows to particular levels of production, it attains economies of scale that decrease the per-unit cost of manufacturing products.
- Some assets can only be purchased in large, discrete amounts, which means that a firm might be required to invest a greater percentage in assets to achieve a smaller percentage increase in sales.

LO.3 Describe and compute (a) operating breakeven and operating leverage, (b) financial breakeven and financial leverage, and (c) total leverage.

- A firm's operating breakeven point is the level of sales that is just sufficient to cover all operating expenses, which include variable costs and fixed costs, so that EBIT = 0. Operating leverage refers to the firm's fixed operating costs. The degree of operating leverage (DOL) indicates by what percent operating income will change if sales change by 1 percent. Firms with higher DOLs experience greater changes in their operating incomes when their sales change, which suggests that such firms (1) have riskier operations and (2) are operating closer to their operating breakeven points than firms with lower DOLs.
- A firm's financial breakeven point is the level of EBIT (operating income) that is just sufficient to cover all financing expenses, which generally include interest payments and preferred dividends, so that EPS = 0. Financial leverage refers to the firm's fixed financing costs. The degree of financial leverage (DFL) indicates by what percent EPS will change if EBIT changes by 1 percent. Firms with higher DFLs experience greater changes in their net incomes when their EBITs change, which suggests that such firms (1) have riskier financing arrangements and (2) are operating closer to their financial breakeven points than firms with lower DFLs.
- Total leverage is a combination of operating leverage and financial leverage. The degree of total leverage (DTL) indicates by what percent EPS will change if sales change by 1 percent. Firms with higher DTLs experience greater changes in their net incomes when their sales change, which suggests that such firms are riskier, and thus have higher costs of capital, than firms with lower DTLs.

LO.4 Discuss how knowledge of leverage is used in the financial forecasting and control process and why financial planning is critical to firm survival.

- The forecasting and control process is continuous. A firm must forecast to plan for its future financing and investing activities. Forecasting is not an exact science, so managers must continuously evaluate and update forecasts to make them more accurate. It is important to learn from past mistakes and incorporate this learning in future forecasts.

Chapter 17 Key Financial Planning and Control Concepts

- Financial planning requires the firm to forecast future operations. A firm forecasts its financial statements (called pro formas) so that arrangements can be made to accommodate expected changes in production, future financing needs, and so forth. A financial plan represents a "road map" for the firm to follow to attain future goals. The process doesn't stop when financial forecasts are completed, because the firm needs to monitor operations as the financial plan is implemented to determine whether modifications are needed.
- A firm evaluates its breakeven points and degrees of leverage to assess the risk associated with its forecasts. In general, a firm with a higher degree of leverage is considered riskier than a similar firm that has a lower degree of leverage. A firm uses the concept of leverage to estimate how fixed costs, both operating and financial, affect its "bottom line" (net) income. Everything else equal, a firm can decrease its risk by decreasing its relative fixed costs, by increasing sales, or by performing both actions. Remember from our discussions in previous chapters that, everything else equal, when a firm reduces its risk, its cost of capital decreases, and thus its value increases.
- Inadequate financial planning is the principal reason businesses fail. As a result, well-run companies generally base their operating plans on a set of well-designed forecasted financial statements. Simply stated, forecasting (planning) is an essential part of successful business.

Key Terms

financial planning The projection of sales, income, and assets as well as the determination of the resources needed to achieve these projections. *p. 296*

financial control The phase in which financial plans are implemented; control deals with the feedback and adjustment process required to ensure adherence to plans and modification of plans because of unforeseen changes. *p. 296*

LO.1

sales forecast A forecast of a firm's unit and rupee sales for some future period; generally based on recent sales trends plus forecasts of the economic prospects for the nation, region, industry, and so forth. *p. 296*

projected (pro forma) balance sheet method A method of forecasting financial requirements based on forecasted financial statements. *p. 296*

spontaneously generated funds Funds that are obtained from routine business transactions. *p. 297*

additional funds needed (AFN) Funds that a firm must raise externally through new borrowing or by selling new stock. *p. 298*

financing feedbacks The effects on the income statement and balance sheet of actions taken to finance forecasted increases in assets. *p. 299*

LO.2

lumpy assets Assets that cannot be acquired in small increments, but instead must be obtained in large, discrete amounts. *p. 302*

LO.3

operating breakeven analysis An analytical technique for studying the relationship between sales revenues, operating costs, and profits. *p. 302*

operating breakeven point (Q_{OpBE} and S_{OpBE}) Represents the level of production and sales at which net operating income is zero; it is the point at which revenues from sales just equal total operating costs. *p. 303*

operating leverage The existence of fixed operating costs, such that a change in sales will produce a larger change in operating income (EBIT). *p. 305*

degree of operating leverage (DOL) The percentage change in NOI (or EBIT) associated with a given percentage change in sales. *p. 305*

financial breakeven analysis Determining the operating income (EBIT) the firm needs to just cover all of its financing costs and produce earnings per share equal to zero. *p. 307*

financial breakeven point ($EBIT_{FinBE}$) The level of EBIT at which EPS equals zero. *p. 308*

financial leverage The existence of fixed financial costs such as interest and preferred dividends; occurs when a change in EBIT results in a larger change in EPS. *p. 309*

degree of financial leverage (DFL) The percent change in EPS that results from a given percent change in EBIT. *p. 309*

degree of total leverage (DTL) The percent change in EPS that results from a 1 percent change in sales. *p. 311*

The Long Night With Financial Analysis

Sudreshan Pale knew this was going to be a long night. The next day at 9 am, the submission of his special paper forming a part of the Financial Analysis course would be due. The instructor for the course Mr. Mirch Phal was a no-nonsense person and had allocated 40% of the total evaluation of the course to this special paper. His words were, "Do not expect to get away with a paper full of mechanical calculation. The correctness of your calculation carries only 10% and the rest of the evaluation is based on your ability to make original analysis".

Sudreshan had put off this work for several days now. The assignment was given 10 days ago, and soon thereafter he had downloaded the crucial figures from the Capitaline database (see Annexure 1 and 2). For several reasons he did not get around to working on the case until now. This, he told himself, is his typical problem of putting off things till the last minute when he would not get enough time to reflect. He vowed to be more systematic in future.

But the immediate problem had to be tackled. The special paper was briefly worded, as was the practice of Prof. Mirch Phal. This read as follows:

"Analyse Bajaj Auto's financial parameters and comment on the financial health of the company with reference to key parameters".

From the discussion in the class, Sudreshan knew that an industry analysis would be expected by Prof. Phal and that was why he had downloaded it (Annexure 3).

Sudreshan realized that he would need to be systematic in his analysis and at the same time, brief. His final comments would need to be unambiguous. He quickly referred some old notes which were assigned as part of the course.

He collected together the portions which he had highlighted.

To begin with, we go back to our discussion on the two systems of accounting that Companies follow – viz. the cash system and the mercantile system. Under the cash system, we take into consideration only those transactions that result in either a cash outflow or inflow. In fact, transactions are recorded in the books of account only if there is either cash coming in or going out. At this point, it must be realised, that the word "Cash" means not just hard currency, but a bank transaction as well. The other system – the mercantile system – not only takes cash transactions into account, but also items where money is payable or receivable. As soon as a transaction resulting in a right to receive or pay takes place, it is recorded in the books. We have also seen that the mercantile system is widely practiced and forms the basic accounting standard in India.

Further, let us recall our discussion on capital and revenue items. Items of expenditure which are deemed as 'capital expenditure' will not be deducted from the income of the company for determining profits. Only the revenue expenses will be considered for this purpose. Of course, an amortised portion of the capital items will also be included as expenditure. It follows that regardless of whether cash has been paid or not, items of revenue expenditure will be considered for determining the profitability, whereas even if cash has been paid in respect of capital expenditure, these will not be considered for profitability purposes.

As seen earlier, depreciation is an "expenditure" in a profitability statement, but does not involve any cash outflow. Similarly, provisions made for bad debts; taxation and other items of anticipated expenditure will go to reduce profits, although not involving any cash outflow.

The following table depicts the impact of various transactions appearing in the profit and loss account of a company on the balance sheet and cash flow statements.

Profit and loss account	Related balance sheet items	Possible cash flow effects
Sales proceeds	Sundry debtors	Cash receipts from customers
Cost of production	Stock of materials, sundry creditors	Cash payments to suppliers
Depreciation expenses	Deduction from asset account concerned	None
Administrative expenses	Prepaid expenses, outstanding payables, appearing on the asset and liability sides, respectively	Cash payments for operating expenses

(1) We know that any item of expenditure incurred in the running of an organization is to be deducted from its income to arrive at the profits, provided the expenditure is "revenue" in nature. We also know that we have to make provisions for depreciation, provisions for bad debts and other known items of expenditure. These expenses, which must compulsorily be deducted from the income, are called "charges" to the profits. In other words, regardless of whether the company makes a profit or loss, these expenses have to be taken into account.

An "appropriation", on the other hand, arises only after the company has made a profit. From the figure of profits, companies set apart a portion for taxation provision, a portion for reserves for equalising dividends, a portion for dividends to the shareholders, etc. These items will be taken into account only if the company makes a profit. Should there be no profits, these deductions or "expenditure" would not be there. Such items are called "appropriation" to profits.

While it is useful to understand the absolute quantum of each asset, liability and revenue item in isolation, far greater understanding of its implication with respect to the trend and performance of the company can be achieved by a "relationship" study. For instance, if we study profits in relation to sales for the current year and compare them with the same relationship for a series of years, greater understanding of the trend and performance can be gained.

The "relationship" study referred above has two facets to it – (1) the relationship of one item to another for the current or previous years, but in respect of the same company and (2) the relationship of these parameters with industry figures or representative figures of competitors or of firms of similar size and operations. The first set enables us to understand the performance of the company in isolation, while the second gives an insight as to where the company stands vis-à-vis the industry or competition.

The intuitive way of arriving at a "relationship" is to develop ratios among key parameters. After the finalized statement of accounts is ready, we ascertain the ratio of one key parameter to another. A large number of ratios are in common use, but some of these are useful only for specific end uses like project appraisal, working capital analysis, securities analysis, etc. We concentrate here only on those ratios which are universal in nature and which can be easily computed.

As seen earlier, liquidity and profitability are two separate yardsticks to gauge a company's performance. The current ratio gives an indication as to the number of times by which the current assets multiply the current liabilities. A judgement based on current ratio should be based only on comparable figures relating to previous years as well as the industry standards. There can be no universal benchmark figure for this. The quick ratio or the acid test ratio is a modification of the current ratio in that only the "quick" assets are considered in the numerator, and inventory, which is the slowest of the current assets, is ignored. The measure gives the extent of fast liquidity enjoyed by the company.

The level of profitability is just as important as liquidity. While absolute figures of profitability may be adequate for some cases, we can have a better understanding of the performance of the company by studying the profits in relation to select parameters like sales, capital employed and equity capital. It may be noted that when we take the return on equity, we have to take only the net income after interest, whereas for return on assets, the net income before interest is taken. This is because in the latter ratio, we are looking at what the total investment fetched and not what is left for the equity holders.

The debt ratio can ascertain the extent of reliance of external financing. The debt-equity ratio gives the proportion of debt to equity. In capital-intensive industries, this ratio can be as high as 4, i.e., debt can be up to four times the equity portion. Normally a debt-equity ratio of 2 is considered acceptable. The times interest earned ratio is a matter or reassurance to the lenders that their interest dues are protected. If the company is doing well in terms of having a high times interest earned ratio, it means that the interest liability is only a relatively small portion of the company's net surplus.

However, if the ratio is small, there is cause for concern for the lender.

The above is not an exhaustive list of ratios that could be drawn up from a company's accounts. Only the most essential and fundamental ratios are considered here. Depending on the specific needs of the user, more ratios could be utilized.

Sudreshan knew that a mechanical application of the above principles would not work. He set out to do as comprehensive an analysis as possible.

Annexure 1

Bajaj Auto Ltd

Balance Sheet (₹ in Millions)			
Year	Mar 13	Mar 14	Mar 15
SOURCES OF FUNDS:			
Share Capital +	2893.7	2893.7	2893.7
Reserves Total +	76125.8	93186.5	104027.8
Total Shareholders Funds	**79019.5**	**96080.2**	**106921.5**
Unsecured Loans +	884.4	591.9	1123.5
Total Debt	**884.4**	**591.9**	**1123.5**
Other Liabilities+	2566.7	2084.2	1400.3
Total Liabilities	**82470.6**	**98756.3**	**109445.3**
APPLICATION OF FUNDS:			
Gross Block +	38288.5	40770.4	41009.1
Less : Accumulated Depreciation +	20244.2	20710	21836.7
Net Block +	18044.3	20060.4	19172.4
Capital Work in Progress+	2935.5	1440.6	2549.4
Investments +	64304.8	85496.3	91533.2
Current Assets, Loans & Advances			
Inventories +	6362.8	6397.2	8141.5
Sundry Debtors +	7675.8	7962.1	7169.6
Cash and Bank+	5588.5	4954.8	5861.5
Loans and Advances +	15240.4	13955.2	16084.5
Total Current Assets	34867.5	33269.3	37257.1
Less: Current Liabilities and Provisions	0	0	0
Current Liabilities +	25086.0	2,8760.9	25666.4
Provisions +	16078.6	18527.0	19095.7
Total Current Liabilities	41164.6	47287.9	44762.1
Net Current Assets	-6297.1	-14018.6	-7505
Deferred Tax Assets	1565.5	1463.9	1371.9
Deferred Tax Liability	2716.5	2895.7	2787.7
Net Deferred Tax	-1151	-1431.8	-1415.8
Other Assets+	4634.1	7209.4	5111.1
Total Assets	**82470.6**	**98756.3**	**10944.5.3**

SOURCE: http://www.capitaline.com

Annexure 2

Company : Bajaj Auto Ltd

Profit & Loss (₹ in Millions)			
Year	Mar 13 (12)	Mar 14 (12)	Mar 15 (12)
INCOME:			
Sales Turnover +	211261.6	211183.2	224790
Excise Duty	11289.1	10094	9092.8
Net Sales	199972.5	201089.2	215697.2
Other Income +	7954.9	7064.1	5824.2
Stock Adjustments +	-240	189	575.6
Total Income	**207687.4**	**208342.3**	**222097**
EXPENDITURE :			
Raw Materials +	143825.7	138955.7	149073.6
Power & Fuel Cost+	1213.3	1061.6	1147
Employee Cost +	6117.6	6964.8	8652.4
Other Manufacturing Expenses +	2607.6	5301.7	6557.3
Selling and Administration Expenses +	7479.9	5211.8	6563.2
Miscellaneous Expenses +	2736.4	3374.2	7117.2
Less: Pre-operative Expenses Capitalised+	628.5	649	600.5
Total Expenditure	163352	160220.8	178510.2
Operating Profit	44335.4	48121.5	4,3586.8
Interest +	5.4	4.9	64.9
Gross Profit	44330	48116.6	43521.9
Depreciation+	1667.7	1796.1	2674
Profit Before Tax	42662.3	46320.5	40847.9
Tax+	11560	13606.5	12580
Deferred Tax+	666.6	280.8	130.5
Reported Net Profit	30435.7	32433.2	28137.4
Extraordinary Items +	345	346.7	-1096.8
Adjusted Net Profit	30090.7	32086.5	29234.2
Adjst. below Net Profit +	0	46	-276.8
P&L Balance brought forward	37051.4	49202.6	61504.5
Appropriations +	18284.5	20177.3	20165.7
P&L Balance carried down	49202.6	61504.5	69199.4
Dividend	13021.5	14468.4	14468.4
Equity Dividend %	4500	5000	5000
Dividend Per Share(Rs)	450	500	500
Earnings Per Share-Unit Curr	975.3	1035.8	872.9
Earnings Per Share(Adj)-Unit Curr	975.3	1035.8	872.9
Book Value-Unit Curr	2730.7	3320.3	3695
Book Value(Adj)-Unit Curr	2730.7	3320.3	3695

SOURCE: http://www.capitaline.com

Annexure 3

Industry: Automobiles-Scooters and 3-Wheelers

Year	2013	2014	2015
No. of Companies	9	6	4
Key Ratios			
Debt-Equity Ratio	0.1	0.07	0.05
Long Term Debt-Equity Ratio	0.1	0.07	0.05
Current Ratio	0.87	0.82	0.85
Turnover Ratios			
Fixed Assets	4.64	4.08	4.38
Interest Cover Ratio	115.05	111.39	593.97
PBIDTM (%)	18.29	22.18	19.47
PBITM (%)	17.46	21.28	18.26
PBDTM (%)	18.13	21.99	19.44
CPM (%)	13.07	15.65	13.83
APATM (%)	12.24	14.75	12.63
ROCE (%)	56.1	49.38	38.06
RONW (%)	44.12	37.01	27.67

SOURCE: http://www.capitaline.com

The Overnight Value Add

Feroz Khan was about to leave office on the evening of January 1, 2015, when the phone rang. As the Management Trainee in Sabkojeet Investments, he was in charge of the Xampher Pharmaceuticals account. Xampher had engaged Sabkojeet for monitoring and advising on its investments, which though currently small in nature were expected to grow in tandem with the growth of Xampher's fortunes. Earlier in the day as a part of a routine review, Feroz was relieved that the account did not have too many complications and was quite "passive" in nature.

The phone rang insistently. Feroz had a fleeting thought to ignore it and just go off, but then decided against it. It was Srirag Xampher, the Head of Finance and nephew of the owner, on the line. He said, "Feroz, I want you to do something urgently. There has been a daylong meeting for a takeover of the company, and we are in the process of negotiating the deal. We have adjourned for an hour and are meeting again over dinner at 8. I want you to tell me the impact this will have on our individual portfolios. You know that we are five owners, and I am just mailing you our holding in bonds and shares. I want you to determine how much the deal will benefit each one of us individually".

Feroz wanted to mutter that he was about to leave office and that he would give the report tomorrow. He knew that Srirag would then say that since the negotiations were to happen later in the day, he would need it straightaway. So, he said, "Okay, let me have the details and I will give you a statement as fast as possible".

Srirag replied, "That will not do. If you do not respond by 8, it will be too late".

Feroz restarted his laptop and got the mail from Srirag. It read as follows:

"The holding by the five shareholders in Xampher Pharma is given below:

Name	Number of shares
Rolloji Xampher	96100
Maline Xampher	89250
Srirag Xampher	46300
Nager Xampher	44350
Sujunior Xampher	29000

Xampher had a share capital *of* ₹ 30,50,000 consisting of 305000 shares of ₹ 10 each, divided among the five stakeholders.

The bond holding by the 5 holders is given below: (all bonds have a face value *of* ₹ 100 and mature on the December 31st of the year indicated, pay coupon on a yearly basis based on rate indicated). The current ytm for 2019 bonds is 7.5%, for 2026 bonds is 5.75% and for 2028 bonds is 6.25%.

Name	6% 2019 bond	5.75% 2026 bond	6.25% 2028 bond
Rolloji Xampher	32100	41000	34000
Maline Xampher	15000	12800	24000
Srirag Xampher	17500	35100	15000
Nager Xampher	14400	26100	23500
Sujunior Xampher	10000	22000	18500

The rough details of the takeover proposal are that the company will pay us ₹ 38 million against our selling the debt to them, and ₹ 22 million for the equity shares. You know, of course, that we are not a listed company and that the shares have been valued so far on book value for wealth purposes and the valuation as on December 31st, 2014 *is* ₹ 22 per share.

Please ascertain the exact benefit that each of the stakeholders will have by virtue of the takeover, clearly demarcating the benefit from the holding of bonds and the holding of shares"

Feroz knew that he had to be accurate and would not be able to offer excuses for mistakes as the deal would be struck later that night.

Rahul's Interest In Interest Rates

Rahul Poochnahe found two customers waiting for him as he entered office. He nervously checked the time and was relieved that he was not late. There has been such a rush of enquiries on personal banking thanks to new schemes introduced in the bank that his day would be full with helping potential investors of various age groups and expectations to meet their ideal investment portfolio.

Rahul had joined the Bank as Personal Investment Officer a couple of months back. After graduating from a leading school, he was picked on campus recruitment for this post. The first month was spent on a series of training programs on the internal procedures in the Bank as well as familiarizing himself with the Bank's sophisticated software. In the second month, he was allotted this post and had a senior officer help him for the first 20 days. Rahul realized that the type of questions that customers raised involved computation and up-to-date information on the present interest rates.

The first customer waiting for him wanted to know the interest rate for a 5 year deposit. He wanted to know the difference between investing in a cumulative deposit and getting periodical interest. The current rate for deposits being 7.75%, the customer wanted to know which would be a better option for him if he wanted his money only after 5 years. Since the compounding in the Bank for deposits was on a quarterly basis, Rahul had to patiently show the calculations involved.

The second customer had a number of questions.

Suppose he took a loan of ₹ 1,00,000, what would be the instalment that he would need to pay every quarter, given that the bank interest rate is 10.25%? Suppose he can pay only a maximum of ₹ 2000 per month, how many months will it take for the loan to be repaid? The customer's friend has informed him that he was paying ₹ 2500 per month as EMI for a loan of ₹ 40,000 for 8 years. What interest would that translate into and whether that interest is higher or lower than the one in Rahul's bank.

At that moment, there was a buzz on the intercom and Rahul was told by the branch manager to urgently answer a mail from a client, which had the following questions:

If the client took a loan of ₹ 5,00,000 repayable through EMI and had a maximum disposable monthly income of ₹ 5000, how many years would it take to have the loan repaid in full?

The client has an uncle who has a bank balance of ₹ 25,47,520. He wanted to know that at the prevailing interest rate of 8.25%, how many more years he can last with this corpus, if he allowed the bank to take an equal monthly instalment of principal and interest.

The client was a director of a company which was building up a corpus of ₹ 50 lakhs for expansion plans after 6 years. Someone had suggested to the company to accumulate yearly instalments with the initial instalment straightaway, so that the company has ₹ 50 lakhs at the end of 6 years. At a going interest rate of 9.75%, how large should the instalment be?

The client has ₹ 1,00,000 available for an education fund he seeks to create for his nephew. If the rate of interest is 8.25%, what will the amount be after 7 years? What if the interest was compounded half yearly or quarterly or monthly? What is the effective interest rate in each case?

Index

Chapter 2
Analysis of Financial Statements

$$\text{Net cash flow} = \text{Net income} + \text{Depreciation and amortization} \quad 2.1$$

$$\begin{aligned} \text{ROA} &= \text{Net profit margin} \times \text{Total assets turnover} \\ &= \frac{\text{Net income}}{\text{Sales}} \times \frac{\text{Sales}}{\text{Total assets}} \\ &= \frac{\text{Net income}}{\text{Total assets}} \end{aligned} \quad 2.2$$

$$\begin{aligned} \text{ROE} &= \text{ROA} \times \text{Equity miltiplier} \\ &= \frac{\text{Net income}}{\text{Total asssts}} \times \frac{\text{Total assets}}{\text{Common equity}} \end{aligned} \quad 2.3$$

$$\begin{aligned} \text{ROE} &= \left[\binom{\text{Profit}}{\text{margin}} \times \binom{\text{Total assets}}{\text{turnover}}\right] \times \binom{\text{Equity}}{\text{multiplier}} \\ &= \left[\frac{\text{Net income}}{\text{Sales}} \times \frac{\text{Sales}}{\text{Total assets}}\right] \times \frac{\text{Total assets}}{\text{Common equity}} \end{aligned} \quad 2.4$$

Chapter 3
The Financial Environment: Markets, Institutions, and Investment Banking

$$\text{Amount of issue} = \frac{\text{NP}}{(1 - \text{F})} \quad 3.1$$

Chapter 4
Time Value of Money

$$\text{FV}_n = \text{PV}(1 + r)^n \quad 4.1$$

$$\begin{aligned} \text{FVA}_n &= \text{PMT}\,[(1 + r)^{n-1} + (1 + r)^{n-2} + \cdots + (1 + r)^0] \\ &= \text{PMT}\sum_{t=0}^{n-1}(1 + r)^t = \text{PMT}\left[\frac{(1 + r)^n - 1}{r}\right] \end{aligned} \quad 4.2$$

$$\begin{aligned} \text{FVA(DUE)}_n &= \text{PMT}\sum_{t=0}^{n-1}(1 + r)^t\,(1 + r) \\ &= \text{PMT}\left\{\left[\frac{(1 + r)^n - 1}{r}\right] \times (1 + r)\right\} \end{aligned} \quad 4.3$$

$$\begin{aligned} \text{FVCF}_n &= \text{CF}_1(1 + r)^{n-1} + \cdots + \text{CF}_n(1 + r)^0 \\ &= \sum_{t=0}^{n-1}\text{CF}_t(1 + r)^t \end{aligned} \quad 4.4$$

$$\text{PV} = \frac{\text{FV}_n}{(1 + r)_n} = \text{FV}_n\left[\frac{1}{(1 + r)^n}\right] \quad 4.5$$

$$\text{PVA}_n = \text{PMT}\left[\sum_{t=1}^{n}\frac{1}{(1 + r)^t}\right] = \text{PMT}\left[\frac{1 - \frac{1}{(1 + r)^n}}{r}\right] \quad 4.6$$

$$\begin{aligned} \text{PVA(DUE)}_n &= \text{PMT}\left\{\sum_{t=1}^{n}\left[\frac{1}{(1 + r)^t}\right](1 + r)\right\} \\ &= \text{PMT}\left\{\left[\frac{1 - \frac{1}{(1 + r)^n}}{r}\right] \times (1 + r)\right\} \end{aligned} \quad 4.7$$

$$\text{PVP} = \text{PMT}\left[\frac{1}{r}\right] = \frac{\text{PMT}}{r} \quad 4.8$$

$$\begin{aligned} \text{PVCF}_n &= \text{CF}_1\left[\frac{1}{(1 + r)^1}\right] + \cdots + \text{CF}_n\left[\frac{1}{(1 + r)^n}\right] \\ &= \sum_{t=1}^{n}\text{CF}_t\left[\frac{1}{(1 + r)^t}\right] \end{aligned} \quad 4.9$$

$$\begin{aligned} \text{Periodic rate} = r_{PER} &= \frac{\binom{\text{Stated annual}}{\text{interest rate}}}{\binom{\text{Number of interest}}{\text{payments per year}}} \\ &= \frac{r_{SIMPLE}}{m} \end{aligned} \quad 4.10$$

$$\begin{aligned} \text{Number of interest periods} = n_{PER} &= \binom{\text{Number}}{\text{of years}} \times \binom{\text{Number of interest}}{\text{payments per year}} \\ &= n_{YRS} \times m \end{aligned} \quad 4.11$$

$$\begin{aligned} \text{Effective annual rate (EAR)} = r_{EAR} &= \left(1 + \frac{r_{SIMPLE}}{m}\right)^m - 1.0 \\ &= (1 + r_{PER})^m - 1.0 \end{aligned} \quad 4.12$$

Chapter 5
The Cost of Money (Interest Rates)

$$\begin{aligned} \text{Yield} &= \frac{\text{Dollar return}}{\text{Beginning value}} = \frac{\text{Dollar income + Capital gains}}{\text{Beginning value}} \\ &= \frac{\text{Dollar income + (Ending value − Beginning value)}}{\text{Beginning value}} \end{aligned} \quad 5.1$$

$$\begin{aligned} \text{Rate of return} = r &= \binom{\text{Risk-free}}{\text{rate}} + \binom{\text{Risk}}{\text{premium}} \quad 5.2 \\ &= r_{RF} + \text{RP} \\ &= r_{RF} + [\text{DRP} + \text{LP} + \text{MRP}] \end{aligned} \quad 5.3$$

$$r_{Treasury} = r_{RF} + \text{MRP} = (r^* + \text{IP}) + \text{MRP} \quad 5.4$$

$$\text{Yield (\%) on an n-year bond} = \frac{R_1 + R_2 + \cdots + R_n}{n} \quad 5.5$$

Equation Card Cont.

$$\text{Value of an asset} = \frac{\hat{CF}_1}{(1+r)^1} + \frac{\hat{CF}_2}{(1+r)^2} + \cdots + \frac{\hat{CF}_n}{(1+r)^n}$$

$$= \sum_{t=1}^{n} \frac{\hat{CF}_t}{(1+r)^t} \qquad 5.6$$

Chapter 6
Bonds (Debt)—Characteristics and Valuation

$$\text{Bond value} = V_d = INT\left[\frac{1 - \frac{1}{(1+r_d)^N}}{r_d}\right] + M\left[\frac{1}{(1+r_d)^N}\right] \qquad 6.1$$

$$V_d = \left(\frac{INT}{2}\right)\left[\frac{1 - \frac{1}{(1+r_d/2)^{2\times N}}}{(r_d/2)}\right] + \frac{M}{(1+r_d/2)^{2\times N}} \qquad 6.2$$

Bond yield = Current yield + Capital gains yield

$$= \frac{INT}{V_{d,Begin}} + \frac{V_{d,End} - V_{d,Begin}}{V_{d,Begin}} \qquad 6.3$$

Chapter 7
Stocks (Equity)—Characteristics and Valuation

$$\text{Stock value} = V_s = \hat{P}_0 = \frac{\hat{D}_1}{(1+r_s)^1} + \cdots + \frac{\hat{D}_\infty}{(1+r_s)^\infty}$$

$$= \sum_{t=1}^{\infty} \frac{\hat{D}_t}{(1+r_s)^t} \qquad 7.1$$

$$\hat{P}_0 = \frac{D_0(1+g)^1}{(1+r_s)^1} + \frac{D_0(1+g)^2}{(1+r_s)^2} + \cdots + \frac{D_0(1+g)^\infty}{(1+r_s)^\infty}$$

$$= \frac{D_0(1+g)}{r_s - g} = \frac{\hat{D}_1}{r_s - g}$$

= Value of a constant growth stock 7.2

$$\text{Expected rate of return} = \text{Expected dividend yield} + \text{Expected growth rate, or capital gains yield}$$

$$\hat{r}_s = \frac{\hat{D}_1}{P_0} + g \qquad 7.3$$

$$\hat{P}_t = \frac{\left(\text{First constant growth dividend}\right)}{r_s - g_{norm}} = \frac{\hat{D}_t(1+g_{norm})}{r_s - g_{norm}} = \frac{\hat{D}_{t+1}}{r_s - g_{norm}} \qquad 7.4$$

$$\text{Economic value added} = EVA$$

$$= EBIT(1-T) - \left[\left(\text{Average cost of funds}\right) \times \left(\text{Invested capital}\right)\right] \qquad 7.5$$

Chapter 8
Risk and Rates of Return

$$\text{Expected rate of return} = \hat{r} = Pr_1r_1 + \cdots + Pr_nr_n$$

$$= \sum_{i=1}^{n} Pr_ir_i \qquad 8.1$$

$$\text{Standard deviation} = \sigma = \sqrt{(r_1 - \hat{r})^2 Pr_1 + \cdots + (r_n - \hat{r})^2 Pr_n}$$

$$= \sqrt{\sum_{i=1}^{n} (r_i - \hat{r})^2 Pr_i} \qquad 8.2$$

$$\text{Estimated } \sigma = s = \sqrt{\frac{\sum_{t=1}^{n} (\ddot{r}_t - \bar{r})^2}{n-1}} \qquad 8.3$$

$$\bar{r} = \frac{\ddot{r}_1 + \ddot{r}_2 + \cdots + \ddot{r}_n}{n} = \frac{\sum_{t=1}^{n} \ddot{r}_t}{n} \qquad 8.4$$

$$\text{Coefficient of variation} = CV = \frac{\text{Risk}}{\text{Return}} = \frac{\sigma}{\hat{r}} \qquad 8.5$$

$$\text{Portfolio return} = \hat{r}_p = w_1\hat{r}_1 + w_2\hat{r}_2 + \cdots + w_N\hat{r}_N$$

$$= \sum_{j=1}^{N} w_j\hat{r}_j \qquad 8.6$$

$$\text{Portfolio beta} = \beta_p = w_1\beta_1 + \cdots + w_N\beta_N$$

$$= \sum_{j=1}^{N} w_j\beta_j \qquad 8.7$$

$$\text{Risk premium for Stock j} = RP_j = RP_M \times \beta_j$$

$$= (r_M - r_{RF})\beta_j \qquad 8.8$$

$$\text{Required return} = \text{Risk-free return} + \text{Premium for risk}$$

$$r_j = r_{RF} + RP_j \qquad 8.9$$

$$r_j = r_{RF} + (RP_M)\beta_j$$

$$= r_{RF} + (r_M - r_{RF})\beta_j \qquad 8.10$$

Chapter 9
Capital Budgeting Techniques

$$NPV = \hat{CF}_0 + \frac{\hat{CF}_1}{(1+r)^1} + \frac{\hat{CF}_2}{(1+r)^2} + \cdots + \frac{\hat{CF}_n}{(1+r)^n}$$

$$= \sum_{t=0}^{n} \frac{\hat{CF}_t}{(1+r)^t} \qquad 9.1$$

$$NPV = \hat{CF}_0 + \frac{\hat{CF}_1}{(1+IRR)^1} + \cdots + \frac{\hat{CF}_n}{(1+IRR)^n} = 0$$

or

$$\hat{CF}_0 = \frac{\hat{CF}_1}{(1+IRR)^1} + \cdots + \frac{\hat{CF}_n}{(1+IRR)^n} \qquad 9.2$$

$$\text{PV of cash outflows} = \frac{TV}{(1 + MIRR)^n}$$

$$\sum_{t=0}^{n} \frac{COF_t}{(1 + r)^t} = \frac{\sum_{t=0}^{n} CIF_t(1 + r)^{n-t}}{(1 + MIRR)^n} \quad 9.3$$

$$\text{Payback period} = \left(\begin{array}{c}\text{The year just}\\ \textit{prior} \text{ full recovery}\\ \text{of initial investment}\end{array}\right) + \left(\frac{\begin{array}{c}\text{Amount of the intial}\\ \text{investment that is } \textit{unrevovred}\\ \text{at the start of the recovery year}\end{array}}{\begin{array}{c}\text{Total cash flow generated}\\ \text{during the recovery year}\end{array}}\right) \quad 9.4$$

Chapter 10
Project Cash Flows and Risk

$$\begin{aligned}\text{Supplemental operating } \hat{CF}_t &= \Delta\text{Cash revenues}_t - \Delta\text{Cash expenses}_t - \Delta\text{Taxes}_t\\ &= \Delta NOI_t \times (1 - T) + \Delta Depr_t\\ &= (\Delta NOI_t + \Delta Depr_t) \times (1-T) + T\Delta Depr_t \quad 10.1\end{aligned}$$

Chapter 11
The Cost of Capital

$$\begin{aligned}\left(\begin{array}{c}\text{After-tax}\\ \text{component}\\ \text{cost of debt}\end{array}\right) = r_{dT} &= \left(\begin{array}{c}\text{Bondholders'}\\ \text{required}\\ \text{rate of return}\end{array}\right) - \left(\begin{array}{c}\text{Tax}\\ \text{savings}\end{array}\right)\\ &= r_d - r_d \times T\\ &= r_d(1 - T) \quad 11.1\end{aligned}$$

$$\begin{aligned}V_d &= \frac{INT}{(1 + YTM)^1} + \cdots + \frac{INT + M}{(1 + YTM)^N}\\ &= \frac{INT}{(1 + r_d)^1} + \cdots + \frac{INT + M}{(1 + r_d)^N} \quad 11.2\end{aligned}$$

$$\begin{aligned}\text{Component cost of preferred stock} = r_{ps} &= \frac{D_{ps}}{P_0 - \text{Flotation costs}}\\ &= \frac{D_{ps}}{P_0(1 - F)} = \frac{D_{ps}}{NP_0} \quad 11.3\end{aligned}$$

$$\begin{aligned}\text{Required rate of return} &= \text{Expected rate of return}\\ r_s &= \hat{r}_s\\ r_{RF} + RP_s &= \frac{\hat{D}_1}{P_0} + g \quad 11.4\end{aligned}$$

$$r_s = r_{RF} + RP_s = r_{RF} + RP_M\beta_s = r_{RF} + (r_M - r_{RF})\,\beta_s \quad 11.5$$

$$r_s = \hat{r}_s = \frac{\hat{D}_1}{P_0} + g \quad 11.6$$

$$r_e = \frac{\hat{D}_1}{NP_0} + g = \frac{\hat{D}_1}{P_0(1 - F)} + g \quad 11.7$$

$$WACC = w_d\,(r_{dT}) + w_{ps}\,(r_{ps}) + w_s\,(r_s) \quad 11.8$$

$$\text{Break point} = \left(\frac{\begin{array}{c}\text{Maximum amount of } \textit{lower} \text{ cost}\\ \text{of capital of a given type}\end{array}}{\begin{array}{c}\text{Proportion of the type of capital}\\ \text{in the capital structure}\end{array}}\right) \quad 11.9$$

Chapter 12
Capital Structure

$$\text{Degree of operating leverage} = DOL = \frac{\%\ \Delta \text{ in NOI}}{\%\ \Delta \text{ in sales}} = \frac{\left(\dfrac{\Delta EBIT}{EBIT}\right)}{\left(\dfrac{\Delta Sales}{Sales}\right)} \quad 12.1$$

$$\begin{aligned}DOL &= \frac{Q(P - V)}{Q(P - V) - F} = \frac{S - VC}{S - VC - F}\\ &= \frac{\text{Gross profit}}{EBIT} \quad 12.2\end{aligned}$$

$$\begin{aligned}\begin{array}{c}\text{Degree of}\\ \text{financial leverage}\\ \text{(no preferred stock)}\end{array} = DFL &= \frac{\%\ \Delta \text{ in EPS}}{\%\ \Delta \text{ in EBIT}} = \frac{\left(\dfrac{\Delta EPS}{EPS}\right)}{\left(\dfrac{\Delta\ EBIT}{EBIT}\right)}\\ &= \frac{EBIT}{EBIT - I} \quad 12.3\end{aligned}$$

$$\begin{aligned}\begin{array}{c}\text{Degree of}\\ \text{total}\\ \text{leverage}\end{array} = DTL &= \frac{\%\ \Delta \text{ in EPS}}{\%\ \Delta \text{ in sales}}\\ &= DOL \times DFL\\ &= \frac{\text{Gross profit}}{EBIT} \times \frac{EBIT}{EBIT - I}\\ &= \frac{\text{Gross profit}}{EBIT - I}\\ &= \frac{Q(P - V)}{Q(P - V) - F - I}\\ &= \frac{S - VC}{S - VC - F - I} \quad 12.4\end{aligned}$$

$$\begin{aligned}EPS_1 &= EPS_0 + EPS_0(DTL \times \%\Delta Sales)\\ &= EPS_0[1 + (DTL \times \%\Delta Sales)] \quad 12.5\end{aligned}$$

Chapter 13
Distribution of Retained Earnings: Dividends and Stock Repurchases

$$\text{Transfer from RE} = \left[(\text{Shrs}) \times \begin{pmatrix}\%\text{ stock}\\ \text{dividend}\end{pmatrix}\right] P_0 \qquad 13.1$$

Chapter 14
Working Capital Policy

$$\begin{pmatrix}\text{Account}\\ \text{balance}\end{pmatrix} = \begin{pmatrix}\text{Amount of}\\ \text{daily activity}\end{pmatrix} \times \begin{pmatrix}\text{Average life}\\ \text{of the account}\end{pmatrix} \qquad 14.1$$

$$\begin{aligned}\text{Inventory conversion period (ICP)} &= \frac{\text{Inventory}}{\text{Cost of goods sold per day}}\\ &= \frac{\text{Inventory}}{\left(\dfrac{\text{Cost of goods sold}}{360\text{ day}}\right)}\\ &= \frac{360\text{ day}}{\left(\dfrac{\text{Cost of goods sold}}{\text{Inventory}}\right)}\\ &= \frac{360\text{ days}}{\text{Inventory turnover}}\end{aligned} \qquad 14.2$$

$$\begin{aligned}\text{Receivables collection period (DSO)} &= \frac{\text{Receivables}}{\text{Daily credit sales}}\\ &= \frac{\text{Receivables}}{\left(\dfrac{\text{Annual credit sales}}{360}\right)}\\ &= \frac{360\text{ days}}{\left(\dfrac{\text{Annual credit sales}}{\text{Receivables}}\right)}\\ &= \frac{360\text{ days}}{\text{Receivables turnover}}\end{aligned} \qquad 14.3$$

$$\begin{aligned}\text{Payables deferral period (DPO)} &= \frac{\text{Accounts payable}}{\text{Credit purchases per day}}\\ &= \frac{\text{Accounts payable}}{\left(\dfrac{\text{Cost of goods sold}}{360}\right)}\\ &= \frac{360\text{ days}}{\left(\dfrac{\text{Cost of goods sold}}{\text{Accounts payable}}\right)}\\ &= \frac{360\text{ days}}{\text{Payables turnover}}\end{aligned} \qquad 14.4$$

$$\text{Cash conversion cycle} = \text{ICP} + \text{DSO} - \text{DPO} \qquad 14.5$$

Chapter 15
Managing Short-Term Assets

$$\begin{aligned}\text{Total inventory costs (TIC)} &= \text{Total carrying costs} + \text{Total ordering costs}\\ &= \begin{pmatrix}\text{Carrying cost}\\ \text{per unit}\end{pmatrix} \times \begin{pmatrix}\text{Average units}\\ \text{in inventory}\end{pmatrix} + \begin{pmatrix}\text{Cost per}\\ \text{order}\end{pmatrix} \times \begin{pmatrix}\text{Number of}\\ \text{orders}\end{pmatrix}\\ &= (\text{C} \times \text{PP}) \times \left(\frac{\text{Q}}{2}\right) + \text{O} \times \left(\frac{\text{T}}{\text{Q}}\right)\end{aligned} \qquad 15.1$$

$$\text{Economic ordering quantity} = \text{EOQ} = \sqrt{\frac{2 \times \text{O} \times \text{T}}{\text{C} \times \text{PP}}} \qquad 15.2$$

Chapter 16
Managing Short-Term Liabilities (Financing)

$$\text{Percentage cost per period} = r_{PER} = \frac{\begin{pmatrix}\text{Dollar cost}\\ \text{of borrowing}\end{pmatrix}}{\begin{pmatrix}\text{Dollar amount}\\ \text{of usable fund}\end{pmatrix}} \qquad 16.1$$

$$\text{Effective annual rate (EAR)} = r_{EAR} = (1 + r_{PER})^m - 1.0 \qquad 16.2$$

$$\text{Annual percentage rate (APR)} = r_{PER} \times m = r_{SIMPLE} \qquad 16.3$$

$$\text{Usable funds} = \text{Principal} - \begin{pmatrix}\$\text{ reductions from}\\ \text{principal amount}\end{pmatrix} \qquad 16.4$$

$$\text{Usable amount} = \text{Principal} \times \left[1 - \begin{pmatrix}\%\text{ reductions from}\\ \text{principal amount}\end{pmatrix}\right] \qquad 16.4a$$

$$\text{Required loan (principal) amount} = \frac{\begin{pmatrix}\text{Amount of funds} \\ \textit{needed} \text{ for use}\end{pmatrix}}{1 - \begin{bmatrix}\text{Reductions from the principal} \\ \text{stated as a decimal}\end{bmatrix}} \qquad 16.5$$

Chapter 17
Financial Planning and Control

$$\text{Estimated AFN} = \begin{matrix}\text{Forecasted} \\ \text{increase} \\ \text{in assets}\end{matrix} - \begin{matrix}\text{Forecasted} \\ \text{increase} \\ \text{in liabilities}\end{matrix} - \begin{matrix}\text{Forecasted} \\ \text{increase in} \\ \text{retained earnings}\end{matrix}$$

$$= [(TA_0 - SL_0) \times g] - [NI_0\,(1 + g) - D] \qquad 17.1$$

$$\text{Full capacity sales} = \frac{\text{Existing sales level}}{\begin{pmatrix}\text{Percent of capacity used} \\ \text{to generate sales level}\end{pmatrix}} \qquad 17.2$$

$$Q_{OpBE} = \frac{F}{P - V} = \frac{F}{\text{Contribution margin}} \qquad 17.3$$

$$S_{OpBE} = \frac{F}{1 - \left(\frac{V}{P}\right)} = \frac{F}{\text{Gross profit margin}} \qquad 17.4$$

$$\text{Degree of operating leverage} = DOL = \frac{\%\ \Delta \text{ in NOI}}{\%\ \Delta \text{ in sales}} = \frac{\left(\frac{\Delta NOI}{NOI}\right)}{\left(\frac{\Delta Sales}{Sales}\right)}$$

$$= \frac{\left(\frac{NOI^* - NOI}{NOI}\right)}{\left(\frac{Sales^* - Sales}{Sales}\right)} \qquad 17.5$$

$$DOL_Q = \frac{Q(P - V)}{Q(P - V) - F}$$

$$= \frac{S - VC}{S - VC - F}$$

$$= \frac{\text{Gross profit}}{EBIT} \qquad 17.6$$

$$EPS = \frac{\begin{pmatrix}\text{Earnings available to} \\ \text{common stockholders}\end{pmatrix}}{\begin{pmatrix}\text{Number of common} \\ \text{shares outstanding}\end{pmatrix}} = 0$$

$$= \frac{(EBIT - I)(1 - T) - D_{ps}}{Shrs_C} = 0 \qquad 17.7$$

$$EBIT_{FinBE} = I + \frac{D_{ps}}{(1 - T)} \qquad 17.8$$

$$\text{Degree of financial leverage} = DFL = \frac{\%\Delta \text{ in EPS}}{\%\Delta \text{ in EBIT}} = \frac{\left(\frac{\Delta EPS}{EPS}\right)}{\left(\frac{\Delta EBIT}{EBIT}\right)}$$

$$= \frac{\left(\frac{EPS^* - EPS}{EPS}\right)}{\left(\frac{EBIT^* - EBIT}{EBIT}\right)} \qquad 17.9$$

$$DFL = \frac{EBIT}{EBIT - EBIT_{FinBE}}$$

$$= \frac{EBIT}{EBIT - I} \quad \text{when } D_{ps} = 0 \qquad 17.10$$

$$\text{Degree of total leverage} = DTL = DOL \times DFL$$

$$= \frac{\text{Gross profit}}{EBIT} \times \frac{EBIT}{EBIT - EBIT_{FinBE}}$$

$$= \frac{\text{Gross profit}}{EBIT - EBIT_{FinBE}}$$

$$\left.= \frac{S - VC}{EBIT - I} = \frac{Q(P - V)}{[Q(P - V) - F] - I}\right\} \text{ when } D_{ps} = 0 \qquad 17.11$$